The making of strategy
Rulers, states, and war

Edited by

WILLIAMSON MURRAY
Ohio State University

MACGREGOR KNOX
London School of Economics and Political Science

ALVIN BERNSTEIN
George C. Marshall European Center for Security Studies

CAMBRIDGE
UNIVERSITY PRESS

CAMBRIDGE UNIVERSITY PRESS
Cambridge, New York, Melbourne, Madrid, Cape Town, Singapore, São Paulo, Delhi

Cambridge University Press
32 Avenue of the Americas, New York, NY 10013-2473, USA

www.cambridge.org
Information on this title: www.cambridge.org/9780521566278

First published 1994
First paperback edition 1996
16th printing 2009

A catalog record for this publication is available from the British Library.

ISBN 978-0-521-45389-9 hardback
ISBN 978-0-521-56627-8 paperback

The making of strategy

To those – comrades, friends, acquaintances, and strangers – who died in Vietnam because their leaders had no patience with history or with the imponderables that are the stuff of history.

Contents

Contributors

Alvin H. Bernstein
Director of the George C. Marshall
European Center for Security
    Studies

Eliot A. Cohen
Professor of Strategic Studies
Johns Hopkins University

Wilhelm Deist
Research Director
Militärgeschichtliches
    Forschungsamt

Robert A. Doughty
Chairman, Department of
    History
United States Military Academy

John Gooch
Professor of History
University of Leeds

Colin S. Gray
Professor of International Politics
Director of Center for Security
    Studies
University of Hull

Mark Grimsley
Professor of History
Ohio State University

Michael I. Handel
Professor of Strategy
Naval War College

Holger H. Herwig
Professor of Strategy
University of Calgary

Donald Kagan
Professor of History
Yale University

MacGregor Knox
Stevenson Professor of
    International History
London School of Economics and
    Political Science

John A. Lynn
Professor of History
University of Illinois/Urbana
    Champaign

William S. Maltby
Professor of History
University of Missouri/St. Louis

Peter Maslowski
Professor of History
University of Nebraska/Lincoln

Williamson Murray
Professor of History
Ohio State University

Geoffrey Parker
Professor of History
Yale University

Brian R. Sullivan
Senior Fellow
Institute for National Strategic
   Studies
National Defense University

Arthur Waldron
Professor of Strategy
Naval War College

Earl F. Ziemke
Professor of History
University of Georgia

Acknowledgments

Many individuals helped make this volume possible, and it would be churlish not to give them the thanks that are their due. The Mershon Center and its director Charles Herman provided the financial support that got this project off the ground and maintained it for six years; equally important was Chuck's moral support of the editors. Along with the Mershon Center, as a co-equal partner, the Smith Richardson Foundation provided matching funding and enthusiastic support. William Brodie and Devon Cross were invaluable supporters as well as friends in keeping the project on course.

Here at Ohio State a number of colleagues devoted considerable time and energy to various aspects of the project. Allan Millett and Don Lair organized and ran the startup conference in Newport and provided support and help throughout the course of the project. At the Mershon Center, Joe Kreuzel and Paul Tiberi were especially helpful. Claudia Riser and Josie Cohagen ran the office of the Program in International Security and Military Affairs at the Mershon Center with efficiency and good humor. Several graduate students participated in making *The Making of Strategy* from its inception through final editing: Steve Glick, Matt Oyos, Al Palazzo, Thomas Arnold, and David Thompson all provided valuable help. A number of student workers at Mershon did the interminable mailing, photocopying, telephone answering, and other duties: of these, Jessica Montgomery, Doug Plummer, Todd Miller, and Anita Limbacher were particularly helpful.

We would also like to thank our contributors. They took our criticisms, editing, and deadlines with great good humor and patient attention to the task at hand. We are profoundly grateful to Cambridge University Press for its willingness to publish a manuscript of this size. And we thank Ronald Cohen, our manuscript editor, whose conscientious editorial hand and eagle eye smoothed out the rough edges in the text and corrected the occasional oversights that inevitably occurred in a work of this extent.

We believe we have achieved a coherence within this volume that is unusual in collective works. But we readily accept responsibility for whatever errors and weaknesses may have crept in during the book's long gestation. This volume's strengths are those of its contributors. Its weaknesses are above all our own.

WILLIAMSON MURRAY   MACGREGOR KNOX   ALVIN BERNSTEIN

Illustrations and tables

MAPS

FIGURES

TABLES

1

Introduction: On strategy

WILLIAMSON MURRAY AND MARK GRIMSLEY

The concept of "strategy" has proven notoriously difficult to define. Many theorists have attempted it, only to see their efforts wither beneath the blasts of critics. B.H. Liddell Hart's well-known definition – "the art of distributing and applying military means to fulfill the ends of policy" – may suggest the limitations of the definitional approach, for this forthright but unhappy example restricts the word strictly to *military* affairs, whereas in practice strategy operates in a much broader sphere.[1]

In fact, such straightforward definitions go fundamentally astray, for strategy is a process, a constant adaptation to shifting conditions and circumstances in a world where chance, uncertainty, and ambiguity dominate. Moreover, it is a world in which the actions, intentions, and purposes of other participants remain shadowy and indistinct, taxing the wisdom and intuition of the canniest policymaker. Carl von Clausewitz suggests that in such an environment, "principles, rules, or even systems" of strategy must always fall short, undermined by the world's endless complexities. While models and categories may assist analysis, they can offer no formulas for the successful framing of strategy or conduct of war. Theories all too often aim at fixed values, but in war and strategy most things are uncertain and variable. Worse, such approaches deflect inquiry toward objective factors, whereas strategy involves human passions, values, and beliefs, few of which are quantifiable.[2]

Consequently, reality weds strategic planning tightly to its larger context. Political objectives play their role, of course, as do diplomatic, economic, and military resources. These elements are obvious, but other factors also influence strategic thinking in subtler but equally vital ways. Geography helps determine whether a given polity will find itself relatively free from

[1] B.H. Liddell Hart, *Strategy* (New York, 1967), p. 335.
[2] Carl von Clausewitz, *On War*, trans. and ed. by Michael Howard and Peter Paret (Princeton, 1976), pp. 134, 136.

threat or surrounded by potential adversaries. Historical experience creates preconceptions about the nature of war and politics and may generate irresistible strategic imperatives. And ideology and culture shape the course of decision-makers and their societies in both conscious and unconscious ways. Not only may ideology and culture generate threats where a different perspective would see none, but their influence usually shapes perceptions about alternatives. Moreover, the nature of a government's organization may largely determine the sophistication of its strategic assessments and the speed with which it can respond to new threats and opportunities.

This essay will explore these factors, and others, later. For now it is enough to note that they exert enormous influences on strategic planning and on the implementation of plans in war. By probing the full dimensions of those influences, this book will attempt to illuminate how they affect the *process* of strategy.

These essays originated at the U.S. Naval War College during the academic year 1985–86, when a number of the contributors met formally and informally to discuss strategy and policy.[3] The participants discerned a need for historical examination of the ways in which political and military leaders evolve and articulate strategies in response to external challenges. They felt that much of the existing literature focused on the influence of individual thinkers[4] or dwelled exclusively on a single polity. Neither approach provided much insight into the various factors that have actually molded the strategies of rulers and states. Consequently, discussions turned increasingly toward the *making* of strategy as the element crucial to understanding the ultimate meaning of that elusive word. Moreover, by the nature of their work as historians (or, in some cases, as historically minded political scientists), they were acquainted in some depth with a number of specific national examples. Consequently, it seemed that a book that included case studies would allow for instructive comparisons, especially if it covered a wide range of historical periods and types of polity.

The resulting book focuses on the making of strategy at its highest level, a level that frequently ranges beyond the military high command. It deals with the use of military power in the pursuit of national interests, but its authors are as interested in periods of peace as in periods of war. It operates from the premise that even stunning operational success cannot overcome defective strategic policy. As a study of military effectiveness in the first half of the twentieth century concluded:

---

[3] The authors of this essay are indebted to Eliot Cohen, Holger Herwig, Steven Ross, John Gooch, Alvin Bernstein, Stan Pratt, and the numerous visitors who came through Newport to lecture in the Strategy and Policy course at the Naval War College.

[4] See in particular, two important volumes: Edward Meade Earle, ed., *Makers of Modern Strategy* (Princeton, 1943); and its revised and expanded successor, Peter Paret, ed., *Makers of Modern Strategy* (Princeton, 1986).

No amount of operational virtuosity . . . redeemed fundamental flaws in political judgment. Whether policy shaped strategy or strategic imperatives drove policy was irrelevant. Miscalculations in both led to defeat, and any combination of politico-strategic error had disastrous results, even for some nations that ended the war as members of the victorious coalition. Even the effective mobilization of national will, manpower, industrial might, national wealth, and technological know-how did not save the belligerents from reaping the bitter fruit of severe mistakes [at this level]. This is because it is more important to make correct decisions at the political and strategic level than it is at the operational and tactical level. Mistakes in operations and tactics can be corrected, but political and strategic mistakes live forever.[5]

The main lines of a state's strategy are frequently easy to discern. But the process by which that strategy has evolved is often extremely complex, and the Mahanian notion that sound strategy might spring forth by the discovery and application of eternal principles falls short of reality. Strategic thinking does not occur in a vacuum, or deal in perfect solutions; politics, ideology, and geography shape peculiar national strategic cultures. Those cultures, in turn, may make it difficult for a state to evolve sensible and realistic approaches to the strategic problems that confront it.

One of the strangest aspects of the nineteenth and twentieth century strategic cultures of European states was the tendency of military men to dismiss the political dimension of strategy as something that got in the way of operational necessities. Sir Henry Wilson's contemptuous dismissal of British politicians as "frocks" typified turn-of-the-century military attitudes. But of all the Europeans, the Germans exhibited the strongest predisposition to regard politics as something that ended when the iron dice rolled.

There was, of course, considerable irony in this, for it had been the extraordinary political and strategic wisdom of Otto von Bismarck that had allowed the Prussian state to unify Germany with only minimal opposition from other European powers. Yet the senior military leaders of the new Reich failed to understand the complexities of Bismarck's diplomacy and strategy. Fascinated by their victories at Königgrätz, Sedan, and Metz, they championed operational requirements above everything else. Moltke put it bluntly: "[I]n the case of tactical victory, strategy submits."[6] Ludendorff, for his part, saw no more than tactics. Questioned about the operational objective of his great "Michael" offensive in March 1918, he commented, "I object to the word 'operation.' We will punch a hole in [their line.] For the rest, we shall see."[7] The German defeat in World War I did not modify this

---

5 Allan R. Millett and Williamson Murray, "Lessons of War," *The National Interest* (Winter 1988), which describes the main findings of a study that its authors edited: *Military Effectiveness*, 3 vols. (London, 1988).

6 Quoted in Hajo Holborn, "Moltke and Schlieffen: The Prussian-German School," in Earle, ed., *Makers of Modern Strategy*, p. 180.

7 Crown Prince Rupprecht of Bavaria, *Mein Kriegstagebuch*, ed. by Eugen von Frauenholz

obsession with the battlefield. Geyr von Schweppenburg, a leading panzer commander in World War II and the first military attaché to London in the 1930s, admitted to Liddell Hart in 1949 that he had never read Haushofer or Delbrück. Clausewitz, he said, struck the German officer corps as too abstract to require serious attention. Even the general staff regarded him merely as "a theoretician to be read by professors."[8]

This dismissive attitude toward strategy proved disastrous for Germany in two world wars. But even when policymakers take strategic analysis seriously, their solutions can still fall well short of the mark. With the benefit of hindsight, of course, the correct course is usually easy to see: to recognize, for example, the flawed strategic visions with which the major powers confronted the outbreak of World War I. As the ensuing catastrophe made clear, something was terribly amiss. But when one views matters as they appeared through the lens of government and public opinion, and above all in the uncertain light of what was actually known at the time, it becomes harder to sort out reasonable from foolish courses of action. This process is not helped by the almost continual shift in currents of power and interest. It proved difficult enough for the United States to navigate in the relatively simple, bipolar world of the post-1945 era; earlier periods were far more complicated. Contrasting British strategic decision-making in the 1930s with that of the United States after World War II, Paul Kennedy has emphasized the "extraordinary *fluidity and multipolarity*" of the interwar period:

> At the beginning of the 1930s, the Soviet Union was widely regarded as the greatest land enemy of the British Empire, while in naval terms the chief rivals were the United States and Japan; Italy was seen as an old friend, France was unduly assertive and difficult (but not hostile), and Germany was still prostrate. Five or eight years later Japan appeared as a distinct challenge to British interests in the Far East, Germany had fallen under Nazi rule and was assessed as "the greatest long-term danger," and Italy had moved from friendship to enmity; whereas the United States was more unpredictable and isolationist than ever.[9]

The end of the Cold War has done much to restore this multipolar world. The great complexity of the new international arena has already begun to supplant the nuclear threat as a major world problem.

The nature of international politics has been the subject of debate among historians since the ancient Greeks. Thomas Hobbes stated the most extreme position when he termed it one of permanent conflict and maintained that so

---

[8] (Munich, 1929), Vol. 2, pp. 322, 372n., quoted in Holger Herwig, "The Dynamics of Necessity: German Military Policy During the Great War," in *Military Effectiveness*, Vol. 1, p. 99.

[8] Leo Geyr von Schweppenburg to B.H. Liddell Hart, 3.8.49, in Liddell Hart Papers, 9/24/61, Kings College Library, London.

[9] Paul Kennedy, "British Net Assessment and the Coming of the Second World War," in Allan R. Millett and Williamson Murray, eds., *Calculations* (New York, 1992).

long as "men live without a common power to keep them all in awe, they are in that condition which is called Warre."[10]

Neither Thucydides nor Clausewitz would have gone so far; both perceived a much larger chasm between the rough-and-tumble of peacetime competition and the violent, blood-soaked reality of war. But Thucydides, whose writings greatly influenced Hobbes, also portrayed the core of international relations as the naked exercise of power. As his Athenians say to the Spartans in 432 B.C.:

> We have done nothing extraordinary, nothing contrary to human nature in accepting an empire when it was offered to us and then in refusing to give it up. Three very powerful motives prevent us from doing so – security, honour, and self-interest. And we were not the first to act in this way. Far from it. It has always been a rule that the weak should be subject to the strong; and besides, we consider that we are worthy of our power. Up till the present moment you, too, used to think that we were, but now, after calculating your interest, you are beginning to talk in terms of right and wrong.[11]

The international environment, then, is one in which struggle predominates. A variety of factors shape that struggle. Clausewitz classified them into three: "a remarkable trinity – composed of primordial violence, hatred, and enmity, which are to be regarded as a blind natural force; of the play of chance and probability within which the creative spirit is free to roam; and of its element of subordination, as an instrument of policy, which makes it subject to reason alone."[12] Although Clausewitz intended this trinity to describe the nature of armed conflict, it applies with equal relevance to the conduct of strategy in peace as well as war. The tension between ideology or religion on the one hand and rational calculations of power on the other, as well as the decisive role of chance, make accurate prediction an impossibility in the affairs of nations. Both internal and external pressures buffet policy-makers seeking to frame national strategies.

Understanding this environment of struggle is essential to the formulation of any sensible strategic policy. And history offers the indispensable key to

---

[10] Thomas Hobbes, *Leviathan*, ch. 13, para. 62.

[11] Thucydides, *History of the Peloponnesian War*, trans. and ed. by Rex Warner (Harmondsworth, UK, 1976), p. 80. The theme is repeated even more starkly in the Melian Dialogue: "Our opinion of the Gods and our knowledge of men lead us to conclude that it is a general and necessary law of nature to rule wherever one can. This is not a law that we made ourselves, nor were we the first to act upon it when it was made. We found it already in existence, and we shall leave it to exist for ever among those who come after. We are merely acting in accordance with it, and we know that you or anybody else with the same power as ours would be acting in precisely the same way." See ibid., pp. 404–5.

[12] Carl von Clausewitz, *On War*, p. 89; Thucydides likewise emphasizes the dominant role of chance. The numerical determinists of the social sciences disagree. Trevor N. Dupuy, for example, comments that "While there is some influence of chance on the battlefield, it generally affects both sides equally, and military combat is as close to being deterministic as it is possible for any human activity to be." See Dupuy, *Understanding War: History and Theory of Combat* (New York, 1987), p. xxv; we are indebted to Barry Watts for calling attention to this passage.

that understanding. Thucydides justified his purpose in writing *The Peloponnesian War* by declaring that past events – human nature being what it is – "will, at some time or other and in much the same ways, be repeated in the future."[13] Providing contemporary strategists with a general understanding of how the strategic policymaking process has worked in the past may help that process to work better in the present and future. But any such understanding will be far different from currently popular checklists of principles and overarching theories of international relations. Reality is far too subtle and complex to accommodate mere theory. At best, theory can provide a way of organizing the complexities of the real world for study. Clausewitz, who thought long and hard on the virtues and deficiencies of theory, concluded:

> It is an analytical investigation leading to a close *acquaintance* with the subject; applied to experience – in our case, to military history – it leads to thorough *familiarity* with it. The closer it comes to that goal, the more it proceeds from the objective form of a science to the subjective form of a skill, the more effective it will prove in areas where the nature of the case admits no arbiter but talent. It will, in fact, become an active ingredient of talent. Theory will have fulfilled its main task when it is used to analyze the constituent elements of war, to distinguish precisely what at first sight seems fused, to explain in full the properties of the means employed and to show their probable effects, to define clearly the nature of the ends in view, and to illuminate all phases of warfare through a thorough critical inquiry. Theory then becomes a guide to anyone who wants to learn about war from books; it will light his way, ease his progress, train his judgment, and help him to avoid pitfalls.[14]

The purpose of this book is therefore not to impart doctrine, but to offer its readers an introduction to the wide variety of factors that influence the formulation and outcome of national strategies. Nothing can provide policymakers with the right answers to the challenges that confront them. But history suggests the questions they should ask.

Understanding the strategic choices that faced past decision-makers requires a grasp of the circumstances, opinions, and assumptions with which all strategists contend. Some of these factors have a definite, objective existence – a nation's geographical position, for example. Others, like ideology or the weight of past historical experience, are intangibles. A few, such as estimates of economic strength, occupy an intermediate position between the two. Some elements may be amenable to quantification, while others resist it. The interplay of factors specific to a given polity will govern the way in which it formulates strategy, so that the way modern-day Israel makes strategy, for example, differs markedly from the way that Bourbon France made it. Yet the strategy-making processes of different states do have substantial

---

13   Thucydides, *The Peloponnesian War*, p. 48.
14   Clausewitz, *On War*, p. 141.

similarities: we do not live in a universe where *all* the variables are independent. Consequently, while variables have different effects from one nation to the next and from one era to another, some of them recur with impressive regularity.

GEOGRAPHY

The size and location of a nation are crucial determinants of the way its policy-makers think about strategy. The importance of these two factors is overwhelmingly obvious, yet their influence can be subtle. In Israel, for example, the pressures of geography have been so overwhelming as to produce an obsession with security. By contrast, the United States was for most of its history so removed from major external threats that it could ignore, and even reject, most of the tenets of balance-of-power politics.

The location of the British Isles offers a convenient case through which to explore many of the ramifications of the geographical factor. The British are close enough to the European continent to participate fully in its economic and intellectual developments, but stand apart behind the shields of the North Sea and English Channel, which since 1066 have successfully barred invaders – although the bloodless 1688 invasion of William III forms a partial exception to the rule. Proximity to the continent made Britain's governments acutely conscious of the threat of invasion. That fear spurred, in part, the development of its navy; it also dictated its historic policy toward the Low Countries, a policy aimed since the days of Elizabeth I at keeping that region outside the control of any major power.

Britain's geographical position also encouraged development of the specious but attractive conception of a "British way in war," argued with great eloquence (and even greater bias) by Liddell Hart. The nub of his argument was that over the centuries Britain had been most successful when it had eschewed heavy land commitments on the continent in favor of a peripheral strategy that maximized the Royal Navy's ability to project power against the enemy's weak points.

Liddell-Hart was, of course, trying to avert a repeat of the 1914–1918 continental commitment that had cost over 700,000 military dead. But in so doing he ignored or distorted a number of vital facts. First, Britain had not in the past avoided continental commitments, as the ghosts of Marlborough and Wellington might have assured him. Second, the extent to which Britain *had* been able to limit its forces on the European mainland depended primarily upon whether it had major continental allies capable of maintaining pressure on the enemy. Third, the peripheral strategy owed much of its success to the exposed position of valuable enemy overseas colonies, which had given the Royal Navy easy targets and the Foreign Office powerful bargaining chips in negotiations. But fourth and most important, Germany, the major continental threat to Britain in the first half of the twentieth

century, fit none of the conditions for a peripheral strategy. As Michael
Howard has pointed out:

> It was . . . precisely the failure of German power to find an outlet and its
> consequent concentration in Europe, its lack of any possessions overseas, that
> made it so particularly menacing to the sprawling British Empire in two world
> wars and which make so misleading all arguments about "traditional" British
> strategy drawn from earlier conflicts against the Spanish and French Empires,
> with all the colonial hostages they had offered to fortune and the Royal Navy.[15]

Even so, it is worth noting that Liddell Hart's reaction against World War I fit
within a larger national pattern of British antipathy to continental commitments. Jonathan Swift's biting essay, *On the Conduct of the Allies,* had
denounced Marlborough's strategy as fiercely as Liddell Hart had attacked
Haig's.

If geography has exerted a dominant influence on threat-assessment and
strategy, it can also shape critical doctrinal decisions. In the 1920s and
1930s, both British and American airmen articulated a pervasive, even dogmatic thesis that air power could gain decisive results independently of
ground and naval forces.[16] The Germans, by contrast, developed a substantially different approach. German airmen did not dismiss the idea of "strategic" bombing because of some misbegotten belief that air forces should be
tied to the "coat-tails of the army." Rather they, unlike their Anglo-American
counterparts, had to contend with the real and constant threat of land invasion. American and British airmen could rhapsodize about leaping over battle lines and tearing the heart from the enemy's society, but German airmen
had to deal with such prosaic matters as the possibility of losing their airfields. Bombing factories and sowing terror in Prague, Warsaw, and Paris was
all very well, but such exploits would avail little if the German army concurrently lost the Rhineland and Silesia. Luftwaffe planners recognized the value
of "strategic" bombing, but they could not afford to view it as the only
proper role for air power. For geographic reasons, German airmen *had* to
think about supporting the ground war as well.[17] For the British and Americans, by contrast, the loss of Belgium, the Netherlands, or even France would
not preclude the possibility of fighting on.

Yet the influences – or constraints – of geography can place severe limits
on the achievements of national strategic aims.[18] Philip II of Spain clearly
aimed at a hegemonic position in Europe; yet his far-flung domains exposed
Spain and its possessions to pressures from so many sides that it often seemed

15 Michael Howard, *The Continental Commitment* (London, 1972), p. 32.
16 For the mindset of American airmen, see Michael Mandelbaum, ed., *America's Defense*
    (New York, 1989); and Williamson Murray, *Luftwaffe* (Baltimore, 1985), Appendix I.
17 Williamson Murray, "The Luftwaffe Before the Second World War: A Mission, A Strat-
    egy?" *Journal of Strategic Studies* (September 1981): pp. 261–70.
18 See Geoffrey Parker, "The Making of Strategy in Habsburg Spain: Philip II's 'bid for
    mastery', 1556–1598," in this volume.

beleaguered. In the Mediterranean, the Ottoman Turks were a constant and powerful threat; in the north, the Dutch rebellion presented a persistent economic and ideological threat that the English delightedly exacerbated; and in the center, the French, despite their internal fractures, represented a latent rival. Finally, as Drake's voyage around the world was to demonstrate, the wealth of the Americas, on which so much of Spain's position in Europe depended, was vulnerable to attack. Admittedly, many of Philip's problems stemmed from his inability or unwillingness to make the diplomatic concessions that might reduce the number of his opponents, but the merest survey of a map (not to mention any knowledge of the realities of communications and travel in sixteenth century Europe) should suggest the severe limitations that geography exerted on Spain's strategic choices.

Finally, the size of a state is a central element in its strategic situation. Israel's compactness and lack of territorial depth have made an offensively oriented preemptive strategy almost imperative; conversely, Russia's sprawling expanse has made possible its historical strategy of trading space for time in a protracted defense. By the same token, doctrinal preferences based on one set of geographical circumstances can prove dangerous when extended arbitrarily into another. For example, interior lines and the relatively short distances and advanced transportation network of central and western Europe shaped the German operational approach to war. But when confronted by the vast steppes of the Soviet Union, that approach soon led to disaster, in part thanks to its cavalier attitude toward logistics. German planners never learned the healthy respect for distance that characterized the ambitious and highly sophisticated manner in which the Americans, for instance, projected and sustained power over great distances.[19]

But geography has an impact beyond that of mere physical distance. In their war against the rebellious American colonies, the British found it impossible to control the military forces they projected across the Atlantic. Admittedly the political preconceptions with which the British embarked on this war made it a dubious proposition almost from the outset. Nevertheless, it is worth noting that of Lord Germaine's approximately sixty-three letters of instruction to General Sir Henry Clinton during the period from 1778 to 1781, six took less than two months to arrive in North America, twelve took approximately two months, twenty-eight took two to three months, eleven took three to four months, four took four to five months, and two took five to seven months.[20] While the wonders of modern technology have removed some of the difficulties involved in communicating orders and projecting power, time and distance and weather still exercise enormous influence on the strategic options and capabilities of states.

[19] See Martin van Creveld, *Supplying War: Logistics from Wallenstein to Patton* (Cambridge, 1977), pp. 142–81; and Klaus Reinhardt, *Die Wende vor Moskau, Das Scheitern der Strategie Hitlers im Winter 1941/42* (Stuttgart, 1972).
[20] Piers Mackesy, *The War for America, 1775–1783* (London, 1975), p. 73.

History

Historical experience influences strategic choices almost as strongly as geography. If the small size and exposed location of Israel weighs heavily on the minds of its policymakers, so too do the memories of the diaspora and the Holocaust. While it is possible (though unlikely) that Israel's Arab neighbors never literally meant their threats to drive the Jews into the Mediterranean, to a nation born from the ashes of six million dead those threats carried more than rhetorical significance. Israeli insistence on holding the occupied territories and willingness to shoot first and ask questions later are manifestations of historical experience, however misguided they may seem to those who see policymakers as dispassionate "rational actors."

In a similar vein, the fate of the Czech people in the aftermath of the Battle of the White Mountain in 1620 (when the Habsburgs entirely destroyed the Czech national army) explains much about Czech behavior in the twentieth century. The victorious Habsburgs proceeded to "Germanize" the Bohemian and Moravian lands to the extent that it is difficult to speak of a national culture beyond that of the Czech villages until the mid-nineteenth century. That memory shaped the behavior of Czech national leadership in September 1938, February 1948, and August 1968: better to surrender than risk national extinction. History has been kinder to others. Even Poland's cruel past never led to anything so catastrophic as the fate of the Czechs after 1620. Perhaps in consequence, the Poles have displayed a willingness to stand up against the greatest odds.[21]

If the lessons of history can be read, they can also be misread, as the Germans demonstrated in two world wars. The unification of Germany was primarily a result of the political astuteness and careful balancing of Bismarck. But neither Wilhelm II nor his generals appreciated or studied the deft statecraft involved. Both concentrated instead on the martial component, a necessary but scarcely sufficient condition of Bismarck's success. The battlefield triumphs over Denmark, Austria, and France convinced them of the primacy of operational requirements over everything else. As a result, Germany fought the war of 1914–1918 with a lack of political sense that contributed heavily to its ultimate defeat. The Schlieffen Plan, which sought to achieve swift and decisive victory at the operational level, had the strategic effect of provoking British intervention. Its inflexibility was likewise the product of military preferences, and made inevitable a two-front war that Germany might conceivably have avoided: until the Germans mobilized, in lock-step conformity to the Schlieffen Plan, France had not yet committed itself to the support of Russia in what was, after all, a crisis initially confined to Central and Eastern Europe. And after war commenced, the German

---

21 For a comparison of strategic situations in 1938 and 1939, see Williamson Murray, *The Change in the European Balance of Power, 1938–1939: The Path to Ruin* (Princeton, 1985). The Poles fought; the Czechs did not.

navy's insistence on unrestricted submarine warfare – again a purely operational recipe for victory – virtually guaranteed American intervention, a strategic disaster so enormous and so obvious that only the complete triumph of blinkered military "necessity" could have caused it.

The peculiar circumstances in which Imperial Germany collapsed in 1918 led to a second, even more dangerous misreading of historical experience. By 1917–18 the German armies had defeated Russia and seemed on the brink of victory over France. Then the sudden German military collapse, coupled with the outbreak of revolution at home, led to an armistice that permitted Germany to escape the full consequences of its actual strategic situation: the crushing military defeat on German territory that had to wait until 1945. Ludendorff and others could thus claim that the Allies had not vanquished the German army in the field; it had been "stabbed in the back" by liberals, revolutionaries, and Jews at home. That argument convinced not only German generals and emergent agitators of the radical right, such as Adolf Hitler, but also many who should have known better. Even Friedrich Ebert, the new Social Democratic president of the Weimar Republic, hailed the returning army as "unbeaten."[22]

Then the German government's civil bureaucracy, much of it still under officials from the former Reich, launched a massive disinformation campaign that distorted Germany's considerable role in starting World War I. Those efforts duped a significant portion of international opinion and scuttled any chance for the German people to reach an accurate understanding of their recent past.[23] Not until 1945, after a second ruinous war, were they in a position to do so. In the meantime, this false reading of historical experience had distorted the German view of the Reich's strategic choices by adding new ideological fixations to the officer corps' still-unexamined cult of operational necessity.

Historical periods themselves may profoundly influence how nation-states make strategy. For the Western democracies in the 1930s, World War I cast a sinister shadow over choices and prospects. In Britain, memories of the trenches helped blind not only politicians but much of the public to the unprecedented nature of the Nazi threat. The British ambassador in Berlin even suggested to the Foreign Secretary that Britain's mediator in the Czech crisis should "not allow himself to be influenced by ancient history or with arguments about strategic frontiers and economics."[24] The reaction at every level of society to the horrors of the Western Front made any true understanding of the nature of the new threat almost impossible. It seemed incon-

---

[22] See especially, Gerhard Ritter, *Staatskunst und Kriegshandwerk: Das Problem des Militärismus im Deutschland*, Vol. 3, *Die Tragödie der Staatskunst: Bethmann Hollweg als Kriegskanzler (1914–1917)* (Munich, 1964).

[23] Holger Herwig, "Clio Deceived: Patriotic Self-Censorship in Germany after the Great War," *International Security* (Fall 1987).

[24] Documents on British Foreign Policy, 3rd Series, Vol. III, Doc. 590, 6.8.38, letter from Henderson to Halifax.

ceivable that any nation would ever again resort to war as an instrument of
national policy, much less that a continental statesman might willfully and
even eagerly unleash a Europe-wide conflagration. As Kingsley Martin noted
in the *New Statesman* in spring 1938: "Today if Mr. Chamberlain would
come forward and tell us that his policy was really one not only of isolation-
ism but also of Little England in which the Empire was to be given up
because it could not be defended and in which military defence was to be
abandoned because war would totally end civilization, we for our part would
wholeheartedly support him."[25]

In France, the mood was little different, but at least the French recognized
that the Nazis were more than a collection of nationalist eccentrics. It is
excessive to ascribe French defeat in 1940 to the impact of World War I on
France's armies.[26] But the diplomatic and strategic decisions of the French
government in the late 1930s were the distinct result of the baleful influence
of the war's 1.35 million dead on the French national consensus. When the
premier, Edouard Daladier, returned from securing "peace for our time" at
the Munich Conference, he ordered his plane to circle Le Bourget airport for
fear that the crowd below had come to lynch him. When he discovered that
they were there to cheer him instead, he could only mutter that they were
"fools" who did not grasp what they were applauding.[27] Yet even those in
France who were aware that war had been at best temporarily averted preferred a few more months of peace to a war they felt would surely be a replay
of 1914–1918.[28] The enormous difference in the *German* reaction to World
War I suggests the gulf that may occur between national evaluations of
collective historical experiences; Ernst Jünger's war memoirs show a savage
delight in combat utterly alien to figures such as Henri Barbusse or Guy
Chapman.

The nature of the regime

A host of further factors influence the making of strategy. Ideology (or
religion, depending on the polity and period), cultural attitudes, organizational and administrative arrangements, the impact and influence of military
and political institutions, the ability of the state to mobilize its economic
resources, and the individual choices and idiosyncratic behavior of statesmen
and military leaders all have an immense impact on the forging of national

---

25 Quoted in N. Thompson, *The Anti-Appeasers* (Oxford, 1971), pp. 156–7.
26 Robert Doughty's book, *The Breaking Point: Sedan and the Fall of France, 1940*
    (Hamden, CT, 1990), underlines that the collapse of May 1940 resulted from *extraordi-*
    nary military incompetence on the part of the French high command – especially General
    Maurice Gamelin, the commander in chief.
27 Telford Taylor, *Munich: The Price of Peace* (New York, 1979), pp. 58–9.
28 And they were to a great extent right; only this time, largely due to their stunning collapse,
    they escaped most of the bloodletting. But the price in national honor, values, and stability
    was close to catastrophic.

strategies. The exact relationship between these factors varies widely from one state to another, and even within a state the removal of a few key individuals can have a significant bearing on the course of policy.

RELIGION, IDEOLOGY, AND CULTURE

Taken together, these three terms comprise something the Germans have captured in a single, expressive word – *Weltanschauung* – the obvious utility of which has led to its adoption in non-German discourse as well. The influence of *Weltanschauungen* upon strategy is elemental, vast, and far stronger than another German borrowing, Realpolitik, would have one believe. Realpolitik suggests that decision-makers can strip strategic calculations of all considerations save those of pragmatism and power. The term exudes a sense of hard-headed sagacity. In fact, however, it is profoundly misleading – and even ideological – for the naked exercise of power for its own sake is seldom the ultimate goal. Power is a means, not an end. It exists to advance or defend the interests of the groups who control it. The fundamental assumptions about the nature of society and even the purpose of human life of those groups in turn shape their perceptions of interest. From a historical perspective, many, if not most, case studies of the making of strategy would make no sense without consideration of the role of belief systems.

This point is especially difficult for Americans to grasp, for they regard themselves as a practical society without an ideological or religious agenda. Yet in fact the United States represents an excellent example of the role of *Weltanschauung* on the making of strategy. Americans have long believed that their nation was uniquely the embodiment and protector of liberal democracy. "Freedom hath been hunted round the Globe," trumpeted Thomas Paine during America's birth pangs. "Asia and Africa have long expelled her. Europe regards her like a stranger, and England hath given her warning to depart. O! receive the fugitive, and prepare in time an asylum for mankind."[29] Echoing this view, Abraham Lincoln called America the "last, best hope of earth."[30] And despite motivations that have often been less than pristine, American policymakers have generally reflected this tradition of exceptionalism. For a century it led them to reject both alliances with the "sordid" houses of Europe and the lust for colonies that seized Europeans during the last third of the nineteenth century. The rejection of colonies was not absolute, of course. Many Americans harbored dreams of "manifest destiny" – dreams that were themselves born of a belief in American exceptionalism – and most learned to feel comfortable when the United

[29] Quoted in Ernest R. May, "America's Destiny in the Twentieth Century," in Daniel J. Boorstin, ed., *American Civilization: A Portrait from the Twentieth Century* (New York, 1972). p. 321.
[30] Roy P. Basler, ed., *The Collected Works of Abraham Lincoln*, 8 vols. (New Brunswick, NJ, 1948–1954), vol. 5, p. 537.

States acquired both "informal" and formal empires of overseas possessions in and after 1898. But the fact that America chose an avenue toward world power relatively unencumbered by colonies reflected deep-rooted ideological and cultural convictions. On several occasions during World War II, Franklin Roosevelt irritated Winston Churchill with meddlesome and seemingly gratuitous urgings that the British dismantle their own colonial network. From the standpoint of Realpolitik, such nagging was pointless and even harmful. But to the leader of the "last, best hope on earth" it had a serious underlying purpose.

Perhaps the most striking restatement of American exceptionalism in the last fifty years occurred, of all unlikely places, in NSC-68, the now famous top-secret blueprint for containment of the Soviet Union. Prepared in 1950, it depicted the emerging Cold War as a mortal confrontation between two diametrically opposed value systems. On one side stood the United States, whose fundamental purpose was "to assure the integrity and vitality of our free society, which is founded upon the dignity and worth of the individual." On the other side lurked the monsters in the Kremlin. "The fundamental design of those who control the Soviet Union and the international communist movement," explained the team who drafted NSC-68, "is to retain and solidify their absolute power, first in the Soviet Union and second in the areas now under their control." "The idea of freedom under a government of laws, and the idea of slavery under the grim oligarchy of the Kremlin" were irreconcilable. A free society valued "the individual as an end in himself" and welcomed diversity; it sought to "create and maintain an environment in which every individual has the opportunity to realize his creative powers." It was tolerant, because it recognized the inherent strength of the guiding ideology of individual liberty. Save in self-defense, it rejected violence as a tool of politics, for "in relations between nations, the prime reliance of the free society is on the strength and appeal of its ideas, and it feels no compulsion sooner or later to bring all societies into conformity with it." Against this enlightened ideal stood the Soviet system. "No other value system is so wholly irreconcilable with ours, so implacable in its purpose to destroy ours. . . ."[31]

NSC-68 remains startling in its Manichean depiction of the clash between the United States and the Soviet Union. The temptation of Realpolitik is to dismiss this section of the paper as mere propaganda aimed at the gullible. Yet it could not have been propaganda. NSC-68 circulated only among the highest echelons of the American government; although well-known in outline, it was not finally declassified until 1975. And it provided the foundation of American national security policy for most of the quarter-century after

---

[31] See "NSC-68: A Report to the National Security Council," reprinted in *The Naval War College Review* 27 (May-June 1975), pp. 51–108. The quoted passages are taken from pp. 54–6.

1950. It reflected accurately the ideological assumptions that underpinned American strategy.

Earlier belief systems affected policymakers no less powerfully. As Geoffrey Parker observes of Spain's Philip II, "[i]f Philip . . . elected to prolong the sufferings of his subjects in order to prosecute his strategic goals, whatever their cost, the explanation lies . . . in his unshakable confidence – to the end of his days – that he was doing God's work and that, in the end, God would provide."[32] Consequently, Philip continued the immensely costly war against the Dutch while fighting an equally ferocious struggle against the Turks in the Mediterranean. In both cases, Philip was fighting for rational strategic purposes, yet at the same time his religious aims were inextricably intwined with his geopolitical goals. And in the midst of his difficulties he also shouldered the burden of destroying Protestantism in England, an obvious overextension of his limited means. Philip would have found completely incomprehensible the Catholic Cardinal Richelieu's support for the Protestant Swedes against the Catholic Austrian Habsburgs in the next century.

Within the Western tradition, religion lost much of its influence on strategy as a result of the disastrous Thirty Years' War (1618–1648). Nevertheless, remnants of that influence survived for some time, and outside the West religion remains a basic strategic motivation. Shortly before he came to power in 1979, for example, the Ayatollah Khomeini championed the notion of a holy war. "Holy war means the conquest of all non-Moslem territories," he wrote. "War will perhaps be declared after the formation of an Islamic government worthy of the name. . . . It will then be the duty of all adult ablebodied men to volunteer for this war of conquest whose final goal is to make Koranic law supreme from one end of the earth to the other."[33] The human wreckage left by the Iranian Revolution has underscored the sincerity of his message only too well.

Yet it is ideology, the secular variant of religion, that has exerted the most potent influence over strategic policy during the past two centuries. The French Revolution and the nearly quarter-century of war that ensued set the tone for the twentieth century. Secular religions particularly plagued the first half of our century and came close to breaking the back of Western civilization during World War II. Hitler's drive to create a unified Europe from the Urals to Gibraltar under German (Aryan) control – a Europe that would be, moreover, entirely *Judenfrei* – provided a dynamism and power that nearly destroyed all his competitors.[34] The other major powers failed to com-

---

[32] Parker, "The Making of Strategy in Habsburg Spain."
[33] Quoted in MacGregor Knox, et al., *Mainstream of Civilization,* 5th Edition (New York, 1989), p. 1052.
[34] For analyses of Hitler's ideological maturation and vision, see E. Jäckel, *Hitlers Weltanschauung* (Tübingen, 1969) and MacGregor Knox, "Conquest, Foreign and Domestic, in Fascist Italy and Nazi Germany," *Journal of Modern History* (March 1984).

prehend the driving force behind German policies. And Hitler's strategic policymaking in the late 1930s made virtually no provision for balancing ends and means. He simply aimed to build the world's most formidable army, a world-class navy, and an air force that – had it been completed in peacetime – would have required 85 percent of the world's production of aviation fuel.[35]

The Soviets made the greatest mis-estimate of the Nazi ideological threat. Undoubtedly influenced by the Marxist perception that revolutions come only from the Left, Soviet leaders refused to take seriously Hitler's talk about the *Lebensraum* in the East. Believing that the Nazi movement was nothing more than the product of "monopoly capitalism," Stalin and his associates looked favorably on Hitler's ascent; throughout the 1930s they made a number of clandestine approaches to Berlin, while playing the "popular front" tune for the benefit of the gullible in the West. In 1939 Stalin apparently achieved his dreams in the Nazi-Soviet Non-Aggression Pact, which guaranteed a war among the capitalist powers. But that war soon left the Soviet Union alone on the European continent with Nazi Germany, and Stalin's faulty perceptions of Hitler's motives once again blinded the Soviets to the inevitability of the coming blow.

Yet while Nazi ideology gave Hitler's movement a revolutionary dynamism that came close to toppling the world order, it ironically played a fundamental role in the failure of the Nazi invasion of the Soviet Union. Not only did the Nazi *Weltanschauung* cause the Germans largely to underestimate their Soviet opponent for much of the war, but it resulted in the Germans – Nazi leaders and soldiers alike – waging a war of extermination that gave the Soviet peoples much of their will to resist.[36] Throughout the war in the East, Hitler held fast to his ideological vision of a crusade waged against the eastern Judeo-Bolshevik threat, whatever the political or military repercussions might be. The result was the survival of one of the most appalling regimes in human history, one that defined its political enemy in terms of class rather than race. Nevertheless, Stalin did prove more adaptable to the harsh strategic necessities, but the cost of educating him out of some of his ideological preconceptions proved extraordinarily high to the Soviet Union.

Closely related to ideology, but less consciously held and usually less dogmatic, are cultural attitudes. Such attitudes help set the style of national leadership as well as a nation's receptiveness to it. As John Lynn demonstrates, Louis XIV's quest for *gloire* explains much about his strategic approach; it also clearly sets him off from the values of most modern statesmen.

---

[35] See Wilhelm Deist, *The Wehrmacht and German Rearmament* (London, 1981).

[36] Recent works that discuss the role of ideology in the German campaign in the East include: Horst Boog, et al., *Das Deutsche Reich und der Zweite Weltkrieg*, Vol. IV, *Der Angriff auf die Sowjetunion* (Stuttgart, 1983); Omer Bartov, *The Eastern Front, 1941–1945: German Troops and the Barbarization of Warfare* (Oxford, 1988) and *Hitler's Army: Soldiers, Nazis, and War in the Third Reich* (Oxford, 1991); Christian Streit, *Keine Kameraden* (Stuttgart, 1978).

Yet in our own century, Hitler's desire to glorify himself as Führer of the German people – chillingly and enthusiastically depicted in Leni Riefenstahl's film *Triumph des Willens* – echoes the past.

But cultural attitudes cut far more deeply than the mere style of national leadership. They can also determine in part a polity's aptitude for strategic calculation. War, for example, lay at the center of the classical Roman *Weltanschauung* – the compound of military glory, paternal authoritarianism, and imperial ambition that helped make Rome a tenacious, ruthless, and resourceful opponent. By contrast, the culture of the Ming Chinese proved to be a profound strategic handicap. Not only did it promote a sense of superiority that kept the Ming from appreciating the Mongol threat, but its Confucian elements subtly encouraged the belief, as expressed by Arthur Waldron, in "states in which cultural and moral norms kept order, means that they considered both more admirable and more potent than mere force."[37] Good rule consisted of the cultivation and preservation of these norms; control over hostile rivals would result only from remaining true to the natural order of things rather than manipulating the environment through coercion. The Ming frowned on naked resort to force, although sometimes taking that path. The consequence of such beliefs – so alien to the combative traditions of the West – was failure to adapt effectively to a shifting strategic environment.

Economic factors

The implementation of any strategy obviously depends significantly on the economic means available. The Spain of Philip II illustrates the difficulties that an early modern state could experience in securing sufficient means to carry out its strategy. The Spanish government's failure to pay its soldiers in Flanders in 1576 triggered a disastrous mutiny and the sack of Antwerp, which undermined the strategic and political policies that Philip had pursued during the previous decade. The Dutch, on the other hand, possessed a thriving commercial economy that enabled them to prevail in their revolt – even though the conflict lasted for eighty years.

Indeed, throughout the early modern period, a state's ability to generate capital was an issue of the highest importance. Chronic difficulties in gathering funds placed a premium on "making war pay for war," an expedient that continually directed armies toward the richest provinces of Europe and spurred the creation of elaborate systems of forced contributions. But such measures were, at best, inefficient. Soldiers wasted or destroyed too much of what they seized, the need to live off the land often acted as a severe brake on operations, and the uncertainty of supply made armies unresponsive to centralized control. Above all, the absence of effective capital mobilization

---

[37] See Arthur Waldron, "Chinese Strategy from the Fourteenth to the Seventeenth Centuries" in this volume.

hindered the creation of sufficiently strong armies and navies. The need for stronger forces helped spur the development of absolutism, as monarchs strove to obtain ever greater control over their revenue base.

Alliances between government and commercial interests were an even better solution. The Dutch foreshadowed this arrangement, but the English, after their revolution and civil war, decisively embraced it. A sharing of power between Crown and Parliament permitted a radical yet voluntary increase in taxation and encouraged wealthy men to lend money to the state on a massive scale. More than any other factor, superior fiscal organization allowed England to challenge and eventually eclipse Bourbon France in the struggle for European mastery.[38]

Eventually, all Western states recognized and adopted this economic advantage. Yet while modern fiscal arrangements eased constraints on strategy, they did not remove them. Indeed, the desire to throw off all economic shackles by achieving autarky helped to drive the European imperialism of the nineteenth century and to create the Anglo-German antagonism that led in part to the catastrophe of World War I. The same basic drives spurred Japanese expansion into Korea, Manchuria, and China. American retaliatory economic measures – a series of embargoes culminating in a complete cutoff of petroleum – goaded Japan into its seizure of the East Indies and its desperate, reckless attack on the United States itself.

Economic factors also deeply affected Japan's nominal ally in World War II. Nazi Germany in the 1930s came close to economic disaster; its rearmament program was wildly extravagant given the resources at hand, although completely in line with Hitler's goals.[39] The pressures of an overheated economy then increasingly forced Hitler's hand, and led him to move before the Reich was fully ready for war. But as he said when told that the German military was not ready for war in 1938, the issue was not the preparedness of the armed forces but rather the balance between the Wehrmacht and its opponents. Luckily for the Third Reich (at least in the short run), the Germans fought not in 1938, when their economic cupboard was bare, but rather in 1939, when they could draw on resources from the defunct Czech Republic and the Soviet Union.

On the other side of the hill, desperate fear of another continental war intersected with two major economic constraints on British strategy.[40] Neville Chamberlain recognized the limits of Britain's economic power and the danger that the government's rearmament program might shatter the public and international financial confidence that British governments had worked so hard to repair since the crisis of 1931. He also feared that another conflict

---

38 The best analysis of this alliance is John Brewer, *The Sinews of Power: War, Money and the English State, 1688–1783* (New York, 1989).
39 See Murray, *Change in the European Balance of Power*, Chapter I.
40 Ibid., Chapter II.

would complete the job of destroying Britain's economic position that World War I had begun. Chamberlain and the analysts in the British treasury were indeed correct on the second count. But on the first count their failure to look beyond their ledgers and comprehend the nature of the Nazi threat came close to destroying Britain's independence.

Since the first third of the nineteenth century, the economic constraints on American policymaking have been considerably less than those on virtually all other modern powers (except from the perspective of the Confederate States of America). In the Civil War, once the national economy had geared up, the federal government was in a position to project immense military power deep into the American South and break the rebellion at its heart. World War I, and especially World War II, embodied "the American way of war"; the economic strengths of the United States proved crucial in creating or sustaining the great coalitions that broke Germany's power. But the world's largest economy did not confer omnipotence: the Vietnam War suggests that even overwhelming economic might is of little utility in implementing a fundamentally flawed strategic vision.

The organization of government and military institutions

The structure of government and military institutions plays a crucial role in the formulation of strategy and its adaptability to actual conditions. The form of government effects the ability of decision-makers to analyze and interpret the external environment. Through the centuries, tyrannies have displayed a notorious tendency to punish the bearers of bad news; consequently, the willingness of their bureaucrats to analyze the world in realistic terms may be less than satisfactory. Officials in any system are highly skilled at telling leaders what they want to hear. And military institutions can display a wide variety of traits that may make them especially suited for the planning and execution of strategy or, conversely, may cripple their effectiveness.

In classical Greece and Rome, the two most important Western political paradigms, governmental and military institutions were intimately intertwined. The Athenian *polis* debated strategic policy and regularly elected generals (*strategoi*) from its own membership. As a result, while leaders of stature and ability could generally impose their own strategic vision, as Pericles did during the early years of the Peloponnesian War, they still had to remain sensitive to the shifting emotions of a willful democratic assembly. The decisions of that assembly, in turn, could sometimes prove disastrous, as in the Athenian expedition to Sicily. The ruling elite of the Roman republic, for its part, consisted entirely of men who had served in active campaigns: combat service was an absolute prerequisite for political office. The identity of citizen and soldier permitted Rome to draw on its entire population and thus to field large and thoroughly trained armies almost continuously. The ferocious discipline of the Roman military, reinforced by the Roman warrior ethic and its conceptions of virtue, made possible an instrument of power unrivaled in the ancient world, enviously studied by Machiavelli, and energetically duplicated by Maurice of Nassau and Gustavus Adolphus during the seventeenth century.

The identification of government and military continued well into the early modern period. Both Maurice and Gustavus Adolphus combined the roles of army commander and head of state, a trait they shared in common with many European monarchs. As late as 1870 King Wilhelm of Prussia accompanied his army against France, took part in the operational decisions of that campaign, and stood on the heights above Sedan while Krupp cannon blasted the French army (itself accompanied by Emperor Napoleon III) into ignominious submission. But among the emerging liberal states, a sizeable gap emerged between governmental and military institutions; and regardless of the nature of the regime, the apparatus of strategic planning steadily expanded as the size and complexity of the modern state created a host of governmental bodies and committees to analyze the strategic environment. One has only to compare the process of making strategy in 1864, when Lincoln, Stanton, and Grant bent over maps in the White House, to what happened only eighty years later, when Roosevelt, the Joint Chiefs of Staff, various intelligence committees, and theater commanders all had their hand in stirring the strategic soup. Roosevelt was undoubtedly as much in control of American strategy in 1944 as was Lincoln in 1864, but the structure of government and its ability to provide carefully considered advice had undergone a revolution.

The expansion of bureaucratic influences has greatly affected strategic decision-making, especially as competing agencies and armed services seek to impose their own parochial interests upon the making of strategy. In the United States, the clash between "massive retaliation" and "flexible response" during the late 1950s reflected as much the budgetary rivalry of the air force and army as it did measured consideration of the most effective approach to national security requirements. Each of the armed forces has already begun to characterize the new post-Cold War environment in ways that will increase, or at least maintain, its traditional share of the fiscal pie.

Making strategy

All of the influences described above go into the making of national strategies. It is a process, as suggested, that involves internal political influences and idiosyncracies of individual behavior as well as the pressure of external events and threats. In discussing the outbreak of World War I, Winston Churchill suggested some of the ambiguities involved in the making of strategic policy:

One rises from the study of the causes of the Great War with a prevailing sense of the defective control of individuals upon world fortunes. It has been well said, "there is always more error than design in human affairs." The limited minds of the ablest men, their disputed authority, the climate of opinion in which they dwell, their transient and partial contributions to the mighty problem, that problem itself so far beyond their compass, so vast in scale and detail, so changing in its aspects – all this must surely be considered before the complete condemnation of the vanquished or the complete acquittal of the victor can be pronounced. Events . . . got on to certain lines, and no one could get them off again. Germany clanked obstinately, recklessly, awkwardly towards the crater and dragged us all in with her.[41]

In the modern era, a comparison of Britain and Germany in the 1930s suggests how extraordinarily differently these processes function from one government to the next. In Britain, a carefully orchestrated and organized system of committees beginning with the Cabinet and working its way down through layers of bureaucracy – the Committee of Imperial Defence (CID), the Foreign Policy Committee, the Chiefs of Staff Committee, the Joint Planning Committee, and the Joint Intelligence Committee – carefully weighed and evaluated every aspect of Britain's strategic situation. The whole process insured careful calculation, thorough analysis, and serious debate over strategic issues at every level of the British government. The various bodies produced strategic surveys that are models of bureaucratic rigor and analysis, in every sense superior products within the limitations of bureaucratic life.

In stark comparison, an almost complete absence of process marked the Nazi system, as it had the preceding Weimar and Wilhelmine regimes. The bureaucracy remained largely uncoordinated; military and civilian leaders hardly ever discussed basic strategic issues; and no process of assessment analyzed the broader economic and political aspects of strategic questions. This lack of system was fully in accord with Hitler's principles of government. And the result left the strategic decision-making process almost entirely under the control, and within the mind, of the Führer.

Yet there is considerable irony in this comparison, for the well-ordered, careful processes of British bureaucracy largely failed in the 1930s to come to grips with the threat that Nazi Germany posed to Britain's survival. Moreover, British assessments displayed a penchant for wild swings in evaluation. Up to 1935 they tended to minimize the threat; then from June 1936 through 1938 they wildly overestimated German capabilities, inflating them far beyond the rather meager successes of Nazi rearmament to date. But in 1939 the evaluation process once again downgraded the German military threat precisely at the moment when the Wehrmacht's military capabilities were finally beginning to realize the potential of the immense resources that Hitler had lavished on it. In the broadest sense, the British failure lay in the inability

[41] Winston S. Churchill, *The World Crisis* (Toronto, 1931), p. 6.

of its bureaucracy to assess the ideological and strategic threat posed by Hitler's final goals. Failure to understand Nazi intentions, which were thoroughly revolutionary in nature, led to a failure to respond effectively to Hitler's actions in 1938 and 1939.

Hitler, using intuition rather than any recognizable system of strategic analysis, in contrast, largely read the situation correctly. He understood what his critics did not: that the British and French leaders and population had little stomach for another great war. This insight allowed him to achieve an extraordinary diplomatic and strategic victory in 1938, although he had nearly pushed his nation into a war that it stood no chance of winning and would have lost more quickly and at far less cost to the world than the war that occurred in 1939.[42]

After Churchill succeeded Chamberlain as prime minister in 1940, the British system of analysis received direction from above, an ability to *judge* the products of the bureaucracy, which it had simply never possessed in the 1930s. It was this system that the Americans largely copied in World War II and generally employed to great effect in the Cold War period. If the American system had some quirks – namely, an independent legislature – that made it function in a less efficient fashion, at least a willingness *existed* to grapple systematically with strategic issues. That had never been the case in Germany, and the German defeat in World War II reflected not only the idiosyncracies of Hitler's *Weltanschauung* but the inability of the German bureaucracy to understand – much less analyze – strategic problems.

Conclusion

Several general points about the making of strategy bear repeating. The first is that those involved, whether statesmen or military leaders, live in a world of incomplete information. They do not know, in most cases, the strategic intentions and purposes of other powers, except in the most general sense, and their knowledge of their own side is often deficient. Second, circumstances often force them to work under the most intense pressures. When a crisis occurs they have little time for reflection. As a result they often focus on narrow issues without looking at large long-term choices; in other words, they will see some of the trees but miss the forest. Few can express their ideas in a logical or thorough fashion, either on paper or face to face. Most merely react to events rather than mold them to their purposes. Like politics, strategy is the art of the possible; but few can discern what is possible. And neither history nor – consequently – strategy has ended with the end of the Cold War. Great storms bring not calm, but rather new struggle between rulers, states, alliances, peoples, and cultures.

---

[42] See Murray, *Change in the European Balance of Power*, Chapter VII.

The essays that follow range across nearly two and a half millennia of human experience. Across such an expanse it is impossible to deal with every significant period and polity; the authors were necessarily forced to choose. The aim, however, was not to provide a comprehensive guide to the making of strategy at all times and places, but rather to show how the factors identified here – geography, history, culture, economics, and governmental systems – have always profoundly affected the strategic process. If these essays succeed in that task, they will have achieved their purpose.

2

Athenian strategy in the Peloponnesian War

DONALD KAGAN

In the last quarter of the fifth century B.C. (431–404) the Athenians and their allies fought a terrible and devastating war, at first against the Spartans and their allies, chiefly from the Peloponnesus, but ultimately also against many of their own rebellious allies and the almost unlimited financial resources of the Persian Empire of the Achaemenids as well. It was the "Peloponnesian War" from the point of view of the Athenians; the Spartans presumably considered it the "Athenian War." But like so much of Greek history we see it from the Athenian perspective. Most of what we know about the war comes from Thucydides the son of Olorus, an Athenian contemporary who served as a general in 424 and was condemned and sent into exile for the rest of the war when a city for which he had partial responsibility fell to the enemy. His personal calamity was a boon to posterity, for his exile enabled him to travel about the Greek world and to talk with participants on both sides. The result was a history of unusual even-handedness and great profundity.

From the perspective of the fifth-century Greeks, the Peloponnesian War seemed as much a world war as the great war of 1914–1918 seemed to the Europeans of the time. Thucydides tells us that he began his history as the war began,

> in the belief that it would be great and noteworthy above all the wars that had gone before, inferring this from the fact that both powers were then at their best in preparedness for war in every way, and seeing the rest of the Hellenic people taking sides with one side or the other, some at once, others planning to do so. For this was the greatest upheaval that had ever shaken the Hellenes,

This essay is based on my four-volume history of the war published by the Cornell University Press between 1969 and 1987. Parts of it are adapted from sections of that history, and sometimes passages are used without alteration.

extending also to some part of the barbarians, one might say even to a very large part of mankind.[1]

The war was a terrible turning point in Greek history, causing enormous destruction of life and property, intensifying factional and class hostility, dividing the Greek states and unsettling their relationships with one another, and ultimately weakening their capacity to resist conquest from outside.

Despite great misfortunes, errors of their own making, and the vast array of enemies gathered against them, the Athenians came remarkably close on several occasions to winning the war, or at least emerging with their independence and power intact. Nor was their final defeat inevitable. Thucydides indeed emphasizes how difficult they were to bring down:

> Even after their defeat in Sicily, where they lost most of their fleet as well as the rest of their force, and faction had already broken out in Athens, they nevertheless held out for ten more years, not only against their previous enemies and the Sicilians who joined them and most of their allies, who rebelled against them, but also later against Cyrus, son of the Great King [of Persia], who provided money to the Peloponnesians for a navy. Nor did they give in before they destroyed themselves by falling upon one another because of private quarrels.[2]

What kind of state fought so hard yet lost the greatest war in the history of ancient Greece?

To understand the situation and character of the Athenian state, it is useful to think of it as the "Athenian Imperial Democracy," with significance connected to each part of the designation. Athens had a unique history that helped shape its character long before it became a democracy and acquired an empire. It was the chief town of the region known as Attica, a small triangular peninsula extending southeastward from central Greece. Attica has an area of about 1,000 square miles, but much of it is mountainous and rocky and unavailable for cultivation. The rest was hardly first-rate farmland; early Attica was relatively poor even by Greek standards. This proved a blessing when invaders from the north swept down and occupied the more attractive lands of the Peloponnesus, but regarded Attica as not worth the trouble of conquest. The Spartan conquerors of the richer lands of the southern Peloponnesus enslaved the far more numerous natives, whom they called helots, and lived off their labors without working the soil themselves. But they paid a price: their state became a single-minded military academy and armed camp, isolated, suspicious of contact with the outside, and ever-fearful of a helot uprising. The Athenians, on the other hand, claimed to be autochthonous, to have sprung from their own soil and to have lived in the same place since before the birth of the moon. They were free to go their way without the burden of oppressing a discontented underclass.

---

[1] 1.1.2. References are to Thucydides unless otherwise indicated.
[2] 2.65.12–13.

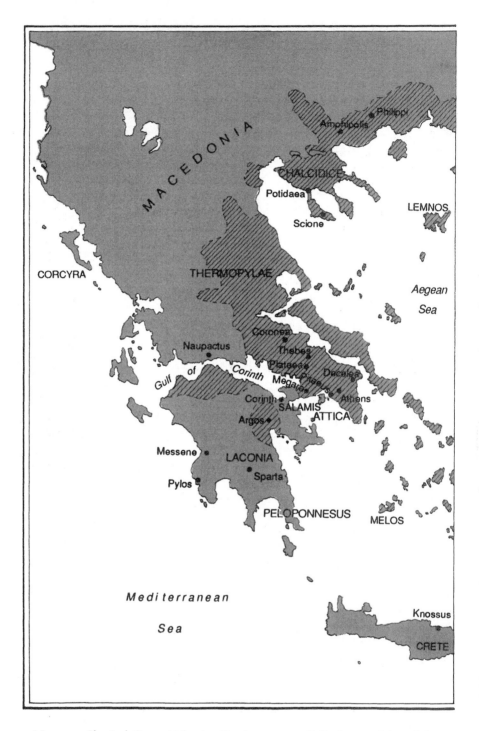

Map 2.1. Classical Greece/Athenian Empire, ca. 450 B.C. *Source.* Adapted from Kagan, Ozment, and Turner, *The Western Heritage,* Volume A: To 1527, Fourth Edition (New York: Macmillan, 1991), 76, 79.

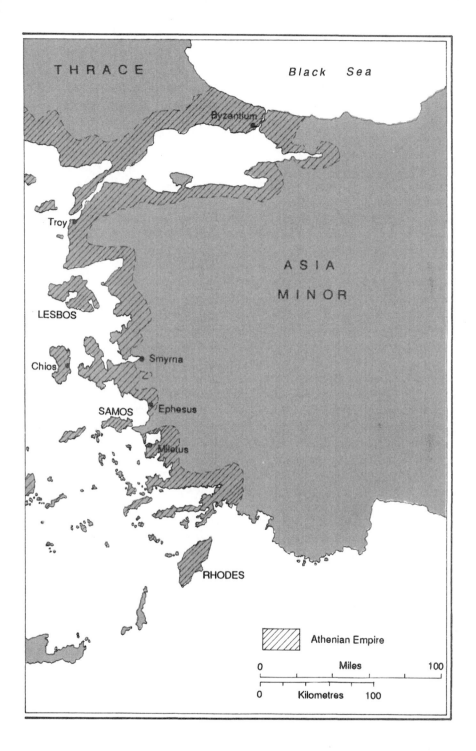

THRACE

Black Sea

Byzantium

Troy

ASIA

MINOR

LESBOS

Chios

Smyrna

SAMOS

Ephesus

Miletus

RHODES

Athenian Empire

0   Miles   100

0   Kilometres   100

Another secret of the rise of Athens was the early unification of the region under Athenian control. Unlike the Thebans who constantly fought for control of Boeotia on the northern frontier of Attica, the Athenians did not become entangled in quarrels and wars with neighboring towns. All the communities of Attica were part of the Athenian city-state, and all their free, native-born inhabitants were Athenian citizens on an equal basis. The absence of intense pressures, internal and external, may help explain Athens' relatively easy-going, nonviolent early history and its emergence in the fifth century as the first democracy in the history of the world. By mid-century, the democratic constitution had basically reached the completion of its development toward the full and direct participation of all adult male citizens in their own government.

The sovereign in Athens was the assembly (*ekklesia*), which made all decisions on policy – foreign and domestic, military and civil. It met no fewer than forty times a year in the open air, overlooking the marketplace and beside the Acropolis. All male citizens were eligible to attend, vote, make proposals, and debate. At the start of the war, about 40,000 Athenians were eligible, but attendance at the assembly rarely exceeded 6,000. This was the body that approved treaties of peace and declarations of war. All strategic decisions were first proposed, discussed, and debated in the open before thousands of people, a majority of whom had to approve every detail of every action. For any expedition, the assembly voted on its target and purpose, the number and specific nature of ships and men, the funds to be spent, the commanders to lead the forces, and the specific instructions to those commanders.

The most important offices in the Athenian state, among the few filled by election rather than by lottery, were those of the ten generals (*strategoi*). Because they commanded divisions of the Athenian army and fleets of ships in battle, they had to be military men; because they needed to secure election for a one-year term with the possibility of reelection without limit, they had to be politicians. In the fifth century, most generals had skills in both areas, although some were stronger in one respect than the other. Although these men could and did impose military discipline while on campaign, they were not very powerful in the city. At least ten times a year, they faced a formal opportunity for complaint against their conduct in office, and at the end of their term they had to make a full accounting of their behavior in office, both military and financial. On each occasion, they were subject to trial if accused of misconduct, and liable to serious punishment if convicted. Thucydides was not alone in suffering harsh treatment from a dissatisfied people.

The ten generals together did not make up a cabinet or a government; the assembly was the government. Sometimes, however, a general would gain so much political support and influence as to become the leader of the Athenians in fact, if not in law. Cimon attained such stature for the seventeen years between 479 and 462, when he appears to have been general each year, to have led every important expedition, and to have persuaded the Athenian assembly to support his policies at home and abroad. After Cimon's departure, Pericles achieved similar success over an even longer period. For three decades before the war, he seems to have been a general each year, to have assisted the election of some of his associates, to have conducted those campaigns he thought necessary, and to have gained the support of the Athenians for his domestic and foreign policies. It is important to note, however, that he never had any greater formal powers than the other generals and never tried to alter the democratic constitution. He was still subject to the scrutiny provided for in the constitution and required a vote in the open and uncontrolled assembly to take any action. He did not always get what he wanted and, on some occasions, his enemies persuaded the assembly to act against his wishes, but Thucydides' description of the Athenian government on the eve of the war was that it was a democracy led by its first citizen. Pericles was influential not because of any hidden power or the control of armed force, for he had none. The Athenians followed his lead because of his reputation for intelligence, wisdom, ability, honesty, and patriotism, because of his remarkable talents as a public speaker, and because of the success and popularity of his policies and leadership. Thucydides introduces him into his history as "Pericles son of Xanthippus, the leading man in Athens at that time and the ablest in speech and in action."[3] Thucydides went too far in saying that Athens in Pericles' time, though a democracy in name, was becoming the rule of the first citizen.[4] In fact, it always remained a thoroughgoing democracy in every respect. But in the crisis leading to war, in the adoption of a strategy to fight it, and into the second year of its conduct, the Athenians invariably followed the advice of their great leader.

The power and prosperity of the Athenian democracy depended on its command of its great maritime empire, centered on the Aegean Sea, the islands in it, and the cities along its coast. Beginning as the Delian League, a voluntary alliance of Greek states that invited Athens to take the lead in continuing the war of liberation and vengeance against Persia, it gradually became an empire under Athenian command functioning chiefly for the advantage of Athens. Over the years, almost all the members gave up their own fleets and chose to make a money payment into the common treasury instead of contributing their own ships and men. The Athenians used the money to increase the number of their own ships and to pay the rowers to stay at their oars for eight months each year, so that the Athenian navy became by far the biggest and best fleet ever known. The imperial revenue provided a considerable surplus beyond the needs of the navy, and the Athenians used it for their own purposes, including the great building program that beautified and glorified their city and gave work to its people. It also

---

[3] I.139.4.
[4] 2.65.7.

allowed them to accumulate a large reserve fund. The navy protected the ships of their merchants in their prosperous trade around the Mediterranean and beyond. It also gave the Athenians access to the wheat fields of the Ukraine and the fish of the Black Sea with which they could supplement their inadequate home food supply and even replace it totally, using imperial money if forced to abandon their own fields because of war. Once they completed the walls that surrounded their city and connected it to the fortified port at Piraeus, as they did in mid-century, the Athenians were invulnerable. They could choose a strategy unavailable to any Greek state, then or before. They could avoid all major land battles against a numerically and tactically superior enemy, stand behind their walls, leave their lands undefended, and maintain themselves indefinitely while striking the enemy from the sea. Pericles persuaded the Athenians to employ this plan when they entered the Peloponnesian War.

To understand Pericles' goals and the strategy that he chose to achieve them, we need to examine the origins of the war. Between 461 and 445, with lapses and interruptions, the Athenians fought a war against the Spartans and their Peloponnesian allies that modern scholars call the First Peloponnesian War. For a good part of that period, the Athenians had control of territory on the mainland that extended from central Greece to the Isthmus of Corinth. While they held it, they could bottle up the Spartans in the Peloponnesus, interrupt the trade of Sparta's allies, especially its chief naval ally, Corinth, and themselves remain protected from attack from any direction. Rebellions in this Athenian land empire, however, opened the road into Attica to the Peloponnesian army, and Pericles was able to avoid a major land battle only by negotiating the Thirty Years' Peace. That peace was quite satisfactory to Pericles and most Athenians, for it recognized the Athenian Empire and divided the Greek world into two spheres of influence, the Athenians controlling the Aegean and the Spartans the mainland. A unique clause in the treaty guaranteed a serious effort at "peaceful coexistence" by providing for compulsory arbitration in case of future disagreements. Pericles' long-range goal was to maintain this peace.

The great war came, very much against Pericles' wishes, when Corinth attacked the neutral island of Corcyra (modern Corfù), and the Corcyraeans asked the Athenians to join them in an alliance against Corinth. The treaty specifically permitted neutrals to join either side, but an alliance with Corcyra against Corinth posed obvious problems. The knowledge that Corinth and Corcyra had the only other sizeable fleets in Greece persuaded Pericles and the Athenians to accept. If the Corinthian and Corcyraean fleets united under a hostile command, the combined force could challenge Athens' control of the sea and therefore its security. The Spartans were not eager to go to war, for they knew that the Athenians had not formally broken the peace, and they were reluctant to be drawn into a major war over quarrels that did not concern them directly. Pericles counted on the Spartans to be sensible and understand that Athens had no designs on them or their allies but was acting defensively. As the crisis wore on, the Corinthians convinced the Spartans that Athens was expansionist by nature and represented a permanent danger and that as a result they must destroy the Athenian empire.

Pericles did not want war, yet he took a number of actions that angered and frightened the Peloponnesians and helped the advocates of war carry the day in Sparta. He supported the Athenian alliance with Corcyra and interfered with the autonomy of Potidaea, an Athenian ally, fearing that it might rebel because of its traditionally close relationship with Corinth. Both actions angered Corinth. He imposed an embargo on Megarian trade with Athens and its empire to punish Megara for helping Corinth against Corcyra and to deter other Peloponnesian states from becoming involved in the quarrel. The angry Megarians joined the chorus of those demanding that Sparta lead the Peloponnesians against Athens. Pericles rejected all Spartan demands and insisted on the letter of the treaty, the submission of all differences to binding arbitration. The Spartans never asked Athens to break off the treaty with Corcyra; at one point they even offered peace if the Athenians would only withdraw the Megarian decree. The decree had no intrinsic importance to Athens, and many Athenians wanted to accept the Spartan offer. Why did Pericles refuse? What threat made him willing to fight an unwelcome war over "a scrap of paper" rather than yield?

Pericles knew that the Spartans had accepted the existence of the Athenian Empire with the greatest reluctance. From its earliest days, a faction in Sparta had resented Athenian power and wanted to destroy it. Normally, this aggressive faction was in the minority, but from time to time, especially when circumstances made Athens seem vulnerable, it used Athenian actions, however innocent in intention, to frighten the Spartan majority into war. It had succeeded on two previous occasions in the last thirty years, and had come close once. For Pericles, the Thirty Years' Peace, especially its arbitration clause, provided a way to prevent a repetition of the threat. Throughout the crisis, however, the Spartans ignored their treaty obligations:

> It has long been clear that the Spartans are plotting against us, and it is even clearer now. The treaty states that differences between us must be submitted to arbitration . . . but they have never themselves asked for arbitration and do not accept it now that we offer it. They want to resolve their complaints by war instead of by discussion, and now they are here, no longer requesting, but already demanding.[5]

That was what troubled Pericles. If the Athenians accepted Spartan demands under threat of force, they would set their city back a half century to a time when Sparta was the unique and unquestioned leader of the Greeks. Athenian power and independence would be at the mercy of the fluctuations of Spartan politics. The Thirty Years' peace guaranteed Athenian equality

---

[5] 1.140.2.

with Sparta and the division of Greece into spheres of influence. That arrangement rested on the principle of mutual noninterference and provided carefully for relations with neutral states and, most importantly, for the arbitration of differences. If the Athenians gave way to the threat of war now, they would abandon their claim to equality and open themselves up to blackmail whenever the Spartans chose. Pericles therefore refused to rescind the Megarian decree. This is how he explained his views to the Athenians:

> Let none of you think that you are going to war over a trifle if we do not rescind the Megarian decree, whose withdrawal they hold out especially as a way of avoiding war, and do not reproach yourselves with second thoughts that you have gone to war for a small thing. For this "trifle" contains the affirmation and the test of your resolution. If you yield to them you will immediately be required to make another concession which will be greater, since you will have made the first concession out of fear.[6]

This was a classic rationale for rejecting appeasement, and admirable in its courage and resolution. But were Pericles' fears justified? In terms of the immediate crisis, no. The specific grievances between Athens and Sparta were not intrinsically important. On the one hand, had the Athenians withdrawn the Megarian decree the crisis would presumably have passed without war. But on the other, Pericles was right about the persistence of an implacably hostile faction in Sparta. Had Athens made the required concession, it might have calmed the fears of the normally cautious and pacific majority for a time, but it might also have led to a harder Spartan line in future conflicts. Pericles believed that he had discovered the one strategy that could guarantee success and convince the Spartans to abandon threats and war. He was certainly right in believing that he was the only one who could persuade the Athenians to adopt it and execute it. He refused to yield, in large part, because of the unique opportunity to set the Athenian Empire and Spartan-Athenian relations on a permanent and sound basis. The availability of such an apparently promising strategy may have helped bring on the war.

Pericles, convinced that the Spartan decision to fight was an aberration, adopted a strategy meant to persuade the Spartans of their mistake and to restore peace on the basis of the status quo ante. He envisaged a world in which the Athenians and the Spartans, each realizing that they had no way of imposing their will on the other, would respect the integrity of the other.

A successful strategy must rest on a clear understanding of the aims of a war and an accurate assessment of the resources available to both sides. It must seek to employ one's own strength against the enemy's weakness, make use of the experiences of the past, and adjust to changes in conditions, both material and psychological. Sound strategy insures in advance that if the first expectations meet with disappointment, an alternate plan is ready. Rarely, however, have states or statesmen embarked upon war in such a fashion.

---

[6] 1.140.5.

Pericles' strategy did not aim to defeat the Spartans in battle, only to convince them that war with Athens was futile. His strategic goals, therefore, were entirely defensive. He told the Athenians that if they "would remain quiet, take care of their fleet, refrain from trying to extend their empire in wartime and thus putting their city in danger, they would prevail."[7] The practical plan to achieve Pericles' goals went as follows: the Athenians were to reject battle on land, abandon their fields and homes in the country to Spartan devastation, and retreat behind their walls. Meanwhile, their navy would launch a series of commando raids on the coast of the Peloponnesus. This strategy would continue until the frustrated enemy agreed to make peace. Pericles meant the naval raids and landings to annoy and to suggest how much damage the Athenians could do if they chose. The strategy was not to exhaust the Peloponnesians physically or materially, but psychologically. Pericles meant to convince the Spartans, the primary enemy, that they could not win a war against Athens. A modern scholar puts it well:

> [Pericles] must first prove that the existence of Athens and of the Athenian Empire could not be destroyed and then that Athens, too, could harm her enemies. . . . It was a reasonable calculation that the nerve and will-power of her opponents might well be exhausted before the treasures on the Acropolis, and that they might admit that the power and determination of Athens were invincible.[8]

No Greek state had ever attempted such a strategy, for no state before the coming of the Athenian imperial democracy ever had the means to try it. The Athenians were in a position to use such an approach in the latter part of the First Peloponnesian War but did not do so, perhaps because Pericles was not yet politically secure enough to persuade the assembly. His task was not easy, for this unprecedented strategy ran directly against the grain of Greek tradition. The most powerful force in the shaping of Greek culture was the epic tradition represented in Homer's Iliad and Odyssey. Centuries of poetry, tales, wars, and athletic contests reinforced this tradition, which placed bravery in warfare at the summit of Greek virtues. By the seventh century, the hoplite phalanx, a closely ordered and highly disciplined block of heavily armed infantrymen, had become the main military force of the Greeks. It depended on the discipline, courage, and fighting spirit of the ordinary citizen. Willingness to fight, bravery, and steadfastness in battle became the essential characteristics of the free man and the citizen. Pericles' strategy of passivity, therefore, ran directly counter to Greek tradition.

Most Athenians, moreover, were farmers whose lands and homes were outside the walls. The Periclean strategy required them to look on while the Spartans destroyed their houses, crops, vines, and olive trees. In the face of

---

[7] 2.65.7.
[8] F.E. Adcock, "The Archidamian War, 431–421 B.C.," *Cambridge Ancient History*, Vol. 5 (Cambridge, 1940), p. 195.

these facts, as well as the power of tradition and its cultural values, it is hard to understand, even in retrospect, how Pericles convinced the Athenians to adopt his strategy. Part of the explanation lies in the uniquely powerful political position he had achieved by 431. No formal constitutional changes had occurred for twenty years, but Pericles' talents, his continuity in office, and his success in defeating challengers gave him unprecedented influence. In 443, he drove the leader of the chief opposition faction into exile, and in the years that followed no effective organized political group challenged him. Pericles was probably the only man with the imagination to conceive a plan that ran counter to such deep and strong prejudices and certainly the only one with the ability to put it into effect. For such deeds, Hans Delbrück awards him a place "among the greatest generals in world history." His greatness lay in conceiving the plan, implementing it decisively by yielding all of Attica instead of taking half measures, but most of all, in putting the plan through a democratic assembly and insuring its implementation by the force of his personality: "The fulfillment of this decision is an act of generalship that may be placed on a level with any victory."[9]

Pericles had reason to believe that his proposed strategy was the best one available and that Athenian resources were adequate to make it succeed. Meeting the enemy on land would have been foolish, if for no other reason than the Peloponnesians' great advantage in numbers. At the beginning of the war, the Athenians could field an army of 13,000 infantrymen of an age and condition to fight a pitched battle and had another 16,000 able to man the border forts and the walls surrounding and connecting Athens and Piraeus.[10] Plutarch tells us that the army that invaded Attica in 431 numbered 60,000.[11] He undoubtedly inflated that number, but Pericles himself admitted just before the war that in a single battle the Spartans and their allies were a match for all the other Greeks put together.[12] Recent history, moreover, had shown that intelligent Athenians recognized the relative weakness of their army. During the First Peloponnesian War, they had fought bravely but lost the Battle of Tanagra in 457, despite the advantage of superior numbers, and they had suffered heavy casualties. When the Peloponnesian army invaded Attica in 446, the Athenians had made a truce and abandoned their land empire rather than fight. That memory must have helped the anti-Athenian party in Sparta convince their fellow citizens to declare war again. If they invaded Attica during the growing season, the Athenians would never hide behind their walls and allow the Spartans to ravage their land and homes. Either they would yield without a battle, as they had in 446, or they

---

[9]   Hans Delbrück, *Geschichte der Kriegskunst*, Vol. 1, *Das Altertum*, (Berlin, 1920, reprinted 1964), pp. 125–26.

[10]   2.13.6–7.

[11]   *Pericles* 33.4.

[12]   1.141.6.

would come out to fight and be destroyed. In either case the war would be short and victory certain.

Pericles went to war to prove the Spartan "hawks" wrong. He made this point quite clear to the Athenians, saying: "If I thought I could persuade you I would urge you to go out and devastate your own property to show the Peloponnesians that you will not take orders from them to save it."[13] He believed that once the Spartans saw the Athenians' willingness to make the necessary sacrifices, avoid land battles, and follow his unprecedented strategy, they would also see the futility of war against Athens and negotiate a peace. The resulting agreement, though no different in substance from the Thirty Years' Peace, would be secure and lasting, because the Spartans would have recognized Athenian invincibility.

To carry out his strategy, Pericles had resources that surpassed those of any previous Greek state and dwarfed those of his opponents. Apart from the subject-states of their empire, which supplied money payments and rowers for the fleet, the Athenians had a number of free allies who provided their own warships and crews, as well as some infantry, cavalry, and money. The power and hopes of Athens rested on its magnificent navy. In its dockyards lay at least 300 seaworthy warships as well as some others that the Athenians could repair and use in case of need. Athens' free allies – Lesbos, Chios, and Corcyra – could also provide ships, perhaps over 100 in all. Against this armada, the Peloponnesians could send about 100 ships, but the skill and experience of their crews were no match for the Athenians, as the first decade of the war proved repeatedly.

Pericles knew that the key to naval warfare, and therefore to his strategy, was money to build and maintain the ships and to pay their crews. Here, too, Athens held a vast advantage. In 431, the annual income of Athens was 1,000 talents, of which 400 came from internal revenue and 600 from tribute and other imperial sources.[14] Although about 600 talents was available for the cost of the war each year, that amount was not enough to sustain the Periclean plan. The Athenians would need to dip into their substantial capital. At the beginning of the war, the Athenians had 6,000 talents of coined silver in the treasury, another 500 in uncoined gold and silver, and 40 talents worth of gold plates on the statue of Athena on the Acropolis that they could remove and melt down in an emergency.[15] The Peloponnesians could not match this extraordinary wealth. The Spartan king spoke for most when he said, "we have no money in the public treasury nor can we easily raise money by taxation." The Corinthians were better off than the others, but they had

---

[13] 1.143.5.
[14] A talent represented a specified weight in silver. It is impossible to give a modern monetary equivalent, but it may be helpful to know that one talent was the cost of paying the crew of a warship for a month, that there were 6000 drachmas in a talent, and that one drachma was a good day's pay for a skilled craftsman in Athens.
[15] 2.13.4–5.

no reserve fund, and Pericles justifiably told the Athenians that "the Peloponnesians have no money, either public or private."[16]

Even the wisest and best-prepared strategy is not likely to succeed unless those who employ it carry out its design faithfully. Pericles' great challenge, as Delbrück pointed out, was to get the Athenians to follow the plan. The first Peloponnesian invasion was purposefully leisurely, in the hope that the Athenians would regain their senses and yield before seeing their lands destroyed. So long as the invaders pushed no further than they had come in 446, the Athenians held back, thinking the enemy might turn away, as before. But when they came close to the city, visibly laying waste to the land, the Athenians could no longer bear it. Thucydides describes their reaction:

> Naturally, it seemed to them terrible to see their land ravaged in full view. The young men had never seen such a thing, and the older men not since the Persian War. It was the general opinion, and especially among the younger men, that they should not stand about and watch but go out and put a stop to it. . . . The city was irritated in every way, and they were angry with Pericles. They completely forgot the warnings he had given them in advance, abused him for being a cowardly general who would not lead them out to battle, and held him responsible for all their troubles.[17]

The leader of his bellicose opponents was Cleon, a politician who had criticized Pericles for some time and would emerge as the leader of the Athenian "hawks" after his death. The comic poet Hermippus gives us an idea of the tone of these attacks in a play probably performed in spring 430 that addressed Pericles as follows: "King of the Satyrs, why won't you ever lift a spear but instead use only dreadful words to wage the war, assuming the character of the cowardly Teles. But if a little knife is sharpened on a whetstone you roar as though bitten by the fierce Cleon."[18]

It is a tribute to Pericles' courage and determination that he held fast to his policy in the face of such pressure, and proof of his extraordinary influence and leadership that he managed to prevent the Athenians from abandoning it at once. All male Athenian citizens of military age participated in both civilian and military decision-making; the modern distinction between civilian and military authority did not then exist in Athens. This sometimes had disadvantages, but the two-sided character of the office of general assisted Pericles' efforts to maintain his chosen strategy despite the instinctive reaction against it. Thucydides describes the scene:

> Pericles saw that they were very angry at the situation in which they found themselves and that their thinking was not at its best. He was confident that his decision not to go out and fight was correct, so he prevented the calling of an assembly or any other meeting, fearing that if the people came together they

[16]   1.80.4; 1.141.3.
[17]   2.21.3.
[18]   Quoted by Plutarch in *Pericles* 33.4.

would make a mistake by acting out of anger instead of using their judgment. He watched over the city and kept it peaceful, so far as was possible.[19]

During a brief but intense, perhaps critical, period, normal political debate and discussion ceased. No law was passed; no emergency powers were granted to Pericles or to the board of generals as a whole. The assembly held regular meetings that did not depend on the actions of the generals, of whom Pericles was just one in ten, with no greater formal power than the others. How was he able to put politics aside long enough to protect his strategy?

The Spartan siege of Athens forms part of the answer, and strategic necessity gave the generals more power than usual. The citizens were under arms, guarding the walls; an assembly meant leaving the city walls undefended, and if the soldiers stayed at their posts the assembly would be peculiarly unrepresentative. These circumstances represented a good reason for canceling the regular meetings, and Pericles' personal influence – his unofficial but powerful position as recognized leader – would have done the rest. No doubt he prevailed on the other generals, some of whom were his political associates, to see the matter his way, and against their combined recommendation no official would have dared call the citizens to assembly. In Roman terms, Pericles achieved his purpose not by *imperium* but by *auctoritas*.

Pericles had selected a strategy, he had the political means to hold the people to it, and he seemed to have the resources to carry it out. So impressive a judge as Thucydides was certain that it was the right strategy and that it deserved to succeed:

> Pericles lived two years and six months after the beginning of the fighting, and after he died his foresight in regard to the war was acknowledged even more. He said that if the Athenians would remain quiet, take care of their fleet, refrain from trying to extend their empire in wartime and thus putting their city in danger, they would prevail. . . . Pericles had more than sufficient reasons at that time for his personal forecast that Athens would win through quite easily in the war against the Peloponnesians alone.[20]

Thucydides attributes the failure of the Periclean strategy to his successors, who "did everything contrary to his plan in every way."[21] But Pericles' strategy remained intact for two years after his death. Even more to the point, in retrospect we can see that it had already failed while he was alive. In the second year of the war the Athenians, against the opposition of Pericles, sent an embassy to Sparta to ask for terms of peace. We are not told what terms emerged, but evidently the Athenians thought them too harsh, for they rejected them and continued fighting. The fact remains, however, that the Spartans could have offered terms good enough for the Athenians to accept while falling short of what Pericles sought. By Pericles' definition, the offer-

---

[19] 2.22.1.
[20] 2.65.6–7; 13.
[21] 2.65.7.

ing and acceptance of any such terms would have meant the loss of the war. The very request for terms and the rejection of Pericles' counsel, moreover, shows that his fellow citizens took a negative view of his strategy. His persistence in it cost him his position of power and much more; in their disappointment and anger, the Athenians deposed Pericles from office, put him on trial, and imposed on him a heavy fine. All of these actions flowed from and were evidence of the failure of his strategy.

Why did the strategy fail? Part of the answer lies in an unforeseen and – given the state of medical knowledge at the time – unforeseeable disaster: the plague. In 430, the second year of the war, a terrible plague fell upon Athens. Nothing like it had ever occurred before, and modern scholars and physicians continue to debate its identity without agreement. With the entire population of Attica crowded into the walled area, the pestilence was especially deadly. Before running its course, it carried off one-third of the Athenian population. No doubt the plague did great harm to the Periclean strategy by weakening the will of the Athenians and encouraging the Peloponnesians to keep fighting. But after negotiations failed, the Athenians' will to fight held, and the Spartans gave no evidence that their determination ever weakened. Doomed from the start, the Periclean strategy was already unraveling before the outbreak of the plague.

To evaluate the plan, we need to know how long Pericles expected the Spartans to fight. Those who regard the outcome of the Archidamian War (431–421) as justification for his strategy do not generally raise this question, but they reason implicitly that a war of ten years was not outside his calculations. This notion rests, in part, on Pericles' speech to the Athenians on the eve of the war. The Peloponnesians, he says, "have had no experience with wars overseas or extended in time; they only wage brief wars against each other because of their poverty."[22] The great majority of the Peloponnesian soldiers, all but the Spartans themselves, farmed their own lands; they could not stay away long and had to bear the costs of an expedition from their own funds. Such men would risk their lives rather than their property, "for they are not sure that they won't use up their funds first, especially if the war lasts longer than they expected, which is quite likely."[23]

Pericles rightly argued that the Peloponnesians lacked the resources to launch the kind of campaign that would have endangered the Athenian Empire, but nothing prevented them from continuing to invade and devastate Attica every year. These invasions lasted no longer than a month, and the soldiers' food represented the only cost. The important question was, how long could the Athenian treasury hold out at the annual rate of expenditure required to sustain the Periclean strategy? Some idea of average annual cost is possible by examining the first year of the war, when Pericles was firmly in

---

[22]   1.142.3.
[23]   1.141.5–6.

control and his strategy applied to the letter. It was as unadventurous a year as any, and Athens was still in good fighting trim. When the Peloponnesians invaded Attica in 431, the Athenians sent 100 ships around the Peloponnesus. A squadron of thirty ships sailed to protect the crucial island of Euboea. Another seventy ships, already blockading Potidaea, brought the total to 200 Athenian ships in service for the year. A ship at sea cost a talent per month, and eight months was the usual period that ships remained at sea (although the blockade probably required the ships at Potidaea to stay the year round). These estimates would result in an expenditure of 1,600 talents for naval expenses. The forces on land required additional expenditure, with Potidaea consuming the greatest portion. No fewer than 3,000 infantry participated in the siege there, and sometimes more; a conservative average is 3,500. The soldiers received one drachma a day and one for a retainer each day, so that the daily cost of the army was at least 7,000 drachmas, or one talent and one-sixth. If we multiply this figure by 360, a round number for a year, we arrive at 420 talents. Other military costs certainly arose but simply the naval expenses and the cost of the troops at Potidaea required over 2,000 talents. Two other calculations, based on different kinds of data, supply a similar figure.[24]

Clearly, Pericles must have expected to spend about 2,000 talents a year to carry on the war. Three years of such a war, then, would cost 6,000 talents. In the second year of the war, the Athenians voted to set aside 1,000 talents from their reserves for use only "if the enemy should make a naval attack against the city and they should have to defend it," and assigned the death penalty to anyone who might propose using it for any other purpose.[25] A usable reserve fund of 5,000 remained; if we add three years of imperial revenue, 1,800, we get 6,800 talents. Pericles, therefore, could maintain his strategy for three years, but not for a fourth.

Pericles could calculate with much greater precision than can we; he could hardly have expected a war of ten years, much less the twenty-seven it ultimately lasted. He wanted to force a change of opinion in Sparta, the true decision-maker in the Peloponnesian League. That hope was not unreasonable in view of the reluctance with which the Spartans went to war in the first place, the long delay between their vote for war and their first action, their attempts to negotiate a peace in the interim, and the reluctance with which Sparta's king went to war.[26] To persuade the Spartans to consider peace required the assent of only three of the five annual officials in Sparta called ephors. To get them and the Spartan assembly to accept peace, the Athenians

---

[24] For these calculations and a fuller discussion of the cost of the war, see Donald Kagan, *The Archidamian War* (Ithaca and London, 1974), pp. 35–40.

[25] 2.24.1.

[26] These matters are discussed in Donald Kagan, *The Outbreak of the Peloponnesian War* (Ithaca and London, 1969). See especially, pp. 286–342.

needed merely to help restore the natural majority that kept Sparta inside the Peloponnesus most of the time.

In light of these facts, Pericles' plan seemed to make excellent sense. The Spartan King Archidamus had warned his people that they had mistaken expectations about the character of the coming war, that the Athenians would not fight a land battle and be defeated, and that the Spartans had no other strategy available at that time. They did not believe him. Pericles aimed to prove to the Spartans that their king had been right. His main tactical problem was the defensive one of restraining the Athenians and preventing them from offering battle in Attica. The offensive naval actions were deliberately unimpressive, intended only to demonstrate that a lengthy war would damage the Peloponnesians. Offensive actions would, in fact, conflict with the plan. Such actions, while unable to bring about victory, might enrage the enemy and prevent the reasonable policy of Archidamus from winning the upper hand. But a policy of restraint at home and abroad would likely bring the friends of peace to power in Sparta sooner or later.

Pericles might have expected such a change in Spartan opinion to come about quickly, possibly after one campaigning season. Perhaps it would take two years of similar actions, surely not more than three, for it would be unreasonable for Sparta to continue to beat its fist against the wall of the Athenian defensive strategy. The plan did not work. The first year brought signs of trouble. Sparta showed no signs of yielding, and Potidaea held out stubbornly, draining the Athenian treasury beyond expectation and dangerously cutting Pericles' margin for error. The next year the plague almost brought disaster. Even before it struck, Pericles had decided to increase the pressure with a major attack on the Peloponnesian city of Epidaurus. He had not changed strategy but merely intensified it to speed the education of the Peloponnesians. When Pericles died, he "left the defensive war as his testament."[27]

Pericles might not have adhered to the same strategy as the war dragged on and discredited his expectations. He was an intelligent and resourceful leader, and he might soon have seen what was necessary and done it. His error, though serious, was common. He expected the enemy to see reason when punished and when the futility of further fighting became clear. In our own time, the failures of strategies based on aerial bombardment, superior firepower, and naval supremacy have shown that the enemy does not always calculate rationally (by our standards of rationality) or suffer psychological collapse, but often becomes more determined as punishment continues or increases. When policymakers are not remote aristocratic professionals but citizens of a state, public opinion is a force, and passion and hatred of the enemy often obliterate rational considerations of self-interest. Sparta and

---

[27] M.H. Chambers, "Thucydides and Pericles," *Harvard Studies in Classical Philology* 62 (1957), p. 86.

Athens were preeminently such states. Small powers in our own century have held out beyond prudence against vastly superior enemies; in the war between Athens and Sparta, where the two sides were roughly equal, stubborn resistance and sacrifice were even more likely. The Periclean strategy failed on that account.

However one judges Pericles' strategy, his death in fall 429 left a terrible void. No towering figure stood ready and able to exercise the enormous influence he had held. "Those who followed him," said Thucydides, "were more equal with one another," and so not able to provide the unified, consistent leadership needed in war. The choices available to Athens in 429 were theoretically three: (1) to seek immediate peace; (2) to adopt a more aggressive strategy, running risks to try to defeat Sparta quickly; (3) to continue the policy of Pericles, avoiding risks, wearing down the Spartans, and working for a negotiated peace on the basis of the status quo ante bellum. Each view had adherents, but the failed negotiations of 430 had totally discredited the peace party. The Athenians were not willing to make peace on Sparta's terms if, in fact, the Spartans had offered any. It seems likely that the peace party was in disgrace, for no leader appeared willing to associate his name with its policy. Cleon led the aggressive faction, but unlike his competitors he had never been a general. His lack of experience as a military leader hampered his attempt to move Athens to a more aggressive strategy. Even more important, the still-raging plague and a depleted treasury further undermined Athens' military strength and morale. The leadership of the moderate faction fell to Nicias, a capable, experienced, cautious, and unimaginative general who clung tenaciously to the Periclean strategy, which held sway without deviation until 427.

Most generals elected in spring 427 continued to adhere to the old strategy, but the election of Demosthenes signaled that some Athenians wanted a change. The new man soon proved himself the most aggressive and imaginative Athenian general in the Archidamian War, the inventor and executor of campaigns that departed completely from the strategy of Pericles. But the shift to a new strategy was gradual and came only as circumstances forced it upon the Athenians. The old strategy had already produced a crisis in 428 when Mytilene, the major city of the island of Lesbos, an autonomous ally of Athens, launched a rebellion with Spartan and Boeotian support. This worst of Athenian nightmares, a revolt in the empire, required the dispatch of an expensive expedition to besiege the island just as the treasury neared exhaustion. To pay for the operation the Athenians imposed on themselves the first direct tax of the war, perhaps the first in their history. The siege lasted until 427, and to relieve it a Peloponnesian fleet entered the Aegean and reached the coast of Asia Minor. For a moment, the enemy penetration threatened to touch off rebellions throughout the empire. However, the Spartan commander, not up to the challenge, panicked at the approach of an Athenian fleet and abandoned Mytilene to its fate.

The episode nevertheless revealed the dangers of the original strategy. Four years of defensive warfare had worn down Athenian resources to the point where the Spartans were willing to risk a naval expedition in the Aegean. A greater Peloponnesian effort coupled with better leadership at this moment might have proven deadly for Athens. By summer 427, most of the ingredients that would produce Athenian defeat more than twenty years later were already at hand. Athens was short of money, part of its empire was in revolt, the undefended coastal cities of Asia Minor were ready to rebel, and Persia stood poised to join the war against Athens. The Spartans, as Thucydides said on a later occasion, were the most convenient of all people for the Athenians to fight.[28] The next time, however, they might find more courage and an abler leader.

In the same year, a civil war in Corcyra threatened Athenian control of that important ally. Failure to act was leading to dangerous defections and threats of collapse. That realization may help explain why the Athenians became more adventurous in 427. They sent the general Eurymedon with a fleet to help the friends of Athens at Corcyra and then to sail on to Sicily in answer to a request for help from Athenian allies there. Syracuse, the island's chief city, was a colony of Corinth and friendly to the Peloponnesian cause. Athens' allies feared a Syracusan attempt to gain control of the whole island, and the Athenians worried that their Peloponnesian enemies would benefit from Sicily's wealth and power.

In 426, even the cautious Nicias carried out punitive raids against the island of Melos, a Spartan colony that had helped the parent city financially, and Boeotia, whose forces had joined in the ravaging of Attica. Both expeditions represented mild escalations within the Periclean strategy. In the same year, Demosthenes took a small fleet around the Peloponnesus on what the Athenians must have intended as a similar mission: to assist the friends of Athens in western Greece and do as much damage to the enemy as was possible without risk. The allies northwest of the Gulf of Corinth urged an attack on the island of Leucas, a Corinthian colony strategically located on the route to Corcyra, Italy, and Sicily. Leucas was a sensible and obvious target, but with some persuasion, Demosthenes decided instead to defend the port at Naupactus by attacking the barbaric Aetolian tribes that threatened it. The Messenians of Naupactus were also allies, and their city was a valuable port on the gulf, but Demosthenes made his decision for other reasons. His bold imagination conceived a plan that might change the course of the war in one stroke. He would land on the north shore of the gulf, move rapidly eastward through Aetolia, gather allies in central Greece, and attack Boeotia from the rear. At the same time, an Athenian army would attack Boeotia's east coast. A variety of mishaps caused the plan to go awry, and Demosthenes found himself fighting a campaign in mountains and forests

[28] 8.96.5.

against natives who knew the territory. The Athenians lost 120 men in the fiasco, and Demosthenes chose to stay in Naupactus rather than face his angry countrymen at home.

Although modern scholars have often criticized him, perhaps unfairly, Demosthenes had good reason to fear an accounting for his actions. An analogy with a more famous military disaster, the Gallipoli campaign of 1915, and its equally famous author, Winston Churchill, helps illuminate the question. On that occasion, as in 426, a great war between powerful alliances had reached deadlock. Each side had tried its original strategy, and each side had failed. Unable to hit on a better idea, each had lapsed into a war of attrition. Churchill, dissatisfied with that situation, thought a better solution might be available. His thoughts seem appropriate to our problem:

> Nearly all the battles which are regarded as masterpieces of the military art, from which have been derived the foundation of states and the fame of commanders, have been battles of manoeuvre in which very often the enemy has found himself defeated by some novel expedient or device, some queer, swift, unexpected thrust or stratagem. In many such battles the losses of the victors have been small. There is required for the composition of a great commander not only massive common sense and reasoning power, not only imagination, but also an element of legerdemain, an original and sinister touch, which leaves the enemy puzzled as well as beaten. It is because military leaders are credited with gifts of this order which enable them to ensure victory and save slaughter that their profession is held in such high honor.[29]

At the strategic level, Churchill was such a leader. He conceived a plan to capture Constantinople, put Turkey out of the war, and so outflank the enemy. The plan failed not because of poor conception but because of poor execution. Had it succeeded, it might have shortened the war considerably, and at least it would have opened a route to Russia that might have kept that country in the war longer.

Was Demosthenes also such a leader? Was the Aetolian campaign the rash, imprudent blunder its critics claim, or was it a brilliant maneuver that would have left the enemy "puzzled as well as beaten"? The answers lie not merely in the failure of the plan. Churchill has set down the general principles that guided him in World War I. They seem helpful in analyzing the strategy of the Archidamian War as well:

1. The Decisive theatre is the theatre where a vital decision may be obtained at any given time. The main theatre is that in which the main armies or fleets are stationed. This is not at all times the Decisive theatre.

2. If the fronts or centres of armies cannot be broken, their flanks should be turned. If these flanks rest on the seas, the manoeuvres to turn them must be amphibious and dependent on sea power.

[29] Winston S. Churchill, *The World Crisis II, 1915* (London, 1923), p. 21.

3. The least-guarded strategic points should be selected for attack, not those most strongly guarded.
4. In any hostile combination, once it is certain that the strongest Power cannot be directly defeated itself, but cannot stand without the weakest, it is the weakest that should be attacked.
5. No offensive on land should be launched until an effective means – numbers, surprise, munitions, or mechanical devices – of carrying it through has been discovered.[30]

Let us test Demosthenes' Aetolian expedition against these principles:

1. No main armies were arrayed against each other in the field. For Sparta, the main theater was the soil of Attica; for Athens it was the territory of Sparta and its allies that the Athenians ravaged in the hope of wearing out the enemy's will to continue the war. Neither turned out to be the decisive theater.
2. There were, of course, no fronts to break through, but the main targets of each side had proven by 426 as invulnerable as the two armies entrenched across western Europe in 1915. The Aetolian campaign was amphibious, making use of the superior mobility of sea power to land an army at a vulnerable point.
3. The western border of Boeotia was a "least-guarded strategic point."
4. The Spartans were not susceptible to direct defeat; the Boeotians, though not the weakest of Sparta's allies, were certainly weaker than Sparta, especially in the west. Their defeat would have made it difficult, if not impossible, for Sparta to execute its annual invasions of Attica. Athenian control of central Greece would have prevented the Spartans from sending an army overland to disrupt the Athenian empire north of the Aegean, as they were able to do in 424. A successful attack on Boeotia would therefore remove every means available to Sparta for hurting Athens; the Spartans would recall Athenian successes in the First Peloponnesian War and be more inclined to negotiate a peace.
5. Demosthenes counted on surprise. He had every reason to think it would be effective. The Boeotians would never expect an attack from the seemingly safe west.

Demosthenes' plan was in fact brilliant, but he had conceived it hastily and executed it sloppily. The main problem was timing; the plan required speed for success, but that very speed prevented the careful preparation needed for a tricky, coordinated operation. Another problem was Demosthenes' unfamiliarity with the terrain and with the tactics of lightly armed guerrilla forces. He perhaps deserves blame for pushing ahead in the face of many uncertainties and even after things began to go wrong. But the legerdemain of which Churchill speaks is not the hallmark of cautious generals afraid to

[30] Ibid., p.50.

run risks, nor do states frequently win great wars without such generals. Finally, Demosthenes was risking very little, for Athens lost only 120 marines. Such a price, though regrettable, was not excessive in light of the great rewards victory would have brought. Demosthenes, moreover, was that rare soldier who could learn from his mistakes. He used what he had learned to good advantage in the future.

Demosthenes stayed at Naupactus when his term of office came to an end. The Messenians there still held him in high regard, despite his failure, and so did Athens' other allies north of the gulf. When the Spartans led a Peloponnesian army into that territory, Athens' Ambracian allies sent for Demosthenes, though now a private citizen, to lead them. Using a joint force of heavy infantry and lightly armed men and the tricks of fighting in wooded and mountainous country that he had learned, he laid a trap for the Peloponnesians, ambushed and routed them, and destroyed Spartan influence in the region.

Rehabilitated and elected general again in spring 425, Demosthenes launched a campaign that changed the course of the war. An Athenian fleet headed west to Corcyra and Sicily. With great difficulty, he persuaded its commanding generals to place him with a small force of soldiers and only five ships at Pylos, at the southwestern tip of the Peloponnesus, in Messenia. He must have noticed this place on previous voyages and asked his Messenian friends from Naupactus about it. It was naturally suited to his plan, which was to build a permanent base on the coast from which the Messenian enemies of Sparta could ravage Messenia and Laconia, receive their escaped helot countrymen, and even, perhaps, stir up a helot rebellion. The plan clearly departed from previous Athenian strategy, and the commanders of the fleet greeted it with scorn. They only agreed to put in to Pylos when a storm forced them; at the first opportunity they hurried on to Corcyra. Demosthenes built his little fort and waited. When the news reached the Spartans, they recalled the army from its annual invasion of Attica, brought back their fleet from Corcyra, and sent an army to attack the fort. Without a blow being struck, Demosthenes' novel action had already forced Sparta onto the defensive.

The Spartans soon found that the Athenian fort was strong and well located. To help with the assault, they landed a force on the island of Sphacteria, just south of Pylos, stretching across the mouth of the Bay of Navarino. This deployment proved to be a serious mistake, for the Athenian fleet, returning from Corcyra at Demosthenes' request, sailed into the harbor and defeated the Peloponnesian navy, imprisoning the Spartan force on Sphacteria. Inhabitants of the twentieth century, accustomed to casualty lists in the millions, may marvel that so tough a military state as Sparta would ask for peace merely to recover 420 prisoners, although at least 180 of them were Spartiates from the best families. But this number represented fully one-tenth of the Spartan army. In a state that practiced a strict code of eugenics, killing imperfect infants, whose separation of men from women during the most fertile years guaranteed effective birth control, whose code of honor demanded of its soldiers death rather than dishonor, and whose leading caste married only its own members, we may readily understand that concern for the safety of even 180 Spartiates was not merely sentimental but extremely practical.

It is impossible to exaggerate the stunning effect and importance of this naval victory. Once convinced that they could not rescue their men, the Spartans immediately asked for a truce while they sent envoys to Athens to negotiate a general peace. Thucydides ascribed the outcome of Demosthenes' plan chiefly to chance, but more than chance was involved. Demosthenes conceived and executed the entire campaign with a keen eye for the special opportunities offered at Pylos and Sphacteria. He could not have been confident that the Spartans would occupy Sphacteria and run the risk of encirclement. If the Athenians could occupy Pylos and damage and embarrass the Spartans by launching raids from it and receiving escaped helots, that would still distract them from their offensive operations, damage their prestige, and cause them concern. Yet one might imagine that they would find the Athenian occupation of a permanent base in Messenia unendurable. Initiative and daring provoke the enemy to make mistakes; a foe is much less likely to err when unchallenged and in possession of the initiative. And credit for the victory must go to the general who devised and executed the plan that forced the enemy to make a mistake.

The Spartans offered peace on the basis of the status quo, and most scholars believe that the Athenians should have accepted. They have deemed it a Periclean peace, but did the Spartan proposal deserve that title? Pericles' aims were largely psychological. He did not hope to render the Spartans incapable of making war on Athens but to make them unwilling to do so. He sought to convince them that they did not have the power to defeat Athens, but the tenor of their speech shows just the opposite. They blamed their troubles on a mistake, which they could reverse at any time. From the Periclean point of view, the Spartans had learned nothing useful. A peace that returned the Spartan prisoners in exchange for nothing but promises of good will for the future certainly raised the questions that one modern scholar has asked: "What guarantee would such a peace give that Sparta would not begin the war again at an opportune time? Was that a goal that would have been worth such a vast sacrifice? And would Athens, and especially, would its allies then be again in a position and be willing to make these sacrifices a second time?"[31]

Nicias nevertheless favored peace. Cleon opposed it, arguing that so long as they held the Spartan prisoners they could have peace whenever they wanted, and he insisted on a peace that would protect Attica from invasion.

[31] K.J. Beloch, *Die Attische Politik seit Perikles* (Leipzig, 1884), p. 23.

His terms included the surrender and removal to Athens of the Spartans on Sphacteria, and the forfeit of both of Megara's ports. The Spartans, of course, refused, and the Athenians followed Cleon's advice and rejected the Spartan offer.

When Nicias proved unable to capture the men on the island, Cleon took on the assignment and, in collaboration with the brilliant Demosthenes, forced the Spartans to surrender and brought the prisoners home in triumph. The victory at Pylos gave the Athenians the whip hand. So long as they held the prisoners, Attica was free from invasion, for they threatened to kill the hostages if a Spartan army entered Attica. The surrender of the prisoners, moreover, was a terrible shock to Spartan self-confidence and prestige. "In the eyes of the Greeks this was the most unexpected event in this war, for they believed that the Spartans would never hand over their arms because of starvation or any other compulsion but would hold on to them as long as they could and then die."[32] Cleon and his associates took advantage of the situation and tripled the imperial tribute, something that Athens could not have dared to do before. This revenue raised permitted the Athenians to continue fighting and even to strive for a decisive victory.

Pylos and Sphacteria finished the Periclean strategy. Cleon's and Demosthenes' definition of victory was not psychological, but tangible. They wanted to control Megara and Boeotia and thereby to recover the invulnerability Athens had enjoyed at the height of its power after it secured Boeotia in 457 when the Peloponnesians left the area following the victory at Tanagra.[33] In 424, Demosthenes conceived daring and innovative plans to achieve these objectives. They involved collaboration between opponents of the regime in the enemy cities and Athenian forces approaching under cover of surprise, and depended on careful coordination and timing. Both came close to success, but ultimately failed. The Megarian venture failed because a Peloponnesian army under the great Spartan general Brasidas happened to be in the neighborhood at the wrong time. Characteristically, Demosthenes' losses were light, despite his failure. The Boeotian venture misfired because the timing went wrong. Even then, the cost should have been low, but one of the Athenian generals, who could and should have avoided battle, fought instead at Delium and suffered a rout with heavy losses.

These reversals did great harm to Athens' new aggressive strategy, and Brasidas applied the coup de grace when he marched an army north to the Thracian region of the Athenian Empire and captured a number of imperial cities, especially the strategically critical town of Amphipolis. These misfortunes deflated the Athenians, and they agreed to a one-year truce in spring 423 in the expectation of negotiating a lasting peace. Peace proved impossible to achieve, and when the truce ran out Cleon took an army north to

---

32 4.40.1.
33 N.G.L. Hammond, *A History of Greece to 322 B.C.*, 2d ed. (Oxford, 1967), p. 294.

recover the lost territories. In the battle to recover Amphipolis, both Brasidas and Cleon perished. That removed the most aggressive leaders in each city, the men Aristophanes called "the mortar and pestle of war." The Athenians were weary of war, while the Spartans had been making peace offers ever since 425. Nicias, with Cleon gone and the aggressive strategy discredited, negotiated a peace for fifty years on the basis of the status quo ante bellum, with a few exceptions. To many it seemed to fulfill Pericles' goals after ten long years of fighting, although it had taken a sharp departure from his strategy to get there.

In fact, the peace was a delusion from the first. It far from satisfied even Periclean requirements, for the Spartans never acknowledged their inability to defeat Athens. To the contrary, when the Athenians dragged their feet in the negotiations, the Spartans threatened to invade Attica, regardless of the fate of the prisoners. The Athenians had yielded in the face of threats. The Spartans, however, in their desperation to get peace, had betrayed their allies. The peace terms left Megara's port and Corinthian territories in Athenian hands and required the Boeotians to return the Athenian fort of Panactum. The disgruntled allies of Sparta therefore worked to renew the fighting. They hoped to involve two significant Peloponnesian states, Elis and Mantinea, both engaged in serious quarrels with Sparta. A major reason for the Spartans' eagerness for peace had been the expiration of their treaty with Argos in spring 421. The Argives had refused to renew it and were making ready to challenge Spartan leadership in the Peloponnesus again. Their ambitions were a further threat to the preservation of peace. At this moment the Athenians were convenient opponents for the Spartans: the Peloponnesian League was in turmoil, the Argives were fresh and eager to challenge Sparta, and the Athenians could cause havoc at will by launching raids from Pylos and the sea. But the Athenians were tired, and the aggressive faction was leaderless for the moment. Athens therefore made peace.

The futility of the peace should have been immediately apparent, for the Spartans never sincerely intended to restore Amphipolis, a provision that the Athenians regarded as essential. Sparta and Athens could not have made peace in 421 without the promise of Amphipolis's restoration, and the peace could not last without the fulfillment of that promise. No Athenian politician, not even Pericles at his strongest, could have compelled the Athenians to restore Pylos until Amphipolis was again in Athenian hands. Unless both things happened, it was only a matter of time until the peace collapsed.

Alcibiades, Pericles' charismatic and ambitious young nephew and ward, quickly emerged as the leading rival to Nicias and as the champion of those who wanted to resume the war. Argos had moved ahead to form its own alliance, a "third force" that included Mantinea and Elis. Alcibiades wanted Athens to join them in a quadruple alliance of democratic states to destroy Sparta's position in the Peloponnesus and thus eliminate its power to threaten Athens. The success of the new strategy would make possible a major victory in a land battle against Sparta with little risk to the Athenians themselves, for the great majority of the soldiers would come from the three Peloponnesian democracies fighting against the Spartans and the remaining Spartan allies. The diplomatic part of Alcibiades' strategy worked perfectly. In summer 418, the Spartans fought their opponents without the aid of their Corinthian and Boeotian allies and with only a small numerical superiority. Alcibiades later boasted that "without great danger or expense to the Athenians, the Spartans had been compelled to stake their hegemony on a single battle."[34]

Incredibly, however, Alcibiades was not part of the battle that crowned his strategy. In the volatile politics of post-Periclean Athens, he failed to win reelection as general for the very year in which his plans came to fruition, while Nicias and his associates, who opposed the plan, shouldered the responsibility for its execution. Athens sent only 1,000 infantry and some cavalry; its navy remained idle. If the Athenians had sent 3–4,000 more infantrymen, as they easily could have, the odds would have swung heavily against the Spartans. If they had made naval raids on the Peloponnesus in the days before the battle, they could have compelled the Spartans to reduce the size of their forces at Mantinea. Even so, the battle was a near thing, and the allies almost ended the war and Spartan power. But they lost their chance with the battle.

Neither Nicias nor Alcibiades emerged from the episode with enough credit to gain the upper hand, and the "phoney" peace dragged uneasily on as the frustrated Athenians cast about for a new policy. That was the situation when ambassadors from Athens' Sicilian allies arrived in 415 to ask for help against the menace of Syracuse and its satellites. "If the Syracusans, they said, who had depopulated Leontini, were not punished and, after destroying their allies who were still left, took power over all of Sicily there was the risk at some time in the future . . . they might send [the Peloponnesians] help with a great force and help destroy the power of Athens."[35] Athens' previous involvement in Sicily had ended in 424 when the Sicilian Greeks agreed among themselves to a kind of Sicilian Monroe Doctrine, rejecting the interference of foreign states in their affairs and politely sending the Athenians home.

The Athenians had no compelling reason to go to Sicily in 415. They could easily have ignored the appeals of their small, far-off allies had they chosen. The threat of Syracuse's gaining control of the entire island and using its power to help the Peloponnesians in a renewal of the war was only a future possibility that required no immediate action. Some Athenians – though how many is hard to say – saw Sicily as a kind of El Dorado. If they could conquer the island and add it to the empire, they would solve Athens' financial

---

[34] 6.16.
[35] 6.6.2.

problems and enrich the Athenian people. Nicias of course opposed an expedition; Alcibiades strongly favored it. He now equalled the popularity and influence of his older rival, the rich and pious Nicias, a distinguished, if careful, general who had never lost a battle and whom the Athenians revered as a favorite of the gods. Alcibiades appears to have sought to surpass the position and achievements of his guardian and uncle, Pericles. A brilliant success in Sicily seemed the road to preeminence in Athens.

His plan was characteristically clever and not risky. He asked for only sixty warships, the same number deployed in Sicily in 424. He would take these ships to southern Italy and Sicily and use his diplomatic skills to win over the cities there to an alliance against Syracuse. With his ships and their men, they could either defeat Syracuse in battle or take the city by siege. With Syracuse under control, no one could prevent the Athenians from having their way in Sicily. An objective evaluation reveals little of value for Athens in Alcibiades' plan. Even if Syracuse fell, as was entirely possible, Athens would still need to gain and keep control of a large island far from Attica with a considerable population. In winter the sea route was unsafe, so rebellions would be easy, and Athens did not have the numbers to maintain an adequate garrison. At the same time, Alcibiades' plan contained little danger for the Athenians. The Sicilians would do most of the fighting, and the Athenians could sail home if the plan failed. In the worst case, even the loss of sixty ships and their full crews, while serious, would have had little strategic consequence. In no way could this original plan have produced the Sicilian defeat that actually occurred.

It was the astonishingly inept political maneuvering of Nicias that led to disaster. Defeated in the first vote, he devised a stratagem to reverse the decision. This time he tried to deter the Athenians from their purpose by magnifying the size of the forces needed for success and safety. The tactic misfired, and the people voted for everything Nicias had specified. A modest expedition at small risk suddenly became a major campaign with vast forces, the destruction of which would bring disaster. Alcibiades, as the chief advocate for the campaign, was to command. But the assembly, suspicious of his youth and impetuousness, also chose the reluctant Nicias as his colleague. Since the two men disagreed and could check each other, the Athenians appointed still a third general to break a tie: Lamachus, a bold and experienced soldier but a much lesser figure with no political support.

This "troika" set off for Sicily, stopping at Rhegium at the toe of Italy. Things began to go wrong at once. Rhegium was important to Athenian success; it was an old ally and strategically located for attacking Messana (modern Messina) across the strait. Alcibiades counted on it to be the main base of operations in that region and to help bring other Italian cities into the alliance. Nicias' misconceived ploy in the Athenian assembly, however, had destroyed the prospects for Alcibiades' plan. The vast size of the Athenian force frightened the Italians and Sicilians more than Syracuse did. The Rhegians refused to allow the Athenians into their city.

The three generals now met to consider their next step. Nicias, who was against the campaign from the first, in essence proposed a show of force and a swift return home. Alcibiades thought such an expedient disgraceful. Instead, he suggested a scaled-down version of his original strategy. He would use his diplomatic talents to win over the Greek cities of Sicily and even the native Sicilians to supply soldiers and food. With them as allies, the Athenians could attack Syracuse. Lamachus proposed that they sail at once and attack Syracuse directly. Thucydides endorsed that plan as the best, and there is no reason to disagree; a swift assault might well have taken the city from the unprepared Sicilians. Lamachus, however, had no chance. Nicias wanted to do nothing, and the thought of an attack on Syracuse undoubtedly appalled him. Alcibiades had his own plan and would consider no other. Unwilling to accept Nicias' feeble plan, Lamachus reluctantly supported Alcibiades.

It does not seem likely that the plan would have worked in the new circumstances, but it became a lost cause when a ship arrived ordering Alcibiades to return to Athens to stand trial. Before the fleet had sailed, Alcibiades stood accused of involvement in a terrible religious profanation, but he had faced no action at the time. After his departure, however, his political enemies engineered his recall to stand trial. Rather than obey, he fled to Sparta, where he was to do his countrymen considerable harm.

After Lamachus died in battle, Nicias, who disliked the entire mission, assumed sole charge when it was already too late to give up the campaign. His dilatory management of the siege of Syracuse caused its failure and allowed the Peloponnesians to send help that proved decisive. Sick and discouraged, he asked for reinforcements in the hope that the assembly would refuse and recall him and the army. Instead the Athenians redoubled their bet and sent all the help requested along with Demosthenes. But it was too late, for the Athenian position had become untenable. Demosthenes tried to persuade Nicias to withdraw while there was still time to save the forces, but Nicias delayed out of fear of his reception at home. Finally, he decided to leave, but an eclipse of the moon made the superstitious general keep his army where it was until escape became impossible.

Thucydides calls the Sicilian expedition "the greatest action of all those that took place during the war and, so it seems to me, at least, the greatest of any which we know to have happened to any of the Greeks; it was the most glorious for those who won and the most disastrous for those defeated. For the losers were beaten in every way and completely; what they suffered was great in every respect, for they met with total destruction, as the saying goes – their army, their ships, and everything were destroyed – and only a few of many came back home."[36]

---

[36] 7.87.5–6.

Almost everyone thought that the Sicilian disaster would bring the immediate defeat of Athens. At the instigation of Alcibiades the Spartans established a permanent fortress in Attica that denied the Athenians their farms and the revenue from their silver mines, and forced them to stand guard at their walls without relief to meet unexpected raids. Thus the Spartan presence acted as a constant drain on the Athenian treasury and on their energy, nervous as well as physical. Even more serious, a wave of rebellions broke out in the empire following news of the defeat in Sicily. These upheavals deprived the Athenians of revenue and drained the treasury even more by forcing them to man ships to put down the rebellions. Finally, the Persian Empire joined the fray, making an agreement with the Spartans to supply money to build a fleet large enough to defeat Athens. In 411, an oligarchic coup took control of Athens, and extremists almost betrayed the city to Sparta before the Athenians overthrew them and restored the democracy.

The last phase of the war was almost entirely naval, as the Spartans took the offensive and moved onto the Athenians' favored element, the sea. To win, they needed to destroy the Athenian navy, but that task was not easy. Despite their current poverty and the intense pressures on them, the Athenians put down almost all the rebellions and regained control of the seas. They defeated the Peloponnesian navy time after time and forced the Persians to replace the losses repeatedly. The Athenians aimed to hold out and keep destroying enemy fleets until either the Spartans or the Persians gave up. Twice the Spartans offered a peace on the basis of the status quo, and the Athenians might have been wise to accept one of these offers. But they had lost all trust in the Spartans after the collapse of the Peace of Nicias in 421, and instead they sought a decisive victory. At last the Spartans found a brilliant admiral in Lysander, while the Athenians lost the services of their ablest naval commanders because of internal political quarrels. In 405, Lysander destroyed the last Athenian fleet at Aegospotami and won the war.

The terrible consequences of the war give rise to the question of whether it might have been avoided or if its course and outcome might have been different. The answers to such questions are not available to the historian in a professional role, but the search for them is irresistible to anyone of normal curiosity and with the hope that history may reward its devoted students with a degree of understanding and even wisdom.

A careful study of Athenian strategic decisions, both political and military, produces a sense of several lost opportunities. Beginning in reverse order, with the last phase of the war, the decision of the Athenian commander Phrynichus to refuse battle with the Spartan navy off Miletus in 412 lost a chance to stamp out the rebellion of Athens' allies before it had spread too far and reached the Hellespont, before the heavy involvement of the Persians, and before the Spartans had found an effective leader in Lysander. The opportunity was great enough to justify considerable risk. But in fact the risk was not unduly great; not surprisingly, the Athenians later blamed Phrynichus and removed him from office.

During the last phase of the war, the Athenians lost another opportunity when the Spartans offered peace twice. Had they accepted, they certainly would have averted defeat in 405, and the death of the Persian king the next year might well have removed the threat to Athens for a long time. Why did the Athenians refuse? Most students of the period blame the demagogues and the foolishness and volatility of the democracy, but demagogues existed in Athens in 421 and the city was no less democratic, yet the Athenians made peace when they were much less hard-pressed. It was precisely the failure of that peace, and the disappointment and suspicion it caused, that helps to explain the Athenians' refusal to accept subsequent Spartan offers.

The advocates of peace in 421 allowed their eagerness to stand in the way of an objective assessment of reality and of sound policy. Had they insisted on the fulfillment of commitments and on actions rather than words, they might have compelled the Spartans to meet their obligations, thereby establishing the basis for a lasting peace. Failing that, at least they would not have sacrificed Athenian interests for no return and destroyed the basis for negotiation in the future. At the time, their desperate longing for peace at almost any price undermined later prospects for negotiation and, still more, for a victorious peace.

In fact, at one point at least the Athenians appear to have had a chance for a complete victory that would have rid them of Sparta's perpetual suspicion and envy. They could have defeated the Spartans at Mantinea in 418 if they had sent a larger army and used their fleet and the Messenians posted at Pylos to distract the enemy. The Athenians failed to do these things in part because the culmination of the strategy of alliance with the Argive group came at a time when the opponents of that strategy held power. Nicias and his associates were in command, however, because most Athenians felt uncomfortable with a strategy of engagement on land against Sparta.

The Peloponnesian War was a classic confrontation between a great land power and a great naval power. Each entered the war hoping and expecting to keep to its own element and to win a victory in a way that conformed to its strength at a relatively low cost. Within a few years, events showed that victory was not possible in that way for either side. To win, each had to learn how to fight successfully in the other's domain. The Athenian disaster in Sicily gave the Spartans the chance to win by making an alliance with Persia and, after many failures, they won the war by destroying the Athenian fleet. There was no other way. To win a true victory rather than a Periclean standoff, the Athenians would have had to find a way to beat the Spartans on land. Sparta's failure to meet its obligation to restore Amphipolis turned the Athenians toward a strategy that could win the war by defeating Sparta on land in the Peloponnesus, but Pericles' strategy, which Nicias continued, had become Athens' natural policy. Democratic Athens could not long sustain a more aggressive strategy that involved fighting on land but did not produce an immediate victory, especially after it had grown accustomed to war at low risk and low cost in lives. By the time Alcibiades' new strategy reached its crisis, the old forces under Nicias again held sway; men who shared Nicias' views were the generals, and they carried out the new aggressive strategy without boldness or conviction, glad to escape disaster as the new policy failed. After the defeat at Mantinea, Nicias and his associates returned gladly to a simulacrum of peace, but real peace remained an illusion. The only question was where and when the war would break out again.

The old strategy could not win even the limited victory that Pericles had sought, much less a victory that would deprive the enemy of the capacity to fight, which Spartan determination had made necessary. For that, the Athenians would have needed to take the offensive, fight a major battle on land, and find a way and a time to win it. But they shrank from such a commitment. Such a response is understandable in a state that had come to think of itself as an invulnerable island. It had developed a way of fighting that avoided much of the danger and unpleasantness of hoplite battle. This style of war allowed the Athenians to concentrate their forces quickly and attack an unprepared enemy; it permitted them to strike others without danger to their own city and population. Success in this style of fighting made it seem the only one necessary, and defeats with great losses on land made the Athenians reluctant to risk other land battles.

Pericles carried the traditional strategy to its extreme by refusing to use the army even in defense of Attic soil. This approach left him with no hope of disabling the enemy but only of punishing the Spartans and their allies to a greater or lesser degree and discouraging them from continuing the fight. The nature of the enemy made "the Athenian way of warfare"[37] inadequate, and Pericles' strategy was a form of wishful thinking that failed.

For a state such as Athens in 431, satisfied with its situation and capable of keeping the enemy at bay, the temptation to avoid the risks of offensive action was great, but it contained dangers. It encouraged the mental rigidity we might call "the cult of the defensive."[38] Such a cast of mind may induce leaders to apply a previously successful strategy or one supported in general theory to a situation where it is inappropriate. It has other disadvantages as well, including a limited capacity to deter potential enemies from provoking a war. Deterrence by standing behind a strong defensive position and thereby depriving the enemy of the prospect of victory assumes the enemy possesses a high degree of rationality and a strong imagination. When the Spartans invaded Attica in 431 they must have thought they risked little. Even if the Athenians refused to fight, even if they persisted in that refusal for a long

---

[37] I adapt the term from B. Liddell Hart, *The British Way of Warfare* (London, 1932).

[38] I adapt the term from "the cult of the offensive," which in the view of some modern scholars dominated European military thought in the years before World War I.

time, both of which seemed unlikely and unnatural, the Spartans would risk little more than time and effort. In any case, their own lands and city would remain safe. Had the Athenians possessed the obvious capacity to strike Sparta at its most vulnerable point, Pericles' strategy of deterrence might have achieved success.

Once the war started, the "cult of the defensive" dissuaded the Athenians from taking the measures needed for victory. They lost their best opportunity in 418, only to make a much greater investment and undertake greater risks in the Sicilian expedition three years later. A connection may exist between the two events. Perhaps the outcome of the battle of Mantinea discredited the cautious traditional policy, encouraging a bolder, more aggressive spirit that the Athenians then inappropriately applied to a peripheral campaign of marginal importance. After the disaster in Sicily, they could only try to hold out until Spartan incapacity and internal divisions led to some kind of acceptable peace. Even then, distrust of the Spartans and confidence in their own naval superiority led the Athenians to reject a peace that would have averted defeat. But Athens had exhausted the treasury on which its naval power relied, and political quarrels had denied the Athenians their best commanders. The Spartans, however, with the support of Persian money and the shrewd leadership of Lysander, learned how to fight at sea well enough to win. The great irony is that the swift, aggressive, innovative Athenians – as the Corinthians compared them to the Spartans before the war – proved less able to adjust to a different way of fighting than the slow, traditional, unimaginative Spartans. The Athenian experience in the Peloponnesian War suggests that during times of war, when open debate must precede decision-making and when the persuasion of relatively uninformed majorities is often required, democracies may find it harder to adjust to the necessities of war than less open societies. Perhaps that lesson is what Thucydides had in mind when he connected the Athenian defeat with the death of Pericles, who alone among Athenian politicians could persuade the people to fight in a way contrary to prejudice and experience.

3

The strategy of a warrior-state: Rome and the wars against Carthage, 264–201 B.C.

ALVIN H. BERNSTEIN

INTRODUCTION

Niccolò Machiavelli, the theorist whose writings defined the modern state, selected the Roman Republic as his ideal polity. His reasons might seem eccentric to most modern readers: the discipline and extraordinary willingness of its conscript army to endure privation; the oligarchy's aggressive drive and thirst for military glory; and Rome's desire for possessions only imperial conquest could confer.[1] These gave Machiavelli a paradigm that stood in sharp contrast to his conception of the Italy of his day. For his own good reasons he may have understated the ruthlessness and lust for power of his fellow Italians, but he was surely right about the capacity of the Roman Republic to build an immense empire in a world of hostile powers, while possessing few natural resources and a marginal geographic position.

Rome began as a small city-state whose existence remained precarious throughout its early history. Etruscans, Latin and Italian tribes, and Gallic invaders all at one time or another threatened the city's existence. Rome's defense depended entirely on its citizen army. Its location did not provide significant protection – the seven hills, at best, represented terrain suitable only for minimal fortification. Without a natural harbor the Romans could not establish themselves as a major seafaring and mercantile city-state.[2] Nor did Rome in the beginning have any significant source of wealth other than

[1] Niccolò Machiavelli, *The Discourses*, see Book I., chs; iv–vi; xxv; xxxi; lx. Book II, chs. i–iii; vi. For a properly skeptical view of a "thirst for possessions" as a motivating force for Roman aggressiveness, see Ernst Badian, *Roman Imperialism in the Late Republic* (Pretoria, 1967).

[2] On the subject of early Roman seapower, see J. H. Theil, *Studies on the History of Sea-Power in Republican Times* (Amsterdam, 1946) and Chester Starr, *The Beginnings of Imperial Rome: Rome in the Mid-Republic* (Ann Arbor, Michigan, 1980), pp. 58ff. For Rome's harbor at the mouth of the Tiber, fifteen miles from Rome, see Russell Meiggs, *Roman Ostia* (Oxford, 1960).

the meager crops that its peasantry scraped from its soil. Rome's early survival was due as much to its poverty as to the success of its military institutions. Like Athens during the Greek Dark Ages, Rome had nothing to attract invaders.[3]

But on this unpromising foundation the Romans built an empire that eventually controlled the entire Mediterranean basin and a substantial portion of the European hinterlands to the north. At the end of its period of expansion, by the time of Christian era, Rome controlled an area approximately two-thirds the size of the continental United States with a population of between fifty and sixty million. Moreover, even with the most conservative reckoning of Rome's decline and fall, the Romans governed this area for a period of six centuries. It was the extraordinary commitment on the part of Roman citizens and leaders, the *Senatus Populusque Romanus,* during the period examined in this essay that set the stage for this achievement. After Rome's triumph in the Second Punic War, no power ever again contested its advance on anything approaching an equal basis.

THE ROLE OF THE ROMAN POPULACE

Carl von Clausewitz, the great nineteenth-century theorist of war, insisted that war was a means and not an end,[4] in complete agreement with the second-century B.C. Greek historian, Polybius.[5] But a Roman of the middle Republic might well have urged them to reconsider their verdicts. In the rarefied precincts of late twentieth-century academia, the man who loves fighting for its own sake is not only unknown but practically unimaginable. But in less cerebral, more primitive, and far more dangerous worlds, violence often enjoys or acquires a legitimacy all its own.[6]

In the early days of the Republic constant external danger and the perpetual need for military action molded an ethos that raised the capacity for violence to the status of virtue, a quality valued as good in itself. Between 327 and 241 B.C., as the Romans emerged as the dominant power on the Italian peninsula, they enjoyed – or perhaps endured – just five years of peace. Only in the most unusual circumstances did Rome *not* go to war. After the out-

---

3 This is what Thucydides (I, ii, 5) says about Athens.

4 Carl von Clausewitz, *On War* (ed. and trans. by Michael Howard and Peter Paret, Princeton, 1976): "No one starts a war, or rather no one in his senses should do so, without first being clear in his mind what he intends to achieve by that war and how he intends to achieve it."

5 Polybius, III, 4, 10–11: "No sane man goes to war with his neighbors simply for the sake of defeating his opponent. . . . All actions are undertaken for the sake of the consequent pleasure, good, or advantage."

6 See Clausewitz, *On War,* Book I, Ch. iii, p. 100: "In any primitive, warlike race, the warrior spirit is far more common than among civilized peoples. It is possessed by almost every warrior; but in civilized societies only necessity will stimulate it in the people as a whole, since they lack the natural disposition for it."

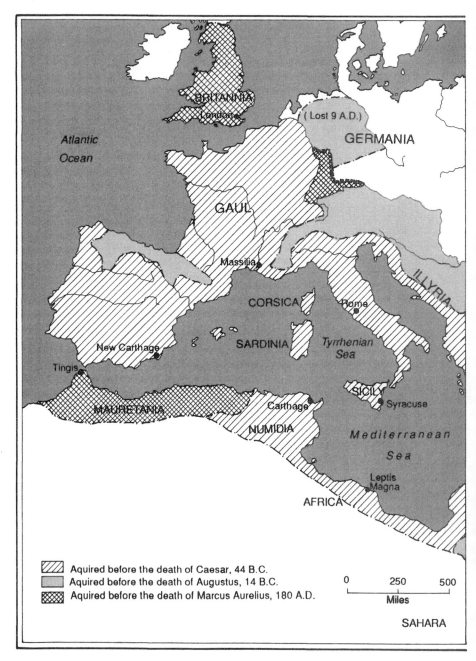

Map 3.1. Roman Expansion. *Source.* Adapted from Wallbank, et al., *Civilization Past and Present*, Volume A to 1600, Seventh Edition (New York: HarperCollins, 1992), 82.

break of the First Punic War, the Roman legionary, if anything, spent even more time on campaign than during the period of expansion in Italy.

What made such war-making possible? Between his seventeenth and forty-sixth birthdays the Roman citizen owed the state sixteen years of active military service. Though a citizen-soldier rarely spent sixteen continuous years on campaign, he might serve in the ranks for periods of six or seven years before returning to civilian life. And since he was by than an experienced soldier, the state invariably soon recalled him to active duty.[7] Moreover, the law allowed the government to extend the legionary's obligation to twenty years; records exist of cases in which this happened.[8]

If conflict was at the center of the Roman *Weltanschauung*, how Romans perceived, prepared for, and waged war says much about the extraordinary broadness of Roman strategy. An uncommon ruthlessness and vindictiveness characterized the Romans. Perhaps nothing makes that clearer than the Roman practice of decimation.[9] Units defeated in battle in a shameful fashion, or disgraced in some other way, received the sentence of decimation, decreed by the consuls and carried out by their centurions, who executed every tenth man. Polybius explains the procedure:

> If it ever happens that a number of men are involved in [cowardly] acts – if, for instance, some entire maniples have quitted their ground in the presence of the enemy – it is deemed impossible to subject all . . . to military execution. But a solution to the difficulty has been found at once adequate to the maintenance of discipline and calculated to strike terror. The tribune assembles the legion, calls the defaulters to the front, and after administering a sharp rebuke, selects five or eight or twenty of them by lot, so that those selected should be about a tenth of those who have been guilty of the act of cowardice. These selected are punished . . . without mercy. The rest are put on rations of barley instead of wheat and are ordered to take up their quarters outside the *vallum* and the protection of the camp. As all are equally in danger of having the lot fall on them, and as all alike who escape are made a conspicuous example of by having their rations of barley, the best possible means are thus taken to inspire fear for the future and to correct the mischief which has actually occurred.[10]

Tacitus elaborates the underlining principle:

> When every tenth man from a defeated army is beaten with clubs, the lot also falls on the brave. Making an example on a grand scale inevitably involves some injustice. The common good is bought with individual suffering.[11]

7   Polybius. vi., 19. The most exhaustive and insightful work on this subject is the hefty volume by Peter Astbury Brunt, *Italian Manpower, 225 B.C.-A.D. 14* (Oxford, 1971).
8   See the calculations of Adam Afzelius, *Die römische Kriegsmacht während der Auseinandersetzung mit den hellenistischen Grossmächten* (Copenhagen, 1944), pp. 48–61, and the reservations of Richard E. Smith, *Service in the Post-Roman Marian Army* (Manchester, 1958), pp. 6–10. See also, Arnold Joseph Toynbee, *Hannibal's Legacy: The Hannibalic War's Effects on Roman Life* (London, 1965), Vol. 2, pp. 79–80; Brunt, *Italian Manpower*, pp. 399–402.
9   The point about decimation is made, and the quotations are cited by Keith Hopkins, *Death and Renewal: Sociological Studies in Roman History* (Cambridge, 1983) Vol. 2, pp. 1ff.
10 Polybius, vi, 38.
11 Tacitus, *Annals*, xiv, 44.

The practice of decimation represented an extraordinary disciplinary measure, especially when imposed on a conscript army. Not until the late seventeenth century did western military organizations punish individual soldiers for cowardice and breaches of military discipline; not until the twentieth, with its mass armies and totalitarian states, do we see the capacity to inflict collective capital punishment on a similar scale.

Historians tend to see Sparta as the warrior state. But in fact it was a *polis* in which a small warrior elite dominated the great helot mass of Laconia's populace. This imbalance made the Spartans reluctant to wage wars of foreign conquest – the helots might revolt – and forced Sparta to isolate itself from the rest of Greece. Foreign campaigns carried with them the danger that exposure to foreign cultures might corrupt Spartan warriors. Moreover, the small numbers of warrior-citizens made the Spartan leadership sensitive to the losses that wars entailed.

In almost every respect the Roman polity stands in stark contrast. The *Senatus Populusque Romanus* could demand service from a great peasant mass of the expanding state year after year, in the manner of modern states since the *levée en masse* of 1793.[12] Consequently, Rome could field large and formidable armies on an almost continuous basis. Unlike modern democracies, it could also accept high casualty rates without changing its strategic goals. In other words, the Romans created a society of warriors based on the citizen soldier. They feared neither the casualties of war nor the internal social perils that so deterred the Spartans. Once involved in conflict, the Romans stayed the course: here was a society indeed willing to "bear any burden, pay any price."

The Roman state's ability to elicit this level of service from both citizens and allies in return for minimal compensation was a remarkable phenomenon. It reflected a value system entirely foreign to that of the liberal societies of the twentieth-century West. The difference between Rome's approach to things military, its view of what strategy comprised, and our own underlines a crucial fact of life: it is dangerous for the West in general, and for Americans in particular, to believe that others view strategy and the nature and uses of force through an Anglo-American lens.

Paternal authoritarianism prepared the ground for Roman military discipline. During the third century B.C., family and state did not yet exist as separate entities. The head of each Roman household maintained absolute authority over his family, and exercised the power of life and death over its members. Domestic Roman politics consisted of alignments and realignments among powerful senatorial families. Family institutions, therefore, retained a public analogue in the extreme power of the annual consular

---

12   Iraq, a country of some seventeen million, could field what has been called the fourth largest army in the world until much of it deserted or was destroyed in early 1991. A similar point could be made about the People's Army of Vietnam (PAVN): see Douglas Pike, *PAVN: People's Army of Vietnam* (Novato, CA, 1986).

magistrates and the collective and awesome authority of the Roman sena-
tors, the *patres*. Their judgments, and above all their authority (*auctoritas*),
helps to explain the extraordinary discipline, obedience, and acquiescence of
the individual Roman legionary.

THE ETHOS OF THE ROMAN OLIGARCHY

The Romans, as the Germans would say, were thoroughly *kriegslustig*. This
quality not only applied to the rank and file, but extended to and no doubt
stemmed from the values of the highest reaches of Roman society. Clausewitz
makes a point that applies explicitly to the highly competitive, aristocratic
Romans:

> Of all the passions that inspire man in battle, none, we have to admit, is so
> powerful and so constant as the longing for honor and renown. The German
> language unjustly tarnishes this by associating it with two ignoble meanings in
> the terms "greed for honor" (*Ehrgeiz*) and "hankering after glory"
> (*Ruhmsucht*). The abuse of these noble ambitions has certainly inflicted the
> most disgusting outrages on the human race; nevertheless their origins entitle
> them to be ranked among the most elevated in human nature. In war they act as
> the essential breath of life that animates the inert mass. Other emotions may be
> more common and more venerated – patriotism, idealism, vengeance, enthusi-
> asm of every kind – but they are no substitute for a thirst for fame and honor.
> They may, indeed, rouse the mass to action and inspire it, but they cannot give
> the commander the ambition to strive higher than the rest, as he must if he is to
> distinguish himself. They cannot give him, as can ambition, a personal, almost
> proprietary interest in every aspect of fighting, so that he turns each oppor-
> tunity to best advantage – plowing with vigor, sowing with care, in the hope of
> reaping with abundance. It is primarily this spirit of endeavor on the part of
> commanders at all levels, this inventiveness, energy, and competitive enthusi-
> asm, which vitalizes an army and makes it victorious.[13]

At least until the second century B.C., Roman aristocrats had an intimate
acquaintance with war. They had little choice; no Roman could stand for
political office until he had served on ten annual military campaigns.[14] As the
Republican authors Polybius and Sallust make clear, Roman aristocrats
placed great value on heroism; hand-to-hand combat and battlefield glory
were essential elements in the attainment of political and social distinction.[15]
One of the highest and almost inaccessible honors was the *spolia opima*, the

---

13 Clausewitz, *On War*, Book I, ch. iii, p. 105.
14 Polybius, vi. 19.4, cited by William V. Harris, *War and Imperialism in Republican Rome
    327 – 70 B.C.* (Oxford, 1979), p. 11 and notes.
15 Polybius, vi, 54, 4: "Many Romans have willingly fought in single combat to decide a
    whole battle, many have chosen certain death." Sallust, *Bellum Jugurthum*, xxxv. 5; xxxix.
    5; lxiii. 2: "Each man hastened to strike an enemy, to climb a rampart, to be seen in the
    doing of such a deed."

spoils offered to a Roman general who had slain an enemy leader in single combat. Though the Romans obviously invented Romulus's victory to credit him with building the temple of Jupiter Feretrius and the institution of custom, epigraphical and literary evidence attests to the victory of M. Claudius Marcellus over Viridomarus in 222 B.C. It is clear that Roman officers, perhaps even including the highest ranking consuls, shared the risks of the ancient battlefield. As a contemporary scholar has noted:

> In ancient conditions it was scarcely possible for the tribunes to maintain any influence over the course of battle, once it had begun, without being very near to the fighting itself. . . . The much scarred bodies of certain veteran officers are some indication of the part this class of person often played in combat.[16]

The Second Punic War suggests the level of sacrifice that the Republic demanded even from its highest leadership. Over a period of ten years, twelve of twenty consuls died in the war, and "possibly two or three tribunes out of the twelve who served in a pair of legions may quite commonly have lost their lives in the most severe battle of a campaign."[17] Consequently, the caste that governed the state and demanded a high level of sacrifice from the citizens made the same demands of its own members. It is not surprising, then, that the Republic soldiered on despite catastrophes such as Trasimene and Cannae.

Along with their willingness to bear the hardships of unceasing war, the Romans possessed as ruthless an attitude toward conflict as any people in history. The younger Scipio Aemilianus, reputedly far more cultured than most second-century B.C. Republican aristocrats,[18] nevertheless responded to a rebellion in the Spanish town of Lutia by cutting off the hands of four hundred young men who had urged resistance to the Romans – for the discouragement of others.[19] At all levels of society, the Roman attitude towards those whom they conquered was typically violent. Scipio was not disciplined for this act but rather awarded a triumph, one of the highest honors the Roman state could confer.[20]

---

16 Harris, *Imperialism in Republican Rome*, pp. 39–40.
17 Ibid.
18 Consider, for example, the words Cicero puts into the mouth of Scipio in his work, *De Re Publica*, I, 36: "I must ask you not to think me entirely ignorant of Greek literature nor disposed, especially in political questions, to prefer it to our own. See me rather as a true Roman, liberally educated thanks to my father's diligence, and eager for knowledge from boyhood, yet trained much more by experience and by the precepts I learned at home, than by any I received from the study of books." See also James Eric Guttman Zetzel, "Cicero and the Scipionic Circle," *Harvard Studies in Classical Philology* Vol. 76 (1972), pp. 173–79.
19 Appian, *The Iberian Wars*, p. 95.
20 Livy xxx, 15, 12: *neque magnificentius quicquam triumpho apud Romanos . . . esse*, ("there is nothing more magnificent among the Romans than the triumph.") See H.S. Versnel, *TRIUMPHUS: An Inquiry into the Origin, Development and Meaning of the Roman Triumph* (Leiden, 1970); also Peter A. Brunt, "Laus Imperii," in (eds. P. D. A. Garnsey and C. R. Whittaker) *Imperialism in the Ancient World* (Cambridge, 1978), p. 163.

Significantly, the word ferocity (*ferox*) has no negative connotation in Latin. The history of the Republic is replete with cities destroyed whether they had surrendered or not. The sack of Syracuse in 212 B.C., where the great Greek scientist Archimedes was slain by a legionary, and the utter destruction of Carthage in 146 B.C., are only the most conspicuous examples of normal Roman practices. As one historian has noted:

> The significance of Roman ferocity is hard to gauge. In many respects their behavior resembles that of many non-primitive ancient peoples, yet few others are known to have displayed such an extreme degree of ferocity in war while reaching a high level of political culture. Roman imperialism was in large part the result of quite rational behavior on the part of the Romans, but it also had dark and irrational roots. One of the most striking features of Roman warfare is its regularity – almost every year the legions went out and did massive violence to someone – and this regularity gives the phenomenon a pathological character. As far as the symptoms are concerned, Polybius gives an accurate description: writing about the First Punic War, but using the present tense, he says that it is a Roman characteristic to use violent force . . . for all purposes.[21]

Despite this emphasis on martial values and virtues, early Roman society felt the need to provide both religious and moral justification for every war that it fought. The ancient fetial law (*ius fetiale*) stated that "no war was acceptable to the gods unless it was waged in defense of one's own country or one's allies."[22] Though the Romans were not unique in maintaining that they acted in response to the needs of their own security, they claimed the moral high ground in a uniquely Roman way. The appeal to the gods, whose authority underlay the fetials' actions, was essential to make Rome's wars appear legitimate in the eyes of the people. By using the protection of Rome's allies as a pretext for hostilities, the law gained a flexibility that later became increasingly necessary to keep religious statute from interfering with imperial ambition.

The *ius fetiale* required an elaborate procedure to justify war (*ius ad bello*). The Romans used these procedures to demonstrate that they waged only just wars (*bella iusta*), and that they would fight only after performing necessary religious and legal rituals. The fetials had the responsibility and the authority to declare war, and as envoys of Rome they had to make three separate journeys to the offending country to recite Rome's grievances (*rerum repetitio*). Only after due procedure (*ad res repetandas*) – which in theory allowed the prospective enemy the opportunity to satisfy Roman demands for redress – could the fetials throw their "magical" spear into the enemy's territory to appease the gods and ensure Roman victory.

But such procedures were simply formal legal prerequisites for a war on which the senatorial leadership had already decided. Roman demands were non-negotiable, and only abject surrender could avert hostilities once the

---

[21] Harris, *War and Imperialism*, p. 53.
[22] Ibid, p. 167.

fetials set out on their journey. The terms were *purposely* set at an unacceptable level, well out of proportion to the nature of the injury reportedly committed. Nor did the fetial procedure in any way dictate that all Rome's wars be objectively defensive. In his discussion of Rome's mission to Queen Teuta's Illyricum in 230 B.C., Polybius explains the value of a pretext for going to war that allowed Rome not to appear the aggressor, but rather the defender of its Italian allies. One of the Roman ambassadors expounded Rome's ethical virtue to the queen. "The Romans have the fine custom of joining together to punish the injustices done to individuals and of helping the victims of injustice."[23] His declaration amounted to a declaration of Rome's mission as "policeman" of the Mediterranean, a role not necessarily compatible with a belief in solely defensive wars. Cicero reports Laelius, a second century B.C. Roman who was the *consigliere* of Scipio Aemilianus, as saying: "Our people have now gained power over the whole world by defending their allies."[24]

THE ALLIANCE STRUCTURE

"Of basic importance [to the Romans in winning their wars] were the people of Rome, the people known as Latins, the peoples from the other parts of Italy associated with it, and its colonies. Thence came the vast number of soldiers which enabled it to fight and to hold the whole world." Machiavelli thus sums up the crucial component that brought victory to the Romans in their numerous wars. The military power that Rome carefully constructed through alliances gave it the power to defeat its most formidable enemies. That power continued to grow and expand until it enabled the Romans to dominate the ancient Mediterranean world.[25]

The army that Rome forged during the third century contained several distinct groups: the Romans themselves; Latins, racially and linguistically akin to the Romans; and a confederation of non-Latin tribes in Italy that contributed more than half of Rome's soldiers. This last network represented the result of centuries of coercive diplomacy and fighting between the Romans and their neighbors on the peninsula. After 338 B.C., many Latin communities became part of the Roman body politic. They received the full Roman franchise, the *civitas optimo iure*. They possessed privileges such as the right to intermarry (*connubium*), and to have contracts concluded with Roman citizens honored in Roman courts (*commercium*). While the Latins could not hold office nor vote in the Roman assembly, they could gain either privilege simply by exercising their right to migrate to (the *ius migrandi*) and

23 Polybius, ii, 8, 10.
24 Harris, *Roman Imperialism*, p. 164.
25 The best book on this subject is the collection of essays by Emilio Gabba, translated by P. J. Cuff: *Republican Rome: The Army and the Allies* (Berkeley and Los Angeles, 1976), especially chapter 1.

live on Roman territory (*ager Romanus*). Incorporated (and related) peoples such as the Campanians enjoyed similar privileges. That they did not receive the full franchise followed naturally from being too distant to exercise that privilege.[26]

Rome's relations with its Italian allies (*socii*) differed significantly from those with the Latins. Including the peoples of northern Etruria, Umbria, southern Italy, and the Apennine highlands, these Italian *socii* did not share a common culture, language, or institutional structure with the Romans. With the exception of a few Apulian and some Umbrian states, they submitted to Rome only after a series of bloody struggles between 327 and 264 B.C. The vast majority of Italian communities and tribes thus concluded treaties – freely or under duress – with Rome that were all clearly to Rome's advantage.

One category of Italian allies enjoyed what they termed the "equal treaty" (*foedus aequum*). Their exemplary conduct in aiding or at least not resisting the Roman advance entitled them to a status that in theory placed their community on a par with the Roman state. In practice, however, Rome recognized no equals. The grant was titular only, guaranteeing that subject allies had no *formal* obligations to fulfill and that Rome would not interfere in their domestic affairs. The informal, implicit obligation of the client state was to bend its foreign policy to suit Rome's will, to regard Rome's friends and enemies as its own, and to supply soldiers for Rome's wars. This was the price Rome exacted for its friendship, for its guarantee of "freedom," and for the favor of protection from outside interference in its client's affairs.

All other treaties with tribes and communities in Italy provided the Romans with the right to call for military contingents. These *socii* could pursue their own forms of government and religion, but Rome did not require them to pay tribute or accommodate Roman garrisons except during wartime (with a few exceptions such as Tarentum). Despite disparities in terms, these agreements worked because they gave the *socius* a guarantee of peace and considerable internal autonomy. As Machiavelli noted, "cities . . . rest more tranquil and content under a government they do not see."[27]

Presumably, the leaders of these allied communities could count on Roman help to quell internal rebellions, and enjoyed the backing of the ever-present threat of Roman retribution for violations. Their agreements did not, however, allow the allies (*socii*) to establish political relations with other states or, more importantly, to avoid fighting in Rome's wars. All had to provide foot soldiers and cavalry, according to the *formula togatorum*.

The precise fashion in which the *formula togatorum* worked is not entirely

---

[26] See Adrian Nicholas Sherwin-White, *The Roman Citizenship* (Oxford, 1973, second edition), pp. 38–118.

[27] See Machiavelli, *The Discourses*, Book I, ch. i, and Sherwin-White, *Roman Citizenship*, pp. 119–33.

clear.[28] Some scholars believe that it fixed for all time the maximum number of men the Romans could legally demand from each ally not covered by "equal treaties" (*foedera aequa*).[29] Others think that each ally, whether or not it had concluded a *foedus aequum,* had to deliver its entire levy on demand and that the *formula togatorum* was merely an administrative device: a sliding scale to designate the number of soldiers Rome conscripted while allowing the number to vary from year to year at its discretion. This last view best fits the interpretation suggested by Polybius.[30]

However the allies satisfied their obligations, Roman citizens were eligible for conscription by possessing a certain minimum property. As the Latin put it, they had to be of *adsiduus* status,[31] which in practice meant that they needed resources sufficient to arm and equip themselves for legionary service. This class probably consisted almost exclusively of the rural proletariat and yeoman farmers.

The same pattern of military obligation presumably marked the allied peasantry. Their military contingents always accompanied Rome's citizen legions into the field. While the ratio of Romans to allies fluctuated throughout the third century – and even more so during the next – there were usually more allied soldiers under arms than Roman. More allies also lived on the Italian peninsula, so that proportionately the burden of military service in the long run probably bore down about as heavily on the allies as on the Romans. The leading demographer in the field estimates that in 225 B.C. there were about 640,000 adult male allies but only about 300,000 Romans available for service.[32]

Hannibal viewed this alliance structure and the military power it placed at Rome's disposal as his enemy's central strength. In prosecuting the Second Punic War, his strategy aimed, above all, at undermining that power by attacking and destroying the alliances on which it rested. The successes he enjoyed resulted in part from the counterstrategy of Rome's temporary dicta-

28 See Gaetano De Sanctis, *Storia dei Romani* Volume II, p. 453, n. 1, (Turin and Florence, 1907) for a full citation of the relevant title from the *lex agraria* of 111 B.C.
29 See Toynbee, *Hannibal's Legacy* Vol. I, pp. 424–37 and Beloch, *Der italische Bund unter Roms Hegemonie*, pp. 201–10.
30 See Brunt, *Italian Manpower*, pp. 545–48 who cites Polybius, Book v, 21, 4. He thinks that the ratio of Romans to allies varied over quite short periods, for different armies and in different years. He traces a broad trend in which the percentage of allies to Romans bearing arms declined during the Hannibalic War owing to defection to the Carthaginians, rose sharply thereafter when the Romans penalized the traitors, but then moved toward parity, reaching it in about 170 B.C. By the end of the century, however, Rome conscripted two allies for every Roman citizen because of discontent with the draft and the decline of *adsidui* qualified for legionary service (cf. Emilio Gabba, "Ricerche sull'esercito professionale romano da Mario ad Augusto," *Athenaeum*, Vol. 29 [1951], pp. 171–272).
31 Rome might call upon the *proletarii*, men below the status of *adsidui*, to serve in the legions in times of emergency, and both they and freedmen (emancipated slaves) regularly rowed in the fleet.
32 Brunt, *Italian Manpower*, p. 84.

tor, Fabius – a strategy that Hannibal's superior operational abilities forced the Romans to adopt. That Roman counterstrategy of refusing battle and harassing the enemy's army could not always protect loyal allies or punish defectors. Hannibal's successes also reflected the allied classifications described earlier: defections during the Second Punic War divided essentially along the lines that the Romans themselves had drawn. Latins, who enjoyed great privileges and close connections with Rome, did not defect, even though Hannibal wooed them vigorously. The sole instance of outright Latin disobedience came from twelve colonies that refused to supply Rome with troops, although in the end they returned to the fold peaceably, as befitted their status as honorary Romans.

The conduct of other groups, including Campanians and non-Latin *socii*, differed sharply from that of the Latins. After Hannibal's staggering victories at Cannae, the Lucanians, Bruttii, Hirpini, Capuans, and many others changed their allegiance to Hannibal. Livy correctly describes this dissolution of loyalties as a frantic attempt at self-preservation at a time when the allies "despaired of the survival of Roman power." It was also the result of the looser ties that Rome had established with these allies.

THE FIRST CONFLICT WITH CARTHAGE

Rome's perception of the Carthaginian threat largely determined its strategy during the Second Punic War. The two western Mediterranean powers had contacts well before the Romans consolidated their control over Italy. The intermediaries were Rome's Etruscan neighbors, whose ports in Italy were open to Phoenician ships. After the Romans drove out the Etruscan dynasty at the end of the sixth century, Carthage made a treaty with the new republic. Polybius in fact read a copy of the treaty engraved on bronze and preserved in the Treasury at Rome. Carthage obviously dictated its terms, since the treaty was wholly in its favor. The Romans agreed to sail neither south nor west of the Gulf of Tunis, and to make no agreements in Libya or Sardinia except in the presence of a Carthaginian herald. At this early date, the Carthaginians clearly aimed to exert control over central Italy and to prevent other powers from offering an alternative to their hegemony. In return, Carthage pledged to abstain from injuring certain towns in Latium.

In renewing the treaty in 348 B.C., the Carthaginians stiffened its conditions considerably. The new agreement excluded Italian traders from Sardinia, Libya, and the western Mediterranean from the Gulf of Tunis to Mastia in Spain. Only Carthaginian Sicily and Carthage itself remained open. Rome was still an agrarian society; throughout the fourth century it focused on the internal affairs of the peninsula while its future rival gradually transformed the western Mediterranean into a Carthaginian lake.

To support its empire, Carthage needed money for both ships and soldiers; that financial support came from customs duties. Its army, unlike Rome's, consisted not of citizens but of mercenaries hired from subject nations in Africa, Sardinia, and Iberia. By the time of the First Punic War (264–241 B.C.), the only Carthaginian citizens serving abroad were officers; Carthaginians joined the rank and file only when war came to Africa itself. This practice indulged the inclinations of a citizenry indifferent to martial virtues, but it had at least one serious drawback: it limited the number of soldiers the Carthaginians could field to the number for which their treasury could pay.

The early treaties between Rome and Carthage delineated separate spheres that reduced opportunities for conflict. The agreement of 279 B.C., when Pyrrhus, king of Epirus, invaded Italy with a formidable professional Greek hoplite army, stipulated that the Carthaginians would stay out of Italian and the Romans out of Sicilian affairs. Rome would hold Pyrrhus in Italy and prevent him from invading Sicily. In return, the Carthaginians may have provided naval support. The pact failed in its object, and Pyrrhus crossed the narrow straits separating Italy from Sicily. When Carthage fought Pyrrhus in Sicily, it neither asked for nor received Roman aid, undoubtedly because the Carthaginians had no desire to see another competing power on the island. For similar reasons, the Romans had not asked the Carthaginians for help against Pyrrhus in southern Italy. Toward the end of the decade, when Pyrrhus left Sicily on his way back to Greece with nothing to show for his efforts, he reportedly described the island as "a cockpit we are now leaving for the Carthaginian and the Roman to fight in."[33]

Subsequent Sicilian history justified that prophecy. A strong Syracuse under its king, Agathocles, had earlier checked Carthaginian expansion on the island, but on his death in 289 B.C., the Carthaginians again advanced until pushed back by Pyrrhus. After Pyrrhus's departure the Carthaginians defeated the Syracusan fleet, recovered their lost possessions, and reduced the Greek cities in central Sicily. By 275, Syracuse's influence had shrunk to eastern Sicily, and even there it met opposing powers.

Some of Agathocles's discharged Campanian mercenaries, hired to fight the Carthaginians, seized Messana in northeastern Sicily. Styling themselves Mamertines after the Sabellian god of war, Mamers (Latin *Mars*), they proceeded to plunder surrounding Carthaginian and Greek territory. In 265 the Syracusans under Hiero, Agathocles's son and successor, defeated the Mamertines and besieged Messana. Carthage now intervened and with the consent of the Mamertines threw a Punic garrison into the town. Hiero had to return to Syracuse. The Mamertines, however, had no desire to keep this new garrison. Some advocated seeking an alliance that would aid them in removing their Carthaginian "liberators." In 264 Rome accepted their offer of alliance and undertook this task.

Polybius explains that the Romans risked war with both Carthage and Syracuse because they feared the geostrategic advantage Carthage might gain if it consolidated its hold on Sicily and kept Messana: it would control all the islands surrounding the Italian Peninsula. Moreover, Messana would provide a convenient base of operations for a move into southern Italy, the most recent and therefore the most vulnerable of Rome's "circle of friends," and would present an alternative to Roman hegemony among the newly incorporated Greek city-states of *Magna Graecia*.

Roman fears of encirclement were legitimate enough. Moreover, since the Greeks of *Magna Graecia* had only lately entered the Roman alliance and not always enthusiastically, they might well respond to Carthaginian blandishments. Nor were the Romans the sort to decline an invitation to continue their annual warring. The Mamertine alliance provided a pretext to remove the Carthaginians from northeast Sicily while satisfying the demands of the *ius fetiale*.[34]

In 264 an advance guard of Roman soldiers arrived in Sicily and forced the commander of the Carthaginian garrison in Messana to evacuate the citadel. The Carthaginian field commander apparently tried to avoid war with the Romans; he neither contested the crossing of the straits nor tried to hold Messana. But Rome's stroke provoked a different reaction from the oligarchy in Carthage. They recalled the accommodating Carthaginian commander and crucified him.

Neither side had yet declared war, but former enemies joined in an unlikely alliance: the Carthaginians and the Syracusans combined against the Romans to remove the newly arrived Italian barbarians from Sicily. A formidable Punic army garrisoned the city of Agrigentum on the southwest coast, then advanced and encamped outside Messana. Hiero brought a Syracusan army to Messana from the south, and the new Roman liberators suddenly found themselves besieged, while the Punic fleet blocked Roman reinforcements from across the straits. In fact, the Romans managed to slip their legions into Sicily at night, and now, with a substantial army of their own at Messana, they sent twin ultimatums to the Carthaginians and Syracusans; they demanded that both raise the siege. With the rejection of these demands, the Roman consul declared a state of hostilities, and the First Punic War began in earnest.

In spring 262, with the Carthaginians recruiting in Spain, Liguria, and Gaul, the Romans sent both their consular armies to Sicily to attack the enemy's base of operations at Agrigentum. After a protracted siege of seven months – protracted because supplies filtered through the blockade – the Punic commander fought his way out of the city, both sustaining and inflicting heavy casualties. The day after the battle, the Romans sacked Agrigentum and sold its inhabitants into slavery, a calculated act of intimidation directed against other Sicilian cities that might support Carthage.

34 Harris, *Roman Imperialism*, pp. 34–5.

The Romans had won an important victory, but they still could not withdraw their legions to Italy confident that the Carthaginians would leave Sicily alone. By 261 Rome therefore resolved – as it may have done from the beginning – to drive the Carthaginians from the island altogether, even though the task presented considerable operational difficulties. The heart of the problem, as Polybius stresses, lay in Carthage's undisputed mastery of the sea. Even after the Roman victory at Agrigentum, only the insignificant inland towns that feared the powerful and ruthless Roman army joined the Roman side: the more numerous and powerful coastal cities remained open and loyal to Carthage. They were fortified against land assault, while Carthage supplied them from the sea. As long as Carthage had this naval access, the Romans could not turn battlefield victories into strategically decisive results. They might defeat the Carthaginians on land, but thanks to its superior naval forces, Carthage could return to besiege Messana and even settle old scores with Syracuse once the Romans withdrew.

Moreover, Carthaginian naval forces now began ravaging the Italian coast while North Africa remained untouched because of Rome's inadequate naval strength. To solve their Sicilian problem, the Romans had to escalate the conflict and choose one of two strategic options. On the one hand, they could have continued operations in Sicily in an attempt to drive the Carthaginians from every city that supported them. On the other, they could have applied pressure for a lasting cessation of hostilities by raising the stakes and threatening Carthage itself with an assault on Africa. Both choices meant challenging Carthage at sea.

While the ancient literature does not describe Rome as a naval power,[35] the alliance they headed did include the seafaring cities of *Magna Graecia* – states such as Tarentum, Locri, Elea, Naples, and Cumae, with centuries of naval experience and formidable navies. The Romans had used only armies for their conquests, because their opponents in Italy were land powers and they rarely needed to make a naval assault. From their new Greek allies in the south, they acquired the bulk of their naval forces, though they expanded their own fleet by building an additional 120 galleys.

In summer 256 a newly organized Roman fleet rounded the east coast of Sicily, encountered the Carthaginian navy off Cape Ecnomus, and won a great naval victory. As a result, Rome could strike at Africa itself and remove the Carthaginian presence from Sicily.

The Romans disembarked on the African shore for the first time at Clupea just east of Carthage. When the Carthaginians realized what the Romans intended, they recalled their forces from Sicily and recruited fresh troops, while the Roman commander, Regulus, besieged Adys. After an initial suc-

---

35 Theil, *Studies on the History of Roman Sea-Power in Republican Times;* Starr, *Beginnings of Imperial Rome,* pp. 58ff.

cess, he advanced to Tunis and encamped for the winter. In spring of 255 he engaged a Carthaginian force that sallied out against him and met disaster. Only two thousand Romans survived the battle, while the Carthaginians captured Regulus along with 500 others. A Roman fleet of about 250 vessels sailed to Africa to rescue the survivors of Regulus's army. Near the Hermaean Promontory they met and defeated the Carthaginian fleet of perhaps 200 ships. Following their second naval victory, the Romans rescued the survivors and set out for Italy. But on their return, off the Sicilian coast between Camarina and Cape Pachynus, a devastating storm destroyed all but 80 of the Roman ships. The African campaign had become a costly failure.

That winter (255–54), having levied more taxes to rebuild the fleet, the Roman Senate reassessed its strategic options. Since Rome had failed to take the war to Africa, it decided to launch a series of campaigns to drive the Carthaginians from those Sicilian cities still willing to provide Rome's enemy with a base. In spring 254, four Roman legions stormed the Punic base at Panormus (modern Palermo) from both land and sea. The operation succeeded, and the Romans sold into slavery the 13,000 citizens who were unable to raise the ransom. Tyndaris and Solus consequently also fell.

The Carthaginians could offer their Sicilian clients little help in resisting this latest Roman offensive since they had recalled their forces to face Regulus, and because they had to suppress a Numidian uprising. The Carthaginians did manage to storm and recapture Agrigentum, but fearing that they would not be strong enough to hold the city, they burned it to the ground. Neither their weakness nor their brutality enhanced their reputation in Sicily, and at the end of this campaigning season, they held only a handful of Sicilian towns.

In 252 the Romans captured Thermae and the Lipari Islands, but repeatedly failed in attempts to take Lilybaeum. Meanwhile, another Roman fleet fell victim to weather. The Carthaginians were nevertheless too focused on their Numidian problems to take advantage of this Roman setback, and made no serious attempt to regain the ground they had lost. The next two years (252–50) passed uneventfully.

Two years of renewed activity followed the lull. The Romans again sailed against Lilybaeum and tried to blockade the town, while an army marched on Panormus. Lilybaeum, however, proved impossible to crack; it was well-fortified and its harbor, though small, was extremely difficult to attack. In 250, the Romans advanced to begin their siege with 120 ships and 4 legions, but the Carthaginians repeatedly ran the blockade – sometimes with the help of their Greek allies from Rhodes – and succeeded in burning the Roman siege-works. There seemed no easy way for the Romans to dislodge the Carthaginian presence at Lilybaeum.

Realizing the ineffectiveness of this blockade, the Romans decided in 249 upon yet a third strategy. Unable to take the war successfully to Africa or to drive the Carthaginians from their major Sicilian strongholds, they resolved to advance into Sicilian waters and destroy the Punic fleet at Drepana, 16 miles north of Lilybaeum. The idea was sound, but the Roman commander executed the plan ineptly; Rome suffered its first major naval defeat of the war, losing 93 out of 123 galleys. Another storm ravaged the remainder. At year's end, only 20 of the 240 galleys with which the Romans had started the year had survived.

There was no question now of continuing the naval blockade of Lilybaeum. Nevertheless, the Romans managed to cut off all roads leading to Drepana. Although Rome had lost control at sea, Carthage held only Lilybaeum and Drepana. This approach at least turned defeat into stalemate, and even though Rome could not build yet another navy, it entertained no thoughts of peace. Moreover, Numidian problems still distracted the Carthaginians.

The stalemate ended with the emergence of a new and energetic Carthaginian leader. In 247 Hamilcar Barca took advantage of Rome's abandonment of a naval strategy to raid the coast of southern Italy. The next year he struck at the rear of Roman armies besieging Drepana and Lilybaeum with a landing west of Panormus. He fortified a position on the mountain behind the city and anchored his fleet at its foot, so that he could collect intelligence and communicate it to Carthaginian commanders at both besieged ports. This was an important achievement, because from his mountain vantage point Hamilcar could direct efforts to thwart Rome's siege tactics. He held the Romans at bay for three years, harassing their forces and raiding the Italian coast as far as Cumae. In 244 he advanced to Mount Eryx to relieve the pressure on Drepana. He captured the town of Eryx on the northern slopes of the mountain, but never managed to break the siege. Details of this struggle, unfortunately, have not survived, though we know that the contest ended only with the conclusion of the war itself.

The long years of Hamilcar's campaigns strengthened the conviction of the Roman Senate that it could only win the war by victory at sea. With the treasury exhausted, a collective loan, repayable only in the event of victory, now financed a fleet of 200 warships and transports.

In summer 242 this fleet set sail for Drepana to attempt once more to destroy the Carthaginian fleet. On arrival it found no Punic navy waiting to face it; the Carthaginians had transferred the crews to support their wars in Africa. An attack on Drepana failed, but the besieged town was running out of provisions. By March 241 the Carthaginians manned a fleet of between 170 and 200 galleys. They intended to land stores in Sicily and then, after embarking Hamilcar and his men, to face their foes at sea. Just off the Aegates Islands they met the Romans. Hampered by makeshift equipment and heavy freight, the Carthaginians lost; the Romans sank fifty ships and captured seventy more. Further resistance was out of the question, and Carthage now gave Hamilcar full powers to negotiate a peace.

THE SPOILS OF VICTORY, THE COST OF DEFEAT

It is easy to overestimate this victory. The Romans had defeated Carthage on both land and sea by a narrow margin. The war had lasted twenty-three years, and only Rome's extraordinary staying power had finally allowed it to prevail. Despite their tactical superiority, the Roman legions did not succeed in driving the Carthaginians from their strongholds; the enemy held its own in Sicily to the end. The final decision came at sea, but the crucial factor in Roman victory was not military or even naval skill so much as dogged persistence. That persistence in turn depended on the support and strength of Roman legionaries and Italian allies. Their alliances enabled the Romans to replace the innumerable fleets wrecked by storms or defeated by the Carthaginians, just as they raised legion after legion in the war against Hannibal a generation later.

In 241 Hamilcar Barca and the Roman consul, Gaius Catulus Lutatius, agreed upon conditions for peace. Carthage evacuated Sicily, returned all Roman prisoners and paid a war indemnity of 2,200 talents in twenty annual installments, a modest sum for an empire so wealthy. Both sides agreed not to attack the allies of the other. In gaining Sicily, Rome had won security for its southern flank, its object in waging war in the first place. The centuriate assembly in Rome, which had the power of ratifying declarations of war and treaties of peace, later altered these terms. At the instigation of those in the Senate who wished to compromise Lutatius's credibility, it voted to add another 1,000 talents to the indemnity and cut the time for repayment to ten years.[36] In addition, Rome gained all the islands between Sicily and Carthage, prohibited Punic ships from sailing in Italian waters, and refused Carthage the right to recruit mercenaries in Italy.

While the war had levied a light toll in blood on Carthage – since most of its soldiers had been mercenaries – the cold war that followed endangered the city's very existence. Twenty thousand mercenaries returned to Africa from Sicily and demanded their back pay. Libyans, Iberians, Celts, Ligurians, Balearic Islanders, and Greeks found a common bond in their claims on the Carthaginians. They marched on Tunis and spread revolt throughout the countryside. The native population rushed to arms against their overlords, while the Numidians swept over the city's western frontier. After capturing Utica and Hippo, the mercenaries marched on Carthage itself. Without command of the sea, however, they had little chance of success. Revolt in Sardinia further exacerbated Carthaginian difficulties. Carthage defeated the mercenaries and recaptured its African territories in the end, but it had paid a price for victory that weakened it thereafter.

During the years of domestic struggle Carthage had little trouble with Rome, even though the Romans could have exploited the rebellion in Sar-

---

[36]   See Ernst Badian, *Foreign Clientelae (264–70 B.C.)* (Oxford, 1958).

dinia. The mercenaries who had revolted from Carthage appealed to Rome for help, probably in 239. Since it looked as though the Carthaginians would subdue the uprising in Africa and could soon concentrate their efforts on regaining control over the island, the Senate rejected the appeal. For the time being, Rome preferred not to involve itself with unpredictable bands of mercenaries, and continued to honor the treaty of 241. In addition, the tribal peoples on Rome's north and east were becoming unruly, and that threat seems to have inhibited Rome from opening a third front.

But in 238 Gaul and Illyria calmed, and the Romans took advantage of a second appeal by mercenaries to declare war against Carthage. There was little likelihood that the battered Carthaginians would have the heart for another conflict, and indeed Carthage suggested that the matter be submitted to arbitration. Rome ignored that request and granted peace only at the price of another 1,200 talents and surrender of Sardinia. Even Polybius remarks that Rome's behavior was "contrary to all justice." In expelling the Carthaginians from Sardinia, the Romans removed another potential base for attack against their own coasts.

Throughout the 230s Rome fought skirmishes with Gallic tribesmen, and though Rome directed its attentions eastward toward Illyria near the end of the decade, Roman attention sharply refocused on the north in 226. The Gallic clans were gathering; memories and tales of the sack of Rome created panic throughout Italy. Rome hastily reached an agreement with Hasdrubal, Carthaginian commander in Spain, whose empire-building was raising visions of new troubles with Carthage.

The Romans hastened north to defend Italy. The Gauls advanced over the Apennines and, devastating the countryside, took the road to Rome and slipped past the two consular legions sent to block their way. These hastened in pursuit, but the Gauls, deciding not to face the legions in battle, retired with their booty to the Etruscan coast, which offered further plunder and forage for their horses. Followed by a consular army, they proceeded northward but found yet another Roman force waiting. These were legions recalled from Sardinia. The Gauls formed two lines back to back to meet the double Roman attack, but this Gallic mob faced a real army. Despite the death of one consul, superior Roman discipline and equipment overcame Gallic ferocity. The Gauls left 40,000 of 50,000 warriors dead on the field, with most survivors taken prisoner. Only a fraction of the Gallic cavalry escaped; never again did a Gallic army cross the Apennines.

While Rome engaged its forces in Cisalpine Gaul and tried to suppress the fierce Illyrians across the Adriatic, Carthage expanded its holdings in Spain.[37] In a swift but deliberate campaign, Hamilcar's successor, Hasdrubal, marched north to the Ebro river. In 226 Rome, concerned over

---

[37] For the wealth the Carthaginians would have exploited in Spain, see H. H. Scullard, "The Carthaginians in Spain," *The Cambridge Ancient History: Vol. 8 Rome and the Mediterranean to 133 B. C.* (Cambridge, 1989, 2nd edition), pp. 40–43.

the restless Gauls, made a treaty in which Hasdrubal promised not to cross the Ebro in arms, and almost certainly received assurances in return that the Romans would not interfere with his conquests south of the Ebro. If the Carthaginians had harbored aggressive intentions toward Italy, now surely was the time to capitalize on Rome's predicament. That they did not constitutes one of the clearest pieces of evidence that war, when it came in 218, stemmed from Roman aggression.

After Hasdrubal's assassination in 221, Hamilcar Barca's twenty-five-year-old son, Hannibal, took his place. This most formidable adversary in Rome's history renewed the expansionist policies of his predecessors. Saguntum, one of the cities south of the Ebro, managed to withstand him. Scholars have debated the affair from antiquity to the present, but Hannibal's subsequent attack, siege, and plunder of the city was the proximate cause of the Second Punic War.[38] Even though Saguntum lay south of the Ebro – the demarcation line between the spheres of influence stipulated by treaty – the Romans had accepted Saguntine fealty,[39] just as they had that of the Mamertines in Sicily a generation earlier, and almost certainly for analogous reasons. Rome's ultimatum to Hannibal to cease his siege of Saguntum clearly violated both the spirit and the letter of the Ebro treaty. The Romans, perhaps genuinely uncertain about Hannibal's long-term intentions, demanded Carthaginian obedience. They must have understood – as must the Carthaginians – how such a retreat would undermine Carthaginian credibility throughout Iberia as other Spanish cities would grasp for the benefits that the "friends" of Rome enjoyed. The Carthaginians undoubtedly saw this as the last straw, incontrovertible evidence that they could never live in peace with the Romans, whose appetites knew no limit.[40]

DURING THE SECOND PUNIC WAR

The Romans probably believed that the Second Punic War would run a strategic course similar to the first, with Spain now playing the role of Sicily.

---

[38] See Alan E. Astin, "Saguntum and the Origins of the Second Punic War," *Latomus* xxvi (1967); and Harris, *Roman Imperialism*, pp. 200–5; and Scullard in the *Cambridge Ancient History* Vol. 8, pp. 25ff.

[39] One ancient source, Dio Cassius (xii. fr. 48) records a Roman embassy sent to investigate Carthaginian activity in Spain as early as 231. Some modern scholars who accept his evidence also place the new agreement with Saguntum in this year, i.e., before the conclusion of the Ebro Treaty in 226. See, e.g., E. Taubler, *Die Vorgeschichte des 2. punischen Krieges* (Berlin, 1921), p. 44; P. Schnabel, "Zur Vorgeschichte des zweiten punischen Krieges," *Klio* xx (1920), pp. 110ff.; W. Otto, "Eine antike Kriegsschuldfrage. Die Vorgeschichte des zweiten punischen Krieges," *Historische Zietschrift* cxlv (1932), pp. 498–516; F. Oertel, "Der Ebrovertrag und der Ausbruch des zweiten punischen Krieges," *Rheinisches Museum für Philologie* lxxxi (1932), pp. 221ff.; M. Gelzer, "Nasicas Widerspruch gegen die Zerstörung Karthagos," *Philologie* lxxxvi (1931), pp. 261–99, and most recently, John Briscoe, "The Second Punic War," in the new, second edition of *The Cambridge Ancient History*, Vol. 8.

[40] See Astin, "Saguntum."

Rome's early preparations for war certainly suggest such an approach. Moreover, in the settlement following the First Punic War and in its subsequent dealings with Carthage, Rome's political strategy was obvious: to deprive the Carthaginians of any base capable of attacking the Italian Peninsula. Rome now controlled not only Sicily, but the islands between Sicily and Africa, Sardinia, and Corsica as well. Since ancient fleets normally followed the coastline, a seaborne attack by the Carthaginians against Italy would put their naval forces at great risk, for Rome controlled the sea routes to Italy. At the outbreak of war, this dominance led the Romans to believe that they alone would decide where the war would take place – on land.

The Senate intended to confine the war to Spain and Africa. It sent one consul with 24,000 men and 60 galleys against the Carthaginians in Spain. The other, with 160 vessels and an army of about 26,000 in Sicily, prepared to attack Africa. The African strategy was not a direct attack on Carthage itself: the forces sent were inadequate for such an undertaking, as the campaigns in the First Punic War had revealed. Instead, Rome proposed to encourage and support a revolt among the native tribes in the interior.

In the face of Rome's naval superiority and control of seaborne access to the peninsula, Hannibal decided to attack Italy by land. He had no intention of fighting on the strategic defensive in Spain or Africa; instead, he invaded Italy with the aim of destroying Rome's center of gravity, the real basis of its naval and military strength: its network of Latin and Italian alliances. But without a siege train to take any of Italy's walled cities, he could accomplish this only by subverting allied loyalty and by defeating the legions in combat.[41]

Hannibal decided to cut his communications, live off the land, and sweep down into northern Italy to establish a base of operations, rather than rely on Spain. It was a bold, dangerous plan, and in the end, a near thing. Hindsight suggests Hannibal might have done better had he adopted a defensive strategy in Spain, and used his operational genius to defeat the legions sent out against him. The lessons of the First Punic War, however, made this an unlikely strategy for a daring Carthaginian commander to adopt. Hannibal therefore left Spain with an army of 40,000 men; only 26,000 reached Italy after their trek across the Alps.

Hannibal crossed the Ebro river early in June and reached the Rhone by mid-August; no Roman army contested his passage. The Boii and Insubres near the new Latin colonies, Placentia and Cremona, had rebelled – almost certainly at Hannibal's instigation – and the legions earmarked for Spain had to put down the insurrection instead. Hannibal marched up the Rhone, but precisely where he crossed the Alps is still a matter of dispute. Most experts think he took the pass between the Little St. Bernard and Mt. Genevre,

41 See Barry S. Strauss and Josiah Ober, *The Anatomy of Error: Ancient Military Disasters and Their Lessons for Modern Strategists* (New York, 1990), pp. 133–61.

though a convincing case has been made that he crossed at the Col de Clapier.[42]

After storming the major settlement of the Taurini (modern Turin), Hannibal found that the Roman legions diverted by the local insurrection had caught up with him. A complicated series of maneuvers followed, leading to the battle of Trebia, south of Placentia, on a bitter December day. At its end, Hannibal had destroyed two-thirds of the Roman army and had won the first real engagement of the war.

The Romans then abandoned the northern plains of Italy, where Hannibal's cavalry and his Gallic allies had proved most useful, and decided to defend central Italy instead. They did not know, however, where Hannibal would cross the Apennines. Having advanced to Bononia (modern Bologna), he could move either southwest or southeast, and the Romans therefore split their forces by posting one legionary group to guard Arretium (modern Arezzo), the other to protect Ariminum (modern Rimini).

In May, when the snow had melted in the passes, Hannibal abandoned his base camp and crossed the Apennines at Collina. He deliberately encouraged one of the Roman armies to attack him by exposing his flank as he marched to Cortona on the road to Rome. Suddenly he swung off this route and headed east toward Perugia along the northern shore of Lake Trasimene. He marched his forces into a narrow divide between hills that descended directly to the lake except for a narrow three-mile-long plain, and posted his troops in ambush on the hills above that plain. The Romans followed blindly, and early on a misty morning they marched in column into the defile. Hannibal's troops rushed down from the hilltops and for two hours the battle raged. The Roman commander died and only some 6,000 of his men cut their way out, only to be rounded up later. The disaster was complete; Rome had lost two legions, although Hannibal did grant the surviving Roman allies their freedom. There was no disguising the seriousness of the occasion. In Rome a praetor gravely announced: "We have been beaten in a great battle."

The catastrophe caused so great a crisis in Rome that the state turned to the traditional remedy, eschewed for thirty years: a dictator. The Senate chose Quintus Fabius Maximus, but also gave him a second-in-command, his *magister equum,* who disagreed with the strategy he had announced: to dog Hannibal's heels and avoid pitched battles at all cost. The failure to anticipate this counterstrategy was the biggest Carthaginian miscalculation of the war. Yet it is tempting to forgive Hannibal because he could not have imagined that the Roman state with its warrior ethos would respond by declining

---

[42] See J. F. Lazenby, *Hannibal's War* (Warminster, England, 1978), pp. 45–46 with notes. He is following Sir Denis Proctor, *Hannibal's March in History* (Oxford, 1971). A variation of the Col de Clapier route was advanced earlier by M. A. Lavis-Tafford in the *Bulletin commemorant le centenaire de la Societe d'Histoire et d'Archeologie de Maurienne,* xiii (1956), pp. 109–200.

to give battle and by hiding behind its walls. Indeed, the evidence suggests that this was not a strategy that came easily to the Romans.

Unable to bring on a decisive battle, Hannibal moved through Samnium into Campania, one of the most fertile regions of Italy. Fabius followed and looked on while Rome's allies had their lands laid waste. At the end of the campaigning season, Hannibal marched back to Apulia, crossing the Apennines for the fourth time that year. None of the towns of Campania had opened their gates to him.

When news came next year that Hannibal had captured the Roman depot at Cannae on the right bank of the Aufidus River, the Romans could no longer resist responding. Under the command of the *magister equum*, they decided to ignore Fabius's operational directions and give battle. Four reinforced legions marched on Cannae. In a brilliant tactical maneuver, the Carthaginians enveloped the advancing Roman legions and cut them to pieces.[43] The Carthaginians slew 25,000 Romans and captured 10,000, while perhaps 15,000 escaped. So ended the greatest battle the Romans had yet fought. The defeat badly shook Italian confidence in Rome's ability to prevail. Many towns in Samnium and Apulia and nearly all those in Lucania and Bruttium went over to what they took to be the winning side – Hannibal's. In the autumn, Capua, the second most important city in Italy, and some other Campanian towns followed suit. But the whole of Latium, Umbria, and Etruria remained loyal to Rome, and the strategy of exhaustion of Fabius Cunctator appeared vindicated.

Since Rome refused to accept defeat, Hannibal had no choice but to persevere in his attempt to break up the Italian Confederacy. Without control of the sea, Carthage could not reinforce or resupply him, so he devised a new strategy aimed at extending the theater of operations and raising up a circle of enemies to surround the Romans. In the west, the war continued in Spain, and Carthaginian forces landed in Sardinia. In the north, the Gauls' continuing hostility provided a threat and a buffer. In the east, the Carthaginians sought an alliance with Macedon, which now attempted to expel Roman forces from Illyria. In Sicily, Hannibal encouraged the Greek cities to turn to Carthage. The continuing superiority of Italian manpower, however, allowed the Romans to operate in all these theaters simultaneously. Their bases of operations throughout Italy enabled them to resupply the armies they fielded, and their superior naval forces limited the effects of enemy operations in the Greek east and Sicily.[44]

43 The literature on Cannae is vast. For bibliographical references, consult F. W. Walbank, *A Historical Commentary of Polybius* Vol. I, (Oxford, 1957), pp. 435f. and *The Cambridge Ancient History Vol. VIII Rome and the Mediterranean 218–133 B. C.* (Cambridge, 1930), pp. 726f. Oddly, the new (second) edition of volume 8 of the *Cambridge Ancient History* contains not a single article or book on the subject of Cannae in its otherwise massive bibliography.

44 Strauss, *The Anatomy of Error*, pp. 133–61.

One of the consuls, Publius Scipio, also understood the supreme importance of holding the enemy at bay in Spain. He sent his brother Gnaeus there in 218 and joined him the next year. Their assigned task was to prevent supplies and reinforcements reaching Hannibal from Spain, but they soon launched an offensive designed to break forever the enemy's power in Iberia.

In his first campaign Publius Scipio not only prevented reinforcements from reaching Hannibal but also won a base of operations and began the conquest of the district north of the Ebro. In 217, another Hasdrubal, Hannibal's brother, approached the mouth of the Ebro with an army and fleet. Although he had fewer ships, Scipio decided to give battle. He wanted to avoid having his flank turned, and understood that he had to have command of the sea both to advance any further and to prevent Hannibal from receiving naval support. Scipio received reinforcements from the people of Massilia (modern Marseille), well known for their naval prowess and eager to safeguard their trade with Spain by checking Carthage at sea. Accordingly, the Romans engaged and defeated the enemy fleet off the mouth of the Ebro. This victory allowed them to cross the Ebro safely, and affected the entire course of the war by destroying Hannibal's hopes for success. After a feeble demonstration off Italy that same year, the Carthaginians abandoned any large-scale naval operations, and left Hannibal in Italy and Rome in control of the sea.

Hasdrubal's advance in 215 put everything at risk. He engaged the Roman army in a pitched battle on the Ebro, knowing that a victory would wrest back control of Spain for Carthage and allow him to join Hannibal in Italy. He failed. The Scipios had won Rome's first victory of the war (presumably to an army much inferior to Hannibal's), an achievement that strengthened Rome's image both in Italy and Spain, where former subject tribes now revolted against the Carthaginians. In 212 Publius Scipio and his brother succeeded in taking Saguntum, and planned further offensives to the south and into the hinterland. In 211 they advanced in two divisions against the Carthaginians, but as they penetrated south, they moved farther from their supply lines and deeper into territory where the natives remained loyal to the Carthaginians. In the end, both brothers were defeated and killed in battle, but their accomplishments were substantial. They had prevented reinforcements from reaching Hannibal; they had inflicted two severe defeats on the enemy's forces – by sea off the Ebro, and by land at Ibera; they had captured Saguntum and advanced farther south. They had wrested from Carthage a considerable part of the Spanish Empire from which it drew so much of its strength.

During the bitter months after Cannae, the Roman people refused to accept defeat, even though the depletion of Roman manpower had been enormous and Southern Italy had rebelled. Clearly, Rome had to avoid open battle with Hannibal at all costs; Fabius's attrition strategy formed the basis of all subsequent Roman operations in Italy. Above all, Rome had to maintain naval supremacy. This involved keeping afloat nearly 200 ships manned by some 50,000 sailors. Moreover, all the legions abroad had to be kept there in order to tie up enemy forces outside Italy. By 212 the Romans had managed to put 25 legions in the field with roughly 5,000 Romans per legion.

Despite Carthage's attempt to encircle Rome with enemies, Hannibal had to remain in Italy without much help, and this guaranteed his failure. Only the arrival of reinforcements from Spain could have changed the course of the Italian campaign, and the Scipios had barred the road. Hannibal, who had vainly tried to take Puteoli and Nola, therefore abandoned his Campanian offensive. He also failed to achieve surprise at Heraclea and Tarentum, and the Roman fleet stationed at Brundisium fled too quickly for him. He could not transmute operational superiority into strategic or political results.

In Campania, Capua, and in Sicily, Syracuse had gone over to the Carthaginian side, as had Tarentum in *Magna Graecia*. But by 211 the Romans had destroyed Capua politically, and they eventually recaptured Syracuse. Meanwhile, news of the Scipios' defeat had come from Spain. Claudius Nero, who served at Capua, went out with reinforcements but took up a purely defensive position to hold the Ebro line. Marcellus, the victor at Syracuse, did not try to reduce Tarentum, for even the Romans were now war-weary. In 210 twelve of the Latin colonies refused to send their military contingents. But the next year the war turned. While two consular armies held Hannibal at bay, Fabius, aided by a fleet and a diversionary attack on Caulonia, moved against Tarentum. The city fell by treachery and was sacked before Hannibal arrived. The Romans' dogged determination also reduced Syracuse and Capua, and penned up Hannibal in Southern Italy. Meanwhile, news had arrived of a brilliant Roman success at New Carthage. The whole complexion of the war was changing.

After the loss of the elder Scipios, the Romans had forfeited all Spain south of the Ebro, including perhaps Saguntum. The fall of Syracuse and Capua, however, allowed them to reinforce Spain. Late in 211 an army commanded by Claudius Nero landed, and in the next year tried to secure the land north of the Ebro. Rome then voted the twenty-five-year-old son of Publius Scipio, Scipio Aemilianus, an extraordinary command of forces in Spain. He had fought in Italy, but since he had held only a junior office, the aedileship (in 213), he was not legally qualified for supreme command. The details of his election are obscure, but the Roman Senate enthusiastically voted him to consular command in Spain. His reinforcements brought Roman forces, including the Spanish allies, to over 30,000 men.

Scipio immediately attacked the enemy's base of operations at New Carthage, which contained the bulk of Carthaginian money and war material as well as hostages from the whole of Spain. Its harbor was one of the best in the western Mediterranean; Scipio had realized that a base of operations that could be resupplied by sea was essential, and that his father had failed because Saguntum, his base, had not been far enough south. Therefore, one morning in 209, the small garrison of New Carthage awoke to find itself besieged by both land and sea. Scipio had marched rapidly south with his main army and arrived simultaneously with his fleet as it made an amphibious assault. Thereafter, Scipio held the key position in Spain. Besides an immense quantity of booty, money, and supplies, he gained control of the local silver mines and cut deeply into enemy revenues. He spent the rest of the year in building up a model army and drilling it in new tactical procedures and the use of new weapons.

He now had a base sufficiently far south to justify an assault on Baetica, which he carried out in 208. Although he allowed Hasdrubal's army to escape and cross into Italy, he had won a great tactical victory. Early in 206 the Carthaginians decided to stake the fate of Spain on a single pitched battle. Scipio met the combined forces of the Carthaginians near Ilipa (near modern Seville), defeated them, cut off their retreat by a rapid pursuit and destroyed most of Carthage's Iberian forces before they could surrender. The last traces of Carthaginian resistance at Gades collapsed, and the remainder of Carthage's forces sailed off to the Balearic Isles. So fell the Carthaginian Empire in Spain. Scipio now prepared for the future by slipping across to Africa to interview Syphax, a Numidian sheikh who had been harassing Carthage, and another Numidian prince, Masinissa. The collapse of Hannibal's offensive in Italy could not be far off.

Hasdrubal's force, which had escaped Scipio in Spain, now arrived in Italy and tried to reinforce Hannibal. The Romans defeated the new army at the battle of Metaurus and killed Hasdrubal. Rome's victory in Italy was almost complete. It had won an open battle on the Italian Peninsula for the first time during this long war, and the first serious attempt to reinforce Hannibal had failed. This was a decisive moment. Hastening south, the successful Roman commander, Nero, catapulted Hasdrubal's head into his brother's camp at Larinum. After learning the bitter news, Hannibal withdrew to Bruttium and held on desperately while another Carthaginian army landed at Genoa and tried, unsuccessfully, to reach him. More Carthaginian reinforcements headed for Italy in 205, only to be driven to Sardinia by a storm. With all hope of victory in Italy now lost, Hannibal received orders in the autumn of 203 to return home to defend Carthage. Having maintained an undefeated army in the heart of enemy territory for fifteen years, he at last evacuated the peninsula and returned to Africa to face Scipio, Rome's most brilliant general.[45]

In 204 a Roman expeditionary force of about 30,000 men sailed for Africa. Scipio landed near Utica where he hoped to establish a base; Masinissa and his Numidian cavalry soon joined him. They pressed the siege of Utica by land and sea, but winter arrived with the city still resisting. The next spring, Scipio handily crushed a relief army by a surprise attack. Then he renewed the siege of Utica and, after yet another battlefield victory, captured

---

[45] See B. H. Liddell Hart, *A Greater Than Napoleon: Scipio Africanus* (Boston, 1927).

Tunis, from which he disrupted Carthage's land communications. The Carthaginians made a desperate attack on his fleet at Utica, but he arrived in time to thwart them.

The situation at Carthage was now critical, and while Hannibal made his way home, the Carthaginians approached Scipio with peace terms. They offered to evacuate and renounce Italy, Gaul, and Spain; to surrender their navy save twenty ships; to pay an indemnity of 5,000 talents; and to recognize the power of Masinissa in the west, as well as the autonomy of the native Libyan tribes in the east. Such terms would have made Carthage a purely African power, nominally independent but in practice a client state of Rome. The Senate declared an armistice after some debate, and in winter 203–202 officially ratified the terms. The war seemed at an end.

When Hannibal finally arrived, he renewed hostilities, despite the recent ratification of the treaty. Learning of this Punic treachery, Scipio stormed up the Bagradas valley and isolated Carthage from its economic base. Hannibal then advanced to Zama; he clearly hoped to cut Scipio's communications and to force him to fight before his Numidian cavalry arrived. Each side fielded some 40,000 men, and at the end of the battle, Scipio's forces had destroyed Hannibal's army.

In a three months' armistice, Carthage agreed to pay reparations for breaking the truce, to give hostages, and to supply grain and pay for the Roman troops over the course of the armistice period. Carthage would retain its autonomy and territory within the "Phoenician Trenches" (roughly modern Tunisia), but effectively fell to the status of a subordinate ally of Rome, prohibited from making war outside Africa, and unable to do so within Africa without Roman permission. This ended its existence as a Mediterranean power and gave it no guarantees against future aggression. Carthage surrendered its navy, returned all prisoners of war to Rome, and agreed to pay an indemnity of 10,000 talents in fifty annual installments, an amount that would keep it weak and dependent on Rome for the foreseeable future. In return, the Romans agreed to evacuate Africa within 150 days.

CONCLUSION

In both the Peloponnesian and Punic Wars, a martial state triumphed over a more sophisticated enemy. There was nothing inevitable about either victory; Sparta and Rome won only after protracted conflicts whose outcomes remained in doubt to the end. Their example proves that states that preserve and cherish the ethos of the warrior do not ipso facto have the military advantage. Wealth, superior technology, attention to logistical detail, and strategic insight count as well. So does operational skill, and here the Roman commanders were greatly inferior to Hannibal. A genuine reverence for the martial virtues does, however, make such a state a tough opponent. Its citizens and leaders are more likely to sacrifice for victory, and they possess more of that prime strategic virtue – persistence.

The discipline of Rome's conscript army and the number of citizens available for service were assets essential to victory. Both grew naturally from the tribal, patriarchal society where state and extended family existed as one. Third-century Republicans could not have conceived of using mercenaries to protect or expand the Roman *imperium*. In the period of the Punic Wars, moreover, military accomplishment was tightly interwoven within the fabric of politics. Competitive Roman oligarchs could attain the glory and renown they needed for political advancement only from proven bravery and successful command in the field. The men who made foreign policy therefore tended to keep the state at war, which offered them and their successors the requisite opportunities to display their manly virtues.

At the same time, Roman strategy provides the most vivid illustration of the instinct for the jugular. The Romans' unerring sense of the prerogatives of power stemmed from a pragmatic ruthlessness unencumbered by competing imperatives. Their brutality was rarely gratuitous; their occasional acts of clemency stemmed from calculated self-interest. When Hannibal's superior operational skill threatened the warrior state, Roman leaders substituted practical discretion for traditional valor and retreated before their enemy in order to avoid a fourth, possibly fatal defeat. Preservation of Rome's ability to exact military vengeance had to come above all else. That ability alone, not any fondness for Roman hegemony, preserved the loyalty of allies and ensured the survival of the commonwealth.

4

Chinese strategy from the fourteenth to the seventeenth centuries

ARTHUR WALDRON

Very ancient and very modern Chinese strategy has attracted much attention. But few scholars have chosen to study the vast period that intervenes between Sun Tzu (fl. B.C. 500) and Mao Tse-tung (1893–1976).

Within that millennium and a half, the fourteenth to the seventeenth century represents a period of considerable importance, one that opened with a series of dramatic military actions. By 1279, the Mongols had completed their conquest of the territories of the Chin (1115–1234), Hsi-hsia (1038–1237), and Southern Sung (1126–1279) states and created, in the Yüan empire, a polity more extensive than any in East Asia since the T'ang (618–907). But the vast Yüan empire proved unstable: succession struggles weakened it, and within less than a century the ethnic Chinese forces of Chu Yüanchang (1328–1398), founder of the Ming (1368–1644), drove the Mongols out of China proper and back onto the steppe. The new dynasty, like the Yüan, initially took an active approach to security: it mounted repeated campaigns into the Mongol steppe, attempted to conquer Vietnam, and sent its fleet to Southeast Asia and beyond under the leadership of Cheng Ho (1371–1433). But in the middle of the fifteenth century the Ming began to turn inward. After 1449, when the Mongols destroyed an imperial expeditionary force under the emperor himself, the Ming no longer campaigned actively, and instead adopted reactive and defensive strategies, perhaps most dramatically manifested in the extensive program of border fortification that created the so-called "Great Wall." The Ming dynasty lasted until the early seventeenth century, when it succumbed to internal rebellion and the invasion of the Manchu founders of China's last dynasty, the Ch'ing (1644–1912).

Obviously, no single "Chinese strategy" guided events during this period. There was not even a single Chinese state; rather, a sequence of states existed, and most were at war with one another. At various times these polities employed a variety of strategies. Investigation of this period must thus disap-

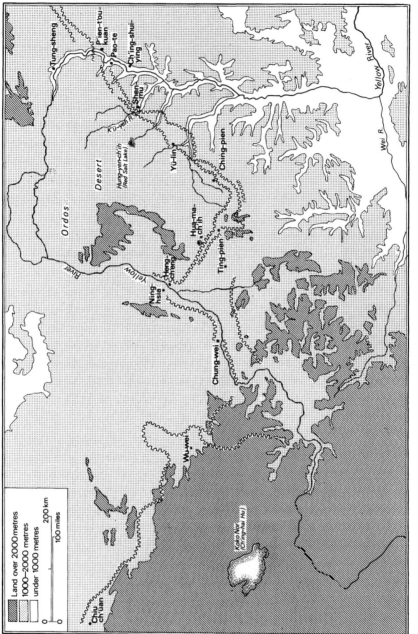

Map 4.1. China's Inner Asian Frontiers: The Yellow River loop and the Ordos. *Source.* Adapted from Arthur Waldron, *The Great Wall of China: From History to Myth* (New York: Cambridge), 106.

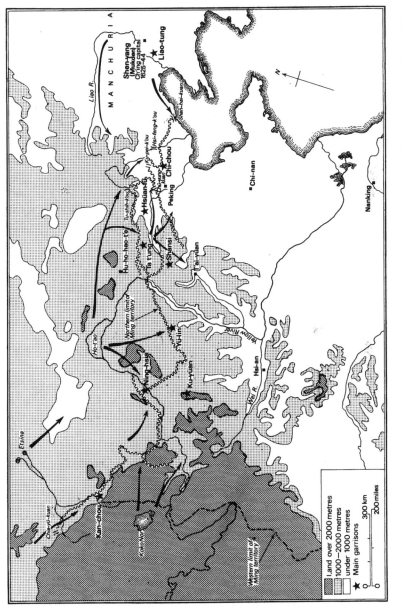

Map 4.2. China's Inner Asian Frontiers: The late Ming defense line. *Source.* Adapted from Arthur Waldron, *The Great Wall of China: From History to Myth* (New York: Cambridge), 162.

point anyone who seeks to identify a consistent "traditional" Chinese approach to strategy; no such thing existed. But it will nevertheless reward the student of Chinese national security policy, for in the course of these three centuries, the Chinese tried most of the different approaches to the problem contained in or at least advocated in their tradition. Essentially these approaches were of two different types, each with distinct cultural origins.

What we think of as "Chinese" culture, and often imagine to be unique and pure, is in fact a complex alloy of elements drawn from two sources: the steppe civilization of the nomads and the settled civilization of the people who are today called "Han." This is certainly the case with military strategy. Until the early modern era, nomads were the masters of war: they fought the brilliant campaigns and made the dramatic conquests. They developed a sophisticated body of military doctrine, never codified or recorded, which some of their settled neighbors nevertheless occasionally understood or attempted to adopt. This nomadic heritage forms one of the two great streams of the Chinese military tradition.

The other is the indigenous stream, which had its origins in warfare among sedentary proto-Chinese states before true horse nomads appeared on the scene. As with the other earth-bound societies whom the nomads threatened along the rim of Eurasia from Europe to Korea, this approach proved inadequate to the new military challenge, yet was so deeply rooted culturally and socially that it proved virtually impossible to discard. The story of Chinese strategy from the fourteenth to the seventeenth centuries is essentially one of the shifting employment of these two traditions by the Ming state, which confronted a chronic nomadic challenge on its northern frontier.

These shifts in strategy were more than intellectual. Changes in security policy mirrored changes in the nature of the regime itself. By its end, the Ming was very much the "traditional" Chinese state. Its economic heartland lay in the rich river valleys and lowlands of the south, where productive farming and expanding commerce supported an elite that perfected the refined culture of the classics, calligraphy, and artistic connoisseurship, and that increasingly thought of itself as uniquely civilized. Even the Ch'ing conquest in 1644 affected that elite's way of life relatively little; historians thus often lump Ming and Ch'ing together as a continuum, "late imperial China," a concept that makes sense in terms of the economy and society of China proper.

But the early Ming had been something quite different. For most of the preceding period, a "Chinese" regime in the south and a nomadically based polity in the north had divided the territory of present-day China. Each had its own methods of rule and of war, and only the Yüan had decisively united the two. When the ethnically Chinese founders of the Ming succeeded in driving the Mongols back to the steppe, they therefore faced a problem on which their own tradition offered little guidance: how to rule a polity that included both the traditional Chinese territories of the south and those of the north, where for centuries steppe influences had predominated.

Patriotically minded Chinese historians have by and large missed this problem. They have portrayed the Ming victory over the Yüan as a national victory, which vindicated Chinese culture and nationhood against nomadic barbarism and imperialism. But far from representing a reassertion of Chinese culture, the early Ming was a continuation of the Yüan empire under new auspices.[1] Although the Ming imperial family was from the south, it adopted nomadic styles of warfare and dress, employed many Mongols in its service, and maintained many Yüan institutions. Although the Ming-Ch'ing regime – typically thought of as the "traditional Chinese state" – may have been "sinicizing in appearances," it in fact perpetuated "the substance of the later Chinese empire as . . . found . . . under the Mongols."[2]

But incorporation of both settled and nomadic elements in a single state internalized those tensions hitherto expressed in external warfare or the building of fortifications. At the Yüan court, some officials advocated a Chinese-style approach to rule and to warfare, while others espoused steppe models.[3] The early Ming was similar; as Edward Dreyer has pointed out, its characterizing struggle was one between a "sense of continuity with the departed Yüan regime" and the powerful feeling of cultural Chineseness, which he calls "Confucianism."[4] As the Ming matured, it became more and more Chinese in flavor. But the same tensions arose once more when the Ch'ing empire again linked the worlds of Inner Asia and China proper. Even today, traces of these tensions exist – for example, in the troubled domination of Peking over Tibet and Sinkiang.

In terms of social architecture, then, the Ming, with its combination of nomadic and Chinese elements under Chinese rule, represented something new. The Chinese tradition provided little in the way of a model for such a structure and its policies. This fact was particularly evident in the formulation of national security policy, which led to repeated and fundamental clashes between the nomadic and Chinese approaches.

Of these two approaches, the Chinese is by far the easier to study. The Ming inherited a tradition of writing about military questions that extended

[1] Frederick W. Mote, "Some Problems of Race and Nation in 14th Century China," Paper presented to the University Seminar on Traditional China: Columbia University, 11 March 1969.

[2] Joseph F. Fletcher, Jr., "Bloody Tanistry: Authority and Succession in the Ottoman, Indian Muslim, and Late Chinese Empires," Paper prepared for the Conference on the Theory of Democracy and Popular Participation, Bellagio, Italy, 3–8 September 1978, p. 78.

[3] John Dardess, *Conquerors and Confucians: Aspects of Political Change in Late Yüan China* (New York and London, 1973). Some interesting comments on the specifically military aspects may be found in Francis Cleaves, "The Biography of Bayan of the Barin in the *Yüan shih*," *Harvard Journal of Asiatic Studies* 19 (1956), pp. 185–303.

[4] Edward L. Dreyer, *Early Ming China: A Political History 1355–1435* (Stanford, 1982), p. 62.

back to the sixth century B.C. At that time no unified Chinese polity existed: warring states divided what today is China and contended for the position of *pa* or "hegemon." As is typical when contenders share a common culture and are roughly equal in technology and resources, these states relied as much on psychology and politics as they did on force or actual fighting. In the classic text of the period, Sun Tzu's *Art of War,* victory without battle represents the supreme achievement: "[T]o fight and conquer in all your battles is not supreme excellence; supreme excellence consists in breaking the enemy's resistance without fighting."[5]

The *Art of War* still has much relevance to the psychological and political aspects of strategy. But even as it was being written, its immediate usefulness was fading for the Chinese, who confronted a new threat. True horse nomads from the Inner Asian steppe were appearing on the frontiers of the Chinese cultural world, and they practiced a mobile warfare that the Chinese simply could not match.

Their arrival made much of previous Chinese political and military theory obsolete. Such defining thinkers of Chinese civilization as Confucius (c. 551–479 B.C.) and Mencius (?372–?289 B.C.) propounded fundamentally cultural theories of the polity: they envisioned agricultural states in which cultural and moral norms kept order, means that they considered both more admirable and more potent than mere force. The *Great Learning* contains the classic statement of this Chinese philosophy:

> The ancients who wished clearly to exemplify illustrious virtue throughout the world would first set up good government in their states. Wishing to govern well their states, they would first regulate their families. Wishing to regulate their families, they would first cultivate their persons. Wishing to cultivate their persons, they would first rectify their minds.[6]

Pacification of society resulted from the extension of this process to the disorganized, largely sedentary, and technically inferior "barbarians" (the words used were *i* and *ti*). The idea that the barbarians might hold their own against such moral influence, that an adversary could be in Chinese terms "barbarous" and yet militarily superior, would have struck such thinkers as self-contradictory.

Yet the new nomads had just such qualities, and their arrival created a gap between cultural theory and military practice that persisted through the Ming and beyond. The classics had plenty to say about the *i* and *ti*, but nothing at all about the horse nomads. The Chinese word *hu*, which denotes them, does not even occur in the great classic texts, including the *Art of War.*[7]

---

5 Sun Tzu *Ping-fa* III.2, Lionel Giles, trans., *Sun-tzu on the Art of War – The Oldest Military Treatise in the World* (London, 1910), p. 75.
6 Wm. Theodore de Bary, et al., comp., *Sources of Chinese Tradition* (New York, 1960), p. 129.
7 Jaroslav Prusek, *Chinese Statelets and the Northern Barbarians in the Period 1400–300 B.C.* (New York, 1971), p. 223. 23.

Yet these *hu* and their descendants constituted the chief military challenge to China right down to the Ch'ing.

A fault line therefore developed at the heart of the Chinese conception of the polity. Where a seamless continuity had existed (as in the *Great Learning*) between individual and familial virtue and the health of the state, a gap now appeared. The morally generated internal order of the classics was not enough: external forces utterly resistant to the sort of cultural suasion might threaten the very survival of society. For purposes of ruling the territories that were culturally Chinese, the classics sufficed. But for dealing with the horse nomads, something quite different was necessary. The result was division in an ostensibly unified and universal tradition, division that nearly crippled the formulation and execution of effective national security strategy during the period under consideration.

Well-educated Chinese of the Ming had remarkably little useful knowledge about the primary strategic threat to their state. The curriculum leading to the civil-service examinations systematically underrated the importance of the nomads and misrepresented the effectiveness of policies for controlling them. Basic information about the nomads came almost exclusively from histories rather than from experience, and these accounts by and large presented caricatures rather than reality. Scholars studied not the Mongols of their own day, or even the history of the Yüan, but took guidance instead from the relationship between the Han dynasty (B.C. 206-A.D. 220) and the Hsiung-nu, a tribal people sometimes identified with the Huns of Europe. They learned to interpret nomad behavior not as the expression of economic or political needs, but rather as a matter of their nature, or even moral character.[8] Thus the *Shih Chi* of Ssu-Ma Ch'ien (B.C. ?145–?86/74) explains nomad attacks, observing that "It is their custom to herd their flocks in times of peace and make their living by hunting, but in periods of crisis they take up arms and go off on plundering and marauding expeditions."[9] In the *Han shu*, a moral judgment is made: the nomads are "covetous for gain, human faced but animal hearted."[10]

Such assessments of the nomads fitted in well with the larger moral basis of Chinese political thought. But because they missed completely the complexity of the nomadic-settled relationship, the classics provided no useful guide to action. Modern anthropologists agree that nomadic polities develop in response to settled states, in order to extort wealth from them.[11] For this reason, a settled society can use economic payments – usually far less onerous than defense costs – to manage nomadic threats in ways understood

---

8 On caricatures of the nomads in a number of sedentary societies, see Ruth I. Meserve, "The Inhospitable Land of the Barbarian," *Journal of Asian History* 16 (1982), pp. 51–89.

9 *Shih Chi* (Chung-hua shu-chü ed.)110.2879.

10 *Han Shu* 94B.3834.

11 For example, A.M. Khazanov, *Nomads and the outside world*, Julia Crookenden, trans., with a Foreword by Ernest Gellner (Cambridge, 1984).

even in the Han. Until the middle of the second century B.C. that dynasty followed a policy that mixed economic and diplomatic methods of nomad management (the so-called *ho-ch'in*) with considerable, though not complete, success.[12]

But the orthodox written tradition of the Chinese tended to play down the success of that policy, stressing instead the virtue of the officials who opposed it on ostensibly moral grounds. In the Han, for example, Chia I (201–160 B.C.) had loudly criticized the court's pragmatic approach to the nomads. He spelled out his views in a memorial whose supremely unrealistic opening words Ming policymakers and intellectuals repeatedly quoted: "The population of the Hsiung-nu does not exceed that of a large Chinese *hsien* or district. That a great empire has come under the control of the population of a district is something your minister feels must be a source of shame."[13] Chia I was one of the first examples of a type of politician who would appear over and over again in Chinese history and greatly complicate the making of national security policy. He was unwilling, for moral reasons, to treat with "barbarian" nomads on anything close to equality. This approach exerted a powerful influence as long as the moral notions that validated it served as the bases of Chinese culture. Repeatedly it overshadowed other, more pragmatic approaches.

But pragmatism was not completely absent from the tradition. The T'ang abandoned the idea of nomad cultural inferiority, and that approach contributed to their brilliant success. T'ang T'ai-tsung (*r.* 626–649), for example, when asked by his ministers why his foreign policy surpassed that of all previous emperors, responded that "since Antiquity all have honored the Hua ["Chinese"] and despised the I and the Ti ["non-Chinese," "barbarian"]; only I have loved them both as one, with the result that the nomad tribes have all held to me as to father and mother."[14]

Rulers who were less ambitious than T'ang T'ai-tsung, or less willing to view nomad and Chinese as equals, could adopt defensive measures that, while limiting Chinese territory, in theory at least could manage the threat from the steppe. Wall building was the most important of these expedients. Since antiquity Chinese had built walls both between their own states and along the steppe border. These early ramparts were of tamped earth. Ts'ai Yung (133–192) explained their purpose: "Heaven created the mountains and rivers, the Ch'in [B.C. 221–207] built long walls, and the Han [B.C. 206-A.D. 220] established fortresses and walls. These all aim to divide the interior from that which is alien, and to distinguish those of different tradi-

---

12 Thomas J. Barfield, "The Hsiung-nu Imperial Confederacy: Organization and Foreign Policy," *Journal of Asian Studies* 41 (1981), pp. 45–61.

13 *Han Shu* 48.2240–2242; Ying-shih Yü, *Trade and Expansion in Han China: A Study in the Structure of Sino-Barbarian Economic Relations* (Berkeley and Los Angeles, 1967), p. 11.

14 *Tzu-chih t'ung-chien* (Peking, 1956) 198.6247. As rendered by Charles Hartman in *Han Yü and the T'ang Search for Unity* (Princeton, 1986), p. 120.

tions."[15] But closing the frontier was not, as is sometimes thought, a fundamental Chinese cultural preference. Many dynasties, the strong ones in particular, had left the frontier open. It was rather a political choice.

Kao Lü, a minister at the court of emperor Hsiao-wen-ti (r. 466–499) of the Northern Wei (386–534, itself of nomadic origin), provided the classic formulation of the advantages of wall building. Kao explained that the northern barbarians were:

> [F]ierce and simple-minded, like wild birds or beasts. Their strength is fighting in the open fields; their weakness is in attacking fortified places. If we take advantage of the weakness of the northern barbarians, and thereby overcome their strength, then even if they are very numerous, they will not become a disaster for us, and even if they arrive, they will not be able to penetrate our territory.[16]

He thus argued that the dynasty should build ramparts to isolate itself from the steppe.

Nowhere did the Chinese written record do real justice to the sophistication of the nomads or articulate a realistic means of dealing with them. Modern scholars have discovered much about how the nomads waged war, and the picture they give is scarcely of the fierce and simple-minded people described by Kao Lü. The Mongols, for example, had their own highly developed (if narrowly adapted) way of life and culture, and sophisticated military operational techniques. They had good intelligence, were flexible and sophisticated in diplomacy, and could coordinate and execute complex military operations, even when large distances separated individual units.[17] Some Chinese defense officials fully understood these facts. They had spent time on the borders, and some knew the Mongol language. But neither the larger culture in which they worked nor the institutional framework of the Ming government allowed them to exert much influence on the formation of security policy.

Power was highly centralized in the early decades of the Ming dynasty. The emperor presided over a dichotomous administration: a prime minister headed the civilian branch and a chief military commission and a commander-in-chief led the military hierarchy. This structure closely paralleled that of the Yüan. But by the middle of his reign, the Ming founder, Chu Yüan-chang (also called the Hung-wu emperor), grew extremely suspicious of both his prime minister and his generals. In 1380, the abolition of the post of prime minister, the division of the chief military commission into five, and the purge of many leading officials left both civilian and military bureaucracies without an executive.

---

15 *Hou Han shu* (Chung-hua ed.) 90.2992.
16 *Wei shu* (Chung-hua edition) 54.1201.
17 Denis Sinor, "On Mongol Strategy," in Denis Sinor, ed. *Inner Asia and Its Contacts with Medieval Europe* (London, 1977) pp. 238–49.

Although a strong and active emperor could fill the vacuum thus created, the crippled bureaucracy had lost any ability to function on its own. And even with a strong emperor, problems emerged. Edward Dreyer has summed the situation up:

> The Ming government after 1380 was . . . characterized by fragmentation of authority at both the central and provincial levels, but more extremely at the center, where the five chief military commissions, the twelve guards, the Six Ministries, the Censorate, and a swarm of lesser agencies competed for the emperor's attention. In order to preserve the security of his position, the emperor determined to act as his own chancellor, and he spent the rest of his reign reading official documents.[18]

A division of authority existed even within the bureaucracy. Two ministers in the hierarchy held responsibility for policy regarding the borders, a task best treated as a single problem. The ministry of war dealt with the military aspects, while the ministry of rites dealt with diplomacy – the question of nomad titles and the circumstances under which nomads could enter China and trade or, as the language of the time put it, "present tribute" at the court. Often the two worked at cross purposes.

These institutional arrangements, made early in the dynasty, meant that without a responsible emperor the Ming government was literally incapable of formulating a security policy. Many different people participated in the process: ministers, generals, imperial friends and relatives, sometimes even the palace servants and eunuchs. Even if all had worked together in perfect harmony, none among them had the authority to make policy alone. And policy became impossible to formulate when, as was usually the case, bureaucratic, personal, and intellectual reasons divided them. Worse, the military capacity of the dynasty declined precipitously in the century after the Ming was established. The founding emperor's systems of raising troops and supplying provisions proved unworkable; expenses for warfare, palace construction, and trade increasingly outstripped revenues. All these factors affected the making of strategy during the period dealt with here.

To some extent these problems were familiar. Since earliest times Chinese courts had claimed a universal sovereignty, but most had understood the impossibility of actually exercising it. The states that existed in south China from the fourth to the seventh centuries, for example, while calling from time to time for the recovery of the north, carefully avoided any attempt to do so and dealt with the northern regimes pragmatically, by means of diplomacy, trade, and strong defense.[19] But when the Mongols withdrew into the steppe in 1368, thus giving the Chinese control of a unified state encompassing both north and south, a hitherto academic question became real: where did China end? What boundaries made sense?

---

[18] Dreyer, pp. 105–106.
[19] Charles A. Peterson, "First Reactions to the Mongol Invasion of the North, 1211–17," in John W. Haeger, ed., *Crisis and Prosperity in Sung China* (Tucson, AZ, 1975), pp. 215–52.

This argument worked itself out in the Ming, and is most clearly seen in the making of border policy for the long sea coast and the steppe frontier. The *Veritable Records* of the dynasty preserve what are, in effect, the position papers of the various participants in the policy debates, as well as substantial information about the decision-making process. In the case of the steppe frontier, the debate has left something more: a physical record as well, in the form of the "Great Wall of China." That system of fortification, usually and erroneously believed to have a continuous history dating back two thousand years, was in fact constructed gradually over two centuries beginning in the mid-Ming. Like the French decision to build the Maginot Line nearly four hundred years later, the building of the Chinese wall involved a shift from an offensive or counteroffensive military posture to the strategic defensive. And as in France, the decision created a great controversy.[20]

In its early years the Ming tended to follow Mongol-style policies on both land and sea frontiers. In the north it sought to take over as much as possible of the old Yüan empire, including the Mongol capital at Karakorum. Mounted Ming expeditionary forces pursued the nomads into the steppe, and in 1372 and 1380 came close to taking that city. After the founding emperor's death, his son Chu Ti (r. 1403–1425), born (of a Mongol mother, the nomads thought) and raised in the north, behaved even more like a Mongol than had Chu Yüan-chang. Following the nomadic practice of tanistry, he had seized the throne from the designated heir in a bloody war. Then, having assumed the reign title Yung-lo, he raised vast armies in an impressive but ultimately futile attempt to eradicate Mongol resistance to his power.[21]

In Southeast Asia and along the coast, early Ming policies were similarly expansionist. Mongol armies had pushed into China's southwest and into Southeast Asia, and the new dynasty secured Yünnan province. Vietnam, invaded by the Yung-lo emperor, remained under Ming control from 1407 to 1427. On the southeast coast, seaborne trade appeared ready to thrive. Just as caravans and traders linked Peking and the north to Inner Asia and ultimately, via the Silk Road, to Europe, so Chinese merchant ships had long enjoyed a maritime trade extending beyond Southeast Asia to the Indian Ocean and the shores of Africa and the Middle East. The Yüan had a strong navy, and this tradition as well carried over into the Ming with the voyages of the great Chinese fleets under the Muslim admiral Cheng Ho (1371–1433),

---

20 On the Great Wall, see Arthur Waldron, *The Great Wall of China: From History to Myth* (Cambridge, 1990), also "The Problem of the Great Wall of China," *Harvard Journal of Asiatic Studies* 43 (1983), pp. 643–663 and "The Great Wall Myth: Its Origins and Role in Modern China," *Yale Journal of Criticism* 2 (1988), pp. 67–104; for the Maginot Line, Judith M. Hughes, *To The Maginot Line: The Politics of French Military Preparation in the 1920's* (Cambridge, 1971). See also Rafe de Crespigny, *Northern Frontier: The Policies and Strategy of the Later Han Empire* (Canberra, 1984), an excellent study, which pays much attention to strategy, of an earlier period in Chinese history.

21 Wolfgang Franke, "Yunglo's Mongolei Feldzüge," *Sinologische Arbeiten* 3 (1945), pp. 1–54; "Chinesische Feldzüge durch die Mongolei im frühen 15 Jahrhundert," *Sinologica* 3 (1951–52), pp. 81–88.

the greatest feats of seamanship anywhere in the world up to that time, which demonstrated Ming power and secured diplomatic relations with Southeast Asian states. For a while it appeared that the dynasty might revive something that resembled the flourishing trade relationship between T'ang and Sung China and Srivijaya, which had dominated the Straits of Malacca until the eleventh century (and indeed the Ming did retain paramount influence in the area until the arrival of the Portuguese in the sixteenth century).[22]

But by the mid-fifteenth century, the dynasty's position had deteriorated on all fronts. Along the coast the founding Hung-wu emperor had distrusted trade, which he sought first to supervise and then to eliminate. But garrisons and patrols only created the large-scale smuggling that bedeviled the dynasty until the sixteenth century. The Yung-lo emperor's attempts to solve problems by military means in the steppe and in Vietnam proved costly and indecisive. A Ming naval force met with defeat on the Hoang-giang [Huang-chiang], one of the entrances of the Red River in 1420; this and subsequent setbacks set in motion the process that led eventually to the evacuation of Vietnam and the abandonment of the great naval expeditions.[23] Gradually the Ming began to reverse the economic, political, and national security policies of the Yüan and of its own early period. Along the steppe frontier, construction of border fortifications began: these works ultimately became "The Great Wall." By the middle of the sixteenth century, the Ming had forbidden all trade along the coast.[24]

The process is perhaps the most important and best documented example of the making of Chinese strategy in late traditional times. It is also of interest in the twentieth century, during which the Chinese have repeatedly shifted from openness and expansion to closure and defensiveness. Just why the dynasty made the decisions it did remains somewhat unclear. But the story appears, in essence, to be one of conflict between the imperatives of Chinese culture and the military and strategic needs of the state.

The strategic reversal took place over many decades. Its most important turning point, however, came about twenty-five years after the Yung-lo emperor's death, with the military disaster of T'u-mu, when the young Cheng-t'ung emperor (r. 1435–1449) attempted to lead an army into the steppe against the Mongol Esen (d. 1455) and fell into a carefully prepared ambush.

---

[22] Dreyer, p. 123; also Jung-pang Lo, "The Emergence of China as a Sea Power During the Late Sung and Early Yüan Periods," in John A. Harrison, ed., *China: Enduring Scholarship Selected from The Far Eastern Quarterly-The Journal of Asian Studies* (Tucson, AZ, 1972) pp. 91–105 (originally published 1952) and "The Decline of the Early Ming Navy," *Oriens Extremus* 5 (1958), pp. 149–168; James Geiss, "Zheng He," in Ainslie T. Embree, ed., *Encyclopedia of Asian History* (New York), vol. 4, pp. 299–300.

[23] Lo, "Decline of the Early Ming Navy," pp. 151–52.

[24] Kwan-wai So, *Japanese Piracy in Ming China During the 16th Century* (East Lansing, MI, 1975); Pin-ts'un Chang, "Chinese Maritime Trade: The Case of Sixteenth-century Fu-chien (Fukien)," Ph.D diss., Princeton University, 1983.

The Mongols destroyed the Chinese army and captured the emperor himself.[25] That debacle eliminated whatever consistency of purpose Ming strategy might once have had.

The Ming was losing the knowledge, the capacity, and the will to maintain an effective security policy for the steppe. The series of campaigns that Khubilai (1216–1294) waged against steppe rivals represents a model of what their strategy might have been. These campaigns combined tactics of economic blockade and military offensive: against Arigh Boke and Khaidu, Khubilai poured Chinese resources into the steppe in support of his own forces, while at the same time denying his rivals any access to sedentary resources. The result, after much attrition, was victory for Khubilai.[26] The influence of Khubilai's example was evident in the approaches of the early Ming emperors, but all traces of it vanished after the third decade of the fifteenth century.

Thereafter, while inconclusive debate raged about the dynasty's strategic posture toward the steppe frontier, none of the alternatives considered attained the subtlety or potential effectiveness of the nomadic approach. Giving the constraints of the Chinese tradition, the argument became a simple choice: whether the right policy should be an active one, which sought to clear the territory and bring it under Ming rule, or whether it should be a defensive posture that settled for some sort of modus vivendi, even at the expense of abstract claims. By and large the military favored the latter, while civilian politicians (perhaps remembering Chia I) preferred the former.

The resources at the dynasty's disposal had an important effect on the decision. Broadly speaking, China's wealth lay in the south, and success in the steppe would depend on the court's willingness to ship enough of that wealth north and expend it in Inner Asia. A key to the Yüan dynasty's steppe policy was its mobilization of resources in the south for use in military campaigns and subsidies in the north.[27]

The Ming inherited most of the military establishment the Yüan had created. The Hung-wu emperor's army of conquest swelled with the many former Yüan soldiers who came over to his side (even as the main Mongol forces withdrew deep into Mongolia, beyond the range of Ming attack). It is estimated that by 1392, approximately 1.2 million men were on active ser-

25   F.W. Mote, "The T'u-mu incident of 1449," in Frank A. Kierman, Jr. and John K. Fairbank, eds., *Chinese Ways in Warfare* (Cambridge, MA, 1974), pp. 243–72; also Philip de Heer, *The care-taker emperor: aspects of the imperial institution in the fifteenth century as reflected in the political history of the reign of Chu Ch'i-yü* (Leiden, 1986).
26   Morris Rossabi, *Khubilai Khan: His Life and Times* (Berkeley, Los Angeles, London, 1988) pp. 56–62; John Dardess, "From Mongol Empire to Yüan Dynasty: Changing Forms of Imperial Rule in Mongolia and Central Asia," *Monumenta Serica* 30 (1972–73), pp. 117–165; also Th. T. Allsen, "The Princes of the Left Hand: An Introduction to the History of the *Ulus* of Orda in the Thirteenth and Early Fourteenth Centuries," *Archivum Eurasiae Medii Aevi* 5 (1985[1987]), pp. 5–40.
27   See Dardess, "From Mongol Empire to Yüan Dynasty."

vice for the Ming.[28] Some of these, including substantial numbers of cavalry, served in Inner Asia and along the steppe frontier, fighting the Mongols after the dynastic founder's death. Others were in garrisons both inland and in the frontier zone.

Such a vast army was extremely expensive to maintain. Purely nomadic auxiliaries, of which there were some, had their own horses and could live easily on the steppe. But Chinese forces had to obtain support from the outside. China proper has never produced good horses, and the Ming used mounts either from Mongolia itself or from Korea. At the start of the dynasty at least, however, the mounted frontier forces of the Ming seem to have been as good as those of the Mongols.[29]

To maintain their standing army, the early Ming turned to expedients the Yüan had also used.[30] The Ming drew soldiers, generation after generation, from registered "military households" designated to provide a fighting man and his equipment. The dynasty also attempted to make border garrisons self-supporting, by having them farm when not actually involved in fighting. This was the system of *t'un-t'ien,* originated in the Han and regularly advocated thereafter.[31] Although the Ming founder boasted that he had "supported an army of one million men without using a single grain taken from the people," the system in fact never worked as intended. By the early fifteenth century, the Ming military was stumbling from one financial crisis to another.[32]

This development was striking because in potential the Ming far outstripped any of its rivals. The Chinese economy was vast, and good water transport made it relatively easy to move men and supplies from south to north. If the Chinese were occasionally short of horses, a nomadic product, the nomads were chronically short of grain, metal, and medicines, along with other products of the settled world. Ming forces were well-equipped: soldiers carried pikes and muskets, some groups had small cannons, and many soldiers wore padded body armor.[33]

Mobilization of resources, however, was probably more difficult for the Ming than it had been for the Yüan. Yüan administration was far more

28 Ray Huang, *Taxation and Governmental Finance in Sixteenth Century Ming China* (Cambridge, 1974), p. 265.
29 For a broad analysis, which touches China, of the sources and role of war horses in the steppe, see Rhoads Murphey, "Horsebreeding in Eurasia," *Central and Inner Asian Studies* 4 (1990), pp. 1–13.
30 Romeyn Taylor, "Yüan Origins of the Wei-so System," in Charles O. Hucker, ed., *Chinese Government in Ming Times: Seven Studies* (New York, 1969) pp. 23–40; also Hsiao Ch'i-ch'ing, *The Military Establishment of the Yüan Dynasty* (Cambridge, MA, 1978).
31 Wang Yü-ch'üan, *Ming-tai ti chün-t'un* (Peking, 1965).
32 Ray Huang, *Taxation and Governmental Finance in Sixteenth Century Ming China* (Cambridge, 1974), also "Military Expenditure in Sixteenth Century Ming China," *Oriens Extremus* 17 (1970), pp. 39–62.
33 Ray Huang, *1587: A Year of No Significance* (New Haven and London, 1981), pp. 156–88.

flexible than that of the bureaucratic Ming. Particularly under a strong ruler like Khubilai, the Yüan could alter rules and reallocate resources without great difficulty. The dynastic founder of the Ming, by contrast, made comprehensive inventories of resources and attempted to match them with specific needs. Just as particular families supplied soldiers for particular units, designated households provided other goods and services in perpetuity. There were craftsmen, entertainers, salt extractors, fishermen – every sort of household. The Ming aimed to establish a comprehensive and self-sustaining equilibrium, but the result was quite different. Within a generation the Ming system had made it impossible to move resources that had been dedicated to this system. Thus, military families that no longer produced soldiers went on being military families, while the dynasty had to hire soldiers through the money economy – paying twice for defense.

The difficulty of mobilization represented only one reason for the Ming's inability to duplicate the Yüan achievement and control the steppe. The fact that the Ming were from the south of China was probably just as important, for the dynasty was far less willing to devote resources to steppe warfare than the Yüan had been. Another is probably that by the fifteenth century, the unwritten secrets of Mongol dominance in the steppe began to vanish. Great Mongol generals knew and understood them, and some Chinese had learned from them. But the Mongol oral tradition could never sustain itself against the vast documentation of other approaches to warfare contained in the Chinese written tradition.

This process was evident in the way the Ming perceived and understood the threats to its security, and not only those from the steppe. The dynasty, as already mentioned, was essentially opening new historical ground, and had little in the way of precedent on which to rely. The warfare that created it occurred mostly within China proper, between insurgent leaders who sought to overthrow the Yüan and other Chinese who were loyal to the Mongols (Kökö Temur, one of the greatest Yüan generals, was in fact a Mongolicized Chinese). This warfare was political rather than territorial. Chu Yüan-chang sought to be leader, but of exactly what he was not sure, and blending everything from orthodox Confucian tenets to messianic strands of Buddhism as it suited him, he went from being an avowed Sung loyalist to a would-be territorial magnate to the founder of a new dynasty.[34] It was only when he had conquered China proper, yet still confronted an undefeated Mongol army in the steppe, that he began to think about national security.[35]

Even so, personal threats to his authority worried him most. He knew that many of his subjects had served the Mongols and might serve them again,

---

[34] In addition to Dreyer's *Early Ming China*, see John W. Dardess, "The Transformations of Messianic Revolt and the Founding of the Ming Dynasty," *Journal of Asian Studies* 29 (1970), pp. 539–58.

[35] Dreyer treats this in *Early Ming China*; also with more detail in "The Emergence of Chu Yuan-chang," Ph.D diss., Harvard University, 1970.

and he feared that the Mongol court in the steppe might be behind intrigues within his own entourage. Such fears contributed to his decisions to execute his prime minister and leading generals, and to build a divided administrative structure that could never pose a threat to the monarch. Chu Yüan-chang, in other words, appears not to have been so concerned with the security of "China" or even of the "Ming dynasty" as he was with the security of his own power. He had purposefully created many of the weaknesses in the Ming that later haunted the dynasty. For Chu, the "threat" could come from anywhere.

Something of the same attitude animated his son the Yung-lo emperor. Enfeoffed as the Prince of Yen (Peking), he had secured nomadic support when he turned against his nephew Chien-wen, the legitimate heir designated by Chu Yüan-chang. This act of "usurpation" (which went against Chinese practices, though it would have been standard in the steppe) meant that the Yung-lo emperor could not rely upon the support of the Confucian literati. Thus, like his father, he became suspicious of everybody. Some suggest that Yung-lo sponsored the voyages of Cheng Ho in response to rumors that the legitimate emperor had somehow survived the burning of his palace and was alive somewhere in Southeast Asia.

In the first two major Ming reigns, or roughly until the 1420s, the sense of collective state identity necessary for the identification of threats did not yet exist. The rulers defined danger according to their own position, and they could as well purge Chinese for intriguing with the Mongols, ally with the Mongols against other Chinese, or enlist Chinese and Mongols alike in their steppe armies. Such a sense of threat remained in keeping with the nomadic tradition. In the steppe, another country or another culture did not represent a threat: individuals and their followers did. After the defeat of that individual, the threat disappeared and his followers might become yours. That fluid and personal sense of security priorities governed the early Ming.

Nevertheless, the Ming created an institutionalized security system as well. Like the Mongols before them, both of the first Ming emperors placed outposts in the steppe transition zone, some new, some already established under the Yüan. Unlike the Yüan, they also built rudimentary fortifications at passes leading to Peking, which Yung-lo had made the capital early in the fifteenth century.[36] Above all, they built lookout and signaling towers. To have any sort of advantage over the nomads, the Ming needed to know of a threat as soon as possible; systems of fire, smoke, and sound signals, relayed from tower to tower across hundreds of miles of desert and mountain, ensured that they did.[37]

The early Ming was also fairly well informed about the internal politics of

[36] Edward L. Farmer, *Early Ming Government: The Evolution of Dual Capitals* (Cambridge, MA, 1976).

[37] Henry Serruys, "Towers in the Northern Frontier Defenses of the Ming," *Ming Studies* 14 (1982), pp. 8–76.

the steppe world. Many ethnic Mongols served in the dynasty's forces, and at least some ethnic Chinese who served on the borders learned the Mongol language and came to understand how politics worked in the north. In the early period, the dynasty took a keen interest in the steppe, actively establishing quasidiplomatic relationships with the nomads, and receiving trade and tribute missions at the capital. In essence, early Ming strategy toward the steppe seems to have followed, in its broadest outlines, that of the Yüan. This process must have depended upon personal knowledge and understanding, for nowhere in Chinese (or Mongolian, for that matter) is there a written guide to such policy.

The personalized basis of Ming strategy proved to be the major weakness of the early security system. An emperor like Yung-lo might have an almost intuitive understanding of how to play the game of steppe politics. But an emperor raised in the palace and educated entirely in the Confucian classical tradition would not, any more than his ministers who shared a similar education. As a result, the more the Ming dynasty became "Sinicized," the more it grew away from its roots as a successor to the nomadic Yüan, and the more it drew political and moral guidance from strictly Chinese sources and precedents the less effective its national security policy became. The increasing incorporation of Chinese approaches – particularly those from the Southern Sung dynasty – did not simply weaken policy: it turned it toward disaster.

This process drew on classical texts for its inspiration. It would be misleading to speak of a "Confucian" foreign or national security policy, given that the classics scarcely address such topics. But certain elements in Confucian thought, which Chinese intellectuals repeatedly applied to foreign policy questions, are perhaps best summed up as "maximal goals and minimal policies." The Confucian classics portray a single world, civilized at the center and shading off toward barbarism at the edges, but nevertheless a unified one, in which the emperor provides the junction of the human and the transcendent realms. Rule, direct or indirect, over everything, is in such political thought a natural consequence of the fundamental order of nature. In other words, conquest or extraordinary feats of diplomacy can not achieve it. It is rather something that will come about of itself provided only that natural processes are allowed to work themselves out. Such a goal was clearly "maximalist." Yet given a truly virtuous emperor, it will occur through inaction, as a result of natural social processes – a "minimalist" policy.

Above all, virtually all strains of Chinese philosophy frowned on the use of force. Even Sun Tzu's description of war and conquest avoids much talk about violence. He uses the word *li*, force, only nine times in his entire *Art of War*, while Clausewitz uses *Gewalt* eight times alone when defining war in the two paragraphs of Book I.2.[38] Furthermore, when Sun Tzu does use the

---

[38] Lionel Giles, *Sun-tzu;* Carl von Clausewitz, *On War*, Michael Howard and Peter Paret, trans. and eds. (Princeton, 1976), p. 75.

word force, he does so almost always to stress the need to conserve it. The words that Samuel Griffith puts in Sun Tzu's mouth in Book III.11 have dazzled more than one Western strategist: "Your aim must be to take All-under-Heaven intact."[39] This, however, is a mistranslation, and what Sun Tzu really says is far more in line with his general caution about the use of force: "keeping his own forces intact he will dispute the mastery of empire."[40] So even traditional China's preeminent military theorist shrank from the use of direct force.

The Taoists, too, rejected force as a means of rule. The *Tao-te-ching* states that "those who aid the ruler with Tao do not use military force to conquer the world," and notes that "after a great war comes the year of adversity."[41] Confucians shared the same predisposition against force and warfare. At one point Confucius commented on the plan of Chi-sun of the state of Lu to attack the small state of Chüan-yü. Aware that the rigors of war might disrupt the stability of the attacking state, he observed "I am afraid that the sorrows of the Chi-sun family will not be on account of Chüan-yü, but will be found within the screen of his own court."[42] The key to creating and controlling a large empire, according to these classics – all of which antedate the appearance of true horse nomads – was virtue and morality.

The increasing dominance of this classical tradition in Ming China made it hard for policymakers to behave rationally. Many believed that dominion over all under heaven was natural rather than simply a difficult challenge, and its nonachievement became a sign of moral failure. Under the influence of the classical tradition, critics of the court also tended to propose unrealistic solutions to the complex problems of border defense. Harking back to the Han dynasty, commentators would write that the Mongols were "no more numerous than the inhabitants of a single Chinese *hsien* or district," and thus ought to be easy to control. The unwritten tradition of steppe politics that had enabled the Yüan and the early Ming to operate fairly successfully gradually dissolved in the vast corpus of written Chinese history and philosophy.

This development inevitably skewed the decision-making processes that governed national security policy.[43] Although the Ming had experts on frontier and defense policy who usually combined a first-rate classical education with common sense and border experience, such people had more and more difficulty in making their voices heard. Foreign policy instead became an

39 Sun Tzu, *The Art of War*, translated and with an introduction by Samuel B. Griffith, with a foreword by B.H. Liddell Hart (New York and Oxford, 1963), p. 79.
40 D.C. Lau, "Some Notes on the Sun Tzu," *Bulletin of the School of Oriental and African Studies*, University of London, no. 28, part 1 (1965), pp. 319–35, esp. pp. 334–35.
41 Paul J. Lin, *A Translation of Lao-tzu's Tao-te-ching and Wang Pi's Commentary* (Ann Arbor, MI, 1977), p. 55.
42 *Lun Yü* ["Analects"] XVI.1. James Legge, trans., *The Chinese Classics* (reprint ed.: Taipei, 1971) Vol. 1, pp. 306–309.
43 On Ming foreign policy, see Jung-pang Lo, "Policy Formulation and Decision-making on Issues Respecting Peace and War," in Charles O. Hucker, ed., *Chinese Government in Ming Times: Seven Studies* (New York and London, 1969), pp. 41–72.

arena for the factional politics of the Ming court. Unqualified people made military proposals, and the ultimate decisions on them reflected intrigue rather than deliberation. This was natural, given that the first emperor had weakened and divided the bureaucratic hierarchies which might otherwise have made policy in a systematic way. A series of erratic or weak emperors in the sixteenth and seventeenth centuries – Cheng-te (1506–1522), Chia-ching (1522–1567), Lung-ch'ing (1567–1573), and Wan-li (1573–1620) – exacerbated the situation. Further complicating matters was the emergence, as southern China grew wealthier, of influential intellectuals who formed learned academies or *shu-yüan,* the most famous of which was the Tung-lin. These intellectuals discussed questions of military strategy and attempted to make their usually aggressive approaches to foreign policy heard at court.[44]

The three cases already noted illustrate the strategic problems facing the Ming. First is T'u-mu, a campaign that offers a classic example of how nonmilitary personnel took over the making of military policy. Second is the debate over long-term policy toward the Mongols, which came to focus on one issue: whether or not to conquer and fortify the crucial territory of the Ordos in the Yellow River loop. The enormously expensive sixteenth-century Ming program of wall-building came out of this debate. Finally, there were the depredations of so-called "Japanese pirates," in fact southeast coast merchants and traders who violated the policy of maritime exclusion.

Esen (d. 1455), the adversary at T'u-mu, was a Mongol leader in the heroic mold. Even under the early and more cosmopolitan Ming rulers, exchanges with the steppe had been diminishing. Although steppe rulers might receive titles from the Ming and engage in a certain amount of trade, the number of exchanges was already much less than under the Yüan, and this destabilized the steppe. A steppe leader might benefit greatly from the reestablishment of the old relationship, and this Esen sought to do. He aimed to restore the unity, power, and prestige of the steppe peoples as the Ming developed, and eventually to change the terms of their relationship with the Chinese state. The Mongols wanted what they had enjoyed earlier, closer diplomatic relations and easier trade, and when these proved difficult to obtain, they threatened to conquer China in the manner of their ancestors. In the little more than a decade before the battle of T'u-mu, Esen made himself hegemon of an area that stretched from modern Sinkiang to Korea and married his daughter to the young khan.

Esen's people, the Oirat, had become tributaries early in the Ming dynasty, and trading missions of Mongols obtained permission to visit the capital several times a year, though strict controls determined the number of their members and their routes. For a variety of reasons, however, the Mongols

44 Heinrich Busch, "The Tung-lin Shu-yüan and its political and philosophical significance," *Monumenta Serica* 14 (1949–55), pp. 1–163; John Meskill, "Academies and Politics in the Ming Dynasty," in Charles O. Hucker, ed., *Chinese Government in Ming Times* (New York and London, 1969), pp. 149–74.

objected to such arrangements. The volume of trade was insufficient and the Ming proved unable or perhaps unwilling to live up to Mongol expectations of the ruler of north China, and play the role of active patron and subsidizer.

Although the Mongols found their relationship with the Ming too limited, many Chinese considered it excessive. Even formal trade and tribute missions were more than they could countenance. Drawing on the xenophobic tradition of southern China, they scorned nomads for moral reasons and believed such beings were beneath the notice of the Chinese emperor. Of course, some Chinese understood that such a policy could lead only to catastrophe, but as we shall see, they were unable to make their views prevail.

Crisis came when an influential eunuch at the court of the young Cheng-t'ung emperor (r. 1435–1449) unilaterally cut the numbers of Oirat permitted to trade in Peking. This action led to a discussion among the nomads, with the khan (according to Chinese accounts) calling for peaceful negotiations, while Esen pushed for attack. As Esen began to deploy his forces outside the passes for attack, a second debate commenced at the Ming court.

The emperor and his immediate circle wanted to raise an army – or "punitive expedition" as they called it – to put Esen in his place. The minister of war, however, K'uang Yeh, spoke out strongly against such an attack. His staff prepared memoranda detailing the problems of supplying a protracted campaign in the steppe, and he himself argued that:

> The Six Armies must not be lightly employed. . . . Armies are instruments of violence; warfare is a dangerous business. The sages of antiquity undertook war with cautious respect, not daring to do so carelessly. The Son of Heaven, although the most exalted of men, would now go personally into those dangers. We officials, though the most stupid of men, nonetheless say that this must not occur.

The advocates of attack, however, carried the day. The Emperor replied to the remonstrances of his officials, saying:

> These words of you Ministers all convey very well your loyalty and patriotism. But the bandits offend against heaven and dishonor our favor to them. They have already violated our borders; they have murdered and plundered our military and civilian population there. The border garrison commanders have repeatedly asked for armies to come to their aid. We have no choice but to lead a great army in person to exterminate them.

The expedition proved disastrous. A huge army passed through Chü-yung-kuan pass in August 1449, on its way to the steppe and a decisive encounter with the nomads. On the thirteenth day out, it passed a battlefield on which thousands of Chinese, killed in an earlier engagement, still lay unburied. A few days later, as the troops became more and more frightened, the eunuch in charge decided to call off the expedition and reversed the march – right into a Mongol ambush. Near the postal relay station of T'u-mu, the Mongols surrounded the entire Ming army and cut it to pieces. Those who could tore off their armor and fled. Many more perished, while the emperor himself, sitting unharmed in the middle of the battlefield, became a Mongol prisoner.[45]

In a number of ways this battle was the turning point for Ming strategy. It marked the last time a Chinese army actually left China proper and headed into the steppe to deal with the nomads, and as such brought a profound shift in the whole strategic stance of the dynasty. Its outcome dissipated completely the military prestige – the *wei*, or "awesomeness," that much valued, if intangible, ingredient of strategic success – that earlier emperors had accumulated by virtue of their active conquests. It underlined also the extent to which the Ming court and its rule had politicized and rendered irrational the process of strategic decision-making.

Defeat at T'u-mu caused the effective collapse of the Ming position on the northern border. Chinese garrisons retreated from outlying posts, while the Mongols, who had hitherto remained well to the north, began to press down into the steppe transition zone. This development in turn created the strategic problem that would remain critical, and unresolved, until the end of the dynasty.

The experience of both the Yüan and the early Ming had demonstrated that it was impossible to secure northern China without powerful influence, if not control, over the steppe. That influence depended on the maintenance of bases and striking forces along the steppe margin. In this connection the single most important territory was the Ordos, the area of northwest China within the great loop of the Yellow River. This territory was mostly desert, and by rights should have belonged to the steppe. But the river made irrigated agriculture possible, which permitted self-supporting or nearly self-supporting Chinese garrisons there. The Yüan had controlled the Ordos, as had the T'ang and other earlier powerful dynasties. But even at the very beginning the Ming had never placed a garrison there, though an outpost at Tung-sheng, just outside the river loop, provided a kind of control. In 1403, however, the Yung-lo emperor withdrew this garrison, along with a number of others along the frontier. As long as this retreat left the overall might of the dynasty unaffected, it was not a major strategic mistake. But as we have seen, in the mid-fifteenth century came the destruction of the main Ming army and Ming prestige. Under those conditions, the lack of outposts in the steppe transition zone was soon sorely felt.

The collapse after T'u-mu occurred in two stages. First came the defeat of the expeditionary force. The second stage came in its immediate aftermath and had long-term implications. The T'u-mu defeat swept the Ming out of the steppe transition zone and brought the nomads into it. The strategic positions and the resources of that region could, if the Chinese turned them

---

[45]   This account follows F.W. Mote, "The T'u-mu Incident of 1449."

northward, contribute to control of the steppe. If the nomads possessed them, however, and turned them southward, these resources could provide an enhanced ability to pressure China proper. That was exactly what happened. Particularly under the leadership of a succession of dynamic khans in the sixteenth century, the nomads turned the tables on the Chinese, built settlements along the Ming's northern frontier, and sent out from them both raiding parties and petitions to court.

The Ming gradually came to understand their new strategic predicament in traditional terms. The importance of the Ordos had been known since pre-Ch'in times, and in the fifteenth century the great encyclopedist Ch'iu Chün (1420–1495) made its significance explicit in his "Supplement to the Extended Meaning of the *Great Learning*" (*Ta-hsüeh yen-i pu*). By the 1460s, a debate was underway at court over whether or not to raise an army to "recover" the Ordos. This debate manifested the better defined traits of mid-Ming strategic policymaking.[46]

As at the time of T'u-mu a few decades earlier, opinion at court had been divided. Drawing directly on the words of Chia I, the senior grand secretary Li Hsien (1408–1467) proposed a policy of recovery. He wanted men, horses, war carts, and provisions on the border in preparation for a campaign in 1467, and the emperor agreed to the scheme.

But the sheer impracticality of the suggestion made it impossible to implement. Generals in command of border regions dragged their feet. The resources required simply did not exist, and furthermore, as T'u-mu had shown, an ill-prepared and unsuccessful campaign could spell disaster. So for a number of years after Li made his proposal, the Ordos recovery policy, though officially adopted, lay dormant.

In the early 1470s, however, the minister of war, Pai Kuei (1419–1475) undertook sponsorship of the Ordos recovery. His family's origins went back to the Yüan army, and he proved an energetic advocate of the forward policy. His support led to the concentration of forces and the appointment of a senior official as *p'ing-lu chiang-chün* ("general who pacifies the barbarians") in 1472.

This serious attempt to put the strategy into practice, however, brought home its impracticality. Commanders on the border sent memorials to Peking explaining the desperate condition of their forces, while those charged with paying for the enterprise worried about the reaction of the peasants taxed to provide the expedition's food and metal.

The outcome was important for China. When the unfeasibility of Ordos recovery became clear, others at court, most notably Yü Tzu-chün (1429–1489), began to call for a strictly defensive policy: wall building. Strong dynasties had never favored this policy. Perhaps T'ang T'ai-tsung delivered

---

[46] The debate is treated in Waldron, *The Great Wall of China*; also in a rather unsatisfactory article, I Chih, "Ming-tai 'Ch'i-T'ao' Shih-mo," in Pao Tsun-p eng, ed., *Ming-tai Pien-fang* (Taipei, 1968).

the classic slur on it when he praised his general Li Chi (584–669) by saying that while Sui Yang-ti [580–618, a famous "bad last emperor"] had spent vast sums building walls to defend his ill-ruled domains, he, T'ai-tsung, had only to appoint his general Li to Ping-chou on the frontier to pacify the nomads.[47]

Yü Tzu-chün, however, argued for a defensive line along the southern margin of the Ordos desert to block off the nomadic invasion routes from the Yellow River loop into China proper. After much inconclusive skirmishing along the frontier and heated politicking at court, Yü's approach carried the day, and the dynasty completed an adobe rampart roughly 600 miles long along the Ordos margin in 1474. This structure was the first installment of "The Great Wall of China," though at the time it was simply a local expedient to deal with a particularly difficult military challenge.

From the completion of Yü's wall to the middle of the sixteenth century, the Ming confronted an increasing strategic challenge. During this period, the Mongols finally began to pull themselves back together after the Chinese victories in the early Ming and the internecine warfare that followed Esen's attempt in the 1450s to usurp the title of khan. In 1488, a descendent of Chinggis proclaimed himself Dayan-khan – khan of the Yüan, a title that suggested irredentist goals. After a long war with rivals in the steppe, the Dayan-khan (Batü Möngke, c. 1464–c. 1532) began raiding the Ming frontier not only in the north, but also in the hitherto quiet west. He repeatedly sought trade and tribute relations with the Ming, but rejection turned him more and more to outright warfare.

The Mongols well understood the geostrategic situation. In Yüan times, Khubilai had built a line of forts in the steppe transition zone from which to control his rivals in Mongolia, and the Hung-wu emperor's deployments in the early Ming had served the same purpose. The Dayan-khan established his own mirror image of these deployments in 1514: a line of permanent camps from which he could project influence southward, harrying the borders of the Ming up to the approaches to the capital. Another similarly gifted leader, the Altan-khan (1507–1582), followed the Dayan-khan, and continued the same approach. The Altan-khan founded the city he called Köke-khota [whence Hu-ho-hao-t'e or Hohhot, its present name] just to the northeast of the Yellow River loop. This settlement exerted pressure along the whole Ming defense line. The Altan-khan, however, appeared not to have envisioned a reconquest of China. He sought instead to obtain official status and trading privileges within the Ming system.[48]

Warfare with the Altan-khan led to a second eruption of the debate over

[47] *Hsin T'ang-shu* (Chung-hua ed.) 93.3818–19.
[48] For the Mongols of the Ming, see Louis Hambis, *Documents sur l'histoire des Mongols à l'époque des Ming* (Paris, 1969) and the works of Henry Serruys, in particular "Sino-Mongol Relations During the Ming, II. The Tribute System and Diplomatic Missions (1400–1600)," *Mélanges Chinois et Bouddhiques* 14 (1969).

Ordos recovery, this time at the court of the Chia-ching emperor (r. 1522–1567). The emperor had come to the throne from a collateral line while still a child; his was arguably the most faction-ridden of all Ming courts, a situation that had a lamentable effect on foreign policy. During this reign, an able and ambitious young official with military duties, Tseng Hsien (1499–1548), once again proposed Ordos recovery. Tseng perhaps really believed it was possible, but debate at court over his proposals quickly lost sight of the military and strategic questions. The question of Ordos recovery became, instead, a personal showdown between two grand secretaries competing for the emperor's favor – Hsia Yen (1482–1548), who favored it, and Yen Sung (1480–1565), who opposed it. Although the court initially welcomed Tseng's proposals, which received strong support from patriotic or xenophobic elements at court, Yen Sung and his faction ultimately triumphed. They not only defeated the policy, but also managed to arrange the executions of both Tseng and his sponsor Hsia Yen.[49]

The resolution of the Ordos debate in favor of a defensive policy strengthened trends already apparent in the early sixteenth century. This period marked the beginning of the great age of Chinese wall building. Earlier dynasties, if they built fortifications at all, had relied upon earth for material and peasants for labor. But in the mid-Ming, for the first time on any large scale, the Chinese began to build fortifications in stone. This greatly increased the cost of defenses, requiring the use of silver from the treasury and the employment of specialized masons and other craftsmen for construction. During this period Shan-hai-kuan, Chü-yung-kuan, Chia-yü-kuan, and other sites along the Ming frontier took their present form.

Finally, there was the coast. Both the maritime prohibition introduced in 1523 at the suggestion of Hsia Yen, and the analogous prohibitions of trade along the northern frontier, led to trouble. Merchants who had hitherto traded with Japan and southeast Asia turned to piracy. Raids, often in search of repayment of bad debts, ravaged the southeast coast, while in the capital, the court was at a loss for a policy. As with the northern frontier, it tended to take a hard line. Hsia Yen secured the appointment of one of his protégés, who attempted to seal off the south China coast (virtually an impossible task even today with radar and fast patrol boats!) and stamp out the pirates' base areas. None of this worked, however, and as was the case with the Ordos, only compromise could solve the problem.[50]

Compromise, however, was difficult to secure through the decision-making apparatus of the Ming court. For most of the sixteenth century, a stalemate existed in Peking between advocates of trade and diplomacy on both northern and southeastern frontiers, and those who, moralistically and

[49]   For details, see Waldron, *The Great Wall of China*.
[50]   Kwan-wai So, *Japanese Piracy in Ming China During the 16th Century* (East Lansing, MI, 1975).

nationalistically, wished to destroy agents of compromise and seal off the frontiers. This outcome was in many ways the worst possible one: both piracy and raiding continued, while an impoverished court spent vast sums against them without effect. The eventual collapse of the Ming dynasty in the early seventeenth century arguably had its roots in this period.

Ming policy, then, was highly ineffective. Chinese history, however, did contain examples of regimes that managed to find security from threats coming from the steppe. Usually, but not always, dynasties that were themselves partially or totally of nomadic origin followed such policies and thus had access to the unwritten traditions of rule and warfare that formed the operations of the Mongols and other nomads. The early Ming are an example in keeping with the Yüan origin of many of the new dynasty's institutions; the first and third emperors, in particular, demonstrated some understanding of war and diplomacy in the steppe. Periods of effectiveness resulted from a secure hold on the steppe transition zone: through garrisons in the Ordos and other key regions; a willingness to transfer resources from China proper northward both to support such garrisons and to subsidize nomadic allies; an understanding of steppe warfare and an ability to wage it in its two forms – the long-term economic blockade of the opponent, and the rapid and decisive strike against an enemy concentration in support of a candidate for leadership at a time of transition. Perhaps above all, effectiveness required a high degree of intellectual flexibility. It was unwise to treat the nomads as if they really were "barbarians." One had to understand their economic and political needs and to make use of those needs as levers to influence developments in the steppe.

The failure to sustain a workable Ming policy on any of these levels stemmed largely from institutional division and cultural conflict. No single official or ministry in the Ming government had the power to make a final decision about national security policy. And no prime minister or commander-in-chief of the armies existed. Rather, a score of officials, palace employees, and eunuchs contended among themselves for control of the emperor. Only when a well-informed and strong emperor was in power could the system produce decisions – right or wrong.

Disagreements among the contenders for power ran deep. A major theme of the Ming period is the gradual ebbing of steppe cultural influence and the ascendancy of the culture of the Chinese deep south: the refined, brilliant, but culturalistic and xenophobic world-view of the wealthy literati of the Yangtze delta and other such areas. Brilliant, moralistic scholars, born and raised in environments of great sophistication, who had never laid eyes on a "barbarian" but rather knew of them only from books a millennium out of date, increasingly revived an inflammatory and exclusivist patriotic rhetoric that proved highly effective when directed against moderate voices at court. Public opinion, such as it was, weighed in powerfully on the side of bad policy.

The disagreements between the two policy factions corresponded only partially to the division between civilians and the military. Among military men (the educated officials who made their careers leading armies), some shared the views of the xenophobic groups, but more probably understood the absolute necessity of compromise with the Mongols. Among civilians, however, a handful really understood the wretchedness of the military situation, and there was no shortage of eloquent and outspoken advocates of potentially disastrous expedients. A good example is Yang Chi-sheng (1516–1555), executed for his bitter attacks on the advocates at the Ming court of compromise with the Mongols, thus becoming a patriotic martyr whose memory the Chinese still honored as recently as 1937 in the face of Japanese aggression.[51] Civil-military alliances formed, in other words, on both sides of the issues, with eunuchs, imperial relatives, and other influential figures distributing themselves in accordance with personal interest rather than any policy stake.

The implementation of policy reflected the ambiguities of its making. The military establishment created at the beginning of the Ming – the system of hereditary military, horse-supplying and other households replenishing a standing army of over one million men, and the system of military farms at which these soldiers supported themselves by growing grain when not fighting – had sounded appealing, but never worked, and was effectively useless by the early fifteenth century. Similarly, the military and civil bureaucracies that should have administered and directed that army swiftly lost effectiveness. Areas of responsibility were unclear, chains of command repeatedly crossed over one another, and at the top no one had the power to make important decisions. This meant that when actual fighting became necessary, the Ming had to improvise and pay its forces outside the comprehensive military structure theoretically still existing, created at the dynasty's beginning.

By the middle of the Ming, its real armies were professional. In effect, top commanders received commissions for particular purposes, and troops assembled *de novo* whenever a threat arose. This arrangement was enormously wasteful, and because it required irregular levying of taxes and other imposts on the people, it could create sudden resistance precisely in the area contemplated for military action. This happened in the 1540s when Tseng Hsien, preparing his Ordos recovery army, confiscated metal cooking pots from the population, and, to their considerable annoyance, melted them down for use as weapons. Indeed, fear of civil unrest was probably one of the factors that led ultimately to the abandonment of the policy.

The cumbersome nature of the Ming military was in turn one of the factors that made it difficult for the state to change its policies in face of a shifting

---

[51] See the biography by Sun Yuen-king and L. Carrington Goodrich in L. Carrington Goodrich, ed. and Chaoying Fang, assoc. ed., *A Dictionary of Ming Biography 1368–1644* (New York and London, 1976) Vol. 2, pp. 1503–1505.

strategic environment. But more important obstacles were bureaucratic and intellectual. As already suggested, no office in the entire government managed security policy, as such an office might threaten the emperor's power. No one took a comprehensive view of policy, either geographically or historically. Intellectual trends, particularly in the latter part of the dynasty, did not favor responsible and realistic consideration of strategic issues. As the old south-Chinese culture revived, more and more intellectuals assumed theatrically "anti-barbarian" poses as part of a larger attempt to bring the policies of the Ming court more in line with their wishes. This climate of opinion soon made it almost sure political death to propose, for example, permitting the Altan-khan to send ambassadors to Peking as his father had once done.

Ultimately the political battles of the intellectuals undermined the dynasty. When the Manchu threat appeared, their arguments prevented an effective response. Chao I (1727–1814) "blamed the empty talk of the scholars. In their early days, he says, the Manchus had no intention of conquering China. Had the Ch'ung-chen emperor [r. 1628–45] made peace with them, he could have concentrated his army on suppressing the rebels instead of having to fight both."[52]

Ming ability to deal with immediate threats was no better than its capacity to make long-range strategy. For almost fifty years, from the mid-sixteenth century until its end, every autumn brought a nomad descent on China. These attacks were not wanton aggressiveness: year in and year out the nomads looked for some kind of normalization of relations. But even the virtual predictability of the nomads' attacks and the routes they would take did not save the Chinese from repeated surprise attacks and defeats.

The institutional reaction was to develop signaling systems and garrisons along the border, and these appear to have worked reasonably well. They were never comprehensive, however, and the northern frontier was vast, as the Altan-khan demonstrated in a raid in 1550 that took him to the gates of the capital. A nomad raid stopped at one point on the frontier could always move quickly to another and break through. Even the Ming's extensive fortifications never had much effect: a positional perimeter defense simply would not work against the nomads.

Of course, the dynasty had never formally adopted such a strategy as a long-term method of defense. The "wall" developed in one place after another, in response, initially at least, to specific challenges. Because provisions for defense were essentially local and fit only imperfectly into any larger strategy, efforts that might have produced a single comprehensive policy dissipated into a host of small-scale initiatives.

---

52 Albert Chan, *The Glory and Decline of the Ming Dynasty* (Norman, OK, 1982), p. 300, apparently citing Chao I, *Erh-shih-erh shih cha-chi* (in *Ts'ung-shu chi-ch'eng chien-pien*, Taipei, 1965–66), 35.739–41.

The only bright spot was the development along the coast and later on the northern frontier of tactical approaches that made good use of Ming strength. The appearance of the "Japanese pirates" in the middle of the fifteenth century had stimulated the creation of a cadre of militarily competent operatives on the coast. Able officials gravitated to the region – notably Ch'i Chi-kuang (1528–1588), who developed new methods of training and new types of tactics. The improvement of firearms and the fortification of coastal cities helped the situation, but most importantly, trading policy changed after 1554, permitting more or less free exchange subject only to a customs duty. A number of men who later served on the northern frontier got their start in the south dealing with the pirates. But the Ming neither institutionalized nor systematized these measures. Strategic success depended upon personalities and their political supporters at the center.

The long-term strategy of the Ming becomes visible only in retrospect, and in three phases. In the first phase, the Ming followed, in effect, the grand strategy of the Yüan dynasty, trying to secure a position in the steppe by bringing Chinese resources to bear up on it and using a mixture of diplomatic, economic, and military means to pressure the nomads. In the second, which lasted from the middle of the fifteenth century until the middle of the sixteenth century, the Ming lacked a single clearly articulated strategy. Rather, as the culture of the dynasty began to shift away from nomadic models, divisions appeared about how best to alter military strategy. The result was inaction. In the third phase, the dynasty took steps that suggested a new grand strategy. This was "The Great Wall," which grew gradually as the dynasty strengthened first one and then another frontier sector.

But, in fact, the Ming managed a really competent national security policy at only one point after the early period. In the 1570s, a single grand secretary who knew what had to be done managed to achieve unquestioned sway over both his colleagues and the emperor. This was Chang Chü-cheng (1525–1582).

Chang understood that the solution to the problems with Mongolia must involve compromise. He followed the model used in dealing with the pirates and brought several of the key originators of that successful policy to the north to deal with the Mongols. He secured peace with the Altan-khan and forced it through the government. In 1571 the Ming agreed to give the khan official status and to permit him to trade. He in return agreed to cease raiding. And astonishingly enough, peace really did arrive. Expenses for the armies dropped dramatically: in 1577 the costs of defense at Hsüan-fu, Ta-t'ung, and other points along the nomadic attack routes near the capital had dropped to only 20 to 30 percent of expenses before the peace. Subsidies to the Mongols under the new system amounted to only one-tenth of previous defense costs. But the success of Chang's policy ended with his death.[53] It had

53 Henry Serruys, "Sino-Mongolian Relations During the Ming (II)," pp. 64–83.

required a strong man to push through such abhorrent compromises, and without Chang, quarrelling began again, this time permitting the Manchus to grow strong, and eventually to conquer the Ming. Strategic success depended, above all, on political unity and coherence.

The student of strategic culture may find this a disappointing harvest. "Late imperial China," it turns out, was politically faction-ridden and as a result incapable of producing anything remotely like a coherent national security policy. The state created many of its own worst problems: the nomads, for instance, would never have made so many destructive raids if the Ming had only allowed them to trade. But powerful cultural and political currents in the society and intelligentsia made such a policy unpopular and difficult to implement.

Yet these are important conclusions. The tendency to homogenize the Chinese past and then overgeneralize continues to be a problem both in the West and in China itself. Although most overgeneralization is about culture and society, it has had a pernicious influence on comparative studies of foreign policy and strategy. Students of China's modern foreign policy tend to imagine that it builds on a single "tradition," and have created a substantial library of scholarship to sustain this contention.[54] Scholars have likewise sought to discover a Chinese tradition of warfare and strategy, or in the language of this book, a Chinese strategic culture.[55] Both of these enterprises have their validity and their usefulness. But they tend to suffer from lack of genuine historical perspective, and to reflect instead the pervasive Western tendency to think of China as a single, homogeneous, and long-extant entity. As in the case of foreign policy, however, the real Chinese past is not a single tradition, but rather several different and competing ones.

Knowledge of these traditions makes it possible to classify the approaches of different Chinese states at different times. Some have been expansionist and have relied on offensive warfare, though that strategy did not work well after the arrival of the nomads without steppe alliance. Others have perforce or by choice been defensive, and have sought to exclude the steppe from their politics by withdrawal to the deep south beyond the range of nomadic horsemen or by wall-building. Still others – and these are perhaps the most interesting – have sought to manage the steppe, making use of culture, economics, and diplomacy as well as force.

The Ming exhibits characteristics of all three, starting as a blend of the first and the third, and ending up as the second. The evolution of Ming strategy

---

[54] Even as he opened up new scholarly territory, John Fairbank created some of these myths: they are well-expressed in the introduction to his *The Chinese World Order* (Cambridge, MA, 1968). For an exhaustive statement, see Mark Mancall, *China at the Center: 300 Years of Foreign Policy* (New York, 1984). A dissenting view is presented in Morris Rossabi, ed., *China Among Equals: The Middle Kingdom and its Neighbors, 10th-14th Centuries* (Berkeley, 1983).
[55] See, for example, Chong-Pin Lin, *China's Nuclear Weapons Strategy* (Lexington, MA, and Toronto, 1988), pp. 17-36.

underlines the importance of culture in general to strategic culture. The shift to a more defensive and xenophobic outlook was not confined to the military sphere but reflected much broader developments in intellectual life. But the Ming also demonstrates that culture was not supreme. Although Chinese tradition worked ever more strongly against strategic rationality, at critical times such as the 1570s individuals who had amassed the requisite political power could decisively affect the dynasty's national security policy.

Similar patterns have emerged in other periods of Chinese history as well, including the present. Even after the end of the Ch'ing, centralized and bureaucratic government continued to rule China, operating in a highly politicized environment. While Confucianism had ceased by the mid-twentieth century to play the political role it had in the sixteenth, nationalistic and xenophobic beliefs had grown in influence, playing an important part in policy formation – though in just what ways remains difficult to specify. At some times they seemed to have taken control. But at others, particularly when governments were strong, rational and pragmatic policies could still take hold. In trying to understand these specific cases, the most useful approach will probably continue to be the one taken here: to examine not merely the content of strategy, but also the process, and the multitude of factors that bear upon it, by which strategy is made.

5

The making of strategy in Habsburg Spain: Philip II's "bid for mastery," 1556–1598

GEOFFREY PARKER[1]

INTRODUCTION

Scholars have claimed that Philip II, ruler of an empire upon which – quite literally – the sun never set, lacked a "grand strategy." "He never outlined a plan or programme for his reign," wrote H. G. Koenigsberger in a penetrating study of 1971, "nor did any of his ministers. . . . [And] for this failure there can be only one reasonable explanation: they had no such plan or programme."[2] The assumption that there was no "blueprint for empire" underlies most writing about the overall policy aims of Philip II.

Paul M. Kennedy wholly accepted this premise in his chapter on "The Habsburg bid for mastery" in *The Rise and Fall of the Great Powers* (1987). "It may appear a little forced to use the title 'The Habsburg bid for mastery' " wrote Kennedy, because "despite the occasional rhetoric of some Habsburg ministers about a 'world monarchy,' there was no conscious plan to dominate Europe in the manner of Napoleon or Hitler." But, as Kennedy shrewdly recognized, the absence of a comprehensive global master plan did not necessarily preclude the harboring of comprehensive global ambitions; for "[even] had the Habsburg rulers achieved all of their limited regional aims – even their *defensive* aims – the mastery of Europe would virtually have

[1] I am grateful to the Research Board of the University of Illinois at Urbana-Champaign for supporting two research assistants – Kathleen M. Colquhoun and Jeffrey M. McKeage— who helped me to prepare this paper. I am also indebted to those who provided comments, ideas, and criticisms: John F. Guilmartin, Edward N. Luttwak, John A. Lynn, William S. Maltby, Williamson Murray, Jane H. Ohlmeyer, and to the history graduate students in my classes at both the University of Illinois at Urbana-Champaign (especially Nancy van Deusen) and at the Ohio State University (especially Brian Greenwald).

All dates are given New Style (unless otherwise stated) and all sums of money are given in Castilian ducats, of which there were between four and five to the pound sterling during the reign of Philip II.
[2] H. G. Koenigsberger, *Politicians and Virtuosi: Essays in Early Modern History* (London, 1986), pp. 80, 82.

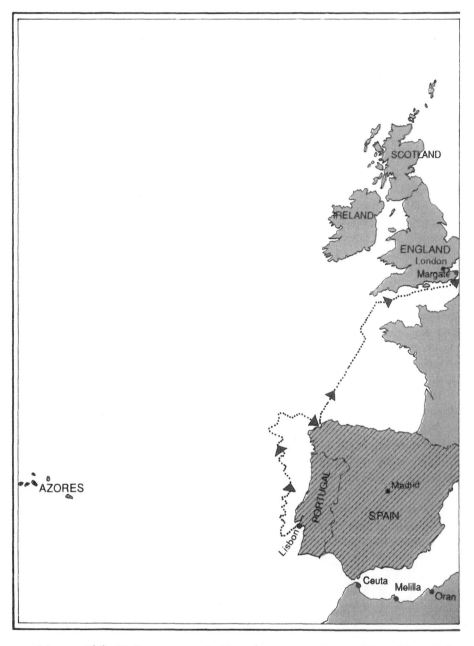

Map 5.1. Philip II's European empire/Armada campaign. *Source.* Adapted from Colin Martin and Geoffrey Parker, *The Spanish Armada* (London: Hamish Hamilton, 1988), endpapers.

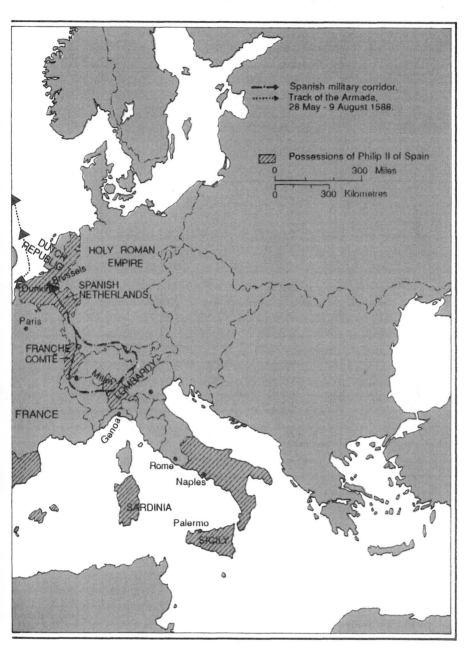

Spanish military corridor.
Track of the Armada,
28 May - 9 August 1588.

Possessions of Philip II of Spain

0   300 Miles

0   300 Kilometres

DUTCH
REPUBLIC

HOLY ROMAN
EMPIRE

Brussels

Dunkirk

SPANISH
NETHERLANDS

Paris

FRANCHE
COMTÉ

Milan

LOMBARDY

FRANCE

Genoa

Rome

Naples

SARDINIA

Palermo

SICILY

been theirs."[3] For although he did not succeed to the Imperial title and the Habsburg hereditary lands in central Europe on the death of his father Charles V in 1558, Philip II nevertheless governed an empire "whose banners and standards have crossed more than one third of the world, from Sicily to Cuzco and to the province of Quito, a distance which includes nine hours of difference. . . . And if we measure its extent, from north to south, it covers one quarter of the earth."[4] That was the situation in 1577. Five years later, with the conquest of the Philippines in full swing and the entire Portuguese overseas empire annexed, Philip II's possessions spanned all twenty-four of the world's time zones.

Paul Kennedy's analysis of the strategic parameters of Habsburg imperialism is by far the best currently available, and it offers a masterly synthesis of published work on the subject. Contemporary documents also support Kennedy's argument. For example, the king himself frequently insisted that he had no desire to add to his enviably extensive domains: he wished merely to conserve them. Thus in 1586 he informed Pope Sixtus V (who had urged him to conquer England):

> I have no reason to be driven by ambition to acquire more kingdoms or states, or to gain reputation, because Our Lord in his goodness has given me so much of all these things that I am content.[5]

If the king chose to go to war with foreign powers from time to time, he always proclaimed that his motive was self-defense – that he only attacked when he was himself attacked. Thus he could truthfully assert that the Habsburgs' wars with France normally began with a French ultimatum or declaration: in 1521, 1536, 1542, 1552, 1556, and even in 1595 – with another projected attack on Spain in 1572 averted only by the assassination of the chief architect of the operation, Gaspard de Coligny. Philip II could likewise claim that his wars against the Ottoman Turks were primarily defensive, with Spain mobilizing only after an attack upon itself or upon one of its allies: after the capture of Tripoli from the Knights of St. John in 1551, and after the conquest of Cyprus from the Venetians in 1570. The very size of Philip II's empire meant that its defenders could almost always plausibly

---

3   Paul M. Kennedy, *The Rise and Fall of the Great Powers: Economic Change and Military Conflict from 1500 to 2000* (New York, 1987), pp. 35f. Precisely the same point was made by H. Lutz, *Christianitas Afflicta: Europa, das Reich und die päpstliche Politik im Niedergang der Hegemonie Kaiser Karls V. (1552–1556)* (Göttingen, 1964), pp. 208f; and by J. H. Elliott, "Foreign Policy and Domestic Crisis: Spain, 1598–1659," in Elliott, *Spain and its World 1500–1700: Selected Essays* (New Haven, 1989), pp. 114–41.

4   From an anonymous astrological tract of 1577 quoted in D. C. Goodman, *Power and Penury: Government, Technology and Science in Philip II's Spain* (Cambridge, 1988), p. 30. The concept of using "time-zones" to measure size seems strikingly modern.

5   Archivo General de Simancas [hereafter AGS], *Sección de Estado* [hereafter *Estado*] 947/110, Philip II to the count of Olivares, Spanish ambassador in Rome, 22 July 1586. See a parallel statement from 1558 in M. J. Rodríguez Salgado, *The Changing Face of Empire: Charles V, Philip II and Habsburg Authority, 1551–1559* (Cambridge, 1988), p. 161.

argue that something or someone threatened the security of one part of the empire or another. As his grandson put it with some eloquence in 1626:

> With as many kingdoms and lordships as have been linked to this crown, it is impossible to be without war in some area, either to defend what we have acquired or to divert our enemies.[6]

But that is not how Spain's neighbors perceived the situation. They, on the contrary, remained unshakably convinced that the Spanish Habsburgs pursued a grand strategy aimed at the subjugation of the entire continent, if not the entire world. They adduced two sets of facts as proof. On the one hand lay the numerous works written in support of the Habsburgs' universalist aspirations. The election in 1519 of Charles V – ruler of Spain, the Netherlands, and almost half of Italy – as Holy Roman Emperor gave rise to a spate of polemics calling upon the new ruler to imitate the achievements of his namesake Charlemagne and unite all Christendom. Juan Ginés de Sepúlveda, who was later appointed tutor to Philip II, wrote one of the more extreme of these appeals and no doubt tried to pass his ideas on to his young charge.[7] Somewhat later, the prince's journey from Spain to the Netherlands in 1548 became the occasion for another outpouring of tracts urging the Habsburgs to acquire the "Universal Monarchy." Many more followed.[8] For its part, the Cortes (parliament) of Castile "rejoiced repeatedly in the fact that God had given His Majesty so many kingdoms and they said quite naively that they hoped he would acquire many more."[9]

The threat of Habsburg domination, as Spain's enemies perceived it, lay not only in literature, however, but also in the hard facts of political geography. The French, German, and English governments all felt the menace of Philip II's powerful army, and not without reason, as it lay just across their borders in the Netherlands after 1567. The army intervened in France in 1569 and in the 1590s, in the Rhineland in the 1580s, and threatened En-

---

6 Archives Générales du Royaume [hereafter AGRB], Brussels, *Secrétairerie d'Etat et de Guerre* 195/64, Philip IV to the Infanta Isabella, 9 August 1626. The strategic culture of the court of Philip III and Philip IV is brilliantly discussed in J.I. Israel, *Empires and Entrepôts: The Dutch, the Spanish Monarchy, and the Jews, 1585–1713* (London, 1990), chs. 6–7; in Elliott, "Foreign Policy and Domestic Crisis: Spain, 1598–1659"; and in Elliott, "Managing Decline: Olivares and the Grand Strategy of Imperial Spain," in Paul M. Kennedy, ed., *Grand Strategies in War and Peace* (New Haven, 1991), pp. 87–104.

7 See J. M. Headley, "The Habsburg World Empire and the Revival of Ghibellinism," in S. Wenzel, ed., *Medieval and Renaissance Studies*, Vol. 7 (Chapel Hill, 1978), pp. 93–127; and A. Losada, *Juan Ginés de Sepúlveda a través de su "Epistolario" y Nuevos Documentos*, 2d ed. (Madrid, 1973), pp. 64ff and 94ff.

8 These publications are surveyed by F. Bosbach, "Papsttum und Universalmonarchie im Zeitalter der Reformation," *Historisches Jahrbüch*, 107 (1987), pp. 44–76; idem, *Monarchia Universalis: Ein politischer Leitbegriff der frühen Neuzeit* (Göttingen, 1988: Schriftenreihe der historischen Kommission bei der bayerischen Akademie der Wissenschaften, Vol. 32), ch. 4, and pp. 166–67 (a list of works on the subject published during Philip II's lifetime); and A. Pagden, *Spanish Imperialism and the Political Imagination* (New Haven, 1990), pp. 2ff and 37ff.

9 See Koenigsberger, *Politicians and Virtuosi*, p. 93.

gland in 1571 and 1587–88. As Lord Burghley, chief minister of Elizabeth I, observed in 1584: "If he [Philip II] once reduced the Low Countries to absolute subjection, I know not what limits any man of judgment can set unto his greatness." England would become a prey to Philip's "insatiable malice, which is most terrible to be thought of, but most miserable to suffer." Seen from Paris, the encircling arms of the Habsburgs – whose embrace extended from Spain through northern Italy and Franche Comté to the Netherlands – seemed even more intimidating. According to Gaspard de Coligny in 1572, "In sight of the wisest" Philip II's ambition was "to make himself monarche of Christendome, or at least to rule the same." A few years later, Henry of Navarre complained of "the ambition of the Spaniards who, having acquired domination of so many lands and seas, believe no part of the world to be inaccessible to them." The judgment of Philip's former secretary Antonio Pérez, during his exile in France in the 1590s, provided scant reassurance on this score: "The heart of the Spanish Empire" he wrote "is France."[10]

Even the popes felt uneasy about the temporal power of Spain, for the Papal States bordered upon Habsburg lands and depended on the grain of Habsburg Sicily. And no pontiff could forget either the Habsburg sack of Rome in 1527 or the ruthless use of hunger and force to defeat the papal war effort against Philip II in 1556–57. Papal support for the "crusades" of the Spanish Habsburgs, whether launched against infidels or heretics, almost always remained muted from fear that any Habsburg success might reinforce, however slightly, the dynasty's stranglehold on Italy.

THE PARAMETERS OF SPANISH GRAND STRATEGY

What is to be made of this mass of contradictory evidence? Unfortunately, the Spanish Habsburgs and their ministers neither wrote nor allowed others to write manuals of strategic analysis on the grounds that such works might compromise national security. So the truth about their strategic vision emerges only from close study of the vast corpus of largely unpublished royal letters and memoranda, formerly conserved in the archive of the counts of Altamira, and now scattered between manuscript collections in Geneva, London, and Madrid. Taken in conjunction with the government's own official records, they somewhat modify Paul Kennedy's analysis by revealing not just "the occasional rhetoric of some Habsburg ministers about a 'world monarchy'" but a recurring discussion of how best to achieve world monarchy.

[10] Quotations from W. Scott, ed., *The Somers Collection of Tracts* (London, 1809), pp. 164–70; W. T. MacCaffrey, *Queen Elizabeth and the Making of Policy 1572–1588* (Princeton, 1981), pp. 338f; N. M. Sutherland, *The Massacre of St Bartholomew and the European Conflict (1559–1572)* (London, 1973), p. 265; and G. Groen van Prinsterer, ed., *Archives ou correspondance inédite de la maison d'Orange-Nassau*, 2d series, Vol. 1 (Utrecht, 1857), p. 11 (Henry of Navarre to the Earl of Leicester, 8 May 1585).

To begin with, the Spanish Habsburgs would surrender nothing, however acquired, that they already possessed, for in strategic terms they viewed their extensive dominions as an integrated and mutually dependent edifice, in which the loss of any part would jeopardize the security of the whole. This perception was particularly relevant to the Netherlands, where frequent revolts and other forms of political opposition led to suggestions that Spain should "cut her losses" and abandon this outlying part of Philip II's extensive empire in order to secure peace for the rest. But three strategic arguments successfully countered such "defeatism." First, Spain's continued possession of the Netherlands seemed vital to the intimidation of France: "I am well aware," wrote Philip in 1558, "that it is from the Netherlands that the king of France can best be attacked and forced into peace"; while in 1582 Cardinal Granvelle, at the time Philip II's chief minister, repeated that "The surest means we have of keeping France in check is to maintain strong forces in the Netherlands."[11] Second, after a bitter civil war broke out in the Low Countries in 1572 and the rebels began to receive assistance from foreign powers, the argument appeared that they served as a sort of "punch ball" for the entire empire, since as long as Spain's enemies fought in the Netherlands, they would lack the resources to attack Spain itself. In the words of a political commentator in the early seventeenth century:

> Those who do not realize that the domestic peace which Spain enjoys derives from the long wars in the Low Countries know little of public affairs. They are only defensive and they further the tranquillity of these kingdoms because the day that Spain removes her armies from those provinces, we would inevitably see theirs in Spain.[12]

Third (and perhaps more convincing), any weakness toward Spain's opponents in the Netherlands might sooner or later compromise the Spanish hold over Italy, America, and even the peripheral kingdoms of the Iberian peninsula. Thus in June 1566, just as the troubles began, one of Philip II's senior advisers warned from Rome that "All Italy is plainly saying that if the rebellion in the Netherlands is allowed to continue, Lombardy and Naples will

---

[11] Quotations from L. P. Gachard, *Retraite et Mort de Charles-Quint*, Vol. 2 (Brussels, 1855), p. 43: Philip II's Instructions to B. Carranza, 5 June 1558; and British Library [hereafter BL] *Additional Ms.* 28,702/96–100, Cardinal Granvelle to Don Juan de Idiáquez, 3 March 1582. See also a discussion of the strategic value of Italy by Charles V's councilors in 1544: F. Chabod, "Milan o los Países Bajos? Las Discusiones sobre la 'Alternativa' de 1544," in *Carlos V (1500–1558): Homenaje de la Universidad de Granada* (Granada, 1958), pp. 331–72; and the general remarks of Israel, *Empires and Entrepôts*, pp. 163–69.

[12] P. Fernández de Navarrete, *La Conservación de Monarquías* (Madrid, 1626), p. 123. The same argument was made in 1574 by Philip II's minister of Finance, Juan de Ovando. Despite Spain's desperate financial plight, he argued, more money must be found for the war both in the Mediterranean and in the Netherlands "in order to restrain and defeat our Muslim and Protestant enemies, because it is certain that if we do not defeat them, they are going to defeat us" (Instituto de Valencia de Don Juan [hereafter IVdeDJ] 76/491–503, "Relación de la Hacienda Real," April 1574).

follow."[13] Eleven years later, when Philip II and his advisers discussed whether to go on with the war in the Netherlands or to make concessions to secure peace, one of the key arguments deployed was that clemency would be taken for weakness, and would "put at risk the obedience of other vassals who, it is greatly to be feared, would take it as an example to rebel themselves."[14] As time passed this "domino theory" expanded to include all parts of the Spanish monarchy: if Spain lost Lombardy, communications to – and therefore control of – Germany and the Netherlands would become impossible; or, more comprehensive still, weakness or defeat in any of these three spheres of interest would inexorably produce a general collapse. As the Count-Duke of Olivares put it in 1635:

> The first and greatest dangers [facing the Spanish crown] are those that threaten Lombardy, the Netherlands and Germany, because a defeat in any of these three is fatal for this Monarchy; so much so that if the defeat in those parts is a great one, the rest of the monarchy will collapse, for Germany will be followed by Italy and the Netherlands, and the Netherlands will be followed by America; and Lombardy will be followed by Naples and Sicily, without the possibility of being able to defend either.[15]

Moments of acute crisis or exhaustion, however, revealed an underlying set of strategic priorities. Most basic was the belief that Spain was the pivot and motor of the entire monarchy. It had not always been so – during the reign of Charles V, Germany and Italy were the center of gravity – but Philip II acknowledged the primacy of the peninsula in 1558–59 by making Spain his headquarters. "We must all seek the remedy [for the current financial crisis]" he told his principal adviser in Brussels, "as I shall do to the utmost of my ability. And since it is not here [in the Netherlands] I shall go to Spain to seek it."[16]

By moving to the Iberian peninsula, Philip II inevitably became dependent on advisers whose view of imperial priorities reflected Spain's traditional strategic outlook. Three basic perceptions had dominated this outlook since

---

13   E. Poullet, *Correspondance du Cardenal de Granvelle, 1565–1586*, Vol. 1 (Brussels, 1877), pp. 314–18: Granvelle to Philip II, 19 June 1566. The argument was accepted by the Council of State, which stated that "If the Netherlands situation is not remedied, it will bring about the loss of Spain and all the rest." (Report of the Council meeting in Archivio di Stato, Naples, *Carte Farnesiane* 1706, Miguel de Mendivil to Margaret of Parma, 22 September 1566: from the transcript made by L. van der Essen.)

14   AGS *Estado* 2843/7, *Parescer* of the Council of States, 7 September 1577, opinion of Don Gaspar de Quiroga, supported by the marquis of Aguilar and the President of the Council of Castile.

15   AGS *Guerra Antigua* 1120, unfol., paper of Olivares written in February 1635.

16   C. Weiss, *Papiers d'Etat du Cardenal de Granvelle*, Vol. 5 (Paris, 1844), p. 606: Philip II to Granvelle, 24 June 1559. On the westward shift of the Habsburg empire's center of gravity during the 1550s, see H. Lutz and E. Müller-Luckner, eds., *Das römisch-deutche Reich im politischen System Karls V.* (Munich, 1982: Schriften des historischen Kollegs, Kolloquien, Vol. 1), pp. 277f; A. Kohler, *Das Reich im Kampf um die Hegemonie in Europa 1521–1648* (Munich, 1990: Enzyklopaedie deutscher Geschichte, Vol. 6), pp. 22–26; and Rodríguez Salgado, *Changing face of Empire*, pp. 339–56.

the days of his great-grandfather, Ferdinand the Catholic.[17] First and most obvious, any threat to the security of the Iberian peninsula must take precedence over any other problem. As one of Philip II's advisers observed during the Portuguese succession crisis of 1578–80: "In terms of the utility, the good and the strength of Spain, and of the grandeur and power of Your Majesty, uniting the crowns of Portugal and Castile matters more than the reconquest of the Netherlands."[18] Second among these strategic traditions bequeathed came a dogged determination to turn back the Muslim tide in the Mediterranean and to protect the Christian outposts in the East. Philip II – one of whose hereditary titles was "King of Jerusalem" – therefore resolved to continue his father's struggle against the Ottoman Turks and refused to consider making peace for several years even when simultaneous campaigns in the Netherlands threatened to cripple his treasury.[19]

The third inherited priority in Philip II's grand strategy was the determination to use any and all means to keep Italy firmly within Spain's orbit – or, as one Spanish viceroy unkindly put it: "These Italians, although they are not Indians, must be treated as such so that they understand that we are in charge of them and never think that they are in charge of us."[20] Force partly achieved that goal: on the one hand, large permanent Spanish garrisons guarded the areas directly under Habsburg rule (Sardinia, Sicily, Naples, and Lombardy), as well as a handful of fortresses in Tuscany, while a substantial fleet of war galleys protected the sea lanes and the coast. On the other, many of the smaller Italian states demilitarized themselves – choosing to disband their own forces and to rely instead on those of Spain for their own defense.[21] But Spanish hegemony rested equally upon a sophisticated "diplomatic system" – perhaps the first of early modern times, and certainly the only one operating in the Age of Philip II. Charles V set out its essential elements in the Instructions which he wrote in 1548 for the guidance of his son and suc-

---

[17] On this heritage, see J. M. Doussinague, *La Política Internacional de Fernando el Católico* (Madrid, 1944); and J. N. Hillgarth, *The Spanish Kingdoms 1250–1516*, Vol. 2 (Oxford, 1978), pp. 534–39 and 570–75.

[18] Quotation from F. J. Bouza Alvarez, "Portugal en la Monarquía Hispánica 1580–1640: Felipe II, las Cortes de Tomar y la Génesis del Portugal Católico," Universidad Complutense de Madrid, Ph.D. thesis, 1987, p. 70: G. B. Gesio. For a seventeenth-century example of the same strategic priorities in action, see Don Miguel de Salamanca's advice to the Count-Duke of Olivares after the revolts of Catalonia and Portugal: "The first concern should be to settle the problems of Spain, rather than to save the other provinces." (Archivo Histórico Nacional, *Estado libro 969*, unfol., Salamanca's letter from Brussels dated 14 July 1641.)

[19] AGS *Estado* 554/84, "Las razones que concurren para no se poder dexar la Jornada de Levante" [early March 1573]; and *Estado* 554/89, Philip II to the Duke of Alva, 18 March 1573. On the start of the war in 1550–51, see Lutz, *Christianitas Afflicta*, pp. 40–42; on its prosecution by Philip II see F. Braudel, *The Mediterranean and the Mediterranean World in the Age of Philip II*, 2 Vols. (London, 1973), part 3.

[20] BL *Additional Ms.* 28,399/7–9, letter from the Governor of Lombardy to Philip II, February 1570, postscript.

[21] This point is well made for the Genoese Republic after 1528 by C. Costantini, *La Repubblica di Genova* (Turin, 1986), p. 52.

cessor, Philip, then just twenty-one years old. The emperor specially commended close relations with the Duchy of Mantua, immediately south of Spanish Lombardy, and with the Republic of Genoa, which was Lombardy's gateway to the Mediterranean and therefore to Spain.[22] The former remained within the Habsburg orbit principally through marriage: the Gonzagas of Mantua were one of the few other dynasties from which the Habsburgs chose spouses.[23] Both commerce and politics bound the patricians of Genoa to Spain. Eighty percent of the Republic's long-distance trade by sea was with the territories of Philip II, and Genoese merchant-bankers were deeply involved in the finances of the Spanish Monarchy. And whenever the oligarchs of the Republic encountered difficulties, whether from their own citizens – as in 1547 and 1575 – or from foreign powers – as in the Corsican troubles from 1551 to 1569 – Spain rushed to their rescue.[24]

Mantua and Genoa, however, were only two of the approximately 300 "imperial fiefs" that comprised northern Italy. Some sixty aristocratic families controlled most of the territories, and Philip II dominated these families through a combination of rewards and threats. On the reward side, he could either offer to cede adjacent Spanish territory to a loyal ally (thus he dangled the restitution of Piacenza before the dukes of Parma and the cession of certain fortresses in Tuscany before the Grand Duke of Florence) or even offer marriage with a member of his family (thus in 1585 Duke Charles Emanuel of Savoy wed Philip II's younger daughter Catherine). There were also plenty of jobs for members of Italy's ruling families in the service of Philip II: Alexander Farnese, duke of Parma, became captain-general of the Army of Flanders for Philip II from 1578 to 1592, and welcomed to his glittering entourage many younger scions from neighboring states. In addition, prominent members of Italy's ruling families (particularly "heirs apparent") often resided for a time in Spain, where Philip II's courtiers fêted, entertained, and encouraged them to see the world through his eyes. Finally, a wide range of other rewards existed – pensions, presents, land, offices, and honors – culminating in a knighthood of the Golden Fleece, the foremost order of chivalry in Europe, whose members Philip II – their Grand Master – called "my cousins."[25]

22 See the "Instructions" of 1548 in F. de Laiglesia, *Estudios Históricos, 1515–1555*, Vol. 1 (Madrid, 1918), pp. 93–120.
23 See details in P. S. Fichtner, "Dynastic Marriage in Sixteenth-Century Habsburg Diplomacy and Statecraft: An Interdisciplinary Approach," *American Historical Review*, 81 (1976), pp. 243–65; and E. Romero García, *El Imperialismo Hispánico en la Toscana durante el Siglo XVI* (Lérida, 1986), part 3.
24 See Costantini, *La Repubblica*, chs. 4 and 8; and R. Emmanuelli, *Gênes et l'Espagne dans la Guerre de Corse, 1559–1569* (Paris 1964).
25 On Philip II's manipulation of the rulers of northern Italy, see M. A. Romani, "Finanza pubblica e potere politico: il caso dei Farnese (1545–93)," in Romani, ed., *Le corti farnesiane di Parma e Piacenza*, Vol. 1 (Rome, 1978), pp. 3–89; and Romero García, *El Imperialismo Hispánico*, pp. 111–56. For the use of the "Tusón" as a reward, see Archivio

When carrots failed, however, out came the stick. For the king of Spain was not only the most powerful ruler in Western Europe, he was also "Imperial Vicar" for Italy, and could thus exercise feudal rights over all the emperor's vassals in the northern half of the peninsula. He served regularly as a court of appeal for their territorial disputes, intervening to support those he favored and threatening those he did not. In 1571 he even ordered his troops to invade and occupy one imperial fief, the marquisate of Finale, whose ruler had offended him, and two years passed before his forces withdrew.[26] He also maintained full diplomatic relations with eleven Italian states and received a constant stream of information from agents, friends, and spies throughout the peninsula.[27]

The Finale episode was an early example of a more aggressive spirit in the strategic culture of the Court of Spain. It became more evident after the death of the childless King Sebastian of Portugal in 1578, which laid his extensive possessions open to Spanish annexation. The tone of a court preacher, Fray Hernando del Castillo, proved typical:

> Uniting the kingdoms of Portugal and Castile will make Your Majesty the greatest king in the world . . . because if the Romans were able to rule the world simply by ruling the Mediterranean, what of the man who rules the Atlantic and Pacific oceans, since they surround the world?

Before long, the unification of the peninsula came to represent a vital step on Spain's road to global mastery, "The gain or loss [of Portugal] will mean the gain or loss of the world" wrote Philip's envoy in Lisbon.[28]

The acquisition of the entire Portuguese empire, successfully accomplished between 1580 and 1583, unleashed a flood of even more ambitious plans. The verses of the soldier-poets Fernando de Herrera, Alonso de Ercilla, and Francisco de Aldana, which circulated widely in the 1580s, all displayed a self-intoxicating rhetoric that called for Spain to conquer the world and – at least in the case of Aldana – suggested detailed strategies for its attainment.[29]

---

di Stato, Mantua, *Archivio Gonzaga: Carteggio Estero* 583/310 and 334, Philip II to the new duke, 19 March and 7 November 1588, about conferring the knighthood.

[26] See Archivio di Stato, Lucca, *Offizio sulle Differenze dei Confini*, 269 unfol., letters from Madrid dated May-August 1586 communicating Philip II's support for the Republic in a territorial dispute with the duke of Ferrara; and F. Edelmayer, *Maximilian II., Philip II., und Reichsitalien: Die Auseinandersetzungen um das Reichslehen Finale in Ligurien* (Stuttgart, 1988: Veröffentlichungen des Instituts für europäische Geschichte Mainz. Abteilung Universalgeschichte, Vol. 130).

[27] Even the chief cipher clerk of the Pope was in Spanish pay in the 1580s according to the evidence quoted in M. Philippson, *Ein Ministerium unter Philipp II: Kardinal Granvella am spanische Hofe 1579–86* (Berlin, 1895), p. 56.

[28] Quotation from Bouza Alvarez, "Portugal en la Monarquía Hispánica," p. 82: Fray Hernando del Castillo.

[29] See the brilliant analysis of the "messianic imperialism" of these three writers in A. Terry, "War and Literature in Sixteenth-Century Spain," in J. R. Mulryne and M. Shewring, eds., *War, Literature and the Arts in Sixteenth-Century Europe* (London, 1989), ch. 4. See also

Meanwhile, in the Far East, Dom João Ribeira Gaio, Bishop of Malacca, advocated in 1584 the pooling of Iberian resources worldwide in order first to conquer Sumatra and Thailand, and then to annex southern China. These areas were "very great and very wealthy. And thus His Majesty [Philip II] will be the greatest lord that ever was in the world."[30] Meanwhile, in the Far West, jubilation at the marquis of Santa Cruz's conquest of the Azores archipelago in 1582 reached such heights that some Spaniards claimed that "even Christ was no longer safe in Paradise, for the marquis might go there to bring him back and crucify him all over again."[31] Santa Cruz himself, only a trifle more modestly, informed his master that "with Portugal pacified, England is ours" and called for a preemptive strike against the Protestant regime of Elizabeth Tudor.

Gradually, as in the case of Portugal in 1578–80, the king and his ministers came to see the conquest of England as the only way of assuring imperial defense. A senior official informed the Duke of Medina Sidonia, commander of the Armada, before he sailed that "All our wars and affairs afoot today are reduced to this one enterprise" – the invasion of England – for it was the unique means of simultaneously preserving the lifeline between Spain and America, of protecting the Iberian peninsula from invasion, and of ending the war in the Netherlands – "that voracious monster which gobbles up the troops and treasure of Spain."[32] But this was not the only justification for the proposed invasion of England. Two others flanked the defensive argument: "reputation" and "religion."[33]

There was nothing unusual about the former in the context of the prevailing norms of sixteenth-century political philosophy. The rulers of every European state believed that to "lose face," whether by failing to make good a claim or through military defeat, damaged their international standing, and the Spanish Habsburgs were no exception. In the stirring phrase of Don Balthasar de Zúñiga, who had sailed with the Spanish Armada and even-

the illuminating essay of F. Fernández Armesto, "Armada Myths: the Formative Phase," in P. Gallagher and D. W. Cruickshank, eds., *God's Obvious Design: Papers of the Spanish Armada Symposium, Sligo, 1588* (London, 1990), pp. 19–39.

30 Quoted, along with other "universalist" projects of the day, in C. R. Boxer, "Portuguese and Spanish Projects for the Conquest of Southeast Asia, 1580–1600," *Journal of Asian History*, 111–112 (1969), pp. 118–36. Not all were fanciful: in 1596, a small party of Spaniards briefly took over Cambodia.

31 Bibliothèque Nationale de Paris *Fonds français* Ms. 16108/365, M. de St. Gouard (French Resident at the Court of Philip II) to Catherine de Medici, 20 August 1582.

32 Quotations from E. Herrera Oria, *La Armada Invencible* (Valladolid, 1929: Archivo Documental Español, Vol. 2), pp. 148f: don Juan de Idiáquez to the Duke of Medina Sidonia, 20 February 1588. See also, similar sentiments in G. Maura Gamazo, Duke of Maura, *El Designio de Felipe II y el Episodio de la Armada Invencible* (Madrid, 1957), p. 167: same to same, 28 February 1587; and AGS *Estado* 2855, unfol., "Sobre el negocio principal: dióse a Su Magestad a 15 de enero 1588" ("[Sending the Armada] is the only way to secure what comes from America, to free our own coasts from invasion, and to secure the Netherlands").

33 See the arguments cited in C. Gómez-Centurión, *La Invencible y la Empresa de Inglaterra* (Madrid, 1988), p. 50.

tually became chief minister of Philip III: "A monarchy that has lost its reputation, even if it has lost no territory, is a sky without light, a sun without rays, a body without a soul."[34] The same consensus prevailed at the court of Philip II. Thus in 1573 the king decided to continue to fight against the Turks after the defection of Venice because to sue for peace would "lose the common esteem of the world." Four years later his ministers advised him that negotiations with the Dutch rebels were incompatible "with the honor and reputation of Your Majesty, which is your greatest asset." Anything but war would "strain Your Majesty's conscience and hazard your honor and prestige."[35] Likewise in 1588–89, the Spanish government refused to make peace with either the English or the Dutch in the wake of the Spanish Armada's defeat, because to do so would "imperil our reputation."[36]

But usually along with the maintenance of Spain's prestige came some mention of the defense of the Catholic faith. An aura of "messianic imperialism" pervaded policymaking at the court of Philip II. The official mind justified difficult political choices on the grounds that they were necessary not only for the interests of Spain but also for the cause of God, and attributed victories to divine intervention and favor, while normally rationalizing defeats and failures either as a Divine attempt to test Spain's steadfastness and devotion – thus providing a spur to future sacrifices and endeavors – or else as a punishment for momentary human presumption.[37]

Of course, an element of "providentialism" lurked in the strategic thinking of almost all states in the century following the Reformation, as religious and political issues became ever more tightly intertwined and the bible came to represent a guide to secular as well as spiritual salvation. Most nations in this period regarded themselves as the new "Chosen People," granted a direct contract by God. Thus, Philip II's archenemies, the English and the Dutch, also regarded their victories as the result of direct divine intervention (the inscription on a Dutch medal struck to celebrate the destruction of the Spanish Armada was a typical example: "God blew and they were scattered"). Likewise they saw their history as predetermined by Providence, and viewed their wars against Spain as a sort of "Protestant Crusade."[38] But

---

34 Even Treasury officials agreed: in 1625 the President of the Council of Finance warned King Philip IV that "the lack of money is serious, but it is more important to preserve reputation." Quotations from Elliott, "Managing Decline," pp. 93, 96.

35 AGS *Estado* 2843/7, *Consulta* of the Council of State, 5 September 1577; for 1573, see the documents cited in note 21 above.

36 AGS *Estado* 2851, unfol., *Consulta* of the Council of State, 2 November 1588; ibid., *Estado* 2855, unfol., "Sumario de los quatro papeles principales," 11 November 1589.

37 See the classic discussion of the origins of Spanish "messianic imperialism" in the 1520s in M. Bataillon, *Erasmo y España: Estudios sobre la Historia Espiritual del Siglo XVI*, 2d ed. (Mexico, 1950), pp. 226–31; and F. Yates, *Astraea: The Imperial Theme in the Sixteenth Century* (London, 1975), pp. 1–28.

38 Various "providentialist" medals of 1588 are reproduced in M. J. Rodríguez Salgado, ed., *Armada 1588–1988* (London, 1988), pp. 276f. For examples of English and Dutch providentialism, see: M. McGiffert, "God's Controversy with Jacobean England," *American Historical Review*, 88 (1983), pp. 1151–74; C. Z. Wiener, "The Beleaguered Isle: A

these sentiments ran particularly strong in Spain, where many felt that an inscrutable yet benevolent Providence was responsible for creating the Habsburg empire through a complex sequence of dynastic accidents – by premature deaths and infertile unions as well as by judicious marriages – and had then made Charles V lord of first Mexico and then Peru. That Providence would then in time humble France, defeat England, and extirpate Protestantism. Friends and foes alike came to see the Spanish monarchy as an almost supernatural force. More than all other states, wrote Tommaso Campanella, "it is founded upon the occult providence of God and not on either prudence or human force"; and the whole of history seemed to be a heroic progression in which disasters – even the Moorish Conquest of 711 and, eventually, the Spanish Armada of 1588 – became mere episodes in Spain's almost miraculous advance toward world monarchy.[39]

Naturally this apocalyptic interpretation gained particular popularity among the numerous clerics who advised Philip II. Thus in 1566, when the Protestant tide reached its height in the Netherlands, an influential Catholic ,preacher warned the king:

> The holy bones of the Emperor your father are complaining and his spirit will demand God's punishment against you if you allow the loss of those states, without which Spain cannot live in safety. Your Majesty inherited not only your states and kingdoms from your ancestors, but also your religion, valor and virtue. I dare to say humbly to Your Majesty that you will forfeit the glory of God if God should lose his honor and his place over there [in the Netherlands] where Your Majesty is his lieutenant.

The king heeded the warning: within a month, preparations commenced for sending a Spanish army of 70,000 men to restore order in the Netherlands. And when the use of force seemed to have backfired, in 1574, another cleric (Philip II's private secretary – and chaplain – Mateo Vázquez) reminded his master that:

> God, who can do anything, is our greatest strength in these troubles, since we have seen that He always looks out for Your Majesty, and in your greatest necessities gives the greatest signs of favor. . . . And since Your Majesty fights

Study of Elizabethan and Early Jacobean Anti-Catholicism," *Past and Present*, 51 (1971), pp. 27–62; D. R. Cressy, *Bonfires and Bells: National Memory and the Protestant Calendar in Elizabethan and Stuart England* (Berkeley, 1989), chs. 7, 9, and 10; D. R. Woolf, *The Idea of History in early Stuart England: Erudition, Ideology and "the Light of Truth" from the Accession of James I to the Civil War* (Toronto, 1991), pp. 4–8; and G. Groenhuis, *De Predikanten: de Sociale Positie van de Gereformeerde Predikanten in de Republiek der Verenigde Nederlanden voor 1700* (Groningen, 1977), pp. 77–107.

39 Campanella quoted by Pagden, *Spanish Imperialism*, p. 51. On Spain's history as a cycle of alternating disasters and miracles, see the penetrating remarks of P. Gallagher and D. W. Cruickshank, "The Armada of 1588 Reflected in Serious and Popular Literature of the Period," in Gallagher and Cruickshank, *God's Obvious Design*, pp. 167–83.

for the cause of God, He will fight – as He has always done – for the interests of Your Majesty.[40]

Philip II was entirely comfortable with this Providential vision. From an early stage in his reign, he seemed to have seen himself as called to save God's Chosen People. In August 1559, as he waited impatiently for a favorable wind to take him back to Spain, he wrote to one of his advisers:

> Everything depends on the will of God, so we can only wait to see how best He can be served. I trust that, because he has removed other worse obstacles, He will remove this one too and give me the means to sustain my kingdoms, so that they will not be lost.[41]

The king constantly equated his own interests, and those of the lands that he ruled, with those of God. Thus in the 1560s he refused to moderate the heresy laws in force in the Netherlands because he believed that "if the Catholic faith is lost, my estates will be lost with it"; and he urged his advisors "To tell me in all things what you think is best for the service of God, which is my principal aim, and so for my service." Before long, the two had become inseparable: "You are engaged in God's service and in mine – which is the same thing," he reassured one of his dispirited commanders in 1573.[42]

In strategic terms, this problem became acute when the king failed to distinguish between "the cause of God" and his own aims abroad. Repressing heresy and improving Catholic devotion among his own subjects was one thing; seeking to impose the same standards upon the subjects of other rulers was quite another. Nevertheless at times Philip II pursued the latter with the same blind and passionate determination with which he pushed the former. When his plan for an invasion of England in 1571 in support of a Catholic rising began to unravel because of the arrest of the chief conspirators, Philip nevertheless insisted upon going ahead:

> I am so keen to achieve the consummation of this enterprise, I am so attached to it in my heart, and I am so convinced that God our Savior must embrace it as His own cause, that I cannot be dissuaded. Nor can I accept or believe the contrary.[43]

The king agreed to cancel the project only with great regret two months later. Likewise, in 1586, when Philip sanctioned Spanish intervention in France to uphold the Catholic faction, he noted on a document:

---

40 AGS *Estado* 531/91, Fray Lorenzo de Villavicencio to Philip II, 6 October 1566 ("humbly" seems curiously incongruous amid such threats!); and IVdeDJ 51/31, Mateo Vázquez to Philip II, 31 May 1574.
41 Weiss, *Papiers d'Etat,* Vol. 6, p. 82: Philip II to Cardinal Granvelle, 24 August 1559.
42 AGS *Estado* 527/5, Philip II to Gonzalo Pérez, undated [March 1565]; and Bibliothèque Publique et Universitaire, Geneva, *Ms Favre* 30/73v, Philip II to Don Luis de Requeséns, 20 October 1573, copy of holograph original.
43 AGS *Estado,* 547/3, the king to the Duke of Alva, 14 September 1571.

Truly, I have only agreed to this because it seems to be the only way available to remedy the religious state of that kingdom. It may mean that we shall encounter other difficulties arising from what we are doing, but the cause of religion is the most important thing of all.[44]

It might have been imperialism cloaked in the guise of religion, but it was imperialism none the less.

SPANISH GRAND STRATEGY IN PRACTICE

This persistent belief in some special divine dispensation for Spain – that, in seventeenth century terms, "God is Spanish" – also influenced strategy on a practical level.[45] As Philip II put it in 1571 in connection with his desire to invade England, his deep conviction that God was on his side "leads me to understand matters differently [from other people], and makes me play down the difficulties and problems which spring up; so that all the things that could either divert or stop me from carrying through this business seem less threatening to me."[46] Likewise in 1587–88, when he again planned the overthrow of Elizabeth Tudor, Philip II was confident that, at the critical moment, God would intervene directly to provide the desired outcome in spite of all the odds. When the commander of the invasion fleet complained about the madness of launching the Armada against England in midwinter, the king replied serenely: "We are fully aware of the risk that is incurred by sending a major fleet in winter through the Channel without a safe harbor, but . . . since it is all for His cause, God will send good weather."[47] And in June 1588, after a storm had damaged some of the ships, driven others into Corunna, and scattered the rest, the king remained serene. When he heard suggestions that these reverses might be a sign from God to desist, the king replied: "If this were an unjust war, one could indeed take this storm as a sign from Our Lord to cease offending Him; but being as just as it is, one cannot believe that He will disband it, but rather will grant it more favor than we could hope." "I have dedicated this enterprise to God," the king concluded. "Get on, then, and do your part!"[48] A better example of cognitive dissonance would be hard to find. Upon such rocks of blinkered intransigence, rational calculations of Spain's strategic advantage foundered.

In the event, however, the Habsburg "bid for mastery" fell short. Philip II

---

44 AGS *Estado K* 1448/43, royal apostil on a letter from Don Juan de Idiáquez to Don Bernardino de Mendoza, 27 April 1586, minute.

45 "God is Spanish and fights for our nation these days" claimed the Count-Duke of Olivares, chief minister of Philip IV in 1625: quoted by J. Brown and J. H. Elliott, *A Palace for a King: The Buen Retiro and the Court of Philip IV* (New Haven, 1980), p. 190.

46 AGS *Estado* 547/3 (see note 43).

47 AGS *Estado* 165/2–3, Philip II to Archduke Albert, 14 September 1587.

48 Quotations from Maura, *El designio,* pp. 258–61, Medina Sidonia to Philip II, 21 and 24 June 1588; and Oria, *Armada invencible,* 210–14, Philip to Medina Sidonia, 1 July 1588.

failed to conquer England in 1571 or 1588; the Turks, though defeated at Lepanto in 1571, did not sue for peace; and France did not become a Spanish satellite. In *The Rise and Fall of the Great Powers,* Paul Kennedy advanced three explanations for these failures. First, he accorded great importance to "the Military Revolution" of early modern Europe. The development of a new generation of powerful gunpowder weapons, he argued, led to a radically different system of star-shaped defensive fortifications that made the capture of major strongholds virtually impossible without prolonged sieges. This, in turn, helped to fuel a prodigious and sustained growth in the size of armies and navies, leading inevitably to a dramatic increase in their cost. Thanks to the escalating expense of war, the Habsburgs "consistently spent two or three times more than the[ir] ordinary revenues provided." That was the principal reason for their failure. But according to Kennedy, two other factors reinforced these problems. The Habsburg empire, in Kennedy's view, was "one of the greatest examples of strategical overstretch in history," for "the Habsburgs simply had too much to do, too many enemies to fight, too many fronts to defend." In addition, they suffered from sustained failure to mobilize available resources in the most efficient way. Instead, they squandered their assets, as in the expulsion of the Jews and Moors, and later of the moriscos; in the maintenance of numerous internal tariff barriers; and in the minting of a disastrously overvalued copper currency.[49]

Yet despite all these liabilities, Philip II still mustered sufficient resources to achieve spectacular successes. His forces managed, for example, to conquer most of the Philippines in the 1570s and 1580s, to annex the entire Portuguese empire between 1580 and 1583, and to recover much of the Netherlands between 1583 and 1587. In 1587–88 he concentrated an amphibious force that cost 60,000 ducats a day to maintain and was, according to friend and foe alike, "the largest that has ever been seen in these seas since the creation of the world." It was "the greatest and strongest combination, to my understanding, that ever was gathered in Christendom."[50] And for the last twenty-five years of his reign he maintained between 70,000 and 90,000 soldiers in the Low Countries – in what some enthusiasts called *Castra Dei* (God's encampment) – as well as perhaps as many men again in garrisons elsewhere around the globe, to say nothing of the capital invested in fleets

49 See Kennedy, *Rise and Fall,* pp. 44–55. Some doubts are expressed about the sufficiency of this explanation for the failure of Spain's "bid for mastery" in G. Parker, "Philip II, Paul Kennedy and the Revolt of the Netherlands, 1572–76: A Case of Strategic Overstretch?" in E. L. Petersen, et al., *Clashes of Cultures: Essays in Honour of Niels Steensgaard,* (Odense, 1992), pp. 50–79.

50 G. Canestrini and A. Desjardins, eds., *Négociations Diplomatiques de la France avec la Toscane,* Vol. 4 (Paris 1872), p. 737: Filippo Cavriana to Belisario Vinta, 3 March 1587; J. K. Laughton, *State Papers Concerning the Defeat of the Spanish Armada,* Vol. 1 (London, 1895), p. 361: Sir John Hawkins to Sir Francis Walsingham, July 31 [O.S.], 1588. See also ibid., Vol. 2 (London, 1900), p. 59: Admiral Howard to Walsingham, 8 August [O.S.], 1588 ("All the world never saw a force such as theirs was.")

Table 5.1. *The cost of Philip II's imperialism, 1571–1577*

	Money received from Castile (in ducats)	
Year	By the Mediterranean fleet	By the Army of Flanders
1571	793,000	119,000
1572	1,463,000	1,776,000
1573	1,102,000	1,813,000
1574	1,252,000	3,737,000
1575	711,000	2,518,000
1576	1,069,000	872,000
1577	673,000	857,000
Total	7,063,000	11,692,000

At this time, Philip II's revenues from Castile totaled roughly 6 million ducats, half of which was required to service the national debt.

Sources: AGS *Contaduri a Mayor de Cuentas*, 2a época 55 (Accounts of F. de Lixalde for the Army of Flanders) and 814 (Accounts of J. Morales de Torre for the Mediterranean fleet).

and fortifications (Table 5.1).[51] Obviously, Spain could support this constant and costly military effort only because the economy of Spain, the hub of the empire, continued throughout the reign to be buoyant and productive – at least in comparison with those of the rest of Europe.[52] Although Philip II worried incessantly about cash flow, the resources necessary to run his empire were clearly available, and for much of his reign he mobilized them adequately.

What his monarchy lacked was the political skill, and above all the political flexibility, to squeeze the maximum return from every advantage. For although the Spanish Habsburgs could win battles, they seemed incapable of winning wars. The problem stemmed from the absence of any organization for high-level strategic planning. The king had no "cabinet," no "war office," and no "Combined Chiefs of Staff." There was – for better or worse – no Pentagon or Net Assessment Office to evaluate strategic possibilities and limitations. Although a complex network of councils – each with its own

51 Details of this achievement are given in G. Parker, *The Army of Flanders and the Spanish Road 1567–1659: The Logistics of Spanish Victory and Defeat in the Low Countries' Wars* (Cambridge, 1972); and I. A. A. Thompson, *War and Government in Habsburg Spain, 1560–1620* (London, 1976). See also J. Schoonjans, "Castra Dei: l'organisation religieuse des armées d'Alexandre Farnèse," in *Miscellanea Historica in Honorem Leonis van der Essen* (Leuven, 1947), pp. 523–40.

52 See, for example, the works surveyed in A. W. Lovett, "The Golden Age of Spain: New Work on an Old Theme," *The Historical Journal*, 24 (1981), pp. 739–49.

president, secretary, and designated councilors – advised Philip II, these bodies dealt only with routine matters. Their principal function lay in discussing incoming letters and memoranda in a given area of responsibility and recommending what action, if any, to take. And strict lines of demarcation defined their duties. Thus, the Council of War considered and reported on letters concerning the crown's armed forces – both naval and military – within Spain; but the supervision of the crown's armed forces in the Netherlands and Italy remained the domain of the Council of State – for all Spain's interests abroad, whether diplomatic, commercial, or military were the exclusive preserve of the Council of State. Likewise, the Council of the Indies dealt with the military affairs of America, while after 1583 another council dealt with the defense of the Portuguese empire and reported directly to the king from Lisbon. Budgets for all military operations underwent review by yet another body, the Council of Finance.

This fragmentation of responsibility constituted a serious obstacle to effective planning, but the king employed three devices in an attempt to overcome it. First, he never depended solely on the councils for advice. On the one hand, a number of key advisers served on several councils: a position on both the councils of State and War, or on Indies and Finance, was common; a seat on State, War, and Finance was not unknown. On the other, Philip II could coordinate the business of his empire by diverting discussion of certain matters away from the conciliar system altogether. In times of crisis, the king might designate a particular minister – or, more usually, a small committee (*junta*) of ministers – to oversee a particular operation. In summer 1571, for example, he established a small committee to review all reports and to recommend actions in the naval campaign that culminated in the battle of Lepanto, while in 1573–75 the "Committee of Presidents" – including up to eight senior councilors – discussed the best solutions to the financial crisis resulting from simultaneous wars in the Low Countries and the Mediterranean. And in 1580–83, while the king and most of his ministers concentrated on the acquisition of Portugal and its empire, Cardinal Granvelle handled all other foreign business.

As a second device for overcoming the fragmentation of his government, the king allowed his ministers – whether at court or abroad – to write to him directly, in effect short-circuiting the conciliar structure. "If you write on the envelope 'To be delivered to the king in person,' it will be done" he decreed. The king's personal private secretary handled all such letters, and the councils never saw them.[53] However, a quick reprimand awaited anyone who abused this privilege and tried to write directly to the king about matters deemed unimportant.[54] But Philip was normally willing to read almost any-

[53] AGS *Estado* 1049/107, Philip II to the Viceroy of Naples, 13 February 1559, minute. It was noted that the same Instruction was being sent to all ministers of the Crown.

[54] Biblioteca de la Casa de Heredía Spínola [hereafter HS], 141/108, Philip II to Mateo Vázquez, 1 May 1586: "This business of sending letters 'for me personally' is getting to be

thing that came across his desk, and the impact of some of the information and advice received in this way – often stemming from people not directly involved in government – frequently influenced subsequent decisions.[55]

Finally, and most important, the king insisted upon seeing for himself all the letters that went out in his name, and on personally reviewing the recommendations of the relevant council on each incoming report. This was an incredible administrative burden: on some days the king claimed to have signed 400 letters, and on average he seems to have considered and resolved thirty individual petitions a day – as well as giving audiences and debriefing ministers and messengers.[56] He also spent hours wrestling with his apparently endless financial difficulties. Part of the problem was, as the king himself confessed, that he did not understand most of the solutions suggested to him: "To be frank," he told the secretary who had just forwarded a particularly complex proposition,

> I do not understand a word of this. I do not know what I should do. Should I send it to someone else for comment, and if so, whom? Time is slipping away: tell me what you advise, or if it would be best for me to see the author [of the memorandum] – although I fear I shall not understand him. But perhaps if I had the papers in front of me it might not be too bad.[57]

And so the bewildered king rambled on, laboring to understand why he had no money left and what he could do about it. In 1588, during the Armada campaign, the shortage of funds again became so acute that the king ordered his financial advisers to draw up a special statement every Saturday to show how much cash remained in the treasury – the grand total was often less than 50,000 ducats – and which obligations were pending. Philip II, generally reputed to be the richest monarch in the world, then spent several hours toiling over the documents in order to decide which of his debts he could afford to pay and which he would have to defer.[58]

Not surprisingly, with so much attention lavished upon detail, the king sometimes fell seriously behind with his paperwork. In 1578, for example, he penned the following complaint on a file one of his secretaries had sent:

---

a nuisance; sometimes I do not even have time to open them" the king complained. Persistent writers were ordered to desist.

55 Two examples may suffice: P. D. Lagomarsino, "Court Factions and the Formation of Spanish Policy towards the Netherlands 1559–1567," Cambridge University, Ph.D. thesis, 1973, shows clearly the influence of Fray Lorenzo de Villavicencio on Philip II's response to the development of heresy in the Low Countries; and A. J. Loomie, *The Spanish Elizabethans: The English Exiles at the Court of Philip II* (New York, 1963), ch. 3, on Hugo Owens.

56 Details from C. Riba García, *Correspondencia Privada de Felipe II con su Secretario Mateo Vázquez 1567–1591* (Madrid, 1959), p. 36: note of 30 March 1576; and IVdeDJ 97 "Libro de memoriales remitidos desde xx de agosto 1583 en adelante."

57 BL *Additional MS* 28,699/103, Philip II to Mateo Vázquez, 22 April 1574.

58 See numerous *Relaciones de sábado* in AGS *Consejos y Juntas de hacienda* 249, carpetas 16–18. Almost all bear tortured royal annotations and computations.

I have just been given this other packet of papers from you, but I have neither the time nor the strength to look at it. I will not open it until tomorrow. It is already past ten o'clock and I have not yet had dinner. My table is full of papers for tomorrow because I cannot cope with any more today.[59]

From time to time Philip II also complained about his health: "Although I am less tired today than yesterday, my eyes can hardly see" he wrote one day, and on another "I am working with my eyes half closed." Shortly afterward, his entire self-confidence seems to have wavered: "The position I hold is a foul one," he exclaimed to his secretary. And a week later: "With the problems I face these days I really do not know how I survive."[60]

Naturally, on the rare occasions when the king's health or spirits collapsed, the decision-making process ground to a complete halt.[61] The records of his secretaries show that on the whole he dispatched documents requiring a decision within a day, and that urgent matters almost always received priority.[62] Moreover, the king's insistence on seeing and checking everything for himself did guarantee a degree of coordination between the work of the various councils, even if the individual councilors remained in the dark. However, Philip II's personalized system of government contained two major drawbacks in the area of strategic planning. First, the monarch's close and constant involvement in the daily routine of government seems to have prevented him from stepping back and considering his affairs from a longer perspective. Admittedly at Lent and sometimes at other times, he went on retreat for a week or more; he routinely held up all business while he attended church; and throughout his life he spent a considerable part of each day at prayer – all activities that might have afforded him the leisure to consider his overall position. But his intense devotion seems instead to have merely reinforced his confidence that "God would provide."

The second weakness in strategic direction created by Philip II's system of "confuse and rule," of deliberately ensuring that no one knew as much as he did, was the incapacity of his administration to shape events rather than simply respond to them. When a new crisis arose or the monarchy required a new policy, Philip's government handled it *de novo*.

Both weaknesses appeared clearly in the planning of the "Enterprise of England," as the Spanish court termed its grand strategy against Elizabeth Tudor in 1585–88, a process that is worth detailed examination for two reasons. First, because the planning process associated with it left behind

59 IVdeDJ 51/162, Vázquez to the king with reply, 11 April 1578.
60 IVdeDJ 51/51, Vázquez to the king with reply, 19 July 1575; ibid., 51/172, idem, undated (= early 1574); ibid., 44/117, idem, 3 March 1575; and ibid., 44/119, the king to Vázquez, 10 March 1575.
61 For a serious example of total breakdown – in the spring of 1587 – see C. Martin and G. Parker, *The Spanish Armada* (New York, 1988), pp. 135–36.
62 See the notations in the registers of Antonio Gracián, the king's patronage secretary in the 1570s, in *Documentos para la Historia del Monasterio de San Lorenzo de El Escorial*, Vol. 5 (Madrid 1962), pp. 19–127, and Vol. 8 (Madrid, 1965), pp. 11–63.

remarkably full records that reveal starkly the disharmonies between the king's strategic aims and his resources, and between his planning methods and the military effectiveness of his armed forces. Second, because the Enterprise marked the high-water mark of Philip II's "bid for mastery": the decision to invade England initiated a war fought on land and sea that lasted until 1604 and caused the failure of Spain's efforts both to suppress the Dutch revolt and to secure the victory of the Catholic party in France.

The sudden and striking volte-face in Spain's policy toward England reflected a sudden and striking change in England's position among Spain's strategic priorities. The immediate sequence of events leading to Philip II's irrevocable decision to launch the enterprise dates back to July 1584, when the death of Francis Hercules, Duke of Anjou, created a major succession crisis in France, by leaving Anjou's childless elder brother, Henry III, as the last of the Valois dynasty. Because of the "Salic Law," only heirs in the male line could succeed to the French throne, and Henry of Bourbon, King of Navarre and leader of the French Protestants was the nearest relative to Henry III in the male line. Since French Catholics found him totally unacceptable, militants among them created a paramilitary organization, the "League," dominated by Henry Duke of Guise and dedicated to securing a Catholic succession. Guise promptly entered an alliance with Philip II, both to secure Spanish military assistance should civil war break out in France, and to acquire Spanish funds to help keep the League's army prepared. The treaty of Joinville of 31 December 1584 guaranteed both objectives. In March 1585 the League mobilized and demanded that Henry III join it in extirpating Protestantism from France. In July, in the treaty of Nemours, he agreed, ceding a number of important towns to the League's control as a pledge of his support.

On the one hand, these events reassured Philip II that for almost the first time in his reign he had absolutely nothing to fear from France. On the other, they terrified Queen Elizabeth: France slid unmistakably into another civil war, the threat of a new Spanish attack on England loomed larger and, with Spain's grip tightening on the Netherlands, the ideal launching pad for invasion would soon become available. The queen had secretly furnished aid to the Dutch for some time, hoping to bolster their resistance, but had always stopped short of offering open and public assistance for fear that it would provoke Spain to declare war.[63]

At precisely this moment, however, when even Elizabeth's most aggressive councilors had reluctantly concluded that they dare not escalate their support for the Dutch, Philip II played into their hands. In response to protests from the prince of Parma, who commanded Spain's army in the Netherlands, concerning the continued clandestine trade of the Dutch with Spain and

---

[63] BL *Harleian Ms.* 168/102–5, "A consultacion . . . touchinge an aide to be sent in to Hollande againste the king of Spaine" (March 18, 1585 O.S.)

Portugal, the king signed a decree on 19 May 1585 confiscating all north European ships and merchandise in Iberian harbors. He instructed his officials to scrutinize the papers of every embargoed vessel, and then to release all but the Dutch. But Queen Elizabeth, hearing only about the arrest of English ships and crews, turned the embargo into an excuse to make war on Spain.[64]

Almost immediately, the queen sent a small squadron to Newfoundland with orders to attack the Iberian fishing fleet; the raid brought back many boats and about 600 mariners to captivity in England. Simultaneously, any of her subjects who could claim losses from the embargo received license, through letters of marque, to recover damages by plundering any ship sailing under Philip II's colors. On 20 August 1585 Elizabeth signed a formal alliance with the Dutch – the treaty of Nonsuch – promising to provide over 7,000 regular troops for their army, to pay for one-quarter of their defense budget, and to dispatch one of her principal councilors to coordinate government in the rebel provinces and to lead their army. Finally, Sir Francis Drake, who already had a naval task force standing by, received authority to sally forth and attack Spanish shipping and possessions in both the Old World and the New. Drake's squadron of thirty-three vessels sailed from Plymouth on 24 September 1585. On 7 October they arrived off Galicia, and for the next ten days raided several villages in the vicinity of Vigo and Bayona and spent their spare time desecrating churches, collecting booty, and taking hostages.

No sovereign state could overlook such an act of naked aggression. Don Diego Pimentel, one of the senior Armada commanders captured in 1588, told his interrogators that "[t]he reason why the king undertook this war [against England] was that he could not tolerate the fact that Drake, with two or three rotten ships, should come to infest the harbors of Spain whenever it pleased him, and to capture its best towns in order to plunder them."[65] The archival evidence bears him out: the harrying of Galicia in the second week of October led Philip to accept the pope's commission to invade England on 24 October. For by then he had heard nothing about the treaty of Nonsuch, though he certainly knew all about the raid on Galicia.[66]

Nevertheless it was one thing to decide to invade England, and quite another to make it happen. The king decided first to commission his leading adviser, Don Juan de Zúñiga, to prepare a wide-ranging strategic review of the problems facing the monarchy. Zúñiga could draw upon a lifetime's

[64] See the text of the embargo in AGS *Guerra Antigua* 180/81, Philip II to Antonio de Guevara, 25 May 1585.

[65] *Breeder Verclaringhe vande Vloote van Spaegnien: De Bekentenisse van Don Diego de Piementel* (The Hague, 1588: Knuttel pamphlet nr. 847).

[66] News of the build up of English forces in Holland following the treaty of Nonsuch was contained in two letters from Parma to Philip II dated 30 September 1585 (AGS *Estado* 589/81 or *Secretarías Provinciales* 2534/212). From letters intercepted between the Dutch and the English Court, Parma also knew that this was part of a new commitment by Elizabeth, but he still did not know that a formal treaty had been signed.

experience of political and military affairs. He had fought in the Netherlands in the 1550s, rising through the positions of ambassador to the papal court and viceroy of Naples to become in 1582 a councilor of war and state in Madrid. Now he presided over the standing committee (the *Junta de Noche* or "night committee") formed to coordinate central government policy and advise the king on major problems. As news poured in concerning the buildup of English forces in the Dutch Republic and the depredations of Drake's fleet in Galicia (and later in the Canaries and the Caribbean), Zúñiga's report identified four major enemies: the Turks, the French, the English, and the Dutch. He reasoned that with the Turks still at war with Persia, a defensive posture would suffice in the Mediterranean, while subsidizing the League would keep France in a state of paralysis. This left England and the Dutch. The latter had posed a constant problem ever since the rebellion of 1572, but the English menace was new. Zúñiga insisted that Elizabeth had openly broken with Spain, and so Philip must respond. "However, to fight a purely defensive war is to court a huge and permanent expense, because we have to defend the Indies, Spain and the convoys travelling between them." An amphibious operation of overwhelming strength, he argued, represented the most effective form of defense, and also the cheapest. The diversion of resources to the enterprise against England might compromise the reconquest of the Netherlands; but Zúñiga felt that this was a risk worth taking because unless threatened directly, England would assuredly attack Spain again.[67] No doubt on the basis of Zúñiga's advice, the king wrote on 29 December 1585 to inform the prince of Parma of his decision to invade, and to ask for suggestions on the appropriate strategy.[68]

Given England's traditional strength by sea, experience has shown that – until the development of air power – only four strategies offered prospects of a successful invasion. The first was a simultaneous combined operation by a navy strong enough to defeat or keep at bay the opposing English navy, and a convoy numerous enough to carry an army sufficient to accomplish the conquest. William I in 1066 and William III in 1688 successfully employed this technique; the French also attempted it in 1692, 1759, and 1779, but failed. The second strategy involved assembling an army in secret near the Channel, while sending out a fleet from some other port as a decoy – to lure away the Royal Navy – so that a squadron of light and nimble transports could ferry the army across the Channel virtually unescorted. Napoleon favored this ploy in 1804–05. The third strategy represented a variant of the second: a diversionary assault on Ireland to lure away England's principal

67 IVdeDJ 32/225, "Parescer" of Don Juan de Zúñiga, undated (late 1585).
68 AGS *Estado* 589/15, Philip II to Parma, 29 December 1585. See also *Estado* 947/102, Philip II to the Count of Olivares, Spanish ambassador in Rome, 2 January 1586, announcing that Parma would command the invasion forces. However this letter also reveals that the king entertained some doubts about how keen the pope *really* was on the invasion of England: this might help to explain the delay in getting the Enterprise under way.

forces, leaving the mainland relatively open to invasion. The French tried this, with partial success, in 1760 and 1798. And, finally, a surprise assault was theoretically possible at a time when England was unprepared – as the French, yet again, attempted in 1743–44.[69] That all four possibilities received consideration in the 1580s is a tribute to the excellence of Philip's advisers; that in 1587–88 the king tried to undertake three of them at once reveals the limitations of his methods of strategic planning!

Confusion began to creep in when the marquis of Santa Cruz, in command of the royal navy at Lisbon, complained to the king on 13 February 1586 about the depredations of Drake and called for a major retaliatory strike against England. Philip replied on the 26th, inviting the marquis to formulate a plan of attack, but omitting to tell him either that he had already decided on invasion, or that he had also asked Parma for ideas.[70] Advised by the Provisioner-General of the fleet Bernabé de Pedroso, Santa Cruz worked fast, and sent a draft proposal to court on 22 March 1586. Unfortunately only the lists of necessary resources appear to have survived, but the immense detail of this document – ranging from the number of capital ships down to the last pair of shoes required – make Santa Cruz's intention perfectly plain.[71] He clearly envisaged the third alternative strategy for the invasion of England: a diversionary attack on Ireland followed by a surprise attack on the mainland. A fleet of some 150 great ships and 400 support vessels, assembled in Iberian ports, would transport 55,000 invasion troops – together with their equipment, munitions, and supporting artillery – directly to a landing point somewhere in the British Isles. The operation would follow the lines of such earlier successes as the relief of Malta in 1565 and the conquest of the Azores in 1582 and 1583.

Early in April 1586 Santa Cruz presented his plans in detail to a group of top advisers at the Escorial. The exact landing area he designated remains unknown, for no minutes of the meeting have survived; but most probably he picked the port of Waterford in southern Ireland since many subsequent papers mentioned the region. The attack was scheduled for summer 1587, and preparations were to center on three areas: Lisbon, where ships and men were to assemble to form a strike force under the personal command of Santa Cruz; Andalusia, where the Duke of Medina Sidonia – who had also attended the planning meeting – was to raise troops and assemble supply vessels to send to Lisbon; and Vizcaya, where eight large merchantmen and four pinnaces were to serve as a new naval squadron under the command of Spain's most experienced Atlantic seaman, Juan Martínez de Recalde.[72]

69 Based upon F. McLynn, *Invasion: From the Armada to Hitler, 1588–1945* (London, 1987), passim.
70 J. Calvar Gross, et al., *La Batalla del Mar Océano* [hereafter *BMO*], Vol. 1 (Madrid, 1988), pp. 564 and 566ff, with revised date in Vol. 2 (Madrid, 1989), p. ix.
71 *BMO*, Vol. 2, pp. 45–74.
72 See AGS *Estado* 2218/43, Don Juan de Idiáquez to Archduke Albert, 2 April 1586 on the preparations at Lisbon; Maura, *El designio de Felipe II*, pp. 145ff, on Medina Sidonia's

However, just as preparations to implement the Santa Cruz plan began, the prince of Parma completed his own strategic assessment. He explained it in a twenty-eight page letter dated 20 April 1586 and entrusted further details to the special messenger who brought the letter to court. Parma began by regretting the lack of secrecy surrounding the king's intentions. According to him, even ordinary soldiers and civilians in Flanders were openly discussing the best way to invade England. Nevertheless, the prince believed that three basic precautions might still save the enterprise. First, the king must have sole charge "without placing any reliance on either the English themselves, or the assistance of other allies." Second, the French must not interfere, either by sending assistance to Elizabeth or by intervening in the Netherlands. Third, sufficient troops and resources must remain behind to defend the reconquered Netherlands against the Dutch even after the assault force had left.

Only after meeting these conditions could the prince detach a force of 30,000 foot and 500 horse from the Army of Flanders and ferry it across the Channel aboard a flotilla of seagoing barges to launch a surprise attack on England. Provided his precise intentions remained a secret, "given the number of troops we have to hand here, and the ease with which we can concentrate and embark them in the barges, and considering that we can ascertain, at any moment, the forces which Elizabeth has and can be expected to have, and that the crossing only takes ten to twelve hours without a following wind (and eight hours with one)," Parma felt sure that the invasion stood a fair chance of success. "The most suitable, close and accessible point of disembarkation [he concluded], is the coast between Dover and Margate," which would permit a surprise march on London. This was, in essence, the fourth alternative invasion strategy: the surprise assault.

Parma devoted only two paragraphs of his letter to the possibility of naval support from Spain, and even then he considered it only in the context of the worst possible scenario: that somehow details of his plan had become known in England. In that case, he suggested, since Drake's exploits forced the king to mobilize a fleet to protect the Atlantic, perhaps this new navy might "either sail suddenly up here in order to assist and reinforce the troops who have already landed [in Kent] and keep open the seaway between the coasts of Flanders and England; or else – if your fleet is large, well-provided, well-armed and well-manned – it could create a diversion which will draw the English fleet away [from the straits of Dover]."[73]

Philip II thus confronted two plausible plans. His foremost naval com-

part; and AGS *Contaduría Mayor de Cuentas* 2a época 1208, on the embargo of ships to form the squadron of Vizcaya between 10 April and 7 May 1586.

73 AGS *Estado* 590/125, Parma to Philip II, 20 April 1586; its arrival is noted in 590/126 "Lo que dixó Juan Bautista Piata de palabra a 24 de junio 1586" (a document which itself contains additional information about the plan).

mander endorsed one; his most experienced general the other. Which was better?

To some extent, the long delay before Parma's strategy arrived at court reduced its appeal. The king had asked for Parma's plan on 29 December 1585 and issued a reminder six weeks later. Finally sent on 20 April 1586, the strategy did not reach the royal cipher clerks until 20 June, and four more days elapsed before the debriefing of the bearer, Giovanni Battista Piatti, by the king's ministers. The proposal prompted questions about the exact amount of shipping currently available in the ports of Flanders to ferry a major army across the open sea, and about the possible advantage of seeking a landing place in the Thames estuary, closer to London. Then Don Juan de Zúñiga took over the whole dossier.[74]

The conflict with the Santa Cruz plan, as already adopted, left Zúñiga totally undeterred. Instead, he sought to amalgamate the two strategies. He proposed that the marquis's fleet sail from Lisbon, carrying all available troops together with most of the materiel needed for the land campaign, directly for Ireland. There it would put ashore its assault troops, and secure a beachhead. This, Zúñiga anticipated, would threaten and distract Elizabeth's naval forces, thereby neutralizing their potential for resistance when, after some two months, the Armada suddenly left Ireland and made for the Channel. The main invasion force of 30,000 veterans, under Parma's leadership, would then sail in a surprise attack from the ports of Flanders to the beaches of Kent in a flotilla of flat-bottomed craft, while the Armada cruised off the North Foreland and secured the local command of the Narrow Seas requisite for a safe crossing. It would then offload the siege artillery and supplies necessary for a swift march on London. Finally, with the two beachheads established and the seas made secure, the fleet of supply ships under the Duke of Medina Sidonia in the ports of Andalusia would bring up further reinforcements and replenishments. This overwhelming military and naval superiority would destroy the Tudor regime, replace it with a Catholic one favorable to Spain, and force the English garrisons in Holland to surrender the places they held to Philip II's forces, effectively ending the Dutch Revolt as well. Spain would thus kill two dangerous birds with a single stone.[75]

One wonders whether Philip II realized the enormity of the proposed change of plan. In retrospect, Santa Cruz's strategy contained much merit. The events of 1588 proved that once they got their Armada to sea, the Spaniards could move 66,000 tons of shipping from one end of the Channel to the other with little difficulty, despite repeated assaults upon it; while the Kinsale landing of 1601 showed how easily an invader could secure and

[74] See AGS *Estado* 589/15, Philip II to Parma, 29 December 1585; and 590/117 and 125, Parma to Philip II, 28 February and 20 April 1586; and 590/126, "Lo que dixó Juan Bautista Piata."

[75] *BMO*, Vol. 2, p. 212, "Parescer" of Don Juan de Zúñiga.

fortify a bridgehead in southern Ireland. Likewise, Parma's concept of a Blitzkrieg landing in Kent also had much to recommend it; time and again, his troops had proved their invincibility under his leadership, and the largely untrained English forces, taken by surprise, would probably have succumbed to the Army of Flanders as it marched on London.[76] The Armada's undoing ultimately resulted from the decision to unite the fleet from Spain with the army from the Netherlands as the obligatory prelude to launching the invasion.

Why did they choose this course? Zúñiga had played an outstanding role in coordinating the naval campaigns of the Mediterranean for almost twenty years; and Philip II had also participated in many victorious campaigns in the past, most notably the conquest of Portugal in 1580. That exploit, too, had involved a combined military and naval operation, and perhaps the king felt that two simultaneous attacks were more likely to succeed than one and that since money seemed available for both he need not choose between them. For the king was, essentially, an *armchair* strategist. He had virtually no firsthand experience of any of the five levels of strategy that Edward Luttwak has noted: technical, tactical, operational, theater, or grand strategy.[77] Worse still, he would not allow anyone else to provide the critical skills that he lacked. For Philip II's secretive system of government ensured that no one but he and his chosen confidants ever subjected the plan to critical scrutiny. No one at the Spanish court could demand how, precisely, two large and totally independent forces under sail, with operational bases separated by more than a thousand miles of ocean, could achieve the accuracy of time and place necessary to accomplish their linkup. Nor could anyone ask how Parma with his vulnerable and lightly armed barges in Flanders, would run the gauntlet of the Dutch and English warships stationed offshore to intercept and destroy them.

On 26 July 1586 Giovanni Battista Piatti returned to the Netherlands with details of a master plan for the conquest of England that embodied, in all essentials, the complex and subtle vision of Don Juan de Zúñiga. A parallel dossier went to Lisbon. But Philip II invited neither Parma nor Santa Cruz to comment on the orders sent to them; he merely commanded them to carry out the plan.[78] The king also instructed all public authorities in Spain, Portugal, Naples, and Sicily to prepare troops, munitions, and other necessary equipment, while Spanish and Italian reinforcements were readied for dispatch to the Army of Flanders, and shipping from all over Europe headed toward Lisbon and Cadiz.[79]

---

[76] This argument is developed in more detail in Parker, *Spain and the Netherlands*, ch. 7.
[77] See E. Luttwak, *Strategy: The Logic of War and Peace* (Cambridge, MA, 1987), part 2.
[78] The Instructions of 26 July have not survived, but can be surmised from AGS *Estado* 2218/52, Philip II to Parma, 18 July 1586; fo 56, Don Juan de Idiáquez to Parma, 27 July 1586; and fo 67, Philip II to Parma, 1 September 1586.
[79] AGS *Estado* 1261/87, Philip II to the Governor of Lombardy, 7 August 1586; and *Estado* 1088/210–212, to the viceroys of Naples and Sicily, 12 November 1586. The towns of

As the troops, ships, and munitions assembled, Philip II took a number of other steps to assure the success of the Enterprise of England. Although Zúñiga died in November 1586, the king continued the diplomatic offensive already underway to ensure that at the crucial moment no foreign power would raise a finger to save Elizabeth Tudor. Almost at once, Elizabeth removed a major diplomatic obstacle from Philip's path: on 18 February 1587 her officials executed Mary Queen of Scots. Within weeks, Philip II's agents abroad were capitalizing to the utmost upon the "murder" of Mary Stuart, using it to justify their master's maturing plans to extirpate the tyrannous "English Jezebel."

In France, Spain's subsidies to the leaders of the Catholic League increased, and in April 1587 their forces seized three towns in Picardy, near the frontier with the Netherlands, and replaced the royal garrisons with League troops. This in effect guaranteed that no aid from Henry III or the French Protestants would reach either the Dutch or the English opponents of Philip II.

The whole strategic scene changed, however, when Queen Elizabeth, upon news of Philip's designs, decided to launch Sir Francis Drake with a powerful flotilla on the preemptive strike soon known as "the singeing of the King of Spain's beard." Neither the sack of Cadiz in May 1587 nor even the destruction of stores and ships represented the critical action, but rather it was Drake's subsequent – and well-publicized – departure to intercept the treasure galleons returning from the East and West Indies. That threat forced Santa Cruz to take his powerful fleet to sea in July, not to Ireland as intended, but to await the returning fleets off the Azores. Although he accomplished this feat brilliantly, losing only one East Indiaman to Drake, he could not return to Iberian waters until October, and then only with storm-damaged ships and sick men. As a consequence, the Armada did not sail against England in 1587, and Spain's grand strategy required rethinking (Table 5.2).[80]

Philip II worked hard. First, he ordered the auxiliary fleet in Andalusia to sail to Lisbon and join forces with the warships of Santa Cruz upon their return from the Azores. Then on 14 September he issued a detailed directive for the Armada. It contained no talk of invading Ireland – indeed two whole clauses of the Instructions explained that because of the delays resulting from Drake's raid and the need to escort the treasure fleets, no time remained to secure a base in Ireland before invading England. The purpose of the Enterprise, the king emphasized, was unchanged; he had altered only the strategy.

Santa Cruz now received orders to sail with the entire fleet "in the name of God straight to the English Channel and go along it until you have anchored off Margate head, having first warned the Duke of Parma of your ap-

Spain were ordered to prepare to levy troops on 7 October 1586 (AGS Guerra Antigua 189/119–68).
[80] On the raid, see Martin and Parker, *The Spanish Armada*, pp. 130–32 and the sources listed at p. 283 note 9.

Table 5.2. *Military strength of Philip II and his enemies, 1587–1588*

PHILIP II

Spain, North Africa, Portugal
On the Armada: 19,000 troops
In garrisons: 29,000 troops
Fleets: 131 ships with the Armada at Lisbon. 22 galleys defending the Mediterranean.

Italy
Milan: 2000 troops
Naples: 3000 troops and 28 galleys
Siciliy: 2000 troops and 10 galleys

Overseas
5000 soldiers in Portuguese Asia
8000 soldiers in Spanish America

Netherlands
27,000 troops ready to invade England
40,000 troops in garrisons throughout the Netherlands
81 ships and 194 barges for the invasion of England

ENEMIES

England
45,000 troops on land at the peak of the Armada crisis
15,000 men with the Royal Navy
6,000 troops in the Dutch Republic
197 ships scattered along the south coast

Dutch Republic
17,500 troops
67 ships scattered between the Flemish and Frisian coasts

proach."[81] Then, the king continued, "[t]he said duke, according to the orders he has received, on seeing the Narrow Seas thus made safe by the Armada being either anchored off the said headland or else cruising in the mouth of the Thames, . . . will immediately send across the army that he has prepared in small boats, of which (for transit alone) he has plenty." Philip II went on to insist that until Parma and his men had made their crossing, the Armada "was to do nothing except make safe the passage, and defeat any enemy ships that may come out to prevent this." He also loftily asserted that "from Margate, you can prevent any junction of the enemy warships in the

[81] After the death of his father in September 1586, Alexander Farnese became Duke of Parma.

Thames and the eastern ports, with those in the south and west, so that the enemy will not be able to concentrate a fleet which would dare to come out and seek battle with ours."

The scheme sounded highly convincing, but at least one crucial question went unanswered: would the Grand Fleet cross to the ports of Flanders to meet Parma's army, embarked ahead of time and ready to go, or did the king expect the invasion barges to put out and meet the fleet in open water? In the former event, how would the deep-draft ships of the Armada negotiate the shallows and sandbanks fringing the Flemish coast; in the latter, how could a fleet cruising several miles offshore protect Parma's vulnerable barges from the heavily gunned Dutch blockade squadron once they left the safety of Dunkirk and Nieuwpoort? The king's silence on this matter was, to say the least, an unfortunate oversight.[82]

But perhaps Philip II did not think it mattered, for he had two more diplomatic tricks up his sleeve: the simultaneous paralysis of both France and the Dutch Republic. At a meeting with the Spanish ambassador in late April 1588, the Duke of Guise, acting on behalf of the League, agreed that he would engineer a general rebellion the moment he heard of the Armada's departure. The immediate payment of 100,000 ducats to the League's leaders clinched the deal. Early in May the Paris Catholics began to agitate for a takeover of the city and when, on 12 May 1588, Henry III deployed his Swiss Guards to preserve order, the entire capital erupted into violence, erecting barricades against the king's troops and forcing him to flee. The "Day of the Barricades" made Guise the master of Paris, and shortly afterward he became "lieutenant-general of the kingdom." Philip II had intended that Guise capture Henry III along with Paris and force him to make concessions – including free access to ports such as Boulogne and Calais – as the Armada entered the Channel. But even without that crowning achievement, the towns of Picardy, as well as Paris, remained under League control, and friendly forces now held the Channel ports.

Spain's diplomacy also ensured – rather more surprisingly – that the Dutch rendered precious little aid to England. As rumors of an imminent invasion multiplied, Elizabeth began serious negotiations for a cease-fire with a team of diplomats that Philip II and Parma had graciously supplied. The queen

---

[82] The Instructions may be found in Oria, *La Armada Invencible*, pp. 33–37: Instructions for Santa Cruz, 14 September 1588. See also the parallel Instructions sent to Brussels: AGS *Estado* 594/5, Philip II to Parma, 4 (sic) September 1588. The oversights in the royal master plan were brought to Philip's attention by Parma, at least, on numerous occasions; but he never received an answer. Cfr AGS *Estado* 592/147–9, Parma to Philip II, 21 December 1587; and *Estado* 594/6–7, 79 and 197, idem, 31 January, 22 June, and 21 July 1588. However perhaps one should not be too critical, for there is a striking parallel here with the planning of Operation OVERLORD (the invasion of Normandy) in 1944. Allied strategic planning dealt with only two objectives: (i) how to get ashore in sufficient strength to secure a bridgehead; and (ii) how to pursue the enemy after breaking out of the bridgehead. No consideration seems to have been given to how to get from (i) to (ii)! (I owe this point to Russell Hart of the Ohio State University.)

begged her Dutch allies to join her in the talks, but her appeal divided the Republic, with the inland provinces – and even some towns in Holland – favoring discussions. However, the States-General held firm and refused to send delegates to the peace talks. In desperation, the English troops in the Netherlands thereupon attempted to seize a number of strategic towns in the Republic. They failed, and England had now totally discredited itself. Following this striking success, Philip II extended the talks with Elizabeth's diplomats, and authorized his agents to hint at concessions. Each time, to his delight, the English took the bait – moving to Spanish territory at Bourbourg (near Dunkirk) in May 1588, even allowing one of their number, Sir James Croft, to discuss terms for a complete English withdrawal from the Netherlands. Once more, Spanish propaganda made much political capital out of "perfidious Albion" with the already suspicious Dutch. It is true that Elizabeth also gained something from the talks – an observation post in Flanders from which to monitor Parma's military preparations; but she lost far more by forfeiting the trust of the Dutch.

AFTER THE ARMADA

In the event it did not matter, for the invaders never managed to join forces. The Dutch blockade of the Flanders coast in July 1588 with thirty-two heavily armed warships kept Parma's transports confined to port, while the fireships, galleons, and guns of the Royal Navy possessed sufficient superiority over those of the Armada to ensure that Medina Sidonia could not remain in the Narrow Seas long enough to rendezvous with Parma. But if the tactical factors were the immediate cause of the defeat of the Spanish Armada in 1588, the defective strategic planning of the Spanish government undoubtedly lay at its core.

No improvement took place in this regard after the Armada's defeat – rather the reverse. Although the king suffered at least one "dark night of the soul" during which he feared that God had abandoned Spain, by the middle of November 1588 he was urging his advisers to come up with a new strategy for the conquest of England. The councilors – as in 1585–86 – unanimously rejected a defensive posture on the grounds that it would cost almost as much as a new offensive but would do nothing to bring the war to an end. Instead they urged the king to build up his forces again in preparation for a new amphibious attack on the Tudor state. This time, however, they explicitly ruled out both a landing in Ireland and the involvement of the Army of Flanders, in favor of an expedition "sailing straight to England and trying to conquer it."[83] The Council also recognized the need for a Spanish High Seas

---

[83] See Martin and Parker, *The Spanish Armada,* p. 258, on the king's remarkable loss of faith on 10 November. But two days later he had recovered and was asking his councilors to discuss how best to attack England again (AGS *Estado* 2851, unfol., "Lo que se platicó en el Consejo de Estado a 12 de noviembre 1588.")

Fleet. The Armada of 1588 had included few royal ships – the galleons of Portugal, inherited in 1580; the Mediterranean galleasses; the escort vessels from the transatlantic convoys – but the following year Spain laid down twelve new galleons of 1,000 tons each in the Cantabrian shipyards. A total of fifty-three royal warships became available for North Atlantic use by 1598. Furthermore the royal arsenals manufactured some 500 tons of ordnance in 1589–90, specifically made to a uniform design that combined range with firepower.[84]

But plans for a new Armada collapsed almost before they began when news arrived at court of Henry III's murder of the Duke of Guise, Philip II's client and ally. The king's advisers immediately realized that the task of defending the Catholics of France now devolved on Spain, even though "the amount of money that will be required will ruin the preparations we are making here." All agreed that aid to the League should remain clandestine, for as one councilor put it: "The temptation to declare war on France is great; nevertheless, when we consider the state of this Monarchy, the open war with England (so powerful at sea), and the pressure that our rebels and enemies will bring to bear on His Majesty, we must not declare war on France under any circumstances."[85] But events soon conspired to undermine this prudent stance. Henry III's murder by a Catholic fanatic in August 1589 made Henry of Navarre the legal king of France, although his title to rule remained unacceptable to most Catholics because of his Protestantism. On 7 September Philip II warned the Duke of Parma of the critical state of affairs in France:

> My principal aim [he explained] is to secure the well-being of the Faith, and to see that in France Catholicism survives and heresy is excluded. . . . If, in order to ensure this exclusion and to aid the Catholics so that they prevail, you see that it is necessary for my troops to enter France openly [then you must lead them in].

Philip realized that this course would require sacrifices in other theaters. In 1588 he had canceled both a plan to conquer Sumatra and a proposal to build a fort at Mombasa in order to save money; he had also withdrawn his support from the Duke of Savoy's surprise invasion of Saluzzo, an enterprise that he had previously approved.[86] Now he recognized the need to scale down the war against the Dutch:

---

84 Details in Thompson, *War and Government in Habsburg Spain*, p. 191f; and idem, "Spanish Armada Gun Procurement and Policy," in Gallagher and Cruickshank, *God's Obvious Design*, pp. 69–84.
85 AGS *Estado* 2855, unfol., "Lo que se platicó en Consejo de Estado a 10 de henero de 1589, entendido el sucesso del duque de Guisa."
86 Details from J. H. da Cunha Riva, ed., *Arquivo Português Oriental*, Vol. 3 (Nova Goa, 1861), pp. 130f and 146, Philip II to the Viceroy of India, 23 February and 14 March 1588; and G. Altadonna, "Cartas de Felipe II a Carlos Manuel II Duque de Saboya (1583–96)," *Cuadernos de Investigación Histórica*, Vol. 9 (1986), pp. 137–90, at pp. 168–71: Philip II to the Duke of Savoy, 23 June, 1 November, and 23 December 1588.

The affairs of France [he told Parma] create obligations which we cannot fail to fulfill because of their extreme importance; and since we cannot undertake too many things at once, because of the risk that they will all fail (and because my Treasury will not allow it), it seems that we must do something about the war in the Netherlands, reducing it to a defensive footing.

Philip ordered Parma to pay off any surplus troops and allocate the rest to garrisons in case the king suddenly required his presence in France.[87]

Still Philip hesitated to strike, however, whether against Elizabeth of England or Henry of Navarre, because for most of summer 1589 a massive – albeit mismanaged – Anglo-Dutch expeditionary force sacked Galicia and menaced Lisbon, while another English squadron lay off the Azores hoping to ambush the returning treasure fleets. The traditional priorities of Spanish grand strategy now came into play: the crown could not denude the Iberian peninsula of the forces required for its defense. Early in 1590, however, the military success of Henry of Navarre, with English and Dutch aid, forced the Spanish government to face the possibility that unless the French Catholics received open and substantial military aid, their resistance might collapse. Three alternative areas for intervention seemed most promising: an invasion by the Army of Flanders in the north, a landing in Brittany in the west, and an advance into Languedoc or Navarre in the south. From the outset it appeared clear that one operation would not be enough to save the Catholic cause, and that three would overtax Spain's resources. As a result the Council of State suggested that the fleet intended for another assault on England should instead convey an expeditionary force to Brittany, while the Army of Flanders, instead of continuing the reconquest of the Netherlands, should invade northern France.[88]

Henry of Navarre's crushing defeat of his Catholic opponents at Ivry on 14 March 1590 decided the matter, for it jeopardized the security of Paris, the League's capital since the Day of the Barricades. On hearing the news of the battle, Philip II informed Parma that "the strategy for assisting the French Catholic cause that I have followed, although the correct one until now, will not do any longer." He commissioned the duke to invade France at once with 20,000 men. They left the Netherlands in late July and entered Paris in triumph on 19 September. Shortly afterward, another expeditionary force sailed from Spain to Blavet in Brittany to reinforce the French Catholic forces there.[89]

87 AGS *Estado* 2219/197, Philip II to Parma, 7 September 1589.
88 See the important policy discussion in AGS *Estado* 2855, unfol., "Lo que sobre las cartas de Francia de Don Bernardino y Moreo hasta las del 6 de hebrero se ofrece" and the Consulta on it.
89 AGS *Estado* 2220/1 fo. 157, Philip II to Parma, 4 April 1590; and fo. 165, confirmation dated 16 April. On the course of Parma's intervention in France, see van der Essen, *Alexandre Farnèse*, Vol. 5. A study of the Spanish expeditionary force in Brittany is urgently needed.

Spain's open intervention was of great short-term importance since without it Navarre would doubtless have won in 1590. As it was, the two sides in the French civil war now stood fairly evenly matched. But Philip II found himself with not one but three "voracious monsters gobbling up the troops and treasure of Spain."[90] When in February 1591 one of his ministers cautiously pointed out the inordinate cost of the wars against France and England, and suggested that "if God had placed Your Majesty under an obligation to remedy all the troubles of the world, He would have given you the money and the strength to do so," the king loftily retorted, "I know you are moved by the great zeal you have for my service to say what you did, but you must also understand that these are not matters that can be abandoned by a person who is as conscientious about his responsibilities as you know me to be. . . . " "The cause of religion," Philip concluded, "must take precedence over everything."[91]

The king, it seemed, had learned nothing and forgotten nothing. Since God's cause seemed to be equally involved in all three theaters, he decided to throw caution to the winds and invest resources in all of them at once. Nor did he neglect other areas of the "Spanish system." In Italy his influence, exercised through bribes and threats, secured the election of four pro-Spanish popes in less than two years, while in the Catholic Swiss cantons that separated Lombardy from Germany, his diplomats concluded advantageous treaties of alliance that facilitated the transfer of men, messages, and money to northern Europe.

As before, Philip II permitted no discussion of his perception of Spain's strategic needs; indeed, if anything he became more intransigent – it was as if, after the Armada, the king suffered a sort of "hardening of the arteries." Courtiers noted that he seemed impervious to ordinary emotions, displaying to the world an almost reptilian composure in the face of joy and sorrow alike. He also spent more time at prayer, more time asleep, and more time sick. Thus the king was too ill to transact business in May and June 1595, in March and April 1596, in spring 1597, and for most of 1598, the year of his death. He spent most of his last three years in the sixteenth-century equivalent of a wheelchair – a sort of lounger with movable positions from vertical to horizontal – in which he ate, worked, and slept, wearing loose garments that did not put pressure on his arthritic joints. But although he allowed others to conduct audiences and other public duties and signed many of his orders with a rubber stamp, the king retained total control of policy, determined that no weakening should occur in Spain's struggle for the cause of religion. Despite the continuing lack of success on all fronts, Spanish treasure and troops poured into France. Two more Armadas sailed against England (in 1596 and 1597), and every Dutch offensive met with stiff resistance.

90 The phrase used by Don Juan de Idiáquez in 1588 about the Low Countries' Wars: see page 126 above.
91 IVdeDJ 51/1, Mateo Vázquez to Philip II, 8 February 1591, and royal reply.

Spanish grand strategy had become no more than a blind determination to keep on fighting on all fronts until either Spain or its enemies collapsed from exhaustion. When the Cortes of Castile protested in 1593 against the heavy expenditure on foreign wars, pointing out that "although the wars against the Dutch, the English and the French are holy and just, we must beg Your Majesty that they may cease," the king rebuked the Representatives of the People for their insolence:

> They should and must put their trust in me, in the love I have for these king-doms, and in the long experience I have in governing them, [and accept] that I shall always do what is in their best interests. Speak to them at length in this vein and advise them that they are never, on any pretext, to come to me with such a suggestion again.[92]

If Philip II elected to prolong the sufferings of his subjects in order to pros-ecute his strategic goals, whatever their cost, the explanation lies not in his ignorance of conditions or consequences, but in his unshakable confidence – to the end of his days – that he was doing God's work and that, in the end, God would provide.

Thus, although Paul Kennedy correctly identified the Military Revolution, strategic overstretch, and shortage of money as the proximate causes of the failure of Philip II's bid for mastery, a messianic imperialism fatally com-pounded them, driving the king to elevate religious principle above common sense. The key, to use Philip's own words, was a "confidence in God" that led him "to understand matters differently" from other people and made him "play down the difficulties and problems which spring up." The great weak-ness in his strategic vision lay in the fact that if God were not Spanish, Spain was bound to fail. "In the end, we cannot do everything with nothing" the Duke of Parma complained to his master in 1586, "and one day God will grow tired of working miracles for us."[93] After 1588, for all the treasure and troops deployed, and for all the prayers and devotions offered, the strategic miracles ceased.[94]

---

[92] Actas de las Cortes de Castilla, Vol. 16 (Madrid, 1890), pp. 169–73: 6 May 1593.
[93] AGS *Estado* 590/23, Parma to Philip II, 28 February 1586.
[94] On Spanish Grand Strategy after 1588, see the forthcoming thesis of Edward S. Terrace, "The Failure of Philip II's Bid for European Mastery, 1589–98" (University of Illinois, 1994).

6

The origins of a global strategy: England from 1558 to 1713

WILLIAM S. MALTBY

Tension between England's naval and imperial commitments and its periodic need to intervene with land forces on the European continent has characterized the making of strategy from the Elizabethan era to the present. This tension arises naturally from the three primary strategic objectives that the makers of English strategy pursued at the beginning of the early modern period. The most immediate was to prevent invasion by maintaining naval control of the Channel. The second was to protect England's overseas trade and to encourage the development of colonies, while the third, which sometimes took precedence over the second, was to prevent any European power from achieving hegemony on the continent. All were interrelated and all were present in the thinking of the Elizabethans, but they did not coalesce into a workable strategic system until the War of the Spanish Succession.

The delay was due in part to a lack of resources and in part to certain features of the Elizabethan heritage itself. That heritage included a fascination with maritime strategies and preconceptions that, because they derived from the heroic example of Drake and Hawkins, rarely underwent the rigors of analysis. Since the Elizabethan example powerfully influenced later strategists, and since it, too, developed partly in response to financial limitations, the relationship between these two issues bears careful scrutiny.

Mercantilist assumptions were a major influence on all early modern strategists. The established tendency to define wealth in terms of specie, and the ancient notion of political economy as a zero-sum game, had made late medieval states acutely conscious of their trade balances. The age of discovery seemed to offer greater opportunities for autarky and for the incremental surpluses needed to sustain the ever-growing cost of war. Though maritime strategy could help ensure the safety of overseas trade or to acquire and defend colonies, no continental state could rely upon seapower for its primary defense. The naval strategies of Spain, France, the Netherlands, and even Portugal remained subservient to the primary strategic aim of gaining or defending territory. The function of seapower was to preserve communications and the unimpeded flow of wealth without which land warfare would be far more difficult.

Despite the subsidiary nature of such strategies, they were neither inadequately thought through nor inexpensive. They consumed vast resources and often aimed in almost Mahanian terms at the naval control of entire regions. From the beginning of the sixteenth century, the Portuguese worked to protect their *carreira da India* both from corsairs off the West African coast and from commercial rivals in the Arabian Sea, where they attempted to establish naval supremacy. The Spanish sought to control the Caribbean and developed a system of convoys to preserve their lines of communication with the New World. They also fought an ongoing struggle for naval mastery in the western Mediterranean, and the revolt of the Netherlands made them acutely aware of the need to control the North Sea.[1] But such efforts were beyond their resources. They achieved command of the sea with occasional interruptions in the Caribbean and sporadically in the Western Mediterranean, but the Dutch rebels seized and kept control of their own coasts. Though the Dutch soon emerged as Europe's leading maritime nation, they tended to rely on convoys for the protection of trade outside home waters, and on commerce raiding to harass their enemies. Their deep commitments on land, much like those of the French and Spaniards, made it impossible for them to consider a purely maritime strategy.

That luxury belonged to the English alone. Like France and the Netherlands, England came late to the colonial game, but by mid-sixteenth century it had a growing overseas trade and felt the first stirrings of imperial ambition. Its unique geographic position encouraged a sense of isolation from the troubles of Europe; a strong English fleet could theoretically protect the island against all threats from the continent. Beginning with the fifteenth century *Libelle of Englyshe Policye,* English writers increasingly opposed continental commitments.[2] Their basic arguments, as set forth in dozens of publications from Hakluyt's *Voyages* to Swift's "Conduct of the Allies," were that a strong navy could defend the realm, protect commerce, and ensure the development of colonies. Modest land forces might be necessary to deal with Ireland or the Scots, but it was folly to commit them to the continent. Should it become necessary to intervene in Europe, the fleet alone could destroy or blockade the enemy's commerce, thereby crippling its ability to pay for war. Cut off from fisheries, colonies, and foreign markets, even Spain or France would be forced to sue for peace.

It was a seductive notion that for some, at least, held out the hope of making war pay for war. During the seventeenth century this early form of

---

[1] I.A.A. Thompson, *War and Government in Habsburg Spain, 1560–1620* (London, 1976), pp. 186–87.

[2] First published 1436. The best critical edition is by G. Warner (Oxford, 1926).

navalism became an article of faith in England, thanks to distrust of standing armies and to the rapid expansion of commerce. Because it aimed at the control of trade routes and colonies, it was by definition a global strategy, though a limited one. Those who disagreed with it usually accepted the need for a powerful navy with transoceanic capabilities, but doubted that sea-power alone could defeat continental states that were virtually self-sustaining in the necessities of war. Many, including Elizabeth I, feared that not even the fleet could save England if Spain or France achieved hegemony in Europe. When the queen sent troops to the Netherlands in 1585, she acted on the theory, generally accepted today, that only armies can break a land power.[3] Unfortunately, the English contribution was too small to accomplish that objective, and the perception that the venture had failed obstructed similar strategies in the future.[4]

The issues that dominated Elizabethan strategic debate were thus not truly bipolar. Everyone agreed that England must be strong at sea, but those who opposed all commitments on land were vocal and bitter. Their efforts were a powerful impediment to the development of coordinated strategies. But to the degree that strategy is a matter of allocating resources, such arguments had considerable force. Until the Revolution of 1688–89, England could not afford to maintain an effective military presence on the continent. Indeed, for most of the period it was incapable of maintaining a fleet beyond the narrow seas; a global maritime strategy was no more attainable than was the development of an army capable of defeating the Duke of Parma or Louis XIV.

England was not poor in absolute terms, though its relatively small population placed it at a disadvantage when compared with France or Spain. The problem lay in its government, a fiscally underdeveloped monarchy chronically unable to exploit the resources of its subjects. Permanent taxation on the French or Spanish model did not exist, and Henry VIII's alienation of the monasteries and their lands symbolized the crown's general failure to maximize domain revenues.[5] The resulting poverty affected every aspect

---

[3] See "Mahan versus Mackinder," in Paul M. Kennedy, *The Rise and Fall of British Naval Mastery* (New York, 1976), pp. 177–202.

[4] Charles Wilson, *Queen Elizabeth and the Revolt of the Netherlands* (London, 1970), p. 136. For a general discussion of Elizabethan strategy, see R.B. Wernham, "Elizabethan War Aims and Strategy," in *Elizabethan Government and Society*, S.T. Bindoff, et al., eds. (London, 1961), pp. 340–368.

[5] Elizabeth's revenues are difficult to calculate on an annual basis. F.C. Dietz, *English Public Finance, 1485–1641* (London, 1964, first published, 1932), pp. 7, 296, 328n, shows crown rents rising from 66,448 pounds to 88,767 pounds during the reign, while customs revenues ranged from about 80,000 pounds to 99,400 pounds. The thirteen parliamentary appropriations during the reign totaled 29 million pounds, or an average annual yield of 64,450 pounds (p. 392n). By comparison, Spanish revenues increased from 8.7 million ducats in 1577 to 12.9 million in 1598. Regardless of how one calculates average yields or the rates of exchange between the two currencies, this is at least six to eight times greater than the funds

of military and naval operations. It was always a struggle to keep adequate numbers of ships and men in service. This difficulty affected both deployment and training, for long-serving personnel were a luxury that England could rarely afford. Underlying all were weak bureaucratic structures that created difficulties of their own over pay, provisioning, recruitment, naval construction, and repairs. The Spanish Habsburgs had long been aware that a global strategy was expensive if for no other reason than that the available technology was barely equal to the task. Such a strategy inevitably consumed men, ships, and treasure at an appalling rate. Only those who could swallow their losses and develop a fiscal and administrative system capable of replacing them could hope to win the imperial game.

Until the Revolution of 1688–89, English statesmen lacked the resources to win. Their failure limited the options available to the strategists and narrowed their field of vision; in any event, they were operating with few useful precedents. The vagaries of wind and sea, the almost complete absence of credible intelligence, and the fiscal pressures for a short campaign all favored dramatic, high-risk ventures, while the lure of prize money sometimes influenced their judgment as it influenced that of their successors for centuries to come.[6] These circumstances were one source of England's perennial fascination with Spain's treasure fleet and its preference for raids or "descents" on enemy ports. Descents, whether as preemptive strikes or as simple harassment, remained popular even after a string of costly failures in the late sixteenth and seventeenth centuries, and in the face of a growing realization that such incursions tended to strengthen enemy resistance.

The hunt for the treasure fleet was even more distracting. The English struggled just to locate the *flota* much less capture it, but it remained a major objective until well into the eighteenth century. This persistence stemmed from the belief that the seizure of one year's convoy would cripple the Spanish war effort and greatly enrich the English, a view based on gross overestimates of the fleet's value both in absolute terms and as a percentage of Spain's revenues. Spain could survive the loss of convoys to both the weather and the Dutch, but was prepared at the same time to devote its entire naval force to protecting them. It is therefore hard to imagine a more difficult target or one less likely to produce strategically decisive results.

The Elizabethan heritage was a mixed blessing to the seventeenth-century strategists who worked in its shadow. If it encouraged global vision and an offensive spirit, its underlying navalism made intervention on the continent

---

available to Elizabeth's government in a normal year – and it was far more predictable. About one third came from the Indies and most of the rest from perpetual taxes imposed on Castile, the population of which was about twice that of England's. For a useful discussion of Spanish revenues in English, see Thompson, *War and Government*, pp. 68–69.

6 Scholars have more often ascribed the strategic lapses of the Elizabethan admirals to temperament. See Garrett Mattingly, *The Armada* (Boston, 1959), pp. 261–62. Kennedy, *Naval Mastery*, p. 32, calls them "volatile, hot-headed, erratic personalities."

politically difficult and some of its most cherished precepts proved misleading. Under the early Stuarts, intellectual barriers of this kind were less important than poverty, a vise the dynasty never escaped. The Stuarts could not "live of their own," and every attempt to increase revenues raised vexing issues of sovereignty. Colonial enterprise made great advances at private expense, but except for a brief interlude during which the Duke of Buckingham engineered the disasters at Cádiz (1625) and Ile de Rhé (1627), foreign policy remained generally unassertive. It was probably just as well. When Charles I, braver though less wise than his father, launched a fleet by extending the payment of ship money to inland counties, the resulting uproar contributed to his ultimate downfall.

Admittedly, the scheme was deceptive. Its real purpose was to cement the Spanish alliance by assisting Spain against the Dutch, and Charles, desperate as always for money, apparently believed that Spain would contribute something toward its costs.[7] Because the government thought the alliance unpopular, it told the public that the fleet would provide commerce protection in the Channel. In the end, the fleet served neither purpose adequately. Spanish assistance was not forthcoming, while the ships, including the massive *Sovereign of the Seas,* were too few to contest the Dutch main fleet and too large for the effective harassment of fishermen and privateers.

The ease with which the government collected ship money at first indicated there was considerable support for strengthening the navy as long as the king's true intentions remained hidden.[8] But Charles's personal and dynastic aims, already at odds with those of Parliament, quickly fueled resistance. Fiscal paralysis ended only with the king's execution, and the vessels of the ship money fleet, with their great size and elaborate decoration, thereafter symbolized royal pride and extravagance.

The Commonwealth and Protectorate of Cromwell reversed this situation temporarily. The triumph of Parliament over the king dissolved its reluctance to finance war since it now controlled both the raising and spending of money. Impelled at first by the need to deal with seagoing Royalists under Prince Rupert and then by broader considerations, Parliament expanded the fleet to force levels far exceeding those of Elizabethan times. The ships, too, were different. Realizing that the massive three-deckers favored in Channel warfare could not cross the Atlantic or remain out after October without peril, Parliament began to commission smaller, more seaworthy vessels known as frigates. Unlike later vessels of the same classification, these two-deckers carried as many as fifty guns and could stand in the line of battle, but their fine lines and minimal superstructure gave them a decided advantage over the great ships in both speed and seakeeping ability. The result was a

7   Simon Adams, "Spain or the Netherlands? The Dilemmas of Early Stuart Foreign Policy," in
    H. Tomlinson, *Before the English Civil War* (New York, 1984), p. 84.
8   Kevin Sharpe, "The Personal Rule of Charles I," in *Before the English Civil War*, p. 70.

formidable instrument that enabled Cromwell and his Generals-at-Sea to think once more in global terms.[9]

Cromwell has been called the last of the Elizabethans, but the situation he confronted differed in important ways from that of his spiritual ancestors. Spain no longer presented a serious threat to England, and internal disorders had again weakened France. For the time being, neither threatened to achieve hegemony on the continent. It was in England's interest to preserve the status quo, but the immediate goals of the Commonwealth and later of the Protectorate lay elsewhere.

The first strategic priority arose from England's growing commercial rivalry with the Dutch. Anglo-Dutch tension did not stem solely from the desires of English merchants who wanted, as Monk was later to put it, "more of the trade the Dutch now have."[10] The Dutch themselves saw England as holding a noose that could one day choke off their lines of communication if they failed to control the Channel. Their behavior was correspondingly assertive. Convinced that if the Dutch succeeded they would threaten not only trade but England's fundamental security, Parliament created a main battle fleet capable of defeating them.

The second priority related more directly to pressure from the merchant community. The Levant trade mandated a naval presence in the Mediterranean. Though some, like Monk and Montagu, realized that this presence would eventually require a permanent base under English control and advanced schemes for the conquest of Gibraltar, their ideas failed to produce action.[11] The Commonwealth fleet conducted its Mediterranean operations from Lisbon by agreement with the Portuguese.

The elevation of Cromwell as Lord Protector revived truly Elizabethan ambitions. Cromwell's motives are not always easy to decipher,[12] but war with Spain was the centerpiece of his strategic policy. His primary objective was to cut Spain off from its American colonies by seizing Hispaniola and Havana. The English could then block the return of the treasure fleets and harvest the profits of the Indies for themselves.[13] The French, with whom he formed an alliance in 1655, would help protect English interests in the Mediterranean and assist in the seizure of Dunkirk, which could serve as a

9   For a good description of the Parliamentary and Cromwellian shipbuilding programs, with illustrations, see Frank Fox, *Great Ships: The Battlefleet of King Charles II* (Greenwich, U.K., 1980), pp 51–72; also A.H. Taylor, "Galleon into Ship of the Line," *Mariner's Mirror*, 44 (1958), pp. 267–85, and 45 (1959), pp. 14–24, 100–114.

10 Quoted in Alfred Thayer Mahan, *The Influence of Sea Power upon History, 1660–1783* (Boston, 1890), p. 107.

11 The idea was first suggested in 1625. See Sir Julian Corbett, *England in the Mediterranean*, Vol. 1 (London, 1904), p. 135.

12 The best attempt is probably Michael Roberts, "Cromwell and the Baltic," *Essays in Swedish History* (London, 1967), pp. 138–94.

13 A full discussion of this strategy may be found in Edward Montagu's minutes of the meeting of the Protector's Council on 20 April, 1654. C.H. Firth, ed., *The Clarke Papers*, Vol. 3 (Camden Society Publications, 61, 1899), pp. 203–206.

bridgehead should it become necessary to send troops to the continent to support the Protestant cause.[14] Through a series of misadventures, Penn captured Jamaica instead of Hispaniola and Blake's efforts to sieze the *flota* were only partially successful. However, England did take Dunkirk and Nova Scotia and maintained a presence in America, the Caribbean, and home waters.[15] Cromwell aimed not at defense but at the enhancement of English wealth and power, and his policy was as close to a global strategy as the interests of the time demanded.[16]

It did not last. The Restoration marked a period of strategic retrenchment during which the English reorganized and strengthened their navy along more professional lines. Charles II and his brother, the Duke of York, were dedicated navalists and enthusiastic supporters of colonization, but the nature of the Dutch wars prevented them from pursuing wider concerns. The economy of the Netherlands was by this time almost wholly dependent on overseas trade.[17] England's geographic position made it theoretically possible to destroy that economy by controlling access to Dutch ports through blockade or through the capture of shipping in the Channel and the North Sea. England required little more than rough equality in the number of fighting ships, for Providence had given it the weather gage and the best harbors. From the strategic point of view, all three of the Anglo-Dutch wars, whether fought during the Commonwealth or under the later Stuarts, are therefore of limited interest. Both sides threw all of their naval forces, including armed merchantmen, into a bitter struggle in home waters. Fleets of as many as 120 ships engaged in battles which for length, tactical interest, and sheer bloody-minded determination have rarely been equaled in the entire history of naval warfare. The Dutch raid on the Medway and "Sir Robert Holmes, his bonfire," also inflicted great damage, but none of these actions was in any sense global. In most the guns were audible on shore.[18]

The restoration of peace again raised the question of sovereignty. The Popish Plot brought a temporary end to cooperation between Crown and Parliament, reduced appropriations for the fleet, and forced the abandonment of Tangier, acquired by marriage at the beginning of the reign. Though the fleet had largely recovered by 1688, the Duke of York, now James II,

[14] This project had been discussed as early as 1651–52. See C.P. Korr, *Cromwell and the New Model Foreign Policy* (Berkeley, 1975), pp. 180–85.

[15] For a good brief description of the Spanish war, see Bernard Capp, *Cromwell's Navy* (Oxford, 1989), pp. 86–106.

[16] Christopher Hill, *God's Englishman* (London, 1970), pp. 166–68.

[17] Kennedy, *Naval Mastery*, p. 51; Capp, *Cromwell's Navy*, p. 78.

[18] Contemporary accounts of these battles may be found in volumes 13, 17, 30, 31, 41, 86, and 112 of the Naval Records Society Publications, and in H.T. Colenbrander, *Bescheiden vreemde archieven omtrent de grote Nederlandsche Zeeorlogen 1672–76*, 2 Vols. (The Hague, 1919). The best modern analyses are in J.C.M. Warnsinck, *Van Vlootvoogden en Zeeslagen* (Amsterdam, 1942). See also, Richard Ollard, *Sir Robert Holmes and the Restoration Navy* (London, 1969).

soon found himself fighting for his throne against the very instrument he had done so much to create. It was not until his departure in 1688 that the English resolved the issue of sovereignty, and therefore of finance, in favor of Parliament.[19]

The results were astonishing. Under Charles II, annual crown revenues normally amounted to between 1.3 and 1.4 million pounds, reaching 2 million pounds only in the war years 1665 and 1666, and rising again to that level with the accession of James II in 1687.[20] In contrast, revenues during the Nine Years' War totaled 32.7 million pounds, and during the War of the Spanish Succession 64.2 million pounds.[21] The largest single source of this increase was the land tax, introduced in 1692. Based on an assessment of 4 shillings per pound of income, it succeeded because those who controlled Parliament supported it. Factionalism and bitter party struggles were by no means dead, but with a king of their own making on the throne, a majority of English gentlemen no longer feared the use of their money to subvert their liberties or their religion.[22] At the same time, they extended the excise, a more regressive tax, to nearly every consumable item.[23]

The willingness of the public to extend credit further expressed confidence in the new settlement. As Walpole noted in his "Debts of the Nation Stated" (1712), investment in tontines, loans, annuities, and other public instruments had covered about one-third of all expenses in the War of the Spanish Succession and still remained popular with investors.[24] Large-scale development of the credit markets began under William III with a series of long-term loans managed by the Exchequer for public subscription. Some of the issues were badly managed, but loans from the chartered companies supplemented them, and they were ultimately covered by the Bank of England. The Bank, founded in 1694, was the first of its kind in Europe and demonstrated its utility almost from the start. In the panic of 1696–97 it helped save the government's credit by accepting depreciated Exchequer tallies in return for stock and by taking over the exchange contracts for the army in Flanders. In the War of the Spanish Succession, the Bank agreed to "circulate" Exchequer bills by cashing them at stated rates, and in 1709 it funded £1.7 million in bills that the government could not discharge. After 1713 the Bank gradually

---

19   J.H. Plumb, *The Growth of Political Stability in England, 1675–1725* (London, 1967), p. 69.
20   P.G.M. Dickson, *The Financial Revolution in England 1688–1756* (New York, 1967), p. 42; C.D. Chandalman, *The English Public Revenue 1660–1688* (Oxford, 1975), pp. 332–33.
21   Dickson, *Financial Revolution*, p. 10.
22   The tax was widely resented, but this appears to have been due to the lack of uniform collection. See W.R. Ward, *The English Land Tax in the Eighteenth Century* (London, 1953), p. 57.
23   P.G.M. Dickson, "War Finance, 1688–1714," *New Cambridge Modern History*, Vol. 4, p. 286.
24   Robert Walpole, "The Debts of the Nation Stated and Considered in Four Papers," (London, 1712), p. 7.

took over the management of all long-term borrowing, but long before this it had assumed a critical role in maintaining public confidence.[25]

By 1700 the English system of public finance was the best in Europe. When combined with diminished resistance to taxation it made the vast proceeds of a century of economic growth accessible to the state as never before. Global strategy was now at last affordable, but its implementation was to be halting, controversial, and at times inadvertent.

The delays were due to England's strategic position in the years immediately after 1689. When William III accepted the English throne, he created a conjuction of forces that was intolerable to Louis XIV. France was at the apogee of its power, with an army that was arguably the best in Europe, and thanks to the efforts of Colbert, a navy capable of challenging the combined fleets of England and the Netherlands for the first time. Based on the Atlantic ports and commanded by the great Tourville, it presented a mortal threat of invasion, whether to Ireland or to England itself. To oppose a French invasion the allies would have to concentrate virtually all naval resources in the Channel, even if it meant neglecting other interests at sea.

On land, William III as king and stadholder was determined to maintain the fortresses in the Spanish Netherlands that protected his native country. The chief attraction of the English crown had been the opportunity it afforded to add England to the Grand Alliance against his arch-rival Louis XIV; the provision of English troops for the continent was virtually a condition of his employment. His supporters among the English elite accepted it as such, but a minority of extreme Tories did not, and used the occasion to revive navalist arguments in their most rigorous form. In this, if in little else, they found themselves allied with merchant interests seeking a more active protection of trade in the Mediterranean, the Baltic, and the Caribbean. Many argued that William's interests remained parochially Dutch and that his policy served no English purpose. His preference for Dutch advisers reinforced this impression, but his supporters invoked the Protestant cause and the time-honored argument that not even the English fleet could save England if France achieved hegemony on the continent.[26] These rather Elizabethan disputes had little immediate impact. William got his English troops – 87,000 of them mustered out in 1697 – but the revival of navalist arguments had unforeseen consequences in the reign of his successor.

The policies of William III were not parochial, but his strategy on land was defensive and traditionally Dutch. He did not realize the full magnitude of the resources now at his disposal, and his campaigns in the Low Countries seem almost timid compared with the later exploits of the Duke of Marlborough. In contrast, his efforts at sea and in driving the French and their Irish and Jacobite allies out of Ireland seem remarkably bold. An attempted

[25]   Dickson, "War Finance," pp. 290–93.
[26]   Henry Horwitz, *Revolution Politicks: The Career of Daniel Finch, Second Earl of Nottingham 1647–1730* (Cambridge, 1968), p. 129.

invasion of England in 1691 was met with an order delivered by Queen Mary to engage the French fleet at once, regardless of the odds. The English commander, Torrington, did so against his better judgment and met defeat at Beachy Head. But the invasion failed, and in the following year Russell crushed a second French effort at La Hogue.

Analysis of these two battles did not affect English planning. Torrington, at least, understood the significance of Beachy Head, and formulated from it a strategic principle that has been widely debated ever since. After engaging a fleet twice as strong as his own, he took refuge in the Thames Estuary. At his subsequent court martial he declared that as long as there was a "fleet in being" the French would not dare invade, even if the fleet in question were substantially weaker than their own. He was right. His adversary, Tourville, returned to port after the victory, presumably because he feared that Torrington, whose professional judgment he respected, might catch him landing troops on a lee shore. In such circumstances, a strong fleet could find itself at the mercy of a weaker one with many of its ships at anchor and few if any of them able to make their way back out to sea.[27]

Torrington, though acquitted, never commanded again, and the possible implications of his doctrine went unheeded. English strategists remained committed to absolute naval superiority in home waters whatever the cost. Their instincts were, in Mahanian terms, correct, but they became an obstacle to the development of global strategies. Several years passed before anyone dared to "divide the fleet" and dispatch major forces to areas of English concern outside home waters. They did so only when the true meaning of what had happened in 1690–92 became apparent.[28]

As noted in Chapter 7, French strategy on land remained the exclusive creation of Louis XIV, who took a personal interest in everything that concerned his army. The reverse was true at sea. The king knew nothing of ships and was prepared to follow his advisers in naval matters, but factions and legitimate differences over policy divided them. Colbert had created the navy in the face of determined opposition from his rival, Louvois, who continued to oppose its expansion during the ministry of Colbert's son and successor, Seignelay. When Seignelay died some months after the battle of Beachy Head, Pontchartrain – who was hostile to the Colbert family – replaced him. Louvois used this opportunity to suggest that France scrap its fleet. But he died shortly thereafter, and Pontchartrain, unwilling as yet to diminish the

[27] This episode is analyzed at some length in Sir Herbert Richmond, *The Navy as an Instrument of Policy* (Cambridge, 1953), pp. 213–21. See also, Michael Lewis, *The Navy of Britain, A Historical Portrait* (London, 1948), pp. 468–69, and John Ehrman, *The Navy in the War of William III* (Cambridge, 1953), pp. 349–54. For La Hogue, see C. de La Roncière, *Histoire de la marine francaise*, Vol. 6 (Paris, 1909–1932), pp. 104–30; Ehrman, *William III*, pp. 394–97, and Mahan, *Influence*, pp. 184–91.

[28] Mahan, *Influence*, p. 194.

importance of his newly won office, opposed his suggestion. The king rejected the advice.[29]

It was a temporary reprieve. The apparently meager results of Tourville's *campagne du large* of 1691, and the following year's disaster at La Hogue, made the navy appear ineffectual against the English whether it won or lost. Meanwhile, the armies of the Grand Alliance pressed ever harder on France's frontiers. Costs mounted, and in 1693–94 a famine that struck much of France caused widespread misery and greatly reduced tax revenues. This combination of events doomed the main battle fleet. Louis had already reduced the naval budget by 45 percent when Vauban wrote his famous *Mémoire sur la course* in which he advocated commerce raiding over seeking to destroy the allied fleet.[30]

The virtues of this idea seemed obvious. French power was based on land. The king had created a great fleet thanks to Colbert's persuasive advocacy of trade and colonies, and because a navy had seemed the most direct means of attacking England. Neither of these objectives was essential to French survival. Ironically, only the need for timber and naval stores kept France from becoming virtually self-sufficient in all but luxuries. It was England, not France, that depended on overseas trade, and disrupting that trade would stanch the flow of English money to the continent. By crippling English commerce, the French would not only relieve the pressure on their army, but do so at a profit through the seizure of English assets.

It was another scheme to make war pay for war. After 1693–94, the size of France's main battle fleet fell greatly, and syndicates of privateers leased royal ships, inflicting great damage to English interests.[31] In the process, men like Jean Bart, Forbin, DuGuay-Trouin, and Chateau-Renault inspired some of the most glorious chapters in French naval history. But this decision, though probably unavoidable, had disastrous consequences.

Mahan and Corbett noted long ago that France thereby gave up any claim to command of the sea, although it could regain that command if it wished as the American Revolutionary War showed. The French turn to commerce raiding made an English global strategy not only possible but necessary. England's wealth depended upon trade, and the new policy threatened it on a worldwide basis as never before. England had to protect its trade at all costs,

29 The best account of French naval policy in these years is Geoffrey Symcox, *The Crisis of French Sea Power 1688–1697* (The Hague, 1974). This episode is described on pp. 105–6. See also Lionel Rothkrug, *Opposition to Louis XIV: The Political and Social and Origins of the French Enlightenment* (Princeton, 1965), pp. 381–83 and J.S. Bromley, "The French Privateering War 1702–1713," *Corsairs and Navies 1660–1760* (London, 1987), pp. 217–20.

30 Vauban was a protege of Louvois and an investor in privateering voyages. The *Mémoire sur la course* was not his first writing on the subject. See Symcox, *Crisis*, pp. 177–87 for a complete discussion, and pp. 234–35 for a summary of French naval expenditures.

31 J.S. Bromley, "The Loan of French Naval Vessels to Privateering Enterprises," *Corsairs and Navies*, pp. 187–212.

and the disbanding of the French battle fleet released English ships from their traditional duties in the Channel. As a spur to English strategic development, this French decision ranked with the contemporary revolution in English taxation and finance.

Because of the inadequacy of early modern intelligence, the nature of the French decision was not fully apparent for several years. A rising tide of commercial losses indicated that a *guerre de course* was in progress, but the English knew little about the condition of the French line of battle and refused to assume that it no longer posed a threat. Russell, the victor at La Hogue, was especially reluctant to divert resources from the Channel. With Ireland secure and the French defeated at sea, William III felt free to resume the offensive, but Russell opposed either an attack on St. Malo or a Mediterranean expedition. His vigorous protests caused his dismissal from office, and ultimately earned him much criticism from Corbett and others.[32] But his obstructionism was not due entirely to a morose and liverish disposition.[33] A descent on St. Malo was probably impossible for technical reasons and would have served little strategic purpose.[34] William's diversion of 102 warships to the Mediterranean in 1693 was successful, but it might have been otherwise. As already suggested, French naval policy followed the ebb and flow of court politics; when the right influences came to bear – for example in 1704 – France could still threaten English sea power.[35] It is now impossible to know what Russell knew, but given the magnitude of French skill and resources, a degree of pessimism was justified. The realization that France could not long sustain such threats developed slowly, and the consequent uncertainty, together with the limitations built into the English strategy-making process, created further misdirection and delay.

Strategy under both William III and Queen Anne developed through consensus. Contemporaries recognized the expertise of William and his military successor, the Duke of Marlborough, but neither could impose his strategic conceptions by fiat. Orders to admirals at sea normally went out as royal warrants countersigned by a secretary of state. The Admiralty Commissioners, who were also members of Parliament, were not necessarily informed, but Parliament exercised oversight through a variety of committees, debated strategy on the floor, and frequently investigated the conduct of individual campaigns or actions.[36] Moreover, Parliament had to be con-

---

32 Ehrman, *William III*, pp. 403–405, 412–13; Horwitz, *Revolution Politicks*, pp. 118–46. The St Malo project was Nottingham's invention, but William had favored a Mediterranean strategy since 1689. He saw it as a diversion to draw French resources away from the Netherlands. See J.C.M. Warnsinck, *De Vloot van den Stadhouder Koningk 1689–90* (Amsterdam, 1934), p. 22.
33 Corbett, *England*, Vol. 2, pp. 162, 179–80.
34 See p. 172. Richmond, *Navy*, p. 233, disagrees, citing the experience of 1758.
35 Bromley, "The French Privateering War," p. 219. French naval construction in fact revived in varying degrees during the years 1702, 1704, 1706, and 1707.
36 Ehrman, *William III*, pp. 304–305.

vinced that a plan of campaign was sound before it would vote the necessary funds. This meant that civilian ministers, party leaders, and other opinion-makers within the English oligarchy entered the decision-making process at every stage. Various groups in turn influenced them: merchants, country gentlemen, and family interests of every kind.[37]

The military men, too, had their say: in part because of their valuable experience and technical knowledge, and in part because they, like other members of the nation's elite, were part of the same clientage systems that dominated all political life. Professionalism had increased, especially in the navy, but most officers still owed their rank to "interest" and enjoyed close ties with the Court or with one or another of the factions in Parliament. The campaign season ran from April to October, and the players developed strategy for the coming year during the London winter season, when they tended to see one another on a regular basis.[38]

Their proximity makes the actual process of strategic formulation almost unrecoverable to the historian, at least in its more interesting aspects. Parliamentary debates and gossip remain, but thousands of other informal discussions in salons, taverns, dinner parties, balls, and random encounters are lost. Unofficial correspondence exists only when key figures retreated to their country estates or were otherwise absent, and official documents tend to reflect decisions rather than the process that created them.[39] The compromises, trade-offs, and private deals characteristic of advanced systems of clientage are often lost to recorded memory. Decisions were usually compromises, and those who dissented could only grumble and criticize until victory dismissed their complaints or misfortune made them next year's policy.

But England was not alone. It was part of the Grand Alliance, and the Dutch and the continental allies had to accept any decisions before action could begin. As Marlborough discovered, this process could lead to modifications that amounted in some cases to near reversal. Each of the allies had its own priorities, and the Dutch, with their interlocking memberships in the provincial estates, the five admiralties, the Estates General, and the great chartered companies, enjoyed a decision-making process that was as at least as complex and as unrecoverable to historians as that of the English.

The formulation of strategy under these conditions precluded Caesarism and ensured that different points of view would be heard, but its disadvantages are obvious. Because the process was political and rooted in compromise, it encouraged multiple objectives that tended to neutralize one another. Moreover, by encouraging civilian participation it gave credence to

---

[37] For a comprehensive, if controversial, analysis of the various "interests" involved, see Robert Walcott, *English Politics in the Early Eighteenth Century* (New York, 1956).

[38] Geoffrey Holmes, *British Politics in the Age of Anne* (London, 1967), p. 288.

[39] The papers of many leading figures have also been lost. For a list, see Holme, *British Politics,* pp. 287–88.

views that professionals might reject and then guaranteed that those same ideas would reappear in later years whether or not they proved successful. In a system of this kind, each year brought a new conjunction of political forces with a subtly different balance of interests and perceptions. Consistency of strategic principle became as elusive as clarity of vision. Only a summary of the great debate that unfolded during the War of the Spanish Succession can throw light on the process and its ultimate result.

Tory navalism, rooted in Elizabethan precedent and party faction, had resisted William III's continental activities throughout his reign, and had secured the premature disbanding of his army. After the accession of Queen Anne, the weight of this obstacle to a balanced strategy diminished, in part because of popular outrage over Louis XIV's attempt to place a Bourbon on the Spanish throne, and in part because the new regime, under Marlborough's influence from the start, managed to coopt the Tories[40] – they could form a government on the condition that they behave as Whigs. This arrangement eventually isolated the Earl of Rochester and other Tory extremists.

The new Tory ministry acknowledged the need for an army on the continent, but many of its members did so with silent reservations, or perhaps with a different understanding of what such an effort would entail.[41] "Whig" strategy continued to favor decisive action on land. "Tory" strategy centered around commerce protection, the Spanish treasure fleet, and quasi-Elizabethan "descents" on French coastal towns. But these were tendencies rather than fixed positions. Consistency existed only at the political extremes, and many strategy-makers modified their views from year to year or even from month to month.

An unwillingness to challenge the technical judgment of admirals further complicated the situation. The great problem of war at sea in the early modern period was neither strategy nor tactics, but the effective management of ships. Seventeenth century men-of-war were works of art and awesome in their power, but by modern standards they were cranky, awkward, and incredibly complex. To manage them was a minor miracle of human organization. Dutch William and the Duke of Marlborough, who had served at sea in his youth, knew this. If Sir George Rooke or Sir Cloudesley Shovell said something was impossible, decision-makers usually accepted their word, though the motives of the sea officers were not always politically pure.[42]

In these circumstances, orders for sea commanders were both comprehensive and remarkably vague throughout the war of the Spanish Succession. In 1703, for example, Rooke received orders to protect the Channel and, if he

[40] Sir Winston Churchill, *Marlborough: His Life and Times*, Vol. 2 (New York, 1933–1938), p. 247; Horwitz, *Revolution Politicks*, p. 168.

[41] Churchill, *Marlborough*, Vol. 3, pp. 66–67.

[42] Corbett, *England*, Vol. 2, pp. 300–301; Churchill, *Marlborough*, Vol. 5, p. 274.

saw fit, to harass the Biscayan ports of the enemy. A second fleet under Sir Cloudesley Shovell was ordered to intimidate the Barbary States, the Grand Duke of Tuscany, and Venice, and to clear French privateers from the Adriatic; it was then to proceed to Malta for no stated purpose. When Shovell asked for clarification, a new set of orders told him to convoy the Levant fleet, after which he was to assist the Imperial troops in Sicily and Naples with his marines. He also received authority to attack Cádiz, Toulon, or any other place in Spain or France including French installations that he might hear of in the vicinity of Genoa.[43] It is little wonder that " . . . when Sir Clodesly at the desire of the Dutch admiral [van Almonde] shew'd him his orders it was with difficulty that he could be persuaded they were the only ones he had. . . ."[44]

Such orders sound like a recipe for chaos, but it may be wiser to regard them as the products of a strategic sensibility more flexible than our own. Technology had advanced little since the days of Elizabeth. As Shovell himself once told the Duke of Savoy: " . . . it is no new thing for us to be sometimes three weeks or a month getting to a place which at other times we may get to in twenty-four hours, which will show Your Highness that our motions are not so regular nor cannot be so timely adjusted as marches by land."[45] Savoy might have responded, as Marlborough probably would have, that marches on land were not very predictable either. Given the limitations of technology, the tyranny of distance, and the complexities of domestic and international politics, the strategists of the day knew that they were prisoners of contingency. Strategy for them was not a master plan, but a series of options, any one of which might develop targets of opportunity.

Despite their emphasis on various options, the English did slowly develop a consensus that ultimately formed the basis of their demands at the Congress of Utrecht, a consensus born of trial and error and held together in the end by the glue of economics. As a host of widely disparate initiatives succeeded on land and sea, it became apparent that "Whig" and "Tory" strategies were not necessarily incompatible and that England – Britain after 1707 – was strong enough to afford both.

An examination of budgets from 1702 to 1713 reveals that whatever the composition of the government, England's primary strategic investment remained the land war on the continent.[46] Though under fire from certain

---

[43] According to Horwitz, *Revolution Politicks*, pp. 170–171, 175, Nottingham was the spirit behind these orders, but they certainly appear be the work of a committee. They are found in British Library, Add. Mss. 29591, ff. 193, 195, 199; H.O. Admiralty, XIII, 71 (April 28), 82 (May); and Admiralty Secretary's Out-Letters, 30 (May 8); and are summarized in Corbett, *England*, Vol. 2, 230–32.

[44] John Knox Laughton, ed., *Memoirs Relating to Lord Torrington* (Camden Society Publications, New Series 40, 1889), p. 119.

[45] Quoted in John Hely Owen, *The War at Sea under Queen Anne* (Cambridge, 1938), p. 167.

[46] Dickson, "War Finance," p. 285.

Tories, the basic principle that seapower could not entirely reduce France remained in force and in fact became more generally accepted as the war progressed.

In the campaigns themselves, the Duke of Marlborough normally made England's strategy, and his views came to dominate the alliance as a whole. They did not, however, become unbreakable precedents for later British policy. Marlborough was the leading advocate of offensive warfare in his day. He preferred wherever possible to seek out, engage, and destroy the enemy's main field army with the ultimate purpose of invading enemy territory. As his Dutch allies were fond of pointing out, it was an appropriate strategy for an island power that could risk its army without risking its borders. They could not do the same, and usually preferred a defensive war of siege and maneuver.[47] The Austrian Empire, too, had its own priorities, and continually thwarted Marlborough's designs during the early years of the war. The Austrians proved difficult, not for the base reasons that Swift imputed to the allies, but because the Duke's strategy did not always suit their legitimate interests and because he was not always right. The ill-fated attempt in 1705 to invade Lorraine by way of the Moselle was a case in point.

After the great victory at Ramillies in 1706, these obstructions diminished and Marlborough's ideas gained regular acceptance, although he continued to seek consensus. His "reckless and ruthless" view of war, as Sir Winston Churchill called it,[48] became an inspiration to later commanders, but the British rarely implemented it thereafter because its success had derived largely from the Duke's unusual personality. A hundred years passed before another British general achieved the rare combination of military and diplomatic skills needed to dominate a pan-European alliance while providing as little as one seventh of its troops. In the meantime, British efforts on the continent, though often distinguished, tended to dissolve into the strategy of the allies or trickle away in peripheral campaigns.

At sea, the strategic situation was far more complicated, both because of its intrinsic difficulties and because no individual emerged from the Admiralty with the overwhelming reputation of a Marlborough. The fundamental problems were still those of the reign of William III. France possessed two battle fleets, one based at Toulon in the Mediterranean and one at Brest in the Atlantic. The decision to adopt the *guerre de course* as a primary strategy had much reduced both fleets, but the English did not know by how much and did not know if they could afford to let the two fleets join. William III

---

[47]   Alice Clare Carter, *Neutrality or Commitment: The Evolution of Dutch Foreign Policy 1667–1795* (London, 1975), pp. 28–35. Carter's views are a corrective to the Churchillian view that the Dutch suffered from a "dyke-mentality," and owe much to the earlier works of J.G. Stork-Penning, "The Ordeal of the States: Some Remarks on Dutch Politics during the War of the Spanish Succession," *Acta Historiae Neerlandica*, Vol. 2, see especially p. 113, and *Het grote werk: vredes onderhandelingen gedurende de Spaanse Successie-oorlog 1705–1710* (Groningen, 1953).

[48]   Churchill, *Marlborough*, Vol. 4, p. 202.

had hoped to prevent such a juncture by controlling the Straits of Gibraltar, and he kept the fleet at Cádiz in 1694 over the protests of Lord Russell. Veterans of the Dutch Wars had learned never to divide the fleet, and without knowing the extent of French strength, Russell felt that such a strategy put England itself at risk while inhibiting the fleet's ability to protect commerce in the Channel. He apparently found little merit in William's subsidiary objective of using Cádiz to gain control of the West Indies trade.[49]

The debate resumed in 1702 on much the same grounds, with Sir George Rooke and his Tory friends in Parliament supporting the position formerly associated with Russell the Whig. Rooke lost. He received orders to take Cádiz with fifty ships of the line while Shovell remained to guard the Channel. A much smaller squadron under Admiral Benbow was already in the Caribbean to halt the depredations of French raiders and to look for the Spanish treasure fleet. The result was an Elizabethan comedy of errors. Rooke failed to take Cádiz. In the meantime, the government had become preoccupied with reports that the treasure fleet was on its way, and reinforced Shovell while sending contradictory orders to Rooke in the hope of intercepting it. In the end, the *flota* made it into Vigo, but Rooke's ships then destroyed it at anchor. Most of the treasure was already ashore, negating the effect of the action, but the victory saved Rooke's reputation. Ignoring the government's wish that he leave a squadron behind, he returned to England.[50]

As already described, the orders for 1703 sent Shovell to the Mediterranean; but he went only because Rooke thought the task beneath his dignity, and preferred to remain with the Channel fleet, which numbered seventy-six ships of the line. Neither accomplished anything of note, but it was becoming obvious that the French Atlantic fleet was not by itself a major threat. In the following year, the emphasis of naval strategy shifted decidedly to the Mediterranean. Shovell's instructions of 1703 indicate English goals – aside from the preservation of the Levant trade, they sought to intimidate such potential French allies as the Barbary states and the Pope, and to encourage the Portuguese, who had signed the Methuen Treaties in 1703. Strong diplomatic pressure came from the Empire to assist the campaign of Eugene of Savoy in northern Italy and to support Imperial designs on Naples and Sicily. Above all, Marlborough continued to believe in the possibility of a diversion that would draw Louis' attention away from the Spanish Netherlands and the Rhine. The idea of an attack on Toulon by land and sea appears to have been in his mind almost from the beginning of the war, though he could not actually attempt it until 1707.[51]

49 Ehrman, *William III*, pp. 412–13.
50 Oscar Browning, ed., *The Journal of Sir George Rooke 1700–1702* (Naval Record Society Publications, Vol. 9, 1897), pp. 230–34.
51 Corbett, *England*, Vol. 2, p. 205.

The achievement of these goals required the establishment of a Mediterranean base. Even in wealthy England, the manning and equipping of a fleet strained the limits of preindustrial organization. The navy was often not ready to sail before July, and it had to be back in port before the October storms. The actual fighting season was therefore too brief for all but the simplest of operations. The primary reason was the design of the ships. English statesmen may have begun to envision a global strategy, but English ships had evolved during the Dutch Wars and usually fought within sight of land. Sheer numbers and the weight of artillery determined victory, and English ships tended to carry more guns per ton of displacement than their French or Spanish counterparts. Naval architecture, like other forms of engineering, is an art based on compromise. More guns meant less stowage space and sacrifices in seaworthiness. The big three-deckers were especially top-heavy. As Sir Cloudesley Shovell said: "an admiral would deserve to be broke who kept great-ships out after the end of September and to be shot if after October."[52] On a foul night in late October, 1707, he proved his point by running the *Association* aground with the loss of all hands.

But the admirals only reluctantly gave up the advantages of firepower, especially in the Mediterranean where the Toulon fleet might appear at any moment. An advanced base was clearly essential, and although Lisbon was now available as a result of the Methuen Treaties, it was more than 1,200 sea miles from Toulon. Moreover, the prevailing winds in the Straits of Gibraltar were westerly and a two-knot surface current ran from west to east. For most of the year, ships could expect to wait for many days while attempting a fair passage out of the Mediterranean. The major exception was in July and August when English fleets were more likely to seek to enter the Mediterranean. But it was at that point that the Levanter, a hot, moist wind from the east, was likely to keep the great ships hanging about Cape Trafalgar for a week or more before permitting them to enter the Straits.

The capture of Gibraltar in 1704 helped to solve this problem, but although Gibraltar provided a base within the Mediterranean and made it possible for England to control the Straits, it was of little use in supporting England's other objectives in the region. Significantly, its acquisition was not the primary objective of the year's campaign. Marlborough had hoped to attack Toulon, or, alternately, to relieve Nice if the French army menaced it. Louis XIV seemed to have anticipated this move, for he ordered his son, the Comte de Toulouse, to take command of the Brest fleet and bring it into Toulon. Toulouse eluded Shovell's squadron in the Atlantic and outran Rooke's in the Mediterranean, but Shovell left his station, and the two branches of the English fleet joined in late June. On land, the French king had thrown his southern army against Prince Eugene in Italy. Nice was now safe but Eugene was too busy to attack Toulon. Contingency had reduced the

---

[52] Quoted in Fox, *Great Ships*, p. 169.

number of options available to the English. They had few soldiers of their own, which ruled out an attack on heavily garrisoned Cádiz, and of the other projects in Rooke's orders only Gibraltar seemed practicable.[53]

The episode illustrates how strategic planning worked in practice. Improvisation was essential and, to a degree, foreseen. Rooke apparently wanted to draw Toulouse into battle by seizing a place of such strategic importance that its loss would devastate Spanish morale. If this was his intent, he succeeded. The capture of Gibraltar and the ensuing sea battle of Málaga created a sensation, but twenty-five years passed before Britain did anything to develop Gibraltar as a base.[54]

Gibraltar, although useful, was not an ideal port; sheltered on three sides, it was still open to southwest gales and the surrounding hills caused disturbing eddies when the wind blew from the east or south. The only secure anchorage for large ships was a relatively small area near the Old Mole in the northeast corner of the bay.[55] Fresh water was – and still is – in short supply, and a fleet in the Straits still had to fill its casks at Tetuan or elsewhere on the Moroccan coast – if the Moroccans approved – or by force at Málaga. Above all, Gibraltar was over 900 miles from Toulon. Because the currents along the coast of Spain run from north to south and the wind there blows from the north, on average, for 150 days each year, mariners customarily set a course northwest from the Straits to Minorca before steering north close-hauled for the final 250 mile run into Toulon. The entire journey normally took at least eight to ten days.

Most naval officers thought that if their task was to attack Toulon or to monitor the activities of the French fleet, they could perform it better from Minorca, whose harbor, Port Mahon, was the finest in the Mediterranean. A fleet based on Gibraltar could not winter there. It might watch the Straits for much of the year but could do little if the French decided to interfere with Imperial designs in Italy or, after 1705, with the Anglo-Habsburg foothold in Cataluña. The admirals argued that if they could seize Minorca, fast ships on picket duty off Toulon could alert the fleet within hours if the French came out. Moreover, Port Mahon was large enough to accommodate the fleet's winter refit, and could therefore provide a year-round base to throttle French trade out of Marseilles.

The argument was not new. William III had demanded Minorca at the Peace of Rijswick, but the diplomacy of Louis XIV had forestalled him. Shovell had long advocated its capture, and in 1706 an influential pamphlet entitled "An Inquiry into the Causes of our Naval Miscarriages" made the case for Minorca to the public at large. But nothing was done about it until

---

[53] Corbett, *England*, Vol. 2, pp. 256–75.
[54] Owen, *War at Sea*, p. 91.
[55] Corbett, *England*, Vol. 2, pp. 256–57, contains a contemporary map and brief description taken from a survey drawn up by Sir Henry Sheere in 1705.

1708.[56] This delay was due in part to Marlborough, who preferred a direct attack on Toulon, and to the Earl of Peterborough's diversion in 1705 at Barcelona, yet another instructive example of the making of strategy in those years.

As far as the English cabinet knew, the Mediterranean fleet of 1705 intended to help the Duke of Savoy in his proposed campaign on the Riviera, or failing that, to do something on the coast of Spain. Shovell was to command at sea and Peterborough on land. When the fleet arrived at Lisbon in June, Archduke Charles, the Habsburg claimant to the Spanish throne, argued strenuously for an attack on Barcelona. After much debate, the English capitulated to their allies, and in due course the capital of Cataluña fell to Peterborough who had initially been the most determined opponent of the project.[57]

The capture of Barcelona, like that of Gibraltar, aroused tremendous enthusiasm among the Tories. The Whigs, winners in the elections of 1705 and reluctant to discourage support from this quarter, wherever it might be directed, made every effort during 1705 and 1706 to protect Barcelona from the inevitable Bourbon counterattack. "No peace without Spain" became the Tory war cry, an attitude that in later years proved a major barrier to the settlement of the war. In the meantime, the defense of Barcelona consumed all energies, and not until 1707 could Marlborough realize his ambition of an attack on Toulon. It failed. Finally, in the following year, Admiral Leake drove the French out of Minorca, and by so doing established British naval control over the western Mediterranean.[58]

The emergence of Britain as a Mediterranean power marked a permanent change in the nation's commitments. As part of the evolution of a global strategy, this change was more important than the army's successes in northern Europe because it involved the establishment of fixed overseas bases and because the future implementation of the policy did not depend upon the prestige of a single individual. Moreover, it was virtually without precedent. Although the idea of a permanent British role in the Mediterranean was an old one, it did not become a national priority until the acquisition of Gibraltar and Minorca.

The process by which this occurred had little to do with any grand design. The strategic conceptions of both Marlborough and the navalists had been implemented piecemeal in the course of their annual strategic debates. The planning process itself was politically messy and intellectually inconclusive. Though most British initiatives bore no fruit, the two that succeeded –

[56] *Harleian Miscellany,* Vol. 9, pp. 5–28.
[57] Churchill, *Marlborough,* Vol. 5, pp. 59–64.
[58] By June 1708 Marlborough had become convinced of the need to capture Minorca, and his intervention turned the tide. Churchill, *Marlborough,* Vol. 5, p. 535. Corbett, *England,* Vol. 2, p. 305, describes the campaign.

Gibraltar and Minorca – produced dividends that nearly every segment of English opinion appreciated. For the navalists, the possession of these bases permitted the English to harass French trade, protect their own, and obstruct any convergence of the French fleets. For the exponents of a continental strategy, Minorca was an ideal advanced base for the great diversions of Marlborough's dream, and Gibraltar prevented the isolation of Minorca from its lines of supply and communication.

The more immediate question in 1707–08 was not whether the Mediterranean strategy was valid, but whether or not England could afford it without sacrificing vital interests in the North Sea and the Channel. By 1713 that question had received a positive answer, but only after a thorough and painful reevaluation of how best to deal with the French *guerre de course*.

It is impossible to determine the actual number of English trading vessels seized between 1702 and 1707, but 3,000 is a conservative guess.[59] Most losses occurred in "home" waters. The merchants saw them as directly proportional to the number of English warships assigned to the Mediterranean, and cited the marked increase in privateering activity during 1704 and 1707 as evidence. The Admiralty itself believed this contention, at least in part, but the differences from year to year were relative, not absolute.

In this kind of warfare the initiative lay almost entirely with the raiders. They could afford to be flexible in their choice of objectives, most of which lay within a few hours of their own well-defended ports, and they quickly developed ships and tactics that made it extremely difficult for large warships to intercept them. Barring carelessness or extremely bad luck, they could decline an engagement if the English appeared in superior force. Their victims failed to develop an effective response to this threat until late in the war, and even then some have argued that the decline of privateering after 1709 had more to do with the economic exhaustion of France than with the success of English measures. The truth probably lies between these extremes.

The record of the Channel fleet in dealing with privateers was at first dismal. Following Elizabethan precedent, large squadrons sailed in 1702 to look for the treasure fleet or for a French convoy said to be carrying the Duke of Albuquerque from La Coruña to Mexico. Ships cruised off Dunkirk and Calais in an effort to contain the privateers, but blockades though never entirely abandoned, proved only moderately effective.

Dunkirk was the greatest of privateering ports. Approachable only through sandy shoals running parallel to the coast, it was a dangerous place in bad weather or when a pilot's knowledge of the shifting sands antedated the last major storm. The English lost more than twenty ships there between 1702 and the end of the war. This costly surveillance reduced privateering but did not end it, for the Dunkirkers monitored their approaches daily and

---

[59] Bromley, "French Privateering War," p. 237.

knew precisely how many hours of night or fog they needed to traverse them in the face of a blockading fleet.[60] The geography of St. Malo, the second French port in value of prizes seized, was different but equally troublesome. Located on the northern coast of Brittany a few miles west of the Cherbourg peninsula, the town lay at the bottom of a deadly pocket created by the prevailing westerlies and a tidal range of nearly forty feet; a blockade by sailing ships seemed impossible.[61] Frustration over these difficulties led navalists to propose amphibious descents on the ports themselves, but the fortifications the French lavished on their exposed towns and the navigational hazards that hampered blockade tended to thwart any such plans. Rooke sought to harass the coast in 1703, but accomplished nothing.

Convoys, perhaps the most obvious response to the problem, met with initial resistance from merchants and naval officers alike. The costly delays involved in assembling fleets persuaded many merchants to take their chances with the French. Naval officers, in the Elizabethan tradition, preferred offensive action wherever possible and saw convoys as a waste of precious resources. They also believed, with some justification, that convoys were ineffective. English merchants had little experience in stationkeeping and the privateers were adept at cutting out stragglers. Moreover, the French could often divine the size of a convoy's escort in time to concentrate superior force against it. Many private vessels were formerly of the line, and the more famous raiders could sometimes count on the assistance of commissioned naval vessels if the prize seemed worth the effort. At least one modern historian has suggested that some of the resulting battles should properly be regarded as fleet actions.[62]

In practice, these doubts and limitations reduced the English navy to playing hide-and-seek with its opponents throughout much of the war, with discouraging results. In the number of individual and squadron-size actions fought, the honors fell more or less equally to both sides. When the English lost, offending captains underwent sensational trials that tended to reinforce a growing perception of naval incompetence. Shipping losses continued to mount. Finally, after a combined force under Forbin and DuGuay-Trouin routed both the Virginia and the Portugal convoys in 1707, Parliament took action. Under pressure from merchant interests and noting the weakness of the escorts of both fleets, Parliament passed the Cruisers and Convoys Act of March 1708.[63] The navy was now obliged to cruise in the Soundings and break up the French "wolf packs" that waited there for inbound merchant-

---

[60] J.S. Bromley, "The Importance of Dunkirk as a Privateering Port," *Corsairs and Navies,* p. 79.

[61] See Russell's comments in *Historical Manuscript Commission Reports-Finch Papers,* Vol. 4, p. 270.

[62] E.H. Jenkins, *A History of the French Navy* (London, 1973), p. 102.

[63] Agitation for the bill was also related to Whig efforts to remove Marlborough's Tory brother, Admiral George Churchill, from his post at the Admiralty. Owen, *War at Sea,* pp. 69–70.

men. It was then to gather the merchantmen into convoys and provide them with much enlarged escorts for the run up the Channel. As the great ships that comprised the major part of the fleet were unsuited to most forms of commerce protection, Parliament ordered the construction of new ships of the fourth and sixth rates for this purpose. No other action better symbolized the shift from a defensive main fleet strategy to one based on the protection of British interests worldwide.

The new methods seemed to work. British losses in home waters declined markedly after 1708, although losses increased in the Western Hemisphere, the Mediterranean, and along the Portuguese coast. This shift in the geography of violence casts doubt on the theory that French economic stress was more important to the decline of privateering than British strategy. The point is important because it reflects on the debate over the success or failure of the *guerre de course*. Commerce raiding provided France with badly needed foreign exchange and greatly enriched parts of the French maritime community. Once established, it generated enough capital to become a self-sustaining industry largely independent of the rest of the economy. By improving its operations in the Channel, the British navy forced the privateers to operate in distant waters at higher cost. If there was a net reduction in losses it was because the British thereby drove smaller entrepreneurs out of business.[64] At the same time, the overall verdict of modern navalists on French strategy stands. The *guerre de course* hurt England badly, and it may have been the best strategy available under the circumstances, but it did not prevent its victims from achieving their most important objectives on land or at sea. The formidable engine of British economic growth ensured that seaborne trade continued to increase despite terrible losses. At best, commerce raiding prolonged the war but did not change its outcome.[65]

Another British initiative in the Channel was underway at this time, but its relationship to trade was tangential. The Earl of Sunderland nominally headed the government in 1708. Though a Whig and Marlborough's son-in-law, he harbored some curiously Elizabethan ideas. At his direction, a force of 5,000 men moved to the Isle of Wight to create diversions for Marlborough by threatening to descend on the French channel ports. He also believed that the seizure of a portion of the Spanish treasure fleet that same year, with the loss of some 15 million pounds in treasure, would end the war. Neither development moved Louis XIV.

After the Channel and the Mediterranean, the most important and controversial of Britain's strategic concerns lay in the Western Hemisphere. Marlborough, focused as ever on continental Europe, saw the region as peripheral, but the Tories and those Whigs attached to the merchant interest

---

64 Bromley, "Privateering War," p. 241.
65 D.W. Jones, *War and Economy in the Age of William III and Marlborough* (Oxford, 1988), pp. 313–17, has argued that the war actually increased net trade receipts by giving England unrestricted access to the Spanish, Portuguese, and Piedmontese markets.

disagreed. Three main issues troubled them, each of which had its own powerful constituency.

The first issue was French privateering in the West Indies and along the North American coast. Cruising for prizes on both sides was the normal pattern of warfare in the Western Hemisphere, but the obstacles to developing an effective strategy against it were almost insurmountable. Distance and poor communications hindered the search for individual privateers, and the diffuse patterns of trade made convoys ineffective. Vindictive raids on enemy colonies did little to solve the problem, for though Martinique harbored a feared nest of corsairs, the more formidable French squadrons came directly from Brest or St. Malo. Caribbean warfare amounted to a series of raids that had little effect on the broader war, but the complaints of merchants and colonists penetrated to the darkest recesses of the Admiralty.

In response to these pressures, a squadron cruised the West Indies in every year of the war, but to little purpose. The only English harbor capable of maintaining or refitting a fleet in those waters was Kingston, Jamaica. From Kingston to Barbados was a long, hard slog to windward that might take weeks. The run from Jamaica to Boston or Nova Scotia was easy, but ships sailing from New England to Barbados often found the going faster by way of Europe. This made a timely response to French raids on British islands unlikely.[66]

Isolation, combined with poverty and economic rivalries, discouraged cooperation between colonies and even between colonial governments and the navy. The history of these years is a tale of obscure and often violent quarrels between naval officers, royal governors, and colonial legislatures.[67]

Above all, the Caribbean squadron was expensive to maintain. Ships and supplies deteriorated at an alarming rate while the crews succumbed to tropical fevers and debauchery. Men and officers alike regarded assignment to the West Indies as a death sentence and behaved with a lack of discipline that undermined military efficiency and made cooperation with the colonists more difficult than it might otherwise have been. As Josiah Burchett put it, "I wish I could . . . make any tolerable Comparison between the Services this Squadron did the Nation, and the Expence which attended it."[68]

The Admiralty solved none of these problems during the War of the Spanish Succession or for many years thereafter, but the Caribbean had become a commitment from which Britain could not afford to shrink. The emphasis shifted gradually away from raiding islands and hunting the Spanish treasure fleet. In the Georgian era, the British attempted to maintain a naval presence that would, at the least, inhibit major French or Spanish initiatives while holding predation to a minimum. Except for a brief and disastrous interval in the American Revolutionary War, they succeeded.

---

[66] Ruth Bourne, *Queen Anne's Navy in the West Indies* (New Haven, 1939), p. 32.
[67] Ibid., pp. 33–34.
[68] Josiah Burchett, *Transactions at Sea, 1688–1697* (London, 1720), p. 607.

A second strategic priority was Newfoundland, whose population at this time was largely seasonal. At stake was access to the Grand Banks fisheries, an issue of great emotional significance for many Englishmen. The cod was a fish whose symbolic value may have equaled its substantial economic worth. A tradition that long predates Elizabethan times held that the fisheries were the nursery of the nation's seamen and the mainstay of its strength. In the minds of Tory navalists, Britain could not surrender them without a fight.

Newfoundland was the scene of raids and the burning of fishing camps throughout the war. As in the Caribbean, the French held their own, but because they lost the war in Europe, Britain won its territorial claims at the Congress of Utrecht. Though France retained fishing rights and its settlement at Placentia, Britain eventually acquired yet another colonial outpost.

Control of Newfoundland was also related to another issue. The St. Lawrence River was the lifeline of French America, and Newfoundland and what is now Nova Scotia straddled its mouth. In the American colonies, figures such as Governor Dudley of Massachusetts believed that only the total destruction of French power in North America could protect New England. The French, masters of forest diplomacy, maintained alliances with the Indians that posed a constant threat to English settlements even well inside the frontiers.

Samuel Vetch, a friend of Sunderland's, hoped to establish a Scottish colony in Nova Scotia in 1709. Marlborough forestalled him by diverting the expedition's troops to Portugal, but Port Royal fell in the following year and formed the basis of later British claims.[69] Meanwhile, the Tories returned to power, and Governor Dudley's vision provided them with inspiration for the attack on Quebec of Rear-Admiral Sir Hovenden Walker. It failed amid bad weather and accusations of corruption, but not before establishing a precedent.[70] Forty-eight years later, Wolfe and Saunders achieved the same objective in a brilliant amphibious campaign.

In a sense, these American struggles symbolized the evolution of British strategy. Conceived by diverse interests and implemented amid the turmoil of party politics, many of these initiatives were more important for what they later became than for what they were at their inception. A British global strategy emerged from the main streams of the Elizabethan tradition at a time when political evolution at last permitted the implementation of divergent views. This development occurred not through agreement but because a series of ministries sought in part to cancel out each other's policies. As each faction launched its own initiatives, it became apparent that the various goals were neither mutually exclusive nor unaffordable. England had

---

[69] J.S. Bromley, "Colonies at War," *Corsairs and Navies*, p. 25.
[70] The scheme was actually Henry St. John's, who forced it through the cabinet in Harley's absence. H.T. Dickinson, *Bolingbroke* (London, 1970), p. 85. See also, Bromley, "Colonies at War," pp. 25–26.

at last become rich enough to achieve the Elizabethan dream of dominion at sea and military balance on the continent.[71]

Louis XIV had helped by dismantling his main battle fleet. Marlborough and William III established a precedent for effective intervention on the continent, and Bolingbroke, the arch-Tory and patron of Swift, enshrined navalist goals in the Peace of Utrecht. Given the character of British politics, this was probably inevitable. Though the high Tories of the October Club wanted peace at almost any price, parliamentary approval depended upon placating every major segment of opinion including the Whigs and those Tories who, like the Earl of Nottingham, wanted the West Indies "secured to a friendly power."[72]

Utrecht therefore marked a "strategic moment," though it is doubtful that anyone fully appreciated it at the time. Its terms – the product of compromise and consensus even within Britain – contained most of the elements of later strategic concerns. Britain kept Gibraltar and Minorca, Newfoundland, Nova Scotia, and St. Kitts. The fortifications of Dunkirk were to be demolished, and Britain's mastery of the seas would go virtually un-challenged for sixty-five years. Before long, the British used that mastery to intervene, not only in the Mediterranean and North Atlantic, but in the Indian Ocean and in the Baltic, where Peter the Great threatened to achieve hegemony after 1712. Expeditions had sailed to these latter regions during the War of the Spanish Succession, but had not committed acts of war.[73]

By 1713 a unified Great Britain had thus developed a global strategy. That it did so through an evolutionary process reflected the peculiar circumstances of an island nation. Because external threats tended to be sporadic and often ill-defined, honest men could differ over their immediacy, and many felt free to think of strategy in largely economic terms. The early modern period was a time of varied opinions and strategic goals. With the threat of absolutism demolished in the revolution of 1688, no single viewpoint dominated strate-gic debate. It was Britain's good fortune and a tribute to the country's mer-chants and financiers that these multiple concerns surfaced at a time when the nation's wealth could simultaneously support divergent courses of ac-tion.

Circumstances resolved the tension between naval and continental strat-egies. Arguments between the navalists and their opponents continued, but

---

71 For an analysis of the currency, trade balance, and the problem of paying for the wars, see Jones, *War and Economy*, pp. 211–48.
72 Horwitz, *Revolution Politicks*, p. 234. For discussions of the political maneuvering sur-rounding the Peace of Utrecht, see Dickinson, *Bolingbroke*, pp. 93–110 and the un-published Ph.D. thesis by A.D. MacLachlan, "The Great Peace: Negotiations for the Treaty of Utrecht 1710–1713," Cambridge, 1965.
73 In 1703, the *Severn* (54 guns) and the *Scarborough* (36) were dispatched to India for two years, and England maintained two or three ships on station off the Guinea coast through-out much of the war. For a survey of English activities in the Baltic, see R.C. Anderson, *Naval Wars in the Baltic, 1522–1850* (London, 1969, first printed, 1910).

the truly hard choices that had faced the Stuarts no longer existed. Because the nation could now afford substantial commitments on land without giving up command of the sea, strategic debate could center in good conscience on the allocation of resources to multiple objectives. In theory at least, the desirability of a global strategy that could protect all of Britain's far-flung interests gained acceptance from all but the most hardened Tories. Policy choices continued to reflect the ebb and flow of partisan government, but until the cataclysms of the twentieth century, Imperial Britain could have its cake and eat it too.

7

A quest for glory: The formation of strategy under Louis XIV, 1661–1715

JOHN A. LYNN

As he lay dying, Louis XIV confided to the frightened boy of five who succeeded him on the throne of France that he had "loved war too much."[1] The aged monarch recognized that war had dominated his reign and that his repeated resort to arms had cost France dearly. He ruled over more years of conflict than of peace; France was at war during thirty-one of the fifty-four years of his personal reign (1661–1715). This included four major conflicts – the War of Devolution (1667–68), the Dutch War (1672–78), the Nine Years' War (1688–97), and the War of the Spanish Succession (1700–1714).

For this proud king who adopted the sun as his emblem, the pursuit of his personal *gloire* drove the formation of strategy. He was an absolute monarch who shaped policy with his own hands, assisted, but not subverted, by bureau chiefs and advisers. This essay introduces the structures, values, limitations, and circumstances that influenced the creation of French strategy. Since the history of no single war offers an adequate sample of French continental strategy from 1661 to 1715, the essay will deal with his entire reign, rather than focus on a single case study.

Over the course of half a century, the strategic situations that confronted the king evolved continually. He had grown up in the shadow of the Spanish colossus. As a young man, he led the armies of a France that had itself become the preeminent power on the continent. In old age he grappled with coalitions that dwarfed even the resources of mighty France. Death found him chastened and repentant. The history of French strategic policy is a story of a larger-than-life monarch and of his quest for *gloire*.

---

[1] Louis in John B. Wolf, *Louis XIV* (New York, 1968), p. 618. His last words to Louis XV are reported in various forms, which generally accord with one another. Saint-Simon reported them as "Do not imitate me in the taste that I have had for buildings, nor in that which I have had for war. . . ." Louis, duc de Saint-Simon, *Mémoires*, Gonzague Truc, ed., Vol. 4 (Paris, 1953), p. 932.

STRUCTURES OF DECISION: KING AND *CONSEIL*

The France of Louis XIV lay somewhere between the medieval and the modern; its logic and values differed markedly from today's. Although authority had become increasingly centralized and bureaucratic, the monarch still dominated, established, and executed policy. While Louis XIV sought to rule in a rational manner, he crafted his bureaucracy not to govern in his stead, but to insure that he alone governed. The fact that French bureaucracy eventually developed into a perpetual motion machine is beside the point. Louis was the godlike creator of that government, and he was an assertive and all-powerful god.

Born in 1638, Louis did not actually take the reins of government into his own hands until 1661, when his first minister, tutor, and surrogate father, Cardinal Mazarin, died. From then until his death in 1715, Louis ruled France directly and actively. He had come to the throne after a quarter century of exhausting warfare, complicated between 1648 and 1653 by the Fronde, a bizarre revolt that threatened the power of the monarchy. The young monarch resolved that never again would the great nobles and privileged law courts challenge his authority. Nor did he ever have recourse to a first minister after the death of Mazarin.

In substance and style, Louis XIV embodied absolutism, but his power was scarcely absolute: it acknowledged tradition and necessity as limits. Nevertheless, in matters over which he claimed authority, he brooked no interference. Paramount among the king's life-long concerns were foreign affairs, his army, and the conduct of war; in these areas he set and managed policy on a daily basis.

He successfully overwhelmed potential competitors for his authority throughout his lifetime. France's medieval representative assembly, the Estates General, had last met in 1614 and did not convene again until 1789. The great sovereign law courts of France, confusingly known as *parlements*, had attempted to assert their authority during the Fronde, but had failed; under Louis XIV they remained relatively docile. Although the Catholic Church in France might become a factor in foreign policy when Louis squared off against the Vatican, it did not exert great influence. Louis also brought his own government servants at the center and in the provinces to heel. He suppressed independent actions, even among his military commanders on campaign. Authority concentrated at court under his direct supervision; power flowed from the top down, and at the top stood a very few individuals.

Louis XIV debated the issues, made the decisions, and monitored their execution. Freed from the influence of traditional rivals, he exercised complete authority for the formulation of foreign policy and in the drafting of

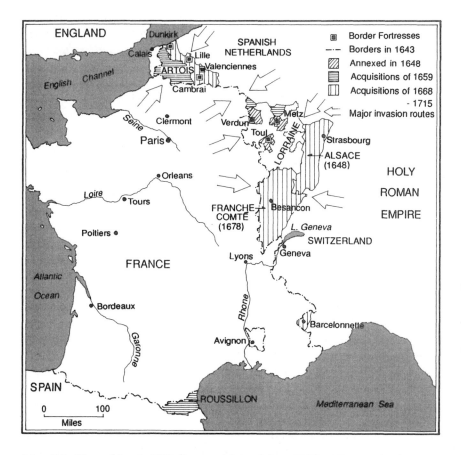

Map 7.1. Wars of Louis XIV. *Source.* Adapted from Willis, *Western Civilization,* Volume I, Fourth Edition (Lexington, Mass.: D.C. Heath, 1985), 653.

strategy. He shared that responsibility only with those rare trusted advisers on whom he called for support.

Louis could not expect to master every detail of government, but he saw his role as one of making decisions based on common sense. For this he needed experts. Five administrative chiefs stood directly below him at the apex of the pyramid: four secretaries of state – foreign affairs, war, navy, and royal household – and one controller-general of finance. While the bureaucratic departments of state, particularly war and foreign affairs, grew and underwent rationalization during his regime, they never threatened Louis' control.

The authority of the small knot of advisers and administrative heads derived not from birth and wealth, but from the fact that Louis called on them to serve. He scrupulously kept powerful nobles of old families, the peers of France, from high bureaucratic posts and from the councils. He once explained that "it was not in my interest to seek men of a more eminent birth because having need above all to establish my own reputation, it was important that the public know by the rank of those whom I choose to serve me, that I had no intention of sharing my authority with them. . . ."[2] With only rare exceptions, he selected men of legal and administrative backgrounds from recently ennobled families.

Because the secretaries and the controller-general commanded considerable patronage, they accumulated networks of clients, who depended on their good will and who in turn became their supporters. This gave Louis' major servants something of an independent power base. While such a network might aid a secretary in rising to power, maintaining himself in office, or in fending off his rivals, it was no defense against the will of the king. By ferociously pursuing and punishing his finance minister Fouquet in 1661 for threatening to dominate royal affairs, Louis gave notice to his principal advisers and administrators that he would not tolerate even the slightest hint of a challenge to his authority.

Louis regularized the decision-making process in councils which he chaired. The most important, the *Conseil d'en haut,* or Council of State, dealt with the most important matters, including issues of war and peace. Those who sat on it could call themselves "ministers" of state. Louis refused to set the membership of this council by ordinance, leaving himself free to choose the three, four, or five who regularly attended its meetings. He kept its size small to insure secrecy. The most common members included the secretaries of state for foreign affairs, war, and navy, and the controller-general of finances. Often the same man held more than one of these offices: Jean-Baptiste Colbert served as secretary of state for the navy and for the royal household, as well as controller-general of finances from 1669 to 1683. But the post of secretary of state did not necessarily carry with it automatic entree into the *Conseil.* One secretary of state for war, the Marquis de Barbézieux, did not receive an invitation to the *Conseil d'en haut,* since Louis preferred the opinions of the Marquis de Chamlay, his personal military adviser. Louis kept control over this council in one further vital way: he expressly forbade his ministers to meet in his absence.[3]

The members of the *Conseil* competed with one another for influence, and Louis was not above playing them off against each other if it gained him leverage and freedom of action. Such conflicts most commonly pitted the two major ministerial families – the Le Telliers and the Colberts – against one another in controversies over turf or policy. Ministers often failed to reach a

---

[2] Louis in André Corvisier, *Louvois* (Paris, 1983), p. 278.

[3] John C. Rule, "Colbert de Torcy, an Emergent Bureaucracy, and the Formulation of French Foreign Policy, 1698–1715," in Ragnhild Hatton, ed., *Louis XIV and Europe* (Columbus, Oh., 1976), p. 281.

consensus at critical times. For example, as the Dutch War approached, the core of the *Conseil* consisted of the old secretary of state for war, Michel Le Tellier, the controller-general of finance, Colbert, and the secretary of state for foreign affairs, Hugh de Lionne. Understandably, Le Tellier regarded the approach of armed conflict without much misgiving, since it would place more power in his hands and in those of his son, the Marquis de Louvois. In contrast, Colbert argued for defeating the Dutch by means short of open warfare. Only through continued peace could he advance his financial reforms and better the economic position of the monarchy. Lionne had his own priorities, hoping that Louis could avoid a war that would jeopardize the 1668 treaty with the emperor that partitioned the Spanish empire of Carlos II (1665–1700) to Louis's advantage. But in this case, neither Colbert nor Lionne could moderate Louis's drive toward war. When the king's mind was set, ministers eventually fell in behind their monarch to further his will and to protect their own positions.

The *Conseil d'en haut* met only at the king's pleasure. Louis used it as he saw fit, and at times he seemed to have viewed it as an annoyance, for his highest civil servants might try to temper or oppose his designs. Inside the council, members discarded court formality: discussions were open and remained strictly confidential, and ministers could criticize the king's positions, though in public they dared not. After the ministers made their opinions known on an issue, Louis usually decided with the majority, although on occasion he overruled it, sometimes for no better reason than to demonstrate his power.

Louis conducted his diplomacy through secret treaties and covert payments, and only the ministers of the *Conseil* knew the details of these arrangements. Even highly placed diplomats remained in the dark about treaties and agreements that the king deemed outside their need to know. When he required military advice, he turned to his leading generals – Turenne, Condé, Vauban, Luxembourg, and Villars. In addition to these individual consultations, Louis also appealed to periodic councils of war, on which leading generals and the minister of war sat.

In the case of the Dutch War, Louis' first war plan evolved in consultation with the *Conseil d'en haut.* He then requested the Prince de Condé to examine its details. Condé sent out his own supporter, Chamilly, on an extended voyage of reconnaissance, and as a result suggested major alterations to the campaign plan. Later, Condé charged his own fortifications expert, Descombes, to scout enemy fortresses. While Sébastien le Prestre de Vauban was the most able military engineer of the day, he was Louvois's protégé, and Condé wanted his own man.

For this system to function under the monarch's control, the king had to possess a great appetite for work, and Louis did. He wrote, "I imposed upon myself the rule of working regularly twice a day two or three hours each time with divers persons of government, not counting the hours I spend myself or the time required for extraordinary affairs."[4] Beyond council sessions, he regularly discussed foreign policy, strategy, and operations privately with his secretaries of state and other experts. Even lesser officials conferred directly with the king on a regular basis.

The Dutch War marked an important change in the level and style of command that Louis, the secretary of state for war, and the *Conseil d'en haut* asserted over operations and strategy. Traditionally, major French commanders had enjoyed considerable independence in the field; as Le Tellier described it in 1650: "The army was a veritable republic and . . . the lieutenant generals considered their brigades like so many cantons."[5] The two great commanders that Louis inherited in 1661, Turenne and Condé, symbolized this independent style of command. As sons of great aristocratic families, they resented directives from the bureaucrats who advised and served the king. These one-time rebels from the Fronde expected a high degree of autonomy and opposed Louis' brand of absolutism. Chafing under orders from the minister of war, Turenne complained that he saw "the direction of armies in the hands of those who better merit the title of valet than that of captain, that the King had resolved to gather for himself alone the *gloire* of all the victories, and that there would remain to the generals only the disgrace of their defeats."[6]

In 1675 both these key players disappeared from the scene: Turenne by death and Condé by retirement. From that point on Louis engaged in *"guerre de cabinet,"* in which he and his civilian advisers, in consultation with military commanders, drafted strategic and operational policy from the seat of government. Generals might lobby for their own plans, but they did not dictate actions. Louis still campaigned on occasion, principally for his own reputation and to raise the morale of his troops, but he did not play the role of warrior-king in the traditional sense. Rather, he was the director, working from backstage.

Louis' system demanded reasonable competence and dependable regularity, not outstanding genius. In a revealing passage written in 1688, Chamlay, confidant of Louvois and later military adviser to Louis, boasted:

> The difference that exists between the present situation of the King's affairs and that of [the Dutch War], is that in those previous times, the fortune of His Majesty and of his kingdom was in the hands of men who, by being killed or by making a bad decision, could lose it in a moment, or at least compromise it in some way by the loss of a battle [from] which it had been difficult to reestablish. Whereas, presently, because of the great conquests that have been made, and because of the advantageous situation of the places that have been fortified, the King finds himself able to grant command of his armies to whomever it pleases

[4] Louis in Wolf, p. 168.
[5] Le Tellier in Corvisier, p. 80.
[6] Remarks of Turenne to Primi Visconti, in Jean-Baptiste Primi Visconti, *Mémoires sur la Cour de Louis XIV*, Jean-François Solnon, ed., (Paris, 1988), p. 63.

him, without having anything to fear from the mediocre capacity of those to whom he confides it.[7]

Protected by his fortified frontier, Louis could control and his bureaucrats could rationalize war.

THE VALUES BEHIND DECISION-MAKING

In a government with so few individuals at its head, the principles of the monarch and his top advisors played a key role in the formulation of policy. Today, it is common to emphasize systems and how they imprison individuals. Institutional constraints did afflict Louis in the areas of taxation and finance, but in international affairs and warfare he still imposed his will. The personality and values of Louis XIV as an individual did much to guide the formulation of the strategic policy of the state. With Louis, it is nearly impossible to separate the monarch from the man. He was groomed from birth to rule France; his person and the state were inseparably linked even if he may never have said "I am the state." And he belonged to the seventeenth century, despite the temptation to see him in twentieth-century terms. As first gentleman of France, the Sun King's values were fundamentally aristocratic, replete with Baroque concepts of war, dynasty, and *gloire*.

The aristocracy did not exceed 2 percent of the population, yet it controlled vast wealth and property and dominated France.[8] Monarchy and aristocracy were compatible: to the political philosopher Montesquieu, monarchy implied aristocracy. The nobility set the values of society and formed those of the king. While the interests of Louis as absolute monarch ran counter to the desire of the aristocracy to retain its independent authority and influence, his opinions on other matters of importance coincided with those of the well-born minority who surrounded him at court. In order to keep the respect of France's privileged elite, a requirement central to maintaining his power, he had to share their values. In the language of modern historiography, he shared the *mentalité* of the aristocracy.

That *mentalité* was central to the king's attitude toward war. For the aristocrat, combat tested his manhood, and for the king, warfare tested his reign. In the *Catéchisme royale*, prepared for him, the boy-king's question "If duels are outlawed, how can the Nobility prove their courage?" receives the answer, "In your armies, Sire."[9] His young courtiers were sure to push for vigorous military action, for they needed an arena in which to win fame. When contemporaries remarked, "He shows the greatest passion for war,

---

[7] Chamlay, 27 October 1688, in Corvisier, p. 459.
[8] Roland Mousnier, *The Institutions of France under the Absolute Monarchy, 1598–1789*, Vol. 2 (Chicago, 1974), p. 147.
[9] Antoine Godeau, *Catéchisme royale* (Paris, 1650), p. 10.

and is in despair when he is prevented from going [to the front] . . . ," it was the highest praise.[10] The thirst for military renown affected women as well as men. Aristocratic young ladies supposedly gave their favors only to soldiers; war, it would seem, was an aphrodisiac.[11] War, "the most important of all the professions,"[12] was sought as a good in itself. Christian virtue fell victim to Roman *virtus* – at least until Louis had proven himself.

Such views run counter to mercantilist notions of war as a struggle over pragmatic economic concerns. Louis disdained the commercial calculations of merchants, and believed the proper prize of war was territory, for land was the supreme good in the aristocratic value system. He never lowered himself to fight over trade. Even the Dutch War, often ascribed to economic competition, was fundamentally territorial from the French point of view; Colbert's arguments lost to those of Le Tellier and Louvois.[13]

Louis also shared the aristocratic concern with family, with the noble "house." It would be anachronistic to see his vision of Europe as "national." He acted for the French state and for the good of his dynasty, the Bourbons: ruling was a family affair. A monarch was both a ruler and the head of a household, who used his power in the first role to exercise his responsibilities in the second. Only his strong dynastic orientation makes Louis' policies immediately before and during the War of the Spanish Succession comprehensible. He ventured French fortune and lives to secure the Spanish throne for his grandson, knowing full well that the crowns of France and Spain would probably never unite. It was enough for a Bourbon to rule Spain.

More than any other, the term *"gloire"* encompasses Louis' aristocratic *mentalité,* and translates best as reputation or prestige. Concern for *gloire* guided the king's actions in a wide range of ventures. It inspired everything from his creation of the Academy of Sciences to his sponsorship of the composer Lully to his war against the Dutch in 1672. Policies that benefited the people and the state added to *gloire.* In linking the monarch with the state, Louis wrote "The good of the one gives rise to the *gloire* of the other."[14]

Louis' concern for *gloire* should not condemn him. He was literally a child of his time and the victim of relentless indoctrination: instructions drafted for his upbringing spoke of *gloire.* For example, he was not to learn methods of hunting that involved deception and trickery, since such practices were unworthy of a prince and did not add to his glory.[15] Mazarin, in his role as

10 Contemporary description in Wolf, p. 78.
11 Primi Visconti, p. 146.
12 Paul Hay de Chastenet, *Traité de la guerre* (Paris, 1668), p. 1.
13 See Paul Sonnino, *Louis XIV and the Origins of the Dutch War* (Cambridge, 1989).
14 Louis in William F. Church, "Louis XIV and Reason of State," in John C. Rule, *Louis XIV and the Craft of Kingship* (Columbus, Oh., 1969), p. 371.
15 Ruth Kleinman, *Anne of Austria* (Columbus, Oh., 1985), p. 122.

tutor and adviser to the young Louis, directed him, "It is up to you to become the most glorious king that has ever been."[16]

The aristocrats of France cared just as much about their own *gloire*. Madame de Sévigné saw the pursuit of *gloire* as a critical and worthwhile element in their education: "Since one constantly tells men that they are only worthy of esteem to the extent that they love *gloire,* they devote all their thoughts to it."[17] The Frondeur, Cardinal de Retz, defined humanity itself in terms of *gloire:* "That which makes men truly great and raises them above the rest of the world is the love of *la belle gloire.* . . ."[18]

A prince's *gloire* rested in large measure on his success in the international arena, and this meant victory in war. *Gloire* predisposed a monarch to desire war – especially a young monarch in need of establishing his own reputation – and Louis admitted that it pulled at him. Accounting for his attack on the Dutch in 1672, he wrote, "I shall not attempt to justify myself. Ambition and [the pursuit of] glory are always pardonable in a prince, and especially in a young prince so well treated by fortune as I was. . . ."[19] With the death of Mazarin, the young man came into his own, determined to try his hand at war. In a 1664 memoir presented to the States, or assembly, of Holland, the Dutch statesman, Johan de Witt, had foreseen the inevitable. France had "a twenty-six year-old king, vigorous of body and spirit, who knows his mind and who acts on his own authority, who possesses a king-dom populated by an extremely bellicose people and with very considerable wealth." Such a king would have to "have an extraordinary and almost miraculous moderation, if he stripped himself of the ambition which is so natural to all princes . . . to extend his frontiers."[20]

The love of *gloire* was of course hardly an exclusively "French disease"; the concern was a European, not a national, obsession. Other rulers also spoke of *gloire* or its Spanish cousin *reputación*.[21] Louis himself employed the term much as modern statesmen speak of national prestige or national interest. Louis defended *gloire* with convincing authority when he wrote, "A king need never be ashamed of seeking fame, for it is a good that must be ceaselessly and avidly desired, and which alone is better able to secure success of our aims than any other thing. Reputation is often more effective than the most powerful armies. All conquerors have gained more by reputation than

---

16   Letter from Mazarin to Louis, in Wolf, p. 89.
17   Letter from Mme. de Sévigné to the Count de Bussy, 23 October 1683, *Lettres de madame de Sévigné,* Gault-de-Saint-Germain, ed., Vol. 7 (Paris, 1823), p. 394.
18   Cardinal de Retz in Gaston Zeller, "French Diplomacy and Foreign Policy in Their European Setting," *New Cambridge Modern History,* Vol. 5 (Cambridge, 1961), p. 207.
19   Louis in Zeller, "French Diplomacy and Foreign Policy," p. 217.
20   De Witt in Ernest Lavisse, *Histoire de la France,* Vol. 7, pt. 2 (Paris, 1906), p. 281.
21   For example, Leopold I, Charles XII, and even William III did so. Ragnhild Hatton, "Louis XIV and his Fellow Monarchs," in Rule, *Louis XIV and the Craft of Kingship.*

by the sword. . . ."[22] *Gloire* was a potent weapon of intimidation and a vital deterrent; Louis was no fool.

Yet the pursuit of *gloire,* of the grandeur of France, did not compel Louis to act in ways that ran counter to the more immediate interests of his dynasty and his state – at least not obviously so. His *gloire* depended on actual achievement. As Vauban once stated, "True *gloire* does not flit like a butterfly; it is only acquired by real and solid actions."[23] The precise role that *gloire* played in the king's actions is therefore difficult to isolate with certainty, for the achievement of *gloire* itself required rationale policies. But it was not so much reason and reward as reputation that ruled.

Historians have long tried to unearth a single principle behind the strategy and foreign policy of Louis XIV. François Mignet identified the pursuit of the Spanish throne, while Albert Sorel found it in a drive for natural frontiers; both theories have weathered the storms of debate poorly. Gaston Zeller did much to define the view held by the majority today. "The quest for glory, then, took the place of a programme for Louis XIV."[24] The realization that Louis did not evaluate his actions in terms of their benefit for the French state or people, but in terms of their effects on his *gloire,* explains his tendency to pursue his wars to excess and his willingness to initiate them when he should have looked for peace.

RESOURCES AND STRATEGY

Louis could only pursue territory, dynastic advantage, and, above all, *gloire,* to the extent that he could mobilize French resources to carry out his strategy. Richelieu's grim observation, written while Louis's father still ruled, haunted the Sun King as well: "There are found in history many more armies perished for lack of bread and discipline [*police*] than by the effort of enemy arms, and I bear faithful witness that all the enterprises that have been undertaken in my time have failed only because of this default."[25]

The problem of marshaling resources lay at the heart of seventeenth-century warfare. On the most obvious level, the king raised funds by taxation and credit; his inability to finance Bourbon military ventures efficiently ulti-

---

22 Louis in Wolf, p. 185. In a similar manner, Vauban, who was little interested in conquest, wrote that, "states maintain themselves more by reputation than by force" (in Michel Parent et Jacques Verroust, *Vauban* (Paris, 1971), p. 78).

23 Vauban, "Pensées diverses," in Albert Rochas d'Aiglun, ed., *Vauban, sa famille et ses écrits,* Vol. 1 (Paris, 1910), p. 627.

24 Zeller, "French Diplomacy and Foreign Policy," p. 207. The erudite and wise Andrew Lossky expresses much the same opinion in more charitable terms: "His aim was quite simple: to increase the grandeur of his State and of his House, so that his own preeminence as 'the greatest king in Christendom' would be beyond dispute." Lossky, "International Relations in Europe," *New Cambridge Modern History,* Vol. 6 (Cambridge, 1970), p. 189.

25 Richelieu, *Testament politique,* Louis André, ed., (Paris, 1947), p. 480.

mately led to frustration and defeat. Perhaps the greatest legacy of the wars of Louis XIV was fiscal exhaustion and debt so profound that the monarchy never really recovered.

Crisis came not because France was a poor region unable to match the wealth of its British and Dutch opponents. On the contrary, seventeenth-century France was the richest and most populous state in Christian Europe. During the last years of the century French authorities compiled the first official census, and Vauban concluded from it that the king's subjects totaled nineteen million souls.[26] Agriculturally, France was rich; only the catastrophic famines of 1693–94 and 1709–10 made the feeding of great armies difficult, but even then the armies remained in the field.

Louis's problem lay not in his realm's poverty, but in his inability to mobilize France's considerable wealth. Finding funds to sustain a major war without exhausting the state proved to be an administrative, political, and social problem too great even for the Sun King. Long wars meant ruin, and Louis regularly backed himself into long wars.

Military success often came down to a question of money; a state with cash could buy men and matériel. French government finances lay in shambles by the late 1650s, although given time and peace some reform was possible. While scholars once credited Colbert with reorganizing the royal finances, his reforms now seem to have stopped short of fundamental changes. Without detracting from his accomplishments, it is clear that whoever occupied the office of controller-general of finances after 1661 could have carried out modest reforms.[27] The sine qua non for success was not Colbert's genius, but the return of peace. Colbert enjoyed the good fortune of serving during more than a decade of peace, interrupted only by the relatively minor crisis of the War of Devolution. The Dutch War cut short much of his progress.

Reform required the ability to tax by regular and rational means and to live within those means; however, warfare quickly outstripped the tax revenues. Increasing tax rates during wartime at best covered only part of the increased need for revenue; at worst, higher taxes led to revolt. Louis consequently paid for wars primarily through borrowing. Colbert's predecessors had survived through expedients: short-term bills of credit, the alienation of future revenues, the wooing of creditors with exorbitant interest rates and kickbacks, and the sale of offices.[28] The purpose of the financial bureaucracies was to hide where the money was really going, not to account accurately for income and expenditure. As Colbert put it, this was a system

---

[26] Ernest Labrousse, et al., *Histoire économique et sociale de la France,* Vol. 2 (Paris, 1970), p. 12.

[27] Peter Jonathan Berger, "Military and Financial Government in France, 1648–1661," Ph.D. diss., University of Chicago, 1979, argues that no real reform occurred before 1659, but that a certain amount of reform was virtually inevitable with the return of peace.

[28] Julian Dent, *Crisis in Finance* (New York, 1973), p. 232.

that "the cleverest men in the realm, concerned in it for forty years, had so complicated in order to make themselves needed [since] they alone understood it."[29] After 1661, Colbert had patched up the system so that it worked tolerably in peacetime. But he failed to rationalize it fully; above all, he failed to make fundamental changes in the government's methods of securing credit. The strain of war immediately brought back the entire range of time-encrusted abuses, with predictable results.

No one could rebuild the foundations of French finance so long as France's strict social hierarchy conceded great privileges, including tax exemptions, to those at the top. Tax privileges protected much of the wealth of the Church and the aristocracy, and Colbert could neither abolish those privileges nor stop the purchase of noble titles and offices that extended those exemptions to ever greater numbers of the wealthy.

The absolutism of Louis XIV may itself have made impossible the creation of a national bank of the kind that had given the Dutch and English such great advantages in managing credit and war. National banks thrived among the maritime powers because their governments by assembly put power into the hands of the very men able to invest in them. Those men could trust in repayment because they could trust in themselves. In contrast, Louis was more inclined to borrow than to repay. He could not govern as firmly as he wished if he abdicated fiscal power to the monied segments of society. Nor, perhaps, would the aristocracy have permitted him to do so. In any case, the absolutist state never effectively mobilized credit through a state bank. The first attempt at a French national bank, that of John Law in 1716, failed miserably. The French had no national bank until 1800; only a revolution made such an institution possible.

The problems of taxation and credit both undermined the monarchy in the long term and cramped the strategic options open to Louis in the short term. The expense of maintaining armies in the field made it strategically wise to send the troops to fight on and eat from enemy territory. This, as we shall see, was a major French strategic technique.

Financial weakness also forced the delay or elimination of offensives. In 1695, though Louis wanted to undertake a major attack in Italy, he had to tell Marshal Catinat that "the only difficulty that presents itself for pursuing offensive war is the considerable sum of money that it requires . . . and after having examined the state of my finances . . . I have, despite myself, been obliged to resolve to pursue only defensive war during the coming year."[30] In Louis' final war, money problems crippled strategy as well as making large-scale offensives impossible after 1709.[31]

---

[29] Colbert in P.G.M. Dickson and John Sterling, "War Finance, 1689–1714," in *New Cambridge Modern History*, Vol. 4 (Cambridge, 1970), p. 298.
[30] Louis to Catinat, Service Historique de l'Armée de Terre, Archives de Guerre (AG), $A^1$1326, no. 1.
[31] Dickson and Sterling, p. 305.

French armies naturally sought to tap resources in the field through requisition. All seventeenth-century forces depended in part on local production and markets, regardless of the wealth and efficiency of their governments, since convoys could not bring up all necessary supplies from remote magazines.[32] But when the Bourbon state proved unable to mobilize the money and goods required to meet the army's needs from within France, as was so often the case, it became doubly necessary for its armies to exploit the food, forage, and funds along and beyond French frontiers. That dependence imposed strategic and operational constraints. French armies occupied enemy territory when possible, laid waste areas that might support the enemy, and protected populations subject to Louis so that they might better supply the sinews of war to his armies.

From the perspective of the French population, Bourbon armies had committed their worst excesses of "self-supply" before Louis's personal reign. Throughout the Spanish war, from 1635 to 1659, Richelieu and Mazarin continually fell short in providing the money and supplies needed to maintain French armies in the field; the army had simply grown faster than the state's capacity to maintain it, and the troops seized food, lodging, and cash for themselves whenever necessary. The resulting pillage produced many a tale of horror.[33]

To be sure, the king and his ministers railed against extortion, pillage, and rape, and sympathized with the sufferings of the population. Yet they did little. Only reductions in the army's battalions and squadrons to a level that the state could support would have achieved results, and that they were unwilling to do. Extortion of money, goods, and even sex by soldiers was not a sign that the French method of maintaining troops in the field had gone awry; it was an integral and necessary aspect of the way in which the Bourbon monarchy tapped resources for its gargantuan forces. As the *Mercure françois* once explained, "One finds enough soldiers when one gives them the freedom to pilfer and the licence to pillage and ravage, supporting them without pay."[34]

This regrettable situation changed during the personal reign of the Sun

---

[32] On the demands of seventeenth-century supply and the need to requisition in the field, see G. Perjés, "Army Provisioning, Logistics and Strategy in the Second Half of the 17th Century," *Acta Historica Academiae Scientiarum Hungaricae* 16, nr. 1–2 (1970). Martin van Creveld, *Supplying War* (New York, 1977), p. 25, writes "In no instance that I have come across is there any question of a force on the move being supplied solely by convoys regularly shuffling between it and its base. . . ." The term "solely" protects van Creveld from being completely off base, but the fact remains that on occasion armies were supplied for entire campaigns primarily from magazines. For example, in 1675 a two-month supply of grain for an entire army of 80,000 men was to be taken from the magazines of Liège and Maastricht, AG, A¹433, letter from Louvois to Estrades, 5 April 1675. I thank my student, George Satterfield, for pointing out this particularly interesting piece to me.

[33] See John A. Lynn, "How War Fed War: The Tax of Violence and Contributions During the *grand siècle, Journal of Modern History,* Vol. 65, June 1993, pp. 286–310.

[34] *Mercure françois,* 1622, p. 445.

King. Much to his credit, Louis was loath to let his armies plunder his own subjects. With the aid of Le Tellier, Louvois, and their successors as secretary of state for war, Louis labored to supply and pay his troops in a far more regular fashion than before. On the whole, he was successful in protecting his subjects from his own forces.

A major explanation for the sharp decrease in abuses against the French population was strategic: Louis fought his wars along the border of France, not in its heart. As much as possible, Louis sent his forces across those borders to exploit enemy territory and populations and expected his commanders to spare his treasury whenever possible by living off enemy resources. He complained to de Lorge during the Nine Years' War, "I am upset to see my army where it is . . . you should cross the Rhine to use up the supplies and forage of Germany and to save Alsace."[35] In drafting plans for 1707, he reminded Marshal Villars on the German front "that one of the great advantages that you can take from this major expedition is that of allowing my army to live at the expense of the enemy country."[36] Thus, for fiscal and logistical reasons, the French favored limited offensives even in fundamentally defensive campaigns.

Local resources were still necessary, but once over the border the king's subjects no longer footed the bill. The result was similar to the earlier ravaging of French villages; it allowed the French to maintain an army larger than taxes and credit could support. The words "courses" and "contributions" describe the two primary methods of extracting local wealth. Courses were raids, involving small parties, of from fifteen to several hundred men. They foraged, requisitioned grain, and seized livestock, in addition to destroying villages and resources that might support enemy forces. Courses were acts of war.

Contributions could be very different. They were payments, usually in money but also in kind, demanded of villages and towns in occupied territory. They were more regular and could function like a tax system. In the much exploited Spanish Netherlands, occupying French administrators established the amount that a locality could afford to contribute to the French treasury, often by reference to prewar tax rolls.[37] They then ordered the population to pay, often by way of printed forms with blanks filled in with the appropriate amounts and dates.[38] The penalty for failing to pay on time was "execution," which meant exactly that. Military units would burn down

---

[35] Louis to Marshal de Lorge, in Wolf, pp. 466–67.
[36] Louis to Villars, 28 May 1707, AG, A¹2015, no. 26.
[37] The best discussion of French contributions exacted in the Spanish Netherlands is provided by Hubert van Houtte, *Les occupations étrangères en Belgique sous l'ancien régime*, 2 vols. (Ghent, 1930). For examples of contributions pegged to taxes, see document apportioning contributions on the basis of aides paid in 1669, Archives du département du Nord (Nord), C 2325, and the decree setting contribution in proportion to the old tax, transport de Flandres, dated 20 April 1676, Nord, C 2326.
[38] See many examples in Nord, C 2333 and C 2334.

the guilty village *pour encourager les autres*. While exact calculations are probably impossible, contributions raised substantial amounts, perhaps as much as 25 percent of the French military budget.[39]

Given that local resources weighed so heavily in the balance, seventeenth-century armies needed not only to exploit base areas for themselves but to destroy those of the enemy. At times, the French compelled an enemy to seek terms by exhausting his territory or pillaging his lands, but such brutal methods usually had less to do with forcing negotiations than with denying him the resources to invade France. Commanded to do so, Turenne ravaged the Palatinate between the Main and the Nechar during the summer of 1674 as converging enemy forces threatened Alsace. While Turenne showed a touching concern for his own men, the ruin they visited on civilians left his conscience undisturbed. The 1674 devastation was an ominous break with the past. Seventeenth-century armies had ravaged areas repeatedly before, but this was the first time that the state had ordered systematic destruction.[40] To protect Alsace in 1676, Louvois wanted the country beyond the Sarre ruined and had the Duchy of Deux Ponts sacked. The Earl of Orrery even argued that in Alsace itself "the French keep but very few Garrisons, and those excellently furnished, and the Countrey generally wasted; so that if the Forces of the Circles of the Empire besiege and reduce one of them the ensuing Summer, that will probably be the most they can aim at, and possibly all things consider'd, more than they can effect."[41]

Of course, France's most notorious recourse to a scorched-earth strategy was the destruction of the Palatinate in 1689. But while perhaps ill-considered for political and moral reasons, it accorded with French strategic practice. Never before was the destruction of a large area more coldly systematic and so complete. The French did display some small restraint; they gave inhabitants time to withdraw with their possessions and struggled to stop pillage by French troops. Yet the destruction by fire of a province, including the ripping down of entire towns stone by stone, was in no way a gracious act.

POSITIONAL WARFARE AND STRATEGY

Louis' interest in fortifications derived in large part from his need to protect his own domains while raiding those of his enemies, but more than this was involved. Louis clearly possessed a taste for "positional warfare," a term that encompasses the construction, defense, and attack of fortifications. This

---

[39] For this estimate, see John A. Lynn, "How War Fed War," and his "Contributions: A Missing Link in the Evolution of War Finance under Louis XIV," *Proceedings of the Annual Meeting of the Western Society for French History*, vol. 18, ed. Gordon Bond (Auburn, AL, 1991), pp. 130–35.
[40] Jean Bérenger, *Turenne* (Paris, 1987), p. 404, makes this point.
[41] Earl of Orrery, *A Treatise on the Art of War* (London, 1677), p. 139.

preference reflected a personality that demanded control, sought to minimize the role of imponderables, and delighted in detail. In addition, positional warfare dominated operations and shaped strategy because it seemed essential to Louis' rigid concept of French security – one that aimed above all at protecting the king's territorial gains from enemy incursions.

Louis' interest in fortification was not unique. Positional warfare shaped war in the seventeenth century, and by mid-century it played a wide variety of roles. Behr exemplified this trend in 1677 when he wrote, "Field battles are in comparison scarcely a topic of conversation. Indeed at the present time the whole art of war seems to come down to shrewd attacks and artful fortifications."[42] This statement contradicted the aged Turenne's robust preference for battle: "In the end the army must fight."[43]

As his focus changed, Louis saw strategy in terms of defensible frontiers, which Vauban so effectively buttressed. This great engineer's influence rose not simply because of his talents, or because he enjoyed the support of Louvois, but because he struck a resonant chord in Louis himself. If he had not had Vauban, Louis probably would have elevated some other engineer; his fortress line was a deeply personal matter.

The shorthand for Vauban's defensive plan for France is the *pré carré*. The term "*pré carré*" is susceptible to two interpretations. On the one hand, the term meant a dueling field; on the other hand, it implied the intent to straighten, or square off, the frontiers to make them more defensible. In a famous letter of January 1673, Vauban proposed the *pré carré* to Louvois:

> Seriously, Sir, the King must think some about creating a *pré carré*. I do not like this pell-mell confusion of fortresses ours and the enemy's. You are obliged to maintain three for one; your men are plagued by it; your expenses are increased and your forces are much diminished.... That is why, be it by treaties, be it by a good war, if you believe what I say, Monseigneur, always preach squaring things off, not the circle, but the *pré*.[44]

This soon became his standard strategic and operational advice. In September 1675, when Vauban urged the taking of Condé, Bouchain, Valenciennes, and Cambrai, he wrote to Louvois that "their seizure would assure your conquests, and create the *pré carré* so much desired...."[45]

His most elaborate plan involved the highly vulnerable frontier with the Spanish Netherlands, the border most dependent on masonry to establish a defense in depth. There he proposed and achieved a defensive frontier that he described as "two lines of fortresses" formed "in imitation of an army's

---

[42] Behr in Christopher Duffy, *The Fortress in the Age of Vauban and Frederick the Great, 1660–1789, Siege Warfare*, Vol. 2 (London, 1985), pp. 13–14.

[43] Turenne in Wolf, p. 79.

[44] Vauban to Louvois, 20 January 1673, AG, A^{1}337, no. 111.

[45] Vauban to Louvois, 21 September 1675, in P. Lazard, *Vauban, 1633–1707* (Paris, 1934), p. 161.

order of battle."[46] In pursuit of his goal, Vauban suggested to Louvois and Louis the fortresses to take in war, and the ones to ignore or bypass. Vauban's strategic ideal thus guided both peacetime construction and wartime operations. He intended his barriers not as flexible defenses, but as seals designed to preserve the sacred land of France.[47] The *pré carré* demanded the rationalization of French frontiers, not just the building of ever more fortifications. Vauban often spoke of abandoning and razing existing fortifications as well as building new ones.

The French budget registered Louis' rising interest in defensive masonry. During the first sixty years of the seventeenth century, the monarchy invested relatively little in fortresses. From 1643 to 1660 the average yearly expenditure inscribed on French accounts was 347,000 *livres*.[48] This figure increased markedly in the 1660s; the average from 1663 to 1667 reached 1,374,000 *livres*. In the period between the War of Devolution and the Dutch War it jumped again to an average yearly expenditure of 3,479,000 *livres*. Expenditures peaked in the 1680s, when the crown budgeted 8,016,000 *livres* annually for fortress construction. Never again did it reach this level under the Bourbon monarchy.

Louis' fortresses played a number of roles in his wars. Most fundamentally, they protected territory; yet they also served an offensive function. The diplomatic and military language of the day spoke of "gates" into the enemy's territory. Fortresses provided bases for offensive operations, as bridgeheads or outposts in enemy areas. This function was particularly critical around Alsace on the Rhine. Thus, what Louis may have intended as defensive actions, his enemies read as offensive.

In addition, fortresses performed critical roles in supplying war. In defending territory they also defended money and goods that constituted the logistical base of the French army. In addition, because it was imperative that armies campaign and winter on enemy territory, fortified "gates" opened up enemy land and populations as a source of supply.

Louis's fortresses also sheltered his magazines, which gave the French considerable advantage in the conduct of warfare, at least through 1691. France's well-ordered system of magazines allowed its armies to take the field earlier in the year than could opponents; an army that worked from magazines could put its horses in the field before the spring grass was high enough to allow grazing. Perhaps no army could entirely support itself from maga-

---

46 Vauban, "Mémoire des places frontières de Flandres," November 1678 in Rochas d'Aiglun, Vol. 1, p. 189.

47 For Provence, he proposed to make it "a fortified country, which by this means would become impenetrable to the enemy." Vauban in Reginald Blomfield, *Sébastien le Prestre de Vauban, 1633–1707* (New York, 1971), p. 127.

48 Archives Nationales, KK 355, Etat par abrégé des recettes et dépenses, 1662–1700. These budgetary figures are also collected in Jean Roland de Mallet, *Comptes rendus de l'administration des finances du royaume de France* (London, 1789).

zines, but well-stocked caches gave an army added flexibility both in campaigning and in changing lines of operation. For example, the Dutch, unable to take the field until May, had to watch the French make opening moves in April. By the time the Dutch could counter them, the French had often achieved major conquests, such as at the siege of Mons in April 1691. But the French did not retain this advantage after the death of Louvois, and logistical calculations, therefore, primarily determined the construction of fortresses and fortified lines.

Beyond supply functions, fortresses and fortified lines were essential to the efficient exploitation of populations through "courses" and "contributions." On the offensive side of the coin, fortresses provided bases for raiding parties that constantly plundered for food and forage. Vauban, for instance, pleaded for a French attack on the enemy stronghold of Charleroi in 1693 since it served as a safe harbor for bands of land-pirates who struck at French territory.[49] On the defensive, permanent fortresses shielded areas from enemy raids.

The king's system of defensive lines evolved gradually. Before the Nine Years' War, Louis tried to deter enemy raids against French preserves by ordering retaliation. If the enemy levied contributions, Louis would retaliate by multiplying those he exacted. If the enemy burnt Louis' villages, he ordered more of the enemy's burnt. These reprisals often served little purpose, but attempts to limit them by treaty failed.[50] Once deterrence and negotiation had failed, prudence demanded the construction of lines to forestall raids, although reprisals remained part of French practice after 1678. Lines appeared as early as the Dutch War, and became more extensive in the Nine Years' War. During the War of the Spanish Succession the French constructed four complete systems of lines to cover the Spanish Netherlands from the Meuse to the sea. These lines of trenches, redoubts, and towers made use of rivers and canals wherever possible. But unlike the trenches of World War I, the lines were not intended primarily to stop field armies, but instead to shelter the rich hinterland from enemy "courses." The value of the territory, and the wealth available to supply French forces in fact determined the siting of the lines.[51] Strategic and operational decisions to hold particular areas and build defensive works rested firmly on logistical considerations.

Positional warfare not only dictated the conduct of campaigns and shaped the geography of war, but even helped to establish force structure. The need to garrison fortresses pushed up army size.[52] Vauban submitted memoranda

---

[49] Letter of 29 June 1693, from Vauban to Le Peletier, in Rochas d'Aiglun, Vol. 2, p. 390.
[50] See Hubert van Houtte, "Les conférences franco-espangnoles de Deynze," *Revue d'histoire moderne*, Vol. 2 (1927), pp. 191–215.
[51] See discussion of lines to cover Alsace in AG, MR 1066, nos. 13–16, and lines to cover north of Spanish Netherlands in AG, MR 1047, no. 9.
[52] See the extensive discussion of this issue in John A. Lynn, "The trace italienne and the Growth of Armies: the French Case," *Journal of Military History*, July 1991.

to Louis arguing that it was fortifications that made the army too large and expensive. In a highly detailed report drawn up early in the Nine Years' War, he presented a table listing 221 fortresses and fortified posts throughout France that swallowed up 166,000 troops.[53] A second report drafted in 1705 increased the number of cities, fortresses, and fortified posts in the tables to 297 that required garrisons of 173,000 infantry and cavalry.[54] The need to man fortresses determined the peacetime size of the French army and contributed to the increase in war strengths, which on paper reached 400,000 men during Louis' last two wars, although these wartime peaks also resulted from the size of the opposing great coalitions.[55] In any case, France needed to abandon and dismantle strongholds to cut the number of troops to more manageable proportions. That explains Vauban's obsession with reducing the number of fortresses.

Thus, the rise in peacetime army size, with all its political and strategic implications, would seem to have been an unintended, almost accidental, consequence of the decision to rely on fortresses. The formation of strategy is often not a rational process; earlier decisions imprison statesmen within the logic of their choices and finally impose policies and actions that these leaders would have preferred to avoid.[56]

THREE ERAS OF FRENCH STRATEGY

The personalities, structures, and policies discussed thus far need to be considered over the fifty-four years of Louis' personal reign, since both international circumstances and the great monarch himself evolved during that half-century. That evolution falls into three eras. In the first, from 1661 to 1678, Louis sought to advance his *gloire* aggressively by conquering new territory. In the second, from 1678 to 1697, French strategy was far more defensive in its goals, though often aggressive in its means. Louis sought to establish defensible frontiers along which French forces would seize the strategic high ground and literally dig in. Louis gained territory to strengthen the wall on his northern and eastern borders. The question of the Spanish succession dominated the last phase, from 1697 to 1714. At first Louis sought peace by bargaining for only part of the Spanish inheritance. However, the will of

---

[53] Service Historique de l'Armée de Terre, Bibliothèque (SHAT, Bib.), Génie 11 (fol.), Vauban, "Les places fortifiées du Royaume avec les garnisons necessaires à leur garde ordinaire en temps de guerre." This document is without date, but marginal notes, apparently by an archivist, analyze the date of the document by the fortresses mentioned.

[54] SHAT, Bib., Génie 11 (fol.), Vauban memoirs, "Etat général des places forts du royaume," dated November 1705.

[55] See John A. Lynn, "The Growth of the French Army during the Seventeenth Century," *Armed Forces and Society,* 6 (Summer 1980); and "The Pattern of Army Growth, 1445–1975," in John A. Lynn, ed., *Tools of War* (Champaign, Il., 1990).

[56] My thanks to Williamson Murray for applying this argument to the relationship between fortresses and garrisons during a presentation I made at Ohio State University in October 1990.

Carlos II gave him little choice but to accept it all for his grandson, Philip of Anjou, knowing that this would lead to war with Emperor Leopold I (1658–1705). In the resulting conflict, the French strategic situation differed from any Louis had faced before; he could establish his armies on friendly land outside French boundaries and fight a holding action.

During the early 1660s, the young Sun King yearned to prove himself in a great war for land and *gloire*. He might reasonably hope to acquire some of the territory belonging to Spain. The enmity between Bourbon France and Habsburg Spain was well established by the time Louis came of age. So long as Spain remained strong, France was under siege. But Spain's long decline and its losing struggle with Richelieu and Mazarin positioned Louis to seize booty. The Spanish Netherlands was a great temptation, and France spent the first period seeking to satisfy this ambition.

The young noblemen at court encouraged Louis in this venture, and his primary military advisers did nothing to dissuade him. In the mid-1660s, Marshal Turenne tutored Louis on military affairs while acting as minister of state with a seat in the *Conseil d'en haut*. Turenne never agreed with Mazarin's decision to end the war with Spain in 1659, for the Spanish Netherlands might have fallen with one more campaign. Now armed force could make amends for diplomatic weakness, and for a time Turenne eclipsed the more conservative Le Tellier and Louvois. The marshal was a great field commander, and Louis could learn from him things he could not from his bureau chiefs.

The death of Philip IV (1621 to 1665) prompted Louis to make his claim. A minor Flemish law held that a daughter from a first marriage could claim a share of her father's possessions despite the existence of a son from a second marriage; thus that property would "devolve" upon her. The daughter in this case was Louis XIV's Spanish wife and queen, the dull and plain Marie-Thérèse. Louis twisted the law to fit French purposes.

Counting on the Dutch to let their old French allies have their way with the Spanish Netherlands, Louis led his armies across the border in 1667, beginning the War of Devolution. But Louis' success frightened the Dutch, and with the end of their war against England in July 1667 they patched together an alliance with the English and the Swedes to forestall further French expansion. Unprepared to meet this unexpected challenge, Louis grudgingly accepted peace after gaining only twelve fortified towns on the border. He planned to return.

He still sought the Spanish Netherlands, but could now only gain it by neutralizing the Dutch, who clearly preferred a declining Spain to an ascending France as a neighbor. Geography took precedence over the history that had allied the Dutch with France against Spain in the sixteenth and early seventeenth centuries. The United Provinces had gained their independence from Spain in 1648 while simultaneously growing into a great commercial and naval power. That independence would now suffer if the French ad-

vanced to their border. In addition, the Dutch and French had become commercial rivals, and while that was of no great concern to Louis, it weighed
heavily in Dutch policy. Louis had another reason for fury at the Dutch; from
his point of view he had stood by them faithfully, and they had repaid him
with "ingratitude, bad faith, and insupportable vanity."[57] A Dutch medal
showing Joshua stopping the sun (read Sun King) in mid-course further
offended his pride.

Louis first isolated them by skillful diplomacy and judicious payments.
Then he "commanded" the army that advanced through the Bishopric of
Liège and crossed the Rhine in 1672, with Turenne and Condé to direct the
troops and Vauban to conduct the sieges. The war began with great successes. But the obstinate Dutch, now under the young William III (1672 to
1702), refused to surrender even though the French occupied many of their
southern towns. Instead, they inundated their land, thus preserving Amsterdam. French aggression soon won the Dutch allies; the Elector of Brandenburg, the Emperor, and the King of Spain joined the struggle against Louis. In
1674, the English concluded another peace with the Dutch. Louis felt compelled to withdraw his forces from the United Provinces. His reluctant withdrawal marked the beginning of the end of his youthful lust for armed
conquest as the road to *gloire*. The death of the bellicose Turenne in 1675
aided this change of focus and tone, as did Condé's retirement that same year.

The return to peace in 1678 ushered in the second era in Louis's policy and
strategy. The king was now "Louis le Grand." He had proven his power and
won his *gloire* by the Treaty of Nijmwegen, and France was greater from the
addition of important cities and an entire province, Franche-Comté. Louis
also believed that he had secured Lorraine, and the French in fact occupied it
for twenty years. He realized that he could never gain the entire Spanish
Netherlands without Dutch acquiescence, and that they would never tolerate
a French presence on their southern border. While he might chip away at the
edge of the Spanish Netherlands, outright conquest lay beyond his means,
and so Louis put aside this goal. His emphasis shifted to holding what he had
already secured while maneuvering diplomatically to obtain what he could
from the inevitable partition of Spanish holdings after the death of the feeble
and childless King Carlos II.

With Turenne and Condé gone, direction of French strategy fell increasingly to the secretaries of state, in particular to Louvois, who gave the generals less leeway. Vauban, the brilliant protégé of Louvois, had the king's ear as
military adviser. Louis saw his strategic problem as predominantly defensive,
and Vauban was the unequalled master of fortifications.

Louis and his advisers came to view France as a beleaguered fortress. In
Vauban's words, "Almost in the middle of the most considerable powers of

---

57   Louis, in a memoir printed in Camille Rousset, *Histoire de Louvois*, Vol. 1 (Paris, 1862–
     64), p. 517.

Christendom, she is equally in range of blows from Spain, Italy, Germany, the Low Countries, and England." A victorious France represented a lightning rod, drawing assaults from all quarters. Vauban believed that "France has today attained a high degree of elevation that renders her formidable to her neighbors, in a manner that they all interest themselves in her ruin, or at least in the diminution of her power."[58] Vauban was by nature a worrier, but so was Louis XIV.

France possessed a long Atlantic and Mediterranean coastline, but the pressures on its extensive land frontiers demanded first priority and denied it anything but fleeting maritime predominance. As a result, Louis never grasped the importance of sea power, and concentrated instead on the many problems of land warfare.

Crucial to French policy in the second era was the continental struggle between Habsburgs and Ottomans. The end of the Thirty Years' War left the Austrian Habsburgs exhausted but able to rebuild. They possessed extensive lands in their own right and still reigned as Holy Roman Emperors, a rump authority perhaps, but still an advantage. However, peace in Germany did not necessarily mean peace for the Habsburgs. A resurgent Ottoman Empire threatened to the southeast. After a brief war in 1663–64, and a twenty-year respite, the Ottomans laid siege to Vienna. In defeating the Turks, Emperor Leopold I acquired resources and created armies to match those of Louis XIV. The Sun King and his advisers recognized this development and believed that time was working against France. The true era of French dominance was thus the brief span between the decline of two empires. Spanish decline allowed the French to assert their preeminence, and Ottoman decline freed the emperor and his forces to challenge the French.

During the second half of his reign, Louis saw the Germans as his major enemies. In a 1684 letter to Vauban, Louvois warned against "the Germans, who from now on ought to be considered as our true enemies and the only from whom we can receive injury if they have an Emperor who wants to mount a horse."[59] Louis therefore adopted a policy designed to block invasion from the east. This defensive strategy was the creation of Louis and Louvois with Vauban as their agent. For all his obsession with *gloire,* the king had more fear of invasion than lust for conquest. Clausewitz concluded that "It had become almost a question of honor for Louis XIV to defend the frontiers of the kingdom from all insult, as insignificant as it might be."[60]

According to Vauban, a system of defensible frontiers required both rationalizing French borders and buttressing them with fortifications. There were two ways to straighten a jagged and confused frontier: sacrifice ad-

[58] Vauban in Alfred Rebelliau, *Vauban* (Paris, 1962), pp. 141–42.
[59] Letter from Louvois to Vauban, 28 June 1684, AG, A^{1}714, no. 807. The full text of this quotation explains more fully that it is Alsace and the defensive line that made the Germans the enemy.
[60] Carl von Clausewitz in Bérenger, p. 514.

vanced position and retreat to a defensible line, or add new pieces of territory to form a defensible line forward. Since the king would not tolerate any violation or loss of his territory, he had only one choice – to fill out his territory to defensible contours by addition, by conquest. This creates a paradox; Louis' ultimate goals were essentially defensive but he pursued them by aggressive means.

Once the emperor became a threat, Louis' attention shifted to the defense of Alsace, which had suffered three invasions during the Dutch War. He believed France needed Strasbourg, Luxembourg, and certain other positions to cover its eastern borders. He grabbed them through the "Reunions," a strange mixture of legality and force. Treaty language tended to define acquisitions in ambiguous terms – one gained a town or area "and its dependencies." The question was always what were those dependencies? Louis established "Chambers of Reunion" to determine what territories conceded to France, historically had dependencies. If this French court found in his favor, he might than choose to enforce his claim. Precedents existed for such legal procedures, and Louis' claims were sometimes fairly strong.[61]

His move on Strasbourg in 1681, however, had little to do with legal niceties. The issue was strategy not justice. By seizing Strasbourg, Louis gained control over two of the three critical bridgeheads spanning the Rhine that offered potential invasion routes to an enemy. (The others were Brisach, already in French hands, and Philippsbourg, which the French lost by the Treaty of Nijmwegen.)

The French thus pursued the strategy of paradox which Corvisier christened "*la défense aggressive.*" While Louis may have viewed his acquisitions as essentially defensive in nature, Europe read them otherwise, for reasons not hard to divine. While Louis desired security, the overbearing monarch acted as if he wanted to conquer or emasculate. And in his first two wars, Louis had acted in ways that suggested an infinite appetite for conquest, although his aim in both did not go much beyond *gloire* and lust for the Spanish Netherlands. The Dutch War cast a brazen image of Louis as a relentless, insatiable conqueror that he never overcame. That conflict convinced contemporary statesmen of his aggressive intent, and this conviction grew stronger following the brutal seizures of land along French borders after 1678. In seeking to deter his enemies by erecting "impregnable" borders during the 1680s, Louis so alarmed his foes that he made the war he sought to avoid virtually inevitable.

Louis never appreciated how his quest for absolute security threatened his neighbors, and how his security must by nature compromise theirs. The same Rhine bridgeheads that denied an enemy the opportunity to attack France gave France avenues to attack its enemies. Louis' fortresses not only covered

---

61 Church, "Louis XIV and Reason of State," p. 389, defends the relative validity of Louis's claims.

his frontiers, they projected French power.[62] It was thus reasonable for those suspicious of the French to read his intentions as offensive.

Alarmed as he might be, the emperor was too busy battling the Turks to resist the French along the Rhine, and he acquiesced to the Truce of Regensburg in 1684, which promised twenty years of peace between France and the Empire. Louis now had a long-term lease on the territories he had seized. But even Regensburg failed to calm Louis' insecurity. As the emperor's forces advanced against the Turks, Louis feared that the emperor would attack France once he had defeated them. He responded by issuing an ultimatum that the Truce of Regensburg be converted into a permanent peace by 1 April 1687. This was a defensive act to be sure, but one carried out in the blustering manner so typical of the 1680s. Finally, in 1688 Louis brought on a general war when he succumbed to what Paul Sonnino has labeled his "fatal predilection for the preemptive strike" by seizing Philippsbourg.[63] In purely military terms this attack made sense because it closed off the Rhine frontier of Alsace. But in political terms it both alienated the Germans and went a long way to convince the Dutch to support William's expedition to England, with all its drastic implications for Louis and France.

Louis refused blame for the Nine Years' War. He believed others had imposed the war upon him and saw his opening moves as essentially defensive – the seizure of Philippsbourg in order to close off the Rhine and the devastation of the Palatinate to undermine any German offensive. It was beyond Louis' intentions, and perhaps beyond his control, that the short defensive war he wanted turned out to be a long and exhausting war of attrition.

The return of peace in 1697 seemed to bring a change. The Nine Years' War had bankrupted the absolutist state, exhausted the French people, and chastised their proud monarch. A once haughty Louis seemed contrite; he pursued a policy of peace at nearly any price. The primary concern of French diplomacy and strategy was now the Spanish succession. Early modern rulers took dynastic affairs into account when calculating international policy, and the late seventeenth century presented Europe with a dynastic crisis of the first magnitude. The fact that the sickly and deformed Carlos II would die childless meant intense competition for position in this crucial race for his possessions. The succession was never far from Louis' mind, and with the return of peace it dominated his thought and policy.

The dynastic marriage game left several contenders holding strong cards – Louis XIV and Leopold I held the best hands, though neither claimed the succession for themselves. Louis put forward his grandson, Philip of Anjou, and Leopold advanced the claim of his second son, Charles. A third candidate, the child Joseph Ferdinand, Electoral Prince of Bavaria, proved to be a

---

62 It was my graduate student, George Satterfield, who first attached the modern strategic term "power projection" to Louis's fortresses.

63 Sonnino, "The Origins of Louis XIV's Wars," in Jeremy Black, ed., *The Origins of War in Early Modern Europe* (Edinburgh, 1987), p. 122.

valuable compromise candidate, at least while he lived. The competition for the Spanish throne doomed Louis XIV and Leopold I to a major confrontation. Both advanced strong claims and were willing to commit considerable resources to the struggle, and neither could allow the other to shift the balance of power in his favor. An early attempt to solve the issue by a treaty of partition in 1668 resulted in Austrian acquiescence to French claims, but the much stronger position Leopold I gained in the late 1680s led him to be more assertive. He signed a treaty with the Dutch and English in 1689 that would have passed on all of the Spanish inheritance to Charles. A more balanced treaty of partition in 1698, when Louis wanted to avoid another war at all costs, gave almost everything to Joseph Ferdinand in order to forestall a clash between Bourbons and Habsburgs. But the untimely death of Joseph Ferdinand scuttled that agreement, and Louis scrambled to draft a new partition treaty with the English and Dutch in order to avert war in 1700. While this treaty would have awarded the lion's share to Charles, leaving Philip with only parts of Italy, Leopold refused it, hoping that Charles would gain the entire inheritance.

Throughout this maneuvering, Louis' goals were dynastic: to secure the throne for his grandson, not to unite the crowns of France and Spain. Philip of Anjou as Philip V of Spain would add more *gloire* to the Bourbon family, making it the preeminent royal house, but would not necessarily allow France to dominate Europe as a dynastic and military power. State goals were two very different affairs, related only through the person of Louis. But the elaborate plans of the great powers collapsed like a house of cards when Carlos II bequeathed the entire Spanish inheritance to Philip. That made war almost unavoidable.

Louis probably had little choice but to accept the will of Carlos II. Had he abided by the treaty of partition of 1700, which the Austrian Emperor had refused to sign, he would have faced a Habsburg succession and occupation in Spain. Louis would have had to fight Leopold for the scraps that the treaty allowed Philip, and he would have had to attack the combined forces of Spain and the Empire to get them. By accepting the will, he would still have to fight Leopold I, but he could fight a defensive war on Spanish territory, with the French and Spanish allied against the Emperor. The trick was to convince the maritime powers that he really had no choice and that his goals were purely dynastic. While Louis could not predict the exact Dutch and English reaction, it was not unreasonable to suppose their agreement, if given reasonable assurances and guarantees.

But the king now misplayed every card. He refused to remove Philip from the French line of succession, leaving open the possibility that the French and Spanish thrones might someday unite. The English and Dutch might have lived with this situation, but Louis went on to insist on sending French troops to take over the Dutch-held barrier forts in the Spanish Netherlands. The forts guaranteed the security of the burgher republic, and Louis' order sent

William III into a rage. In a third reckless act he granted French merchants special trading rights over their English and Dutch competitors in the Spanish colonies. This action particularly infuriated the English. These last two unnecessary moves were apparently a throwback to the self-assertiveness of an earlier Louis.[64]

The strategic challenges of the War of the Spanish Succession differed from those of the earlier wars. Then Louis' armies had either been the aggressors or had tried to hold the *pré carré*. In this last war, his soldiers were once more on the defensive, but beyond the *pré carré*. They were to hold in the Spanish Netherlands, Piedmont, and Spain. Only defeat could drive them back to the French borders, but French defeat was precisely what the War of the Spanish Succession had in store.

CONCLUSION: LOUIS AND THE PHANTOM OF THE SHORT WAR

The course of the Sun King appears dazzling at first glance, but much of his brilliance proved illusory. The great monarch and his ministers pursued disastrously flawed strategies; the Sun King brought not only the dawn of French preeminence but its twilight as well.

Again and again, Louis naively accepted the promise of a short war. He persistently failed to predict the magnitude and length of the conflicts that he precipitated. None of his four wars went as expected, and only one of them, the War of Devolution, was brief. In that conflict, his arms proved successful but Dutch diplomatic maneuvers frustrated his aims. The Dutch War, intended to last but a single campaign, dragged on for six years. Louvois believed that war in 1688 would last only four months, because his goals were modest. But the four month "blitz" he expected turned into the Nine Years' War. The War of the Spanish Succession was even worse; what might have been only a brief contest between Louis and Leopold ravaged western Europe for fourteen years. Why did the great king go wrong so often?

The short answer is that Louis and his ministers expected to fight wars against isolated enemies, or at most small and weak coalitions, but by 1674 powerful alliances always opposed France. Louis had studied interstate relations under Cardinal Mazarin, and he could hardly have had a better teacher. But while Mazarin had relied on supple alliances to preserve French security, Louis tried to vault into a predominant position by French wealth and arms alone. Despite his diplomatic preparations for the Dutch War, Louis was soon isolated, facing William of Orange, the Elector of Brandenburg, the Emperor, and the King of Spain. In 1688 Louis prepared to meet only Ger-

---

[64] As Wolf, p. 513, commented, after seeking peace diligently and even meekly after 1697, Louis once again acted like the Sun King, and paid a terrible price. Paul Sonnino, "The Origins of Louis XIV's Wars," p. 129, sees these acts of 1700 and 1701 as the King "casting off his penitential robes and reverting to his old self."

mans on the field of honor and believed he could win the duel with a single shot. Yet by May 1689 he faced the Dutch Netherlands, England, Spain, and Savoy, in addition to the Emperor and his German allies. In 1700 Louis knew that in accepting the will of Carlos II, he must at least fight the Emperor. But he need not have faced a renewal of the Grand Alliance. Yet in September 1701 the maritime powers united with the Emperor, and Prussia, Savoy, and Portugal ultimately joined as well.

The impact of these miscalculations was immense. Louis XIV drained France by bumbling into wars he did not anticipate. Playing what he perceived as a winning hand, he could afford the initial ante, but when the stakes rose far beyond expectations, he stayed, unwilling to fold his cards, while the odds turned. As the French pursued these struggles with military establishments of unprecedented size year after year, wars for quick gains became wars of attrition. In each of his three great conflicts sheer exhaustion drove Louis to the bargaining table. The strain on French government, finances, and society was monumental. To meet the unexpectedly high demands of warfare, Louis pushed the bureaucratization of absolutism even further. In order to collect and disburse the necessary resources, government bureaus expanded at the center and increased the authority of the king's representatives in the provinces. Faced with the demands of seemingly endless war, an inequitable and inefficient tax system, and poor fiscal management, the monarchy undermined itself. The government tapped resources with rapacious energy and with expedients that wrecked any possibility of rationalizing the monarchy's finances.

The monarch who admitted on his deathbed that he "loved war too much" did not leave his young successor with continental hegemony and domestic prosperity, but rather with a weakened France burdened with astronomical debt and a financial system incapable of discharging it. In a real sense, the end product of Louis's strategy was not his greater *gloire* but the revolution that brought down his dynasty seventy-five years after his death.

8

To the edge of greatness: The United States, 1783–1865

PETER MASLOWSKI

In the 1830s, an inquisitive French magistrate visited the United States to observe democracy in action. After wide-ranging research and travel, Alexis de Tocqueville returned to France, pondered what he had read and seen, and then wrote two volumes describing what he had learned. At the end of the first volume, Tocqueville noted that two great states, the United States and the Russian Empire, had "grown up unnoticed" and "suddenly placed themselves in the front rank among the nations, and the world learned of their existence and their greatness at almost the same time." While admitting differences between the countries, Tocqueville was sure that "each of them seems marked out by the will of Heaven to sway the destinies of half the globe."[1]

The ascent of the United States toward great power status in barely half a century would not have surprised the Founding Fathers, who had envisioned the United States as a great territorial and commercial empire. Within another few decades, their dream was nearly fulfilled as the United States reached the edge of greatness. The country moved toward that exalted position in three phases. First, between 1783 and 1815 the United States struggled to preserve its independence. It not only had to form a government that could generate sufficient military power to survive in a hostile world but also had to fight France in the Quasi-War and England in the War of 1812. Second, after 1815 the United States underwent astonishing economic and population growth, aggressively completed its continental expansion, and extended its commerce into the farthest reaches of the globe. Third, the Civil War guaranteed that the United States would indeed become a great power, by preserving the country as a single entity and confirming the federal government's sovereignty over the individual states.

Throughout this three-stage evolution strategists wrestled with profound

[1] Alexis de Tocqueville, *Democracy in America* (New York) Vol. 1, p. 452.

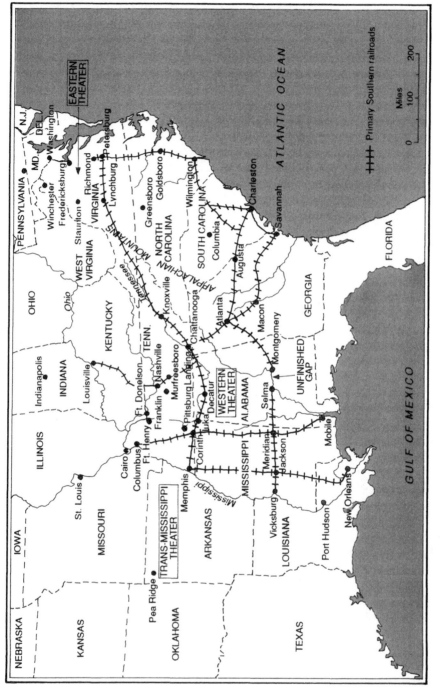

Map 8.1. U.S. Civil War. *Source.* Adapted from Allan R. Millett and Peter Maslowski, *For the Common Defense: A Military History of the United States of America* (New York: Free Press, 1984), 157.

paradoxes. Most fundamentally, the American *Weltanschauung* contained an intense, seemingly moral imperative to expand the country's "experiment" in liberal democratic government beyond its original borders, which required an aggressive strategy along the western frontier. Yet simultaneously strategists also recognized their paramount duty to safeguard the expanding continental homeland from European adversaries, which necessitated a defensive strategy along the eastern seaboard. Compounding this paradox between offensive and defensive strategic concerns was the startling contrast between the vision that most strategists had of the nation's future greatness, and the country's military weakness for approximately fifty years after its founding. Policymakers understood that the feeble federal government could exert so little coercive power on its intensely individualistic citizenry that it would have difficulty in raising adequate manpower and money to wage a war, especially one that became long and large.

Both civil and military leaders also realized the difficulties confronting them in formulating and prosecuting a truly *national* strategy. The country's enormous expanse, primitive communications, and often vitriolic political disputes fostered a fractured regional or local outlook rather than a cohesive national one. As a result, strategy-making frquently contained a "populist" dimension. The desire of political leaders to allay regional concerns, and to maintain popular support and win elections, sometimes determined the timing and location of operations, thereby confounding the military's invariably more narrow focus.

Despite these weaknesses, policymakers and strategists also knew that the country had three strategic advantages. One was that to fulfill its expansionist *Weltanschauung* the United States only had to defeat adversaries who were even weaker than it was – Indians, Spain, and Mexico. As a result, the frontier readily "crumbled" before the onrushing Americans. A second advantage was that in preserving the continental domain from foreign threats, the United States enjoyed a favorable geographic situation. The Atlantic Ocean served as a 3,000-mile wide moat; even the mightiest European nation could not project much military strength across it. And when Britain made near-heroic efforts to send reasonably powerful forces to the New World late in the War of 1812, the United States, like Russia, had such tremendous strategic depth that foreign conquest was virtually impossible. Finally, many strategists perceived that the country's astounding growth was a vital strategic asset. Throughout the late eighteenth century and the first half of the nineteenth century, the longer the United States survived, the stronger – and hence more secure – it became. As it expanded in geographic size, population, and economic strength, the prospect of national extinction (or even crippling damage) from a foreign adversary became progressively less likely.

One last significant point was the personalized, pragmatic nature of American strategy-making. Although the War and Navy Departments developed tiny, permanent *administrative* structures, the military bureaucracy contained no permanent organization that systematically studied potential wartime strategic concerns. From President John Adams and Secretary of War James McHenry during the Quasi-War to President Abraham Lincoln and General Ulysses S. Grant during the Civil War, strategy-making was virtually devoid of institutional influences.

THE ARTICLES OF CONFEDERATION, THE CONSTITUTION, AND MILITARY SECURITY

As avid students of antiquity and as recent members of the British Empire, the men who emerged from the Revolutionary War as "nationalists" – those who favored a strong central government – were familiar with the concepts and practices of empires, and mused about the possibility of the United States becoming one. "However unimportant America may be considered at present . . . ," wrote George Washington, "there will assuredly come a day, when this country will have some weight in the scale of Empires."[2]

Washington and other nationalists not only had a vision, but also a problem. Under the Articles of Confederation adopted during the Revolution, the United States might be hard-pressed to maintain independence, much less achieve greatness. Although encompassing a domain that was gigantic by European standards, the Confederation lacked a strong central authority and was a military dwarf. The reasons were obvious. The states refused to yield any of their sovereignty to the central government, and in particular refused to grant it the right to tax. After the Revolution's successful conclusion, peacetime military preparedness did not seem essential for security – after all, Americans had virtually no mobilized military strength when the Revolution had begun. The United States also confronted severe postwar economic problems. Thus the Confederation sold the Continental Navy's last ship in 1785 and maintained as its "army" only the 1st American Regiment, at an authorized strength of 700 men.

With no navy and a minuscule army, the Confederation was incapable of resolving its numerous acute security problems, both internal and external. In the Northwest, the British refused to evacuate a number of forts from which they conducted a lucrative fur trade, meddled in Indian affairs, and threatened to block American expansion westward. From Florida and the Louisiana Territory Spain exerted similar influences, and kept a stranglehold on the Mississippi River. Powerful Indian tribes also contested the white settlers' westward path. In the Mediterranean, Barbary pirates ravaged American commerce and compelled the government to buy protection with tribute. A domestic crisis further exposed the Confederation's weakness. In

[2] John C. Fitzpatrick, ed., *The Writings of George Washington* (Washington, 1931–44) Vol. 2, p. 520.

fall 1786 a Revolutionary War veteran named Daniel Shays led a revolt of western Massachusetts farmers against debts and taxes; the Confederation could raise neither men nor money to intervene in the crisis. Massachusetts volunteers ultimately quelled Shays' Rebellion, but nationalists seethed with humiliation at the national government's ineptitude and feared that the country was degenerating into anarchy.[3]

The military weakness of the Confederation provided nationalists with incentive to seek a stronger union. Without an infusion of central "coercive power,"[4] the United States would remain impotent and probably fragment into warring republics. The status quo was intolerable to those who envisioned a mighty state seated amidst the great powers. But simply asserting that the government needed more power left a fundamental question unresolved. Could the nationalists devise a governmental structure with sufficient power to provide security against foreign and domestic enemies without transforming the government into a despotic regime that would extinguish state sovereignty and individual liberty? That is, could they reconcile demands for greater cohesion and security with American localism and ideological hostility to government power?

Americans possessed an intense attachment to their local communities, dating back to the earliest colonial period when the English monarchs authorized New World settlements but expected the colonists to defend themselves. Colonial charters and proprietorial grants were specific on this point, and the colonists recognized their situation.[5] Although the Revolution had nationalized the outlook of some citizens, few eighteenth-century Americans acknowledged bonds of loyalty that stretched beyond the borders of their own state.

The bedrock of American ideology was an emphasis on "natural rights," which found consummate expression in the Declaration of Independence with its assertion that "all men" had "certain unalienable Rights, that among these are Life, Liberty and the pursuit of Happiness." The idea of "liberty" had particularly powerful connotations, for civilized people could have no more cherished possession. But liberty's existence was precarious. Its two worst foes were tyranny – arbitrary power exercised at a government's whim – and licentiousness – too much liberty. The protection of liberty from these twin threats required the "rule of law," from which flowed the belief in representative government. The people imposed laws through their elected representatives, and these laws provided the best chance of preserving freedom by checking excesses, either of arbitrary authority or unbridled liberty.

---

[3] For representative Washington statements lamenting the Confederation's weakness and expressing the fears that Shays' Rebellion aroused, see ibid., Vol. 26, pp. 298, 483–96; Vol. 27, pp. 48–52, 305–7; Vol. 28, pp. 289–92; Vol. 29, pp. 27, 52, 184, 238.

[4] Ibid., Vol. 28, p. 502. Also see Vol. 29, pp. 190–91.

[5] For examples, see The Selective Service System, *Backgrounds of Selective Service. Military Obligation: The American Tradition. A Compilation of the Enactments....* (Special Monograph No. 1) Vol. 2, part 6, pp. 137, 285.

Americans especially believed in laws to restrain government, leaving them as free as possible in their "pursuit of Happiness," which meant the pursuit and security of property.[6]

When combined with a lack of traditional restraints on individual behavior such as an established religion and a hereditary class hierarchy, this ideology fostered an unregimented, unrestrained, individualistic, capitalistic society. Americans, Tocqueville marveled, "owe nothing to any man, they expect nothing from any man; they acquire the habit of always considering themselves as standing alone, and they are apt to imagine that their whole destiny is in their own hands." They had "a restless disposition, an unbounded desire of riches, and excessive love of independence" and "a passion for wealth."[7]

American political culture, with its parochialism and ideological distrust of centralized power, shaped strategic culture. In simplest terms, it undermined military preparedness at the federal level by prohibiting large standing forces and organized military planning. Limited coercive powers, a reluctance to deprive citizens of their property via taxation, and a concern for the voters' approbation hampered the government's ability to mobilize military resources. Moreover, the prevalent ideology conflicted with the central military values of subordination, discipline, strict obedience to a hierarchical chain of command, and selfless sacrifice.[8]

The prevailing ideology gained a lustrous gloss from a belief in a special destiny under Providence's divine guidance. Americans thought their society was unique because only the United States had translated the concept of liberty into practice. They also believed they had a mission to uphold – and spread – their novel experiment. Washington wrote that an "Invisible Hand" conducted the affairs of the United States, whose every move "seems to have been distinguished by some token of providential agency." He asserted that "the preservation of the sacred fire of liberty and the destiny of the republican model of government are justly considered, perhaps, as *deeply*, as *finally*, staked on the experiment intrusted to the hands of the American people."[9] He deplored the Confederation because it would be "a triumph for the

---

6 For an extended discussion of these points, see Yehoshua Arieli, *Individualism and Nationalism in American Ideology* (Cambridge, MA, 1964) and John Phillip Reid, *The Concept of Liberty in the Age of the American Revolution* (Chicago, 1988). Thomas Jefferson defined "the sum of good government" as "a wise and frugal Government, which shall restrain men from injuring one another, shall leave them otherwise free to regulate their own pursuits of industry and improvement, and shall not take from the mouth of labor the bread it has earned." See James D. Richardson, ed., *Compilation of the Messages and Papers of the Presidents, 1789–1897* (Washington, 1907), Vol. 1, p. 323.

7 Tocqueville, Vol. 1, pp. 306, 331; Vol. 2, pp. 105, 144.

8 Washington recognized the gulf between civil and military life and the difficulty of instilling military values in an American army; see, Fitzpatrick, Vol. 6, p. 111. Also see *The New American States Papers, Military Affairs* (henceforth cited as *NASP*) (Wilmington, DE, 1979), Vol. 14, p. 204.

9 Richardson, Vol. 1, pp. 52–53.

advocates of despotism" if the United States proved incapable of governing itself, thereby demonstrating "that systems founded on the basis of equal liberty are merely ideal and fallacious!"[10]

Rather than see the experiment in liberty fail, the Founders drafted a new framework of government. They knew of the dilemmas and paradoxes they faced in trying to devise a structure that would "insure domestic tranquility" and "provide for the common defence," and yet "secure the blessings of liberty to ourselves and our posterity." In the Constitution they sought to preserve liberty from excessive power that led to tyranny, and yet surround liberty with enough guardians that it could avoid feebleness and licentiousness. Phrased another way, the Founding Fathers strove to devise a formula that would provide maximum cohesion and security consistent with minimum coercion of the states and individuals.

The Constitution solved the puzzle of balancing liberty and power through a separation of powers and a system of checks and balances that diffused power throughout the governmental structure: between the states and federal government, between the latter's three branches, and within the two houses of the legislative branch. The document's military provisions exemplified this fragmentation of authority. It divided power between the federal government and the states, but unlike the Confederation, it gave paramount authority to the former. To guard against one person or a small group accumulating too much power, it divided control of the military between Congress and the President. By giving national forces two masters, the Constitution insured that neither attained despotic preeminence.[11]

Congress could "declare war," "provide and maintain a navy," and "raise and support armies," and to ensure money for these purposes it could "lay and collect taxes, duties, imposts and excises," and "borrow money." However, no army appropriation could "be for a longer term than two years." It could "grant letters of marque and reprisal, make rules concerning captures on land and water," and "make rules for the government and regulation of the land and naval forces." Congress was to provide for "calling forth the militia to execute the laws of the union, suppress insurrections and repel invasions," and for "organizing, arming, and disciplining" the militia and for governing the militia when in national service. While these were extensive powers, Congressional tyranny was unlikely since the President was the commander in chief of the army and navy, and of the militia "when called into the actual service of the United States." He also appointed military officers, although only with the Senate's advice and consent.

As for the states, the Constitution placed limitations on their military power. Without Congressional consent, they could not maintain nonmilitia troops or warships in peacetime, form alliances with other states or foreign

---

[10] Fitzpatrick, Vol. 28, p. 503.
[11] Gordon S. Wood, *The Creation of the American Republic, 1776–1787* (Chapel Hill, 1969) discusses these complex matters.

powers, or engage in war "unless actually invaded, or in such imminent danger as will not admit of delay." Juxtaposed against these constraints was the national government's pledge to guarantee the states a republican form of government and to protect them from invasion and domestic violence. States also retained their militias, their right to do so being implicit in the states' authority to appoint militia officers and train the militia "according to the discipline prescribed by Congress." The Second Amendment made the states' militia authority explicit.

Three points about the Constitution warrant attention. First, the Founding Fathers perceived that military power had a dual purpose, to provide both external security *and* internal stability. One of the Constitution's fundamental purposes was "to insure domestic tranquility," and the government pledged to protect the states against "domestic violence," and could call out the militia to "suppress insurrections." In *The Federalist,* which Alexander Hamilton, John Jay, and James Madison wrote to explain the Constitution, the theme of preserving domestic harmony recurred frequently, and a number of the essays referred to the specter of Shays' Rebellion.[12] But the army's foremost domestic role was to police the so-called Indian frontier, "that most disagreeable duty in times of profound peace."[13]

Second, the Constitution embodied the United States' complex military heritage, which derived from a mixture of ideology and experience. Two strands of British ideology regarding armies had crossed the Atlantic. Most Americans embraced the Radical Whig view that regular standing armies were tyrannical institutions that posed a constant threat to liberty. As an alternative to a professional army, Radical Whigs endorsed the militia concept, the idea that citizen-soldiers were the safest form of defense because they had no reason to deprive themselves of their liberties. Despite Radical Whig arguments, England did maintain a small standing army, commencing in 1645 with the New Model Army that in the end imposed Cromwell's dictatorship. By the late seventeenth century, Moderate Whigs, representing a second strand of British ideology, argued that a regular army was nevertheless compatible with liberty so long as constitutional safeguards constrained its despotic potential. Moderate Whigs also argued that a standing army was *necessary* to preserve liberty; with the emergence of disciplined regular armies, militias no longer had sufficient expertise to provide external security. While Radical Whigs emphasized the necessity of political reliability, Moderate Whigs stressed the need for military efficiency.[14]

---

[12] For examples, see Jacob E. Cooke, ed., *The Federalist* (Middletown, CT, 1961) pp. 14, 31, 35, 131, 146–47, 162–63, 176, 293, 502.

[13] Cooke, p. 156. As late as 1899, the Secretary of War referred to the army's "police duty against Indians"; see Elihu Root, *The Military and Colonial Policy of the United States* (New York, 1970), p. 352.

[14] Lawrence Delbert Cross, *Citizens in Arms: The Army and Militia in American Society to the War of 1812* (Chapel Hill, 1982) contains an excellent discussion of these ideological debates.

The military experiences of the colonial, Revolutionary War, and Early National periods revolved around a "dual army" of citizen-soldiers and regulars, with the phrase "citizen-soldiers" embodying a confusing melange of common militia, volunteer militia, and nonmilitia volunteers. In the initial stages of colonization, a common militia system, based on universal, obligatory service, had taken root. With manpower in short supply, a pervasive sense of insecurity, and an obvious need for short-term local defense, that system accorded with conditions. Every man was in fact a soldier, and for a few decades Radical Whig ideology and military reality meshed. But as the population grew and the frontier pushed westward, the common militia decayed. By the late seventeenth century, the militia was useful only as a local police force or standby posse comitatus, and for the next century it lived on as an effective military force only in impassioned anti-army rhetoric. However, during the Revolution the common militia experienced a dramatic renaissance and played an essential role in defeating the British. Following the Revolution the image of virtuous citizen-soldiers defending their local communities remained a powerful rhetorical symbol, but the common militia's actual military utility virtually disappeared.

With the militia little more than a rhetorical ideal by 1675, the colonists had turned to volunteer forces of two basic types. As the common militia atrophied, volunteer militia companies emerged. Composed of men who enjoyed soldiering and willingly devoted time and money to it, these exclusive units of relatively affluent volunteers had their own uniforms, equipment, organization, and esprit de corps. Although relatively few such companies existed during the eighteenth century, they underwent explosive growth in the first half of the nineteenth century, and evolved into the National Guard in the post-Civil War era.

A second type of volunteer force also arose. To perform regular garrison duty, patrol the frontier, and undertake campaigns against either Indian or European foes, colonies raised ad hoc expeditionary forces composed of volunteers, usually men from the lower social classes. Serving for extended periods rather than the three months that was typical for the militia, these expeditionary forces sometimes took on the attributes of professional armies. For example, during the French and Indian War, Washington commanded the Virginia Regiment, a unit raised, supplied, and officered under Virginia's auspices. The regiment became so proficient that he tried to have it incorporated into the British regular army.[15] During the Revolution, Washington's Continental Army – a multistate national force that in essence consisted of many equivalents of the Virginia Regiment – became expert enough to match the British army in battle. Despite its skills, the Continental Army was not a regular army that existed in war *and* peace. Instead, it stood in a

---

[15] W.W. Abbot, et. al., eds., *The Papers of George Washington, Colonial Series*, Vol. 4 (Charlottesville, 1983), pp. 112–15, 120–21.

long line of ad hoc, volunteer, expeditionary forces that disbanded when the emergency ended. Between the early 1790s and World War I, the primary method of manpower mobilization was to call for volunteers.

The final element in the complex heritage was a regular army. The Continental Army had convinced Washington and other nationalists that Moderate Whig ideology was valid. Firmly subordinated to civilian control, the Continental Army had *defended* liberty. After independence the United States could no longer rely on the British army and navy, but would need its own military establishment. As the postwar era began, nationalists set forth a preparedness argument that echoed throughout the nineteenth century. In his "Sentiments on a Peace Establishment" of 1783, the seminal statement of nationalist post-Revolutionary War military thought, Washington called for a standing force of 2,631 officers and men to "awe the Indians," garrison the West, and guard against attacks from Spanish Florida or British Canada. Since neither the colonies nor the fledgling United States had maintained a professional army, he realized that "a peace establishment may be considered as a change in, if not the Commencement of our Military system. . . ."[16]

The Constitution permitted all the strands of this heritage to continue. The states retained common militias, from which volunteer companies could be formed, and the central government could mobilize volunteer expeditionary forces and maintain a peacetime army. All these "armies" became so embedded in tradition that in 1824 President James Monroe could routinely justify building coastal fortifications because they would "retard the movement of the enemy into the country, and give time for the collection of our *regular troops, militia, and volunteers* [emphasis added]."[17]

A third important feature of the Constitution was that its military provisions represented a stunning nationalist victory. The new government had ample power to create not merely a standing army, but all the other military elements that Washington's "Sentiments" had suggested, including a navy, seacoast fortifications, and a "respectable and well established Militia." Contrary to the tradition whereby each colony monopolized its own militia, the general insisted that the militia be at least partly nationalized, with the federal government imposing uniformity in arms, organization, and training. In each state he also wanted "a kind of Continental Militia," modeled after the Revolution's minutemen and under national control. Thus Washington proposed a three-tiered land force consisting of a small regular army, a ready reserve similar to the colonial volunteer militia, and an improved common militia. To support the military establishment, he suggested building arsenals, factories, laboratories, and military academies.

To men who imbibed deeply of Radical Whig thought, the Constitution's military provisions looked dangerous. Antinationalists accused the national-

---

16   This document is in Fitzpatrick, Vol. 25, pp. 374–98.
17   *NASP, Naval Affairs*, Vol. 1 (1981), p. 108.

ists of raising bogus fears about foreign wars, Indian wars, and anarchy to impose a tyrannical government. Virginia's Patrick Henry argued that the Confederation had been energetic enough to defeat England; should Americans abandon a government that survived that test? The proposed government had *unlimited* power to maintain a regular army in peace, and such armies had always been the "bane of a republican government; by a standing army most of the once free nations of the globe have been reduced to bondage." Let the new government take effect, and the United States would soon have "a *military king*, with a *standing army* devoted to his will," which he would use "to suppress those struggles which may sometimes happen among a free people, and which tyranny will impiously brand with the name of sedition." The states and the people would be defenseless because the Constitution deprived them of sole control over their militias, the only effective counterweights to national oppression. Equally serious was the absence of a bill of rights protecting many fundamental liberties, especially "the liberty of the press, that grand palladium of liberty and scourge of tyrants."[18]

Nationalists vigorously countered the opposition's arguments. A navy, regular army, and some national control over the militia were necessary. "Safety from external danger," insisted Hamilton, "is the most powerful director of national conduct."[19] Since the United States was economically weak, depended on overseas commercial interests that might collide with those of the great powers, and had European colonies for neighbors, it needed to be prepared for war. Fortunately, the country's natural assets – its vast territory, its distance from Europe, and the predatory European balance of power – meant it needed only a *small* peacetime establishment.

Federalists argued that a navy was essential to defend America's maritime commerce, the Atlantic coast, and American neutrality in European wars. Although they did not propose to compete directly with the great powers in naval strength, the Federalists believed that a navy of even "respectable weight" could exert a decisive influence in the West Indies, allowing the United States "to become the Arbiter of Europe in America, and to be able to incline the balance of European competitions" in North America "as our interest may dictate."[20]

The militia alone would not suffice on land, but one that was *well-regulated* would allow the government to maintain a regular army of minimal size. To insure a competent militia that meshed with the army, the government had to impose uniform standards. The states' right to appoint officers and conduct the training prescribed by Congress would guarantee that the militia retained a strong orientation toward the individual states.

---

[18] For antinationalist documents, see Morton Borden, ed., *The Antifederalist Papers* (1965) and Cecelia M. Kenyon, ed., *The Antifederalists* (1966). The quotations are from Borden, pp. 19, 212, and Kenyon, pp. 361, 363.

[19] Cooke, p. 45.

[20] Ibid., p. 68.

Although the regular army might suppress an occasional mob, it would "be unable to enforce encroachments against the united efforts of the great body of the people."[21] The separation of powers insured that the President could never become a despot with a standing army at his beck and call. And at least once every two years Congressmen had "to deliberate upon the propriety of keeping a military force on foot; to come to a new resolution of the point; and to declare their sense of the matter, by a formal vote in the face of their constituents."[22]

True, the Constitution gave the government a theoretically unlimited power to raise armies and to tax, but how could it be otherwise? The "circumstances that endanger the safety of nations are infinite; and for this reason no constitutional shackles can wisely be imposed on the power to which the care of it is committed." "The *means*," argued Hamilton, "ought to be proportioned to the *end;* the persons, from whose agency the attainment of any *end* is expected, ought to possess the *means* by which it is to be attained."[23] Since money formed the sinews of national defense, the taxing and borrowing powers also had to be unlimited.[24] Finally, to assuage antinationalist fears, the Founders promised to add a Bill of Rights – an explicit guarantee of individual liberties – as amendments.

TESTING THE CONSTITUTION'S MILITARY PROVISIONS, 1789–1815

When the government assembled in 1789, the nationalists (who became known as Federalists) needed to translate the Constitution's military provisions into policy in four areas. They had to establish an agency to administer military affairs, implement its militia responsibilities, and decide whether to raise a regular army and create a navy. On the first of these issues, Congress acted expeditiously by establishing a Department of War in August 1789. The militia presented an issue less easily resolved, since it lay at the heart of the struggle between state and national power. Federalists hoped to create an effective militia as the cornerstone of their military establishment. Secretary of War Henry Knox argued that an energetic national militia was "the *capital security* of a free republic, and not a standing army," which in peacetime could not "be considered as friendly to the rights of human nature." An effective militia required "classing," and Knox proposed three classes: an advanced corps of men from eighteen to twenty, a main corps of men between twenty-one and forty-five, and a reserve corps of older men.[25]

---

21 Ibid., p. 48.
22 Ibid., p. 168.
23 Ibid., p. 147.
24 Ibid., p. 276.
25 *NASP, Military Affairs,* Vol. 14, pp. 167–69.

Not until 1792 did Congress enact the Uniform Militia Act, which foiled Federalist aspirations. The law established the principle of a universal military obligation. But it made no provision for classing, did not impose uniform standards of arms, training, and tactical organization, and gave the states control over exemptions. The most energetic part of the militia remained the elitist volunteer companies, which retained their special status. The government had virtually abdicated its responsibility, letting the states respond to the law according to their diverse impulses. For decades the successors of Washington and Knox pursued the chimera of a well-regulated militia, but not until 1903 did Congress fundamentally revise the feeble structure erected in 1792.

The failure to forge reliable militias made a standing army imperative, and the Federalists inched toward that goal. The government adopted the 1st American Regiment and an artillery battalion formed during Shays' Rebellion, and augmented the 1st Regiment with four companies. But a campaign against the Indians in the Old Northwest in 1790 demonstrated the inadequacy of the new force. In response, Congress created a second regiment and authorized the President to enlist 2,000 "levies" for six months – the first use of federal volunteers who were neither militiamen nor regulars. But when this composite army of militia, volunteers, and regulars ventured into enemy territory in 1791 it suffered a stunning defeat.

The government thereupon authorized three more regular regiments, and Knox reorganized the expanded army into the Legion of the United States under the command of Revolutionary War veteran Anthony Wayne. Reinforced by 1,500 mounted volunteers, the Legion routed the Indians at the Battle of Fallen Timbers in 1794. The Legion had demonstrated the government's ability to provide for the common defense, at least against the Indians.

That same summer the government also showed more competence in insuring domestic tranquility than had the Confederation. Yet another tax protest, the Whiskey Rebellion, erupted in western Pennsylvania. When the rebels defied a presidential command to disperse, Washington ordered four states to provide 12,500 militiamen. Although several states had difficulty mobilizing their quotas and the assembled force was often unruly, the Whiskey Rebellion evaporated as this citizen-soldier army marched into western Pennsylvania. The militia had performed its traditional role as a police force, but this time under national rather than state control.

By applying two kinds of force – an enlarged regular army and a nationalized militia – the new government had overcome domestic crises against Indians and rebels; Federalists believed it had proven the validity of their preparedness argument. However, their use of military power frightened Republicans – the opposition party – and showed that military policy had become a partisan issue. Republicans viewed the Whiskey Rebellion episode as an example of a strong government's armed tyranny, and also insisted that with the end of the Indian campaign in the Northwest the nation could reduce the regular army. In 1796 Congress passed an act that both sides considered a victory. It abolished the Legion and substantially reduced the army, which pleased Republicans. Yet in a sense the Federalists gained more, for a standing army survived, and ever since Washington's "Sentiments," this had been a primary objective of their policy. The act committed the nation to maintaining a peacetime force that served as a frontier constabulary for the next century.

By 1796, two foreign crises had cemented other elements in the Federalist military program in place. The most serious crisis arose in 1793 when France declared war on England, Spain, and Holland, and the belligerents, especially England, began interfering with American commerce. The strongest of the Barbary states, Algiers, posed a lesser threat. No longer bottled up in the Mediterranean by the European powers who were at war, corsairs from Algiers sailed into the Atlantic to prey upon American commerce.

The United States responded to British depredations with negotiations and passive defense. Washington sent to London the diplomatic mission that concluded Jay's Treaty (1795) and restored amicable Anglo-American relations. But in 1794 Congress also voted to create three or four regional arsenals, to build coastal fortifications at twenty-one locations, and to form a Corps of Artillerists and Engineers. Although seaboard fortifications existed from the colonial and Revolutionary eras, those authorized in 1794 were the first for which the national government appropriated money.[26]

Ostensibly to combat the Algerians but with an eye on the European powers, the administration also established a navy in the Naval Act of 1794. The navy's primary role was to foster and protect commerce, but it served other purposes as well. For example, naval officers during peacetime acted as adjuncts to the State Department by transporting diplomats and by personally negotiating treaties. In wartime the navy not only protected commerce but also became "the Sword of the State" and attacked enemy commerce.[27] In cooperation with the army and the coastal fortifications, the navy guarded against invasion. Considering the country's distance from Europe, the dangerous gales, fogs, and shoals along its coastline, and the availability of numerous safe havens for American ships, policymakers believed "the power and efficiency of an American navy must be double its nominal proportion to that of an assailing enemy."[28] Preserving refuges for the navy became a prominent argument for coastal fortifications, as most strategists believed that navies and fortifications complemented one another.[29]

As with the army, the navy became a political issue. Republicans feared that a navy, instead of deterring aggression, might provoke it by so alarming

---

[26] Robert S. Browning III, *Two if by Sea: The Development of American Coastal Defense Policy* (Westwood, CT, 1983), pp. 5–7.
[27] *NASP, Military Affairs*, Vol. 2, p. 143.
[28] *NASP, Naval Affairs*, Vol. 1, p. 69. Also see p. 70.
[29] For example, see ibid., p. 147.

a European nation that it "would crush us in our infancy."[30] A navy would also invite imperialism and adventurism, leading the United States into the sticky web of European politics. Worst of all, it would be expensive. Republicans preferred to shun European affairs and devote national resources to developing the West.

When Washington retired in 1797, the Federalists had not infused as much military vigor into the republic as they desired. Yet they had made great strides in implementing Washington's "Sentiments"; and the institutions and policies they established remained basically intact for a century. The Federalists had failed to establish a well-regulated militia and military academies, but had nevertheless forged a permanent, comprehensive peacetime establishment.

But had the nation developed sufficient cohesion to remain a single republic, and had the Federalists generated adequate military strength soon enough? These became urgent questions shortly after Washington's retirement as the United States struggled to survive the cataclysm ignited by the French Revolution. When war between France and England began, Washington issued a proclamation of neutrality, and in his "Farewell Address" he urged the country to "steer clear of permanent alliances" with other nations and "to have with them as little *political* connection as possible."[31] But declaring neutrality was not identical to maintaining it. The war ensnared the United States, which was not surprising since the military affairs of Europe and North America had been linked since 1689.

The war between France and England completed the fracturing of the American political elite along party lines. Federalists hated the French Revolution's radical nature, believed the United States was too weak to fight England again, and stressed the importance of Anglo-American commercial connections. Republicans emphasized the Revolution's anti-monarchical nature and the Treaty of Alliance of 1778 that bound France and the United States. Jay's Treaty pleased Federalists by preserving peace with England, but angered both the Republicans and France. The French considered it an Anglo-American alliance, and in retaliation increased their depredations against United States commerce. Hoping to avert war, President John Adams sent a commission to France. But France rebuffed it, resulting in the Quasi-War that began in the spring of 1798 and ended in the fall of 1800.

The Quasi-War was in several respects a prototype of many future American wars; it remained undeclared, was limited, and provoked intense domestic dissent. The United States fought for the narrow goal of persuading France to stop harassing commerce, which did not require an ideological crusade to compel the enemy's unconditional surrender, but only "mitigated

---

[30] Quoted in Marshall Smelser, *The Congress Founds the Navy* (Notre Dame, IN, 1959), p. 13.

[31] For the "Proclamation of Neutrality," see Richardson, Vol. 1, pp. 156–57, and for the "Farewell Address," see pp. 213–24 (the quotes are on pp. 222–23).

hostility."[32] In matching military means and political ends, the administration rejected the Francophobes' demand for an alliance with England and imposed restrictions on the use of force. In May 1798 Congress authorized the navy to capture French *warships in American coastal waters,* and in July allowed warships and privateers to take *armed French vessels anywhere.* But the government always limited the navy to action against *armed* ships. Despite pressure from pro-war Federalists and numerous laws expanding the land forces, Adams also restricted the fighting to the sea.

One reason for these limitations was Republican opposition, which hampered the government's ability to mobilize militarily and seemed to portend civil war. Secretary of War James McHenry warned Adams of the "very general indisposition" to war on the part of "a considerable part of the community." Most Federalists believed the country confronted both a foreign threat and a domestic menace.[33] They worried about invasion, but also feared that French agents were conspiring with the Republicans to ignite a civil war if the United States and France declared war.

To deal with the dual danger of French invasion and French-inspired insurrection, Federalists enacted a large preparedness program and branded dissent as disloyalty in the Alien and Sedition Acts. The most repressive was the Sedition Act, which embodied the British common law practice of punishment after-the-fact for seditious libel. Republicans asserted that the Sedition Act was unconstitutional since it violated the First Amendment. They also denounced the notion of seditious libel, arguing that all political debate should be exempt from legal restrictions. The Republican argument ultimately prevailed; thus the Quasi-War established a United States tradition that dissent – even if pernicious and intemperate – was not necessarily disloyalty.[34]

The Quasi-War also prompted the first major reorganization of the military bureaucracy. In 1798 Congress transferred the navy from McHenry's domain to a new Department of the Navy, and revived the United States Marine Corps, which had existed during the Revolution but had expired in the postwar demobilization. Adams appointed the ardent navalist Benjamin Stoddert as the first Secretary of the Navy. Stoddert immediately called for a navy of twelve 74-gun ships of the line and more than thirty smaller vessels, a force that would "make the most powerful nations desire our friendship – the most unprincipled, respect our neutrality."[35] Even the Federalist-dominated Congress would not authorize that many new ships, but during the war Stoddert assembled a respectable force of more than fifty warships

---

32 *NASP, Military Affairs,* Vol. 1, p. 18.
33 Ibid. Also see pp. 39–40, 62, 66.
34 Leonard Levy, *Emergence of a Free Press* (Oxford, 1985) contains a splendid account of these matters.
35 *NASP, Naval Affairs,* Vol. 1, p. 11.

(including converted merchantmen) and more than a thousand privateers. Throughout the conflict the navy worked closely with the British and, in a sense, reinforced them; between January 1798 and December 1800, the Americans never had more than thirty-two ships deployed at any one time in North American and Caribbean waters, while the Royal Navy never had fewer than ninety.[36]

Finally, the Quasi-War was significant because it gave rise to the only purely political army in American history. In 1798, Congress authorized a New Army, as distinct from the "old" army on the frontier.[37] Washington agreed to command both the old and new armies, but would not take the field until war began. Meanwhile, his ranking subordinate, Hamilton, actually commanded the New Army. Hamilton craved military glory and was eager to repel a French invasion, crush a Republican rebellion, and conquer Florida, Louisiana, and perhaps all of South America. He naturally excluded Republicans from the New Army officer corps.

Fortunately for the Republicans, who saw the new force as a threat to liberty, the New Army never matched Hamilton's grandiose expectations. Insistence on each officer's political purity delayed its formation as Hamilton and Washington reviewed each applicant's file. President Adams distrusted Hamilton and undermined his efforts, especially by sending another peace mission to France. Renewed peace prospects slowed the recruiting effort, and when negotiations resulted in the Convention of 1800 ending the Quasi-War, Hamilton's hopes for the New Army vanished.

The end of the Quasi-War ensured Jefferson's election in 1800, since the sudden evaporation of the crisis with France made the Federalist preparedness program look excessive and despotic. It seemed doubtful that Federalist military institutions could survive the transition since Jefferson had been one of the foremost critics of the preparedness program. Yet despite his inclination toward Radical Whig ideology and insistence on governmental economy, Jefferson knew that the international arena was predatory and that military weakness invited aggression.

Once in office the Republicans tilted toward the Moderate Whig position. Although they abolished many of the forces authorized during the Quasi-War, they preserved the Federalist permanent military apparatus. They did not want to destroy the army, which Jefferson now viewed as essential, but merely to relax the Federalist grip on the officer corps. In 1802 his administration founded a Military Academy to produce Republican officers[38];

36 Michael A. Palmer, *Stoddert's War: Naval Operations During the Quasi-War with France 1798–1801* (Columbia, SC, 1987), appendix A, pp. 240–41.
37 Congress also created a Provisional Army, a Volunteer Corps, and an Eventual Army, but the government tried to organize only the New Army. See Captain A.R. Hetzel, U.S. Army, ed., *Military Laws of the United States. . . .* (1846), pp. 72–78, 80–82, 85–88.
38 Theodore J. Crackel, *Mr. Jefferson's Army: Political and Social Reform of the Military Establishment 1801–1809* (New York, 1987) emphasizes this point.

however, not even the Republicans were able to establish a well-organized militia.[39]

In 1807–08, in response to deteriorating relations with England, the Jefferson administration initiated a "Second System" of coastal fortifications more extensive than the Federalists' "First System." The Republicans also maintained a navy, although during Jefferson's administration it focused on small gunboats rather than warships. Gunboats were cheap, simple enough so that maritime militiamen could man them, and incontrovertibly defensive. One thing "this species of naval armament" could not do, Jefferson realized, was protect "our commerce in the open seas, even on our own coast."[40] For a nation so dependent on overseas commerce, this was no small defect, as events leading up to the War of 1812 demonstrated.

No single issue led to the War of 1812. Its causes fall into major and subsidiary categories, and the two major causes both revolved around the United States' inability to protect seaborne commerce. In the war between France and England, both sides resorted to economic warfare that hurt neutral commerce. England was inevitably the worst offender because of its superior seapower. To Americans, it seemed as if England were plundering their commerce. A second maritime issue was impressment. Between 1793 and 1812, British naval commanders impressed nearly 10,000 American seamen. From the American perspective, impressment struck at the heart of national integrity; if the United States could not protect its citizens, what loyalty did they owe it? Compounding these major maritime grievances were three lesser problems. When an agricultural depression hit the West in 1808–09, farmers blamed Britain's restrictive trade policies. In 1811 Indian warfare wracked the Old Northwest again, and Americans castigated the British in Canada for supporting the Indians. Finally, an undercurrent of aggressive expansionism caused some Americans to eye Canada and Florida.

By 1812 the failure to extract concessions from England through "economic coercion" had led many Americans to conclude that the choice was surrender of national honor and sovereignty, or war. The War Hawks, a group of young Republican Congressmen, railed against submission. Their aggressiveness prevailed. Despite the seemingly equal division of war powers by the Constitution, President James Madison took the lead by asking Congress to declare war. From that point on, Congress in essence responded to presidential initiatives rather than initiating its own measures. Nowhere was the executive branch's superiority more evident than in devising strategy.

---

39 Jefferson repeatedly suggested militia reform to Congress, but a typical response was "that it would be improper, at this time, to innovate on the present system of organization of the militia of the United States." See *NASP, Military Affairs*, Vol. 14, p. 194.

40 *NASP, Naval Affairs*, Vol. 1, p. 43. In a classic statement emphasizing that policy should determine force structure, Secretary of the Navy Paul Hamilton argued that the gunboats could be useful or useless, depending "on the species of policy which, in the event of war, may be adopted." See ibid., p. 56.

Madison made the important strategic decisions in consultation with his cabinet.[41]

The Madison administration realized that *the* crucial strategic task was to invade Canada, which had become vital to British commercial and naval power. With Canada occupied, England would have to yield to American demands to avoid damaging its war effort against Napoleon. Since the United States had slight hope of attacking Halifax and Quebec, Canada's two greatest bastions, the best remaining invasion route was up the Hudson River-Lake Champlain-Richelieu River corridor to Montreal.

Unfortunately for Madison, several factors made it impossible to invade Canada successfully. One constraint was limited forces. The government could never entice enough men into the regular army, and neither volunteers nor militia forces were completely subordinate to national authority because the states organized and officered them. An ever-present restraint on manpower mobilization was financial weakness. Approaching bankruptcy by mid-war, the government could not offer pay and bounties high enough to lure men from the civilian economy.

A second difficulty lay in tension between national and regional or local strategic concerns. An invasion of Canada may have been Madison's foremost goal, but coastal towns worried more about naval raids, while the Southwest considered the Creek Indians the primary threat and the Northwest viewed Tecumseh's revived Indian confederacy as its foremost adversary. Governmental weakness and primitive means of transportation and communication made the war so regionally oriented that national strategy was often irrelevant. The administration could rarely impose its will on distant theaters; state and local politicians and generals often ignored its injunctions. Moreover, on several occasions the government deviated from its main strategic task to undertake operations designed to appease local constituencies and thereby shore up support for the war by allowing pro-war candidates to win elections.[42] But regionalism was a strength as well as a weakness. Local leaders understood regional realities and could adopt appropriate measures, while disasters elsewhere did not infect them with defeatism.

A final strategic constraint was the factionalism that pervaded the war effort at all levels. Generals in the same theater rarely cooperated; in the Great Lakes region, naval and army officers fought separate wars. No government agency existed to plan, much less impose, interservice coordination.

[41] The best history of the War of 1812 is J.C.A. Stagg, *Mr. Madison's War: Politics, Diplomacy, and Warfare in the Early American Republic 1783–1830* (Princeton, 1983). Much of the following discussion is based on his book. Also see Marcus Cunliffe, "Madison (1812–1815)" in Ernest R. May, ed., *The Ultimate Decision: The President as Commander in Chief* (New York, 1960). Madison's war message is in Richardson, Vol. 1, (pp. 499–505.)

[42] For example, Secretary of War John Armstrong's strategy in spring 1813 made sense only in terms of the need to influence elections in New York. See Stagg, pp. 285–86, 335.

Personal and political rivalries rent the cabinet. But the most serious factional problem was the rival Federalist Party's almost unanimous opposition to the war, especially in New England. Use of the preferred route to Canada depended on cooperation from New England, but when Madison asked that region's governors to mobilize their militias, they refused.[43] New Englanders also carried on an extensive illicit trade with England and withheld financial assistance from the government. In contrast to New England, support for the war was strong in the South and West. Harnessing that enthusiasm meant attacking Canada through the Great Lakes region. Although this was the least effective road to success in Canada, Madison adopted it because he could not assemble requisite forces in the main theater. Having once committed this strategic mistake, the administration found it impossible to correct it, and from 1812 through 1814 it failed to achieve a decision to the north.

The Treaty of Ghent that ended the war on 24 December 1814 was a curious document. It reestablished the prewar territorial status quo and set up joint commissions to settle American-Canadian boundary disputes, but it mentioned none of the issues that had caused the war. If American achievements are measured against the original prewar objectives, the War of 1812 was a failure. But for three reasons the Treaty of Ghent was a diplomatic triumph. First, the original causes were no longer urgent issues. The end of the European war in 1814 rendered the maritime causes moot since Britain's neutral rights violations and impressment ceased.[44] And although the United States had neither conquered nor occupied Canada or Florida it virtually eliminated the two major Indian threats by killing Tecumseh in 1813 and defeating the Creeks in the Southwest in 1813–1814.

Second, American war aims had changed dramatically, from forcing concessions from England to national survival without loss of territory. Political objectives frequently expand or contract during a war and may, as Clausewitz noted, "change entirely *since they are influenced by events and their probable consequences.*"[45] For America's leaders, conditions deteriorated as the war progressed. One adverse element was escalating Federalist dissent. Not only did the Federalists force an unwise strategy upon Madison, but their dissent also threatened national unity. Events seemed to indicate a movement from resisting the war toward formal neutrality and perhaps a separate peace, followed by secession and the formation of a New England confederation.

---

43 For a selection of New England Federalist sentiment regarding the militia question, see Herman V. Ames, ed., *State Documents on Federal Relations: The States and the United States* (Philadelphia, 1906), pp. 56–65.

44 As Secretary of War James Monroe wrote, "it must be admitted that the effect of the peace in Europe, laid the foundation for the peace between the United States & Great Britain. . . . As soon as these wrongs ceased, the causes of war ceased and the United States were willing to put an end to it." See *NASP, Military Affairs*, Vol. I, pp. 78–79.

45 Carl von Clausewitz, *On War*, edited and translated by Michael Howard and Peter Paret (Princeton, 1976), p. 92.

A Federalist secret meeting at Hartford, Connecticut, in mid-December 1814 induced acute anxiety among Republicans. The administration prepared to use force to crush a secessionist movement. However, moderate Federalists dominated, and instead of calling for secession they proposed a series of Constitutional amendments, including one that required a two-thirds vote (instead of a simple majority) for any declaration of war. Had such a provision existed in 1812, the Federalists could have prevented a declared war. The convention's report meant that the Union would remain intact – for now. But the convention merely adjourned indefinitely; it might still reconvene, perhaps under the control of pro-secessionists.

Another depressing development was that the United States had endured an almost uninterrupted succession of military failures from the war's beginning. For two years the government had been so weak and the country so divided that the administration could scarcely generate any military power. In 1814 Napoleon went into exile, releasing Britain from the immediate demands of the European war. The United States soon faced a punishing three-pronged British offensive that compelled it to fight a desperate defensive war.

But all three British offensives failed, which leads to the third reason why the Treaty of Ghent was an American triumph. Britain achieved none of its grandiose war aims, which included compelling the United States to endorse British doctrine regarding neutral rights, to accept additional restrictions on fishing rights off Newfoundland, to permit the formation of an Indian buffer in the west, and to grant England free use of the Great Lakes, access to the Mississippi, and land to build a military road from Halifax to Quebec. But the Americans showed more ability repulsing attacks than in conducting them: at Plattsburg, Baltimore, and New Orleans they turned back the British.

These failures demonstrated that Britain could not project power into North America any more effectively than during the Revolution. No technological innovations had simplified the task of maintaining armies across the Atlantic, the cost of waging war in North America was still enormous, and the British still had to worry about Europe. The anti-French coalition was unstable, and Napoleon, exiled on Elba, was awaiting an opportunity to return. British policymakers, fearing a renewed European war, concluded that they *must* have peace with the United States. In fighting England a second time and surviving intact, the United States confirmed its independence and the staying power of its institutions, and gained a measure of respect in Europe.

AN EXPANDING EMPIRE, 1815–1860

Reflecting its increasing wealth and power, the United States rapidly expanded across the continent after the War of 1812. Although the country became the dominant power in the western hemisphere during the antebellum era, expansion created new security problems and exacerbated old ones. Instead of one coast, the country now had two coasts to defend. The border with Canada stretched westward, offering greater opportunities for clashing interests. In the southwest, the lengthy boundary with Spain and later with Mexico became a source of friction that ultimately burst into war. European powers retained Caribbean bases from which they could menace the coast, and at least a few of these colonies seemed tempting targets for further American expansion. Throughout the continental domain, Indians remained a threat. If in retrospect the United States appeared increasingly secure (at least from foreign threats) during the decades before the Civil War, policymakers were never sanguine about the prospects for prolonged peace.

The War of 1812 was a revelation to the Republican policymakers who had tried to mobilize forces in the midst of war and had endured the shocks of repeated defeats. After the war they reaffirmed the Federalist vision of moderate preparedness by building upon and refining the existing military institutions.[46] Ideally, the elements in this refined establishment would include a small regular army, a well-disciplined militia, permanent coastal fortifications, a network of interior communications, a relatively large navy, and, as a few perceptive policymakers realized, a well-organized bureaucracy. Strategists hoped these preparations would serve the defensive purposes of protecting the country's continental domain and democratic institutions, and also promote overseas commerce. Because the nation's "providential geographical position" gave "it all the defensible advantages of a remote insular position, in respect to the other great military nations of the world," the armed forces did not have to match the size of those in Europe.[47]

Secretary of War James Monroe suggested a postwar regular army of 20,000 troops. Congress agreed to 12,000, but even that dwarfed any previous army except in wartime or acute crisis. However, the financial panic of 1819 caused Congress to ask Secretary of War John C. Calhoun to cut the army in half. In response, he delivered a ringing call for preparedness. He belittled reliance on the militia as the main line of defense, insisting that a standing army was both indispensable and compatible with liberty. He recommended an army organized on the "expansible" principle so that when war came "there should be nothing either to new model or to create" either in the line or staff.[48] Congress rejected the expansible concept and instead eliminated regiments and reduced the number of officers. Yet no one now questioned the necessity for a standing army, and Calhoun's idea that regulars should be the foundation for war planning during peace prevailed.[49]

---

[46] Richardson, Vol. 1, p. 553; NASP, *Military Affairs*, Vol. 11, p. 55.
[47] NASP, *Military Affairs*, Vol. 3, p. 156; Vol. 11, p. 287; Vol. 14, p. 229.
[48] Calhoun's plan is in, ibid., Vol. 11, pp. 125–28.
[49] NASP, *Military Affairs*, Vol. 14, p. 231; Root, p. 351.

Although he failed to convince Congress to establish an expansible army, Calhoun was instrumental in improving the general staff created during the War of 1812 and in establishing the position of commanding general. The general staff was not a war planning organization. Instead, it consisted of autonomous bureau chiefs reporting to the Secretary of War. The chiefs' purpose was to give the secretary, who was usually a civilian lacking military knowledge, advice on technical, logistical, and administrative matters. Since no single officer commanded the entire army during the War of 1812, district and department commanders had acted independently. When the secretary tried to coordinate their activities, officers resented his "interference." In 1821, when Congress mandated that the army have only one major general and two brigadier generals, Calhoun ordered the sole major general to Washington and designated him the commanding general. Theoretically, the secretary could now direct operations through this officer.

Most officials considered the general staff and the commanding general important reforms, but administrative chaos persisted. The bureau chiefs, who held commissions for life, often refused to cooperate among themselves, defied the secretary, and confused their own bureau's welfare with the army's well-being. A rivalry developed between line officers and those assigned to the staff bureaus. Finally, the commanding general had no clear responsibilities. He could not really command the army, for that would usurp the secretary's duty as the president's appointed deputy. What did he command? No one knew for sure, but the bureau chiefs were certain that he exercised no control over them. The secretary, bureau chiefs, and commanding general struggled for primacy, the secretary received no unified professional advice, and no agency had clear responsibility for mobilization planning.

Militia reform, as usual, fared poorly. Reform proposals periodically appeared, but "classing" systems that might transform the common militia into a reliable reserve met vehement objections. Critics charged that the best class would evolve into a regular army while the remainder of the militia would decay, and that a widespread martial spirit was as essential as widespread voting to preserve liberty.[50] Regulars reinforced by volunteers had replaced the militia as the foundation for defense. Many of these volunteers would come from volunteer militia companies, which proliferated in the antebellum era and pushed for an enhanced role as an organized reserve.[51]

As for coastal fortifications, few could forget Fort McHenry's role in repulsing the British at Baltimore. The war scares of 1794 and 1807 had prompted fortification programs, but now strategists proposed a methodical, permanent peacetime program. The Madison administration established a Board of Engineers and Fortifications to study the subject. Its first report (February 1821) was equal in importance to Calhoun's expansible army

---

[50] NASP, Military Affairs, Vol. 2, p. 77–78; Vol. 14, p. 331–32.
[51] For examples of the volunteer militia seeking an enhanced role, see NASP, Military Affairs, Vol. 14, pp. 367–68, 391.

plan, for it outlined a theory of defense that prevailed until the 1880s. The navy was the first line of defense, declared the board; but since it would probably remain small, seacoast fortifications must support it. The board recommended fortifying fifty positions at a cost of almost $18,000,000. While admitting that the price was high, it emphasized that the cost would be spread over several years and that "the final result is to endure for ages."[52] The program went forward, but slowly and beset by difficulties; yet by the 1850s a substantial system was nearing completion, although the works remained inadequately armed and garrisoned.[53]

The War of 1812 also exposed the handicaps that poor transportation imposed on war-making. In the pre-Civil War era, the army helped to improve the nation's rivers and to build railroads and canals. These investments furthered commerce – but as strategists recognized, in war *time is power* and an increasingly dense transportation system would facilitate military operations.[54]

In 1816, for the first time, the United States undertook a long-range peacetime program of naval construction. Congress authorized nine 74-gun ships of the line, twelve 44-gun frigates, and three steam batteries. Most of these large warships were eventually completed but were often less useful than the host of smaller ships that Congress periodically authorized. No great nation threatened America's growing maritime commerce, but pirates and fast privateers did, and catching them with ships of the line and frigates was difficult. To protect commerce, the navy did not organize battle fleets but instead divided its ships into small squadrons that sailed in geographic areas called stations.

From 1815 to 1842 a Board of Navy Commissioners composed of three captains helped the Secretary of the Navy administer the service. The board provided him with technical assistance on matters such as the procurement of naval stores, but it had no direct policy functions. The board was conservative and lagged behind the rapid changes occurring in maritime technology, prompting Congress to replace it with a bureau system in 1842. Like their War Department counterparts, the bureaus provided specialized management with each chief acting independently and reporting to the secretary. Congress also created a Corps of Engineers to service the navy's few steam warships, thus acknowledging steam's growing importance. As with the army's bureaucratic changes, these innovations were reformist in intent but led to administrative fragmentation and bitter staff-line controversies.

Because of the navy's unsystematic growth and the relative antiquity of its ships compared to European models, critics were soon arguing that it was inadequate to protect the seacoast and the nation's commercial interests. By the 1850s, for instance, American commercial tonnage ranked first in the

---

52 Ibid., Vol. 3, pp. 142–56.
53 Ibid., Vol. 2, p. 27; Vol. 3, p. 237–38, 318; NASP, *Naval Affairs*, Vol. 1, p. 140.
54 NASP, *Military Affairs*, Vol. 14, pp. 244–45.

world, yet its navy ranked fifth.[55] Despite its comparatively small size, the navy played an aggressive role in expanding commerce. Between 1798 and 1883 it conducted more than 130 punitive expeditions, primarily in support of commerce. Naval expeditions combining scientific, commercial, and diplomatic purposes scoured the globe, and naval officers negotiated treaties opening up new opportunities. The most famous such officer was Matthew C. Perry, who negotiated a treaty in the mid-1850s that opened two Japanese ports.[56]

The naval-commercial alliance produced astonishing results. Total exports (including re-exports) increased from $20,000,000 in 1790 to $334,000,000 in 1860.[57] Tocqueville toured the United States amidst this stupendous maritime commercial expansion and could not help but be impressed. "When I contemplate the ardor with which the Anglo-Americans prosecute commerce, the advantages which aid them, and the success of their undertakings," he marveled, "I cannot help believing that they will one day become the foremost maritime power of the globe. They are born to rule the seas, as the Romans were to conquer the world."[58]

The Romans were not the only avid territorial conquerors. Americans proved adept at using war or the threat of war to conquer a continental empire, primarily at the expense of the Indians, Spain, and Mexico. Although raw power fueled this expansion, Americans cloaked their aggressiveness in self-righteousness and masked their rapaciousness with a two-sided argument summed up by the phrase "Manifest Destiny." Since expansion was the nation's destiny, the process was *inevitable*. The North American continent was the country's "proper dominion," said John Quincy Adams. "From the time when we became an independent people it was as much a law of nature that this should become our pretension as that the Mississippi should flow to the sea."[59] Expansion was also *beneficial* because merely preserving liberty was not enough; others must be brought under its beneficent sway. "To arrest our peaceful and onward march," said a congressman, "would be treason to the cause of human liberty. . . ."[60]

Although hardly peaceful, the march went onward and always entailed pushing aside Indian tribes that inhabited areas coveted by whites. In the 1830s, the government established a permanent Indian Territory west of

---

55 *NASP, Naval Affairs*, Vol. 1, pp. 179, 200. Also see pp. 189, 191. Among the navy's foremost critics was President Franklin Pierce; see Richardson, Vol. 5, pp. 288, 339.
56 John H. Schroeder, *Shaping a Maritime Empire: The Commercial and Diplomatic Role of the American Navy 1829–1861* (Westwood, CT, 1985) and David F. Long, *Gold Braid and Foreign Relations: Diplomatic Activities of U.S. Naval Officers 1798–1883* (Annapolis, 1988) both stress the navy's active role in expanding commerce.
57 Bureau of the Census, *Historical Statistics of the United States: Colonial Times to 1970* (Washington, 1975) part 2, pp. 885–86.
58 Tocqueville, Vol. 1, p. 447.
59 Charles Francis Adams, ed. *Memoirs of John Quincy Adams: Comprising Portions of His Diary From 1795 to 1848* (1874–77), Vol. 4, p. 438.
60 Norman A. Graebner, ed., *Manifest Destiny* (Indianapolis, 1968), p. 73.

Missouri and Arkansas and compelled tribes in the east to exchange their traditional homelands for land there. Despite President Andrew Jackson's promise to the Indians that Indian Territory would be theirs forever, it endured for only about thirty years. In the post-Civil War era, it vanished under a deluge of land-hungry and gold-seeking whites, who pressured the government into a policy of concentrating the Indians on reservations, usually in areas settlers did not want. The army had enforced removal, and now enforced the reservation system.

Spain also felt American power. The United States acquired the Floridas in part by fomenting a local revolt and demonstrating Spanish weakness through repeated invasions. The Adams-Onis Treaty (1819) resulted from assertive diplomacy against a debilitated adversary, and not only put the seal on America's possession of the Floridas but also established a favorable western boundary for the Louisiana Purchase, including Spain's claims to Oregon territory.

Mexico also blocked the path of "Manifest Destiny." Americans draped the Mexican War in soothing rhetoric about Mexico's "destiny" to become part of the United States and thereby become "free and happy."[61] But the purpose of President James K. Polk was to acquire Mexico's northern provinces, especially California and New Mexico, and an unquestioned claim to Texas statehood. In May 1846, having found a pretext to proclaim that "Mexico has passed the boundary of the United States, has invaded our territory, and shed American blood upon American soil," Polk asked for and Congress declared war.[62]

Although a neophyte in military matters, Polk dominated the war effort. Aided by growing national wealth and population, by the relatively new military bureaucracies, and by improved transportation and communications (especially steamships and the telegraph), Polk imposed his will on the war in ways unavailable to Adams in the Quasi-War and Madison in the War of 1812. In consultation with his cabinet, Polk even had contingency orders drafted eight months before the war began – the country's first example of *prewar* strategic planning. Once fighting began, he grasped the diverse reins of war – strategy, military appointments, finances, diplomacy, and federal-state relations – and held them tightly for the duration. All he wanted from his "friends in Congress and elsewhere" was that they allow him "to conduct the War with Mexico as I thought proper, and not plan the campaign for me & without consulting me."[63]

Polk devised a strategy appropriate to his limited ends of acquiring Mexico's two northernmost provinces and securing American claims to Texas.

61 Ibid., pp. 137, 213.
62 Milo Milton Quaife, ed., *The Diary of James K. Polk During His Presidency 1845 to 1849* (Chicago, 1910), Vol. 1, 496–97. Polk's war message is in Richardson, Vol. 4, pp. 437–43.
63 Quaife, Vol. 1, pp. 8–12, 427–28. Also see Leonard D. White, "Polk (1845–1848)" in May.

The strategy was a peripheral one, designed to achieve his policy goals without striking at the heart of enemy power in Mexico City. The president established a blockade to exert economic pressure and forestall foreign aid to Mexico, and ordered the conquest of California and New Mexico. With relatively little difficulty the blockade tightened and United States forces occupied the desired provinces and penetrated into three other provinces. Despite this stunning success, the strategy failed because Mexico refused to capitulate. Responding to this unforeseen circumstance, the administration applied greater pressure by capturing Vera Cruz and then driving on Mexico City. The new direct strategy was seemingly successful; in September 1847 General Winfield Scott's army captured the enemy capital.

But to Polk's intense frustration, the enemy still refused to negotiate. As the toll in blood and treasure increased, Polk believed the United States should take as an indemnity more territory than he had originally contemplated. Some expansionists even demanded "All Mexico." However, an emissary dispatched before Polk escalated his war aims finally secured the original territorial demands in the Treaty of Guadalupe Hidalgo of February 1848. Although many of Polk's supporters thought the nation should hold out for additional land, Polk and the Senate accepted and ratified the treaty.

One reason that Polk may have accepted less than he wanted was that the war, like the Quasi-War and War of 1812, sparked domestic dissent. Since a decision for war is a *political* act, it involves political *judgment,* which may or may not be wise or just. Many Americans questioned Polk's judgment. The rival Whig Party was almost unanimous in its opposition, and a small group of "Conscience Whigs" was especially vituperative. Joining the Whigs were pacifists, abolitionists, and two dissident Democratic factions, the followers of Martin Van Buren and those of John C. Calhoun.

Anti-war activists hammered at many themes. Almost all of them considered "Mr. Polk's War" iniquitous and unnecessary, an unprovoked war of imperial conquest. They ridiculed "Manifest Destiny" as a transparently false claim that Democrats used to try to make an unjust war palatable. Many dissenters detested Polk's pro-southern orientation and feared the war would lead to the expansion of slavery, which some considered morally wrong and others viewed as a political issue so explosive that it might rip the Union apart. A few disliked the thought of annexing Mexican territory with its "impure races" supposedly unfit for liberty. Polk's vigorous exercise of executive powers revived Radical Whig fears about despotism. Critics denounced the Democrats' use of a few "perverted phrases," such as "*Our country, right or wrong,*" as gibberish.[64] Still others opposed the war simply because they loathed Polk. Many anti-war advocates supported the cause of Mexico: "We only hope that, if blood has had to flow, that it has been that of the American," an abolitionist newspaper wrote, "and that the next news we

[64] Graebner, pp. 239, 241.

shall hear will be that General Scott and his army are in the hands of the Mexicans. . . . We wish him and his troops no bodily harm, but the most utter defeat and disgrace."[65]

As America expanded from 888,811 square miles in 1790 to 3,022,387 in 1853, it also experienced astonishing population and economic growth. The country had a population of fewer than 4,000,000 in 1790; by 1880 it exceeded 50,000,000.[66] In the mid-1840s, a Senator predicted that among those yet alive some "will live to see our Confederacy numbering a population equal to the Chinese empire." Although not of Chinese proportions, by the late nineteenth century the population of the United States had surpassed that of the United Kingdom, France, or Germany.[67]

Agricultural efficiency, economic productivity, and transportation improvements matched the population explosion. In 1839, farmers grew 378,000,000 bushels of corn; forty years later they produced 1,755,000,000 bushels.[68] In industry, Americans harnessed their individual entrepreneurship and acquisitiveness to ambition and technology; unhindered by government restrictions, they transformed the United States into the second leading economic power by 1860 (Great Britain was first). Between the Civil War and World War I the United States became the world's leading industrial nation. By 1890 its pig iron production was 1,300,000 tons greater than Britain's, and exceeded the combined total of France, Russia, Germany, Austria-Hungary, Italy, and Japan.[69]

One factor fueling the surging economy was what the British called the "American system of manufactures," which meant goods that were mass produced by specialized machines, highly standardized, and consisted of interchangeable component parts. By the 1830s this new system began to replace home manufactures because the United States enjoyed extensive natural resources and a society (at least in the North) that emphasized individual risk-taking, ingenuity, mass education, and widespread literacy, which were attributes that encouraged the creative thinking that led to organizational and technological innovations.[70]

Some policymakers believed the country's latent military assets, combined with its geographic location, made the United States so secure that it could

---

65   Quoted in John H. Schroeder, *Mr. Polk's War: American Opposition and Dissent 1846–1848* (Madison, WI, 1973), p. 105.
66   *Historical Statistics of the United States*, part 1, p. 8.
67   Graebner, p. 158; B.R. Mitchell, *European Historical Statistics, 1750–1970* (New York, 1975), p. 20, 24.
68   *Historical Statistics of the United States*, part 1, p. 512.
69   Paul M. Kennedy, "The First World War and the International Power System," *International Security*, 9 (1984), p. 13.
70   Many aspects of the "American system" remain controversial; see Otto Mayr and Robert C. Post, eds., *Yankee Enterprise: The Rise of the American System of Manufactures* (Washington, 1981). Merritt Roe Smith, ed., *Military Enterprise and Technological Change: Perspectives on the American Experience* (Cambridge, MA, 1985) is a superb collections of essays.

nearly eliminate military preparations and expenditures. A proponent of this viewpoint was Jackson's Secretary of War, Lewis Cass, who argued that "no nation would embark in the Quixotic enterprise of conquering this country." Even if war occurred the United States would have time to mobilize its resources and to use its rapidly growing transportation network to concentrate overwhelming force on a threatened position. Only on the seaboard was the nation exposed to even a minimal threat, and the best defense was a larger navy and modest fortifications to protect coastal cities from a coup de main or escalade.[71]

Many strategists were less optimistic than Cass: "A country exposed as ours is upon every side to the assaults of an enemy by sea and land," wrote Secretary of War John C. Spencer, "can not be defended by small means. And the wisdom of that economy which would postpone the preparation of adequate means for such a purpose may well be doubted."[72] Pessimists feared a third war with England, a second with France, or a conflict with Spain over many long-standing clashing interests. Especially worrisome was the application of steam to naval warfare, which negated the influence of winds, currents, and tides, and had "in point of time, deprived the Atlantic of two thirds of its width, and in certainty of movement and accuracy of calculation has narrowed it still more."[73] The possibility of a surprise attack had seemingly increased dramatically.

During the mid-1830s a war scare arose when France was slow to fulfill a treaty concerning spoliations claims. President Jackson talked of injustice and a stain on the national honor, a rhetoric hauntingly similar to that before the War of 1812, and called for reprisals.[74] No sooner had the French scare dissipated than a crisis arose with England. From the late 1830s until the mid-1840s British and American interests clashed over the Canadian border, Oregon, California, Texas, and Mexico. Policymakers took the possibility of war seriously enough to begin preparations; only in retrospect does it appear obvious that a third Anglo-American war was most unlikely.[75]

Exacerbating such war scares was the post-1815 revolution in military

---

71 *NASP, Military Affairs,* Vol. 1, pp. 207–49. Tocqueville also believed Americans were perfectly secure; see Vol. 1, pp. 299, 331, 405. One of America's most eminent historians argued that between 1815 and 1941, this nation's "security was not only remarkable effective, but it was relatively free." See C. Vann Woodward, "The Age of Reinterpretation," Publication Number 35, Service Center for Teachers of History (Washington, D.C., reprinted from *The American Historical Review,* Vol. 66).

72 *NASP, Military Affairs,* Vol. 11, p. 233.

73 Ibid., Vol. 3, p. 292. Also see Vol. 2, pp. 92, 163–64, 175, and *NASP, Naval Affairs,* Vol. 1, pp. 139–45, 199.

74 John M. Belohlavek, *"Let the Eagle Soar!" The Foreign Policy of Andrew Jackson* (Lincoln, NE, 1985), p. 11. *NASP, Military Affairs,* Vol. 1, pp. 182–84, 191; Vol. 3, pp. 194–95.

75 Two excellent studies of Anglo-American tensions are Howard Jones, *To the Webster-Ashburton Treaty: A Study in Anglo-American Relations 1783–1843* (Chapel Hill, 1977) and Reginald C. Stuart, *United States Expansionism and British North America 1775–1871* (Chapel Hill, 1988). Also see *NASP, Naval Affairs,* Vol. 1, pp. 160, 163.

technology, which caused anxiety among strategists as they pondered a bewildering range of developments. "A period of ten years has become sufficient, in point of duration," wrote Secretary of War John Bell, "to mark an epoch in the onward progress of modern invention and improvement. Even five years may modify, materially, plans of defense now reputed wisest and most indispensable."[76] So swiftly did technology become obsolete that a congressional committee suggested building a disposable navy. Instead of using iron, the navy should rely on cheaply built vessels of white oak, sell them when they decayed, and build new ships "so as to keep the navy up with all the improvements of the day, and in a condition to introduce, without sacrifice, any new invention."[77]

Ironically, the next crisis came not from a European invasion or technological breakthrough, but within America. The Civil War that began in April 1861 seemed to confirm the Federalists' worst fears: that the United States would splinter into several governments and kill the experiment in liberty. President Abraham Lincoln squarely confronted the problem. The war, he said, "forces us to ask: 'Is there in all republics this inherent and fatal weakness?' 'Must a government, of necessity, be too *strong* for the liberties of its own people, or too *weak* to maintain its own existence?'"[78]

THE CIVIL WAR

To capture the Revolutionary generation's attention, Thomas Paine could not have done better than to label his thoughts as *Common Sense* and to offer "nothing more than simple facts, plain arguments, and common sense." As Paine understood, the American character, a product of intense individualism and minimal institutional constraint, was pragmatic and flexible. Revolutionary War military leaders, for example, recognized that experience was often "the best of schools and the safest guide in human affairs"; yet they rejected slavish adherence to European maxims and introduced a pragmatic element into the American military tradition – as exemplified by Washington's abundant common sense and practicality.[79] Dennis Hart Mahan, who taught "The Science of War" at the Military Academy, followed in this tradition. Cadets called him "Old Cobbon Sense" (a nasal infection impaired his pronunciation) because of his injunctions to use judgment and common sense rather than rely on the rote application of so-called principles of war.

---

[76] *NASP, Military Affairs,* Vol. 2, p. 173.
[77] *NASP, Naval Affairs,* Vol. 1, p. 171–79.
[78] Roy P. Basler, ed., *The Collected Works of Abraham Lincoln* (New Brunswick, NJ, 1953), Vol. 4, p. 426.
[79] Irwin Glusker and Richard M. Ketchum, eds., *American Testament: Fifty Great Documents of American History* (New York, 1971), p. 25; Richard K. Showman, ed., *The Papers of Nathanael Greene* (Chapel Hill, 1976-) Vol. 2, p. 232; Don Higginbotham, *George Washington and the American Military Tradition* (Athens, GA, 1985), pp. 78–79, 89.

And Lincoln, whose policy often was to have no policy, had little concern for consistency or doctrinaire solutions.[80]

Strategy-making reflected the national character. The nation had no institutions or systematic procedures to devise formal doctrines, and the military establishment's institutional linkages were so weak that, for example, a commanding general could simply move his peacetime headquarters away from Washington.[81] When a problem arose, strategists thought it through and responded in a pragmatic, flexible manner. The Union's strategy illustrates the personal, noninstitutionalized nature of strategy-making.

Although space limitations preclude a discussion of Confederate strategy-making, such a discussion would simply reinforce this point. The North was fortunate to have men of considerable intellect – not necessarily of the formally educated type, but of the common sense species – in important positions when the war began and others rose to high positions as the war continued. The Union faced such daunting strategic tasks that only men with the ability to think clearly and profoundly could master them.

Since antebellum population growth and economic modernization centered in the North, its *quantitative* resources were superior. In 1861 the Union had a white population of 20,000,000 and the South 6,000,000. Immigration and the recruitment of black men replenished the North's manpower supply, while the South's remained static, although slave labor allowed it to put practically its entire adult white male population into uniform. The Union dwarfed the Confederacy in financial and industrial resources. In 1860 the North had 110,000 manufacturing *establishments*, the southern states had 110,000 industrial *workers*, and the states remaining in the Union manufactured more than nine-tenths of the country's industrial goods. Nor could the Confederacy's raw materials base support much industrial expansion. The unequal tale was the same with railroads; in 1861 the North had 22,000 miles of track, the South 9,000.[82]

The disparities in men, money, and matériel were not as daunting as they seemed for two reasons. First, many imponderables could reduce the disparities. One uncertainty was the border slave states. If Delaware, Maryland, Kentucky, and Missouri joined the Confederacy, the resource imbalances would be substantially redressed. Another uncertainty was the war's length. Both sides began with little mobilized strength. If the South won a quick victory, the North would never have the time to convert its resources into actual military power. European intervention on the Con-

---

[80] James L. Morrison, Jr., *"The Best School in the World": West Point, the Pre-Civil War Years 1833–1866* (Kent, OH, 1985), pp. 95–96; David Donald, *Lincoln Reconsidered: Essays on the Civil War Era* (New York, 1956), Chapter 7 ("Abraham Lincoln and the American Pragmatic Tradition").

[81] Commanding General Winfield Scott moved his headquarters to New York; after the Civil War, Commanding General William T. Sherman went even further – to St. Louis.

[82] For a brief overview of the statistical balance, see E.B. Long, *The Civil War Day by Day: An Almanac 1861–1865* (Garden City, NY, 1971), pp. 700–28.

federacy's behalf, which statesmen in both sections considered a possibility, could negate most Northern advantages. And what about high-level leadership? A comparison of the commanders in chief, Lincoln and Jefferson Davis, seemingly favored the South. The former's military service consisted of a few months in the militia, while the latter's included a West Point education, a gallant Mexican War record, and four years as Secretary of War. By training and experience, Davis appeared well-qualified to lead a wartime nation; Lincoln seemed equally unqualified. A final unanswered question was whether Union or Confederate morale would be more durable. History apparently favored the South. Many Southerners believed that since they were following in the Revolutionary forefathers' footsteps by fighting for home and hearth against a tyrannical government, victory would inevitably be theirs.

Britain's experience in the Revolution indicated a second reason why numerical disparities did not unduly discourage the Confederates. Despite immense advantages over the colonies in resources and manpower, Britain had lost. Now the North was cast in the conqueror's role, and would have to seize an enormous area – the Confederacy was larger than the combined size of Germany, France, Spain, Portugal, and the United Kingdom. When matched against the prospect of occupying and patrolling such immense spaces, the North's manpower resources looked inadequate.

Failure to destroy Confederate armies in one or two great battles made the North's task even more difficult. Except for the invasion of Pennsylvania in 1863, the South operated on friendly soil; Confederate commanders could depend on the local population to pinpoint the enemy's location and to conceal their own. The North could rarely achieve overwhelming numerical superiority on the battlefield. A study of sixty battles revealed that the Union armies averaged only a 37 percent numerical advantage over the Confederates. The North's armies became weaker the farther they advanced as commanders detached troops for garrison and guard duty along ever-lengthening supply lines. The South understood the North's dependence on large-capacity logistical lines and made raids against railroads and telegraph wires part of its strategy. By early 1864 almost half of Union troops in the field were occupying captured territory and guarding communication and logistical lines. And the situation could only get worse.[83]

Conquering the South required complex planning and timing, and no one immediately perceived how to fit the pieces together. Union strategy evolved slowly, with the ultimate result being the total exhaustion of the South's logistical resources and the near-annihilation of its armies. In general, the North stressed exhaustion in the vast western theater between the Appalachian Mountains and the Mississippi, where its armies had room to

[83] James M. McPherson, *Ordeal By Fire: The Civil War and Reconstruction* (New York, 1982), pp. 186–87; Richard E. Beringer, et. al., *Why the South Lost the Civil War* (Athens, GA, 1986), pp. 249–50.

maneuver and the rivers provided good initial penetration routes. In the eastern theater – constricted between Chesapeake Bay and the Blue Ridge Mountains, and with Robert E. Lee's Army of Northern Virginia blocking any southward advance – the emphasis was on annihilation. Not surprisingly, ten of the war's fourteen bloodiest battles occurred between the Union Army of the Potomac and Lee's army.[84]

For the Confederacy, the North's simultaneous pursuit of exhaustion and annihilation produced a vicious cycle. As Union armies in the West occupied territory, severed rail lines, and captured cities, they gradually exhausted the South's ability to make war and weakened Confederate morale, especially on the home front. In both theaters the North hammered at the enemy's armies, and eventually nearly annihilated Lee's army and the Army of Tennessee. As Confederate morale ebbed and Union forces advanced, the South was less able to defend its remaining resources and communications networks. By late 1864 the South's capacity for defense was so reduced that the Union could send massive raids into its shrinking domain with impunity.

Northern strategy emerged from the combined thought of Winfield Scott, Lincoln, Ulysses S. Grant, and William T. Sherman. Scott devised the first coherent strategic proposal, the so-called "Anaconda Plan," named after the giant snake that slowly crushes its victims. The strategy was one of exhaustion, relying "on the sure operation of a complete blockade" and "a powerful movement down the Mississippi" by an expedition of up to twenty steam gunboats and a 60,000-man army to "envelop the insurgent states and bring them to terms with less bloodshed than by any other plan." Scott knew that "the greatest obstacle in the way of this plan" was "the impatience of our patriotic and loyal Union friends," who would urge immediate, vigorous action. As Scott envisioned it, his plan would seal the Confederacy off from Europe and isolate the trans-Mississippi West. The eastern part of the Confederacy would become a peninsula surrounded on three sides by naval power and confronted on the landward side by Union armies. Having grasped the victim in its constricting coils, the North would wait for the Confederacy to suffocate.[85]

Scott's plan meshed with Lincoln's perception of the rebellion and his original war aim. Lincoln believed pro-Union men were the majority in every seceded state except South Carolina but that secessionist minorities had temporarily overwhelmed them. He hoped for sectional reconciliation through a reassertion of Southern Unionism. Under Scott's plan, the North would follow an indirect, stand-off policy that involved little of the bloodshed that would complicate the task of restoring national harmony. But Lincoln's belief in widespread Southern Unionism was wrong, and too many people, as Scott feared, preferred to kill the Confederacy with a rattlesnake's

[84] McPherson, p. 479.
[85] *War of the Rebellion: A Compilation of the Official Records of the Union and Confederate Armies* (Washington, 1880–1901), series 1, Vol. 51, part 1, pp. 369–70.

quick strike rather than the anaconda's slow squeeze. Scott nevertheless had pinpointed two tasks that the Union had to accomplish: blockade, and control of the Mississippi.

To Scott's insights Lincoln added an astute perception. Nothing better illustrated the noninstitutionalized, personal nature of strategy-making than the president's performance. Knowing nothing about warfare – and knowing enough to know he knew nothing – Lincoln taught himself the subject, borrowing military works from the Library of Congress and pouring over them whenever time permitted. Diligent study, a powerful intellect, and remarkable common sense made Lincoln a superb strategist. While many commanders focused on capturing key territory such as Richmond, Lincoln grasped that the Confederate armies were equally vital objectives. He urged his generals to destroy them if possible and suffered near-depression when they routinely failed. Above all, he pressed commanders to undertake the relentless simultaneous advances that the North's greater resources made possible and which negated the South's use of interior lines.[86]

The idea of successive, simultaneous advances ran afoul of mid-nineteenth century principles of mass and concentration, which demanded one offensive at a time. In the winter of 1861–62, the Army of the Potomac's commander, George B. McClellan, developed a plan that was the antithesis of Lincoln's insight. A single massive army (his own) of 273,000 men and 600 artillery pieces would flatten the South in one campaign.[87] Not until 1864 did Lincoln find a general, Ulysses S. Grant, of sufficient intellectual prowess and flexibility to perceive the virtue of simultaneous advances. Grant's 1864 campaign plan demonstrated a strategic vision equal to Lincoln's; it embraced all theaters, put simultaneous pressure on all fronts, and worked "all parts of the Army together, and, somewhat, towards a common center."[88]

Grant also resolved a limitation inherent in simultaneous advances. Rivers were convenient invasion routes, but once the North controlled the Cumberland, Tennessee, and Mississippi, it would have to depend on railroads. And wherever railroads supported penetrations, Confederate guerrillas or cavalry could destroy tracks and bridges, creating insuperable logistical problems. Grant's response becomes clear only by extrapolation and interpolation since he never wrote it down (another example of informal strategy-making, nineteenth century style); he sent army-sized raids to devastate the rebels' remaining logistical base. The raiding strategy eliminated the need to garrison more territory and to protect supply lines since the raiding force moved rapidly

---

[86] Basler, Vol. 5, p. 98.
[87] Stephen W. Sears, *George B. McClellan: The Young Napoleon* (New York, 1988), pp. 98–99.
[88] John Y. Simon, *The Papers of Ulysses S. Grant* (Carbondale, IL, 1967-), Vol. 10, p. 251. The opening paragraphs of Grant's report of his operations from 9 March 1864 until the end of the war explain how completely he agreed with Lincoln's idea of simultaneous advances; see ibid., Vol. 15, pp. 164–66.

and lived primarily off the land while destroying everything of military value in its path.[89]

The raiding strategy's foremost example was Sherman's "March to the Sea." In November 1864, Sherman left Atlanta with a 62,000-man army that cut a 250-mile swath to Savannah. An intensely cerebral man, Sherman added another purpose to these raids: psychological warfare. Instead of devastating only resources with an unmistakable military purpose, he also warred against morale by consciously making the entire population – old men, women, children, the rich and the poor – directly feel the weight of the war.

Several ad hoc boards supplemented the individuals who made Union strategy. As Secretary of the Navy Gideon Welles expanded the navy to tighten the blockade, he appointed a Strategy Board to advise him on ways to make it most effective. And when Welles learned that the Confederates were building an ironclad, the *Virginia* (ex-*Merrimack*), to raise the blockade by sinking the Union's wooden ships, he convened an Ironclad Board, which recommended that the Navy Department let contracts for three different experimental ironclads. One of them, the *Monitor,* arrived at Hampton Roads in March 1862 just in time to fight the *Virginia* to a tactical stalemate in the world's first ironclad duel.

In the War Department, Secretary of War Edwin M. Stanton sought to improve logistical coordination through a War Board of bureau chiefs chaired by Ethan Allen Hitchcock, whom Lincoln and Stanton appointed as their personal military adviser. Although the board soon ceased formal meetings, it did foster interbureau cooperation. Another ad hoc administrative arrangement had modern overtones. When Lincoln appointed Grant to replace Henry W. Halleck as commanding general in March 1864, the War Department improvised the position of chief of staff to facilitate communications between Lincoln and Grant and between Grant and his department commanders. Halleck ably filled that position. But like the Strategy, Ironclad, and War Boards, this new command arrangement was an expedient. At war's end the department returned to its awkward prewar system.

As in other wars, the Union's objectives were adaptable. In suppressing the South, Lincoln had hoped to avoid "a violent and remorseless revolutionary struggle," yet he emphasized that he would employ "all indispensable means" to preserve the Union.[90] As the war assumed a magnitude and duration that neither belligerent had foreseen, Lincoln believed that preserving the Union required the addition of a second war aim – emancipation – which gave a revolutionary purpose to the North's war effort. Emancipation was necessary to forestall English intervention, infuse a moral dimension into the war and invigorate northern morale, and tap a new and vital manpower

[89] Herman Hattaway and Archer Jones, *How the North Won* (Champaign-Urbana, 1982) is the best account of Northern strategy.
[90] Basler, Vol. 5, pp. 48–49.

reservoir: the slave population. Ultimately, almost 180,000 black men, most of them former slaves, donned Union blue.[91]

So great was the manpower pinch that the government overcame traditional inhibitions about impinging on individual liberty and state autonomy, and imposed conscription. But the intrusion was a limited effort to spur volunteering rather than to raise men directly. The law worked as intended. The draft produced only 120,000 enlistments (6 percent of the total). Yet in the war's last two years the North enlisted more than 1,000,000 men, mostly volunteers motivated by the fear of conscription and the lure of lucrative bounties.[92] Conscription, like the ad hoc boards in the Navy and War Departments, was an expedient. In its next two major wars, against Spain and in the Philippines, the nation relied on volunteers.

As in earlier conflicts, support for the war was far from unanimous. From the beginning some Democrats argued that coercion was unjust and unwise; novel exercises of governmental power such as emancipation and conscription fueled anti-war sentiment. Peace Democrats (Copperheads to their enemies) urged resistance to emancipation and to the draft, discouraged volunteering, encouraged desertions, and even advocated resistance to the war itself. They were not without influence. More than 161,000 men eligible for the draft failed to provide substitutes, pay the commutation fee, or report when summoned.[93]

To suppress anti-war activity, Lincoln curtailed civil liberties, allowing military authorities to arrest thousands of people, occasionally repress newspapers, and censor reporters' telegraphic dispatches. He also suspended the writ of habeas corpus, an act Congress sanctioned. Copperheads accused "King Lincoln" of despotism. Republicans countered these accusations of tyranny with charges of treason, and Lincoln assured northerners that infringements of liberty during an unprecedented crisis did not mean they would be denied their liberties "throughout the indefinite peaceful future which I trust lies before them. . . ."[94]

Wise Union strategy and the bravery of northern soldiers ensured that the United States would have an indefinite though far from peaceful future. By mid-summer 1863 the Mississippi was in Union hands, splitting the Confederacy and depriving the eastern half of supplies from Texas and also from Europe through Mexico. With great difficulty the North fought through

91 On the role of black troops, see Ira Berlin, ed., *Freedom: A Documentary History of Emancipation 1861–1867*, series 2, *The Black Military Experience* (Cambridge, MA, 1982) and Joseph T. Glatthaar, *Forged in Battle: The Civil War Alliance of Black Soldiers and White Officers* (New York, 1990).
92 Eugene C. Murdock, *One Million Men: The Civil War Draft in the North* (Madison, 1971) and James W. Geary, *We Need Men: The Union Draft in the Civil War* (De Kalb, IL, 1991) discuss Union conscription.
93 Peter Levine, "Draft Evasion in the North during the Civil War, 1863–1865," *The Journal of American History*, 67 (1981), p. 819.
94 Basler, Vol. 6, p. 267. An excellent study of this topic is Mark E. Neely, Jr., *The Fate of Liberty: Abraham Lincoln and Civil Liberties* (New York, 1991).

Tennessee to Chattanooga, where it severed the South's best east-west rail line, and then struggled on through the ghastly summer of 1864 to Atlanta. From there Sherman marched to Savannah, bisecting the South a second time and savaging its logistical base. In the Virginia theater, with its long roll call of spectacular battles, northern armies ground Lee's army into oblivion. As combined land and naval forces opened the Mississippi, as Union armies cracked the Appalachian barrier, ravaged southern logistics, and battered the Armies of Northern Virginia and of Tennessee, the Union navy tightened the blockade. If it never quite became a noose, it certainly had the South worried about the hangman.

In a mighty display of military prowess, the North was growing *stronger* after fighting an enormous war for four years. As Lincoln pointed out in December 1864, the Union could continue the war indefinitely because it had more men and matériel than when the war began, and its resources were apparently inexhaustible.[95] Despite the extreme difficulty of the North's strategic task, the mobilized strength of half the nation had not only utterly defeated the other half, but had also forestalled foreign intervention.

Lincoln and many other northerners believed the Union had fought a war of cosmic significance, transcending national boundaries into the infinite future. He believed, as had the Founding Fathers, that the United States had a special destiny to nurture its democratic institutions as an example for the world. In 1862 he said that the North "shall nobly save, or meanly lose, the last best, hope of earth," a theme that he repeatedly emphasized.[96] Whether the United States has a special destiny is beyond objective proof, but the war definitely delivered a deathblow to secession and considerably weakened state sovereignty. Within the federal system, the balance of power shifted from the states to the federal government. People no longer said "the United States *are*" but "the United States *is*."

By mid-1865 the United States had achieved the preconditions for great power status. The Founding Fathers had established a government that, as the Civil War proved, would endure as a single entity, one with a huge territory fabulously rich in natural resources, a large and enlightened population, and unparalleled economic strength. The nation had also demonstrated its ability to generate enormous military power. That power stood ready should ambition or necessity impel United States leaders to "sway the destinies" of the world.

[95] Ibid., Vol. 8, pp. 150–51.
[96] Ibid., Vol. 6, p. 537.

9

Strategic uncertainties of a nation-state: Prussia-Germany, 1871–1918

HOLGER H. HERWIG

Leopold von Ranke likened the state to an individual possessing a personality of its own and an idea that guided its actions and development. This analogy applies to the German military as well: its "personality" was a peculiarly Prussian strategic culture and its "idea" was its dual function as guarantor of domestic stability and executor of foreign policy. The army, in a word, served both monarch and state. Its primary function was to maintain order in a conservative Prussian monarchy and, concurrently, to identify and protect the national interests of a polyglot German Empire. The army prided itself on its pursuit of efficiency, but a host of institutional and socioeconomic fetters restrained it in that quest. The army's duality of purpose imposed constraints not only on its composition and recruitment, but also upon strategy – constraints that emerged clearly during the dramatic budgetary debates of 1912–13. This essay rejects the sterile debates about the "primacy" of either domestic or foreign affairs; both interact constantly and eventually combine to produce policy. Neither reigns supreme.[1]

The Prusso-German army was an institution at once simple and complex, with a strategic culture largely shaped by the three short wars of unification against Denmark, Austria, and France. To most outside observers, these were classics taken from the pages of Prussia's foremost military thinker, Carl von Clausewitz: the strong political leadership of Otto von Bismarck used armed force under Helmuth von Moltke for specific, limited political objectives and terminated operations upon attaining those objectives. When friction arose between soldier and statesman, the executive, Wilhelm I, exercised a moderating influence, usually in favor of the latter.

But in Prussian history, Bismarck was the exception rather than the rule. Successive chancellors either succumbed to military pressures or simply re-

---

[1] On the domestic and external functions of the armed forces, see Wolfgang Petter, "Armee und Flotte in Staat und Gesellschaft," in Dieter Langewiesche, ed., *Das deutsche Kaiserreich 1867/71 bis 1918: Bilanz einer Epoche* (Freiburg and Würzburg, 1984), pp. 117–26.

fused to "interfere" in the soldier's domain. Even the elder Moltke, a well-educated and broad-minded man, rejected the teachings of Clausewitz and instead espoused the notion that once war had broken out, politicians should recede from view until the achievement of a battlefield decision, whereupon they could reemerge to hammer out the peace. Moltke's successors took an almost perverse pride in not having read *Vom Kriege*.[2] Moreover, the victorious wars of 1864 to 1871 created a certain mythology: German commentators played down Bismarck's diplomatic preparations for war, if not altogether ignoring them; the decisive role of the general staff became sacrosanct, its officers revered as "demigods," and the regular army received credit for victory, with little acknowledgment of the contribution of the reserves. For all intents and purposes, the "blood and iron" of a royal standing army had forged unification under the leadership of an infallible general staff. After 1871, the almost universal emulation of the Prussian staff system merely reinforced well-established feelings of military superiority, if not downright arrogance. Only a few perceptive contemporary observers noted that the army remained an institution that walked a precarious tightrope between pre-industrial Prussian and industrial German ideals and needs.

The "making of strategy" in Germany evolved through a highly complex and diffuse process. Actually the Reich never possessed an overall military planning institution akin to the Committee of Imperial Defence in Britain or the *Conseil supérieure de guerre* in France. Instead, formulation of military policy devolved upon the Kaiser and through him upon the Prussian War Ministry, military cabinet, general staff, navy office, admiralty staff, and chancery.

The war minister held an impossible position entailing great responsibility but little power. As an active officer he was directly responsible to the Prussian king for the combat readiness of the Prussian army, yet as a minister he was a plenipotentiary to the Bundesrat (Federal Chamber) and as such had to answer to the Reichstag (Parliament) on fiscal matters. The Reichstag, for its part, exercised no control over the military beyond its right either to approve or to reject budgets every five or seven years. The military cabinet, acting solely as an agent of the Crown, was responsible for the army's personnel and appointments. The general staff enjoyed great power and prestige by tradition and example. Constitutionally, it was but "the first advisor of the Imperial Supreme Commander" and possessed no legal or constitutional power to impose its will even upon other agencies of the Prussian army.

With regard to the navy, the State Secretary of the Navy Office was both an active officer and a *federal* official who had to defend budgetary policy before the Reichstag. The chief of the admiralty staff, at least in theory, was

---

[2] For example, General Leo Geyr von Schweppenburg informed B.H. Liddell Hart as late as 1949: "The opinion on Clausewitz in our general staff was that he was a theoretician to be read by professors." Cited in Williamson Murray, "JCS Reform: A German Example?," in *JCS Reform: Proceedings of the Conference* (Newport, 1985), p. 82.

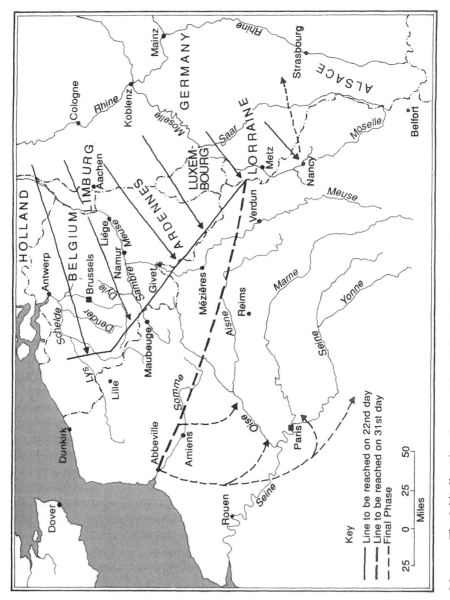

Map 9.1. The Schlieffen Plan. *Source.* Adapted from Paul M. Kennedy, ed., *The War Plans of the Great Powers,*

entrusted with formulating the nation's maritime strategy; in reality, the forceful personality of the head of the Navy Office, Admiral Alfred von Tirpitz, sharply curtailed his powers. Finally, the Imperial Chancellor as the only true *Reichsminister* held ultimate responsibility for all governmental affairs – except those pertaining to the emperor's jealously guarded powers of military command (*Kommandogewalt*). While the chancellor had to countersign imperial decrees and to present military and naval budgets to the Reichstag, he rarely, if ever, took an active part in strategic planning. Like the professional soldiers, he answered only to the Kaiser.

At least in theory, all differences of opinion or policy among the nation's soldiers and statesmen fell to the king-emperor to resolve. However, Wilhelm II was patently unable to fulfill such a central role, and consequently joint services planning remained largely unknown in the Second Reich. Indeed, only in the byzantine world of German military administration could the general staff – an office utterly devoid of constitutional power – have exercised de facto control over national strategy and command over all land forces.[3]

The Prussian army never lost sight of the fact that, in the words of Eckart Kehr, it was above all a "Praetorian instrument of power," and it jealously guarded its special social and constitutional position in the regime. On the one hand, it fought a sustained rearguard action against liberal reformers who wished to transform it into a national militia in accordance with the views of early nineteenth century reformers such as Hermann von Boyen, Neithardt von Gneisenau, and Gerhard von Scharnhorst. On the other hand, it resisted the efforts of conservative reformers, such as War Minister General Julius von Verdy du Vernois, to exploit universal military service to the fullest and make the army truly the training school of the nation. Concurrently, the Junker nobility, whose numerical and financial strength was eroding rapidly in the face of industrialization and urbanization, sought to maintain its privileged status in the officer corps, particularly with regard to staffing prestigious Garde and cavalry regiments as well as the general staff. Its noncommissioned officer corps and enlisted men continued to come from the supposedly reliable, conservative country men: as late as 1911, when only 42 percent of the population lived in rural areas, the countryside supplied 64 percent of all recruits and large urban centers a paltry 6 percent.[4]

Thus by 1900 the Prussian army found itself on the horns of a dilemma. While recognizing the need to fight a modern industrial war with million-man armies dependent upon urban industrial production, its leaders nevertheless refused to reform the Prusso-German social and constitutional system to reflect that necessity. Instead, they sought year after year to balance

3   See Holger H. Herwig, "The Dynamics of Necessity: German Military Policy during the First World War," in Allan R. Millett and Williamson Murray, eds., *Military Effectiveness* (Boston, 1988), Vol. 1, pp. 80–82.
4   Hans-Ulrich Wehler, *Das Deutsche Kaiserreich 1871–1918* (Göttingen, 1973), p. 162.

the external strategic needs of the state with domestic political considerations. In the process, they satisfied neither detractors nor supporters.

THE DOMESTIC CONSTRAINTS ON STRATEGY

Otto von Bismarck possessed a clear political and diplomatic concept after
German unification in 1871. In Europe, he was content to maintain the
pentarchy of great powers; overseas, he rejected calls for an aggressive colonial policy. He fully recognized the Balkans as the potential flash point of
European affairs and hence sought to deny both Austria-Hungary and Russia power and influence there. As late as 1874, the military force requisite to
these goals stood at just over 400,000 soldiers. Under the so-called "iron
law" of 1867, the nation strove to maintain 1 percent of the male population
under arms and automatically to allocate 225 thaler per man to this force.[5]
The ensuing debate over the army thus revolved not so much around resource availability and allocation as around the question of how much influence the Reichstag was to wield over the army.

Constitutional and bureaucratic infighting over the overall conduct of
military policy reached a climax in 1883. In that year, the army moved to
emasculate the single agency that accounted for it in the Reichstag, the
Prussian War Ministry. General Emil von Albedyll, head of the military
cabinet, appointed General Paul Bronsart von Schellendorf to the post of war
minister on condition that the latter accord the chief of the general staff the
right to direct audience with the king-emperor. In addition, the war minister
had to abolish his own Division of Personnel and transfer its functions to an
enlarged military cabinet. A future head of the war ministry, Verdy du Vernois, likened this reform to committing suicide.[6] Not only did these two
reforms destroy the administrative unity that the army had enjoyed since the
early nineteenth century, but they effectively removed all personnel matters
from public perusal. The single army officer responsible to the Reichstag, in
the words of Gordon Craig, was thus "rendered impotent."[7] The general
staff no longer kept the Prussian War Ministry abreast of strategic planning.

A second major organizational reform came in 1889, when Wilhelm II
gathered his military advisers into a *maison militaire* officially entitled "royal
headquarters," with a commanding general at its head – something hitherto

5 Gordon A. Craig, *The Politics of the Prussian Army 1640–1945* (Oxford, 1955), pp. 178,
   220. The conscripts served three years with the line, four years in the active reserve, and five
   additional years in the reformed *Landwehr*.
6 Verdy to Waldersee, 24 February 1889, in H.O. Meisner, ed., *Aus dem Briefwechsel des
   Generalfeldmarschalls Alfred Grafen von Waldersee*, Vol. 1 (Berlin and Leipzig, 1928), pp.
   224ff.
7 See Manfred Messerschmidt, "Die Armee in Staat und Gesellschaft – Die Bismarckzeit," in
   Michael Stürmer, ed., *Das kaiserliche Deutschland: Politik und Gesellschaft 1870–1918*
   (Düsseldorf, 1970), pp. 100–101.

reserved for wartime. A host of special adjutants, generals *à la suite,* and aides-de-camp furthered the diffusion of military authority into a myriad of special interest groups. The growing importance of the roughly forty officers with direct access to the emperor, especially the commanding generals of army corps, helped the emperor in his firm desire to uphold the facade of the royal command authority against parliamentary scrutiny and reform.[8]

First and foremost, the German army was an instrument for domestic stability. As early as 1877, General Alfred von Waldersee, later to become chief of the general staff, demanded the forceful overthrow of the constitution (*Staatsstreich*) to guard against the growing strength of non-noble elements. He awaited in vain an order "to gun down the rabble."[9] Such radical views received great impetus on 20 February 1890 when the German Social Democratic Party (SPD), undoubtedly benefiting from repeal of the infamous Anti-Socialist Law of 1878, received a plurality in the national election. The military treated this as a call to battle. On 20 March, War Minister Verdy du Vernois ordered the heads of most army corps, as well as of the prestigious Garde, to maintain close scrutiny of the SPD, to ready forces to smash its various organizations, and to arrest its leaders in case of domestic unrest. The order remained in effect for the next two decades and was renewed as late as November 1908.[10]

Wilhelm II fully shared these views. In October 1890, he issued a cabinet order giving the military governor of Berlin carte blanche to use both the Garde and III Army Corps as he saw fit against the "internal enemy," Social Democracy. One year later, Wilhelm II publicly acknowledged his determination to use the army chiefly as a domestic police force when, while administering the oath of allegiance to Garde recruits at Potsdam, he reminded the new soldiers that they must be ready, if need be, "to gun down relatives and brothers." The Prussian Ministry of the Interior established an elaborate spy network as well as blacklists of potential SPD recruits in order to keep socialist influence out of the army.[11] The formation of a National Union Against Social Democracy under the guidance of General Eduard von Liebert was therefore not surprising.

An imperial decree of 23 March 1899 attests that these sentiments and

---

8   Wilhelm Deist, "Die Armee in Staat und Gesellschaft 1890–1914," in Stürmer, ed., *Das kaiserliche Deutschland,* pp. 313–16. The royal *Kommandogewalt* was laid down in Article 44 of the Constitution of 1849.

9   Waldersee to Edwin von Manteuffel, 8 February 1877, in Gerhard Ritter, *Staatskunst und Kriegshandwerk: Das Problem des "Militarismus" in Deutschland,* Vol. 2 (Munich, 1965), p. 361.

10 Reinhard Höhn, *Sozialismus und Heer,* Vol. 3 (Bad Harzburg, 1969), pp. 67–68; also Deist, "Armee in Staat und Gesellschaft," pp. 317–18.

11 Stig Förster, *Der doppelte Militarismus: Die deutsche Heeresrüstungspolitik zwischen Status-Quo-Sicherung und Aggression 1890–1913* (Wiesbaden, 1985), pp. 25–26; comments of November 1891 cited in Höhn, *Sozialismus und Heer,* Vol. 3, pp. 71–72; and ibid., pp. 108–115.

measures had not been born simply in the heat of the elections of 1890. The new decree, which was to have serious repercussions at Zabern in 1913–14, left local military commanders with discretion to choose the appropriate moment for supplanting civilian authority, deploying armed force against civilians, and suspending constitutional guarantees of civil liberties.[12] And while the Prussian Ministry of Justice admitted the unconstitutionality of the order, the decree nevertheless remained in effect for the duration of the Second Reich.

Budgetary deliberations of military bills are a useful vehicle to monitor the army's view of itself as a domestic "corps royal." In August 1892, Wilhelm II informed the general staff that he would not hesitate to reject the Reichstag's offer – suggested, in fact, by Chancellor Leo von Caprivi – to increase military expenditures in return for lowering active service from three to two years. The monarch bluntly stated that he preferred a small, well-disciplined, and reliable army to constitutional concessions, even if the latter resulted in a larger army. In other words, Wilhelm II was quite prepared to forego a more powerful instrument of national policy in favor of a reliable domestic police force.[13]

Nor was the volatile monarch alone in this sentiment. Seven years later, the Prussian War Ministry informed a Reichstag budget committee that it sought to strengthen Garde battalions "in order to be prepared for any eventualities, given the large population of Berlin."[14] Again, debating the army bill of March 1904, War Minister Karl von Einem conceded that he preferred "a loyal monarchical and religiously-oriented soldier . . . to any Social Democrat." One month later, Einem warned the chief of the general staff, Alfred von Schlieffen, against expanding the army as this would open officer billets "to democratic and other elements." Questions of strategy did not even surface during the 1904 debate. The general staff, for its part, prepared a treatise on how to suppress civil rebellion in urban centers in 1907. Social Democracy was the enemy; "war to the death" and "merciless" rigor against insurgent socialists the remedy.[15]

Stig Förster in his recent analysis of the German army under Wilhelm II suggests that even the process of military training involved efforts to combat socialist influences in the ranks. The purpose of the "merciless drilling" of troops was to instill blind obedience and thereby stifle individual initiative.

[12] Förster, Der doppelte Militarismus, p. 93.
[13] J. Alden Nichols, Germany After Bismarck: The Caprivi Era 1890–1894 (New York, 1958), p. 212.
[14] Cited in Förster, Der doppelte Militarismus, p. 105.
[15] Germany, Reichstag, Stenographische Berichte 1903/04, Vol. 198, p. 1529, session of 4 April 1904; Einem to Schlieffen, 19 March 1904, cited in Germany Reichsarchiv, Der Weltkrieg 1914 bis 1918: Kriegsrüstung und Kriegswirtschaft: Anlageband (Berlin, 1930), p. 91; and Wilhelm Deist, ed., Militär und Innenpolitik im Weltkrieg 1914–1918 (Düsseldorf, 1970), Vol. 1, pp. xxxv–xxxvi.

Furthermore, the army's tactic of marching troops in heavily massed columns – which contributed to the slaughter of 1914 – stemmed directly from such domestic considerations.[16]

In December 1905, even while Schlieffen was drafting his famous memorandum on fighting a two-front war against a numerically superior coalition, Wilhelm II informed Chancellor Bernhard von Bülow that the Reich could not risk war in the immediate future since it "dare not dispatch a single soldier from German soil" for fear of endangering the safety and property of its citizens in the face of the mounting "red menace." The emperor cogently connected the army's domestic and security functions in his New Year's epistle: "First gun down the socialists, then behead them and render them harmless – if need be by a bloodbath – and then war outside our borders. But not the other way around and not too soon."[17] Three weeks later, General Wilhelm von Hahnke, commanding the Berlin military district, issued an order of the day instructing his troops to disregard parliamentary immunity in case of domestic unrest – an order corps commanders repeated at Münster (General Moritz von Bissing) in 1907 and at Magdeburg (General Paul von Hindenburg) in 1908.[18]

The close tie between the army's domestic function and its national strategic objectives perhaps became most clear in 1913. General Helmuth von Moltke the younger, the new chief of the general staff, recognized that he lacked the requisite force with which to implement Schlieffen's bold encirclement strategy, and had demanded an increase of 300,000 men. War Minister Josias von Heeringen vehemently opposed such an expansion of the army by one-half, reviving General von Einem's argument that this action would open officer billets to "undesirable circles" and thereby expose the army to "democratization."[19] The next day, Heeringen issued an army order decreeing the immediate use of armed force in domestic disturbances since only through "unrestricted force could one achieve the goal that the revolution not remain victorious in even a single place for even a few hours."[20] In the eyes of the Prussian War Minister, the army's domestic function received priority even as the prospect of a general European war drew ever closer. Indeed, fears of the "red specter" convinced Schlieffen that Germany needed to avoid a protracted war at any price.[21]

---

[16] Förster, *Der doppelte Militarismus,* pp. 133–34.

[17] Cited in Bernhard von Bülow, *Denkwürdigkeiten,* Vol. 3 (Berlin, 1930), pp. 197–98.

[18] Deist, "Armee und Gesellschaft," pp. 318–19; Förster, *Der doppelte Militarismus,* pp. 191–92. In February 1912, the Prussian War Ministry passed Hindenburg's order on to other corps commanders.

[19] Heeringen to Moltke, 20 June 1913, in *Kriegsrüstung und Kriegswirtschaft: Anlageband,* p. 180.

[20] Cited in Bernd F. Schulte, *Die deutsche Armee 1900–1914: Zwischen Beharren und Verändern* (Düsseldorf, 1977), p. 278.

[21] Alfred von Schlieffen, "Der Krieg in der Gegenwart," in *Gesammelte Schriften,* Vol. 1 (Berlin, 1913), p. 17.

THE EXTERNAL THREAT

To be sure, national security did represent the other major concern of the army. The establishment of the German Empire in 1871, according to Benjamin Disraeli, constituted a veritable revolution, one even more profound than the French Revolution of 1789. Central Europe was now united for the first time in modern history under the Hohenzollerns, who commanded the finest army in Europe and the world. The elder Moltke, even as he returned victorious from Paris, foresaw that the most dangerous future threat the Reich might face would be a Franco-Russian alliance that would force a multifront war. The war of 1870–71 had amply confirmed Clausewitz's warnings about friction, interaction, and the fog of war, and had weakened the general's faith in the possibility of quick victories in the future: "Germany dare not hope to free itself in a short time from the one enemy by a quick and successful offensive in the west, in order thereafter to turn against another [enemy in the east]."[22] By the late 1870s, Moltke proposed to counter his perception of a two-front threat by a defensive-offensive strategy: Germany would mobilize 360,000 men against Russia and 300,000 against France. In the west, he hoped to defeat French forces from forward positions in Lorraine and the Saar; in the east, he would seek to disrupt Russian forces assembling around Kovno and Warsaw. In both cases, only limited victories were possible; "it must be left to diplomacy to see if it can achieve a peace settlement."[23]

Moltke's calculations complemented Bismarck's position. The Iron Chancellor persistently viewed France rather than Russia as Germany's most likely future adversary. In the 1870s, as during the wars of unification, he sought to assure his military the best possible diplomatic configuration in the event of war. Having rejected territorial aggrandizement as well as continental hegemony in the famous Bad Kissingen *Diktat* of 1877, Bismarck set out to spin a web of alliances that made Berlin the diplomatic center of Europe: Austria-Hungary in 1879, Italy in 1882, Rumania one year later, and Russia in 1887. While Moltke had little faith in alliances and doubted Vienna's ability to undertake major offensives, in 1882 he nevertheless instituted staff talks with General Friedrich Baron Beck-Rzikowsky to coordinate Austro-German strategy in case of war.[24] In the final analysis, Moltke clearly recognized two things. Diplomacy alone could not secure Germany's tenuous position of semihegemony in Central Europe, wedged in between two potential enemies, France and Russia. And no simple strategic-operational solution could resolve the dilemma of a two-front war. This assessment accounts

22   Cited in Ritter, *Staatskunst und Kriegshandwerk*, Vol. 2, p. 244.
23   See Graf Moltke, *Die deutschen Aufmarschpläne 1871–1890*, Ferdinand von Schmerfeld, ed. (Berlin, 1928), pp. 64–66.
24   See Gunther E. Rothenberg, *The Army of Francis Joseph* (West Lafayette, IN, 1976), pp. 113ff.

for his pessimistic as well as prophetic warning in the Reichstag in 1890 that a future war could last seven or perhaps even thirty years. "Woe to him that sets Europe on fire."[25]

The accession of Wilhelm II to the throne, the cancellation of the Reinsurance Treaty with Russia in 1890, and the emergence of a small group of offensive-minded generals in the general staff drastically changed the nature of strategic planning in Berlin. Closely associated with Schlieffen, these officers advocated a renewed search for a rapid decision and studied past battles of encirclement in order to give weight to their arguments. They counseled full exploitation of German manpower reserves and demanded greater emphasis on advances in weaponry and technology. Above all, they rejected diplomacy as a means toward their ends and instead began planning for the next war in virtual isolation.

The "demigods" of the general staff, to use Bismarck's term, were indeed a new breed. Unlike the elder Moltke, they ignored great philosophical questions and studiously avoided deep analysis of statecraft and historical forces. Instead, they drew their experiences from Prussia's victories over Denmark, Austria, and France. They resented Bismarck's political "interference" in those campaigns, glorified the role of Moltke and the regular army, and insisted on the primacy of the military in time of war. They worshiped the goddess "efficiency" as the logical culmination of nineteenth-century rationalism and positivism. Theirs was a narrow world of technical marvels: cartography, railroads, communications, weapons systems. They mastered statistical tables, devised intricate mobilization schedules, formulated complicated plans – and denied civilian experts such as Hans Delbrück a voice in military matters. Blinded by *Fachidiotie*, they never sought to devise a concept of "grand strategy" that encompassed the political, diplomatic, economic, and psychological components of the national polity. They failed even to establish the equivalent of the British Imperial Defence College or the French *Centre des hautes études militaires*. In time, they succumbed to simplistic and dangerous racial stereotypes concerning the threat to the "Germanic center of Europe" from both the "Romance west" and the "Slavic east." Above all, they produced what Wolfgang Mommsen has called "the topos of the unavoidability of a general European war," perhaps the classic example in modern times of a "self-fulfilling prophecy."[26]

---

[25] Cited in Eberhard Kessel, *Moltke* (Stuttgart, 1957), pp. 747–48. See also Gunther E. Rothenberg, "Moltke, Schlieffen, and the Doctrine of Strategic Envelopment," in Peter Paret, ed., *Makers of Modern Strategy from Machiavelli to the Nuclear Age* (Princeton, 1986), pp. 306–311.

[26] Messerschmidt, "Armee in Staat und Gesellschaft," pp. 103–105; Detlef Bald, "Zum Kriegsbild der militärischen Führung im Kaiserreich," in Jost Dülffer and Karl Holl, eds., *Bereit zum Krieg: Kriegsmentalität im wilhelminischen Deutschland 1890–1914* (Göttingen, 1986), p. 151; and Wolfgang Mommsen, "The Topos of Inevitable War in Germany in the Decade before 1914," in Volker R. Berghahn and Martin Kitchen, eds., *Germany in the Age of Total War* (London, 1981), pp. 23–45.

Moreover, this new breed jettisoned Clausewitz. While Bismarck had proclaimed his "shame at never having read Clausewitz," Wilhelm II crowed that "politics keeps its mouth shut during war, until strategy permits it to speak again." The younger Moltke encouraged his son not to read *Vom Kriege* but rather Schlieffen's *Cannae* in order to prepare himself for the entrance exams to the war academy. Even a "progressive" German such as General Wilhelm Groener admitted that he was "more occupied with books of the practical service, than with books on high strategy." Other generals simply proved unable to comprehend Clausewitz. Colmar von der Goltz argued that "it behooves us . . . to guard against . . . the interference of political considerations with the strategic and tactical decisions." Hindenburg, who briefly taught at the war academy, concluded that Clausewitz had "warned against encroachments of politics upon the conduct of war," and the Austrian General Alfred Kraus learned from *On War* that "policy must not interfere with the conduct of war."[27]

An obsession with "worst-case" scenarios went hand in hand with this blinkered professionalism of military specialists. Two examples will suffice. Bismarck's successor Caprivi set the tone for the next two decades in 1892 when he asked the Reichstag to implement conscription, arguing that French threats of *revanche* combined with Russian distrust of Germany rendered a general European war unavoidable, "sooner or later."[28] During the debate over the army bill one year later, Caprivi spoke of mounting Slavic racial animosity – words that Chancellor Theobald von Bethmann Hollweg revived under similar circumstances twenty years later. Berlin ascribed the most sinister, aggressive intentions to its potential adversaries, while concurrently depicting its own policies as peaceable and beneficial to Europe. In the process, German planners closed the door to diplomacy as an effective tool of statecraft. Caprivi's 1892–93 position began the long process whereby German leaders sought security solely through armed strength, "a devil's circle of armaments and counter-armaments, coalitions and countercoalitions, in a climate of mistrust and fear."[29]

Caprivi's worst-case prognostications reached their climax under Schlieffen. Four years after his retirement, the former chief of the general staff published a highly influential article entitled "On Contemporary War," wherein he developed what was to become the standard threat perception among German planners. Schlieffen depicted the chivalrous and peaceable nations of Austria-Hungary and Germany surrounded by devious and warlike neighbors: the French yearned to avenge the defeats of 1870–71; the

---

27   Jehuda L. Wallach, *The Dogma of the Battle of Annihilation: The Theories of Clausewitz and Schlieffen and Their Impact on the German Conduct of Two World Wars* (Westport, CT, and London, 1986), pp. 196–98.

28   Caprivi to the Prussian War Ministry, 27 August 1891, in *Kriegsrüstung und Kriegswirtschaft: Anlageband*, pp. 45–50.

29   Förster, *Der doppelte Militarismus*, pp. 39, 55–56.

Russians wrestled with the "racial antipathy between Slavs and Teutons"; the British seethed with jealousy over German trade; and the Italians, whom the general numbered among the Reich's enemies despite their alliance with Germany, acted from naked lust for territorial aggrandizement. "At the given moment, the gates will be opened, the drawbridges let down, and the [enemy] armies of millions of men will pour into Central Europe across the Vosges, the Meuse, the Königsau, the Niemen, the Bug, and even across the Isonzo and the Tyrolean Alps in a wave of devastation and destruction."[30] This paranoid "worst-case" mentality certainly helped solidify Germany's fatalistic belief in and acceptance of the unavoidability of war. It also lent credence to the general staff's planning for "preventive" war as well as to its subsequent demands for vast annexations.

These prophecies of doom also influenced the frantic activities of pro-military and veterans associations before 1914. The *Wehrverein* with its 300,000 members and the various *Kriegervereine*, united in the *Kyffhäuserbund* at the turn of the century and boasting nearly 3 million members on the eve of the Great War, took up Schlieffen's call for enhanced military expenditures and adopted his bleak vision of Germany's future. General August Keim, who founded the *Wehrverein* in 1912, demanded expansion of the army in order to blunt the threat from France, Russia, Britain, and Italy.[31] That same year, General Friedrich von Bernhardi gave full vent to vulgar social Darwinist notions about the "biological necessity of war" and the "nation's right to conquest" in his popular book, *Germany and the Next War* – and concluded by postulating the dire alternative of "world power or destruction" for the Reich. Heinrich Class, head of the Pan-German League, in another best-selling work of 1912 entitled *If I Were Emperor,* bitterly attacked the prevailing concept that a nation's armed forces existed for defense. Instead, he encouraged his countrymen to embrace the notion of war for the survival of the German race and people. Class's use of words such as "*Lebensraum*" and "*Führerdiktatur*" clearly suggests the emergence of a new form of virile, radical, middle-class "militarism."[32] Military pageantry, Sunday sermons in army garrisons, memorial-day speeches, and regimental histories served to bond the army to these extraparliamentary lobbies.

No doubt such worst-case perceptions stemmed partly from Germany's

---

[30] "Der Krieg in der Gegenwart" was written about 1908; the original is in Bundesarchiv-Militärarchiv, Freiburg, Nachlass Schlieffen, N 43, Vol. 101. The article appeared in the *Deutsche Revue* in 1909.

[31] See Dieter Fricke, ed., *Die bürgerlichen Parteien in Deutschland: Handbuch der Geschichte der bürgerlichen Parteien und anderer bürgerlicher Interessenorganisationen vom Vormärz bis zum Jahre 1945,* Vol. 1 (East Berlin, 1968), p. 574; Messerschmidt, "Armee in Staat und Gesellschaft," pp. 109–10; Deist, "Armee in Staat und Gesellschaft," pp. 330, 333; and Roger Chickering, "Der 'Deutsche Wehrverein' und die Reform der deutschen Armee 1912–1914," *Militärgeschichtliche Mitteilungen,* 25 (1979), pp. 7–34.

[32] Friedrich von Bernhardi, *Deutschland und der nächste Krieg* (Stuttgart, 1912), passim; and Daniel Frymann [Heinrich Class], *Wenn ich der Kaiser wär': Politische Wahrheiten und Notwendigkeiten* (Leipzig, 1912), pp. 74–76.

abysmal diplomatic record after dropping the "pilot," Bismarck, in 1890. In the span of a few years, Berlin went from being the diplomatic capital of continental Europe and the anchor of a web of alliances to self-imposed isolation and "encirclement." France and Russia took advantage of the cancelation of the Reinsurance Treaty in 1890 to forge first a military convention and then a formal alliance in 1894. Britain reacted to the rapid construction of a German battle fleet by settling colonial differences with France in the "entente cordiale" of 1904, which Russia joined three years later. Italy gravitated ever closer to the Entente.

Germany's heavy-handed attempts to dynamite this hostile "ring" through the personal diplomacy of Wilhelm II and Nicholas II at Björkö in 1905 or the blustering saber rattling of German diplomats during the Bosnian crisis of 1908 and the Moroccan crises of 1905 and 1911 resulted instead in diplomatic isolation. Moreover, the Balkan war in 1912 brought defeat to Germany's friend, Turkey, and victory to the Balkan alliance supported by Germany's enemy, Russia. In the process, the unsuspected strength of the Serb army became evident. Viewed from Berlin, that meant fewer Austro-Hungarian forces available for deployment against Russia in a future war. Moltke the younger, Schlieffen's successor, perhaps best expressed the dominant mood in the military circles of Berlin after the second Moroccan crisis when he reduced the Reich's future to a simplistic either-or situation: either Germany stopped "dragging its tail between its legs" and declared its willingness to "draw the sword" in order to back its demands, or it ought simply to "abolish its army and place itself under Japanese protection in order to make money and to grow silly undisturbed."[33]

Moltke's outburst evidenced his frustration over the direction of German policy. A number of factors combined to block the formulation of a coherent national strategy: concern over the army's domestic reliability, mounting naval expenditure, Reichstag parsimony, vacillation by chancellors in pushing for major army bills, failure by successive governments to restore Germany's diplomatic position in Europe, and the resulting need to press into service every available male recruit. Attempts to square this vicious circle of conflicting interests and policies dominated all administrations from Caprivi to Bethmann Hollweg.

THE MAKING OF STRATEGY: A TEST CASE

From 1890 to 1897, planners in Berlin pursued a policy of gradual and moderate army increases designed to keep up with Franco-Russian strength. In March 1890 War Minister Verdy du Vernois demanded 150,000 addition-

---

33 Moltke to his wife, 19 August 1911, cited in Eliza von Moltke, ed., *Helmuth von Moltke. Erinnerungen, Briefe, Dokumente 1871–1916: Ein Bild vom Kriegsausbruch, erster Kriegsführung und Persönlichkeit des ersten militärischen Führers des Krieges* (Stuttgart, 1922), p. 362.

al troops at a cost of 117 million marks, arguing that Berlin and Vienna could only muster 730,000 soldiers against 1.4 million for Paris and St. Petersburg. The French army by itself was numerically superior to that of Germany.[34] Most radically, Verdy demanded the induction of all eligible recruits to produce a "nation in arms" (*Volk in Waffen*). The Reichstag, under the leadership of Ludwig Windthorst of the Center Party, firmly rejected Verdy's concept as too costly – the Reichstag's stance for the next twenty-two years.

In 1893, Caprivi secured passage of an army bill that added 60,000 troops. Yet once again the debate over military outlays raised a central question: was the army to function primarily as a domestic "corps royal," or was it to provide a strategic solution to the problem of a two-front war? In the latter case, 468,000 men were not enough. Moreover, Caprivi argued, failure to exploit the nation's manpower pool would reduce the Reich's value as an alliance partner. In the end, the chancellor insisted that Germany could conduct only a short war without risking domestic stability. Waldersee, chief of the general staff, played no part in drafting the army bill.[35]

The *Quinquennat* of 1893 satisfied the military for the next five years. Verdy's concept of full national mobilization remained a dead letter: the War Ministry estimated that the army was unable to train between 30,000 and 40,000 eligible men annually.[36] Given the government's failure to define a long-range military posture and given the increasing numerical preponderance of the Franco-Russian camp (1.56 million men in 1897–98) over the Germanic coalition (888,000 men), the central issue of how to meet the requirements of national security remained unresolved.

Qualitative considerations further aggravated the army's problems. The costs of creating independent machine-gun companies, adding 210 batteries of field artillery between 1890 and 1899, and expanding the horse-drawn heavy artillery by the late 1890s required 27.5 million marks annually as well as a one-time expenditure of 132.8 million marks. Caprivi's decision to offset the Franco-Russian manpower advantage partially by upgrading the reserves to front-line combat units further intensified the search for already scarce funds.[37]

Ironically, a veritable stagnation in army outlays occurred between 1897 and 1911: three small army bills brought a meager increase of 35,000 men. The reason lay not in a lessening of the perceived threat, but rather in a shift in German interests away from the continent to overseas. This "new course" of *Weltpolitik* and navalism was closely associated with Admiral Tirpitz of

---

[34] Ludwig Baron Rüdt von Collenberg, *Die deutsche Armee von 1871 bis 1914* (Berlin, 1922), p. 36.

[35] Förster, *Der doppelte Militarismus*, pp. 36–56.

[36] *Kriegsrüstung und Kriegswirtschaft*, Vol. 1, *Die militärische, wirtschaftliche und finanzielle Rüstung Deutschlands von der Reichsgründung bis zum Ausbruch des Weltkrieges* (Berlin, 1930), p. 52; Rüdt van Collenberg, *Die deutsche Armee*, p. 50.

[37] *Kriegsrüstung und Kriegswirtschaft*, Vol. 1, p. 54; Michael Geyer, *Deutsche Rüstungspolitik 1860–1980* (Frankfurt, 1984), p. 58.

the Navy Office and Foreign Minister (later Chancellor) Bülow, who cast overboard Bismarck's cautionary stance that Germany was territorially "satiated." Bülow sought to unite the nation behind him through populist Anglophobia and sought an eventual understanding with Russia against "perfidious Albion." Overseas acquisitions would raise Germany to the rank of a world power while securing the throne at home. Tirpitz for his part strove to construct a fleet of about sixty battleships stationed in the North Sea within striking distance of the Royal Navy. Moreover, he secured automatic replacement of the ships every twenty years in order to "remove the disturbing influence" of the Reichstag from the naval program. By challenging Britain's maritime supremacy, Tirpitz and Bülow ushered in both the first modern arms race and the first "cold war" of the twentieth century. Unfortunately for Germany, no diplomatic realignments accompanied this shift in national strategy; Bülow's attempts to woo the Russians failed miserably. From the standpoint of strategy, *Weltpolitik* made no sense whatsoever. Germany, in the words of Alfred Thayer Mahan, lacked access to the world's "great thoroughway," the Atlantic Ocean, for the British could easily turn the North Sea into a "dead sea" if they closed the Dover-Calais and Scotland-Norway passages. German "navalism" made more sense as an internal poltical move than as a maritime strategy.

The "new course" strained the budget to the limit. The federal government could levy no direct taxes, and its primary income came from tariffs, railroad tickets, post and telegraph transactions, and consumer taxes on luxury items such as tobacco, cognac, champagne, theater tickets, and the like. In case of a fiscal emergency, the Reich could either secure loans on the bond market or seek special voluntary donations from the German states; the latter never amounted to much more than 50 million marks per year. Any major expansion of either army or navy thus threatened the Reich's delicate fiscal structure.

During the first three years of Tirpitz's stewardship of the Navy Office, naval expenditures increased by 13.7 percent annually from 114 million to 176 million marks; those of the army rose at a modest annual rate of 2.1 percent from 614 million to 655 million marks. From 1900 to 1913, the navy budget as a percent of the army budget climbed dramatically: 25 percent in 1900, 35 percent in 1905, and 55 percent in 1911; it fell back to 33 percent only after the great army bill of 1913, which increased the senior service's outlay from 929 million to 1,467 million marks. In particular, the so-called "dreadnought revolution" added not only incidental costs of lock, dock, and canal expansion, but doubled the unit cost of battleships from 24 million to 49 million marks between 1905 and 1913. Overall military spending from 1901 to 1913 accounted for 90 percent of total Reich expenditures. In contrast, the individual states bore the brunt of social expenditures such as health care and education. The army's share of military spending hovered between 58 and 61 percent and the navy's between 18 and 20 percent.[38] The vast outlays on the "hated and ugly fleet," as the Conservatives viewed it, eventually forced upon the government fundamental decisions about strategic priorities.

The result was the crisis of 1912–13.[39] A national debate, punctuated with hysterical outbursts by right-wing pressure groups, highlighted the threats the German leadership perceived: diplomatic isolation, "encirclement" by a hostile coalition, fatalistic visions of unavoidable war in Central Europe, "worst-case" operational planning, and stereotypical notions of racial showdowns between Slav and Teuton. It sufficed to add 124,000 men to the peacetime strength of the army. Two groups squared off in the official debate: on the one side stood the Prussian War Ministry, supported by the Conservatives, which desired mainly *qualitative* improvements for the army; on the other side stood the general staff, supported by popular lobbies, which demanded immediate *quantitative* increases in land forces. Chancellor Bethmann Hollweg initially stood above the debate, arguing naively that "grand strategy" did not fall within his domain; thereafter, he lamely sought (according to Tirpitz) to use the army as a "battering ram" against naval estimates. The crux of the debate centered around the possibility of achieving Verdy du Vernois's twenty-year-old call for a "nation in arms" without destroying the conservative monarchical Prussian state.

Schlieffen, the epitome of professional narrowness, had come to his post in 1891 firmly convinced that a two-front war was unavoidable. Within a year, he expressed the view that France was the most dangerous opponent, that Germany could ill afford a protracted war, that only a real *Entscheidungsschlacht* (decisive battle) such as Cannae, Leuthen, or Sedan could break the iron ring of the coalition that "encircled" Germany, and that offensive operations in the west alone promised success.[40] For Schlieffen, the keys to victory lay in rapid mobilization and numerical superiority at the decisive point. The "hammer," or right wing, of the German army must march through Holland, Belgium, and northern France before descending into the Seine basin west of Paris in order to drive the French, Belgian, Dutch, and British armies against the "anvil" of German forces stationed in Lorraine; it needed to be seven times as strong as the left wing. It was a concept born of despair. One throw of the dice on the battlefield would determine the nation's future. Mesmerized by visions of a gigantic *Kesselschlacht*, Schlieffen, in the words of Gordon Craig, "disregarded not only the

---

[38] Hans Ehlert, "Marine- und Heeres-Etat im deutschen Rüstungs-Budget 1898–1912," *Marine-Rundschau*, 75 (1978), pp. 316–18, 321.

[39] Much of the following has been gleaned from Hans Herzfeld, *Die deutsche Rüstungspolitik vor dem Weltkriege* (Bonn and Leipzig, 1923).

[40] Still basic; Gerhard Ritter, *Der Schlieffenplan: Kritik eines Mythos* (Munich, 1965); see also L.C.F. Turner, "The Significance of the Schlieffen Plan," in Paul M. Kennedy, ed., *The War Plans of the Great Powers, 1880–1914* (London, 1979), pp. 199–221.

demographic, technological, and industrial factors which affect the war effort of Great Powers in the modern age, but also the political and psychological forces which are apt to make peoples fight even against hopeless odds."[41]

It is important to remember that the so-called Schlieffen Plan developed in relative isolation. The German navy was not part of the planning process, and no joint discussions explored the interdiction of British cross-Channel troop transports in case of war. Each service pursued its own strategy, and the eve of war in 1914 found Germany's continental military strength weakened rather than enhanced – despite a doubling of defense outlays between 1900 and 1910.[42] The Prussian War Ministry, which was to provide the requisite manpower and material resources for the operation, remained ignorant of the plan until December 1912. Bethmann Hollweg, for his part, merely noted that "the political leadership was not involved in the creation of the war plan," and that "there never took place during my entire period in office a sort of war council."[43] He also learned of the plan only in December 1912.

Above all, the Reich failed to consult its sole firm ally, Austria-Hungary. Quite apart from his general dislike for and distrust of alliances, Schlieffen had grave misgivings about the efficiency of Habsburg forces. He so distrusted Vienna's top military leadership that after 1896–97 he limited contacts to annual festive greetings. Battle along the Seine, not the Bug, would decide the fate of Austria-Hungary. Neither Schlieffen nor his successor, Moltke, ever discussed the creation of a unified military command in what, after all, could only be a coalition war.[44] Berlin and Vienna instead jealously pursued independent operational objectives.

Given his view of Germany's strategic position, Schlieffen faced a rude awakening in June 1899, when General Heinrich von Gossler informed him that in the view of the War Ministry, Germany "had already gone beyond the limits of a healthy [military] development," and that present land forces were too large for effective wartime leadership. Gossler warned of the deleterious qualitative effect of using reserve formations alongside regular forces. The war minister bluntly demanded a *reduction* in force by 144 battalions through the disbanding of all reserve and Landwehr units. The position paper ended by stating that the War Ministry considered that peacetime

---

41 Craig, *Politics of the Prussian Army*, p. 281.

42 See Christian Stahl, "Der Grosse Generalstab, seine Beziehungen zum Admiralstab und seine Gedanken zu den Operationsplänen der Marine," *Wehrkunde* (January 1963), pp. 6–12; and Holger H. Herwig, "From Tirpitz Plan to Schlieffen Plan: Some Observations on German Military Planning," *Journal of Strategic Studies* (March 1986), pp. 53–63.

43 Theobald von Bethmann Hollweg, *Betrachtungen zum Weltkriege* (Berlin, 1919), Vol. 1, p. 167; and Vol. 2, p. 7.

44 Moltke to General Franz Baron Conrad von Hötzendorf, 10 February 1913, in Österreichisches Staatsarchiv-Kriegsarchiv, Conrad Archiv, B. Flügeladjutant, Vol. 3; and Franz Conrad von Hötzendorf, *Aus Meiner Dienstzeit 1906–1918* (Vienna, Leipzig, and Munich, 1923), Vol. 4, p. 259. "The matter of a common supreme command was never brought up before the war."

expansion, especially of the infantry, was at an end![45] The War Ministry remained ignorant of the resource demands inherent in Schlieffen's grand design – which, in fact, still were unknown to the chief of staff himself.

Gossler's views must have incensed Schlieffen. He would need all available reserve formations not only as garrison forces in France but also to cover the advancing regular army's flanks at Antwerp and Verdun. Gossler's demand for a reduction in available manpower and his insistence that German infantry forces were already too large boded ill for the success of Schlieffen's operational plan. When the general staff demanded an additional twenty-four to twenty-five battalions (40,000 men), Gossler responded that as in 1870–71, Germany would have to force a decisive victory with available active units.[46] General von Einem, Gossler's chief aide and successor, joined the fray: "But this armaments race must come to an end at some point and the time must come when . . . the chief of the general staff must remain content with what the army provides him." Never in history, Einem lectured, had a great captain commanded twenty-three army corps, an undertaking that lay in the "realm of fantasy." Gossler's deputy concluded sarcastically: "It is really not the task of the war ministry to pass this piece of wisdom on to the chief of the general staff." Einem agreed fully with Gossler that the German army had reached optimal strength: "If he [Schlieffen] does not think such an army sufficient for an offensive, then a few corps will hardly suffice to give him a feeling of confidence."[47]

Relations between the general staff and the War Ministry reached their nadir in 1905. At the moment when Schlieffen was drafting his famous memorandum on fighting a two-front war and was demanding thirty-three new infantry battalions, the War Ministry informed the general staff that it could condone an increase of only 10,000 men, and these mainly for the cavalry. Moreover, Einem sought to curry favor with the Reichstag by resuscitating Caprivi's 1893 offer to lower the active duty obligations of Germany's conscripts to two years. The war minister once again reminded Schlieffen that army increases translated into new officer billets which the army could only fill at the cost of "democratization" of a corps that was already only half noble. The Kaiser's support for a small, reliable "corps royal" decided the issue.

To be sure, Schlieffen had good reason for concern. Austro-Hungarian-German forces lagged fully 600,000 men behind those of France and Russia. And the alpha and the omega of Schlieffen's strategy was that the war must be short. Neither financially nor economically could Germany afford a pro-

---

[45] Gossler to Schlieffen, 8 June 1899, in *Kriegsrüstung und Kriegswirtschaft: Anlageband*, pp. 57–59.

[46] Schlieffen to Gossler, 19 August 1899, in ibid., pp. 60–67; Gossler to Schlieffen, 19 October 1899, in ibid., pp. 68–72.

[47] Cited in Ludwig Baron Rüdt von Collenberg, "Graf Schlieffen und die Kriegsformation der deutschen Armee," *Wissen und Wehr*, 10 (1927), pp. 624ff.

tracted struggle: "A strategy of attrition will not do if the maintenance of millions [of men] costs billions [of marks]."[48] A long war, Schlieffen feared, would raise the ever-present "red specter" and entail radical social and political change. Far from embracing the concept of the "nation in arms," Schlieffen sought instead to conduct a traditional nineteenth-century "cabinet war" by dictating the movements of millions of men with mechanical schematism. A modern industrial war involving millions of men seemed inevitable, but the general preferred to guide it according to hallowed Prussian concepts. National mobilization for "total war" was anathema to this conservative monarchical soldier.

Prussia's peculiar strategic culture helps explain the failure of top military planners to resolve this apparent impasse between the War Ministry and the general staff. If Schlieffen had really considered the creation of new army corps to be absolutely critical to his operational design, why did he not force the issue by appealing to the All-Highest, the supreme commander, Wilhelm II? Instead, the chief of the general staff remained content to exchange letters across town with the Prussian War Minister. Schlieffen apparently did not even demand a face-to-face confrontation with Gossler or Einem. It was not the Prussian "style" to seek consensus in the realm of operational planning.

The inescapable conclusion is that Schlieffen drafted plans for a two-front war against a numerically superior coalition without regard for available force size. The decisive right wing of the "wheel" that was to sweep the English Channel with its right sleeve required thirteen army corps alone – at a time when Schlieffen could commit but five corps! Schlieffen left it to his successor to resolve the shortfall of eight army corps on the eve of the outbreak of war. Driven by a fanatical belief in a Cannae miracle, Schlieffen blithely ignored anticipated British forces on the continent, overestimated the combat-readiness of German reserves, rejected Clausewitz's principle of the "diminishing force of attack," and contemplated a siege of Paris requiring seven or eight army corps – forces that as yet existed neither in reality nor on paper. Had the chief of the general staff conveniently overlooked the fact that in 1870 the elder Moltke had enjoyed a numerical advantage of seven infantry divisions over the French? Grandiose visions of German troops marching through the Arc de Triomphe with brass bands playing the "Paris Entrance March" substituted for Bismarckian Realpolitik.[49]

Schlieffen, in short, possessed no eye for broad strategic and political issues. He allowed no room for Clausewitz's notion of the "genius of war"; his rigid operational studies permitted no free scope for command; his widely acknowledged operational expertise had evolved only in war games, staff

48 Schlieffen, "Der Krieg in der Gegenwart," in Hugo von Freytag-Loringhoven, ed., *Cannae* (Berlin, 1925), p. 280. Austro-German forces were set at 930,000, those of France and Russia at 1.6 million. Rüdt von Collenberg, *Die deutsche Armee*, p. 61.
49 Ritter, *Staatskunst und Kriegshandwerk*, Vol. 2, pp. 256–58; Wallach, *Dogma of the Battle of Annihilation*, p. 58.

rides, and theoretical exercises without a battlefield test. The plan bearing his name was a pipe dream from the beginning. It was criminal to commit the nation to a two-front operational gamble with the full knowledge that the requisite forces did not exist and that, given the mood of the Reichstag and War Ministry, they were not likely to materialize in the near future.

The younger Moltke was hardly the man to change the nature of either the army or the state by demanding full mobilization of manpower and material resources. While he harbored doubts about certain aspects of the Schlieffen Plan – notably the march through neutral Holland – Moltke nevertheless accepted its basic military-political concept. A follower rather than a leader, Moltke assumed only a marginal role in setting army estimates in 1907: thereafter, the War Ministry consulted him only sporadically about resource availability. Not surprisingly, it was not Moltke but the explosively energetic chief of the second division (mobilization) of the general staff, Colonel Erich Ludendorff, who precipitated the confrontation with the War Ministry over the shape of the German army.

For 1911, Moltke and Ludendorff demanded an immediate increase of 10,000 men as well as an additional 113 machine-gun companies, eighteen artillery batteries, and four battalions of foot artillery. To cover the increase, they asked the Reichstag for a onetime expenditure of 69 million marks and ongoing outlays of 15.5 million marks.[50] For 1912, the general staff requested an additional 39,000 men as well as a onetime outlay of 144 million marks and ongoing costs of 296 million marks. Even with these two sharp increases, Berlin and Vienna could field little more than one million men – still 800,000 soldiers less than France and Russia.[51]

In fact, by 1912 the general staff was in a state of near panic. While the Reich's population had climbed from 30 million in 1870 to 65 million by 1913, and its budget had risen from 340 million marks to 3,400 million marks during that same period, the army had grown only from approximately 400,000 to 600,000 men. France, with a population smaller by nearly 20 million, managed to field a numerically equal force. Whereas in 1870–71, Prussia had enjoyed a clear superiority of 100 battalions over France, by 1913 the Germans would face a French, British, and Belgian advantage of 142 battalions in the west. In the east, the situation was bleaker: even if Rumania honored its alliance with Berlin and Vienna, the Central Powers would confront a Russian superiority of 1,374 battalions. At home, the army's restricted size meant that 38,000 eligible men escaped military service in 1913.[52] The Schlieffen Plan, in other words, was utterly divorced from reality.

[50] *Kriegsrüstung und Kriegswirtschaft,* Vol. 1, pp. 93, 99; Schulte, *Die deutsche Armee,* pp. 61–66.
[51] Rüdt von Collenberg, *Die deutsche Armee,* p. 95; Förster, *Der doppelte Militarismus,* p. 225.
[52] Herzfeld, *Deutsche Rüstungspolitik,* pp. 47, 58, 146, 155.

This dismal *Kriegsbild* emboldened Moltke and Ludendorff to revive General Verdy du Vernois's concept of the *Volk in Waffen*. In October 1912, they called for a 33 percent increase in troop strength; the next month, they formally demanded full implementation of universal male conscription. "Once again, we must become a nation in arms. . . . In this, there is no going backward but only forward for Germany."[53] General von Heeringen felt both surprised and betrayed by this bold initiative, and sought to head it off by requesting an additional 300 million marks from the Reichstag for qualitative improvements before the current *Quinquennat* expired in 1916.

Before reaching a decision, Wilhelm II called a "war council" on 8 December 1912 in the wake of an official communiqué from the British Secretary of State for War, Richard Haldane, that London would never tolerate a repeat of 1870–71 leading to possible German hegemony on the continent.[54] Wilhelm expressed his firm belief in the inevitability of war with the Entente in the immediate future. Moltke concurred. "I regard war as inevitable. The sooner the better." Admiral von Tirpitz pleaded lamely for postponement of war for eighteen months in order to ready the fleet for battle with the Royal Navy. Tirpitz also suggested that the government use the time remaining to enhance Germany's land forces and to exploit available manpower reserves – a radical departure from his customary insistence on naval priority in armaments spending.

War Minister von Heeringen, excluded from the "war council," reacted to news of Moltke's belligerence by reminding the general staff that training facilities were already strained to the maximum and that the armaments industry could not keep up with existing orders.[55] The "war council's" vivid expression of the prevailing fatalistic notions of the inevitability of war and the "worst-case" scenarios rampant in Berlin was symptomatic. Moltke felt that time was working against Germany. Within months, he instructed his staff to cease contingency planning for deployment in the east. Wilhelm II ordered the War Ministry to prepare a new army bill at once. Bernhardi, Class, and Keim mobilized their pressure groups to lobby the government for increased military expenditures.

Moltke and Ludendorff fired their formal broadside on 21 December 1912 in the so-called "great memorandum."[56] Echoing Schlieffen's bleak prog-

---

53 Moltke to Heeringen, 25 November 1912, in *Kriegsrüstung und Kriegswirtschaft: Anlageband*, pp. 146–48.

54 See John C.G. Röhl, "Die Generalprobe: Zur Geschichte und Bedeutung des 'Kriegsrates' vom 8. Dezember 1912," in Dirk Stegmann, Bernd-Jürgen Wendt, and Peter-Christian Witt, eds., *Industrielle Gesellschaft und politisches System: Beiträge zur politischen Sozialgeschichte: Festschrift für Fritz Fischer zum 70. Geburtstag* (Bonn, 1978), pp. 357–73.

55 Bernd F. Schulte, "Zu der Krisenkonferenz vom 8. Dezember 1912," *Historisches Jahrbuch*, 102 (1982), p. 196; and Heeringen to Moltke, 9 December 1912, in *Kriegsrüstung und Kriegswirtschaft: Anlageband*, p. 156.

56 Moltke to Bethmann Hollweg, 21 December 1912, in *Kriegsrüstung und Kriegswirtschaft: Anlageband*, pp. 158–74. Most of the documents pertaining to the 1912–13 army debate

nosis of 1908, they depicted a peaceable, defensive-minded Germanic alliance that harbored no expansionist ambitions "encircled" by a devious and aggressive "triple entente" that sought territorial expansion at the expense of Berlin and Vienna. Incredibly, this was the first time the chief of the general staff informed both the chancellor and the war minister of the basic contours of the Schlieffen Plan. Probably also for the first time, Moltke and Ludendorff notified Bethmann Hollweg and Heeringen that Germany would violate Belgian neutrality with its offensive in the west and that a British expeditionary corps would probably appear on the continent. The general staff also conceded that in the event of war, it now no longer counted on the arrival of the Italian Third Army to defend the Rhine. Finally, Moltke and Ludendorff warned that Vienna's need to hold down the Serbian army in the south made it unwise to expect Austria-Hungary to hurl its main forces against Russia.

The second part of the document listed the general staff's demands: "Manpower reserves are available in sufficient quantity for army increases." The army was currently calling slightly over 50 percent of eligible German males to the colors; in France, the corresponding figure was an impressive 82 percent. Simply by adopting the French quota, Moltke and Ludendorff argued, Germany could call up no less than 300,000 young men – an increase in peacetime strength of almost one-half. Further requests included raising battalion strength from 600 to 800 men, giving regiments their "missing" third battalions, and creating three new army corps.

The general staff thus revealed the gulf that existed between operational goals and force structure. Its demands for a 50 percent increase in troop strength stemmed neither from hysteria nor from bureaucratic infighting. Rather, Moltke, at the urging of Ludendorff, sought with one stroke to make up for the "lost years" in army expansion – 1897 to 1905 – and to realize Verdy du Vernois's call for the "nation in arms."

The War Ministry, for its part, realized fully that the general staff's program would revolutionize the fragile social, economic, political, and constitutional fabric of the Empire. Creation of a modern, mass army in an industrial age would entail jettisoning the army's preeminent function as guarantor of domestic stability. The vast expenditures required to train every available recruit would make the army still more dependent upon the goodwill of the Reichstag, which controlled the budget and in which the dreaded Social Democrats were by far the largest single party. The need to expand the pool of potential officer recruits, General von Heeringen stressed yet again, would further lessen the presence in the corps of offspring from "desired circles." Clearly, the War Ministry was not about to revolutionize the Bismarckian state. Alternative strategies demanding full mobilization of the nation, possible only in a democracy, were precisely what the War Ministry

have recently been reprinted by Volker R. Berghahn and Wilhelm Deist, eds., *Rüstung im Zeichen der wilhelminischen Weltpolitik: Grundlegende Dokumente 1890–1914* (Düsseldorf, 1988), pp. 371ff.

desperately sought to avoid. What Arno Mayer has aptly termed "the persistence of the old regime" thus militated against radical reform of the Prusso-German state. One of the War Ministry's bureau chiefs, General Franz Wandel, pointedly admonished Ludendorff: "If you continue with these armaments demands, then you will drive the German people to revolution."[57]

With the Kaiser's backing, General von Heeringen triumphed. Creation of the three army corps met with postponement until a new army bill came due in 1916. Like Schlieffen before him, Moltke refused to push his program to the point of offering his resignation, and instead remained content to exchange letters with the War Ministry. Once more, the strategic culture of Prussia-Germany foreclosed consensus politics even in military circles. For his troublemaking, Ludendorff received a transfer from the general staff to a regiment at Düsseldorf.

In February 1913 the Reichstag accepted an increase of 137,000 recruits at annual ongoing costs of 183 million marks as well as a onetime outlay of 884 million marks. While this constituted less than half of what Moltke and Ludendorff had demanded, the army bill of 1913 nevertheless was the largest in German history. The French reacted by introducing compulsory three-year military service and raised their active force by 160,000 trained soldiers, with the result that 2.1 percent of its population – double that of Germany – would be under arms. Russia increased its military expenditures to 965 million rubles, thus outspending all the states of Europe.[58] The expectation that the Entente would implement these measures fully by 1916–17 prompted the planners in Berlin to assume that a general European war would break out at that point.

THE IMPLEMENTATION OF STRATEGY: THE GREAT WAR

In light of the planners' fatalistic mood, it is no surprise that they welcomed the outbreak of war in 1914. The German historian Fritz Fischer notwithstanding, 1914 was not a bid for world power or even a *premeditated* war to secure German hegemony on the continent; rather, it was an aggressive attempt to break out of self-imposed encirclement, to revise the European diplomatic alignment by force, and to secure the gains of 1871. From Moltke's point of view, it was better to strike now rather than later: "We shall never hit it again so well as we do now with France's and Russia's expansion of their armies incomplete." The general also reminded his chancellor of the "deeply rooted sentiment of allied loyalty" between Berlin and Vienna, and

---

57 Cited in Herzfeld, *Deutsche Rüstungspolitik*, p. 77.
58 William C. Fuller, Jr., *Civil-Military Conflict in Imperial Russia 1881–1914* (Princeton, 1985), p. 227.

encouraged the Habsburgs to strike quickly against Serbia.[59] Moltke discerned "an atmosphere of happiness," and the Bavarian military plenipotentiary to Berlin, General Karl von Wenninger, informed his government upon visiting the War Ministry: "Everywhere beaming faces, shaking of hands in the corridors; one congratulates one's self for having taken the hurdle." Only the "Hamlet-like" Bethmann Hollweg worried about Germany's "leap in the dark." Admiral Georg Alexander von Müller, Chief of the Navy Cabinet, attested that "the mood is brilliant" because the government had made Russia appear the aggressor.[60]

Müller had hit the nail on the head. Decades old fears of the "red specter" proved groundless. Wilhelm II stood alone in his desire to arrest the leaders of the Social Democratic Party; the government dismissed this precaution as needless on 24 July 1914. Bethmann Hollweg cleverly used Russian mobilization on 30 July to rally the Social Democrats behind the war effort and presented its leaders with a documentary "White Book," designed to show that "the ring of entente politics" had in recent years "encircled us ever more tightly."[61] One-half of the book's thirty documents were forgeries, yet it did the trick: the Social Democrats' parliamentary caucus voted 78 to 14 in favor of war credits on 3 August. This apparent closing of ranks behind a civil truce or *Burgfrieden* spared the army its feared role as domestic police force, although the wartime state of siege laid down in the Prussian law of 1851 left the maintenance of domestic tranquility in the hands of twenty-six deputy corps commanders and about thirty fortress commanders.[62]

Was Germany well prepared in 1914 to meet a sustained long-term conflagration? The answer is a resounding no. First and foremost, Berlin and Vienna had failed to hammer out a systematic war plan. Neither power appreciated that the struggle would be an industrial coalition war. Each pursued independent political goals and drew up operational studies with scant reference to the other. While the Austrians had sought to commit Moltke to deploy specific numbers of troops in the east, to offer precise dates for full force intervention against the Russians, and to define specific military operations, the Germans refused to make firm promises and instead sought total commitment to the war against Russia from their ally in Vienna.

To be sure, relations between the two general staffs had improved dra-

59 Cited in Imanuel Geiss, ed., *Julikrise und Kriegsausbruch 1914* (Hanover, 1964), Vol. 2, p. 299.
60 Bernd F. Schulte, "Neue Dokumente zu Kriegsausbruch und Kriegsverlauf 1914," *Militärgeschichtliche Mitteilungen*, 25 (1979), p. 140; J.C.G. Röhl, "Admiral von Müller and the Approach of War, 1911–1914," *The Historical Journal*, 12 (1969), p. 670; *Julikrise und Kriegsausbruch*, Vol. 2, document 1000c; Karl Dietrich Erdmann, ed., *Kurt Riezler: Tagebücher. Aufsätze. Dokumente* (Göttingen, 1972), pp. 182–83.
61 See Dieter Groh, *Negative Integration und revolutionärer Attentismus: Die deutsche Sozialdemokratie am Vorabend des Ersten Weltkrieges* (Berlin, 1973), pp. 626–27, 642, 651, 670, 684, 692; and Holger H. Herwig, "Clio Deceived: Patriotic Self-Censorship in Germany after the Great War," *International Security*, 12 (1987), p. 8.
62 Deist, ed., *Militär und Innenpolitik*, Vol. 1, pp. xxxi, xl.

matically after Schlieffen's retirement. Moltke and his counterpart, Franz Baron Conrad von Hötzendorf, regularly exchanged letters, arranged personal meetings, attended each other's maneuvers, and shared intelligence. Yet neither man was willing to bare his innermost thoughts and plans to the other. Conrad never fully informed the Germans of his secret intent to tackle Serbia concurrently with Russia; Moltke refused to commit himself on the details of his eastern deployment. Both preferred instead to issue romanticized assurances of standing "shoulder-to-shoulder," to pledge legendary loyalty (*Nibelungentreue*). Thus it is not surprising that the Reich's military plenipotentiary to Vienna, Count Karl von Kageneck, lamented on 1 August 1914 that "everyone has been relying on the belief that the two chiefs of staff had worked out these most intimate agreements between themselves,"[63] whereas, in fact, nothing of the sort had occurred.

Part of the problem was personal. While Moltke was fundamentally shy and introverted, Conrad was an indefatigable bundle of raw energy. While Moltke delegated staff work to senior associates, Conrad stood alone at his writing desk and drafted countless highly imaginative operational studies – against Serbia, Italy, Montenegro, Rumania, Russia, or any combination of these – which he then rushed to the Hofburg and the Ballhausplatz in vain hopes of immediate implementation. While Moltke adamantly refused to engage in political discussions, Conrad sought to push the government into radical diplomatic initiatives and preventive wars. "The fate of nations, peoples, and dynasties," Conrad lectured his emperor and government, "are decided not at diplomatic conference tables but on the battlefield."[64] Armed force alone could retard the centrifugal forces of nationalism in the multinational empire and reverse the Habsburg army's cultural pessimism, which stemmed from its nineteenth-century defeats at the hands of France and Prussia. For Conrad, war was the *only* means of politics.

Nor were Germany's army, industry, or finances geared toward a long war. The Reichstag passed war credits in August of 155,000 million marks, or about 100 million marks per day. The fabled war chest of the Hohenzollerns, sequestered in the Julius Tower at Spandau and containing the last of the French reparations from 1871, amounted to 205 million marks – enough to sustain the war effort for two days! No stockpiles existed of nitrates for munitions, manganese, or rubber (of which Germany imported fully 100

63 Cited in Gordon A. Craig, "The World War I Alliance of the Central Powers in Retrospect: The Military Cohesion of the Alliance," *Journal of Modern History*, 37 (September 1965), pp. 337–38. See also Ludwig Beck, "Besass Deutschland 1914 einen Kriegsplan?," in Hans Speidel, ed., *Studien* (Stuttgart, 1955), pp. 102ff; and Gerhard Ritter, "Die Zusammenarbeit der Generalstäbe Deutschlands und Österreich-Ungarns vor dem Ersten Weltkrieg," in *Zur Geschichte und Problematik der Demokratie. Festgabe für Hans Herzfeld* (Berlin, 1958), pp. 523–49.
64 Ritter, *Staatskunst und Kriegshandwerk*, Vol. 2, pp. 282–86. Rothenberg, *Army of Francis Joseph*, p. 178, noted: "On paper Conrad's plans always had an almost Napoleonic sweep, though he often lacked the resolution to carry them out and also forgot that he did not have the instruments to execute them."

percent in 1913); cotton, wool, or copper (90 percent); leather (65 percent); and iron ore (50 percent). In August 1914 the army belatedly sought to remedy its utter lack of raw materials planning by forming a Raw Materials Supply Division in the War Ministry under the industrialist Walther Rathenau. But Rathenau's attempts to introduce centralized control of Germany's scarce resources remained more theory than reality. At no time did Germany confiscate private capital, property, or investments to pay for the war. A special Food Supply Office, created in May 1916 in the wake of serious demonstrations, merely guaranteed 170 grams of bread per person per day. Lack of proper nutrition and medical care cost 763,000 German civilians their lives during the war. Child mortality, in fact, rose 50 percent starting in 1914. Even the effective exploitation of manpower reserves for the army, which increased the size of the military from 5 million soldiers in 1914 to 11 million by the end of the war, or from 7.5 to 16.5 percent of the total population, severely compounded the shortage of skilled workers. Berlin did not mobilize the female labor force to offset this labor drain.[65] Only about 700,000 females entered the labor force between 1914 and 1918 – compared with 1.6 million in Britain.

Ultimately the nation's fate rested on the success or failure of Schlieffen's grand design. Since the army bill of 1913, Moltke had added two new active army corps and six reserve divisions to his forces, an increase of thirteen divisions since Schlieffen's days. The much-neglected "technical" side of the German army had been upgraded through the introduction of motor-transport companies and a growing concern with logistics. Upon mobilization in 1914, Moltke was able to deploy nine divisions in the east and seventy in the west, of which sixteen were in Lorraine.[66] In forty-two days, this force was supposed to march 300 miles and deliver a crushing defeat to seventy-four French, twenty British, and six Belgian divisions. Mesmerized by Schlieffen's vision of the decisive battle of encirclement and buoyed by the euphoric "spirit of 1914," the army marched on Paris. It ground to a halt at the Marne within a month.

The hard reality was that Germany embarked upon a war of total mobilization with the tools of the nineteenth century: men and horses. Strategic goals and available resources were in disharmony. Martin van Creveld has shown that the sheer size and weight of the German advance eventually assured defeat.[67] Ammunition tables were forty years out of date. Since 1870, the number of wagons required to supply a corps, which took up twenty miles of road and consumed 130 tons of food and fodder daily, had doubled to 1,168. Despite the efforts of 28,000 railroad construction troops, the railheads of the advancing German armies often lagged eighty to one

[65] Wehler, *Deutsche Kaiserreich*, pp. 200–203.
[66] Wallach, *Dogma of the Battle of Annihilation*, p. 66.
[67] Martin van Creveld, *Supplying War: Logistics from Wallenstein to Patton* (Cambridge, 1977), pp. 109–141.

hundred miles behind the front. Men and horses, especially on the right wing, slowed from exhaustion. It would have required 18,000 trucks to carry these combat forces – at a time when Germany possessed but 4,000, of which 60 percent broke down before they reached the Marne. It was something of a miracle that 1.5 million men, or 85 percent of the German army, even arrived in the west within ten days over thirteen railroads.

In strategic terms, the halt at the Marne meant that the nation's sole contingency plan shipwrecked. Neither the so-called "race to the sea" in Flanders nor the spectacular victories at Tannenberg and the Masurian Lakes in the east could obscure this fact. By 18 November the war had become a stalemate: the bloody offensive at Ypres had bogged down in the Flanders mud, and the Russians had blunted the eastern thrust around Lódz. Moltke's successor, General Erich von Falkenhayn, informed Bethmann Hollweg that a German victory leading to a "decent peace" was no longer attainable, and counseled peace without annexations. Deeply depressed by battlefield setbacks, the chief of the general staff prepared to return to the *status quo ante bellum*.

That did not happen. Bethmann Hollweg, the allegedly "moderate" civilian, now inserted a new element into the making of German strategy: war aims. On 19 November 1914 the chancellor informed the Foreign Office of Falkenhayn's position and rejected the general's pessimism. Bethmann Hollweg conceded that the war now would certainly be long, but claimed that its prolongation could be "regarded as a victory for Germany." The nation, he argued, needed "rewards for its incredible sacrifice," and this meant that most of Poland must remain in German hands. The war aims of the Reich's allies also dictated continuation of the struggle. Finally, in an action that further illuminated Germany's strategic culture, the chancellor declined to seek an audience with the emperor even over matters affecting national survival for fear that Wilhelm II would view this as "civilian" usurpation of his military *Kommandogewalt*.[68]

Thus instead of pausing at this critical juncture in winter 1914 to reassess the national-strategic situation in terms of manpower and resources and possibly to contemplate a change within the existing strategic culture, Germany opted to fight on in a war of attrition – despite the fact that it was vastly inferior to its adversaries in manpower and material reserves. Schlieffen's offensive strategy of encirclement and annihilation yielded without debate to a defensive strategy of the diagonal – exploiting interior lines as in the days of Frederick the Great in order to meet the most dangerous enemy thrust of the moment. The transformation of the war of movement into *Materialschlachten* brought with it the degeneration of the art of generalship into what Hans Delbrück termed the strategy of "exhaustion" or "attrition" (*Ermattungsstrategie*). It reached its nadir at Verdun.

[68] Ritter, *Staatkunst und Kriegshandwerk*, Vol. 3 (Munich, 1964), pp. 59–61, 597.

Verdun in many ways serves as the crowning illustration of what was wrong with the making of strategy in Germany. In his famous Christmas Memorandum of 1915, Falkenhayn identified Britain as the ringleader of the hostile coalition that "encircled" Germany and suggested a twofold indirect blow against "perfidious Albion": at sea, he planned to launch unrestricted submarine warfare to deny Britain much-needed overseas supplies; on land, he would hurl a devastating assault "against England's tools on the Continent." Specifically, the chief of the general staff proposed to win a war of attrition against Britain, France, and Russia by bleeding France's forces white in the west.

In planning the campaign, Falkenhayn rejected not only Schlieffen's panacea of the battle of encirclement but also what he termed the "uncertain method of a mass break-through." The chief of the general staff settled instead upon "an operation limited to a narrow front" – that is, a conventional frontal assault hurling men against entrenched positions. Falkenhayn identified the fortified salient of Verdun "behind the French sector of the front" as an object *"for the retention of which the French General Staff would be compelled to throw in every man they have."* It was immaterial, the general averred, "whether we reach our goal or not." The objective of the operation was to bleed the French Army *"to death"*; Falkenhayn later admitted that he "never had the intention of capturing Verdun." The city would simply serve as a gigantic suction cup designed to drain France's lifeblood. French morale was Falkenhayn's *Schwerpunkt;* victory lay not on the Meuse but in Paris, in the minds of the French politicians. Recollections of the capital's political turmoil in 1870–71 may have inspired Falkenhayn's cheerful prediction that "the moral effect in France will be enormous."

The chief of the general staff fully expected the carnage of what he later described as the "Meuse mill," or "Meuse grinder." Despite the advantages of troops defensively deployed in well-fortified positions, the general rosily forecast a kill ratio of five French to every two German soldiers. In reality, the tally amounted to 362,000 French against 336,800 Germans. Falkenhayn's ultimate "trump card" was the expected reaction of the British forces to the north: by enticing General Douglas Haig to stage relief attacks on other parts of the Western Front, or, better still, to suck the British into the Meuse grinder, he would multiply the losses of the Entente. However Haig reacted, one thing was clear – French forces *"will bleed to death."*[69]

Falkenhayn disdained any outside input into his new and atrocious strategy: only Wilhelm II saw the Christmas Memorandum – and approved it. Neither Bethmann Hollweg, nor the Quartermaster-General of the Army,

---

[69] Erich von Falkenhayn, *General Headquarters 1914–1916 and Its Critical Decisions* (London, 1919), pp. 209–218; and German Werth, *Verdun, Die Schlacht und der Mythos* (Bergisch Gladbach, 1979), passim. On Delbrück, see Arden Bucholz, *Hans Delbrück & The German Military Establishment: War Images in Conflict* (Iowa City, 1985), pp. 94–110.

Hugo von Freytag-Loringhoven, nor Crown Prince Wilhelm's chief of staff, General Constantin Schmidt von Knobelsdorf – the very men who would have to bear responsibility for the offensive – learned of the nature or specific direction of the assault. Nor did Falkenhayn coordinate the plan with Vienna. In fact, the Austrians, for their part, quietly withdrew their best units from the Russian front for an independent "punitive expedition" against Italy. As a result, the Russians pierced Austro-Hungarian positions in Galicia and the Habsburg offensive in Tyrol failed miserably.[70] Neither Berlin nor Vienna yet grasped the cooperative nature of coalition warfare.

Falkenhayn's gamble shattered both French and German armies in the Meuse hills. Position warfare continued. More than any other battle, Michael Geyer has argued, Verdun showed "the complete disjuncture between strategy, battle design, and tactics, and the inability to use the modern means of war. But most of all, it showed, at horrendous costs, the impasse of professional strategies."[71] At the moment that Falkenhayn unwillingly yielded to the duumvirate of Hindenburg and Ludendorff as a consequence of the Verdun fiasco, the German navy appeared on the scene with the only German strategic idea of the Great War: unrestricted submarine warfare against all maritime traffic bound for the Entente.

Tirpitz was not a strategic thinker. A modern bureaucratic manager and manipulator, a publicist and propagandist of the first order, he had rallied large segments of the German middle class after 1898 to build a battle fleet second only to that of Britain. At the "war council" of December 1912, as noted, Tirpitz pleaded for eighteen more months in which to prepare for war: twenty months later, the High Sea Fleet entered the First World War fully eight battleships and thirteen cruisers behind schedule. The admiral had in effect adapted Schlieffen's Cannae mentality to the sea: a single, decisive engagement in the south-central North Sea would decide the issue between "perfidious Albion" and Germany, with the former forced to offer battle owing to its strategic culture – national pride, sporting instincts, and historical tradition. Tirpitz's unanswered query to Fleet Chief Admiral Friedrich von Ingenohl during the spring maneuvers of 1914, "What will you do if they do not come?," laid bare the Imperial Navy's dearth of strategic insight.[72]

Not surprisingly, the British distant blockade caught the navy off balance. The High Sea Fleet undertook no major effort to support the army advancing into Flanders or to interdict British cross-Channel troop transports. Periodic "tip-and-run" raids on the British coast brought no strategic relief. The High

---

[70] Wallach, *Dogma of the Battle of Annihilation*, pp. 170–77.

[71] Michael Geyer, "German Strategy in the Age of Machine Warfare, 1914–1945," Paret, ed., *Makers of Modern Strategy*, p. 536.

[72] Cited in Albert Hopman, *Das Logbuch eines deutschen Seeoffiziers* (Berlin, 1924), p. 393. See also Rear Admiral Karl Hollweg to Rear Admiral Wolfgang Wegener, 15 March 1919, in Bundesarchiv-Militärarchiv, Nachlass Wegener, N 607, Vol. 2.

Sea Fleet remained penned up in the "dead" North Sea. The Germans claimed tactical victory when the two battle fleets met – for the first and last time – off the Skagerrak on 31 May 1916. But that action had no effect upon the strategic balance. On 4 July, the German fleet commander, Admiral Reinhard Scheer, informed Wilhelm II that not even "the most successful outcome of a fleet action in this war" could "*force* England to make peace." Britain's favorable "military-geographical position" and its "great material superiority" militated against success. There remained but one alternative: "the defeat of British economic life – that is, by using the U-boats against British trade."[73] The concept of *Materialschlacht* thus reached the war at sea.

In deciding for submarine warfare, Germany manifested none of the secrecy inherent in the grand designs of Schlieffen and Falkenhayn. The decision followed intensive public debate, exhaustive feasibility studies by naval officers and economists, and a genuine war council held at Pless on 9 January 1917, which included Wilhelm II, Bethmann Hollweg, Hindenburg, Ludendorff, and Admiral Henning von Holtzendorff, chief of the admiralty staff. At Pless, the debate included the critical issue of likely American intervention as a result of the U-boat offensive: Wilhelm II dismissed America's entry into the war as "irrelevant" to its outcome. Ludendorff agreed to "accept the risk," and Captain Magnus von Levetzow deemed it to be of "no importance to the fleet." The German navy assured the participants of the Pless conference that the U-boats could sink 500,000 tons of shipping a month for six months and scare about 2 million tons of neutral shipping off the seas through soaring maritime insurance rates; the naval leadership "guaranteed" victory over Britain "with good conscience."[74] Here was a national strategy forged on the unlikely anvil of public opinion, professional naval counsel, academic economic forecasts, and grand strategic deliberations among the nation's highest dynastic, political, and military planners. It also reflected a fascination with a new technology. How realistic was the making of this strategy? First and foremost, it was utterly irresponsible to gamble the nation's future on an untested new weapon, one certain to tip the balance by adding the most powerful neutral to Germany's "world of enemies." In addition, the German experts analyzed the economic factors too narrowly. Naval leaders failed to appreciate the enormous shipbuilding potential of the United States and miscalculated the total tonnage available to Britain – which included German merchant shipping interned in neutral ports. Nor did they possess a clear perception of the precise number of ships per month Britain required to sustain its industries and to feed its subjects. German economists generally overestimated the importance of wheat, failed to take into account substitute grains, and dismissed rationing and price controls as incompatible

---

73 Bundesarchiv-Militärarchiv, Nachlass Levetzow, N 239, box 19, Vol. 2.
74 See Bernd Stegemann, *Die Deutsche Marinepolitik 1916–1918* (Berlin, 1970), pp. 71ff.

with the British "national character." They failed to foresee that Britain could easily increase food production by turning to land not currently in use and by relying on American grain reserves – which were sufficient to compensate for the poor Entente harvest of 1916. Planners also misjudged the ability of the United States to raise a large modern army in record time.[75] These miscalculations, combined with the British decision to convoy merchant shipping, accounted for the failure of the U-boat offensive. In its wake, responsibility fell to Hindenburg and Ludendorff to devise an eleventh-hour strategy to snatch victory from impending disaster. Not surprisingly, Ludendorff reached back to the same notion of total national mobilization that had cost him his post at the general staff in 1912–13.

Hindenburg and Ludendorff planned a two-pronged thrust: mobilization of German manpower and material reserves, and a new offensive strategy. In the process, they virtually swept away the last remnants of the old Prussian army and monarchy.

In August 1916 the general staff presented the War Ministry with the Hindenburg Program, which called for doubling or tripling production of vital raw materials such as coal and steel as well as ammunition, heavy artillery, and machine guns within six months. Four months later, an Auxiliary Service Law sought to mobilize all able-bodied males and females between the ages of fifteen and sixty for the war effort. The army sponsored "patriotic instruction" both at home and at the front to uplift morale. A special Weapons and Munitions Procurement Office, later transformed into a "war office" under General Wilhelm Groener, in effect pushed aside the old Prussian War Ministry. Schemes for boundless territorial aggrandizement and financial reparations surfaced in order to show the nation that its sacrifices were not in vain – as well as to shore up the monarchy against resurgent demands for domestic political and social reform. At the front, recently established "storm-troop" units and assault divisions learned the new infiltration tactics. As the official German history of the war put it, emphasis now lay on "war machines" rather than on "men and horses." Soldiers became the "workers" of war. The Kaiser virtually disappeared as "Supreme War Lord," and the general staff became the de facto nerve center of the entire war effort. One of its leading denizens, Colonel Max Bauer, went so far as to suggest the creation of a "military dictatorship" under Ludendorff in order to mobilize the nation for war.[76] Efficiency became the god of total war.

The bold attempt to create a *Volk in Waffen* failed. The Reichstag proved unwilling to draft females in vast numbers or to surrender its budgetary powers. Industry achieved autonomy, setting its own standards, quotas, prices, and wages, thereby reducing the army to merely another consumer of

75 Holger H. Herwig, *"Luxury" Fleet: The Imperial German Navy 1888–1918* (London and Atlantic Highlands, NJ, 1987), pp. 197–198.
76 See Herwig, "Dynamics of Necessity," pp. 96–97; and Wehler, *Deutsche Kaiserreich*, p. 213.

war materials. A "symbiosis between the military and industry" existed only in theory. Labor, while initially willing to support the program, quickly turned against it: strikes rose from 240 in 1916, to 562 in 1917, and to 499 during the first nine months of 1918.[77]

The gambler's throw on the Western Front in spring 1918 also failed. For all its new emphasis on machine warfare, the German army suffered from lack of mobility: its horses had died; the 30,000 available trucks ran mainly on wooden and iron tires, in contrast to the 100,000 Allied trucks, mostly on rubber; the twenty new A7V tanks on hand proved no match for the Allies' 800 tanks; and an effective anti-tank gun had not even gone into production. By mid-summer, the Allies had blunted the German offensives, and the army had invented a new term, *abgekämpft* – "fought out" – to describe its condition. Strategy now meant fighting on for the sake of fighting, without direction or purpose; Ludendorff even forbade his staff to use the term.[78] Germany drifted toward shipwreck, while its Austro-Hungarian ally shrank to a mere client state.

The war destroyed the Prussian "corps royal" physically as well as morally. Ironically, one of its domestic enemies, Friedrich Engels, had in 1887 proved himself Germany's most percipient prophet of modern war by predicting that in the future the Reich could conduct only a world war of hitherto unknown dimension and intensity. "Eight to ten million soldiers will strangle each other and in the process decimate Europe as no swarm of locusts ever did. The ravages of the Thirty Years' War [will] be telescoped into three or four years and extended to the entire Continent." Engels accurately predicted that "hunger, plagues, and the barbarization of armies as well as peoples" would be the logical outcome of this world war, which would transform "trade, industry and credit" into "general bankruptcy" and sweep away the "old states" of Europe and their "old statecraft." "Dozens of crowns" would "roll in the streets," without new takers.[79] Here was an accurate *Kriegsbild* of the Great War.

CONCLUSION

The making of strategy in the German nation-state between 1871 and 1918 was both difficult and unsuccessful. The *Kriegsbild* of Germany's military planners rested on irrational and eccentric perceptions that Britain, France, and Russia had nefarious designs upon Central Europe. The result was a flawed operational product – the Schlieffen Plan – which failed to achieve the nation's most rudimentary goal: survival.

77 Geyer, *Deutsche Rüstungspolitik*, pp. 104–105; and Wehler, *Deutsche Kaiserreich*, p. 206.
78 Herwig, "Dynamics of Necessity," pp. 94–95, 99.
79 Friedrich Engels's introduction to Sigismund Borkheim, "Zur Erinnerung für die deutschen Mordspatrioten. 1806–1807," dated 15 December 1887, in Karl Marx and Friedrich Engels, *Werke*, Vol. 21 (East Berlin, 1969), pp. 350–51.

National policy, that unique fusion of power politics and culture, never received a clear definition. Slogans such as *Weltpolitik* and *Mitteleuropa* were opaque. The Reichstag had no voice in formulating policy. The military rebuffed harshly civilian critics such as Hans Delbrück when they sought to address national-strategic issues. Divergent perceptions of the external threat – a Franco-Russian continental combination for the army and an Anglo-Saxon maritime union for the navy – went unresolved by the nation's highest leaders. For a century it was peculiarly German to conscript young men as instruments of a national policy that remained stubbornly undefined.

The making of German strategy rested upon an extremely small cadre of planners. At the top stood the king-emperor, "Supreme War Lord" in name if not in reality. Wilhelm II proved patently unable to fulfill his historic and constitutional right to exercise *Kommandogewalt* at the grand strategic level or any other. Bethmann Hollweg, for his part, hid behind an ostrich-like refusal to play a direct role in determining defense policy or in coordinating army-navy strategies and resources. Left without higher guidance, the general staff and War Ministry struggled bitterly over the nature and the goals of the military establishment. The bureaucratic reforms of 1883, designed to remove army personnel policies from Reichstag perusal, destroyed the army's administrative unity and thus imperiled coordinated planning. The Imperial Navy, at best a "satellite" in the army's view, never participated in strategic discussions, and hence in 1914 no interservice contingency plans existed. Distrust of Germany's only steadfast ally, Austria-Hungary, prevented serious interallied planning for a struggle that would inevitably pit one coalition against another. Germany entered the war without a grand strategic plan.

The military either misinterpreted historical experience, or perverted it to buttress its own perception of the threat and to justify a "preventive war." The strategic culture of Wilhelmine Germany, that complex of strategic perceptions and preferred methods, stemmed basically from the wars of unification: the ascendancy of the regular army over the reserves, the infallible central planning role of the general staff, the unquestioned cult of the offensive, the emphasis upon operational solutions to strategic problems, the predetermined nature of modern war as brief battles of encirclement and annihilation, and the primacy of the military over civilians. It is indeed ironic that Schlieffen's and Tirpitz's fascination with *Entscheidungsschlachten* derived from studying Delbrück's analysis of the battle of Cannae – but neither leader apparently noticed that while winning the battle, Hannibal lost the war, or drew the deeper lesson that Carthaginian land power eventually succumbed to Roman sea power![80]

German planners harbored an obsession with "worst-case" scenarios. From Caprivi to Schlieffen, military and political leaders depicted potential

[80] See Bucholz, *Hans Delbrück*, pp. 63–64.

adversaries as devious and aggressive in contrast to the trusting honesty and love of peace of Germany and Austria-Hungary. When sheer numbers failed to make the case that Germany was threatened, racial stereotypes served to underline the imagined danger. Self-fulfilling prophecies of "encirclement" and eventual decline translated into the planning of "preventive" war. In July 1914 visions of this kind convinced the military that only a general European war would shore up the Reich's precarious position in Europe. In place of a civil-military symbiosis in the making of national strategy, the general staff kept its operational plan secret from chancellor and war minister alike from 1905 to 1912. The general staff precipitated the crisis surrounding the army bill of 1913 when it realized that the army's force structure was incompatible with operational goals.

After Bismarck's dismissal in 1890 Germany failed to adapt to a changing strategic environment. Traditional nineteenth-century "cabinet wars" gave way to protracted, industrial mass warfare – as the American Civil War demonstrated and as the elder Moltke predicted. Yet the Prussian army's historical role as guarantor of domestic stability militated against mobilizing the nation for modern warfare. Full exploitation of universal male conscription would mean expansion of the Junker-dominated officer corps, which would in turn entail opening officer billets to "democratic" and other "undesirable circles." The very existence of the "corps royal" was at stake.

An obsession with the "red specter" placed further domestic constraints upon expansion of the army. Not only did this fear help dictate a short-war strategy to avoid social upheaval, but it also reinforced the War Ministry's determination to draft the bulk of the army's recruits from the "reliable" but shrinking rural populace. Only by drawing upon the vast manpower pool of the great urban centers, the bastions of Social Democracy, could planners have met the sustained long-term threat of the numerically superior Anglo-French-Russian Entente. General Verdy du Vernois's ideal of the *Volk in Waffen* meant revolution to much of the military elite of the Prusso-German military-bureaucratic state. Ludendorff's attempts to realize this ideal in 1913 and again after 1916 brought only partial results.

After Bismarck, means and objectives remained disproportionate in the making of German strategy. Schlieffen in particular clung to the delusion of adequacy in his operational calculations. The grand design of 1905, based upon nonexistent forces, left his successors to create as best they could the "missing" eight army corps at the start of a war. Logistics received scant attention; Schlieffen apparently expected troops to live off the land. Mobilization of manpower and material reserves for a protracted industrial war met with rejection; such an effort represented the potential destruction of the delicate social and political fabric of the Second Reich. The Schlieffen Plan was thus a policy born of despair from the start. Buoyed by the operational success of 1870–71 and driven by a distorted *Kriegsbild,* Schlieffen gambled the nation's future on a single throw of the dice in the west. Only in the peculiar Prussian-German strategic culture could a purely military plan of operations, originating in an office devoid of constitutional power, have become national strategy without thorough discussion at the highest levels of policymaking. It was again peculiarly German that the plan remained a secret for seven years from both chancellor and war minister, the two individuals responsible for its political and material success.

When the gamble failed on the Marne in September 1914, no reassessment of national and strategic objectives took place. The issue of war aims injected itself and distorted the making of strategy at this critical stage. Even as the chief of the general staff, Falkenhayn, recognized that Schlieffen's plan had miscarried, that the army was "a broken instrument," and that Germany's chances of victory were slipping away, Bethmann Hollweg refused to draw the consequences from this admission of defeat and instead urged continuation of the war for the sake of annexations and indemnities. Thereafter, strategic goals were inextricably linked to war aims. That the chancellor declined to request an audience with the emperor in November 1914 in order to reassess the situation for fear of thereby "usurping" Wilhelm's "command authority" speaks volumes for the nature of national strategic planning at Berlin.

The making of German strategy reached its nadir at Verdun. Falkenhayn rejected both of the hallowed operational concepts of his predecessors – encirclement and breakthrough – in favor of a strategy of bleeding the French army white. Informing only the Imperial Supreme Commander of his intentions, the chief of the general staff destroyed a good portion of his own army in the "Meuse grinder" in a barbaric attempt to wear the French down and thereby strike an indirect blow at the "real enemy," Great Britain. His strategy of attrition worked only too well – on both sides!

The Imperial navy's bold strategic initiative in the form of unrestricted submarine warfare likewise suffered shipwreck. While based upon exhaustive economic statistical analysis and enjoying input from a host of governmental and private sources, the campaign floundered owing to serious miscalculations. An old remedy – the convoy – blunted the technological innovation of the U-boat. The navy's guarantees of victory over "perfidious Albion" within six months backfired when success failed to materialize; the nation lost its childlike faith in the naval leadership. Far worse, failure to foresee that the major neutral, the United States, could and would retaliate effectively against Germany led to final defeat.

Ludendorff and Hindenburg of the Third Supreme Command wrote the final chapter in the making of German strategy after mid-1916. In reality, Ludendorff forbade the use of the terms "strategy" and even "operations" at general-headquarters; the quartermaster-general permitted use only of the concept of "tactics" among his staff. The arena of choice remained constant: victory in the west, despite the collapse of Russia in the east. The infiltration tactics of the *Michael* offensive in France in spring 1918 proved temporarily effective, but no strategic design lay behind the assault. With the exhaustion of the offensive thrust and with his staff recommending cessation of the fighting, Ludendorff replied lamely that the war must go on, for only a program of vast annexations and indemnities could save the Hohenzollern monarchy from the forces of reform at home.[81]

German strategy failed because it was conceived in purely military terms. Andreas Hillgruber offered a cogent if complex formula for strategic effectiveness. National leaders at all levels, he suggested, need to coordinate and to integrate domestic and foreign policy, strategic and psychological war planning, and economic and armaments production in order to arrive at a coherent ideological, power-political conception of modern strategy.[82] German planners after Bismarck failed in that endeavor. They were unwilling to revolutionize the conservative Prussian-German state in order to mobilize the nation for total war. That attempt devolved upon a later generation, one schooled in the experiences of the Great War.

[81] See Holger H. Herwig, "Admirals *versus* Generals: The War Aims of the Imperial German Navy 1914–1918," *Central European History,* 5 (September 1972), pp. 208–33.
[82] Andreas Hillgruber, "Der Faktor Amerika in Hitlers Strategie 1938–41," in Wolfgang Michalka, ed., *Nationalsozialistische Aussenpolitik* (Darmstadt, 1978), pp. 493–525.

10

The weary titan: Strategy and policy in Great Britain, 1890–1918

JOHN GOOCH

In 1890 Alfred Thayer Mahan affirmed the historic primacy of the Royal Navy in British strategy. He concluded his survey of British sea power from 1660 to 1783 with words of comfort for his Anglo-Saxon readers. For two hundred years, England had reigned as "the great commercial nation of the world" through its maritime hegemony. It still possessed the two requisites that power rested on: "a wide-spread healthy commerce and a powerful navy."[1] Mahan looked back upon a century during which Britain had enjoyed undisputed commercial dominance over every rival. So, too, did Joseph Chamberlain when, three years later, he coined the term Pax Britannica to characterize the consequences of British rule in India. The phrase quickly came to define an era – the years after 1815 when Britain, thanks to its maritime supremacy, had been the greatest of the Great Powers. But by 1890 that moment of predominance had passed.[2] Thereafter strategic and economic realities forced the British to question, challenge, and modify their strategic presumptions.

In the mid-Victorian years, circumstances had permitted the British to avoid hard strategic choices. As Britain slowly declined from the peak of its relative productive power in the 1860s, "new" powers both within and beyond Europe gathered strength. The strategic significance of these trends was increasingly obvious after 1890 and inescapable by the end of the century. Incapable of shoring up its position anywhere and everywhere, Britain had to make difficult global choices. Shortly thereafter, the ambitions of post-Bismarckian Germany, no longer content with its semihegemonial position in Europe, forced Britain to develop a strategy for intervention on the continent. That change consequently exposed the strategic ideas of the two services in detail for the first time. Finally, after August 1914, the British con-

---

[1] Alfred Thayer Mahan, *The Influence of Sea Power upon History 1660–1783* (1890; London, 1965), pp. 539, 540.
[2] G.S. Graham, *The Politics of Naval Supremacy* (Cambridge, 1965), pp. 121–5.

fronted a war of enormous complexity that raised issues to which strategy appeared to have no effective answer. Britain's policy during the years under review thus passed through three phases: a period of revision and readjustment of its global strategic position between 1890 and 1904–05, followed by a decade of more precise and detailed strategic debate, and finally by four years of cataclysmic war characterized by daunting and largely unforeseen strategic problems.

The key to understanding British strategy in the years after 1890 lies in the relationship between the broad goals of diplomacy, the fluctuations in the European and world balance of power, and the strategic options available to support the one and cope with the other. Military strategies in turn depended upon the orientations and preferences of the services and on the resources available. British strategy, like British policy, was a series of pragmatic responses meant to safeguard British interests. Since those interests gradually changed, strategy also changed.

Shifting pressures on its global possessions coupled with tradition shaped British strategy. "There are no settled principles of policy in relation to any part of the world," Lord Curzon had complained in 1899.[3] He exaggerated; there existed well-established general principles from which British foreign secretaries deviated only with great caution. The first was the need to preserve the status quo, and Britain faced considerable problems in achieving this goal, since after 1890 no such thing as the status quo existed. The rise of Japan and the United States to great power status in 1894–95 and 1898, respectively, shifted the global balance against Britain first in the east and then in the west. With established powers jockeying for position around the globe, imperial strategy had to continually remake the status quo. This required an ongoing effort to stretch limited resources further, and both formal and informal arrangements to shield Britain's slow imperial retreat.

This process resulted in constant reorientations as changing relations with other powers created new areas of diplomatic and strategic sensitivity. Between 1882 and 1898, rivalry with France caused Britain to focus on Egypt and the Sudan. The long-term threat of Russian expansion moved the spotlight to the eastern Mediterranean, Persia, and India. Russia's seizure of Port Arthur in 1898 raised the specter of a partition of China, where British trading interests were paramount. Britain had interests everywhere, and great power rivalries meant that the focal point of its strategy must continually shift: as Lord Salisbury plaintively remarked, when he had left the Foreign Office in 1880 no one gave a thought to Africa; when he returned five years later, no one thought about anything else.[4]

A second principle of British policy was the maintenance of the European

3 Curzon to Lord George Hamilton, 6 September 1899, quoted from J.A.S. Grenville, *Lord Salisbury and Foreign Policy: The Close of the Nineteenth Century* (London, 1970), p. 297.
4 Muriel E. Chamberlain, *"Pax Britannica"? British Foreign Policy 1789–1914* (London, 1988), p. 146.

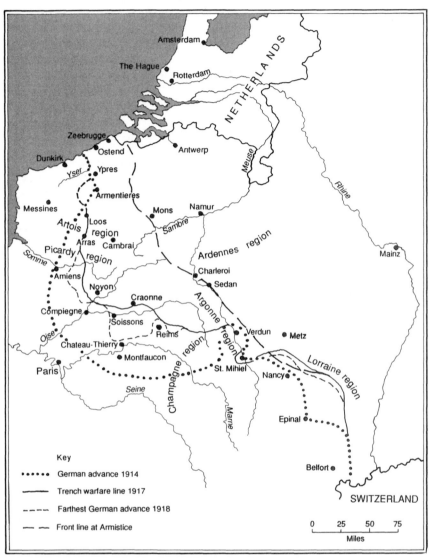

Map 10.1. World War I: The Western Front. *Source.* Adapted from John Laffin, *Brassey's Battles: 3,500 Years of Conflict, Campaigns and Wars from A–Z* (London: Brassey's, 1986), 464.

balance. Whitehall may never have weighed the balance of power in any true military or political sense.[5] But successive foreign secretaries had a clear idea of what it was and shaped their policies to maintain it.[6] With a small standing army and no firm allies, Britain could not realistically threaten direct military intervention on the continent, as Palmerston's humiliation in 1864 had demonstrated. Yet forty years later British statesmen, soldiers, and sailors confronted the question of what strategy to pursue against Germany's drive for hegemonic power in Western Europe. That issue sparked an open contest between sea power and land power advocates that ended with a significant shift of the center of gravity of British strategy from the navy to the army.

The third principle that guided British policy during these years was the belief in "a free hand for a free people."[7] The First Lord of the Admiralty, G. J. Goschen, interpreted this in February 1896 to mean "the freedom to act as we choose in any circumstances that may arise."[8] It rested on a deep conviction that no government could bind the hands of its successors over when and in what circumstances to declare war.[9] Any such declaration demanded overwhelming public support, although the government could never predict the extent of that support since public opinion might be divided or even oppose the preferences of the official mind. As Lord Salisbury suggested:

> Tell me what is the *casus belli* and I may be able to give a guess at the conduct which England will pursue. But without such information we not only cannot guess what England will do, but we cannot determine beforehand her course by any pledges or any arguments derived from general interests.[10]

Salisbury had good reason to take note of British public opinion. Clamor over the massacres of the Armenians by the Turks in 1895–96 had been so great that it would have been impossible to persuade the country to follow Turkey into a war against Russia to protect the Straits.

Despite many pronouncements about the merits of "Splendid Isolation," Britain did make foreign commitments before 1902, when it entered into formal alliance with Japan. An incomplete report to parliament in 1899 – that omitted Britain's obligations under the Treaty of Paris (1856) and the vital multilateral treaty guaranteeing Belgium's territorial integrity (1839) –

5 Paul M. Kennedy, "Great Britain before 1914," in Ernest R. May, ed., *Knowing One's Enemies: Intelligence Assessment before the Two World Wars* (Princeton, 1984), p. 194.
6 See Keith Robbins, *Sir Edward Grey: A Biography of Lord Grey of Falloden* (London, 1971), p. 154.
7 A phrase coined by Sir William Harcourt on 13 April 1897. See Christopher Howard, *Splendid Isolation: A Study of ideas concerning Britain's international position and foreign policy during the later years of the third Marquis of Salisbury* (London, 1967), p. 37.
8 Ibid., p. 22.
9 Chamberlain, *"Pax Britannica"?*, pp. 80–81, 160; Grenville, *Lord Salisbury*, pp. 8, 167, 354; Robbins, *Sir Edward Grey*, p. 152. For a contrary view – that the "free hand" was a convenient fiction of British foreign policy – see Keith M. Wilson, *The Policy of the Entente: Essays on the Determination of British Foreign Policy, 1904–1914* (Cambridge, 1985).
10 Grenville, *Lord Salisbury*, p. 364.

revealed that Britain had accepted the responsibility to defend Sweden and Norway, the Asian territories of the Ottoman empire, Portuguese overseas territory, and all or part of Prussia, Greece, Serbia, Moldavia and Wallachia, and Luxembourg![11] The British gave no serious thought to the strategic difficulties they might encounter in making good these commitments. When in March 1902 the War Office asked what were the government's treaty obligations, it received the offhand answer that there was little profit in meditations of this kind.

The general principles of British foreign policy therefore provided little help in formulating strategy, nor were they designed to do so. But the British could define their strategic interests in particular localities remarkably quickly and precisely. Thus, in July 1898 Goschen, supported by Balfour and Lansdowne, but not the First Sea Lord, Admiral Richards, believed that any attempt by Spain to install guns at the Queen of Spain's Chair, near Algeciras, would be tantamount to a *casus belli*.[12] Constantinople provides another example. It had been a fixed point in an otherwise fluctuating strategic universe, but after 1896, Britain simply ceased to protect the Straits. Egypt and the Nile took their place as a vital area, and in July 1911, Asquith defined the strategic and commercial interests that Britain had to safeguard in Morocco.[13]

As a great imperial and commercial power, Britain had interests everywhere. Physical geography was of some importance in determining strategic policies and placed a premium on naval power, not only because of the scattered nature of imperial possessions and dependencies, but because of the distance between British possessions and those of potential enemies. But while physical geography was fixed, strategic geography was not. British strategy-makers faced many difficulties in that the significance, value, and strategic vulnerability or defensibility of particular parts of the globe varied, depending on political configurations and the level of sophistication of local communications. Politics thus dictated that the Moroccan coast be kept out of French hands only so long as France was a potential enemy. Technology likewise dictated the end to any residual thoughts of repeating the Crimean War; the completion of the Trans-Caspian railway line placed the Russian supply route to Afghanistan beyond the reach of any British expedition to the Black Sea.

Broader issues also affected imperial strategy, often limiting options or making difficult tasks yet more taxing. Without Turkish cooperation, the navy informed Salisbury in 1892, it could not force the Straits and protect

---

[11] C. 9088: "Treaties containing guarantees or engagements by Great Britain in regard to the territory or government of other countries," *Accounts and Papers* CIX, 1899. For a full discussion, see Howard, *Splendid Isolation*, pp. 44–67.
[12] Thomas J. Spinner, Jr., *George Joachim Goschen: The Transformation of a Victorian Liberal* (Cambridge, 1973), pp. 207–10.
[13] Robbins, *Sir Edward Grey*, p. 241.

Constantinople against Russia. Three years later, Salisbury again tried to shape strategy to policy. Reminding the First Lord that "the keeping of Constantinople out of Russian hands has . . . been made a vital article of our political creed," he remarked that everyone except the Admiralty believed the navy could force the Straits.[14] Goschen replied tartly but accurately that only those ignorant of the defenses of the Straits thought so. Finally, in February 1907, faced with the futility of attempting a landing on the Gallipoli peninsula, Grey acknowledged that the Foreign Office would henceforth note the limits on possible strategic action against Turkey. Britain, although bound by the Mediterranean Agreements of 1887 to uphold the independence of Turkey and the freedom of the Straits, eventually recognized that there were certain things its naval and military forces simply could not do.

Strategic geography exerted its influence on Britain indirectly; some powers could exert pressure in one area of the globe in order to make gains in another. This was particularly true of the Russians. In 1900 Lord Salisbury summed up the difficulties Russia could cause: "when her Siberian railway is ready, she will want to be the mistress of the greater part of China, and if Afghanistan is unprotected she can force us to give way in China by advancing upon India."[15] Britain might also face the necessity of retreating in one area to face a threat in another. Thus, in July 1893 Rosebery, then prime minister, informed his First Lord, Earl Spencer, that "You must, I am afraid, increase your Mediterranean strength . . . the present disposition and ethics of the French make anything possible."[16] In that case Rosebery was prepared to weaken the Pacific station in order to add strength in the Mediterranean. The rise of Japan and the United States as regional naval powers further complicated the indirect pressures on Britain.

The complexity of the strategic problems facing Whitehall eventually resulted in a coordinated administrative system that brought together civilians, soldiers, and sailors. The Hartington Commission report of 1890 called for the creation of a Council of Defence, preferably under the prime minister, the abolition of the post of commander-in-chief of the army, and the introduction of a continental style chief of staff. The internal organization of the navy, run by a board system, was to remain unaltered.[17] Strengthening the administrative structures in this way would in theory improve the quality of strategic advice available to ministers.

The services – and their political heads – drew back from such drastic steps for two reasons. Liberal ministers disliked the notion of warlike continental-

[14] Salisbury to Goschen, 3 December 1895, quoted in Spinner, *George Joachim Goschen*, p. 198.
[15] Salisbury to Northcote, 8 June 1900, quoted in Grenville, *Lord Salisbury*, p. 296.
[16] Rosebery to Spencer, 29 July 1893, quoted in Peter Gordon, ed., *The Red Earl: The Papers of the Fifth Earl Spencer 1835–1910*, Vol. 2 (Northampton, 1986), p. 226.
[17] The best brief summary of this subject is still John Ehrman, *Cabinet Government and War 1890–1914* (Cambridge, 1958), especially pp. 6–66.

style structures that might give the military too much influence; the services themselves were too jealous of their autonomy to cooperate. The British did take some steps, such as creation of a Joint Naval and Military Committee in 1891 and the narrowing of the Colonial Defence Committee to local defense issues after 1893.[18] But this was merely tinkering with a system that failed to provide a forum to debate strategic problems and devise solutions.

The advent of Lord Salisbury's government in 1895 produced a step in the right direction when the Duke of Devonshire (who, as the Marquess of Hartington, had produced the report in 1890 advocating just such a body) became chief of a new Defence Committee of the Cabinet that included the service ministers and the chancellor of the exchequer. The duke regarded the committee as responsible for improving the cooperation and functioning of the services. Its work, he thought, would compel the War Office and the Admiralty "to face more directly than they need do now, the question of what it is which they undertake to do, and what are their resources for doing it."[19] The involvement of politicians in the making of strategy nevertheless remained an ideal rather than a reality.

Imperial strategy was the business of both cabinet and military, but the ministers took little account of the new body. Seven years later the duke noted with disenchantment that "merely to bring our best military and naval experts together to discuss a complicated problem of defence will not ensure a solution."[20] By that time, the outbreak of the Boer War in 1899 had exposed the shortcomings of the system for devising imperial strategy and the need for an effective politico-military forum, as Salisbury readily acknowledged the following year.[21] The First Sea Lord greeted the re-creation of the Defence Committee as the Committee of Imperial Defence in 1902 enthusiastically: "It is a first rate idea bringing the Cabinet Council of Defence into immediate relations with the services and Int[ernational] Departments who will thus rub off their sharp corners and have the benefit of knowing the political aspect of problems which must of course govern decisions."[22] With the addition of a permanent secretariat in 1904, the Committee of Imperial Defence became the body that discussed and resolved problems of imperial strategy. Although it could not resolve all issues to everyone's satisfaction, it did reach consensus on many important questions facing Britain as it reoriented its strategy from the wider world toward Europe and the growing German threat.[23]

---

18 Luke Trainor, "The Liberals and the Formation of Imperial Defence Policy 1892–5," *Bulletin of the Institute of Historical Research* 42 (1969), pp. 188–200.
19 Minute, 3 November 1895, quoted in Spinner, *George Joachim Goschen*, p. 192.
20 Selborne Papers, Devonshire to Selborne, 24 November 1902, Bodleian Library: Selborne Box 30.
21 Franklyn Arthur Johnson, *Defence by Committee: The British Committee of Imperial Defence, 1885–1959* (London, 1960), p. 52.
22 Selborne Papers, Lord Walter Kerr to Selborne, 31 December 1902, Selborne Box 31.
23 The literature on the Committee of Imperial Defence is considerable, and no consensus has

Gross expenditures on the navy and army were roughly equivalent from 1890 until 1898; then army expenditure outran that of its sister service between 1899 and 1903. Nevertheless, the navy remained the premier service in strategic terms throughout the 1890s.[24] The Naval Defence Act of 1889 allocated 21,500,000 pounds to build eight first-class battleships and sixty-two other ships, and established a "Two Power Standard" as the stated aim of Britain's naval building program. Reaffirmed in 1893 in the face of French and Russian competition, that aim held good until world events forced a general reassessment in 1901. Declaratory naval strategy began by setting a goal for force levels under the assumption that Britain could use its forces effectively against its putative enemies.

The Two Power Standard and the Royal Navy's strategic preeminence derived from the inescapable fact that the sea lanes were the nation's vital arteries. Britain's position as a commercial and industrial power overwhelmingly dependent on imported food and raw materials meant that the navy's primary task was defense of that traffic in wartime. The need for a strategy of trade protection became inescapable after naval maneuvers in 1889 revealed that the navy could not safeguard Britain's oceangoing traffic against French attack. Successive Directors of Naval Intelligence were keenly aware of the centrality of this strategic issue.[25]

The navy also had to command the Channel and protect the United Kingdom against invasion (an obligation the army also claimed as its own). In addition, the navy had to defend the seaways to overseas territories, maintain its bases, prepare to blockade potential enemies, and be ready to give battle in any quarter of the globe where foreign challenges might imperil British interests. This helps explain why sea power lay at the heart of British strategy and why Selborne could claim in 1903, in the face of mounting international naval competition, that "to all other nations a navy is a mere luxury."[26] Unlike any of its rivals except Japan, Britain could not afford a single defeat at sea without jeopardizing its very existence.

Under these circumstances, the navy's somewhat offhanded approach to

yet emerged on its political or strategic effectiveness. In addition to the works by Ehrman and Johnson already cited, see especially N.H. Gibbs, *The Origins of Imperial Defence* (Oxford, 1955); J.P. Mackintosh, "The Role of the Committee of Imperial Defence before 1914," *English Historical Review* 67 (1962), pp. 490–503; Stephen Roskill, *Hankey: Man of Secrets*, Vol. 1, (London, 1970); Nicholas d'Ombrain, *War Machinery and High Policy: Defence Administration in Peacetime Britain 1902–1914* (London, 1973); John Gooch, *The Plans of War: The General Staff and British Military Strategy c. 1900–1916* (London, 1974); John Gooch, "Sir George Clarke's career at the Committee of Imperial Defence, 1904–1907," *Historical Journal* 18 (1975), pp. 555–69; John W Coogan & Peter F. Coogan, "The British Cabinet and the Anglo-French Staff Talks, 1905–1914: Who Knew What and When Did He Know It?" *Journal of British Studies* 24 (1984–5), pp. 110–31.

24 See Jon Tetsuro Sumida, *In Defence of Naval Supremacy: Finance, Technology, and British Naval Policy 1889–1914* (London, 1989), Table 15.

25 Arthur J. Marder, *The Anatomy of British Sea Power: A History of British Naval Policy in the Pre-Dreadnought Era 1880–1905*, (Hamden, CT, 1964), pp. 84–104.

26 Ibid., p. 13.

strategy and planning in these years may seem surprising – but for much of the nineteenth century it had maintained its supremacy by mere tactical shows of force.[27] The result was substantial areas of professional ignorance. For example, since it did not take much to frighten Asian and African potentates back into line, the real extent of the damage a ship could inflict on shore installations remained a matter of conjecture. Other issues also pushed strategic thinking to one side, among them the fact that the navy was experiencing a dramatic technological revolution that transformed the capital ship during the last quarter of the nineteenth century.[28] There was thus little to stimulate what Julian Corbett later called "the unused organs of naval officers" to strategic speculation, and little that was of much value to guide thought about the wider aspects of his profession until Mahan's first book appeared in 1890.[29]

As a result, sailors took a cavalier line toward war. In 1901, Lord Walter Kerr dismissed the idea of holding naval exercises to meet the menace of the new German fleet with an airy wave of his pen: "It is no use speculating on what might happen in an unforeseen future."[30] In December 1903, alarmed at a possible clash between Japan and Russia, Selborne asked Kerr what action the government should take during the period of neutrality. "I have thought much on the situation," read the reply, "but do not think that there is anything special to be done, except to be ready for anything."[31] The First Sea Lord was clear on the circumstances that might require British intervention, but apparently had no clear idea of what the Royal Navy should actually do – nor did he feel it necessary to examine the possibilities for the benefit of his civilian masters.

If plans did exist, they were frequently unknown to the man on the spot, as Admiral Sir Michael Seymour complained to Earl Spencer from the Mediterranean in September 1893. In this respect, the advent of Admiral Sir John Fisher as First Sea Lord in 1904 changed matters little, since Fisher's theory of war consisted of a few aphorisms ("Hit first, hit hard, and hit anywhere"), written in capital letters and heavily underlined to emphasize their importance.[32] When the navy found itself forced to develop strategic plans for war against Germany after 1904, its tendency to confuse strategy with tactics and

27 C.I. Hamilton, "Naval Power and Diplomacy in the Nineteenth Century," *Journal of Strategic Studies* 3 (1980), pp. 74–88.
28 Bernard Brodie, *Sea Power in the Machine Age* (Princeton, 1941) [reprint, Greenwood Press, 1969]; Karl Lautenschlager, "Technology and the Evolution of Naval Warfare," *International Security* 8 (1983), pp. 12–16.
29 Admiral Sir Reginald H. Bacon, *A Naval Scrap-Book 1877–1900* (London, n.d.) [1925], pp. 264–5; *From 1900 Onwards* (London, 1940), p. 33.
30 Quoted from Marder, *Anatomy of British Sea Power*, p. 463.
31 Kerr to Selborne, 21 December 1903, quoted in Keith Neilson, "'A Dangerous Game of American Poker': Britain and the Russo-Japanese War," *Journal of Strategic Studies* 12 (1989), p. 64.
32 See Marder, *Anatomy of British Sea Power*, p. 347.

its lack of a staff – not created until 1912 – made it ill-prepared to contest the army's case.

Military strategy was in many ways easier to formulate in the late nineteenth century than naval strategy, for points of concentration were easier to identify. The War Office considered its most commanding tasks as the defense of the United Kingdom against invasion by the French and the defense of India against invasion by the Russians. These two problems exposed a fundamental fact around which all military strategy revolved: tradition and inclination combined to limit the army to a small force of regulars backed by an even smaller reserve. For a long time, the army reacted to the evident disproportion between ends and means with disgruntlement; "The student of British military history is well aware," commented one authority in 1904, "that we rarely commence a war with adequate force."[33] But by 1911, when army and navy debated the lineaments of a possible war in Europe, Major-General Henry Wilson had devised a continental strategy that faced up to the awkward fact that Britain could never go to war with a large, continental-style army.

Throughout the nineteenth century, fear of invasion disconcerted British society, and it was to allay these fears that the government introduced the Naval Defence Act of 1889. Denied primacy in national defense by the navy, the army instead turned its attention to the need to fortify London and defend the country against raids. The military problems thus posed, such as whether to meet an attacker on the beaches or conduct a "hedgerow defence" inland, were fairly small beer. It consequently proved impossible to make much of a case for army expansion on the needs of home defense until after the outbreak of the Boer War in 1899.[34]

Fielding a force sizeable enough to fight the Boers meant stripping the United Kingdom of all but a single regular battalion. Not surprisingly, the resulting situation created great public alarm. Anxiety mounted the following year when French, German, and Russian army exercises all included naval cooperation, and in the case of France involved amphibious landings. The first task of the Committee of Imperial Defence was to resolve the issue of who should claim primary responsibility for defending the United Kingdom, the army or the navy. It decided in the navy's favor in 1903, with the prime minister, Arthur Balfour, providing the authoritative strategic survey on which the decision rested. Two more enquiries followed in 1908 and 1913–14 before the matter was laid to rest, but both confirmed Balfour's

[33] Lt. Col. Walter H. James, *Modern Strategy: An outline of the principles which guide the conduct of campaigns to which is added a chapter on modern tactics* (Edinburgh & London), 1904, p. 21.
[34] The authoritative study of the invasion question is H.R. Moon, "The Invasion of the United Kingdom: Public Controversy and Official Planning 1888–1918," Ph.D. University of London, 1968; see also I.F. Clarke, *Voices Prophesying War 1763–1984* (London, 1966).

finding that the navy could protect the country against major invasions and that home defense meant only protection against small raids.

As Russia advanced to Merv in 1884 and Penjdeh on the Afghan frontier the following year, an invasion of India looked far more likely than a cross-channel attack. In 1890, the War Office concluded that checking the Russians required an advance into Afghanistan to meet an invasion on the Kabul-Kandahar line; to defeat it would require another Crimea, which in turn depended on Turkish support.[35] Within a few years, hopes of any such support finally evaporated. Thereafter, as strategy for the defense of India focused on the subcontinent itself, India sent home continually inflated estimates of the numbers required in the event of war – in 1903 it demanded 100,000 men within four months. The secretary of the Committee of Imperial Defence, Sir George Sydenham Clarke, responded by computing the number of camels necessary to keep British forces in the field. By 1905, as Kitchener trumpeted the need to maintain 155,000 troops in Afghanistan, the number of camels necessary to supply such a force exceeded 5 million, far more than local resources could ever produce.[36]

Viceroy Lord Curzon's choice of a forward strategy in India to expand British power into southern Persia was of less significance than the question of whether Indian defense and its enormous manpower requirements would become the benchmark for British military policy. The army made much of its Indian needs as a weapon in the competition for money.[37] The requirements of the subcontinent appeared to reinforce the lessons of the Boer War delineated by Field Marshal Lord Roberts in January 1903: "1. That in future campaigns we must expect demands on a vast scale for infantry drafts. 2. That our reserve is not large enough and must be increased. . . ."[38] But alongside issues of interdepartmental politics, Whitehall felt a genuine fear of what Russia might do once it possessed a rail network in the region.[39]

At the core of British strategy-making lay the perpetual need to weigh one threat against another and to balance the demands of defense against the requirement for economy. Between 1900 and 1914 Britain faced two strategic dilemmas in rapid succession. The first involved concessions in some quarters of the world and negotiating security in others. The second entailed devising plans for military intervention in Europe, something Britain had avoided for almost a hundred years. Political agreement secured the first; naval and military squabbling characterized the second.

In the same years, the anti-Russian strategy favored by Roberts and Kitch-

---

[35] Public Record Office, Memorandum by Lt. Gen. Brackenbury and Maj. Gen. Newmarch, 30 April 1890, W.O. 106/48/E3/2.

[36] For a detailed discussion of Indian strategy see Gooch, *The Plans of War*, pp. 198–237.

[37] On military plans for war in Canada see John Gooch, *The Prospect of War: Studies in British Defence Policy 1847–1942* (London, 1981), pp. 52–72.

[38] Balfour Papers, Roberts to Sandars, 17 January 1903, B.L. Add. Mss. 49725.

[39] Beryl J. Williams, "The Strategic Background to the Anglo-Russian Entente of August 1907," *Historical Journal* 9 (1966), p. 364.

ener in India collided with the rise of Japanese, American, and German naval power. Selborne summarized the problem in a letter to the viceroy that aimed to educate him on wider strategic issues: "It is a terrific task to remain the greatest Naval Power when Naval Powers are year by year increasing in numbers and in naval strength, and at the same time to be a Military Power strong enough to meet the greatest Military Power in Asia."[40]

The Russo-Japanese war of 1904–05 diminished but did not eradicate the Russian threat. The defense of India, as Sir George Clarke remarked, remained mainly a matter for the Foreign Office; he dismissed the Russian threat as improbable on logistical grounds. Others recognized that if the Russians actually invaded Afghanistan, Britain could not hope to meet them, since the country would neither pay for nor produce the vast numbers of troops needed. Diplomacy rescued strategy from its dilemma in 1907 with the conclusion of the Anglo-Russian entente.

By that point, Britain had completed a period of strategic and diplomatic reorientation symbolized by the alliance with Japan and the ententes with France and Russia. The process began in 1901 with the recognition that Britain could not maintain a two-power standard at sea if it included the United States in its calculations. As a result, Britain continued to proclaim a general two-power standard in public, but privately aimed at a reasonable certainty in preparing for war against France and Russia alone. Within a year, the mounting German naval threat made this new posture even more necessary.[41]

In choosing to overlook American naval expansion, Britain bowed to the inevitable. "It is very sad," Lord Salisbury remarked in March 1902, "but I am afraid America is bound to forge ahead and nothing can restore the equality between us."[42] The decision rested on a wide variety of considerations ranging from the much-vaunted "racial brotherhood," to the economic penalties that a war with the United States would inevitably entail.[43] The outcome was a rapid retreat; between 1904 and 1906, the army and navy withdrew their garrisons from Canadian and Caribbean bases and in effect admitted frankly that in a war with the United States, Britain could do nothing to prevent the loss of Canada.[44] Strategic rationalization and withdrawal of British garrisons to economize was nothing new: Earl Grey conducted an imperial retreat in 1846 and had reduced the Canadian garrisons

40 Selborne to Curzon, 4 January 1903, quoted in Christopher Wyatt, "Military and Strategic Defence Considerations in the Making of the Anglo-Russian Entente," B.A. dissertation, Leeds University, 1989, p. 27.
41 Aaron L. Friedberg, *The Weary Titan: Britain and the Experience of Relative Decline, 1895–1905* (Princeton, 1988), pp. 178–9.
42 Selborne Papers, Salisbury to Selborne, 13 March 1902, Selborne Box 4.
43 Stephen R. Rock, "Risk Theory Reconsidered: American Success and German Failure in the Coercion of Britain, 1890–1914," *Journal of Strategic Studies* 11 (1988), pp. 342–64.
44 S.F. Wells, "British Strategic Withdrawal from the Western Hemisphere, 1904–1906," *Canadian Historical Review* 49 (1968), pp. 335–56.

six years later.[45] But this was not partial withdrawal, but rather complete strategic abandonment. It embarrassed some British politicians, and Canada never received official notification that Britain now regarded it as indefensible.

By 1905 the Royal navy could not oppose the U.S. navy close to its own bases, and the same was true of Japan. The Japanese naval victory at Tsushima signaled both the demise of Russian naval power in the Far East and the rise of the Japanese as the dominant regional sea power. Japan posed no immediate threat, for the alliance signed with Japan in 1902 had restored a favorable balance in the Far East. The ententes with France in 1904 and Russia in 1907 likewise brought with them strategic advantages. In Sir Michael Howard's words, they added up to "a quite remarkable diplomatic feat of pacification."[46] It is worth noting that Britain realized considerable strategic gains between 1902 and 1907 by departing from long-established diplomatic principles.

In 1900, Naval Intelligence decided that Germany was Britain's most likely antagonist in a future war, and in 1902 the War Office independently concurred. Britain's experiences as a world power in the nineteenth century had not equipped it to deal with a continental power possessing both military and naval strength *and* seeking European hegemony; the British possessed no agreed strategy to meet the challenge. In the space of twelve years an intense competition between rival strategies developed, and only the existence of the Committee of Imperial Defence allowed something approaching resolution.

In 1897, Major Charles Callwell challenged the view that the army and the navy were rivals and that sea and land represented two distinct spheres of war bearing little relationship to one another. He believed instead that command of the sea was essential for the successful employment of Britain's land forces: "The great strategical principle that in virtue of supremacy upon the ocean bodies of troops, insignificant as compared with the legions which Continental Powers can put into the field, may sometimes decide tremendous issues, is becoming a basis of our national policy."[47] This was less a fact than an aspiration, but Callwell did urge adoption of an amphibious strategy by citing the lessons of the Sino-Japanese War of 1895, the Spanish-American War of 1898, and the Russo-Japanese War of 1904–05, in which naval operations had played "a prominent part in the struggle" and yet "the question of final maritime control [had] been decided by land operations."[48]

---

45 Hew Strachan, "Lord Grey and Imperial Defence," in Ian F.W. Beckett and John Gooch, *Politicians and Defence: Studies in the Formulation of British Defence Policy* (Manchester, 1981), pp. 8–10.
46 Michael Howard, *The Continental Commitment: The Dilemma of British Defence Policy in the Era of the Two World Wars* (London, 1972), p. 30.
47 C.E. Callwell, *The Effect of Maritime Command on Land Campaigns since Waterloo* (Edinburgh & London, 1897), p. 3.
48 C.E. Callwell, *Military Operations and Maritime Preponderance: Their Relations and Interdependence* (Edinburgh & London, 1905), p. 128.

The idea that an amphibious strategy might be the most effective way of dealing with the German threat appeared officially in summer 1905, when the navy expressed interest in exploring the prospects for combined operations through a special sub-committee of the CID. Callwell, then a member of the military operations section of the War Office, enthusiastically supported the scheme: the east coast of Schleswig-Holstein lent itself to such a landing, and if France were an ally, then occupation of the province could draw 400,000 German troops away from the French frontier.[49] Cooler heads concluded that the project was operationally unrealistic, since the forces available were insufficient against strong German defenses. The landing was simply not worth the risk, and on 3 October 1905 the War Office pulled out of the scheme.

The amphibious strategy resurfaced three years later when Major-General Spencer Ewart, director of military operations, and Rear-Admiral Edmond Slade, director of naval intelligence, agreed to cooperate with one another. Slade wanted to keep open the passage into the Baltic so that the navy could operate against German trade and naval forces if they took shelter there by seizing the island of Zealand.[50] Ewart's staff, as opposed to their chief, regarded the operation as a risky one and preferred direct intervention by British forces in France or Belgium.[51] The amphibious strategy included plans for small naval raids by the army against the enemy coastline but drew little attention from the CID in 1909 when it examined alternative strategies in a war with Germany. The potential gains from Baltic operations seemed insignificant compared with the dangers of a direct German attack on France.

The Admiralty's support for amphibious warfare owed something to the strategic ideas of Julian Corbett, who was close to Slade and had some influence over Fisher.[52] The notion that the army was a projectile to be fired by the navy – Sir Edward Grey's phrase, gleefully adopted by Fisher – lay at the heart of Corbett's book *Some Principles of Maritime Strategy*, published in 1911. It received further publicity that year when Major-General George Aston, a Royal Marine, published a set of lectures to the army staff college that reiterated Callwell's arguments.[53] But when subjected to searching analysis at the celebrated CID meeting on British strategy for a war against Germany held on 23 August 1911, an amphibious strategy offered little. The war would probably be over, and France, upon whose partnership Britain

[49] Public Record Office "British Action in Case of War with Germany," 28 August 1905, W.O. 106/46/E2/10.
[50] National Maritime Museum, Slade Diary, 15 January 1908, MRF 39/3.
[51] Public Record Office, "Considerations affecting the operations of a British military force in Denmark in the event of war between the U.K. and Germany," 12 June 1908, W.O. 106/46/E2/15.
[52] Marder, *Anatomy of British Sea Power*, p. 385.
[53] G.G. Aston, *Letters on Amphibious Wars* (London, 1911).

depended to defeat Germany, might be crushed before peripheral operations exercised any effect.

The Admiralty's second strategic option, the blockade of Germany, met with the same objections. During the 1890s, when the navy had focused on protecting British commerce rather attacking enemy seaborne trade, an active blockade seemed the ideal strategy, although it required numerical superiority and appropriate supporting bases for success. But blockade became a more pressing issue after 1902, when war with Germany moved up the strategic agenda. Naval officers saw an Anglo-German conflict as the clash of two commercial and economic systems, a perspective that led to blockade as the basis of strategy.

In 1903, giving evidence about the protection of overseas trade to the royal commission on food supply, the director of naval intelligence expressed moral outrage at the idea of other powers using blockade as a weapon of war against the United Kingdom: " . . . there is the larger question of humanity. You cannot condemn forty millions to starvation on the ground that they assist in defending their country, because you include women and children."[54] At the same time as Prince Louis of Battenberg uttered these words, another Admiralty study suggested that Germany and France were more vulnerable to blockade than Britain because of their higher expenditures on bread. A shift in perspective now took place: blockade ceased to be a defensive preoccupation and became instead an offensive weapon. And as the German threat mounted, scruples such as Battenberg's rapidly became an unaffordable strategic luxury.

By 1908 a group of naval officers were pressing for blockade. They argued that Britain's geographic position and preponderant sea power could throttle Germany: as one wrote, once unleashed, a blockade "would sooner or later [cause grass to] grow in the streets of Hamburg and [inflict] widespread dearth and ruin. . . ."[55] Although the navy attempted to amass the detailed trade statistics to support this contention, Germany was much more self-sufficient than supposed.

The navy failed to emphasize economic warfare over its other suggested courses of action, and thus weakened the impact of its proposals. Blockade also had innate and irremediable defects: the director of naval intelligence, Admiral Slade, admitted in 1908 that a continental blockade against Germany would never be wholly effective so long as Belgium and the Netherlands remained neutral. At the 23 August 1911 meeting of the CID, Admiral Sir Arthur Wilson, the First Sea Lord, presented the case for blockade as one part of an ill thought-out melange of strategic possibilities; a weak case

---

[54] Quoted in Avner Offer, *The First World War: An Agrarian Interpretation* (Oxford, 1989), p. 272.
[55] Ottley to McKenna, 5 December 1908, quoted in Arthur J. Marder, *From the Dreadnought to Scapa Flow*, Volume 1: *The Road to War 1904–1914* (London, 1961), p. 379.

coupled with poor presentation lost the argument.[56] The Admiralty soon dropped the idea, although thanks to Hankey it apparently survived for a while longer in the bowels of the CID.[57]

The blockade strategy possessed two fundamental weaknesses. First, it overestimated the extent of German reliance on overseas trade and the effect that interruptions of trade might have on the Reich's war effort. Second, it was a strategy for the long haul. It might deter Germany from starting a war, but only if it became declaratory strategy, which never happened. It would be of little immediate use if it failed as a deterrent, for France might collapse and Western Europe fall under German control before its effects could be felt. Contemporaries failed to perceive the first point, but the second was inescapable.

In the decade before 1914, strategic unanimity in the naval high command was absent – and this contributed to its loss of ascendancy in British defense policy. Nevertheless, most naval officers preferred a simple strategy: that of decisive battle. Mahan provided a rationale for these hopes, and the navy adopted him with great enthusiasm. "Naval history demonstrates the truth of this general principle," the Admiralty stated in 1904, " . . . the command of the sea is essential for the successful attack or defence of commerce, and should therefore be the primary aim."[58] The means of attaining that command, Mahan had argued, was decisive battle. As a strategy, this was implicit in every part of Fisher's reforms and explicit in Admiralty instructions to fleet commanders. "The principal object," ran the 1908 war orders for the commander-in-chief, Channel fleet, "is to bring the main German fleet to decisive action, and all other operations are subsidiary to this end."[59]

But some naval circles regarded the theory that "the only thing that the British fleet has to do is go for the enemy fleet & destroy it" as extremely dangerous.[60] Its weakness lay in the fact that it was not strategy at all, for it ignored the crucial issue of how to bring the High Sea Fleet to battle. The position of the battle as the ark of the naval covenant disadvantaged the navy, for it meant that the Admiralty saw amphibious operations and blockade, viable alternatives to the "strategy of battle," only as means of luring the enemy into the North Sea. Wilson, who succeeded Fisher as First Sea Lord and spoke for the navy on 23 August 1911, did not believe that blockade could have any real effect on the German economy, but thought that it might force the Germans out into open waters.

The navy was thus unable to propose a course of action to achieve its chosen objective – the destruction of the High Sea Fleet. Nor could it offer

56 For a description of the meeting of 23 August 1911 see Samuel A. Williamson, *The Politics of Grand Strategy: Britain and France Prepare for War, 1904–1914* (Cambridge, MA, 1969), pp. 187–93.
57 Offer, *The First World War*, pp. 293–8.
58 Marder, *Anatomy of British Sea Power*, p. 84.
59 Marder, *From the Dreadnought to Scapa Flow*, Vol. 1, p. 367.
60 National Maritime Museum, Slade Diary, 28 March 1908, MRF 39/3.

rapid assistance to Britain's continental allies threatened with quick defeat in a massive land campaign. The army, by contrast, nursed two alternatives that offered help to the hard-pressed French.

The War Office turned its attention to the problem of meeting possible European commitments in 1902; the first Moroccan crisis of 1905–06 further stimulated its planning for a land campaign on the continent. When confidential military conversations began between Britain and France in December 1905, the army was in no danger of being caught unprepared: earlier that year it had conducted a war game that became the basis of its strategy. The army approach to strategy-making contrasts strongly with the intuitive reasoning favored by Fisher and his admirals.

The 1905 war game produced two results that served as the foundation for British military strategy in succeeding years. Analysis of the game suggested that in the event of war, the Germans would not violate Belgian neutrality at the outset but would first attack the common frontier, and that if and when Germany did invade Belgium, it would not move its forces north of the Meuse. The game also exposed Belgium's military weakness and led to the inescapable conclusion that "unless powerful military aid is afforded her, it seems absurd to think that Belgium can stem the tide of invasion with the resources at her disposal."[61] From this point, strategies for land warfare branched out in two separate but related directions; a strategy of concentration at the decisive point competed with a strategy of diversion. Strategic principles played an important part in the debates that ensued, although the participants used them to justify widely differing proposals.

Concern about Belgium focused on the need to provide wartime assistance, and by April 1906 plans existed to send military forces directly to the Low Countries. But a military visit to Belgium that summer disclosed its unpreparedness, and no additional planning took place over the next five years. Belgium reemerged during the CID meeting of 23 August 1911, when Churchill and Lloyd George pointed out the likelihood of a French retreat after early reverses and the opportunities a Belgian landing offered to divert German forces away from the main front.

The director of military operations, Major-General Henry Wilson, who had hitherto favored direct support for France, took up the idea with alacrity. "The larger the force detached by the Germans from the decisive point the better it would be for France and ourselves," he wrote in September 1911.[62] The six-division expeditionary force would therefore create the optimum impact by concentrating alongside the Belgian army on the Germans' right flank. Unlike most of his contemporaries, Wilson willingly left the narrow realm of military affairs for the enticing arena of politics and went on to propose an Anglo-French defensive alliance that would include Belgium,

---

61   Public Record Office, Strategic War Game, 1905, pp. 13–14. W.O. 33/364.
62   Quoted in Wilson, *The Policy of the Entente*, pp. 130–31.

Denmark, and Russia. This he considered a necessary – even essential – adjunct to military policy.

In making this proposal, Wilson stepped beyond the traditional boundaries of strategy to which both soldiers and sailors had previously adhered, and received a quick reprimand. The Chief of the Imperial General Staff, General Sir William Nicholson, pointed out that Belgium had no motive for entering into such an alliance, and that the British army was too small to defend France in the crucial frontier battles and at the same time aid the Belgians.[63] Consequently, Britain's ability to field only six regular divisions was a major constraint on the making of military strategy. But Wilson planned to remedy this by transferring troops from India, until this idea ran into opposition from the viceroy.[64] By the following summer he had dropped it, although it reemerged on 5 August 1914, when Sir John French proposed sending British troops to Antwerp.

The Belgian option, although it enjoyed brief periods of resuscitation, always yielded to the strategy of direct support for France. In considering this problem, the military quickly fell in with the diplomatic *bouleversement* that had occurred between 1902 and 1907 and accepted the new diplomatic and strategic position that Britain had created for itself. General Spencer Ewart, Wilson's predecessor as director of military operations, believed that "the entente ought to be the cornerstone of our policy; the only alternative is a selfish isolation which would lead to a combination of all Europe against us under the dictatorship of Germany."[65] Ewart concluded that Britain must be ready to help France on land as well as at sea and believed that close cooperation with the French field armies might be the most effective way of protecting Belgium.[66] Despite his brief flirtation with the "Belgian option," Wilson believed the same thing, and concentrated his energies as director of military operations on perfecting the detailed arrangements for transporting Britain's expeditionary force to France.

Along with identifying the optimal strategic location for the British regulars went the question of timing. Initially, official opinion did not think that British military intervention in a Franco-German war must be immediate. Sir George Clarke, first secretary of the Committee of Imperial Defence, did not believe that the outcome of opening battles on the frontier "would . . . be a foregone conclusion by any means"; British intervention would therefore be "a formidable factor."[67] This conception implied some delay between the outbreak of Franco-German hostilities and involvement in the conflict. But by winter 1908–09, when the CID examined the problems of war, opinions

63 Imperial War Museum, Minute, 1 September 1911, Wilson 2/70/16.
64 Imperial War Museum, Wilson Diary, 26 August & 7 November 1911, Haig to Wilson, 7 September 1911, Wilson 2/70/17.
65 Ewart Diary, 7 February 1908.
66 Public Record Office, "Our Position as Regards the Low Countries," 8 April 1907, Cab. 18/24.
67 Public Record Office, Clarke to Kitchener, 5 January 1906, P.R.O. 30/57/34.

had changed. Sir William Nicholson, who had originally argued that the first battles in a war would not be decisive, now emphasized the crucial nature of the first encounters on the frontiers. The reasons were psychological rather than material; the presence of even a small British force might be important at the outset, he believed, because its presence would infuse the French with confidence. That proposition derived from a certain Clausewitzian strategic logic and had the added advantage of conforming with the political objectives of Grey, Haldane, and Asquith, all of whom supported uncompromising British support for France against Germany.

There remained one further ingredient in the "With France" strategy (military plans all bore the letters "WF"): the strategic arithmetic suggested that six British divisions could tip the scales. After estimating German forces probably committed to the west, the numbers that might be deployed on the main front, and the carrying capacity of roads in the region – which he personally reconnoitered by bicycle – Wilson calculated that the Germans could concentrate forty divisions against thirty-nine French divisions. Six British divisions would therefore give the Entente a clear – though small – numerical advantage.

Underlying his plans was an operational assumption that Wilson did not confide to the politicians but which he explained in Staff College lectures before the war. It formed the bridge between the "With France" strategy and the limitations imposed by the size of the British regular army. If, by prior arrangements and by careful training that stressed mobility, the expeditionary force could become a mobile "Flying Column" then, Wilson believed, "we give ourselves every chance not only of defeating even numbers, but of annihilating the enemy's force."[68]

The fact that its strategy apparently rested on careful calculations rather than unsupported maxims won the day for the army in August 1911. The army's proposals also conformed far more closely than the navy's to politicians' conception of British interests in Europe and how best to defend them. In reaching such an outcome, the army conjured up at least one new strategic "principle" – the importance of rapid intervention. Not surprisingly, the mathematics of Wilson's assumptions were hardly realistic. But on the eve of World War I, the naval predominance that had characterized British strategy in the nineteenth century had given way to military preeminence. The war ultimately proved everyone's calculations wrong and demonstrated that only a combined strategy could defeat a powerful continental coalition.

The test of the coherence and suitability of British strategy came in summer 1914. In political terms, it was necessary to compare the situation of July and August against previously agreed principles in order to decide when and under what circumstances the nation should take military action. This meant

---

[68] Imperial War Museum, "Lecture on Initiative & on Power of Manoeuvre," December 1909, Wilson 3/3/15W.

identifying an incontrovertible threat to British interests so that a majority of the cabinet would agree to go to war. Once Britain had answered the political questions, soldiers and statesmen had to agree on fundamental questions of practical strategy: when, where, and how to put British forces on the Continent, and whether or not to send the entire expeditionary force.

The political and military debates between 29 July and 12 August 1914 substantially undermine the claim that "The Cabinet's decision to intervene in the war in August 1914 and the policies they pursued in the next two months did not represent any fundamental departure from the strategic or political principles they had evolved before the war."[69] There was relative clarity in the political sphere, but the tone was decidedly negative rather than positive. The Grey-Cambon letters of November 1912 made it clear that Britain's commitment to support France in a war against Germany was not firm. And even the 1839 treaty guaranteeing Belgian neutrality was open to interpretation. British strategy rested on no firm principles capable of translation into unambiguous prescriptions for action, and led to the reopening of the decision taken in 1911 to commit the British army to the French left wing. Under these circumstances, the processes of semipublic debate and behind-the-scenes "fixing" required to reach a decision established a pattern of civil-military decision-making that soon had unfortunate consequences.

The cabinet initially accepted no political or moral obligations to either France or Belgium. On 29 July 1914, it completely rejected any continental commitment. At a subsequent meeting two days later it reaffirmed the "free hand" as its guiding principle and national interest as its beacon. But at the first of two cabinet meetings held on 2 August, Sir Edward Grey persuaded his colleagues that since the French had stationed the bulk of their fleet in the Mediterranean under the terms of the 1912 Anglo-French naval agreement, moral obligation and practical self-interest dictated that Britain warn Germany that it would not tolerate any German naval action in the Channel or against northern French coasts. This was a remarkable departure from established "principles," for as Samuel Williamson has pointed out, it was "the sole clear-cut instance in which the staff talks exercised a crucial influence upon the Cabinet's deliberations about war or peace."[70] At a second meeting the same day, Grey focused on the issue of the violation of Belgian neutrality, and in a speech to the House of Commons on 3 August he presented this as the *casus belli* – although without using that term.[71] Many – but not all – of the prewar political principles on which diplomacy rested had held, but both the cabinet and the Commons had had to be persuaded of the meaning placed upon them.

With the German violation of Belgian neutrality and the subsequent Brit-

69   David French, *British Strategy and War Aims, 1914–1916* (London, 1986), p. 20.
70   Williamson, *The Politics of Grand Strategy*, p. 355.
71   For the speech, Viscount Grey of Falloden, *Twenty-Five years 1892–1916*, Vol. 2 (London, 1925), pp. 294–309.

ish declaration of war on 4 August, attention switched from diplomatic to strategic policy. The discussion of land strategy at a specially convened war council on 5 August revealed deep differences of opinion on three fundamental issues: whether Britain should pursue an independent or a cooperative strategy, where it should deploy its forces, and when they should fight. In these discussions, strategic principles were of little help. As Chief of the General Staff, French had set his name to at least one memorandum based on the principle of the concentration of the greatest numbers at the decisive point, and Sir James Grierson, a former director of military operations and one of two designated corps commanders for the BEF, spoke up for it at the meeting on 5 August. But both men had quite different ideas as to where this decisive point was.[72]

The war council included the leading members of the cabinet, one sailor (Battenberg, still First Sea Lord) and no fewer than thirteen soldiers. Among the latter were Lord Kitchener, soon to become secretary of state for war; Sir John French, commander-in-chief designate of the BEF; Sir Douglas Haig and Sir James Grierson, the two corps commanders; and Field Marshal Lord Roberts, the senior soldier in the army and a man whom Asquith had regarded four months earlier as "in a dangerous condition of senile frenzy. . . ."[73]

The gathering was partly the consequence of the unusual circumstances prevailing in the army in the aftermath of the Curragh "Mutiny" of March 1914, when Asquith had temporarily taken over the War Office. At that time, French had resigned as Chief of the Imperial General Staff to be replaced by Sir Charles Douglas (also present at the War Council on 5 August), a soldier in whose judgment few put any faith. The meeting probably expressed the politicians' desire to transfer their pragmatic process of decision-making to strategy, and also an awareness of the deep divisions over strategic matters that existed within the British high command. One historian has described it as "a dismal foretaste of the strategic talking-shops which were to govern British policy for the first two years of the war."[74]

The meeting opened with French outlining the General Staff's plans to concentrate the BEF at Maubeuge, although he then instead suggested abandoning them for a concentration at Antwerp. Contrary to appearances, sound strategic principles did underlie this apparently "improvised and ambitious" scheme.[75] French believed that the guiding doctrine behind British

72 "Memorandum by the General Staff on the Effect of the Loss of Sea Power in the Mediterranean on British Military Strategy" (1 July 1912), in E.W.R. Lumby. ed., *Policy and Operations in the Mediterranean 1912–14* (London, 1970), pp. 53–55. For Grierson's intervention see Wilson Diary, 5 August 1914.
73 Asquith to Venetia Stanley, 21 March 1914, Michael & Eleanor Brock, eds., *H.H. Asquith Letters to Venetia Stanley* (Oxford, 1985), p. 59. The cause was the Curragh Incident, in which Roberts was deeply involved.
74 Richard Holmes, *The Little Field Marshal: Sir John French* (London, 1981), p. 196.
75 George H. Cassar, *The Tragedy of Sir John French* (Newark, 1985), p. 84.

strategy should be strategic independence: this would provide the flexibility to redefine national interests according to the threat. He also believed in the value of the BEF as a strategic reserve rather than as an element of the French field army, and in 1909 had suggested delaying any commitment to await events.[76] What French proposed was a soldier's equivalent to the "free hand" favored by British diplomats. But Churchill's assertion that the navy could not protect transports above the Dover-Calais line cut the ground from under French's feet.

The collapse of the Antwerp option meant that the BEF would concentrate either at Maubeuge, as Wilson wanted, or further back at Amiens as Kitchener suggested. But Haig introduced yet another strategic principle, against the run of military opinion: British intervention should only come later in the campaign. He seems to have had in mind a delay of some two or three months during which imperial forces could mobilize and train before being merged with the expeditionary force.[77] Once again, fundamental strategic issues complicated apparently simple and pragmatic questions; in this case, they involved choosing between a cooperative strategy or an independent one, and also whether the British contribution should only amount to a strategic reserve. In the latter respect, Haig's concern was timing, while French's was location.

The principle that early intervention was strategically vital had by now achieved almost universal acceptance; Haig lost the argument. Eventually the meeting adopted Roberts' suggestion that the French should decide where the BEF would concentrate. It also decided to send all six divisions. But the following day, fearful of civilian disturbances and German raids, the cabinet reversed this decision and agreed only to transport four divisions to France, with a fifth following when circumstances permitted. Six days later, on 12 August, with the help of French pressure skillfully orchestrated by Henry Wilson, Kitchener agreed to concentrate the BEF at Maubeuge as the General Staff had originally proposed.

The "strategic moment" that occurred at the end of July 1914 had two preeminent features. First, it demonstrated that British soldiers and sailors had no right of strategic authority and would always have to "sell" their preferred strategy to civilian politicians. Second, it revealed that the soldiers had neither an agreed strategy nor even an agreed reading of strategic principles. The ambiguities of peace thus carried over into the fires of war.

Britain began the conflict by despatching the bulk of its regular army to fight on the French left wing. A fervent and wholly unexpected surge of patriotism produced no fewer than 478,893 volunteers between 4 August

---

[76] For a stimulating "revisionist" discussion of French as a strategist, see William J. Philpott, "The Strategic Ideas of Sir John French," *Journal of Strategic Studies* 12 (1989), pp. 458–78.

[77] Haig to Haldane, 4 August 1914, in Gerard J. De Groot, *Douglas Haig 1861–1928* (London, 1988), p. 146; Wilson Diary, 5 August 1914.

and 12 September 1914; that enthusiasm thereby cemented Britain's strategy in place and provided a reservoir of manpower large enough to postpone conscription until 1916.[78] But since the war took a new and unexpected form and since it undermined almost every prewar strategic assumption, operational and political issues soon exerted influences on strategy that no one had foreseen.

With the appearance of stalemate along a continuous front in northwest Europe by December 1914, the British confronted the necessity of devising a strategy to cope with a long war, a contingency not addressed in prewar planning. The traditional parameters of strategy widened as politicians confronted the novel problems involved in the medium-term management of national resources. Asquith's government held fast to its laissez-faire liberal principles and tried to run the financial and industrial side of the war on the basis of "business as usual." Meanwhile, Kitchener resorted to a strategy of attrition that appeared to aim at conserving his "New Armies" of volunteers through 1915 by active defense – or what Winston Churchill termed "nibbling and gnawing" at the enemy lines. Despite pressure from his field commander and the French that led to the battles of Neuve Chapelle, Festubert, and Loos, Kitchener clung to a strategy of wearing down the enemy. He apparently hoped to continue this approach into 1916 before launching a decisive offensive.[79]

Kitchener's strategy may have aimed at letting Britain's allies bear the brunt of the fighting for the first two years of war, thus making the United Kingdom the dominant power at its conclusion, or it may have been a practical solution to the problems of preparing huge numbers of civilians for battle. Whatever its rationale, it had a major defect. As Sir William Robertson pointed out in December 1915, "We have no guarantee that the enemy will attack us if we sit still."[80]

If Britain waited too long before committing its strength against the Germans, the fighting might so weaken its allies that they could collapse. As Chief of the Imperial General Staff, Robertson counseled the politicians to concentrate the nation's military effort on the Western Front, which he regarded as the decisive theater. It was only there, he believed, and with hard fighting, that the Allies could break German military power.

In adopting this stance, Robertson took sides in a crucial debate over whether Britain should focus its energies and resources on the Western Front or adopt a "peripheral" strategy. The "Easterners" – led by Winston Churchill and Maurice Hankey, secretary to the war cabinet, with intermit-

[78] Peter Simkins, *Kitchener's Army: The Raising of the New Armies, 1914–1916* (Manchester, 1988), pp. 75, 325. For a full survey of this question see Keith Grieves, *The Politics of Manpower, 1914–1918* (Manchester, 1988).

[79] David French, "The Meaning of Attrition, 1914–16," *English Historical Review* 103 (1988), pp. 385–405.

[80] Sir William Robertson, *Soldiers and Statesmen 1914–1918* Vol. 2 (London, 1926), p. 200.

tent support from Kitchener – argued that without the development of new tactics or inventions, the war in France and Flanders would slaughter hundreds of thousands without result. They maintained that a flank attack on the Central Powers, away from its strength, the German army, would make proper use of British sea power and undermine Germany's weaker allies, thereby precipitating German collapse.[81] But the failure of the Dardanelles campaign (April 1915-January 1916) showed that a peripheral amphibious strategy exceeded Allied tactical and operational capabilities, whatever its putative strategic merits.

The "Westerners," led by Haig and Robertson, based their calculations on two classical strategic principles: that concentration of force led to victory, and that decisive victory resulted from the defeat of the main enemy armed force. For one year, 1916, they had their head. Thereafter, under Lloyd George's premiership and in the face of the manpower costs of a "western" strategy, attention turned to peripheral campaigns in Palestine and Italy. In the end, the German offensive of March 1918 dictated a "western" strategy. Although perhaps correct in an abstract sense, the proponents of this "western" strategy could not convert their theoretical formulations into operational success.[82]

In France the new field commander, Haig, undertook a series of costly and fruitless offensives in 1916 and 1917 in the belief that traditional principles – engaging the enemy on a wide front, drawing in his reserves, wearing him out, and finally launching a decisive blow – would work in the new conditions of trench warfare.[83] In obstinately sticking to this operational approach, Haig ignored the realities of military technology; not until 1918 did the British army develop a tactical doctrine that emphasized collaboration between arms.[84] Haig also ignored alternatives such as "bite and hold" tactics that Sir Henry Rawlinson developed in 1916. And Haig also ignored a series of increasingly blunt warnings from Robertson in London against pushing on regardless of casualties. "The best plan seems to me to go back to one of the old principles, that of defeating the enemy's army," Robertson suggested in April 1917. "In other words instead of aiming at breaking through the enemy's front, aim at breaking down the enemy's army, and that means inflicting on him heavier losses than one suffers oneself. If this old

---

[81] For Hankey's important "Boxing Day Memorandum," see Lord Hankey, *The Supreme Command 1914–1918,* Vol. 1 (London, 1960), pp. 244–50; also S.W. Roskill, *Hankey,* 1: 244–50.

[82] The best brief summary of this debate is still Robert Blake, ed., *The Papers of Douglas Haig 1914–1919* (London, 1952), pp. 31–32.

[83] Tim Travers, *The Killing Ground: The British Army, the Western Front and the Emergence of Modern Warfare, 1900–1918* (London, 1987), pp. 86–97; De Groot, *Douglas Haig,* pp. 172, 201–2.

[84] On the whole question of military technology and doctrine, see the excellent study by Shelford Bidwell & Dominick Graham, *Firepower: British Army Weapons and Theories of War 1904–1945* (Boston & London, 1982).

principle is kept in view . . . the casualty bill will be less."[85] Sticking to his own version of prewar principles, Haig ignored this advice. With the political support of the king and of leading conservative politicians, he survived the war. Many of the men under his command were not so fortunate.

Although both Haig and Robertson regarded the Western Front as decisive, it was impossible to concentrate exclusively upon it. With France, Russia, and a number of other minor powers as allies, Britain had to commit itself to their goals as well as to its own.[86] Britain also had to commit troops outside Europe. "Fancy our fighting on a front from Calais to Constantinople," Robertson reflected with some surprise in March 1915.[87] But it was not a single front. From the time Turkey entered the war in November 1914, Britain had to fight two wars, one in Europe and the other in the Middle East; by 1916, British troops were in action in Egypt and Salonica as well as in France and Flanders.

Because of their alliances, the British could not determine their strategy autonomously, and the French in particular exerted military and political pressures to which Britain had to accede. Thus the Somme campaign aimed to relieve the French armies engaged at Verdun, and Robertson could never conclude the Salonica campaign, despite the fact that he regarded its dispersion of allied strength as "unsound from every point of view. . . ."[88] The need to support Russia was a powerful factor in launching the ill-fated Dardanelles campaign, another unwelcome diversion of resources; and Lloyd George's appetite for morsels of the Turkish empire also forced Robertson to accept a further dispersion of British efforts.

It is here that some major deficiencies in the British army's prewar strategic thought and planning become apparent. The British made little effort to cooperate with their continental land allies and preferred to retain strategic independence. The abandonment of the decision reached at the Chantilly conference of December 1915 to launch simultaneous Allied offensives the following year looks, in retrospect, to have been one of the major strategic errors of the war. Nor did Britain capitalize on the opportunities offered by a multitheater war to deploy its forces to divert enemy resources to less critical theaters, as Robertson's attitude toward Salonica demonstrates.

[85] Robertson to Haig, 20 April 1917, quoted in David R. Woodward, ed., *The Military Correspondence of Sir William Robertson* (London, 1989), p. 179.

[86] On the development of British war aims and their relationship with those of Britain's allies, see M.G. Ekstein-Frankl, "The Development of British War Aims, August 1914–March 1915," Ph.D. University of London, 1969; V.H. Rothwell, *British War Aims and Peace Diplomacy 1914–1918* (Oxford, 1971); David French, *British Strategy and War Aims 1914–1916* (London, 1986).

[87] Robertson to Wigram, 24 March 1915, quoted in Woodward, *Sir William Robertson,* p. 10.

[88] Robertson to Mahon, 6 March 1916, quoted in ibid., p. 38. See also David Dutton, "The 'Robertson Dictatorship' and the Balkan Campaign in 1916," *Journal of Strategic Studies* 9 (1986), pp. 64–78.

Naval strategy in 1914 aimed at commanding home waters, at closing the enemy's routes to the world's oceans, and at seizing the most favorable position for a general fleet engagement should the High Sea Fleet leave its bases. In operational terms, this was a preventive role. After the battle of the Falkland Islands in December 1914, no German surface raiders remained on the open seas; protecting British trade now merely meant bottling up the enemy's surface fleet. Geography greatly assisted that defensive strategy, but it also hindered the offensive. The destructive capability of mines and torpedo boats in narrow waters meant, as Admiral Sir George Callaghan concluded on the eve of war, that "we are debarred by geographical reasons from executing any strong offensive against an enemy unless they seek battle in the open sea. . . ."[89]

If geography made the navy's primary strategic task difficult, technological developments rendered it unacceptably hazardous. The sinking of the cruisers *Cressy, Hogue,* and *Aboukir* by a single U-boat on 22 September 1914 provided unambiguous evidence of the vulnerability of surface vessels to submarine attack. Six days later Admiral Jellicoe informed the First Lord, Churchill, that he intended to keep the Grand Fleet well out of harm's way until the submarine menace had been overcome.[90] A month later Jellicoe went further. If the British and German battle fleets ever came into contact and if "the enemy battle fleet were to turn away from an advancing Fleet," he told Churchill, "I should assume that the intention was to lead us over mines and submarines, and should decline to be so drawn."[91]

After several minor sorties in the war's early months, the High Sea Fleet at last met the Grand Fleet at Jutland on 31 May 1916. Jellicoe first turned away from the enemy to position his guns better and then, meeting the enemy for a second time, turned away from an enemy torpedo attack after a six-minute engagement in which the Germans suffered the heaviest bombardment ever delivered at sea. At Jutland, Jellicoe put the strategic need to preserve his fleet – Britain's dominance at sea – ahead of the operational need to risk it in order to defeat his adversary.

Even if Jellicoe had inflicted a Mahanian defeat on the Germans, the victory probably would not have decided the general course of the war in Britain's favor; at least that is what Churchill felt when he first drafted his war memoirs (although he later changed his mind). German victory, however, would have ended Britain's command of the North Sea and might conceivably have cost it the war. The actual outcome merely confirmed the stalemate to which surface warfare had been reduced. The failure of the

[89] "Admiral Sir George Callaghan's Review of the War Plans after Manoeuvres, 1913," in B. McL. Ranft, ed., *The Beatty Papers,* Vol. 1 (London 1989), p. 85.
[90] Jellicoe to Churchill, 30 September 1914, in, A. Temple. Patterson, ed., *The Jellicoe Papers* (London, 1966), pp. 71–72.
[91] Jellicoe to Churchill, 30 October 1914, in ibid. p. 76.

German fleet to venture out into the North Sea again caused the Royal Navy considerable strategic frustration; as Admiral Beatty remarked after the war, "[the enemy] did not give us what we hoped for – a good stand-up fight."[92]

At the outbreak of war, the navy reintroduced its traditional strategy of blockade; for a variety of reasons it had only limited effect. Technically, the development of mines, submarines, and coastal artillery meant that a close blockade was now impossible; instead, a distant blockade involved stopping merchant vessels in the Dover Straits or off the north of Scotland. Diplomatic obstacles were more limiting. Despite eagerness to redefine "conditional" and "absolute" contraband and to extend the doctrine of "continuous voyage," Britain bowed to neutral pressure and thereby diminished the effectiveness of the strategy.[93] Only after the United States's entry into the war on 6 April 1917 did the blockade become fully effective.

On the eve of America's entry, the British naval high command split over the importance of blockade. Beatty thought it might win or lose the war; Jellicoe believed that only the defeat of the enemy's armed forces – "certainly on land, and probably at sea" – would be decisive.[94] In autumn 1917, with a decisive sea battle looking unlikely, the navy accepted that it must shape its sea strategy to achieve two objectives; "firstly, to bring pressure to bear on the enemy people so as to compel their Government to come to terms, and secondly, to resist the pressure applied by them so that we may carry on the war undisturbed."[95] By then, it was the latter task that preoccupied both service and civilian minds.

The effects of blockade were cumulative, but Germany's access to continental sources of raw materials partially offset them. Not until 1916–17 did food shortages and food prices cause serious internal difficulties in Germany and generate demands for peace and reform that in turn caused the authorities to react with repressive measures.[96] A gradual decline in food intake resulted partly from poor harvests and partly from organizational failures: Germany did not put food production and distribution on a war footing until 1917. By 1918, blockade had decreased the volume of imports by approximately 25 percent compared with prewar levels with consequent drastic effects on morale. Contemporaries believed in the efficacy of the blockade of Germany, and in the postwar years it became almost an article of faith in Britain, although a recent study has concluded that German people "were

92 "Address given by Admiral Sir David Beatty . . . 24 November 1918," quoted in Ranft, *The Beatty Papers*, pp. 571–72.
93 A.J. Marder, *From the Dreadnought to Scapa Flow*, Vol. 2, *The War Years: To the Eve of Jutland 1914–1916* (London, 1966), pp. 372–77.
94 A.J. Marder, *From the Dreadnought to Scapa Flow*, Vol. 3, *1917: Year of Crisis* (London, 1969), pp. 40–41.
95 A.J. Marder, *From the Dreadnought to Scapa Flow*, Vol. 5, *1918–1919: Victory and Aftermath* (London, 1970), p. 298.
96 G. Feldman, *Army, Industry and Labor in Germany 1914–1918* (Princeton, 1966), pp. 334–43.

often cold and hungry . . . [but] whatever their complaints, Germany did not starve."[97]

If surface naval warfare frustrated prewar strategic calculations, submarine warfare entirely upset them. In the years before the war, the naval staff saw the submarine as an adjunct to the main battle fleet. This was partly the consequence of a complete failure to imagine that submarines acting as commerce raiders might disregard traditional rules of cruiser warfare, which required warning of an attack and the safe removal of passengers and crew before sinking merchant vessels. The development of oceangoing submarines and the obvious vulnerability of Britain to commerce warfare inspired the Germans to declare "total" naval war on 4 February 1915. Protests from the United States helped end the campaign in summer 1915, but Germany resumed it again on 1 February 1917.

The Admiralty met the German U-boat strategy with conventional operational techniques, but was unable to defeat the enemy because it could not locate him. Patroling trade routes and despatching ships to hunt for submarines – the traditional method for dealing with surface raiders – simply wasted assets: in one week in September 1916, three U-boats operating in the English Channel sank thirty ships in an area patrolled by 572 surface vessels without loss to themselves.[98] The solution, much to First Sea Lord Jellicoe's despair, was ocean convoys. The navy's resistance to convoying, finally overcome in 1917, was the result of two factors: a gross overestimation of the number of vessels requiring escorts, and the belief that civilian masters could not keep their ships in formation.[99] The U.S. navy's participation played a major role in the success of convoying, although the turning point did not come until July 1918, when the tonnage of shipping launched finally exceeded that lost.

CONCLUSION

In 1890, Britain was a great imperial power without an imperial grand strategy. Strategic wisdom amounted to little more than local defense schemes and a limited awareness of the difficulties inherent in defending particular parts of a farflung empire. The diplomatic management of the challenges presented by the United States, Japan, France, and Russia between 1900 and 1907 was a pragmatic adjustment to unavoidable realities. British diplomats made up British strategy as they went along.

---

[97] Offer, *The First World War*, p. 53. Note also Jay Winter's observation that "it was the failure of the German war economy which lost Germany the Great War": J.M. Winter, *The Great War and the British People* (London, 1985), p. 19.

[98] Paul M. Kennedy, "Britain in the First World War," in Allan R. Millett & Williamson Murray, eds., *Military Effectiveness*, Vol. 1 (Boston & London, 1988), p. 58.

[99] On the introduction of convoying and Hankey's putative role in it, see Stephen Roskill, *Hankey*, 1: 353–8, 379–82.

The resort to political solutions to solve strategic dilemmas was one striking feature of the making of British strategy before 1914. The absence of a consensual naval and military strategy was another. The creation of the Committee of Imperial Defence did much to sustain the adversarial nature of strategic debate between the services and little to eradicate it. The war years revealed the extent to which the strategic preferences of army and navy rested upon unproven or untested operational capabilities and exposed the deficiencies in their strategies. The searing feud between Lloyd George on the one hand and Haig and Robertson on the other demonstrates the extent to which Britain failed during the war to devise a political and military strategy acceptable to both civilians and military.[100]

In retrospect, it seems clear that Britain needed two strategies between 1890 and 1918: one for peace and one for war. In peacetime, a determination not to relinquish the empire and to limit expenditure on armaments to the lowest feasible levels meant that the British had only two alternatives – to juggle inadequate resources in an impossible attempt to make imperial ends meet, or to enter into diplomatic commitments aimed at reducing the array of possible enemies. After following the first course for a decade, British policymakers briefly departed from the established canons of policymaking between 1902 and 1907, thereafter falling back into the traditional framework. The lack of clear evidence that a firm commitment to France before 30 July 1914 might have deterred Germany ensured that Britain did not reverse its diplomatic practices after the war. In this respect, the relationship between policy and strategy in Britain emerged fundamentally unchanged from the experiences of 1890–1914.

British strategy for war traditionally revolved around the strength and virtuosity of the navy and the historic constraints on the power of governments that had left Britain with only a small professional army. The consequence was a preference for indirect pressure rather than direct shock – a preference strongly reinforced by the bloody debacles on the Somme and at Passchendaele. The apparent success of the blockade in bringing about Germany's internal collapse – and Haig's apparent failure to bring it about externally – combined to set the strategic parameters within which interwar thinkers proposed strategies for using the aircraft and tank. Thus the world war shaped the making of future military strategy, but left imperial strategy broadly unchanged.

[100] For the best recent account, see David Woodward, *Lloyd George and the Generals* (Newark, NJ, 1983).

11

The strategy of the decisive weight: Italy, 1882–1922

BRIAN R. SULLIVAN

In late 1918, Italy finally acquired European great power status. Austria-Hungary had disintegrated, military defeat had severely diminished the power of Germany, war and revolution had crippled Russia, and the cost of victory had drained France and Britain. Yet once these surviving states recovered, Italy faced major challenges to its status. Unfortunately for Italy, its leaders drew few correct conclusions from recent history. The Italian failure to sustain the bases for continued success suggests a number of somber lessons. Most striking, perhaps, are the disastrous consequences that can attend the use of force as the principal tool of national strategy without the union of people, military, and government that Clausewitz described as necessary for the successful prosecution of war.[1]

Five wars between 1848 and 1870 under a highly centralized Liberal constitutional monarchy created the Kingdom of Italy. The king, the prime minister, and the foreign minister alone directed foreign policy. Military affairs, by the constitution and precedents established during the recent wars, remained the preserve of the monarch and his war and navy ministers. This compartmentalized and incoherent system nevertheless unified the peninsula.

But after Cavour's death in 1861, the fragmented direction of Italian national strategy led to military disaster during the war of 1866, and almost did so in 1870, when Vittorio Emanuele II nearly declared war on Prussia. The Italians nevertheless persuaded themselves that they could look back to the Risorgimento as an unmitigated triumph – so long as they did not look too closely. Indeed, by allying with France in 1858, with Prussia in 1866, and by shifting sides periodically, the Italians had accomplished much with little. As

---

[1] Carl von Clausewitz, *On War,* Michael Howard and Peter Paret, eds., (Princeton, 1984), p. 89; Michael Howard, *Clausewitz* (Oxford, 1988), pp. 72–3.

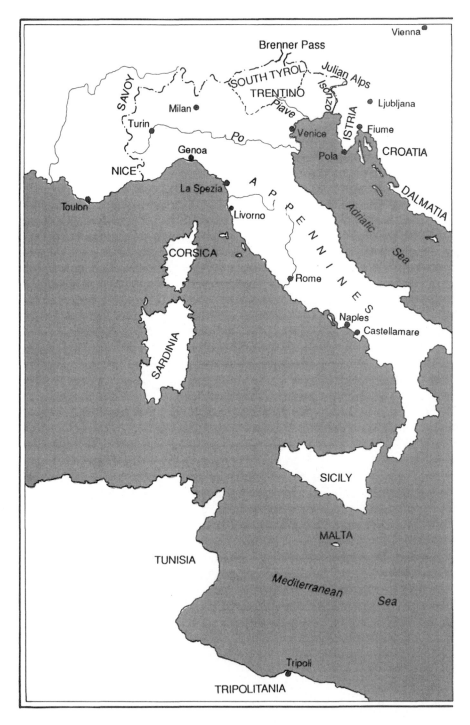

Map 11.1. Italy/Mediterranean in World War I.

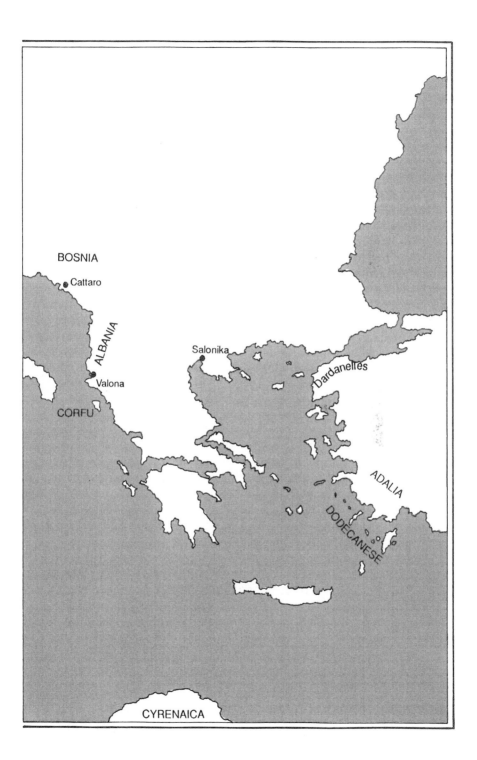

a result, their inefficient system for coordinating foreign policy, military policy, and national strategy remained substantially unchanged until 1915.[2]

THE SEARCH FOR AN ITALIAN NATIONAL STRATEGY, 1882–1900

Inquiry about the ends and means of national strategy in the decades after unification would have puzzled the ruling class. Put in Clausewitzian terms, the question presupposes some understanding of the need for matching resources to policy ends and for close coordination between political and military leaders. That understanding, however, was as lacking in Italy as knowledge of Clausewitz himself.[3] And any such question would have required the definition of a national goal.

After 1870, knowledgeable Italians felt vulnerable to attack from either France or Austria-Hungary. But beyond national survival, many hoped for the acquisition of the *terre irredente,* the Italian-inhabited "unredeemed lands" of Trentino and Istria still controlled by the Habsburg Monarchy. Some dreamed of gaining Dalmatia, for Venice had controlled that strategic coast until Austrian annexation in 1796. A few extended Italy's national claims to include Nice and even Savoy, both surrendered to France in 1860, and possibly to Corsica or British-controlled Malta.

But for several decades after unification such aspirations had little direct influence on the actual policies of the one man who exercised control over both Italian foreign and military policy – the king. Article 5 of the 1848 *statuto* of the Kingdom of Sardinia, which became the Italian constitution in 1861, stated that "the executive power is reserved to the King alone. He is the supreme head of state; he commands all the armed forces on land and sea; he declares war, makes treaties of peace, of alliance, of commerce, and of other kinds, giving notice of them to the Chambers [of parliament] as soon as the interest and security of the state allow. . . ."[4]

Until 1945 the three kings who ruled Italy and their ministers took full advantage of these powers of war and secret diplomacy. For centuries, the House of Savoy had relied on war and intrigue as the major instruments of its foreign policy. Until his death in early 1878, Vittorio Emanuele II sent out emissaries in search of military glory and territorial aggrandizement in any promising direction, although without success after 1870. While less crude

---

[2] Denis Mack Smith, *Italy and its Monarchy* (New Haven, 1989), pp. 3–6, 23–34; Christopher Seton-Watson, *Italy from Liberalism to Fascism: 1870–1925* (London, 1967), pp. 34–5.

[3] John Gooch, "Clausewitz Disregarded: Italian Military Thought and Doctrine, 1815–1943" in Michael I. Handel, ed., *Clausewitz and Modern Strategy* (London, 1986).

[4] Shepard B. Clough and Salvatore Saladino, *A History of Modern Italy: Documents, Readings, and Commentary* (New York, 1967), p. 67.

than his warlike, scheming, and somewhat stupid father, Umberto I inherited his thirst for prestige and power through conquest.[5]

The notion that the unification of Italy would be the first step toward the recreation of the Roman Empire had inspired several of the most important figures of the Risorgimento, particularly Giuseppe Mazzini. The Italian conquest of Rome in 1870, followed by the transfer of the capital to that city, greatly strengthened these imperial tendencies. But the weakness of the Italian economy discouraged expansion; payments on the cumulative debts of the wars of the Risorgimento consumed an average of 34 percent of impoverished Italy's budget until 1897. But the desire to emulate the Romans, known as *Romanità*, combined with inability to do so, plagued the nation for the next seven decades.[6]

Tunisia was the first aspiration of Italian imperialism because of its proximity to Sicily, its strategic location, the increasing numbers of Italians settling there, and its identification with ancient Carthage. French occupation of that North African kingdom in 1881 both infuriated and frightened the Italian ruling class. National outrage prompted an increase in the size of the army, led to the appointment of the army's first chief of staff actually empowered to draw up war plans, and provoked Umberto I into seeking anti-French alliances with Germany and Britain. The king and his small group of advisers hoped that Italy, under the protection of Europe's most powerful land and sea powers, could pursue imperial aims in the Balkans, the Mediterranean, and Africa regardless of French opposition.

Only the alliance with Germany proved feasible. But while Bismarck agreed to the Italian proposal, he insisted that Italy join the existing military and diplomatic pact between Germany and Austria-Hungary. Italian resentment of France outweighed hostility toward the Dual Monarchy, and King Umberto's admiration for the Germans helped overcome his antipathy toward the Habsburgs. Italy therefore entered into what became the Triple Alliance in May 1882. In turn, the Italians received assurances that the alliance would never force them into conflict with Britain.

Umberto hoped that alliance would lessen the Habsburg Monarchy's anxiety over its frontiers with Italy and encourage Austro-Hungarian expansion into the Balkans. Italy would then be able to claim compensation in the form of some of the *terre irredente*. But Italy's constitutional system allowed the monarchy to conceal these plans and even the very existence of the treaty from public and parliament.[7]

[5] Denis Mack Smith, *Victor Emanuel, Cavour and the Risorgimento* (London, 1971), pp. 367–8; idem., *Italy and its Monarchy*, passim; Gaetano Salvemini, *La politica estera dell'Italia dal 1871 al 1914* (Florence, 1944), pp. 34–49.

[6] Seton-Watson, *Italy*, p. 16; B.R. Mitchell, *European Historical Statistics 1750–1970* (London, 1978), p. 5; Federico Chabod, *Storia della politica estera italiana dal 1870 al 1896*, 2 vols., (Bari, 1976), vol. 1, pp. 289–313; Giorgio Rochat and Giulio Massobrio, *Breve storia dell'esercito italiano dal 1861 al 1943* (Turin, 1978), p. 71.

[7] Chabod, *Storia della politica estera*, vol. 2, pp. 602–4; Massimo Mazzetti, *L'esercito* ·

Until 1915 the Triple Alliance proved more a leash than a shield for Italy. Bismarck, his successors, and the Austro-Hungarians recognized Italy's weakness and generally treated it with contempt. With reason, the Germans discouraged Italian colonialism as a dissipation of Italian military resources. In the 1870–1908 period, the Italian government, despite its best efforts, still spent a yearly average of only one-seventh of what the French lavished on their army, and barely one-half of what the Austro-Hungarians expended. Until 1915, far more male Italians reached eligibility for military service each year than the government could equip.

Yet the fundamental weaknesses that afflicted the *Regio Esercito* were mental rather than material. Despite the creation of a general staff in 1867 and the appointment of a true chief of staff in 1882, Italy largely failed to develop a body of military thought. Thanks in part to the traditions of the Sardinian army, the Italian army maintained a decidedly anti-intellectual atmosphere, discouraged contact between its officers and civilian society, and treated independent thinking with hostility. The high command of the Sardinian army had prized obedience above creativity, and the *Regio Esercito* retained that attitude, thanks in part to its police tasks in a new nation suffering from regionalism, banditry, and political and economic discontent.[8]

These weaknesses justified Bismarck's fears about Italian colonial aspirations. The influence of *Romanità* on successive Italian governments nevertheless proved powerful. Bismarck vetoed Italian attempts to join Britain in its occupation of Egypt in July 1882, but failed to prevent an Italian expedition to East Africa in January 1885.[9] Replying to critics of the landing of Italian troops at Massawa, Italian Foreign Minister Pasquale Stanislao Mancini had retorted, ". . . in the Red Sea, the closest to the Mediterranean, we can find the key of the latter, the way that leads us to effective security against any new disturbance of its equilibrium . . ."[10] Mancini argued that from the

italiano nella triplice alleanza (Naples, 1974), pp. 22, 30; Zaghi, *P.S. Mancini*, pp. 31–76; Salvemini, *La politica estera*, pp. 63–9; Seton-Watson, *Italy*, pp. 31, 106–14, 202; Ugoberto Alfassio Grimaldi, *Il re "buono"* (Milan, 1980), p. 164; William A. Renzi, *In the Shadow of the Sword: Italy's Neutrality and Entrance Into the Great War, 1914–1915* (New York, 1987), pp. 1–5; Mack Smith, *Italy and its Monarchy*, p. 79; Rinaldo Petrignani, *Neutralità e alleanza: Le scelte di politica estera dopo l'Unità* (Bologna, 1987).

8 Filippo Stefani, *La storia della dottrina e degli ordinamenti dell'esercito italiano*, 3 vols., (Rome, 1984–85), vol. 1, *Dall'esercito piemontese all'esercito di Vittorio Veneto*, pp. 259–62, 293, 569–70; Ferrucci Botti and Virgilio Ilari, *Il pensiero militare italiano dal primo al secondo dopoguerra (1919–1949)* (Rome, 1985), pp. 37–41; Brian R. Sullivan, "A Thirst for Glory: Mussolini, the Italian Military and the Fascist Regime, 1922–1936," Ph.D. dissertation, Columbia University, 1984, pp. 34–47; Virgilio Ilari, *Storia del servizio militare in Italia*, 4 vols., (Rome, 1989–91) vol. 2, *La "nazione armata" (1871–1918)*, pp. 91–344.

9 Ottavio Barié, "Italian Imperialism: the First Stage," *The Journal of Italian History*, Winter 1979; Petrignani, *Neutralità e alleanza*, pp. 358–60.

10 Roberto Battaglia, *La prima guerra d'Africa* (Turin, 1958), p. 180.

Red Sea, Italy could expand into the Sudan against the Mahdi's empire, while the British advanced from Egypt. A joint expedition could establish the foundations of an Italo-British alliance in the Mediterranean.

Mancini nourished even more grandiose ambitions. He envisioned expansion from the Red Sea to the Nile, then across the Sahara into North Africa. This could lead to Italian domination of Tripolitania and the recovery of Tunisia, giving Italy a swathe of Africa from the Mediterranean to the Indian Ocean. Although Britain would still control Suez, Italy would have outflanked Egypt and escaped from Mediterranean capitivity.[11]

But Mancini's plans collapsed when Britain decided against the reconquest of the Sudan and the Italians failed to adopt the more practical goal of moving along the Red Sea coast to gain control of the strategic Bab al Mandeb. Instead, they turned their attention inland to Ethiopia. This led to a successful war in 1887–88 and the formal establishment of the Italian colony of Eritrea, an adaptation of the Roman name for the Red Sea. In 1889, the Italians assumed protection of a desolate stretch of the Indian Ocean coast and developed the colony of Somalia. They thus controlled areas to both the northeast and southeast of the simultaneously expanding Ethiopian Empire. But they also had begun a conflict for which they lacked a realistic strategy.

The Triple Alliance required increased military spending and costly railroad expansion. Combined with neo-Roman imperialism, these placed the Italian economy under heavy strain. Giovanni Giolitti warned parliament in November 1887 that Italy could either pursue grandeur, with increases in military spending and declining individual freedom, or work for democracy and the hope of better lives for ordinary Italian peasants. Umberto I and Prime Minister Francesco Crispi chose imperialism.[12]

The Italian national strategy-making process had remained basically unchanged since the Risorgimento. Foreign policy remained the secret preserve of the king, prime minister, and foreign minister. One man, Crispi, held both portfolios in 1887–91. Military policy, free from parliamentary influence save approval of the budget, was controlled by the monarch and his senior generals and admirals. Only the king could coordinate diplomacy and military strategy, and approve the passage of relevant intelligence between civilian and military leaders. Umberto I buttressed his authority by keeping information to himself, but lacked the intellect and education to coordinate national strategy himself.

Crispi failed to gain Bismarck's approval for war with France to win back Tunisia. The Germans and British also thwarted Crispi's designs on Morocco

---

[11] Carlo Zaghi, *P.S. Mancini, l'Africa e il problema del Mediterraneo, 1884–1885* (Rome, 1955), pp. 89–112; Petrignani, *Neutralità e alleanza*, pp. 381–93; Sidney Sonnino, *Diario 1866–1912*, Benjamin F. Brown, ed., (Bari, 1972), pp. 516–7.

[12] Rochat and Massobrio, *Breve storia*, pp. 66–83; Nino Valeri, *Giovanni Giolitti* (Turin, 1972), pp. 88–9.

and Tripolitania. Crispi's failure to gain German support for Italian expansion and the collapse of the Italian economy led the king to dismiss Crispi in 1891, but recall him two years later.[13]

Crispi also attempted to conquer Ethiopia, but Italy's allies refused support. They saw no advantage for the Triple Alliance in an Italian empire in East Africa. Meanwhile, France had formed an alliance with Russia in 1894, and the two new allies proceeded to arm the Ethiopians because a great East African Italian colony would block French plans for a trans-African empire. The British refused to allow the Italians to land troops in British Somaliland and march inland to divert and divide the Ethiopian forces. Increasing Anglo-German antagonism and British movement toward an understanding with the French and Russians dissuaded the British from cooperating with Germany's ally. Any chance of an Italian-British-German alliance died.[14]

Even under ideal circumstances, the conquest of Ethiopia lay beyond Italian resources. Yet Crispi thought his power, and Umberto I his prestige, dependent on a great victory in Africa. The Sicilian prime minister also believed that he could settle landless southern peasantry on the East African plateau, thus bleeding off Italy's chronic social unrest and harnessing emigration to imperialism. Whether such motivations can be considered national strategy is another matter. Neither Umberto nor Crispi understood the force required to subdue Ethiopia. The inadequate army they had sent to Eritrea stumbled to military disaster at Adowa on 1 March 1896. Crispi resigned immediately, his power and Italy's ambitions shattered.

Between 1887 and 1896, the Italian army lost 9,500 dead in East Africa, losses proportionately comparable to American casualties in Vietnam, over roughly the same period of time. These dead represented a heavy price for two arid colonies totally unfit for large-scale settlement, and only useful as springboards for future aggression against Ethiopia. In the months after Adowa, the king failed to generate enthusiasm for a war of revenge, and in October 1896 he reluctantly signed a treaty that recognized the independence of Ethiopia.[15]

The worst consequences of the Italian defeat were domestic. Though Italy suffered a severe depression between 1888 and 1896, Umberto refused to reduce military expenditure even to create a better-armed, smaller army. Internal security, and what remained of Italian prestige, required a large army and continued high taxation. In 1898–99, post-1896 industrial expansion

---

[13] Seton-Watson, *Italy,* pp. 80, 154, 161–3; Renato Mori, *La politica estera di Francesco Crispi (1887–1891)* (Rome, 1973); Sonnino, *Diario 1866–1912,* p. 153; Battaglia, *La prima guerra,* pp. 395–7.

[14] Seton-Watson, *Italy,* pp. 176–81; C.J. Lowe, "Anglo-Italian Differences over East Africa, 1892–1895, and their Effects upon the Mediterranean Entente," *The English Historical Review,* April 1966.

[15] Alfassio Grimaldi, *Il re "buono",* pp. 319–329; Battaglia, *La prima guerra ,* pp. 563–807; Sonnino, *Diario 1866–1912,* pp. 183–264; Stefani, *Dall'esercito piemontese,* p. 264; Seton-Watson, *Italy,* pp. 182–5.

generated the first budget surplus since unification, the king appeared vindicated. He nevertheless recognized that the African debacle had revealed serious shortcomings in his military command system. Therefore, in July 1899 he established a Supreme Commission for the Defense of the State under Crown Prince Vittorio Emanuele that consisted of the highest ranking members of the armed forces (although not the war and navy ministers). For the first time, the army and navy chiefs of staff revealed to each other their strategic planning. However, disclosure did not lead to strategic coordination, nor did the king press for such coordination. Lack of coherence continued to afflict Italian military planning.[16]

REACHING FOR GREAT POWER STATUS,
1900–1908

In June 1900 an anarchist murdered Umberto I. The new king, Vittorio Emanuele III, showed devotion to the parliamentary system and determination to defuse Italy's social crisis. After fresh labor unrest in 1900–01, the king appointed a government dominated by its interior minister, Giovanni Giolitti. Giolitti became prime minister in November 1903 and dominated Italian politics until March 1914. He enjoyed three advantages over his immediate predecessors. First, he was the greatest master of Italian politics since Cavour. Second, the failures of Umberto I and Crispi had discredited their methods, allowing Giolitti to seek accommodation with the newly-emerging working and lower middle classes. Third, and above all, Giolitti's years in power coincided with Italy's most intense period of sustained economic and industrial growth until the 1950s.

To encourage stability and check French influence, the Germans invested heavily in Italian industry from the 1890s. Emigrants' remittances brought in additional capital. A 50 percent increase in agricultural prices after 1896 greatly raised landowners' incomes and even brought some prosperity to the peasantry. Italy's growth rate after 1898 was the highest in Europe. And despite heavy emigration, Italy's population rose from 25 million to 34.7 million between 1861 and 1911, while France's population barely advanced, from 37.4 to 38.8 million.[17] Yet by 1913–14, Italy was still a poor and largely agricultural nation, and Italian income per capita averaged half that of Germany and a third that of Britain.

In 1882, the Russian ambassador had remarked that Italy was treated as a

---

16 John Gooch, *Army, State and Society in Italy, 1870–1915* (New York and London, 1989), pp. 110–1.
17 Seton-Watson, *Italy*, pp. 284–97; Alberto Acquarone, *L'Italia giolittiana (1896–1915)* vol. I, *Le premesse politiche ed economiche* (Bologna, 1981), pp. 39–41; Mack Smith, *Italy and its Monarchy*, p. 184; Mitchell, *European Historical Statistics*, pp. 4, 5, 47; Richard Bosworth, *Italy and the Approach of the First World War* (New York, 1983), pp. 8–16.

great power only out of courtesy; no one really believed it. By 1914, thanks to its economic growth, Italy approached that status, although by the barest of margins. In the decade before World War I, their surging industrial base enabled the Italians to expand greatly their military and naval power. When added to geographic position and a relatively large population, this new strength enabled the Italians to "arm the prow and sail toward the world," as the nationalist poet Gabriele D'Annunzio urged in his immensely popular 1908 play, *La nave*. It became increasingly difficult for Italian leaders to place reasonable limits on their ambitions. But how powerful Italy had become and where its true interests lay remained obscure.[18]

The opening of the Suez Canal in 1869 had restored the Mediterranean as a major trade route, dominated geographically by Italy. Informed Italians realized that if their nation could acquire an adjacent part of North Africa, a strong Italian fleet could interdict British and French communications to the east and hinder Russian expansion to the west. That recognition intensified Italian interest in Tunisia and Tripolitania. Another opportunity beckoned in the Adriatic, for Italian possession of Albania or Corfù could cut Austria-Hungary's maritime lifeline running from Trieste and Fiume.

But the growing importance of the Mediterranean also provoked Italian maritime insecurity. The Triple Alliance soothed Italian fear of attack by land but raised the prospect of war against a superior French navy. Italian admirals decided to concentrate their limited resources on construction of the maximum possible number of large battleships. Although Italy could not match French numbers, a concentrated battle fleet could defeat any single French squadron, especially if individual Italian battleships equaled or surpassed French warships. Italian naval thinkers thus rejected the ideas of the *Jeune École* and came heavily under the influence of Mahan. The *Regia Marina* leadership emphasized the primacy of the battleship.

Crispi therefore spent recklessly on the navy; by 1890 it ranked third in size after those of Britain and France. But by 1900, after the collapse of Crispi's megalomaniacal dreams, the *Regia Marina* had fallen to sixth place. Its share of the budget relative to that of the army nevertheless increased from only 21 percent of the army's funding in 1880 to 39 percent in 1890 and 51 percent in 1900, a level it retained thereafter. Given the rise in government revenues after 1898, the navy thus enjoyed increasing budgets until the outbreak of World War I. Vittorio Emanuele III favored the navy and insisted on superiority over the Austro-Hungarian fleet. The advent of the dreadnought allowed the Italians to seek battleship parity with the French and to strengthen their advantage over Austria-Hungary. The *Regia Marina* laid down its first dreadnought in 1909 and nine more by 1915. But weaknesses

---

[18] R.J.B. Bosworth, *Italy, the Least of the Great Powers* (New York, 1979), pp. 2–5; idem., *Italy and the Approach of the First World War,* pp. 51–76; Denis Mack Smith, *Italy: A Modern History* (Ann Arbor, 1969), p. 253.

in the steel industry and tightly stretched budgets resulted in long construction times.[19]

Italy's land frontiers offered the *Regio Esercito* both advantages and problems. The Alpine passes gave Italy contact with Western, Central, and Eastern Europe. While a major European war would be decided north of the Alps, Italy remained capable of opening or closing alternative invasion routes into Southern France, Austria, or the Balkans. Italy could also pin down significant enemy forces. Finally, proximity to the Balkans, combined with Italy's identification with nationalism since the Risorgimento, gave physical and psychological access to the restive nations in the Ottoman and Habsburg Empires. But Italy's mountainous borders with France and Austria-Hungary were difficult to defend, since the foreigners held the higher slopes. A breach in the frontier defenses would expose the rich Po Valley and the industrial Turin-Milan-Genoa triangle. The Italian coastline was long and extremely vulnerable, as were those of Sardinia and Sicily. And the rugged Apennines forced construction of the major north-south railroad lines on the vulnerable narrow plains between the mountains and the seas on either side of the peninsula. The length of the peninsula and the inadequate Italian rail net made mobilization slow; interdiction by naval bombardment might actually halt it.[20]

Additional military problems came from deficiencies in frontier fortifications, particularly in the east, and a shortage of field artillery. These weaknesses made successful defense or offense problematical without a powerful ally. Italy's post-1896 prosperity did allow increases in army budgets from some 240 million lire per year in the early 1890s to 370 million lire in 1910–11. But with the cost of weaponry soaring and all Europe engaged in a frenzied arms race, the *Regio Esercito* remained weaker than the army of any other continental great power – despite unprecedented military spending after 1906.[21]

While the Triple Alliance offered Italy compensation for its weaknesses, the nation had acquired none of the territory to which Umberto I and his

[19] Ezio Ferrante, *Benedetto Brin e la questione marittima italiana (1866–1898)* (Rome, 1983); idem., *Il pensiero strategico navale in Italia* (Rome, 1988), pp. 13–9; idem., "The Impact of the Jeune École on the Way of Thinking of the Italian Navy," *Marine et technique au XIXe siècle: Actes du colloque international: Paris, École militaire, les 10, 11, 12 juin 1987* (Paris, 1988); idem., "Potere marittimo" *Storia militare d'Italia 1796–1975* (Rome, 1990), pp. 192–8; Paul G. Halpern, *The Mediterranean Naval Situation, 1908–1914* (Cambridge, MA, 1971), pp. 187–93; Mack Smith, *Italy and its Monarchy*, pp. 178, 180–1.

[20] Salvemini, *La politica estera*, pp. 17–20; John Gooch, "Italy Before 1915: The Quandary of the Vulnerable," in Ernest R. May, ed., *Knowing One's Enemies: Intelligence Assessment Before the Two World Wars* (Princeton, 1984) pp. 205, 217–26.

[21] Lucio Ceva, *Le forze armate* (Turin, 1981), p. 97; Gooch, "Italy Before 1915," pp. 224–8; Rochat and Massobrio, *Breve storia*, pp. 69, 71, 153–4; Stefani, *Dall'esercito piemontese*, pp. 301–2, 538–82.

ministers had aspired in 1882. The twenty years of rivalry with France had cost Italy dearly. In the aftermath of Adowa, Umberto had therefore agreed to a rapprochement. Foreign Minister Emilio Visconti-Venosta, who had last held that post in 1869–76, conducted the negotiations for Italy. He had refused Italian aid to the French during the Franco-Prussian War and had specified possession of Tunisia as a major Italian aspiration.

In October 1896 he surrendered that dream and recognized Tunisia as a French protectorate. The French in turn agreed to talks over Tripolitania. These negotiations resulted in an exchange of notes in December 1900. The Italians recognized that French interests were paramount in Morocco, and the French accepted an Italian occupation of Tripolitania should France move into Morocco. More important than these agreements was the weakening of Italy's principal motivation for participation in the Triple Alliance.[22]

Another new trend in Italian foreign policy flowed from the understanding that Visconti-Venosta reached with Austria-Hungary in November 1897: should Turkish rule in the Balkans collapse, an independent neutral Albania would emerge. Given Italian internal distress and external weakness after Adowa, this arrangement was the best possible. But it suggested that a stronger Italy would seek greater influence in the Balkans.[23]

This change in course of Italian diplomacy accelerated under Vittorio Emanuele III, due to Italian economic growth and intense royal interest in foreign policy. While Vittorio Emanuele III accepted Italy's domestic democratic stirrings, he insisted on his constitutional prerogatives in foreign affairs. As the king remarked to the British Ambassador, he regarded himself as "somewhat in the relation of a permanent Under-Secretary [for foreign affairs] to succeeding governments."[24] After Giolitti became prime minister in November 1903, royal influence in diplomacy increased, for social reform absorbed Giolitti and he considered a strong monarchical role in Italian foreign policy entirely proper. But even before Giolitti's rise, the king had encouraged movement toward equidistance between the Triple Alliance and France.[25]

After 1900 the expanding detente with France occupied the small Italian foreign policy establishment. In June 1902, the Italians and French advanced their 1900 understanding to allow each to proceed in Morocco and Tripolitania. Each promised neutrality should the other be forced into a war to defend its security. In an exception to the rule that diplomacy was outside the army's purview, chief of staff General Tancredi Saletta learned of this agreement. Whether he was deliberately informed is unclear.[26]

22 Seton-Watson, *Italy*, pp. 35–6, 202–13.
23 Enrico Serra, "Note sull'intesa Visconti Venosta-Gulochowski per l'Albania," *Clio*, July–Sept. 1971.
24 J. Rennell Rodd, *Social and Diplomatic Memories*, 3 vols., (London, 1922–25), vol. 3, p. 25.
25 Mack Smith, *Italy and its Monarchy*, pp. 156–63, 175–6.
26 Seton-Watson, *Italy*, p. 329; Sergio Romano, "Il riavvicinamento italo-francese del 1900–

The 1904 British-French *Entente Cordiale* created a partnership that could offer or deny more African territory to Italy. Then came the Moroccan Crisis of 1905 and the 1906 Algeciras Conference, which revealed how balanced between France and Germany Italy had become. Italy could hardly support Germany's claims to Morocco without forfeiting its own claims to Tripolitania under its agreements with France.[27] In December 1906, the Italians, French, and British signed an agreement over East Africa. The British and French recognized the Ethiopian territory adjacent to Eritrea and Somalia as an Italian sphere of influence and agreed that Italy could join the two colonies with a strip of Ethiopia should the latter disintegrate.[28]

The reasons that had prompted Italy to join the Triple Alliance had now diminished or vanished. Italian aspirations in Africa could be satisfied almost completely, protection against French attack guaranteed, and cooperation with Britain achieved outside the alliance. Italy had advanced these aims by violating the spirit of its pact with Germany and Austria-Hungary. But the Triple Alliance no longer granted Italy the security it once had.

As their rivalry in the Balkans intensified after 1900, so did the possibility of war between Italy and Austria-Hungary. Furthermore, the improvement of relations with France brought Italy a large dividend. In 1906, the *Banca d'Italia* and a group of Paris banks agreed to convert the 8 billion lire Italian national debt from 5 percent interest to 3-¾ percent, dropping to 3-½ percent in 1911. While German finance remained important for Italy, it lost the overpowering influence it had previously enjoyed.[29] But despite the growth in Italian power, the Germans and Austro-Hungarians kept their old contempt for Italy. Whenever disputes between Italy and Austria-Hungary flared, the Germans invariably favored their stronger, more reliable Germanic partner. In turn, the Austrians saw little reason to accommodate Italian complaints.

Austro-Hungarian material superiority to some extent justified such attitudes. Between 1890 and 1913, the Dual Monarchy expanded from 42.6 to 52.1 million inhabitants, a 22.3 percent increase, while Italy, drained by emigration, grew only from 30 to 35.1 million, an increase of 17 percent (not counting the 1.5 million subjects in its African colonies). Italy's gross national product, which had stood at 71 percent of that of Austria-Hungary in 1880, had dropped to 61 percent in 1890 and to 55.6 percent in 1900. A severe industrial recession in 1907–08 dropped Italian GNP even lower, to

1902: diplomazia e modelli di sviluppo," *Storia contemporanea*, Feb. 1979; Enrico Decleva, "Giuseppe Zanardelli: liberalismo e politica estera" in Roberto Chiarini, ed., *Giuseppe Zanardelli* (Milan, 1985), pp. 265–79; Massimo Mazzetti, *L'esercito italiano*, pp. 201–3.

27 Luigi Albertini, *The Origins of the War of 1914*, 3 vols., (Oxford, 1952–57), vol. 1, pp. 162–75.
28 Seton-Watson, *Italy*, p. 362.
29 Seton-Watson, *Italy*, p. 293; Paul Kennedy, *The Rise and Fall of the Great Powers. Economic Change and Military Conflict from 1500 to 2000* (New York, 1987), p. 206.

only 52.5 percent of that of Austria-Hungary in 1910. Average Austro-Hungarian GNP growth outstripped that of Italy in 1860–1910 by 1.76 percent to 1.05 percent annually. In the decade before World War I, the Habsburg Monarchy enjoyed an industrial potential nearly double that of Italy, an advantage accentuated by Italian industry's near-total dependence on imported ores and coal.[30] Italian economic strength did rebound with vigor after 1910, raising the nation's GNP to 60 percent of that of Austria-Hungary by 1913. The growth of the Italian economy seems more impressive compared with that of France: from 46.8 percent of French GNP in 1910, Italian GNP shot up to 57 percent of that of France by 1913.[31]

In military spending, however, the Italians nearly matched the Austro-Hungarians. Between 1900 and 1913, the Italians spent some 1.22 billion current dollars, 84 percent of Austria-Hungary's $1.46 billion. The Italians far outstripped the Habsburg Monarchy on naval armaments: $425 million to $205 million. But even on armies, the Italians spent $799 million or 64 percent of Austria-Hungary's $1.256 billion. At a time when Italy's GNP averaged about 55 percent of Austria-Hungary's, this was impressive. Beginning in 1908, the Austro-Hungarians reacted with notable increases in defense spending, but the Italians responded in kind. By 1914, the Italians had 345,000 men under arms, 78 percent of the Habsburg Monarchy's 444,000, although Italy's population was only 67 percent of Austria-Hungary's.[32]

Significant domestic improvement added to Italian strength after 1900. Problems that had nearly torn Italy asunder in 1896–1900 greatly abated, thanks in part to Giolitti's reforms, while social and ethnic unrest in the Habsburg Monarchy grew worse each year. As a result, the general mood in Italy during the first decade of the twentieth century offered a markedly optimistic contrast to that within Austria-Hungary. It was precisely this upsurge of the economy and of Italian patriotic spirit that helped to drive Italy toward a clash with Austria-Hungary in the Balkans.

---

[30] Kennedy, *The Rise and Fall*, 199, 204; *The Statesman's Yearbook* (London, 1914), pp. 1041–3; Paul Bairoch, "Europe's Gross National Product: 1800–1975," *Journal of European Economic History*, 5 (1976), pp. 281, 283; idem., "International Industrialization Levels from 1750 to 1980," *Journal of European Economic History*, 11 (1982), pp. 284, 292, 299; David F. Good, *The Economic Rise of the Habsburg Empire, 1750–1914* (Berkeley, 1984), pp. 238–41.

[31] Bairoch, "Europe's Gross National Product," pp. 281, 283.

[32] Rochat and Massobrio, *Breve storia*, p. 68; Walter Wagner, "Die K. (U.) K. Armee – Gliederung und Aufgabenstellung" in Adam Wandruszka and Peter Urbanitsch, eds., *Die Habsburgermonarchie 1848–1918*, vol. 5, *Die bewaffnete Macht* (Vienna, 1987), p. 591; Kennedy, *The Rise and Fall*, p. 199; Gunther E. Rothenberg, "The Austro-Hungarian Campaign Against Serbia in 1914," *The Journal of Military History*, April 1989, pp. 127–9. These figures exclude Italian Libyan War expenditures of some 1.7 billion lire (roughly $330 million) but include Austro-Hungarian expenditures on the annexation of Bosnia-Herzegovina.

THE COLLAPSE OF THE TRIPLE ALLIANCE, 1908–1914

Serious friction resulted from the 1907–08 recession. To recover, Italian business began an aggressive campaign to increase exports to the Balkans. But the Austro-Hungarians impeded this effort by sponsoring a railroad project to tie the Balkan peninsula to their own economy. They also failed to offer the compensation Rome expected for Vienna's 1908 annexation of Bosnia-Herzegovina. One of the Triple Alliance's chief attractions, the chance to gain some of the *terre irredente,* had been gravely diminished. At the time, the Italian government could do nothing. But hatred of Austria reawakened, and Italian desire for the Trentino, Istria, and Dalmatia intensified. After 1908, the growing force of public opinion compounded political and economic influences on Italian national strategy.[33]

Giolitti aimed his reforms at creating a stable, prosperous society before introducing a democratic political system. Italian constitutional and parliamentary practices could be adapted to that change. But the royal prerogatives in foreign and military affairs were incompatible with democracy. Even attempts by the predemocratic parliament to influence military affairs had met with rebuffs from the king. Giolitti and his foreign ministers correspondingly kept the generals and admirals ignorant of the new direction of Italian diplomacy. Oddly, perhaps due to respect for the constitutional system, the king did not pass on his own knowledge of foreign affairs to his military leaders. The failure of the Italian political-military system to accommodate itself to the changes created by mass politics and changes in foreign policy led to disaster.

In 1904 Giolitti defused Leftist accusations of poor naval administration by agreeing to a parliamentary commission of investigation. Three years later, he did the same with the army. In anticipation of this parliamentary interference, the king had already reduced the powers of the war minister by decree in March 1906 in favor of the army chief of staff. The chief of staff reported to the king, the war minister answered to parliament. In December 1907, Severino Casana became Italy's first civilian war minister. In early 1908, two royal decrees further amplified the army chief of staff's authority. At the same time, Casana expanded the Supreme Defense Commission, adding the war and navy ministers and making the prime minister its chairman.

By early 1908 the ill health of General Tancredi Saletta, army chief of staff since June 1896, required his replacement. General Luigi Cadorna seemed Saletta's likely successor. But Cadorna demanded total control over the army.

---

[33] Edoardo Del Vecchio, "Penetrazione economica italiana nell'area degli slavi del sud (1878–1896)," *Storia delle relazioni internazionali,* 1985, vol. 2; Seton-Watson, *Italy,* pp. 342–6.

Vittorio Emanuele III and Giolitti balked. Instead, they agreed on a Germanophile, General Alberto Pollio, who took command of the army at this time of growing disjunction between Italian foreign and military policy.[34] Italian popular opinion, economic interests, and diplomacy all pointed toward the growing possibility of a clash with Austria-Hungary. In October 1909, for example, Italian diplomats had tried to repair relations with Vienna in the wake of the Bosnian crisis; both had agreed that neither would come to any understanding with the Russians over the Balkans without consultation. Yet a few days later, Czar Nicholas II and his foreign minister visited Vittorio Emanuele III and revealed that Vienna had extracted a promise from them in 1904 to remain neutral during any war between Italy and Austria-Hungary. This led the Italians to accept a Russian proposal to coordinate Balkan policies. The Italians also agreed to back Russian efforts to open the Straits to their warships, while the Russians accepted Italy's claims on Tripolitania. These agreements were known only by both countries' monarchs, prime ministers, and foreign ministers.[35]

Despite his ignorance of these matters, Pollio recognized the need to prepare for possible war; reports from Vienna revealed that the Austro-Hungarian army leadership favored preventive war with Italy. After initial opposition from Giolitti, parliament voted to improve the defenses and military railroads along Italy's northeastern frontier. Pollio's foresight included preparations for defending the line formed by Monte Grappa and the Piave River, which proved crucial in 1917–18. In case of war with Austria-Hungary, the navy planned to seize a base in Dalmatia to compensate for the absence of fleet anchorages on the Italian side of the Adriatic. Although Saletta had refused to provide a corps for an amphibious operation, Pollio and the war minister, General Paolo Spingardi, prepared plans for a 40,000-man force to seize a Dalmatian fleet base.

Pollio nevertheless still planned for war against France, thus continuing Italy's strategic balance between Triple Alliance and Triple Entente. But the bifurcation of military planning reflected the vacuum in which the government kept the army high command. Pollio apparently never learned of the 1902 neutrality agreement with France; both king and government may have been using their military leaders as camouflage for Italy's increasing detachment from the Triple Alliance. This may even have led to Vittorio Emanuele III's choice of Pollio for army chief of staff, as the general was unusual in being pro-German and pro-Austrian, having an Austrian wife, and speaking fluent German.

---

[34] Ceva, *Le forze armate*, p. 97; Marco Meriggi, "Militari e istituzioni politiche nell'età giolittiana," *Clio*, Jan.-March 1987, pp. 63–84; Gooch, *Army*, pp. 129–32; idem., "Italy before 1915," p. 208; Lucio Ceva, "Ministro e Capo di Stato Maggiore," *Nuova Antologia*, Oct.-Dec. 1986; idem., "Capo di Stato Maggiore e politica estera al principio di secolo," *Il Politico*, Jan. 1987.

[35] Seton-Watson, *Italy*, pp. 338, 347–8.

In 1910–11 a third set of contingencies arose, shifting Italian attention away from Europe. The right wing of the educated Italian public had begun calling for the occupation of Tripolitania even if it meant war with Turkey.[36] Giolitti and his foreign minister, Marchese Antonino di San Giuliano, decided to act by mid-1911. Their decision reflected the mixture of the old and new influences on the making of Italian national strategy. As foreign minister under three prime ministers, between March 1910 and October 1914, Di San Giuliano established the broad outlines of Italian foreign policy for the following quarter of a century. Like Crispi, Di San Giuliano's Sicilian origins had impressed upon him Italy's need to acquire fertile lands and rich resources abroad. He also believed in *Romanità*, and in October 1910 wrote to then Prime Minister Luigi Luzzatti that it was incumbent upon them to think "of that greater Italy which, with different methods but, we trust, not dissimilar results, will emulate ancient Rome, spread through all the regions of the world and enrich them with her own labor."[37]

Di San Giuliano first worked to preserve Italy's balance between France and Austria-Hungary. While he disliked the French, he recognized that Italian weakness counseled further rapprochement. He also worried about the possible decline or breakup of the Habsburg Monarchy, leading to either an alliance between a Greater Serbia and Russia or creating a vacuum into which Germany could move. Either event would exclude Italy from the Balkans.

Di San Giuliano respected German power and recognized Italian dependence on it. Like Crispi, he tried to use the Triple Alliance as an instrument for Italian expansion. Di San Giuliano sought Italian control over Albania, Tripolitania, Ethiopia and, with the disintegration of the Ottoman Empire, southwestern Turkey. Such an empire would allow Italy to dominate the eastern Mediterranean, and would guarantee the basis for a strong economy. The foreign minister favored abandoning claims to the *terre irredente* in return for the cooperation of Italy's allies in reaching his other territorial goals. But after he failed to gain that help, he became more hostile toward Austria-Hungary. He also began to think that Britain, not Germany, might provide Italy with the means to reach his goals.

Di San Giuliano soon converted the king to his views. Vittorio Emanuele III considered colonial expansion per se a luxury that Italy could ill afford, but the king approved any acquisition of Mediterranean territory that might improve Italy's strategic position. Domestically, Di San Giuliano's anti-democratic attitudes stood in marked contrast to Giolitti's policies, and were even somewhat at odds with the king's constitutionalism. In theory, the

---

36 Gooch, *Army*, pp. 134–9; idem., "Italy before 1915," pp. 209–10; Stefani, *Dall'esercito piemontese*, p. 595; Renzi, *In the Shadow*, pp. 34–5, 39; Mack Smith, *Italy and its Monarchy*, pp. 179–80, 194–5.

37 Gioacchino Volpe, *Italia moderna, 1815–1915*, 3 vols., (Florence, 1943–52) vol. 3, p. 322.

separation between internal and external politics enshrined in the Italian constitution should have let Giolitti and Di San Giuliano work toward their goals in harmony. In reality, this old dichotomy between foreign and domestic politics had already eroded by the time Di San Giuliano became foreign minister. The application of his outdated methods in Italian diplomacy therefore had fateful consequences in domestic politics.

By 1911 Giolitti had prepared Italian society for a democratic political system. Giolitti regarded the Socialist Party, whose supporters had increased considerably due to industrial expansion, as both the greatest obstacle and the most promising recruit to his projected democracy. While the Socialists rejected his offer of a cabinet seat, they indicated interest in a tacit political alliance in a democratic system. In June 1911 Giolitti had a near-universal male suffrage bill introduced.[38]

But Giolitti's consensus politics required concessions both to the Left and the Right. The latter included not only the Nationalists, Italy's chief theorists of empire, but also the far more important conservative wing of Giolitti's parliamentary coalition. Under existing circumstances, that meant Italian acquisition of Tripolitania. The second Moroccan crisis in the early summer of 1911 goaded Giolitti and Di San Giuliano into action. If France seized Morocco before Italy gained Tripolitania, Paris would no longer need Rome's diplomatic support and might ignore the 1902 agreements. In August, Giolitti ordered Pollio to study the matter, and the general redrew plans for the Dalmatian expedition to fit this new contingency. But Giolitti indicated no imminent action and Pollio did not expect immediate war.

Only a chance encounter by Di San Giuliano with the naval deputy chief of staff precipitated action. To his surprise, the foreign minister learned that sea conditions imposed a November deadline on any landing in Tripolitania; thereafter, an expedition would be impossible until April 1912. Di San Giuliano and Giolitti decided to move while the international situation was favorable. Parliament was in recess, freeing Giolitti from any outcry by pacifist Socialist deputies. After Giolitti informed Pollio, active preparations began in mid-September without consideration of a twelve-year-old army study warning of the difficulties of an invasion of Tripolitania. The chief of staff encouraged the prime minister in his assessment that the 5–6,000-man Ottoman garrison presented no serious obstacle to rapid conquest. After France and Germany reached an accord over Morocco on 23 September, Giolitti received permission from Vittorio Emanuele III to issue an ultimatum to the Turks.[39]

38 Seton-Watson, *Italy*, pp. 263–71, 281–3, 349–65; Mack Smith, *Italy and its Monarchy*, p. 185; Bracalini, *Il re "vittorioso"*, pp. 64–5, 98; Renzi, *In the Shadow*, pp. 36–43, 55–6; Bosworth, *Italy and the Approach*, pp. 110–2; Bosworth, *Italy*, pp. 1–39, 299–376, 418–9.
39 Francesco Malgeri, *La guerra Libica* (Rome, 1970), pp. 25–140; Gooch, *Army*, pp. 138–40; Fortunato Minniti, "Gli Stati Maggiori e la politica estera italiana" in Richard J.B. Bosworth and Sergio Romano, eds., *La politica estera italiana (1860–1985)* (Bologna,

Giolitti and Di San Giuliano believed that they had acted with the proper mixture of prudence and daring. They had made effective diplomatic preparations and had chosen the last possible moment to act before their agreements with the French might lose their validity. But neither man was educated in military affairs, or had access to those who were. Thus neither could accurately gauge prospects for success in war. Even worse, the government continued to lack an integrated council to assess the range of diplomatic, military, economic, and domestic implications of the shock that the Libyan War might inflict on Italy and Europe. And despite his superiority over his grandfather and father in such matters, Vittorio Emanuele III himself could not adequately analyze such complicated issues. And even had he possessed the ability to integrate national strategy effectively, the king's respect for the constitutional process would have deterred him from so doing.

The war, which began with an impromptu landing by 1,700 sailors at Tripoli on 3 October, was one of the crises that led to World War I. The precariously balanced European alliance system that allowed Italian maneuver in the middle could not survive wars waged to increase Italy's national power. Perhaps if Giolitti had rejected aggression and had tried to achieve his goals by diplomacy, his policy of playing the decisive weight might have brought gains while preserving European peace.

Yet the use of force by great powers to achieve their goals was considered legitimate. Furthermore, in the Italian case, the darker side of the Risorgimento heritage influenced Giolitti, Di San Giuliano, and Vittorio Emanuele III to emulate their predecessors' use of war – but under far different circumstances. The constitutional autonomy in foreign and military policy enjoyed by the king, the prime minister, and the foreign minister freed them from parliamentary and popular restraints. But war was a risky matter for a state as relatively weak and internally unstable as Italy. As it turned out, the initiation of the Libyan War set off a period of crisis for the nation – and its makers of strategy – that lasted until 1949.

War for possession of Tripolitania quickly turned into a struggle with the native Arabs for control of their homeland. The 44,000 men of the Italian expeditionary corps and their commander, General Carlo Caneva, proved ineffective in fighting a guerrilla war that quickly became a jihad. Caneva's force did occupy the main coastal towns of Tripolitania and those of the neighboring province to the east, Cyrenaica. But beyond that, Caneva did nothing – until ordered by Giolitti to occupy the entire coast and the nearby inland oases. Caneva's forces slowly fought their way across the barren landscape, batting away elusive columns of Bedouin hovering on their flanks. But these operations did not bring victory. Recognizing the wisdom of presenting a fait accompli, Giolitti had persuaded Vittorio Emanuele III to

1991), pp. 106–7; David G. Herrmann, "The Paralysis of Italian Strategy in the Italian-Turkish War, 1911–1912," *English Historical Review*, April 1989.

annex Tripolitania and Cyrenaica as Italian colonies on 5 November. Meanwhile, deep in the Sahara, the Turks withdrew their garrisons from Borku, Ennedi, and Tibesti to meet the Italian threat in the north. After the Ottomans left, the French moved in, acquiring what is now the northern half of Chad. The news took months to reach Rome.

As the war dragged on, Giolitti grew increasingly desperate. Reinforcements swelled Caneva's forces to 100,000, but brought the war no closer to an end. Giolitti agreed to expand naval operations to the Red Sea and eastern Mediterranean, including an attack on the forts guarding the entrance to the Dardanelles, and sanctioned the seizure of the Dodecanese Islands in the southern Aegean in May 1912. Fearing an explosion in their Balkan provinces and realizing that the European powers were not coming to its aid, the Ottoman government finally agreed to negotiate.

Turkish difficulties had encouraged the Serbs, Montenegrans, Greeks, and Bulgars to form the Balkan League and drive the Ottomans from Europe. The League mobilized on 30 September. As a result the Turks signed the Treaty of Ouchy on 18 October and granted Italy Tripolitania and Cyrenaica. The Italians promised to vacate the Dodecanese Islands once the Turks evacuated Libya. But the Turks did not complete withdrawal until 1918 and Italy remained in control of these Greek-inhabited islands thereafter. Ongoing operations in North Africa against the Bedouin and their Turkish advisers tied down 60,000 troops – almost 25 percent of the Italian peacetime army – in the two new colonies. The struggle against the Bedouin continued intermittently until 1932.[40]

Italian losses had been light: 3,500–4,000 dead and 4,300–5,000 wounded. But the financial cost was heavy, probably about 1.7 billion lire. In comparison, total spending on the army and navy for fiscal year 1910–11 had been 577 million lire. The war had quickly exhausted the army's stocks of weapons, ammunition, and equipment. The need to provide reinforcements for the Libyan campaign had seriously disrupted the training and force levels of almost every unit in the army. The war had also cost the *Regia Marina* much of its ammunition stocks and subjected Italian warships to considerable wear. But its first significant action since 1866 had given the navy valuable operational experience.[41]

---

[40] Gooch, *Army,* pp. 140–7; John Wright, *Libya, Chad and the Central Sahara* (Totowa, NJ, 1989), pp. 118–9; Halpern, *The Mediterranean,* pp. 193–6; Giorgio Rochat, "L'esercito italiano nell'estate 1914," *Nuova rivista storica,* May-Aug. 1961, p. 312; Rochat and Massobrio, *Breve storia,* p. 165.

[41] W.C. Askew, *Europe and Italy's Acquisition of Libya, 1911–1912* (Durham, NC, 1942) p. 249; Sergio Romano, *La quarta sponda: La guerra di Libia, 1911/1912* (Milan, 1977), p. 254; Rochat and Massobrio, *Breve storia,* p. 162; F. Coppola d'Anna, *Popolazione, reddito e finanze pubbliche dell'Italia dal 1860 ad oggi* (Rome, 1946), pp. 85–8; Ceva, *Le forze armate,* pp. 104, 112–3; Halpern, *The Mediterranean,* pp. 195–6, 198–201; Francesco Malgeri, "La campagna di Libia (1911–1912)," in *L'esercito italiano dall'unità alla grande guerra,* p. 325.

The war also had detrimental influences on the coordination of Italian foreign and military policy. Giolitti and Di San Giuliano had run the campaign in North Africa by direct orders to Caneva, informing neither Pollio nor the king's chief aide, General Ugo Brusati. Pollio complained in June 1912 that after nine months of war he remained completely ignorant of the diplomatic situation. An additional actor entered the confused civil-military relationship in November 1912 with the creation of the Ministry of Colonies. Thereafter, the army contended with two civilian-led ministries capable of involving it in military operations – without any requirement to consult beforehand. Vittorio Emanuele III came to the conclusion that Cadorna had been right after all. The army must be run by a chief of staff free from interference by civilians. When the opportunity presented itself, the king proposed to redress the situation.[42]

Another result of the Libyan War was the apparent strengthening of the Triple Alliance. The war damaged relations with the French, whom the Italians mistakenly believed had helped the Turks reinforce their garrison in North Africa. Di San Giuliano also considered the 1902 entente effectively ended with the annexations of Morocco and Tripolitania-Cyrenaica. With much of the Italian army still pinned down in North Africa, Italy was in no position to risk trouble with Austria-Hungary. Di San Giuliano therefore renewed the Triple Alliance in December 1912. The army and navy chiefs of staff were kept ignorant of the terms, but they did receive promises of information if war appeared imminent. Since the service chiefs were unaware of the 1902 neutrality agreements, they continued war planning against France.

In the aftermath of the war, Pollio feared that the weakening of the armed forces exposed Italy to a French amphibious landing on its western coast. The expression of his private concerns to the Germans resulted in two conventions between the armed forces of the Triple Alliance. After lengthy negotiations, a naval agreement went into effect in November 1913. This convention, with later supplementary agreements, established the procedures under which the Italian and Austro-Hungarian fleets, along with the German Mediterranean squadron, would concentrate under Austro-Hungarian command against the French navy and disrupt convoy traffic between French North Africa and France's Mediterranean ports. Talks among Triple Alliance army representatives concluded with renewal of old Italian plans to send an army to the Rhine in case of war with France. Neither an Italian landing in Provence nor an offensive across the French Alps, both of which the Italians had considered from time to time, seemed feasible any longer. In February 1914, Vittorio Emanuele III consented to plans to dispatch three corps – one quarter of his army – to march alongside the Germans should they invade France. Acting on his own, Pollio even discussed with the Austro-Hungarians the use of Italian troops against the Russians. Despite these

---

[42] Meriggi, "Militari e istituzioni politiche," pp. 89–90; Bosworth, *Italy*, pp. 423–35.

talks, the Italian military leadership remained concerned about signs of Austro-Hungarian hostility, including military preparations along their mutual borders.[43]

The Second Balkan War created even greater instability in the peninsula than before. In July and October 1913 the Austro-Hungarians threatened the Serbs with military action. Both times, the Italians informed Vienna that they were not bound to aid the Austro-Hungarians under such circumstances. At the same time, the Italians adopted Austro-Hungarian methods with the Greeks. They demanded Greek withdrawal from southern Albania, yet inflamed Greek public opinion by their obvious intention of remaining in the Dodecanese. For the Italians, possession of the Greek-inhabited islands represented a springboard for penetration into southwestern Turkey and its rich mineral resources.

Beneath these crises lay a deepening rivalry between Austria-Hungary and Italy in the Balkans. Austria-Hungary's continuing oppression of its Italian minority made relations between the two states even worse. By mid-1914, Di San Giuliano himself warned the German ambassador that unilateral Austro-Hungarian expansion in the Balkans would lead to war with Italy. But it was already apparent that the Libyan War had helped provoke Balkan instability. That in turn had increased the likelihood of a conflict between Italy and Austria-Hungary.

The Libyan war had also sundered the delicate political consensus Giolitti had been building with the Socialists. Socialist Party hotheads, among them Benito Mussolini, had organized violent protests against mobilization in October 1911. The revolutionaries exploited Socialist anger over the war to regain control of the party and renew their call for the violent revolution. Positions hardened at the opposite end of the political spectrum as well. Later that year, the Nationalists resolved to fight for increased armaments, economic autarky, protectionism, and the outlawing of strikes. Years earlier, Giolitti had warned that Italian liberty could not survive in an atmosphere of militarism and imperialism. The increasing polarization of Italian politics as a result of the Libyan War suggested that Giolitti had brought his own prophecy closer to fulfillment. The restive chamber that resulted from Giolitti's crowning domestic reform – the introduction of near-universal suffrage in 1912 – soon induced him to resign in hope of returning to office at a better time. In his place, the king selected Antonio Salandra to head a new government. Salandra boasted of his anti-democratic Liberalism and fervent patriotism. Di San Giuliano found it easy to remain as his foreign minister.[44]

43 Halpern, *The Mediterranean Naval Situation*, pp. 226–63; Gooch, *Army*, pp. 134–55; Mazzetti, *L'esercito italiano*, pp. 265–414; Minniti, "Gli Stati Maggiori e la politica estera," p. 111.
44 Seton-Watson, *Italy*, pp. 381–410; Albertini, *Origins*, vol. 1, p. 523.

NEUTRALITY AND INTERVENTION, 1914–1915

The day Archduke Franz Ferdinand was assassinated in Sarajevo, General Pollio had a heart attack. He died on 1 July. In his place, Vittorio Emanuele III appointed Luigi Cadorna as army chief of staff and supreme army commander in wartime. Cadorna took up his post on 27 July. By then, war between Austria-Hungary and Serbia appeared almost certain. By 31 July a general European conflict was probable. Cadorna assumed Italy would fight on the side of the Triple Alliance and prepared to send all the troops he could to Germany, despite exposure of the Po Valley to a French invasion. But at a cabinet meeting on 1 August the Italian government secretly chose neutrality.

Salandra's diplomatic inexperience allowed his foreign minister great latitude. Di San Giuliano had anticipated that Austro-Hungarian action against Serbia would provoke a European war. The foreign minister did not wish such a conflict nor did he want Serbia crushed. But he realized that this time, unlike 1913, the Germans were backing the Austro-Hungarians unconditionally. The best course of action for Italy, he believed, was to stay out of a general conflict, which might bring blockade or attack by the Royal Navy, and seek compensation should Austria-Hungary acquire Balkan territory. Di San Giuliano hoped for the Trentino or at least the Albanian port of Valona.[45] The unexpected Austro-Hungarian ultimatum to Serbia allowed Italy to refuse to support its allies; the Triple Alliance treaty required prior consultation in such cases. The treaty also guaranteed Italy compensation. Di San Giuliano gave his advice to Salandra on 26 July: "No immediate decisions are necessary . . . we must leave everyone, at home and abroad, in doubt about our attitude and our decisions, and, in this way, try to obtain some positive advantage."[46]

But Vienna refused any quid pro quo unless Italy joined in war against Serbia. On 2 August, shortly after the king had approved Cadorna's plans to send troops to support the German army, the government announced Italian neutrality. Public opinion overwhelmingly supported this decision but the announcement stunned Cadorna. He had to take the initiative to approach Salandra, who told Cadorna to cease war preparations against France and to begin planning for possible conflict with Austria-Hungary.

Di San Giuliano disagreed with Salandra and Cadorna about the best course of action. The foreign minister expected a long struggle of attrition, with German power ultimately prevailing. But Di San Giuliano knew that Italy could not survive lengthy hostilities with Britain. Italy received nearly

---

[45] Albertini, *Origins*, vol. 2, pp. 225–320; Gooch, *Army*, pp. 158–9; Angelo Gatti, *Un italiano a Versailles (Dicembre 1917 – Febbraio 1918)* (Milan, 1958), pp. 355–9, 438; Renzi, *In the Shadow*, pp. 59–82; Mack Smith, *Italy and its Monarchy*, p. 199; Ezio Ferrante, *Il Grande Ammiraglio Paolo Thaon di Revel*, (Rome, 1989), pp. 53–4, 184–7.

[46] DDI, (4), XII, no. 560.

90 percent of its energy needs from imported coal. Much of this coal arrived by sea. Once Britain entered the war on 5 August, Di San Giuliano knew that Italy was at the mercy of the Royal Navy. While awaiting events, he urged remaining in the Triple Alliance as a nonbelligerent. Only if one bloc gained the upper hand should Italy intervene on the winning side; the best outcome would be a severe weakening of *both* France and Austria-Hungary.

Salandra and Cadorna believed that Italy's declaration of neutrality had ended the Triple Alliance. Both expected a short conflict if Italy entered the war against Austria-Hungary. Cadorna wished to begin full mobilization at once. If Italy did not enter the conflict immediately, he reasoned, it would be despised by both sides and isolated at war's end. If Italy's former allies won, Cadorna expected an attack from Austria-Hungary soon afterward. Whatever happened, an isolated Italy would have to assume an even heavier burden of armaments than previously. But if Italy supported the Entente, Cadorna argued it would tip the balance and gain immense power.

But Di San Giuliano and Salandra agreed that the army was too weak to carry out Cadorna's plan. Salandra held a low opinion of the army officer corps, and in March 1914, Pollio had warned him about the army: severe shortages of officers, NCOs, artillery, and machine guns crippled its effectiveness. In July, the prime minister had learned that due to the Libyan War, full equipment existed for only 730,000 of the 1,260,000 men of the fully mobilized army. He therefore refused Cadorna permission to mobilize and waited on events. When the British and French won on the Marne, Salandra and Di San Giuliano came close to intervention. But by late September they recognized that stalemate had set in. Even Cadorna decided it was preferable to wait for spring.[47]

Di San Giuliano died on 16 October. Salandra replaced him with Sidney Sonnino, a far less able diplomat or strategist. Unlike his predecessor, Sonnino was willing to intervene immediately on either side but remained determined to use the war to enhance Italian power. He began talks in early November with both British and Germans, whom he considered the leaders of the two warring alliances. By early 1915 both Sonnino and the king had begun to favor intervention with the Allies, although talks went slowly until early March. By then Sonnino had come to expect few concessions from Austria-Hungary. He had also learned of Allied plans to land at the Dardanelles. If the Allied landing should lead to an Anglo-French invasion of the Balkans, Italy would already have to be in the war.

Sonnino instructed his ambassador in London to present terms for an alliance. Influenced by Cadorna, Sonnino expected a short war, and did not

[47] Bosworth, *Italy and the Approach*, pp. 17, 122–33; Rochat, "L'esercito italiano," pp. 319–48; Gooch, *Army, State and Society*, pp. 153–4, 159–63; Bracalini, *Il re "vittorioso"*, p. 118; Luigi Mondini, "La preparazione dell'esercito e lo sforzo militare nella prima guerra mondiale," in *L'esercito italiano dall'unità alla grande guerra*, pp. 333–6; Gatti, *Un italiano*, pp. 356, 438–9; Renzi, *In the Shadow*, pp. 83–102.

insist on loan agreements or promises of naval or military assistance. By late March, the British had persuaded their allies to accept most of Sonnino's demands. Meanwhile, under German pressure, the Austro-Hungarians had agreed to cede a substantial portion of the Trentino to Italy in exchange for a neutrality guarantee. That disappointed Sonnino, and after Vienna refused to increase its offer, he chose the Allies. On 24 April 1915 British and French troops landed at Gallipoli. Two days later, Italian and Allied representatives signed the secret Treaty of London, binding Italy to enter the war within one month. On 3 May the Italians left the Triple Alliance, which shocked the Austro-Hungarians into additional territorial offers. But it was too late. The king and his ministers wanted war – but only Salandra's chance remark on 5 May informed Cadorna that Italy would enter the war in three weeks. "What? I knew nothing!" the chief of staff exclaimed. Cadorna at once began a belated mobilization.[48] Italy's lack of machinery for the formulation of strategy and for the coordination of the armed forces had once again led to confusion and delay.

The chief of staff had prepared his operational plans by the end of 1914: a penetration of the Austro-Hungarian frontier defenses and an advance of forty to sixty miles into Istria in the first two weeks, then a major battle, another leap of forty to sixty miles to the Ljubljana Gap, and a second great clash by the end of the second month of war. Then an offensive to the northeast along the edge of the Hungarian plain would bring Italy to the gates of Vienna and total victory by early fall 1915.[49]

Cadorna's plans rested upon four assumptions. First, he disregarded warnings from the attachés in Paris and Berlin that modern weaponry had drastically tipped the tactical advantage to the defense. Therefore he believed that the Italian army could break through the mountainous terrain along the Italian border by frontal assault. Second, Cadorna expected simultaneous converging Russian, Serb, and, possibly, Romanian attacks on the Hapsburg Empire in conjunction with his own offensive. In 1914, Austro-Hungary could mobilize only forty-eight divisions, compared with forty-six for Italy, eleven for Serbia, ten for Romania, and ninety-three for Russia. The Russians had suffered extremely heavy casualties in 1914 and had to divide their army to deal with the Germans. But by spring 1915, the Austro-Hungarian army had lost one-third of its professional cadre and suffered heavy troop losses. Third, Cadorna anticipated beginning operations twenty-five days after mobilization. Fourth, he intended to practice extreme economy of

[48] Sonnino, *Diario 1914–1916*, Pietro Pastorelli, ed., (Bari, 1972), pp. 22–129; Bosworth, *Italy and the Approach*, pp. 133–5; Seton-Watson, *Italy*, pp. 426–31; Mack Smith, *Italy and its Monarchy*, pp. 203–14; David Stevenson, *The First World War and International Politics* (New York, 1988), pp. 51–5; Gatti, *Un italiano*, pp. 441–2 (Cadorna quotation). Renzi, *In the Shadow*, pp. 103–269, depicts Italian diplomacy more favorably.

[49] Rochat, "L'esercito italiano," p. 332, n. 2; Mondini, "La preparazione dell'esercito," pp. 346–7; Gatti, *Un italiano*, pp. 440–2.

force, concentrating every available resource on his grand offensive. Every assumption save the last proved false.[50]

The planning of the *Regia Marina* chief of staff, Admiral Count Paolo Thaon di Revel, was more cautious. Although he had learned of the signing of the Treaty of London (but not its specific contents), Thaon di Revel had in other respects been kept even more ignorant than Cadorna. Even after begging in mid-May, the admiral had been refused the date of Italian intervention. Sonnino informed him only on 23 May that hostilities would commence at midnight.[51]

The admiral had nevertheless done his best. After studying the Libyan War and the naval operations of 1914–15, Thaon di Revel decided that the Italian navy had underestimated the utility of light craft, submarines, and aircraft. He also realized how vulnerable dreadnoughts were to mines and torpedoes. After becoming naval chief of staff in March 1913, the admiral had attempted to reorient warship construction toward smaller vessels. Yet he also persuaded parliament to order four budget-busting 34,000 ton superdreadnoughts of the *Caracciolo* class.

Italy's last pre-dreadnoughts had each cost 40 million lire, its first dreadnoughts 70 million lire, and the *Caracciolo* class was estimated at 100 million lire each. Yet even the 1912–13 naval budget, enlarged to pay for the Libyan War, was only 362 million lire. Clearly, Thaon di Revel could not build all types of warship in the numbers he wanted. By so trying, he slowed construction considerably, and left his navy short of new vessels.

Even after the 1913 naval convention, the chief of staff believed Italy remained vulnerable to French attack. All four major Italian naval shipyards, at Genoa, La Spezia, Livorno, and Castellamare, lay on the west coast; the first three were dangerously close to the French Mediterranean naval base at Toulon. Thaon di Revel warned the government that Italy needed either a larger fleet or a change of alliance; his warnings had helped persuade the cabinet to declare neutrality in August 1914. An Adriatic war against Austria-Hungary presented fewer challenges than a Mediterranean war against the Allies. Thaon di Revel nevertheless lacked the necessary light craft, and the Allies refused to reinforce the *Regia Marina* with the destroyers he requested in May 1915.[52]

These limitations and the subordination of Thaon di Revel's plans to those of Cadorna constrained the admiral. He concentrated his battle fleet in the lower Adriatic and relied on light craft to operate in the upper reaches of that sea and along the Dalmatian coast. Thaon di Revel hoped to damage or

50 Stefani, *Dall'esercito piemontese*, pp. 504–22; Gooch, *Army*, pp. 164–9; Gunther Rothenberg, *The Army of Francis Joseph* (West Lafayette, IN, 1976), pp. 184–5; idem. "The Austro-Hungarian Campaign," p. 129; Holger H. Herwig, "Disjointed Allies: Coalition Warfare in Berlin and Vienna, 1914," *The Journal of Military History* (July 1990), p. 265.
51 Renzi, *In the Shadow*, pp. 212, 261–2.
52 Ferrante, *Il Grande Ammiraglio*, pp. 50–4, 178, 195; Aldo Fraccaroli, *Italian Warships of World War I* (London, 1970), pp. 42, 51, 71–2, 99–100, 116; Renzi, pp. 212–4.

destroy as many major enemy warships as possible with light units, then engage the Austro-Hungarians in a major fleet action with superior forces. But he doubted that the enemy battle fleet would venture from its base at Pola unless forced by an advance of the Italian army. Meanwhile, the Italian dreadnoughts would remain at Brindisi or Taranto in case the Imperial navy used the cover of the Dalmatian islands to strike south against Italian coastal towns or merchant shipping. Once the army closed on Pola, the Italian fleet would steam to Venice and protect Cadorna's seaward flank from naval bombardment or engage the enemy fleet if it fled the army's advance.

Thaon di Revel also planned an amphibious attack on the enemy naval base at Cattaro. That operation might also provoke a fleet engagement, while use of that harbor would give the *Regia Marina* control over the southern end of the Adriatic. Italian possession of a Dalmatian city would also strengthen Italian claims to the eastern shore of the Adriatic at war's end and help prevent the emergence of a powerful South Slav state. Thaon di Revel wanted the war to end with total Italian naval security along its eastern coast. But Cadorna refused to give the navy more than a single artillery battery for the proposed Dalmatian operation because he regarded any major amphibious operation as a dangerous dispersion of his forces. Thereafter, army and navy planning developed with very little coordination for the remainder of the war.[53]

Cadorna took a similar view of the colonies. Both in 1914 and 1916, when it appeared that the Ethiopians would attack Eritrea and Somalia, he opposed sending reinforcements to East Africa. Cadorna considered Libya no more important. Beginning in October 1914, Arab attacks nearly pushed the Italians into the sea.

After belatedly learning of the French occupation of Tibesti, Italian columns had moved into the Sahara to limit these encroachments. But unsubdued Bedouin cut the Italian lines of communication and then launched a counteroffensive. Cadorna not only refused help, but withdrew troops from Tripolitania to serve in Italy. By mid-1915, the Italians held only a few coastal towns. But those they held tenaciously as bases for eventual reconquest and to deny supply points to German submarines.

As a result, Sonnino considered as absurd the aspirations of the Italian Colonial Ministry: the extension of Libya to Lake Chad and possibly to the Gulf of Guinea, total control of Ethiopia, an Italian-British co-dominion over Arabia, and, in case of their division, an equal share of Portugal's African colonies. He had refused to present such demands in the London negotiations.[54]

53 Minniti, "Gli Stati Maggiori e la politica estera italiana," pp. 103–4, 109–10, 115–6; Paul Halpern, *The Naval War in the Mediterranean, 1914–1918* (London, 1987), pp. 84–92; Ezio Ferrante, *La grande Guerra in Adriatico nel LXX anniversario della vittoria* (Rome, 1987), pp. 29–33.
54 Angelo Del Boca, *Gli italiani in Africa Orientale. Dall'unità alla Marcia su Roma* (Bari,

Lack of consultation, cooperation, and mutual comprehension between military and civilians as well as between the army and navy thus made the achievement of Italian aims unlikely even before Italy entered the war. Cadorna's strategy and Colonial Ministry plans for colonial expansion were mutually contradictory. Sonnino doubted that Cadorna could drive deep into Austria-Hungary, for like Di San Giuliano and Salandra, he had a low opinion of the army. The foreign minister believed that the best that Cadorna could do would be to seize pieces of the *terre irredente* adjacent to the Italian frontier.

Sonnino relied on diplomacy, not military operations, to gain territory for Italy, and had little interest in colonial booty. As he noted on 3 April 1915: ". . . the only serious reason for our participation in the war . . . is to assure our military predominance in the Adriatic. . . ." It would be best, Sonnino reasoned, to avoid conflict with the British over demands for African and Middle Eastern territory. He dreaded Russia's postwar naval and political presence in the Mediterranean that its projected control of the Straits would bring. He therefore wanted British support should France and Russia place Italy between two hostile powers. Influenced by Thaon di Revel, Sonnino aimed at gaining control of the Adriatic as an impregnable base for the navy. The foreign minister hoped that Austria-Hungary would survive as a bulwark against Russia. But he also wanted Adriatic supremacy for Italy, especially if the Dual Monarchy disintegrated and a powerful Serbia, allied with Russia, emerged from the war.

Sonnino also asked for and received Allied promises of European and Mediterranean territory: the Trentino and South Tyrol to the Brenner Pass; Istria and territory to the north up to the peaks of the Julian Alps (but not Fiume); Dalmatia; Valona and its hinterland with a sphere of influence in central Albania, despite its recent Serbian occupation; permanent Italian control over the Dodecanese; and, finally, the province of Adalia on Turkey's southwest Mediterranean coast. In contrast, the Treaty of London's single clause about colonial territory was vague. It promised only "some equitable compensations" along the borders of Eritrea, Somalia, and Libya, if Britain and France gained German colonies. Italy also promised to make war "jointly with France, Great Britain and Russia against all their enemies."

Advocates of a Yugoslav state learned of the Treaty of London before its signing, and accepted all Sonnino's Balkan aspirations except for Dalmatia. Yet despite pleas from the British and French, Sonnino refused to reconsider

1976), pp. 844–54; Sonnino, *Carteggio, 1914–1916,* Pietro Pastorelli, ed., (Bari, 1974), pp. 75–7, 326, 521; Robert L. Hess, "Italy and Africa: Colonial Ambitions in the First World War," *Journal of African History,* 1963, no. 1; Giovanni Buccianti, *L'egemonia sull'Etiopia* (Milan, 1977), pp. 1, 15; MacGregor Knox, "Il fascismo e la politica estera italiana" in Bosworth and Romano, *La politica estera italiana,* p. 288; Wright, *Libya, Chad and the Central Sahara,* p. 120.

that aim. He thus alienated not only the Serbs, but also the Slovenes and Croats, who preferred the rule of Vienna to that of Rome. Sonnino had added to the fighting power of Italy's enemies.[55]

Even before Cadorna's first offensive, any chance of quick victory had disappeared. In early May, Germany's Gorlice-Tarnow offensive had smashed the Russians. Simultaneously, the Turks contained Allied landings at the Dardanelles. Russian objections to Romanian territorial aspirations meanwhile prevented Romanian intervention in the war. Italo-Serb military cooperation foundered over Italian designs on Balkan territory. The plan for converging Allied attacks on Austria-Hungary collapsed. Cadorna's forces alone fell far short of those needed for his strategy. Worse, in view of the coming war, Italian public opinion had swung decidedly against intervention by early May, despite noisy demonstrations for war by a determined minority. When Giolitti returned to Rome in spring 1915, he gathered so much support that the Salandra government, unnerved by the Gorlice-Tarnow breakthrough and the Dardanelles failure, resigned on 13 May.

At this decisive moment, Vittorio Emanuele III acted. While crowds in Rome and Milan demanded war, he refused Salandra's resignation and vowed to abdicate if parliament did not back intervention. Giolitti recognized that the vast majority of the country wanted peace but concluded that only the collapse of the monarchy could prevent war. Unwilling to provoke revolution, he therefore withdrew into silence. The loss of their only capable anti-war leader forced the Liberal parliamentary majority to meekly accept the guidance of the king and his ministers. Salandra ordered Cadorna to resume mobilization; a precious week had been lost. On May 24, after Vienna rejected an ultimatum, the king declared war.[56]

Despite Italy's Treaty of London undertaking to fight Germany, parliament voted merely to sever diplomatic relations. For the next fifteen months, Italy maintained close economic ties with Germany, where hundreds of thousands of Italians continued to work; trade between the two countries via Switzerland remained brisk. When Royal Navy officers requested confidential German naval documents held by the *Regia Marina* staff, Thaon di Revel refused. In these ways, as in Cadorna's strategy, the Italians sought to conduct their war as an isolated duel with Austria-Hungary.[57]

[55] Ferrante, *La grande guerra in Adriatico*, pp. 14–6; Clough and Saladino, *A History of Modern Italy*, pp. 308–10; Sonnino, *Carteggio 1914–1916*, pp. 51–63, 364–9 (quote, 365), 375–7, 383–8; idem., *Diario 1914–1916*, pp. 114, 121–4; Minniti, "Gli Stati Maggiori e la politica estera," pp. 114–5; William I. Shorrock, *From Ally to Enemy: The Enigma of Fascist Italy in French Diplomacy, 1920–1940* (Kent, OH, 1988), p. 9; Seton-Watson, *Italy*, pp. 435–6.
[56] Seton-Watson, *Italy*, pp. 436–49; Renzi, *In the Shadow*, pp. 221–8; Gooch, *Army*, pp. 169–70; Gatti, *Un italiano*, pp. 442–4.
[57] Gerd Hardach, *The First World War 1914–1918* (Los Angeles and Berkeley, 1977), p. 240; Mack Smith, *Italy and its Monarchy*, pp. 217, 224; Ferrante, *Il Grande Ammiraglio*, pp. 57–8.

ITALY IN THE GREAT WAR, 1915–1918

By late May 1915 Cadorna had assembled thirty-five infantry divisions along the frontier, facing fourteen under-strength Austro-Hungarian divisions and a division-equivalent of German mountain troops. The Austro-Hungarians had known of the signing of the Treaty of London since late April. But exploitation of the Gorlice-Tarnow breakthrough had delayed their despatch of reinforcements. It nevertheless took Cadorna's troops a month of hard fighting merely to reach the Isonzo River. Nowhere did they breach the major enemy defenses. The government's failure to warn Cadorna of the date for war, the abrupt halt to mobilization when Salandra briefly resigned, and the army's administrative dysfunctions had lengthened Italian mobilization to six weeks rather than the planned twenty-five days. The bravery of the infantry did not compensate for poor tactical leadership, sketchy staff work, and lack of artillery and ammunition. The army thus lost its best chance to break its enemy's main line of resistance. The realities of trench warfare soon revealed the absurdity of Cadorna's plans.[58]

Beginning in late June 1915 Cadorna ordered four successive offensives until the autumn rains made further assaults impossible: despite 400,000 Italian casualties, these attacks gained little ground. Curtailing its successful offensive against Russia, the Austro-Hungarian high command transferred sufficient troops from the east to halt the Italians. Heavy Italian losses only led Cadorna to oppose diversion of any of his forces from the Italian Front. When Sonnino urged the seizure of territory in Albania, Cadorna suggested the use of some of the hard-pressed garrison in Tripolitania. Finally, the chief of staff grudgingly agreed to send an expedition to Valona after the Allied landings at Salonica and the Serbian collapse of late 1915.[59]

Cadorna failed to win victory on the battlefield, but he did defeat the civilians in Rome. The government suffered the consequences of decades of ignoring and abusing its generals. Salandra discovered that Cadorna would brook no interference from Rome in either strategy or operations. With the full backing of the king, he ruled the northeastern corner of Italy as a dictator. No politician could enter the war zone without Cadorna's permission, and initially he even refused to inform the cabinet of his plans.

By fall 1915 Cadorna nevertheless recognized the need for some cooperation with Rome. His contacts with the cabinet, however, resembled diplomatic relations between sovereign states. Cadorna rejected military subordination to civilians, and no interpretation of the Italian constitution

---

[58] Seton-Watson, *Italy*, pp. 450–1; Renzi, *In the Shadow*, p. 219; Gatti, *Un italiano a Versailles*, p. 441; Ceva, *Le forze armate*, pp. 117–79; John Gooch, "Italy during the First World War" in Allan R. Millett and Williamson Murray, eds., *Military Effectiveness*, 3 vols., (Boston, 1988), vol. 1.

[59] Ceva, *Le forze armate*, pp. 122–3; Seton-Watson, *Italy*, pp. 450–5; Stefani, *Dall'esercito piemontese*, 624–5; Sonnino, *Carteggio 1914–16*, pp. 576–80, 585–6, 592–6, 601–5, 610–5, 640–2.

contradicted him. Salandra considered asking the king to dismiss the chief of staff but always changed his mind when he could discover no adequate replacement or be certain that Cadorna's successor would behave differently. As a result, Cadorna's power grew, and he used it to concentrate every possible resource along the edge of the Istrian plateau.[60]

Cadorna seemed to justify himself in 1916. He stopped a counteroffensive from the Trentino in June, thanks in part to the diversion of enemy forces to meet the Brusilov offensive. The Italians rebounded with their first significant victory, the capture of Gorizia in August, and at last declared war on Germany. Cadorna's coolness under pressure had impressed Sonnino. Salandra, however, publicly criticized Cadorna for being unprepared to stop the spring counter-offensive. Cadorna now commanded such respect that it was Salandra who fell. An aged nonentity, Paolo Boselli, replaced him.

The 1916 operations showed that Italy did not possess the forces to push the Austro-Hungarians back on the Isonzo while simultaneously seizing booty in the Balkans, the Middle East, and Africa. Cadorna rejected the idea that Italy could use his forces better elsewhere; he did not differ in this respect from his colleagues on the Western Front. But Cadorna's near-total independence from the government gave him the power to impose his personal strategy on the entire nation. He proposed the Italian Front as the focus of Allied efforts in 1917, gaining the support of the British prime minister for diverting major British reinforcements from France. But when Lloyd George raised the idea at a conference in Rome in January, opposition from French and British military leaders killed the project. Italy remained alone.[61]

Due to Cadorna's refusal to release forces for amphibious operations and the Austro-Hungarian admirals' refusal to seek a fleet action, the Italian Navy accomplished little during the first two years of the war. Meanwhile, thanks to their excellent Adriatic harbors and the cover offered by the Dalmatian islands, the light craft of the Austrian Navy and a German submarine force attacked or withdrew at will. Italian rejection of a unified Allied naval command in the Mediterranean or Adriatic further hampered maritime operations.

Within the Italian Navy, Thaon di Revel clashed with Luigi di Savoia, the Duke of the Abruzzi, whom the king had appointed as commander-in-chief of the fleet. The duke argued for aggressive fleet operations to provoke the Austrians into a major engagement. Thaon di Revel thought it foolhardy to risk expensive larger units except in particularly favorable circumstances. Instead, he proposed using smaller vessels for offensive sweeps. But the

60 Meriggi, "Militari e istituzioni politiche," pp. 91–2; Seton-Watson, *Italy*, pp. 457–8; Bracalini, *Il re "vittorioso"*, 119; Gordon A. Craig, *The Politics of the Prussian Army 1640–1945* (Oxford, 1964), pp. 195–6; Gatti, *Un italiano*, pp. 260, 386–7, 428.
61 David Lloyd George, *War Memoirs*, 6 vols., (London, 1934), vol. 3, pp. 1434–52; Ceva, *Le forze armate*, p. 127; Llewellyn Woodward, *Great Britain and the War of 1914–1918* (London, 1967), p. 261.

scarcity of such Italian ships restricted such actions. After the unopposed bombardment of a number of Italian Adriatic sea towns and the loss of three major warships to sabotage and submarine attacks, Thaon di Revel was forced to resign as chief of staff in October 1915. He assumed command of the Venice squadron, while the Duke of the Abruzzi became the de facto head of the navy.

At Venice Thaon di Revel further refined his strategy of striking at the Austrians with aircraft, torpedo boats, and submarines. Meanwhile, the Italian Navy had evacuated the defeated Serbian Army after it retreated to the Albanian coast and had transferred it to Corfú in December 1915-April 1916. But the conquest of Serbia and Montenegro gave the Austro-Hungarians and Germans even firmer control of the eastern Adriatic and easier access to the Mediterranean. As a result, their submarine successes mounted and the lack of Italian-Allied naval cooperation made an effective response impossible.

By early 1917 the Duke of the Abruzzi's strategy had clearly failed, while the fleet had lost a pre-dreadnought to mines and a dreadnought to sabotage. The battle fleet was dangerously vulnerable to mines and torpedoes, and lacked sufficient numbers of escorts. Italian dreadnoughts spent only one day out of every hundred at sea, and never met their Austro-Hungarian counterparts in battle. In February 1917, Vittorio Emanuele III pressured the Duke of the Abruzzi into resignation and appointed Thaon di Revel as both chief -of staff and commander-in-chief of the fleet. Once the necessary numbers of light craft became available, the king intended that Thaon di Revel put his strategy into practice. In the meantime, the main focus of the war effort remained on land.[62]

Cadorna resumed his offensives on the Isonzo in May 1917. He had built up the army to sixty-one infantry and four dismounted cavalry divisions and added four more understrength infantry divisions over the summer. He also shattered much of that army within the space of six months. In his eleventh offensive of the war, from mid-August to mid-September, Cadorna's forces nearly forced the collapse of the Austro-Hungarians. Yet the greatest successes of the offensive came in the first two weeks; thereafter, certain that the enemy was cracking, Cadorna persisted despite 680,000 casualties between May and October and the total exhaustion of his troops. And the Germans refused to allow their major ally to crumble. Since Russia had collapsed, they could send seven divisions to Italy by October 1917. The Central Powers agreed to mount an offensive of their own.

By fall 1917 Cadorna's troops had advanced a maximum of eighteen miles

---

[62] Halpern, *The Naval War*, pp. 118–9, 125–64, 333–8; Ferrante, *Il Grande Ammiraglio*, pp. 56–74; idem., *La grande guerra in Adriatico*, pp. 35–65; Montanari, *Le truppe italiane in Albania*, p. 53; Rodrigo Garcia y Robertson, "Failure of the Heavy Gun at Sea, 1898–1922," *Technology and Culture*, July 1987, p. 551.

from the prewar frontier at a cost of over 300,000 killed, 700,000 wounded, and 1.8 million sick or injured. They had accomplished this by their valor and by Cadorna's ruthlessness. By the end of the war the army had court-martialed 340,000 soldiers (one out of twelve) and executed thousands by firing squads. In a revival of Roman practices, Cadorna even subjected certain units to selective executions when their enthusiasm in the attack was judged wanting. By the eve of the Battle of Caporetto, the *Regio Esercito* was physically and spiritually spent.

The majority of Italians had never supported the war, only passively accepted it. By mid-1917 the population suffered from acute weariness. Food and coal supplies were perilously low. Inflation had reduced both industrial and agricultural wages for many Italians to near-starvation levels. On 1 August 1917, Pope Benedict XV, fearing Austro-Hungarian collapse as a result of Cadorna's imminent offensive, urged Europeans to end their "useless slaughter." In late August bread riots in Turin expanded into full-scale revolt, requiring the army to restore order. In September, part of the Socialist leadership, which had publicly advocated a negotiated peace, urged an attempt to end the war by winter; some even encouraged mass desertion.

Cadorna became increasingly worried by what he regarded as treason on the home front. In the spring of 1917 he rejected pleas from Mussolini, who had recently been invalided out of the army, to establish a military dictatorship. But by the summer Cadorna was warning the government that if it did not stop the spread of subversion, he would. Italy had always lacked mechanisms to ensure that military operations were conducted in pursuit of political objectives. By late 1917 the situation had reversed. Cadorna's autonomy and dictatorial powers allowed his narrowly military views to dominate political direction of the war.

In the midst of this crisis, the Central Powers broke the Italian front at Caporetto on 24 October 1917. Parts of the *Regio Esercito* collapsed. To their surprise, the Germans and Austro-Hungarians realized that they might knock Italy out of the war. The immediate causes of Italian defeat were German tactical and operational superiority, coupled with gross defects in the Italian defenses. But the resulting Italian rout and mass desertions arose from Cadorna's strategic errors, from his brutal methods of leadership, and from the government's failure to control him. Cadorna excused his defeat by publicly accusing some units of cowardice and implying that Socialist anti-war propaganda and papal peace efforts had led to a "military strike." Worse, he nearly panicked the government by first exaggerating the extent of the disaster and then privately advising a separate peace.

Cadorna recovered his nerve and rallied the remnants of his army after a seventy-mile retreat to the Piave River-Monte Grappa line. But Allied pressure and recognition by the king that Cadorna had lost the confidence of army and nation led to his replacement with the more politically astute

General Armando Diaz. Italy had already gained a strong prime minister with the appointment of Vittorio Emanuele Orlando on 30 October. Vittorio Emanuele III and Orlando decided Italy must remain in the war. The Italian economy could no longer function without Allied aid, and defeat after so much suffering might bring revolution.[63]

Against all expectations, the army held the Monte Grappa-Piave line east and north of Venice, while the politicians bickered in Rome and the high command wavered. In January 1918 Diaz began rebuilding his army after the loss of 320,000 casualties, 350,000 deserters or stragglers, and 3,800 of 6,900 artillery pieces. Simultaneously, the national majority united politically for the first time in Italian history. No government had ever sought popular support for a war. But the shock of Caporetto and the heroic defense of the Piave had created a cause that average Italians could understand and support: the defense of *la patria*. For those Italians most aware of deep divisions within the country, among them the ex-Socialist Mussolini, this spontaneous surge of unity emphasized both the nation's latent strength and the inability of conventional politics to mobilize it.[64]

Orlando and Diaz nevertheless recognized the need to enhance civilian and military morale. The army introduced a propaganda service; the government promised its peasant soldiers that victory would bring land ownership to those who had previously tilled it for others. The Orlando government also proved more efficient than its predecessors in concentrating Italian economic resources in support of the war. By June 1918 the army had restored its artillery firepower to the pre-Caporetto level; by November, it counted 9,000 artillery pieces. But only massive aid from its allies made Italy's 1918 achievements possible.

Austro-Hungarian steel production remained triple that of Italy; only Allied coal, steel, and ore allowed the Italians to stand up to their enemy on the battlefield. Conscription of 5.9 million men, most of them peasants, caused a drastic decline in food production. Allied wheat, carried in Allied shipping, fed the Italian army and nation, especially in 1917–18. Even so, Italian soldiers and workers subsisted on far lower nutrition levels than the British and French.

In 1913–14, the government had spent 2.5 billion lire, 92 percent covered by revenues. In 1917–18, government expenditures reached 25.3 billion lire, of which revenue covered only 23 percent. Internal loans raised 15.3 billion lire in 1915–18, while Allied and American loans supplied another 14.5

63 Ceva, *Le forze armate*, pp. 127–43; Seton-Watson, *Italy*, pp. 465–85; Bracalini, *Il re "vittorioso"*, pp. 124–5; Rochat and Massobrio, *Breve storia*, p. 186; Stefani, *Dall'esercito piemontese*, pp. 626–33, 678; Ilari, *La "nazione armata"*, p. 444, 462–7; Vittorio Emanuele Orlando, *Memorie 1915–1919* (Milan, 1960), pp. 229–30, 254, 312–3.
64 Ceva, *Le forze armate*, pp. 143–6; Renzo De Felice, *Mussolini il rivoluzionario* (Turin, 1965), pp. 362–418; Gatti, *Un italiano*, pp. 16–7.

billion lire. These debts hobbled Italian freedom of action until the 1930s.[65]

Italy's weakness after Caporetto persuaded many, even extreme nationalists like Mussolini, of the wisdom of collaboration with nationalist groups seeking to break Austria-Hungary apart. Political warfare thus belatedly entered Italian strategy. But exploiting Austria-Hungary's ethnic cleavages required Italian renunciation of Dalmatia in favor of a Yugoslav state. At the Rome Congress in April 1918, Polish, Czech, Romanian, Serb, Yugoslav, and Italian representatives agreed on the national dismemberment of Austria-Hungary. But Sonnino refused to give up Dalmatia and only reluctantly accepted formation within the Italian army of a Czech Legion made up of Austro-Hungarian prisoners. He vetoed a similar Yugoslav Legion, despite pleas from Diaz. Orlando thought his foreign minister foolish but feared the political consequences of dismissing him. Finally, in September 1918, Diaz persuaded the cabinet to discuss the issue. As a result, the government announced its support for the Yugoslav movement. But despite the enormous improvement in Italy's strategic position, Sonnino still refused to renounce Dalmatia. Italy's leadership thus failed to promote national revolt in Austria-Hungary.[66]

Italian and Allied efforts restored the strength of the *Regio Esercito* by late spring 1918. That allowed the Italians to repulse the Austro-Hungarian "Peace Offensive" across the Piave in June 1918 while inflicting some 150,000 casualties on the enemy. But the exhaustion of the army and of its supply of shells, coupled with continuing doubts about its offensive capabilities, dissuaded Diaz from a counter-offensive. These hesitations continued over the next four months, despite Allied successes in France, increasing signs that the Austro-Hungarian army was crumbling, and growing political pressure on the Italians to attack. It was only in late September 1918, after the Allies smashed the Hindenburg Line on the Western Front and French-led forces broke out of the Salonika enclave – threatening Austria-Hungary from the south – that Diaz realized that the war might end before 1919. Sonnino feared that the French would advance into Albania and hand it over to the Greeks and Serbs, and that the Serbs themselves would seize Dalmatia. He finally resigned himself to the destruction of Austria-Hungary. Even then, only a warning from Orlando to Diaz that continued military inaction threatened the government with a "true disaster" in its relations with the Allies pushed Diaz and his staff into action.

Diaz ordered a hastily organized offensive on the first anniversary of Caporetto. After three days, the attack foundered due to heroic Austro-

65 Ceva, *Le forze armate*, pp. 144–7, 167–70, 175–9; Seton-Watson, *Italy*, pp. 485–9; Hardach, *The First World War*, pp. 133, 136; Mitchell, *European Historical Statistics*, p. 224; Coppola d'Anna, *Popolazione*, p. 85.
66 Seton-Watson, *Italy*, pp. 495–7; Sonnino, *Diario 1916–1922*, pp. 262–4, 291–8; idem., *Carteggio 1916–1922*, Pietro Pastorelli, ed. (Bari, 1975), pp. 392–3, 410–2, 483.

Hungarian resistance. But the collapse of the Habsburg state and national revolutions across the empire had spread mutiny to rear area Austro-Hungarian units. Trapped between the Italian offensive and revolt behind the trenches, the Austro-Hungarian front gave way on 29 October. The Italians swept forward to victory and a dictated armistice on 4 November.

The *Regia Marina* also brought its war to a triumphant end. After returning to command, Thaon di Revel stressed antisubmarine measures. He recognized that 70 percent of the material vital to the Italian war effort arrived by sea via the Gibraltar-Genoa route. Yet the admiral practiced a naval version of *sacro egoismo*. While he insisted that the British and French protect Italian shipping, he concentrated Italian destroyers in the Adriatic. Thaon di Revel wanted to seize Albania and Dalmatia when the opportunity arose.

The Italian naval leadership engaged more in political skirmishing with Italy's allies than in warfare. Italian recovery from Caporetto and Russian departure from the war convinced Thaon di Revel that Italy could indeed dominate the Adriatic after the end of the war. The admiral successfully opposed American suggestions for an amphibious landing in Dalmatia, French plans to station their dreadnoughts at Corfú, and British attempts to create a single Mediterranean naval command, suspecting that each represented a plot against Italian supremacy in the Adriatic. Furthermore, despite Allied and American pressure, the chief of staff refused to risk his battleships in operations. He wanted to preserve the Italian battle fleet for postwar contingencies.

Innovative naval weapons nevertheless gave the Italians notable victories over their official enemies. In December 1917 an Italian motor torpedo boat assault on Trieste harbor destroyed an Austro-Hungarian pre-dreadnought. In early June 1918 a sortie by the Habsburg battle fleet against the Otranto barrage was cut short by another Italian motor boat attack that torpedoed and sank an Austro-Hungarian dreadnought. These successes validated Thaon di Revel's stress on light craft and buttressed his arguments against the need for non-Italian major warships in the Adriatic.

From March 1918, with assistance from the allied navies, the *Regia Marina* slowly gained the upper hand over enemy submarines in the Adriatic. By October, Italian light craft dominated all but the upper reaches of that sea. On the night of 1 November two Italian swimmers guided a demolition device into Pola naval base. The warhead sent to the bottom the former Austro-Hungarian dreadnought that the naval leadership probably knew was the flagship of the new Yugoslav navy. The *Regia Marina* controlled the Adriatic. By mid-November the navy had landed forces along the entire Dalmatian coast. Both the Italian army and navy had ended the war with impressive successes.[67]

[67] Halpern, *The Naval War*, pp. 307–411, 426, 567; Ferrante, *La grande guerra in Mediterraneo*, 70–121; idem., *Il grande ammiraglio*, pp. 69–76; Frank Freidel, *Franklin D. Roosevelt. The Apprenticeship* (Boston, 1952), pp. 362–4.

THE BITTER FRUITS OF PEACE, 1918–1922

The Italians had won their war at enormous cost. The battlefield struggle had devoured about 680,000 Italian lives; another 30,000 succumbed to wounds or war injuries in coming years. The financial cost for war in the 1914–19 period alone was about 26.5 billion lire; another 10.8 billion lire in war-related expenses came due in 1919–24.[68] But the Treaty of London seemed to guarantee a huge return on this investment: Italy's great victory would make it a world power. By early 1919 a situation unforeseen in 1915 – the collapse of Imperial Russia, the Dual Monarchy, and the Ottoman Empire – encouraged these expanded Italian ambitions. Italians began planning for control over the oil, grain, and mines of Romania, the Ukraine, and the Caucasus, and for protectorates over Croatia and the eastern Red Sea coast.

Disillusion came swiftly. At the peace conference, the Italians found that their aspirations far exceeded Allied and American perceptions of Italian strength or achievements. Britain, France, and the United States all opposed the creation of another world power. Sonnino worsened matters by suggesting that Italy needed Dalmatia to fight a future French-Yugoslav alliance. As a result, the Allies decided that whatever territory they did not want for themselves was better left to client states such as Greece and Yugoslavia. Far from gaining its new postwar goals, Italy failed even to acquire what had been promised by the Treaty of London. These disappointments directly affected the Italian army high command. Thanks to the new relationship created by Orlando and Diaz in late 1917, the military leadership had for the first time become intimately involved in the determination of foreign policy. The general staff participated in the formulation of the territorial demands presented at Versailles, and had sent a military staff to advise Orlando and Sonnino.

In late 1918 the army had reinforced the naval occupation of Dalmatia, Fiume, and parts of Montenegro, and had expanded its control over Albania. Despite British opposition, the Italians landed at various points in Turkey between March and May 1919. As the French supported the Greeks and Yugoslavs against Italian expansion, the *Regio Esercito* general staff considered war with both, and drew up plans for the destruction of Yugoslavia as early as December 1918. By spring 1919, war between Italy and Greece over control of Asia Minor also seemed possible, with the Allies and Americans backing the Greeks. By November 1918 Italy also had plans to reconquer its North African colonies. In January 1919, the Italian army began sending troops to Libya.[69]

---

68 Ilari, *La "nazione armata"*, p. 443; Ceva, *Le forze armate*, p. 166; Francesco A. Répaci, "Le spese delle guerre condotte dall'Italia nell'ultimo quarantacinquennio (1913–14 – 1957–58)," *Rivista di politica economica*, April 1960, table 10. All figures are calculated using the pre-inflationary 1913 lira, worth one-fifth of a 1913 American dollar.

69 R.A. Webster, "Una speranza rinviata. L'espansione industriale italiana e il problema del petrolio dopo la prima guerra mondiale," *Storia contemporanea*, April 1980, pp. 221,

Italian expansion reached its apogee in early 1919. When the Allies and Americans refused to accept Italian demands for Fiume, Dalmatia, and western Asia Minor, Orlando and Sonnino walked out of the conference. They expected to be called back immediately. Instead, the conference proceeded without them. After a week, Orlando and Sonnino realized their mistake and returned. But the weakness of the Italian position lay exposed and the British and French divided the German colonies in Africa between them. They offered the Italians only scraps of arid territory on the borders of Libya and Somalia. Meanwhile, recognizing that reconquest would prove too costly, the Italians granted the Libyan Arabs autonomy in return for accepting Italian sovereignty.

In compensation for their territorial disappointments, Lloyd George offered the Italians a protectorate over the Caucasian republics that had emerged from the ruins of the Russian and Ottoman Empires. Orlando ordered Diaz to prepare a 100,000 man expeditionary force for service in Georgia and Azerbaijan, in the hope of exclusive access to an increasingly important source of energy: the Baku oil fields. But these possibilities could not save the Orlando cabinet from public outrage over its Versailles failures. It fell after a vote of no confidence on 19 June 1919. Francesco Saverio Nitti replaced Orlando.[70]

Nitti canceled the Caucasus expedition and reduced the Italian garrison at Fiume. He abandoned any annexations in Turkey and began the withdrawal of most troops there in spring 1920. The Allies granted Italy a mandate over most of Albania, but insurgency and malaria forced the Italians to commit hundreds of thousands of troops in order to maintain 120,000 men there at any one time. By summer 1920 the Italians had withdrawn to Valona after spending nearly 2 billion lire in vain.

Nitti had acted from political compulsion as well as financial weakness. In the postwar elections in November 1919 the Left had increased its strength in parliament. The near-collapse of the economy made it impossible for the government to redeem its post-Caporetto promises to Italy's veterans. Unemployment, soaring inflation, and the example of the Bolshevik Revolution brought the Socialists ever more recruits. At the same time, the Church helped form the reformist Catholic "People's Party" to combat the appeal of the revolutionary Left. These two mass parties gained 256 of the 508 seats in

225–34; Raffaele Guariglia, *Primi passi in diplomazia* (Naples, 1972), pp. 64–7; Sonnino, *Diario 1916–1922*, pp. 308–13, 316–20, 326, 331–2; Ivo J. Lederer, *Yugoslavia at the Paris Peace Conference* (New Haven, 1963), pp. 71–5; Stevenson, *The First World War*, pp. 283–5; Vincenzo Gallinari, *L'esercito italiano nel primo dopoguerra 1918–1920* (Rome, 1980), pp. 48–9, 74; Angelo Del Boca, *Tripoli bel suol d'amore 1860–1922* (Bari, 1988), pp. 360–1.

70 Seton-Watson, *Italy*, pp. 528–36; Enrico Serra, *Nitti e la Russia* (Bari, 1975), pp 17–9; Matteo Pizzigallo, *Alle origini della politica petrolifera italiana (1920–1925)* (Varese, 1981), pp. 8, 99–100; Gallinari, *L'esercito italiano*, pp. 103–7; Del Boca, *Tripoli*, pp. 361–9.

the Chamber of Deputies. Only mutual antagonism prevented them from forming a coalition government. To many on the Right it seemed that the two groups that had allegedly undermined the army before Caporetto might now gain power. Throughout the 1919–20 period, the Left displayed its self-confidence by scorning those who had supported the war. Soldiers, especially officers, soon found it dangerous to appear in uniform. The Nitti government had great difficulty defending public order. Strikes and demonstrations swept Italy.[71]

Economic and social chaos forced Nitti's resignation in June 1920. Giolitti returned as the hoped-for savior of Italy and continued the painful chore of matching Italian foreign policy to Italian weakness, in the process infuriating the Nationalists, the new Fascist movement, and many veterans. Giolitti abandoned Valona in August 1920. His foreign minister, Carlo Sforza, negotiated a settlement that secured a land frontier with Yugoslavia more favorable than the Treaty of London line. In return for abandoning other claims to Dalmatia, Italy received Zara, its immediate hinterland, and four Dalmatian islands, while Fiume became a free state territorially contiguous to Italy.

Sforza negotiated understandings with Greece and Turkey as well. Italy agreed to cede the Dodecanese to Greece when Britain did the same with Cyprus, although Sforza obtained a secret British promise that Cyprus would remain British for the indefinite future, giving Italy permanent de facto possession of the Aegean islands. In return for economic concessions from the Turkish Nationalists, Sforza agreed to evacuate the remaining Italian troops from Turkey in February 1921. In June the last Italian forces withdrew. Italy's postwar imperial dreams seemed over.[72]

But despite the outraged cries from the Right the Nitti and Giolitti governments had not abandoned expansion. Instead, they had adopted more realistic aims than Orlando or Sonnino. Italy had emerged from the war with a major military resource: a modern armaments industry, vastly expanded during the war. But this industry and Italian industry in general could only survive with access to raw materials and markets.

Before World War I, Giolitti had sought to shift Italy from a coal-based economy to a petroleum-based one, ordering the conversion of the state railways and the navy from coal to oil power. But by the early 1920s, imported coal, mostly British, still supplied 83 percent of Italian energy needs and imported petroleum 4 percent. Nitti and Sforza looked to the Balkans, Turkey, and the Caucasus as sources for petroleum. Realizing that Italy lacked the means to conquer oil-producing areas, they decided that Italy could still pursue a policy of economic penetration in regions outside of

71 Seton-Watson, *Italy*, pp. 547–53; Montanari, *Le truppe italiane in Albania*, pp. 183–230, 388–9; Gallinari, *L'esercito italiano*, pp. 163–79.
72 Roberto Vivarelli, *Il dopoguerra in Italia e l'avvento del fascismo* (Naples, 1967), pp. 465, 520, 593–4; Lederer, *Yugoslavia*, pp. 135–6, 176, 240–1; Seton-Watson, *Italy*, pp. 579–84.

British or French control by exchanging manufactures and arms for oil and raw materials.

Between late 1918 and mid-1921, the lira's value had declined sharply due to Italy's economic woes. But this sharply lowered the price of Italian goods for export. In essence, a policy of eastward expansion through peaceful collaboration would have continued the tradition established shortly after Italian unification. At some future date, of course, a reinvigorated Italy might again seek territorial aggrandizement to its east.

Finally, despite Right-wing cries that Italy had accepted a "mutilated victory" in 1919–21, it had in reality gained much from the peace settlement. Across its border, France still faced Germany; a wounded enemy but one bound to recover. A weakened Britain confronted the immediate challenges presented to its empire by the United States and Japan, and likely future threats from Germany and Bolshevik Russia. Italy by contrast now enjoyed land frontiers along the high peaks of the Alps. To the west France lay too bloodied to pose any threat to Italy, and to the north and east there remained only the ruins of Austria-Hungary. With the collapse of the Habsburg, Ottoman, and Romanov Monarchies and the defeat of the Hohenzollerns, Central Europe and the Balkans lay open to Italian political influence and economic penetration. Germany would revive eventually. Italy could thus hope to offer the decisive weight to either side, once the victors and vanquished of the Great War resumed their rivalries.[73]

Unfortunately, Italy lacked the means to integrate its new democratic political system with its old authoritarian strategic decision-making process. Even the old power centers clashed. The admirals wanted Dalmatia. Colonial officials demanded African expansion. The wiser generals considered defense of Dalmatia an impossibility, and knew that more colonies meant fewer troops to defend the Alps. Postwar prime ministers lacked both a coordinating body to resolve these disputes privately and control over public opinion to settle them publicly. Divisions between Right and Left, aggravated by the tremendous strain of war, made the creation of consensus extremely difficult, and prevented public opinion from moderating military, diplomatic, and colonialist pressure for dangerous imperial undertakings. Worst of all, the king reluctantly but decisively turned against Italy's democratic experiment.

---

[73] Bosworth, *Italy*, p. 419; R.A.Webster, *Industrial Imperialism in Italy, 1908–1915* (Berkeley, 1975), p. 334; idem., "Una speranza rinviata," pp. 219–21; Sonnino, *Diario 1916–1922*, p. 339; Serra, *Nitti e la Russia*, pp. 25–35; Pizzigallo, *Alle origini*, pp. xi, 12, 19–20, 23–47; Giorgio Petracchi, "Italy at the Genoa Conference: Italian-Soviet Commercial Relations" in Carole Fink, Axel Frohn and Jürgen Heideking, eds., *Genoa, Rapallo, and European Reconstruction in 1922* (Washington and New York, 1991), pp. 167–70; Carlo Sforza, *Contemporary Italy. Its Intellectual and Moral Origins* (New York, 1944), pp. 226–7; Bracalini, *Il re "vittorioso"*, p. 141, n. 5; Mack Smith, *Italy*, p. 319; *Documents on British Foreign Policy*, First Series, vol. IV, no. 4 [hereafter, DBFP, followed by series, volume and document number]; ibid. XIII, nos. 66, 98, 193; ibid., XVII, nos. 69, 82, 403; ibid., XXII, nos. 147, 198.

A national strategy based on reality proved too subtle for the Italian Right. By late 1919 Nationalists were urging alliances with Hungary, Bulgaria, Turkey, and Germany as the first step toward a war of revenge against Italy's former allies. This attitude soon spread to the army officer corps and influenced the king. As Mussolini's Fascist movement grew into a national political force, he too adopted these policies. But while some younger officers in the *Regio Esercito* supported an alliance with Hungary, others considered another European war a mistake. They urged renewed Italian expansion in Africa, and by early 1920 some were discussing a new war against Ethiopia.

Revived Italian imperialism predated Mussolini's March on Rome. In August 1920 Sforza and Sonnino agreed that recent foreign policy had weakened the army's loyalty to the government. Sforza listened sympathetically while Sonnino advocated an alliance with Hungary, Bulgaria, and Turkey. In mid-1921, when Ivanoe Bonomi replaced Giolitti, a new national belligerence emerged. Having destroyed Austria-Hungary, some Italian leaders now contemplated an eventual war with France and its new client state, Yugoslavia. In January 1922 Bonomi ordered the abandonment of the 1919 accords with the Arabs and the start of operations for the reconquest of Libya. This campaign expanded under Bonomi's successor, Luigi Facta.[74]

The military leadership had already begun planning for a future war. But the mismatch between forces desired and resources available widened as the government faced bankruptcy. Under these circumstances, the navy gained a major victory over its prospective French opponents at the 1921–22 Washington Naval Conference, thanks to false British assumptions of continued cooperation with Italy. In August 1914 the French navy had possessed 689,000 tons of warships to the 286,000 tons of the *Regia Marina*. Most French naval construction had stopped in 1914–18, but recognition of Italian hostility prompted renewed building after the war, including the construction of as many as nine battleships. And despite the continued faith of Italian admirals in battleships, poverty had forced them to abandon the construction of the four ships of the *Caracciolo* class.

The conference rescued the *Regia Marina* from a hopeless building race with the French. The best that Italian admirals had expected was a warship ratio of 80 percent of that of the French navy; but to their astonishment Britain's support brought them parity. Thereafter, the *Regia Marina* could concentrate on the construction of submarines and light craft. These new warships could block French access to the Yugoslavs in the Adriatic, prevent a French blockade of the vulnerable Italian coast, and cut French lines of

74 Giorgio Rochat, *l'esercito italiano da Vittorio Veneto a Mussolini (1919–1925)* (Bari, 1967), pp. 174–5; Alexander De Grand, *The Italian Nationalist Association and the Rise of Fascism in Italy* (Lincoln, NE, 1978), pp. 102–5; Giorgio Rumi, "Mussolini, 'Il Popolo d'Italia' e l'Ungheria 1918–1922," *Storia contemporanea*, Dec. 1975; Seton-Watson, *Italy,* pp. 535–9, 554 n. 3, 602–3; Buccianti, *L'egemonia sull'Etiopia*, pp. 197–200; Sonnino, *Diario 1916–1922*, pp. 357–63; Sergio Romano, *Giuseppe Volpi* (Milan, 1979), pp. 103–8; Del Boca, *Tripoli*, pp. 390–411; Shorrock, *From Ally to Enemy*, pp. 15–8.

communication in the Mediterranean and Atlantic. Italian admirals began to dream of surpassing the French in warship tonnage and of a future Mediterranean war. But *Regia Marina* thinking had already grown even more ambitious. The experience of World War I, combined with knowledge of the goals of the Italian Right, convinced Thaon di Revel that the British might attempt to blockade Italy within the Mediterranean. In August 1922, the admiral warned the senate that British bases at Gibraltar and Suez threatened Italy. The naval staff began planning how to deal with those obstacles to Italian expansion.[75]

New thinking also developed in the army. Some planners suggested scrapping the prewar model of a large, poorly equipped army in favor of some fifteen permanent divisions with heavy firepower, superior mobility, and a high level of training. Such an army would not serve as the basis for wartime expansion, but would strike independently at Italy's enemies at the outbreak of war. Other military thinkers proposed a system based on a small regular army supplemented by universal military training and service along Swiss lines to provide a "nation in arms" of as many as sixty-five divisions.

After much debate the generals rejected both ideas. The conservative high command preferred a peacetime army of thirty skeleton divisions, even if badly trained, poorly equipped, and vastly understrength due to lean budgets. These generals remained skeptical about new theories of warfare based on tanks or aircraft. They neither understood such innovations nor believed that Italy could afford them. Instead, they planned an army based on infantry and artillery supported by horse cavalry as in 1915. An army constructed along traditional lines would remain under professional officer corps control but offered the foundation for expansion, as in 1915–17, in order to deal with the French, Yugoslavs, or some future German threat to Austria.[76]

By spring 1922, however, the Italian political leadership was planning for more than Alpine trench warfare. In April 1922, Chaim Weizmann came away from lobbying the Italian government to support Zionism convinced that the Facta government sought to expel Britain from the Mediterranean and to make that sea Italy's *mare nostrum*. Discussions between British and Italian diplomats in June 1922 left the British with the same impression. They also noted Italian determination to conquer Ethiopia. The British considered the extent of Italian ambitions astonishing, given that Italy lacked the economic and military resources needed for such conquests.[77]

75 Ferrante, *Il Grande Ammiraglio*, p. 203; Giovanni Bernardi, *Il disarmo navale fra le due guerre mondiali (1919–1939)* (Rome, 1975), pp. 42–8, 60, 72–3, 83–4, 107, 130–3, 142–4; Knox, "Il fascismo e la politica estera italiana," p. 297.
76 Gallinari, *L'esercito italiano*, pp. 163–79; Virgilio Ilari, *Storia del servizio militare in Italia*, vol. 3, *"Nazione militare" e "Fronte del lavoro" (1919–1943)* (Rome, 1990), pp. 32–63; Botti and Ilari, *Il pensiero militare*, pp. 26, 44–66; Filippo Stefani, *La storia della dottrina e degli ordinamenti dell'esercito italiano*, vol. 2, tomo 1, *Da Vittorio Veneto alla 2a guerra mondiale* (Rome, 1985), pp. 51–66, 111–23, 153–64, 432–9, 517, 565–8, 599–629.
77 Chaim Weizmann, *The Letters and Papers of Chaim Weizmann*, Bernard Wasserstein, ed.,

These initiatives failed to convince the military leadership that traditional policies could return Italy to the path of greatness. The postwar governments seemed impotent before the revolutionary threat posed by the Socialists and the specter of papal rule symbolized by the Catholic "People's Party." In fact, before his government fell in June 1921, Giolitti had outmaneuvered both opposition parties and returned the country to a semblance of normalcy. But to the Right and many officers it seemed that liberal democracy promised only weak government.

Only the Fascists seemed capable of dealing effectively with the Left, while the inability of the Bonomi and Facta governments of 1921–22 to halt the Fascist onslaught underscored the impotence of the Liberal politicians. By mid-1922 the army and navy leadership believed that the Fascists alone could maintain domestic peace and carry out a foreign policy worthy of a great power. Once Mussolini made clear his willingness to preserve the monarchy, any doubts on the part of Diaz, Thaon di Revel, and other leading generals and admirals receded. After Diaz informed the king during the Fascist "March on Rome" that the army preferred Mussolini as prime minister, Vittorio Emanuele III felt forced to call the Black Shirt leader to Rome and entrust him with the formation of a government. By early 1925 Mussolini had imposed a dictatorship and had began his march toward war.[78]

Mussolini planned to make Italy the decisive weight in Europe. As he told Fascist Party Secretary Augusto Turati in March 1930: "Between 1936 and 1940 the second European war will inevitably explode. It will be necessary to be strong and ready for that day. Because of its geographic and historical position, if Italy will know how to remain alone, it will be the arbiter of the huge conflict . . . That day Italy will be truly great."[79]

Mussolini appreciated that failure to coordinate foreign, military, and economic policy had crippled previous attempts to implement a national strategy. He understood the need to mobilize popular support for national goals. In over fifteen years of tyrannical rule, he gathered all necessary powers in his hands. But despite his ambitions and pretensions, he lacked the qualities of personality and intellect to succeed as a modern Caesar.

Mussolini failed to learn the real lessons of Italian history. Clausewitz had warned of modern war's unpredictability and of the great dangers inherent in its use as an instrument of policy. This was particularly true for a country such as Italy, hobbled by national poverty, a limited military potential, and a

(New Brunswick, NJ, 1977), vol. 11, Series A, pp. 80–1; Public Record Office FO 371/19983 Palestine 1938 E4842, Weizmann to Ormsby-Gore, 15 July 1936; DBFP(1), vol. 4, nos. 5, 126; ibid., vol. 5, no. 87; ibid., vol. 6, nos. 244, 258, 309; ibid., vol. 22, no. 698; ibid., 24, nos. 1, 2, 4, 6, 7, 8.

78 Adrian Lyttelton, *The Seizure of Power: Fascism in Italy 1919–1929* (Princeton, 1988), pp. 1–93; Rochat, *L'esercito italiano*, pp. 397–408; Ferrante, *Il Grande Ammiraglio*, pp. 83–4.

79 Augusto Turati, *Fuori dell'ombra della mia vita. Dieci anni nel solco del fascismo*, A. Fappani, ed., (Brescia, 1973), p. 21.

brittle, conservative military leadership. With increasing harshness, this reality already had manifested itself to the Italians in 1895–96, 1911–12, and especially 1915–18. Each of those wars had developed in a totally unexpected manner, had unleashed uncontrollable popular forces, and had cost Italy far more than its leaders had initially calculated.[80]

From Mussolini's perspective in the early 1930s, however, the strategy of the decisive weight offered great advantages. In practical terms, the strategy aimed at extracting colonial concessions from France in return for tipping the balance of power in Europe against Germany. The strategy had gained Libya for Italy before World War I. In 1935–36 Mussolini used the same methods as his Liberal predecessors to acquire Ethiopia. But just as the Libyan War had seriously weakened the Italian military while helping to push Europe into the Great War, the Ethiopian War bankrupted Italy and severely drained Mussolini's forces, while providing Hitler with the distraction he needed to remilitarize the Rhineland. The supine reaction of the Allies to this and other German breaches of the Versailles settlement helped persuade Mussolini to tilt strongly toward Hitler. Hoping to gain new concessions from the French and British, however, Mussolini continued to waver between Germany and the West in 1936–39. In September 1939 Hitler plunged Europe into another general conflict at a time when the Italian armed forces had barely begun to recover from the Ethiopian and Spanish Wars.[81] Intoxicated by dreams of glory, Mussolini ignored the massive impediments to their realization. After ten months' hesitation he led Italy into war in June 1940. At the time, it seemed that he had intervened at the ideal moment and would gain a vast empire for Italy at a small fraction of the cost paid in 1915–18. In fact, Mussolini had blundered far worse than the Italian leaders of 1915. Nothing underscores Mussolini's folly so much as the contrast between Italian statecraft in 1911–19 – granting all its failures – and Mussolini's conduct of affairs in 1935–43. For even if the Axis had won World War II, how would Fascist Italy have fared in a Europe dominated by Nazi Germany? In terms of Italian interests, the post-1919 settlement imposed by Britain, France, and the United States was infinitely preferable to Hitler's "New Order."

Only fools believe in huge profits from tiny investments. In war, great success requires a vast infusion of wealth or blood – usually both. To play

---

[80] Brian R. Sullivan, "The Impatient Cat: Assessments of Military Power in Fascist Italy, 1936–1940" in Williamson Murray and Allan R. Millett, eds., *Calculations, Net Assessment and the Coming of World War II* (New York, 1992); Clausewitz, *On War*, pp. 585–94.

[81] Arianna Arisi Rota, "La politica del 'peso determinante': Nota su un concetto di Dino Grandi," *Il Politico*, Jan. 1988, pp. 105–6, 112–3; Knox, "Il fascismo e la politica estera italiana," pp. 312–4, 330; Giuseppe Maione, "I costi delle imprese coloniali," in Angelo Del Boca, ed., *Le guerre coloniali del fascismo* (Bari, 1991), pp. 412–7.

decisive roles in major conflicts, nations must pay heavily. The illusory strategy of the decisive weight nearly led to Italy's ruin in 1915–18 and actually did so in 1940–45. As the Italians have learned since, there are far more effective methods to achieve their national goals than war, even for a country as rich as theirs has finally become.

12

The road to ideological war: Germany, 1918–1945

WILHELM DEIST

In Prussia and Imperial Germany, strategy – the use of armed force to maintain or change the external status quo and to preserve internal stability – was the domain of the military. Neither civilian executives after Bismarck nor Germany's parliament, the Reichstag, influenced strategic planning or decision-making.[1] The military monopolized even the historical interpretation of strategic decisions and vehemently defended that privilege against encroachment by academic historians such as Hans Delbrück.[2] In Imperial Germany, it was Helmuth von Moltke, Alfred von Schlieffen, Alfred von Tirpitz, and Erich Ludendorff who dominated strategic thought. Thereafter the industrialization of warfare and defeat in 1918 undermined the military control of national strategy that had stood in such sharp contrast to developments in France, Britain, and the United States. A long and often indirect process ultimately brought political control over strategy even in Germany.[3]

---

[1] See the article by H. H. Herwig, "Strategic Uncertainties of a Nation-State: Prussia-Germany 1871–1891," in the present volume, pp. 242–77.

[2] Arden Buchholz, *Hans Delbrück and the German Military Establishment: War Images in Conflict* (Iowa City, IA., 1985), pp. 19–51; Gordon A. Craig, "Delbrück: the Military Historian," in Peter Paret, ed., *Makers of Modern Strategy from Machiavelli to the Nuclear Age* (Princeton, 1986), pp. 326–53; Andreas Hillgruber, "Hans Delbrück," in Hans-Ulrich Wehler, ed., *Deutsche Historiker*, Vol. 4 (Göttingen, 1972), pp. 40–52.

[3] See especially the stimulating article by Michael Geyer, "German Strategy in the Age of Machine Warfare, 1914–1945," in Paret, *Makers of Modern Strategy*, pp. 527–97. Geyer's interpretation and that of the present article differ in the weight they attribute to essential factors; used together they give the reader a more complete picture; Dennis E. Showalter, "German Grand Strategy: A Contradiction in Terms?" in *Militärgeschichtliche Mitteilungen*, 48 (1990), pp. 65–102, provides a superb summary of the strategic considerations in Prussia in the eighteenth and nineteenth centuries; however, the effects of industrialization and ideology in the conduct of wars in the twentieth century are barely mentioned. For a differing interpretation, see also Manfred Messerschmidt, "German Military Effectiveness between 1919 and 1939," in Allan R. Millett and Williamson Murray, eds., *Military Effectiveness*, Vol. 2, *The Interwar Period* (Boston, 1988), pp. 223–37; Jürgen Förster, "The Dynamics of *Volksgemeinschaft*: The Effectiveness of the German

Yet none of Germany's military or political leaders – from Ludendorff to Blomberg and from Bethmann Hollweg to Hitler – based their policies on rational strategic calculations. On the contrary, they rejected calculation and followed principles of their own, with startling and often disastrous consequences for Germany and the world.

THE CONSEQUENCES OF DEFEAT

Ludendorff's replacement, after Wilhelm II at last dismissed the Quartermaster General on 26 October 1918, was an officer with proven organizational talents in areas far beyond the purely military. From the beginning General Wilhelm Groener realized that he had become trustee of a bankrupt firm, a task in which he could win no laurels.[4] When he assumed his duties, negotiations with the Allies left no doubt that the Germans faced a disastrous political and military defeat. They had lost the "semi-hegemony" in Europe that Bismarck had achieved, while at home the "upheaval that will transform everything," predicted by Bethmann Hollweg in July 1914, seemed imminent.[5] Portions of the German armies fighting in the west had reacted with a "disguised strike" to Ludendorff's grandiose miscalculation of spring 1918, his attempt to force a strategic turn in the war through mere tactics and operations in order to preserve the traditional German power structure.[6] War and collapse had thoroughly disrupted order and obedience while destroying the homogeneity of the army's heart, its officer corps.

The situation required action, not far-reaching plans. Groener's policies, based on an assessment of Germany's position, took existing realities into account. That was remarkable if only because Groener's predecessors – Ludendorff, Falkenhayn, Moltke the younger, and Schlieffen – had neither understood such realities sufficiently nor mustered the courage to act on them.[7] But the pressure imposed by an unusual situation forced Groener to

Military Establishment in the Second World War," in ibid., Vol. 3, *The Second World War,* (Boston, 1988), pp. 191–99.

4 On Groener see Wilhelm Groener, *Lebenserinnerungen,* Friedrich Freiherr Hiller von Gaertringen, ed. (Göttingen, 1957), and his printed diary entries and memoranda from Kiev between 26 February 1918 and 25 October 1918, in Winfried Baumgart, ed., *Von Brest-Litovsk zur deutschen Novemberrevolution: Aus den Tagebüchern, Briefen und Aufzeichnungen von Alfons Paquet, Wilhelm Groener und Albert Hopman, März bis November 1918* (Göttingen, 1971). See also Friedrich Freiherr Hiller von Gaertringen, "Groener," in *Neue Deutsche Biographie,* Vol. 7 (Berlin, 1966), pp. 111–14.

5 Kurt Riezler, *Tagebücher, Aufsätze, Dokumente,* Karl Dietrich Erdmann, ed. (Göttingen, 1972), p. 183 (7 July 1914).

6 Wilhelm Deist, "Der militärische Zusammenbruch des Kaiserreichs. Zür Realität der 'Dolchstoßlegende,'" in Ursula Büttner, ed., *Das Unrechtsregime,* Vol. 1 (Hamburg, 1986), pp. 101–29. Cf. also Herwig, "Strategic Uncertainties," p. 276–77.

7 On Falkenhayn, see above all, K.-H. Janßen, *Der Kanzler und der General: Die Führungskrise um Bethmann Hollweg und Falkenhayn (1914–1916),* (Göttingen, 1967); Ekkehart P. Guth, "Der Gegensatz zwischen dem Oberbefehlshaber Ost und dem Chef des

Map 12.1. World War II: German Offensives, 1939–1942. *Source.* Adapted from Michael J. Lyons, *World War II: A Short History* (Englewood Cliffs, New Jersey: Prentice Hall, 1989), 73.

make hard decisions. In addition to his clear sense of reality, Groener's aims permitted him to craft a strategy in defeat and revolution. Internally, he sought to maintain the armed forces as an instrument of stabilization; externally, his goal was to preserve Germany's territorial unity.

As Supreme Warlord, the discredited Emperor, Wilhelm II, presented a serious obstacle to both goals during the period of political and military disintegration. Groener solved this problem in a manner both dramatic and matter-of-fact: he forced Wilhelm to abdicate. The road to an understanding with the representatives of the new, still vulnerable political order in Germany was now open, and Groener was perhaps the only general officer

Generalstabes des Feldheeres 1914/15. Die Rolle des Majors v. Haeften im Spannungsfeld zwischen Hindenburg, Ludendorff und Falkenhayn," *Militärgeschichtliche Mitteilungen,* 35 (1984), pp. 75–111.

capable of winning the trust of the leaders of the majority Social Democrats.[8] When he assumed his duties as head of the War Office in November 1916, he had expressed the view that Germany could not win an industrialized war without the cooperation of the workers.[9] He held to that view despite a conflict with Ludendorff that had led to Groener's relegation to field command in mid-1917.[10] His November 1918 understanding with the majority Social Democrats, however weak it seemed at times, represented the first and decisive step toward maintaining the domestic political function of the armed forces. Despite the compromises Groener accepted during the revolutionary months, given the rapid disintegration of the old army and his own limited influence over the new Reichswehr, he provided the continuity between the military leadership of the Empire and that of the Republic while safeguarding the military's special position within the state.[11]

The attitude toward the future of the Emperor that Groener took at German headquarters at Spa on 9 November 1918 further illuminated the political convictions that he maintained until his retirement in autumn 1919. Not only did he categorically reject the notion that Wilhelm II and the army should march on Berlin to suppress the revolution. He also opposed – as potentially fatal to German unity – the retention of the Emperor as King of Prussia. The central principle in Groener's strategic thought was the *Reichsgedanke,* the idea of Germany as a single entity, with all its political and emotional connotations. Groener played a decisive role in preventing separatist forces from gaining the upper hand during the unrest that followed defeat. He also successfully opposed those senior officers who argued that renewed resistance based on eastern Germany would improve the peace conditions. Groener forced his senior service opponents to acknowledge strategic reality both at home and abroad: Germany was beaten, and further fighting would worsen rather than improve its position. His contacts with Colonel Conger, an American officer, may have misled Groener about pros-

8   Gerhard W. Rakenius, *Wilhelm Groener als Erster Generalquartiermeister: Die Politik der Obersten Heeresleitung 1918/19* (Boppard, 1977), pp. 1–85. On Wilhelm II see John C. G. Röhl and Nicolaus Sombart, eds., *Kaiser Wilhelm II: New Interpretations* (Cambridge, 1982) and John C. G. Röhl, *Kaiser, Hof und Staat: Wilhelm II. und die deutsche Politik* (Munich, 1987).
9   See the report on the confidential session of the Bundesrat on 9 November 1916, in Wilhelm Deist, ed., *Militär und Innenpolitik im Weltkrieg 1914–1918,* Vol. 2 (Düsseldorf, 1970), Doc. 198, p. 513.
10   See Gerald D. Feldman, *Army, Industry and Labor in Germany 1914–1918* (Princeton, 1966), pp. 373–404. On 28 October 1918, Colonel-General von Einem, a former Prussian minister of war, wrote that Groener had been "anointed with a drop of socialist oil, very clever but with a worker's cap (Ballonmütze) in his traveling bag." See Deist, ed., *Militär und Innenpolitik,* Vol. 1, pt. 2, p. 1346.
11   See Rainer Wohlfeil, *Reichswehr und Republik (1918–1933),* (Frankfurt/M., 1970), pp. 42–91 and 117–19; Francis L. Carsten, *Reichswehr und Politik 1918–1933,* 3d ed. (Cologne, 1966), pp. 13–56. In this connection, see also Ulrich Kluge, *Soldatenräte und Revolution: Studien zur Militärpolitik in Deutschland 1918/19* (Göttingen, 1975); Wolfram Wette, *Gustav Noske: Eine politische Biographie* (Düsseldorf, 1987).

pects of a lenient peace, but when the German government deliberated in June 1919 over whether to sign the Treaty of Versailles unconditionally, Groener advised the Reich President and the government with a sober sense of responsibility. Military resistance had no chance of success.[12] Field Marshal Paul von Hindenburg's comment that "as a soldier" he would prefer "an honorable end to a shameful peace" illuminates the mentality of a military caste that attached little importance to the nation's vital interests.[13] That caste never forgave Groener his break with their traditional notion of honor.

Between October 1918 and June 1919, Groener successfully opposed all adventurism at a time of military defeat, rebellion against order and obedience, and violent political upheaval. His was an immense strategic achievement in the face of the obdurate self-indulgence of his fellow officers. He based his decisions on sober, realistic military calculations and thereby preserved the political position of the military and the unity of Germany. Groener's strategic aims were those of a military officer. His determination to preserve the traditional leadership of the armed forces was in opposition to the aims of the revolutionary forces, although both groups sought to preserve German unity. In retrospect, Groener's success in achieving the latter aim was as desirable as his success with regard to the former was regrettable. From a historical perspective, however, they were intertwined.

The strategic consequences of the Treaty of Versailles – the territorial amputations in east and west and the resulting loss of economic resources – presented German political and military leaders with new and for the moment insoluble problems. In addition, Germany had to accept drastic restrictions on its sovereignty. Those restrictions, combined with a state of general exhaustion after four and a half years of war, placed an increasing drain on material, human, and spiritual resources. Mere survival required enormous sacrifices in all areas. The allies forced Germany to accept the economic exactions spelled out in the Treaty at a time when the domestic consolidation of the Weimar Republic was far from complete. In that way, the Treaty of Versailles made a significant contribution toward discrediting the new order.

The political, economic, and administrative leaders of Weimar confronted three overriding tasks: dealing with the economic consequences of war, coping with the political and economic effects of Versailles, and establishing a strong foundation for the Republic. All Weimar governments pursued the aim of revising the Treaty, although initially without success.[14] Germany's

---

12 See Rakenius, *Groener,* pp. 165–234. For Groener's memoranda and directives, see Heinz Hürten, ed., *Zwischen Revolution und Kapp-Putsch: Militär und Innenpolitik 1918–1920* (Düsseldorf, 1977), Docs. 15, 20, 32, 35, 53, 75.

13 Rakenius, *Groener,* pp. 218, 224.

14 For a general account, see Karl Erich Born, "Deutschland vom Ende der Monarchie bis zur Teilung," in Theodor Schieder, ed., *Handbuch der europäischen Geschichte,* Vol. 7, pt. 1 (Stuttgart, 1979), pp. 523–49; Karl Dietrich Erdmann, "Die Zeit der Weltkriege," in Bruno Gebhardt, *Handbuch der deutschen Geschichte,* Vol. 4 (Stuttgart, 1973); Hagen

situation did not permit a foreign policy with a military accent or the development of any strategy that included the use of armed forces.

In the first years of the Republic the armed forces – the Reichswehr – functioned merely as the necessary though not completely reliable instrument through which the Republic's leaders mastered domestic unrest.[15] Apart from the "normal" problems of the demobilization of a wartime army of approximately 7 million men[16] and its consolidation to the permitted peacetime strength of 100,000, the military provisions of the Treaty of Versailles[17] precluded active participation of the armed forces in the development of strategy. The reduction of the army, the elimination of general conscription (the indispensable foundation of Prussian and German power in Europe), the prohibition of mobilization planning, the restrictions on modern weapons systems, and the exacting limitations on heavy weapons crippled the army as a military instrument. The same was true of the navy, severely shaken by mutiny in 1918. The treaty restrictions on the number and kinds of ships reduced it to a coastal defense force and placed in question its survival as an independent service. Comprehensive inter-Allied inspection and surveillance ensured German compliance with most Treaty provisions.[18]

These rigorous limitations on German military sovereignty condemned the Reichswehr to passivity when French troops occupied the Ruhr in 1923. A comparison with the 1925 peacetime strength of the armies of Germany's neighbors (France: 750,000 men; Poland: 300,000 men; Czechoslovakia: 150,000 men)[19] clearly shows that the Reichswehr had little chance of defeating the ground forces of even one of these states, particularly under the handicap of the 50-kilometer-wide demilitarized zone east of the Rhine[20] and the prohibition against construction of new installations or the alteration of existing fortifications in other border areas.[21] A decade after the outbreak of World War I, the Allies, especially France, seemed to have elimi-

Schulze, *Weimar Deutschland 1917–1933* (Berlin, 1982), and Wohlfeil, *Reichswehr und Republik.*

15 For a critical survey of literature on the history of the Reichswehr, see Michael Geyer, "Die Wehrmacht der Deutschen Republik ist die Reichswehr. Bemerkungen zur neueren Literatur," *Militärgeschichtliche Mitteilungen,* 14 (1973), pp. 152–99.

16 See Wolfram Wette, "Die militärische Demobilmachung in Deutschland ab 1918/19 unter besonderer Berücksichtigung der revolutionären Ostseestadt Kiel," *Geschichte und Gesellschaft,* 12 (1986), Issue 1, pp. 63–80.

17 Specifically Part V, Articles 159 to 212 of the Treaty. See *Der Vertrag von Versailles,* 2nd ed., (1924) published by the German Foreign Ministry.

18 See Michael Salewski, *Entwaffnung und Militärkontrolle in Deutschland 1919–1927* (Oldenburg, Munich, 1966); Jürgen Heideking, "Vom Versailler Vertrag zur Genfer Abrüstungskonferenz. Das Scheitern der alliierten Militärkontrollpolitik gegenüber Deutschland nach dem Ersten Weltkrieg," *Militärgeschichtliche Mitteilungen,* 28 (1980), pp. 48–68.

19 See Von Löbells Jahresberichte über das Heer- und Kriegswesen, von Oertzen, ed., 43 (1926), pp. 61, 95, 141.

20 Articles 42 to 44 and 180 of the Treaty of Versailles. See note 17 above.

21 Article 196 of the Treaty of Versailles. See note 17 above.

nated any German military threat for the foreseeable future. But French military experts would have emphatically rejected that statement by pointing to the German demographic preponderance and the military potential of the German economy. That attitude was one more barrier to Franco-German understanding.

STRATEGY IN THE WEIMAR REPUBLIC

Factors other than the Treaty provisions played a decisive role in the German military situation at the beginning of the 1920s. World War I had demonstrated that military force by itself could no longer decide war. The 1914–1918 conflict was the first industrialized war on European soil. Potential and actual mobilization of the material and spiritual resources of entire nations played a more important role than the operational decisions of army commanders. This change in the nature of warfare found its expression in the works of German military analysts attempting to foresee the requirements of future wars through assessment of World War I.[22] Their thoughts, in numerous variations, formed the basis for future strategic planning.

German military writers in the interwar period often broke the discussion of future war down into three parts. They naturally devoted considerable attention to innovations in weapons technology.[23] Precisely because the Treaty of Versailles forbade German possession of poison gas, tanks, and military aircraft, theoretical interest in these weapons acquired a special significance. The new weapons appeared as instruments for solving the traumatic problems that positional warfare and the battles of matériel had raised in 1914–1918. Their use suggested a return to a war of movement and decisive battle. But all previous experience with innovations in weapons technology underlined the danger of overestimating individual factors in war. The theorists generally only saw the aircraft as capable of revolutionizing warfare, although some of Guilio Douhet's wilder notions met with skepticism.[24] Interestingly, the submarine, one of the most significant developments in weapons technology during World War I, received little attention.

Some military theorists, more concerned with emphasizing the importance of broad areas of national life in future wars, played down the importance of weaponry. Schlieffen's intimations had become reality in World War I: weap-

22 See Michael Geyer, "Die Landesverteidigung: Wehrstruktur am Ende der Weimarer Republik" (unpublished thesis, Freiburg, 1972), pp. 7–29; Wilhelm Deist, "Die Reichswehr und der Krieg der Zukunft," *Militärgeschichtliche Mitteilungen*, 45 (1989), pp. 81–92.

23 See especially, Max Schwarte, ed., *Kriegstechnik der Gegenwart* (Berlin, 1927), and idem, *Der Krieg der Zukunft* (Leipzig, 1931).

24 See Hans Ritter, *Der Luftkrieg* (Berlin, Leipzig, 1926); idem, "Der Luftkrieg der Zukunft," *Militär-Wochenblatt*, 116 (1931–32), pp. 569–73; O. Groehler, "Probleme der Luftkriegstheorie zwischen dem Ersten und dem Zweiten Weltkrieg," *Zeitschrift für Militärgeschichte*, 9 (1970), pp. 406–19.

ons and their use were only one component of total war. Economic resources and the ability to mobilize them had become decisive factors with extremely complex political and military consequences.[25] In a memorandum on "The Importance of the Modern Economy for Strategy" written in the mid-1920s, Groener raised the provocative question of whether "the modern economy with its many problems," did not exert "an irresistible pressure for peace."[26] In 1930 retired Lieutenant General Max Schwarte soberly concluded that the industrialization of war had placed "the production of weapons by workers" on the same level with "the use of weapons" by soldiers.[27] These examples clearly show that military analysts had at least recognized the fundamental change in strategic conditions revealed in World War I.

German military pundits explored yet another new topic with even greater earnestness. Interest in and overestimation of the effects of Allied propaganda against Germany led to the claim that psychological warfare was as necessary as armed conflict and economic warfare.[28] But unlike Allied propaganda in World War I, which had aimed primarily at the enemy, German theorists argued that German propaganda should concentrate on the home front and front line. The intensity of this preoccupation in German military writing reflected the trauma of the revolution, which had confronted military leaders at all levels with the collapse of their authority. That shock, along with a growing realization of their dependence on the economy, had demonstrated to the military caste that political factors determined the conditions under which it exercised its profession.

In the view of military leaders, this fact constituted the real break with Prusso-German military tradition. Theoretical attempts to find a solution to this problem extended from an odd suggestion by Friedrich von Bernhardi to Kurt Hesse's future-oriented publication, *Der Feldherr Psychologos*. Bernhardi was strongly attached to the Wilhelmine tradition and proposed to maintain the morale of the fighting army by, "in a certain sense," isolating it "internally from the homeland."[29] Hesse hoped to solve all problems through the unlimited power of a charismatic leader, a "ruler of men's souls" able to guarantee the unity of the nation and the concentration of its will on one goal.[30] But in general military pundits supported the complete militarization of society in peacetime as a precondition for the effective conduct of war.

25 See Adolf Caspary, *Wirtschafts-Strategie und Kriegführung* (Berlin, 1932).
26 Dorothea Fensch und Olaf Groehler, "Imperialistische Ökonomie und militärische Strategie. Eine Denkschrift Wilhelm Groeners," *Zeitschrift für Geschichtswissenschaft*, 19 (1971), pp. 1167–77, here p. 1175.
27 Schwarte, *Krieg der Zukunft*, pp. 34–35.
28 See Hans Thimme, *Weltkrieg ohne Waffen: Die Propaganda der Westmächte gegen Deutschland, ihre Wirkung und ihre Abwehr* (Stuttgart, 1932).
29 Friedrich von Bernhardi, *Vom Kriege der Zukunft: Nach den Erfahrungen des Weltkrieges* (Berlin, 1920), p. 155.
30 Kurt Hesse, *Der Feldherr Psychologos: Ein Suchen nach dem Führer der deutschen Zukunft* (Berlin, 1932), especially pp. 206–207. See also George Soldan, *Der Mensch und die Schlacht der Zukunft* (Oldenburg, 1925).

The seemingly inescapable necessity of preparing for war economically and technologically in peacetime mandated the militarization of the nation to supply the necessary material and human resources.

With the publication of Ludendorff's *Der totale Krieg* in 1935, discussion about preconditions and characteristics of a future war reached its high point and conclusion. Ludendorff's work, the product of his intense interest in the history of the Great War, presented his conclusions and lessons learned. Significantly, Ludendorff devoted considerable attention to the problem of motivating the armed forces and people.[31] In his view, the "emotional unity of the nation" had become the decisive factor in war. Therefore everything had to be done to create and maintain that unity. Ludendorff proclaimed emphatically that the unity of the nation rested on its ethnic, racial unity – a "native religion" could and must support it. Although Ludendorff believed it vitally necessary to educate the nation thoroughly on the purpose and aims of a war, he left no doubt that propaganda, indoctrination, and education alone would not achieve unity. Preventive measures, similar to protective custody, had to be taken against "dissatisfied elements" that might endanger national unity. Ludendorff directly named the internal enemies of the militarized *Volksgemeinschaft* (the national racial community): the Jews, the Roman Catholic Church, and the Socialists.[32] Ludendorff's notion of a military leader with dictatorial powers and a "defense staff" to prepare the united *Volk* community and lead it in a total war aimed at annihilation of the enemy was a final attempt in Germany to place strategy and the conduct of war under the sole authority of the military.[33]

Apart from his demand for power to the military, Ludendorff, like other theorists before him, offered an extreme picture of an industrialized war requiring the nation's entire resources as well as comprehensive planning and preparation in peace: in effect, a militarized society. Such a view of war necessitated a broad concept of strategy, which one can define as "the integration of domestic and foreign policy, of military and psychological war planning and execution, of defense economy and armaments, by the top leadership of a state in order to carry out a comprehensive ideological and political plan."[34] That definition makes clear the profound change, the enormous expansion in the determining factors, which the concept of strategy had experienced since the nineteenth century. The launching and conduct of

---

31 Erich Ludendorff, *Der totale Krieg* (Munich, 1935), pp. 11–28.
32 Colonel-General Werner Freiherr von Fritsch, dismissed as commander in chief of the army in 1938, held similar views of the internal enemy. See Nicholas Reynolds, "Der Fritsch-Brief vom 11. Dezember 1938," *Vierteljahreshefte für Zeitgeschichte*, 28 (1980), pp. 358–71.
33 See Hans-Ulrich Wehler, " 'Absoluter' und 'totaler' Krieg: Von Clausewitz zu Ludendorff," in Ursula von Gersdorff, ed., *Geschichte und Militärgeschichte: Wege der Forschung* (Frankfurt/M. 1974), pp. 273–311.
34 Andreas Hillgruber, "Der Faktor Amerika in Hitlers Strategie 1938–1941," in Wolfgang Michalka, ed., *Nationalsozialistische Außenpolitik* (Darmstadt, 1978), pp. 493–525, here p. 493.

wars was no longer the exclusive prerogative of political and military leaders, and the population at large now figured centrally in military calculations. In the event of armed conflict, the changed nature of war would inevitably lead to a shift in the weight of political and military leadership, even in Germany. Ludendorff offered one extreme solution. Hitler provided the opposite. Both had the same objective.

In the Weimar Republic, the political and military consequences of Germany's defeat in World War I dominated planning for an uncertain future. A strategy in the sense demanded by Ludendorff was not possible during the first ten years of the Republic. The state sought above all an elusive domestic consolidation and stability; the revision of the Versailles Treaty represented the one common aim of all political forces in the Republic.[35] But though this aim determined the nature of Germany's foreign policy and the activity of its diplomats, a planned, coordinated strategy was impossible under existing conditions. Even the Reichswehr was not in a position to fulfill its responsibilities for national defense.

Despite this situation, German military leaders began in the mid-1920s to think systematically about the necessary preconditions, conditions, and consequences of a possible war. A survey of the early, hesitant attempts to develop a strategy capable of overcoming the existing situation highlights the importance of the first comprehensive strategic conception developed under Wilhelm Groener, returned to power as Reichswehr Minister from January 1928 to April 1932.

In the turbulent days of December 1918 a group of senior officers met at the General Staff building in Berlin to discuss Germany's prospects and future plans. Despite the early date, the two principal strategic concepts of the Reichswehr period emerged.[36] Kurt von Schleicher, then a major, argued vigorously for a three-phase program based on internal consolidation, economic recovery and, only then, "regaining power and influence abroad." Schleicher's views were those of Groener, who in memoranda throughout 1919 stressed repeatedly the priority of domestic policy.[37] Groener's program implied that the armed forces would again be in a position to perform their actual function only after the third phase, "after many years of hard work."

35 See Peter Krüger, *Die Außenpolitik der Republik von Weimar* (Darmstadt, 1985); Michael Salewski, "Das Weimarer Revisionssyndrom," in "Aus Politik und Zeitgeschichte," supplement to the weekly newspaper *Das Parlament*, B 2, 1980; Gaines Post, Jr., *The Civil-Military Fabric of Weimar Foreign Policy* (Princeton, 1973); Michael Geyer, "The Dynamics of Military Revisionism in the Interwar Years, Military Politics between Rearmament and Diplomacy," in Wilhelm Deist, ed., *The German Military in the Age of Total War* (Leamington Spa, 1985), pp. 100–51.

36 See the "Bericht des Hauptmanns v. Rabenau über Besprechungen von Generalstabsoffizieren über die politische Lage," printed in Hürten, ed., *Zwischen Revolution und Kapp-Putsch*, Doc. 11, pp. 30–31.

37 Ibid., Docs. 32, 35, 53, 75, pp. 113–15, 121–25, 158–61, 193–97.

Schleicher's opponent, Major General Hans von Seeckt, described internal consolidation as something that could "be taken for granted." He was convinced that the aim of the state and the Reichswehr must be to make Germany "an acceptable alliance partner" once more. Only a strong international position could guarantee a solid foundation for reconstruction and economic recovery. Seeckt's remarks, like his use of the Tirpitz catch phrase about alliance partnership, showed that he remained a partisan of the Wilhelmine foreign policy that had ended in war against a "world of enemies" in July 1914.[38] In Seeckt's vision, the armed forces would exercise a decisive influence from the beginning. The programs of Schleicher and Seeckt, though based on different assessments of Germany's situation, were typical of the two generations of officers who led the Reichswehr in the following years.

In November 1919 Seeckt became head of the *Truppenamt*, the successor to the old general staff, and in June 1920 army commander. He thus had the chance to implement his program. Until his dismissal in October 1926, the domestic and foreign policy aims he had laid down in December 1918 clearly determined his actions. Reestablishing government authority and internal order proved to be a lengthy process, although the Reichswehr did finally emerge as the decisive power factor as Seeckt had wanted.[39] He strengthened the loose military contacts with the Soviet Union that the Reichswehr had established in 1920, despite the ideological chasm between the two states.[40] He believed that Germany could win the Soviet Union as an alliance partner and could resume its old role in European power politics with Soviet help. With that aim in mind, Seeckt coordinated his Soviet links at least in part with the policies of successive chancellors and of the Foreign Ministry.

Regardless of whether German-Soviet ties – from the Treaty of Rapallo (1922) to the Treaty of Berlin (1926) – enhanced Germany's overall position as Seeckt had expected, German-Soviet military cooperation in that period failed to produce the desired results. Cooperation at first involved only the participation of German firms, with state support, in building up the Soviet armaments industry. Seeckt hoped thereby to transfer abroad German production of arms such as aircraft and heavy artillery forbidden under Versailles, but was unsuccessful. Collaboration with the Red Army after the mid-1920s in testing modern weapons such as aircraft, tanks, and poison gas

---

[38] See the article by Holger H. Herwig, "Strategic Uncertainties," in the present volume, pp. 263–64.

[39] See in this connection, in addition to the standard works by Wohlfeil (*Reichswehr und Republik*) and Carsten (*Reichswehr und Politik*), the study by Hagen Schulze, *Freikorps und Republik, 1918–1920* (Boppard, 1969); Klaus-Jürgen Muller and Eckart Opitz, eds., *Militär und Militarismus in der Weimarer Republik* (Düsseldorf, 1978); Heinz Hürten, *Reichswehr und Ausnahmezustand: Ein Beitrag zur Verfassungsproblematik der Weimarer Republik in ihrem ersten Jahrfünft* (Opladen, 1977).

[40] See Carsten, *Reichswehr und Politik*, pp. 141–57; and especially Rolf-Dieter Müller, *Das Tor zur Weltmacht: Die Bedeutung der Sowjetunion für die deutsche Wirtschafts- und Rüstungspolitik zwischen den Weltkriegen* (Boppard, 1984).

at joint training centers established in the Soviet Union proved far more important. The knowledge gained proved of great value to Reichswehr, Wehrmacht – and Red Army.[41] Seeckt accomplished the foreign policy objectives of his strategic plan only imperfectly, but he did preserve the internal political independence of the armed forces and demonstrated it energetically throughout the first years of the Republic.

Seeckt's efforts to achieve a semi-autonomous role for the military, a legacy of the Prussian army's position in Imperial Germany, also influenced his ideas about the conduct of future wars.[42] In his view, a relatively small but highly mobile operational army equipped with modern weapons would play the decisive role in achieving victory. The mass army was only of secondary importance. This idea reintroduced the "renaissance of the classical [operational] art of warfare," that other military thinkers had discarded as a result of the battles of matériel of World War I.[43] With an operational army always available, such a plan offered the advantage of avoiding two main problems of modern warfare: the motivation of the population and the readjustment of industry. Such factors were irrelevant to Seeckt's preferred kind of warfare.

Although Seeckt was open to the use of modern weapons and assigned to air power a decisive role in the opening phase of war, his insistence that the military must enjoy sole responsibility for the conduct of warfare and his assumption of the continued primacy of actual combat show how deeply rooted in tradition his thinking remained. His attempt – based on the ideas that he had expressed in December 1918 – to create the strategic preconditions for revision of the Treaty of Versailles failed. The industrialization of warfare, which Seeckt ignored in its political as well as its military implications, was irreversible.

During the crisis years of the Republic, military and political realities rather than theories determined the thinking and actions of the officers of the *Truppenamt*. The dominant reality was the inability of the Reichswehr to fulfill its primary duty of defending Germany from attack. For military reasons alone, the Reichswehr was unable to respond to the French occupation of the Ruhr in January 1923.[44] The contradiction between the Reichswehr's claim to sole responsibility for national defense and its inability to fulfill that responsibility created an opening for the conception that Lieutenant Colonel Joachim von Stülpnagel presented in February 1924 to officers of the Reichswehr Ministry. His "Thoughts on the War of the Future" were significant because of their noteworthy realism about the military situation and their

41 See Michael Geyer, *Aufrüstung oder Sicherheit: Die Reichswehr in der Krise der Machtpolitik 1924–1936* (Wiesbaden, 1980), pp. 148–60.
42 See the comprehensive article by Heinz-Ludger Borgert, "Grundzüge der Landkriegführung von Schlieffen bis Guderian," in *Handbuch zur deutschen Militärgeschichte 1648–1939*, Vol. 5, pt. 9 (Munich, 1979), pp. 529–55.
43 Hans Meier-Welcker, *Seeckt*, (Frankfurt/M., 1967), p. 636.
44 Geyer, *Aufrüstung*, pp. 23–27, 76–82.

acknowledgment of factors that Seeckt had completely neglected.[45] The lecture was one of the first Reichswehr reactions to the changed nature of warfare.

The central issue for Stülpnagel was how Germany could fight its western and eastern neighbors, France and Poland. Stülpnagel first described the international situation, which was central to Germany's chances in view of the obvious inferiority of the Reichswehr. In Stülpnagel's opinion, benevolent British neutrality and active Soviet support were essential, but domestic factors were even more vital. World War I had shown that future wars would require "the use of the strength of the entire nation." And Stülpnagel drew an additional, more radical conclusion: the preparations of the state and of the armed forces could only achieve their aims if those aims " . . . harmonize[d] with the national will of the majority of the *Volk*." That was the only possible conclusion to draw from the trauma of 1918. Logically enough, Stülpnagel was ready to go to any length to ensure popular support. He considered a "complete change" in domestic politics necessary, and recommended the "elimination of the abnormal parliamentary conditions" and the "incitement of hatred against the foreign enemy" along with corresponding measures in the schools and universities. Above all, he supported introduction of general, obligatory national labor service and a determined struggle against the "[Socialist] International and pacifism, against everything un-German."[46] Stülpnagel's "war of liberation" required the transformation of the Republic into an ultramilitaristic nationalist regime.

In view of the Reichswehr's inferiority, Stülpnagel developed the idea of a "national war"-in-depth in the border areas. The Reichswehr must obstruct, disrupt, and halt the French and Polish advance, and contest areas already occupied. The aim of this defensive phase, to be achieved through mobility, was to weaken and unnerve the attacking enemy in order to give the German army time to strengthen itself and then defeat the enemy decisively.[47] In Stülpnagel's view, the conduct of the "national war" required a coordinated approach; the preparatory measures he desired would require the cooperation of many institutions of the civilian executive.

Stülpnagel's ideas, marked by a radicalization of warfare, also imputed to the French a "long prepared, sadistic plan" to intimidate the German civilian population by brutal measures, and argued that "national hatred should be raised to a fever pitch" and "must not shrink from using all forms of sabotage, murder, and poison."[48] On the whole, Stülpnagel knew that starting

[45] For the manuscript of the lecture "Gedanken über den Krieg der Zukunft" see Bundesarchiv-Militärchiv (BA-MA) N 5/10. An extract appears in Heinz Hürten, ed., *Das Krisenjahr 1923: Militär und Innenpolitik 1922–1924* (Düsseldorf, 1980), Doc. 184, pp. 266–72.

[46] Ibid., p. 270.

[47] BA-MA N 5/10, pp. 18–22.

[48] Ibid., pp. 12, 39.

such a war would only be a "heroic gesture" for the foreseeable future.[49] Nevertheless, he believed that preparations would require five years or so rather than ten. Even then the situation would be "desperate," but means had to be found that, "born of desperation," would prove so powerful that they would "guarantee us either victory or destruction together with the enemy."[50]

The contrast between Stülpnagel's ideas and Seeckt's "renaissance of the classical [operational] art of war" is striking. Stülpnagel's realism found its expression in his assessment of Germany's situation and in his analysis of domestic and international preconditions for a "war of liberation." That realism made him weaken or even abandon Seeckt's demand for military autonomy in the conduct of war. Without the close cooperation of the civilian authorities, a "war of liberation" would be impossible; in the following years Stülpnagel was one of the most active supporters of such collaboration. His lecture also devoted considerable attention to the functions of the air arm and the navy.[51] But Stülpnagel's realism had limits where the aims of the supposedly inevitable war were concerned.

He remained uninterested in limited political or military objectives: the only choice was all or nothing, total victory or the "heroic gesture" and "destruction together with the enemy." His war plan contained no genuine strategic calculation; despite its realistic elements it remained a desperate attempt to escape a situation perceived as unbearable. Stülpnagel's combination of realistic assessment and irrational aims was no accident; it was a tendency with a future in the German armed forces.

Retired Vice Admiral Wolfgang Wegener's ideas on naval warfare offered a comparable synthesis of realism and unreason. He had concerned himself with the theoretical side of naval warfare since 1915, and published his views under the title "The Naval Strategy of the World War" in 1929.[52] Wegener's realism consisted of a dispassionate analysis of Germany's naval situation and suggestions for improving it based on the experience of the High Seas Fleet in World War I. It was relevant to the current situation not only because of Wegener's suggestions for the future, but primarily because of his devastating criticism of Tirpitz's theory of decisive battle in the North Sea. Wegener described the prewar German fleet, the showpiece of German imperialism, as a coastal defense fleet. He could not have found a more caustic term. His main aim was to demonstrate that a fleet alone, however powerful it might be, could not win the struggle for naval supremacy at the intersection points of world trade. In his view, sea power rested on two principal factors:

[49] Ibid., p. 39.
[50] Ibid., p. 14.
[51] Ibid., pp. 16–18, 36–38.
[52] In 1941, a second edition of the book was published. See Wolfgang Wegener, *The Naval Strategy of the World War*, translated with introduction and notes by Holger H. Herwig (Annapolis, Maryland, 1989).

a fleet and – a new, equally important consideration – geographic position.

Wegener's criticism of the axioms of the Imperial German navy touched a raw nerve in Admiral Erich Raeder and the navy high command. From their point of view any discussion about the function of the fleet could only harm the navy.[53] Limiting naval activities to the Baltic and its approaches was incompatible with the navy's self-image. Naval warfare in the North Sea or the Atlantic, however, could only involve Britain and the Royal Navy, the victor over the German fleet in World War I. At the beginning of the 1930s, however, conflict with Britain was scarcely in Germany's interest.

Raeder therefore reacted to Wegener's book by seeking to smother controversy[54]; Wegener's constructive suggestions seemed even more dangerous than his criticisms. Wegener had pointed out that Germany enjoyed no secure access to the Atlantic, the main world trade route. From this fact he deduced the need for a German window on the Atlantic as a prerequisite for a future naval war. He demanded that the Reich establish bases on the French Atlantic coast (Brest), on the Danish and Norwegian coasts, and even in the Shetlands, the Faeroe Islands and Iceland, in order to control the North Atlantic trade routes.[55] Wegener's criticisms of the Imperial German fleet in the First World War were realistic and his military arguments for obtaining far-flung naval bases convincing. But the political and military implications of his program remained unclear and unaccompanied by corresponding rational strategic goals.

Wegener's book appeared at a time when a faction in the Defense Ministry had gained the upper hand and had begun to lay the foundations for creation of the first comprehensive strategic program in the history of the German state. This development accompained the renewed ascendancy of Groener, now returned to power as Reichswehr Minister, and of his deputy Schleicher. They had learned in World War I that force was only one aspect of war. Germany could not fight an industrialized war without a solid domestic political base and careful consideration of economic factors. Military analysts had also reached similar conclusions and had popularized them. And the Defense Ministry itself had closely studied the problems of national defense since spring 1924; Groener and Schleicher simply drew the logical strategic conclusions from the ideas developed there.[56]

---

[53] On the political and military development of the navy, see Jost Dülffer, *Weimar, Hitler und die Marine: Reichspolitik und Flottenbau 1920–1939* (Düsseldorf, 1972); Werner Rahn, *Reichsmarine und Landesverteidigung 1919–1928: Konzeption und Führung der Marine in der Weimarer Republik* (Munich, 1976); Gerhard Schreiber, *Revisionismus und Weltmachtstreben: Marineführung und deutsch-italienische Beziehungen 1919/1944* (Stuttgart, 1978).

[54] See Dülffer, *Weimar*, pp. 187–88; Wegener, *Naval Strategy*, pp. xxxvii–xxxix.

[55] See Wegener, *Naval Strategy*, pp. 186–98.

[56] This change in Reichswehr policy from Seeckt to Groener is one of the two main themes in the definitive study by Geyer, *Aufrüstung*, pp. 19–236.

Those conclusions, based on a realistic assessment of Germany's position and a determination to create the preconditions for an adequate national defense, impelled a "Fronde" of officers around Stülpnagel to argue for close civil-military cooperation. The dismissal of Seeckt and the appointment of Lieutenant General Wilhelm Heye as chief of the army in October 1926 removed an important obstacle to new strategic input. The Reichswehr's initiatives now concentrated on three main points. Cooperation with the Foreign Ministry intensified, above all with an eye to the defense of German interests at the coming disarmament conference.[57] At home, civil-military cooperation in national defense needed to be widened and strengthened, especially in the organization of border guards and local defense units. The attitude of the Social Democratic government of Prussia was the most important factor in this area.[58] Finally, the national military-industrial base required improvement.

The Defense Ministry proved most successful in the armaments sector, and the government kept itself informed about the size of the secret weapons stocks and the illegal armament programs.[59] Clandestine contacts with industry intensified, thanks in part to the withdrawal of the Interallied Military Control Commission at the end of January 1927.[60] More important, the ministry began to work out a modest middle-term armaments program while Groener, who became Reichswehr Minister in January 1928, obtained financing for armaments expenditures.[61] The government took the initial step in a basic reorientation of Germany's military policy with an appropriation for a first four-year armaments program in October 1928.

But opposition to this policy by members of the ministry and, above all, of the Reichswehr, grew as time passed.[62] The policy of Groener and his Ministerial Office contradicted both Prusso-German tradition and Reichswehr policies under Seeckt. The Reichswehr leaders had accepted in principle – though with qualifications – the political leadership's authority to issue directives and supervise the military, even in a republic headed by a Social Democrat. But it proved difficult to explain the reasons for Groener's support of the Republic and the necessity of limiting the Reichswehr's autonomy to an

---

57 Ibid., pp. 119–88. See also the memorandum "Die Abrüstungsfrage nach realpolitischen Gesichtspunkten betrachtet," which Stülpnagel sent to the Foreign Ministry (Legation Councilor von Bülow) on 6 March 1926, printed in *ADAP*, Series B, 1925–1933, Vol. 1, pt. 1 (Göttingen, 1966), Doc. 144, pp. 341–50.
58 See Carsten, *Reichswehr*, pp. 287–96, 337–39.
59 Ibid., pp. 282–90.
60 Ernst Hansen, *Reichswehr und Industrie* (Boppard, 1978).
61 Michael Geyer, *Aufrüstung*, pp. 198–201; idem, "Das Zweite Rüstungsprogramm (1930–1934)," *Militärgeschichtliche Mitteilungen*, 17 (1975), pp. 125–72.
62 Examples of the growing criticism can be found in Carsten, *Reichswehr*, pp. 326–36 and in Geyer, *Aufrüstung*, pp. 141–48. See also the study by Edward W. Bennett, *German Rearmament and the West* (Princeton, 1979).

officer corps repeatedly strengthened over the years in its attachment to its traditions.[63]

Groener's draft strategic concept, "The Tasks of the Wehrmacht," sent to the chiefs of the army and navy as a directive in April 1930, represented the high point of the Reichswehr's reorientation.[64] The first, promising steps had been taken in previous years to improve national defense capability. Now Groener wanted to establish binding principles to cover the employment of the armed forces. His directive began with two sentences that were self-evident yet incompatible with the traditional self-image of the Reichswehr. The first sentence read: "The tasks given the armed forces by the responsible political leadership constitute the basis for their build-up and use." One may doubt that this principle led to immediate changes, but even the Defense Minister's clear statement of the Reichswehr's position and function was a novelty. Even more radical was Groener's observation that "*definite* prospects of success" were the precondition for the military use of the Reichswehr. That amounted to a rejection of the widespread belief that a two-front war with Poland and France was the most likely conflict Germany faced[65] and restated Groener's conviction, already expressed in the fall of 1928, that Germany must reject from the outset "even the idea of a big war."[66]

In accordance with these premises, Groener considered use of the Reichswehr to be justified only in self-defense or to exploit a "favorable political situation." But he qualified even that statement. The Reichswehr, for example, should act in self-defense only in the event of "illegal border violations (by criminal gangs)" if the army of the state concerned refused to help. In the event of "normal" attacks by enemy armed forces, the Reichswehr should only fight if the enemy were "strongly tied down elsewhere," or if resistance would serve to prevent a fait accompli or unleash "the intervention of other powers or of international bodies." Equally rigorous restrictions governed the employment of the Reichswehr in a "favorable political situation." Use following "a decision of its own leaders," the last of the five possibilities Groener described, would only be possible in a "favorable international constellation." Even under those circumstances the decision to engage the Reichswehr required "*definite* prospects of success." In preparing his directive, Groener gave the two self-defense scenarios the code names "Korfanty" (leader of the Polish irregulars in the postwar fighting over Upper Silesia) and

---

63 On the Reichswehr officer corps, see the articles by Heinz Hürten (*Reichsheer*) and Michael Salewski (*Reichs- und Kriegsmarine*), in Hanns Hubert Hofmann, ed., *Das deutsche Offizierkorps 1860–1960* (Boppard, 1980), pp. 211–45; the literature mentioned by Hürten; and Keith W. Bird, *Weimar, the German Naval Officer Corps, and the Rise of National Socialism* (Amsterdam, 1977).

64 BA-MA M 16/34072. A handwritten draft can be found in the papers of Bredow, BA-MA N 97/9. See also Post, *Civil-Military Fabric*, pp. 231–37: Geyer, *Aufrüstung*, pp. 213–18.

65 See in this regard the spring 1929 conflict between the chief of the Truppenamt, Blomberg, and Groener and his chief of the Ministerial Office, Schleicher: Geyer, *Aufrüstung*, pp. 191–95, 207–13.

66 Memorandum of October 1928, BA-MA N 46/147.

"Pilsudski" (Poland's generalissimo) – a sign that in his view, Poland was the immediate threat.[67]

Groener did not, however, confine himself to a general description of the political factors determining possible employment of the Reichswehr. He drew the logical military conclusions and analyzed the matériel and readiness requirements of each contingency in detail, with special emphasis on logistics and on the ability of German industry to deliver the necessary equipment.

Indicative of Germany's current position and typical of the views of Groener and his immediate subordinates was his frank admission that "the responsible Reich government might, under certain circumstances," have to refrain from using the Reichswehr. Groener's directive also envisaged preparatory planning for communications, evacuations, and demolitions in the border areas in the event that Germany chose not to fight.

Groener regarded war between states as an instrument of policy, but only within the framework of an international system – in contrast to Stülpnagel and Wegener. He completely rejected both Stülpnagel's "heroic" war of national liberation and the notion of total war with its supposedly inherent peacetime requirements. In placing its emphasis on Germany's eastern borders, Groener's directive reflected the policy of revision by stealth that had evolved since Gustav Stresemann had signed the Treaty of Locarno and had taken Germany into the League of Nations. Military planning for national defense was now subordinate to the directives of the political leadership. Equally important was Groener's attempt to overcome the persistent rivalry of the two independent armed services; his directive set missions for both army and navy within the framework of a joint national strategy.[68] Groener, aware that directives alone would not change traditional forms of behavior, had nevertheless taken the first step toward integrating armaments policy and operational planning.

The period between autumn 1926 and autumn 1930 represents an almost unique moment in German strategic history: both state and armed forces had a strategy. The aim of revising Versailles and regaining unrestricted military sovereignty transcended all ideological, political, economic, and social divisions. It was merely the choice of methods for pursuing revision that generated bitter political conflict. After Seeckt's departure, the Reichswehr adjusted to the government's policy of revision by stealth, not because Reichswehr leaders had become convinced supporters of the Republic but because they recognized that accomplishing the Reichswehr's missions required the cooperation of the state. Thus the Reichswehr leadership developed a modest yet integrated armament program and flexible operational planning that fit the requirements of government policy. Groener's

---

[67] Geyer, *Aufrüstung*, pp. 214–17 (emphasis in original).
[68] Ibid., pp. 219–24.

"Tasks of the Wehrmacht" represented the high point of that development.

But these promising first steps remained only an episode. Advocates of Groener's approach came under increasing pressure thanks to the worsening domestic and international situation and the negligible results achieved.[69] Attempts to revise the military provisions of Versailles at the preparatory disarmament conference failed in December 1930: the conference's draft convention expressly sanctioned existing armament limitation treaties, including the Treaty of Versailles. An understanding with France, despite Groener's shift of German military activity and planning to the eastern border, seemed out of reach. The preparatory disarmament conference appeared to preclude international acceptance even of the modest German buildup on which the Reichswehr had planned.[70]

Domestically, the Reichswehr failed to reach an agreement with the government of Prussia on the organization of the border guards and local defense units. At the same time, pressure grew on the Reichswehr leadership to exploit the manpower of the nationalist paramilitary organizations.[71] The Reichstag elections of 14 September 1930, in which the National Socialists enormously increased their share of the vote, played a decisive role in increasing the strain on Groener. Domestic polarization made the political line of the Reichswehr – itself determined by cabinets operating under presidential decrees – increasingly difficult to explain to the officer corps.

Finally, the world depression with its drastic effects on state finances threatened the Reichswehr's buildup, although Groener and Schleicher did succeed in protecting the centerpiece of their policy from serious damage.[72] After engineering Groener's fall in mid-May 1932, Schleicher attempted single-handedly, first as Reichswehr Minister and later as chancellor, to create the domestic and international conditions for carrying out his predecessor's military policy, which he had helped to design. The Geneva Five Power Declaration of 11 December 1932 did offer Schleicher international recognition in principle of Germany's "equality of rights" to armaments. The declaration represented an important partial revision of the military provisions of the Versailles Treaty, but it was far from the international acceptance of the manpower and matériel buildup of the Reichswehr that Schleicher desired. His manifold attempts to secure broad domestic political support for his policy remained unsuccessful.[73] The armed forces once again proved too narrow a base for developing and carrying out national policy. The resignation of Schleicher and his cabinet at the end of January 1933 marked the

---

[69] Ibid., pp. 141–48. See also idem, "Dynamics," pp. 100–51.
[70] Geyer, *Aufrüstung*, pp. 243–55.
[71] Carsten, *Reichswehr*, pp. 392–400.
[72] Geyer, "Rüstungsprogramm," pp. 132–34, 152–56.
[73] Geyer, *Aufrüstung*, pp. 271–97; Carsten, *Reichswehr*, pp. 418–43; Axel Schildt, *Militärdiktatur mit Massenbasis? Die Querfrontkonzeption der Reichswehrführung um General von Schleicher am Ende der Weimarer Republik* (Frankfurt/M., 1981).

definitive failure of the strategy of reestablishing German great-power status within the framework of collective security.

REARMAMENT AND THE MILITARY: THE ECLIPSE OF STRATEGY

No one who considers the years following the National Socialist "seizure of power" (*Machtergreifung*) from a strategic perspective can doubt that the "top leadership" (*Führungsspitze*) of Germany was identical with the person of Adolf Hitler. The fact that President Paul von Hindenburg remained in office until his death in mid-1934 or that competing centers of power continued to exist in Germany did not change this situation. All such centers remained subordinated to the charismatic Führer until 1945.[74] As head of the National Socialist Party and movement, Hitler determined the guidelines of policy and thus of strategy. The leaders of the Reichswehr and the Wehrmacht never questioned his fundamental claim to a monopoly of power. Although historians often speak of an "entente" or even of an "alliance of the [old] elites" with the new leaders, such statements do not call into question Hitler's undisputed claim to political authority as Führer of his movement and chancellor.[75] The "partial identity of aims" of the military leadership and National Socialist regime flowed from agreement at many levels on basic issues of foreign and domestic policy. Conflicts between the regime and its military organizations stemmed primarily from the doggedly defended claims of the military leaders to comprehensive organizational authority in areas directly related to national defense.[76]

The *Machtergreifung*, therefore, confirmed the primacy of the political leadership in questions of strategy, in sharp contrast to the earlier Wilhelmine tradition. For military leaders, however, the conditions of strategic subordination to the political leadership had improved considerably since Groener's time as defense minister. The general aim of German foreign policy – reestablishing unrestricted military sovereignty and Germany's position as a great power in Europe – remained the same as under the Republic, but Germany now presented its demands with far greater emphasis and more effective publicity. The change in methods was decisive, especially in military policy. The appointment of an active duty officer, General Werner von Blom-

---

[74] On the hotly debated subject of the structure of the National Socialist regime, see Gerhard Hirschfeld and Lothar Kettenacker, eds., *The "Führer State": Myth and Reality, Studies on the Structure and Politics of the Third Reich*, introduction by Wolfgang J. Mommsen (Stuttgart, 1981); Hans-Ulrich Thamer, *Verführung und Gewalt: Deutschland 1933–1945* (Berlin, 1986), pp. 338–83; Ian Kershaw, *The Nazi Dictatorship: Problems and Perspectives of Interpretation* (London, 1985).

[75] See Klaus-Jürgen Müller, *Armee, Politik und Gesellschaft in Deutschland 1933–1945* (Paderborn, 1979), especially pp. 30–33; Fritz Fischer, *Bündnis der Eliten: Zur Kontinuität der Machtstrukturen in Deutschland 1871–1945* (Düsseldorf, 1979).

[76] See Manfred Messerschmidt, *Die Wehrmacht im NS-Staat. Zeit der Indoktrination* (Hamburg, 1969); Müller, *Armee*, pp. 33–38.

berg, as Reichswehr Minister, and his installation before the rest of Hitler's cabinet on 30 January 1933 seemed a positive sign for the future development of the Reichswehr. Blomberg, a member of the German delegation to the Geneva Disarmament Conference, was thereafter the driving force behind the change in German disarmament policy.[77]

Prepared by Blomberg, Hitler's decision at the beginning of October to withdraw from the League of Nations and the Disarmament Conference abandoned an essential element of Groener's strategic conception, the claim that Germany could defend itself under existing circumstances only through the support of international institutions and the assistance of other great powers. Hitler's decision represented the first step toward a policy, pursued consistently in the following years, of extricating Germany from the post-1918 collective security system and of regaining unrestricted military sovereignty by breaking with both Versailles and Locarno. Hitler's policy mirrored the hopes, wishes, and demands of those military leaders prepared to accept the dangers involved in achieving what they supposed to be a shared aim – the reestablishment of Germany's position as a great power. And the ever-greater dangers that their efforts summoned up served as justification for the constant acceleration of rearmament.[78]

In his frequently quoted address to Reichswehr leaders on 3 February 1933, Hitler announced how he intended to create the domestic preconditions for his future strategy.[79] He thus freed the military from a problem that, as they had long realized, they themselves could not solve. Already at the first cabinet meeting on 30 January, Blomberg had renounced the traditional but detested military role in preserving domestic order.[80] Now Hitler described the Reichswehr as "the most important institution of the state" and announced a "tighter, authoritarian leadership" as a prerequisite for "regaining political power," which he called the sole objective of his policy. This "reversal" aimed at promoting a general "remilitarization" of the nation and at "strengthen[ing] the readiness to serve in the armed forces and defend the country" by all available means.

---

[77] Wilhelm Deist, "The Rearmament of the Wehrmacht," in Wilhelm Deist, et al., *Germany and the Second World War*, Vol. 1, *The Build-up of German Aggression* (London, 1990), pp. 401–403, and Manfred Messerschmidt, "Foreign Policy and Preparation for War," ibid., pp. 581–86.

[78] See Geyer, *Aufrüstung*, pp. 325–63; Müller, *Armee*, pp. 73–91; idem, *General Ludwig Beck: Studien und Dokumente zur politisch-militärischen Vorstellungswelt und Tätigkeit des Generalstabschefs des deutschen Heeres 1933–1938* (Boppard, 1980), pp. 142–225.

[79] Thilo Vogelsang, "Neue Dokumente zur Geschichte der Reichswehr 1930–1933," *Vierteljahreshefte für Zeitgeschichte*, 2 (1954), pp. 397–436, here pp. 434–36.

[80] Carsten, *Reichswehr*, pp. 447–48; Wolfgang Sauer, "Die Mobilmachung der Gewalt," in Karl Dietrich Bracher, Wolfgang Sauer, and Gerhard Schulz, *Die nationalsozialistische Machtergreifung: Studien zur Errichtung des totalitären Herrschaftssystems in Deutschland 1933/34* (Frankfurt/M., 1974), pp. 41 ff; Günter Wollstein, *Vom Weimarer Revisionismus zu Hitler: Das Deutsche Reich und die Großmächte in der Anfangsphase der nationalsozialistischen Herrschaft in Deutschland* (Bonn, 1973), pp. 23–25.

The National Socialist regime, with the active assistance of the Wehrmacht, proceeded to execute this "remilitarization" of the nation with unprecedented intensity. Although conflicts of authority developed between the military and the National Socialist movement in both state and party arenas, the Wehrmacht never doubted the necessity of the domestic political measures that Hitler had announced.[81] Logically enough, the officer corps and its highest ranking representatives refrained from criticizing the concentration camp system that held 26,000 people by July 1933. The Wehrmacht did not even object seriously to the murder of Generals Schleicher and Bredow in 1934.[82] In the military view, strongly influenced by the experiences of World War I, basic criticism of the forms, methods, and content of Hitler's remilitarization could only jeopardize the essential conditions for practicing the military profession.

Hitler acted decisively both at home and abroad in pursuit of his strategy. But initially he left to the military the manpower buildup and rearmament of the Wehrmacht, the main prerequisite for conquest. That step had serious strategic consequences, though the results impressed contemporaries and historians alike. For example, within six and a half years, the 115,000 man Reichswehr grew into a modern Wehrmacht with a peacetime strength of 1.1 million men and a wartime strength of 4.5 million.[83] Such statistics long concealed the shortcomings of the rapid rearmament process.

In spring 1933, a few weeks after Blomberg took office, the head of the *Truppenamt*, General Wilhelm Adam, described the military situation of Germany as hopeless in the event of armed conflict.[84] The armed forces could stop a Polish advance toward Berlin, but a shortage of ammunition meant that Germany could only resist for a limited time. That sobering reality marked the starting point of a rearmament process directed by the military. The milestones of this process for the army – the December Program of 1933 and the rearmament program of August 1936 – remained the basis for all related measures.[85] The December Program of 1933 called for a threefold increase in the *Reichsheer* to twenty-one divisions by March 1938.

The purely military objective of the program was clear: the twenty-one division army should enable Germany to conduct "a defensive war on several fronts with some prospects of success."[86] This meant the abandonment of Groener's policy, which had tied any use of the Reichswehr to "*definite*

81 See, in addition to Messerschmidt, *Wehrmacht*, Klaus-Jürgen Müller, *Das Heer und Hitler: Armee und nationalsozialistisches Regime 1933–1940*, 2nd ed. (Stuttgart, 1988).
82 See Hans Buchheim, et al., *Anatomy of the SS-State*, Vol. 2 (London, 1968), p. 25 (31 July 1933). On the reaction to the Röhm Affair see Müller, *Heer*, pp. 125–33.
83 Bernhard R. Kroener, et al., *Das Deutsche Reich und der Zweite Weltkrieg*, Vol. 5, pt. 1, *Organisation und Mobilisierung des deutschen Machtbereichs* (Stuttgart, 1988), p. 731.
84 Deist, "Rearmament," pp. 405–408.
85 Ibid., pp. 413–16, 437–56.
86 The memorandum of the *Truppenamt* of 14 December 1933, is printed in Hans-Jürgen Rautenberg, "Drei Dokumente zur Planung eines 300.000 Mann-Friedensheeres aus dem Dezember 1933," *Militärgeschichtliche Mitteilungen*, 22 (1977), pp. 115–17.

prospects of success," in favor of a far riskier military policy. As head of the *Truppenamt* in 1929, Blomberg had failed to prevail against Groener's more cautious course.[87] But now it was Blomberg who shaped military policy, with the complete support of the new head of the *Truppenamt*, Lieutenant General Ludwig Beck. The Wehrmacht leadership's determination to defend Germany solely through military might achieved by massive rearmament – against rather than within the existing system of collective security – helped lead Germany swiftly into harm's way. But recognition of danger led not to caution, but to ever-greater readiness to assume new and greater risks.

This increasing international tension was obvious to Hitler and his generals; it led to a constant stream of concepts, drafts, and plans from the military leadership for further acceleration of rearmament through measures such as the reintroduction of universal conscription in 1935 and the occupation of the Rhineland in 1936. The military planning that preceded and accompanied Hitler's foreign policy coups offers further evidence of rearmament's centrality in German strategy. In 1935–36, discussions within the army general staff about "increasing the fighting power of the army" led to a complete reorganization of the ground forces. That development in turn determined the nature of the rearmament program of August 1936, which remained in effect until 1939.[88] The phrase "increasing the fighting power of the army" necessarily covered the question of how and to what extent to incorporate armored units into the army's structure. In a basic memorandum of 30 December 1935, Beck revealed himself as an advocate of the operational use of armored divisions. But he also suggested that the army had not abandoned its aim of being able to conduct a European war on several fronts. The new weapons system would permit "strategic defense," which in Beck's view could only be successful if conducted "in the form of an attack." "Strategic defense" through armored forces opened the road to a revival of the classical operational art of Schlieffen and Moltke the elder.[89]

The rearmament program of August 1936 envisaged the creation of thirty-six infantry divisions (of which only four were completely motorized), three armored divisions, three light divisions, one mountain division, and a cavalry brigade. The planned peacetime army would have a strength of 830,000 men; the wartime army, 4,620,000 men. Compared with the original strength of the Reichswehr and even with the twenty-one division December Program of 1933, these figures represented a staggering increase in military power over an astonishingly short period. The Wehrmacht's great leap forward would raise the already heightened anxieties of Germany's neighbors and place the German economy under severe pressure – a prospect that the officers planning the program in summer 1936 clearly understood.

---

[87] See Geyer, *Aufrüstung*, pp. 191–95, 207–13.
[88] Deist, "Rearmament," pp. 431–37.
[89] The memorandum of 30 December 1935, is printed in Müller, *Beck*, pp. 469–77.

The chief of the General Army Office, Major General Fritz Fromm, explained to the army's commander-in-chief, Colonel General Werner Freiherr von Fritsch, that the program would make extraordinary demands on Germany's already depleted reserves of raw materials and foreign exchange. Fromm had no illusions: the program was justifiable only if the German leadership had the "firm intention" to use the Wehrmacht at a "certain, already determined point." Fritsch simply ignored the issue that Fromm had raised and approved the program in December 1936.[90] But Fromm's forebodings were justified. Shortages led to raw materials quotas in 1937; by spring 1939, equipment for the wartime army had fallen well below planned figures.

These economic difficulties played an important role in the decisions to move against Austria and Czechoslovakia in 1938.[91] Foreign exchange and strategic raw materials seized in the resulting annexations in turn significantly improved the outfitting of the Wehrmacht for war. This was a paradoxical development: since 1933 an army ready for a European war on several fronts had been the aim of German rearmament; now only the actual use of that army would permit the swift continuation of rearmament. The most serious weakness in the buildup of the army was precisely the failure to match rearmament targets to economic realities; the result was a series of severe bottlenecks after 1936.[92]

Nor was the army the only source of major demands on the economy: the Luftwaffe and navy also had decisive voices in the rearming of the Wehrmacht. An impressive group of competent and influential individuals directed the Luftwaffe buildup from its beginning until 1936.[93] Reich Aviation Minister Hermann Göring, seldom concerned with the details of armaments in the first years, relied on a capable and enthusiastic staff – especially his state secretary, General Erhard Milch. Göring's staff used their master's political influence and their own close connections with industry skillfully; they helped rescue the especially hard-hit aircraft industry from the world depression and swiftly laid the foundation for a Luftwaffe build-up and expansion. They promoted rapid expansion of capacity and pressed for

---

[90] Deist, "Rearmament," pp. 440–47.

[91] Hans-Erich Volkmann, "The National Socialist Economy in Preparation of War," in *Germany and the Second World War,* Vol. 1, *The Build-up of German Aggression* (London, 1990), pp. 323–36.

[92] See ibid., pp. 353–72; Deist, "Rearmament," pp. 451–56. On the problems that rearmament caused the officer corps, see ibid., pp. 425–29, 439–40.

[93] On the buildup of the Luftwaffe, see ibid., pp. 480–504; Edward L. Homze, *Arming the Luftwaffe: The Reich Air Ministry and the German Aircraft Industry, 1919–1939* (Lincoln, 1976); David Irving, *The Rise and Fall of the Luftwaffe: The Life of Luftwaffe Marshal Erhard Milch* (London, 1973); Richard James Overy, "The German Pre-war Aircraft Production Plans: November 1936-April 1939," *English Historical Review,* 90 (1975), pp. 778–97; Williamson Murray, *Strategy for Defeat: The Luftwaffe 1933–1945* (Washington, 1983); Horst Boog, *Die deutsche Luftwaffenführung 1935–1945: Führungsprobleme, Spitzengliederung, Generalstabsausbildung* (Stuttgart, 1981).

rationalization of production, while accepting that the first production models could not incorporate the latest aviation technology.

The new service branch nevertheless fulfilled its foreign policy function. The German government gradually confirmed the existence of the Luftwaffe only after February 1935, but long before that Germany could hardly hide the Luftwaffe buildup, which caused increasing anxiety among neighbors such as Britain. At the end of July 1934, the British Prime Minister, Stanley Baldwin, stated in the House of Commons that Britain could no longer defend itself at the cliffs of Dover, but only on the banks of the Rhine. That confession suggested that the infant Luftwaffe was providing an umbrella of deterrence during the initial buildup of the army.[94]

In its second phase, from 1936 to 1939, the expansion of the Luftwaffe encountered difficulties. Apart from the general bottlenecks in the defense economy and Göring's increasing and often erratic interventions, especially in personnel appointments, the Luftwaffe encountered increasing problems in controlling technological development and industrial planning. Reequipping with new models such as the He 111, Do 17, and Ju 86 bombers took much longer than originally planned, and was not complete until 1937. By then the Aviation Ministry was already planning a second phase of reequipment that would start in 1939 and end in 1940. The He 111 and the Do 17 would give way to the Ju 88 fast bomber, developed after 1936 and undergoing flight tests by summer 1937. Planning for this second phase took place at a time when Britain, the state most disturbed by the buildup of the Luftwaffe, had become a potential enemy. Yet in their previous armaments planning, neither Luftwaffe nor navy had assumed British hostility. The Ju 88 became a victim of this change of course in military policy. The aircraft required innumerable changes and modifications to make it suitable for an air war against Britain, and thus caused delays in the entire reequipment program. Despite the best efforts of the Luftwaffe and industry, the Ju 88 was not available on time, and Germany fought the air war against Britain largely with the He 111 and the Do 17. Technological factors, particularly the development of aircraft engines and the complexities of development, testing, and production, finally imposed limits on the rapid arming of the Luftwaffe.[95] These limits did not change significantly during the war despite technological progress in individual sectors.

Britain's new status as a potential enemy also decisively influenced the navy's armament planning.[96] Since the failure of the Tirpitz Plan, the Ger-

---

[94] See Deist, "Rearmament," pp. 484–85; Messerschmidt, "Foreign Policy," pp. 599–601.
[95] See also Horst Boog, "Luftwaffe und Technik 1935–1945," *Truppenpraxis*, 31 (1987), pp. 65–73.
[96] On naval rearmament, see Deist, "Rearmament," pp. 457–80; Dülffer, *Weimar*, pp. 370–512; Michael Salewski, *Die deutsche Seekriegsleitung, 1935–1945*, Vol. 1 (1935–1941), (Frankfurt/M., 1979); idem, "Marineleitung und politische Führung 1931–1935," *Militärgeschichtliche Mitteilungen*, 10 (1971), pp. 113–58; Carl-Axel Gemzell, *Organization,*

man navy had regarded discussion of a new confrontation with Britain as taboo. Wegener had been aware of this inhibition, but his example also shows that naval officers frequently ignored it. The dream of Germany as a world sea power remained very much alive within the *Kriegsmarine*.

Hitler made new funds available for ship construction, and "parity" with France became the navy's initial aim. For Admiral Erich Raeder, the navy's commander-in-chief, the support of the new chancellor for his service seemed vital. Hitler had, after all, denounced German naval policy under Wilhelm II in *Mein Kampf* for adding to Germany's enemies without accomplishing a useful strategic purpose. Raeder, through his personal contacts with Hitler, was astonishingly successful, for Hitler found the demand for parity with France plausible. But the extent to which British sea power continued to be the decisive measure of the German navy became evident when the naval leadership linked that "parity" with the strength of the Royal Navy. The German construction program of early summer 1934 made parity equivalent to 50 percent of British strength.[97] Such a fleet would serve to prevent the French from entering the Baltic in wartime and could disrupt French sea links in the Atlantic and perhaps even the Mediterranean, areas vitally important to Britain. In notes for a conversation with Hitler on 27 June 1934, Raeder summarized the consequences of his construction plans in one prophetic line: "Development of the fleet, later perhaps against England."[98]

German navy leaders interpreted the Anglo-German Naval Agreement of 18 July 1935, which permitted a further expansion of the German navy, as merely a "provisional" fixing of the two powers' relative naval strength. But this cautious and concealed turn against Britain did not impel the naval staff to examine the likely shape of an Anglo-German conflict. The persistent lack of clarity of political aims gave German naval rearmament a peculiarly uncertain character. In addition, the long lead time characteristic of shipbuilding made naval force planning dangerously inflexible amid the rapidly changing political and military conditions of the Third Reich. Moreover, limited capacity, insufficient recent experience in building warships, and the bottlenecks in the economy after 1935 prevented German shipyards from meeting the navy's construction targets. Not surprisingly, in September 1939 the German navy lacked the ships needed to fulfill the hopes placed in naval rearmament.

The culmination of naval armament planning, the gargantuan "Z-Plan" of January 1939, developed under Hitler's strong urging following his own turn

---

against Britain after 1937.[99] The "Z-Plan" expressed to the fullest the naval officer corps' fantasy of making Germany a world sea power. But the navy could only realize that dream against Britain, and therefore required above all else ships for an Atlantic naval war. The navy's situation by 1939 was similar in its consequences to that of the Luftwaffe: reorientation against Britain came too late to give Germany the forces necessary to fight with full effectiveness at the outbreak of war.

This survey has shown that German rearmament encountered economic difficulties from 1936–37 on, in part because each of the three services planned and implemented rearmament according to its own methods, priorities, and aims. Hitler's approach abandoned Groener's goal of comprehensive armaments planning; in the area of rearmament, the unity of the Wehrmacht had become an illusion. From 1936–37 on, bottlenecks led to raw material quotas that further aggravated competition among the services.[100] From this competition, in existence from the beginning, the rearmament programs developed a momentum that even Hitler could not ignore in his policy decisions. Even within each service, coordination of rearmament programs with the plant capacities and technological skills of the manufacturers was often lacking. The inevitable financial constraints, the constant struggle for foreign exchange and raw materials, and the absence of comprehensive planning made German rearmament chaotic as well as unprecedented in pace and scale.[101]

Several additional factors help explain the bizarre fact that no strategic plan governed this gigantic process. Although the second four-year armaments plan designed under Weimar had already begun by 1933, all three services entered the Third Reich deeply conscious of their weaknesses.[102] They sought above all else to overcome this condition as soon as possible; the menacing situation they perceived was not conducive to cool-headed strategic or force planning. Moreover, in spite of his supposedly great authority, Blomberg, the Reich Minister of War and commander-in-chief of the Wehrmacht, achieved only modest success in imposing policy on the commanders-in-chief of the army, navy, and Luftwaffe. This was especially true in the armaments sector, where Göring's[103] and Raeder's[104] special relationship with Hitler blocked any effort to develop a comprehensive program for the Wehrmacht as a whole.

The development of the Office of Defense Economy and Weapons Affairs

99 Deist, "Rearmament," pp. 472–80.
100 Ibid., pp. 505–508.
101 Michael Geyer, "Rüstungsbeschleunigung und Inflation: Zur Inflationsdenkschrift des Oberkommandos der Wehrmacht vom November 1938," *Militärgeschichtliche Mitteilungen,* 30 (1981), pp. 121–86.
102 As reflected in the memorandum of the chief of the *Truppenamt*, General Wilhelm Adam, in spring 1933. See Deist, "Rearmament," pp. 405–408.
103 See especially Irving, *Rise and Fall.*
104 Salewski, "Marineleitung," passim.

in the War Ministry represents an excellent example of the decentralized, uncoordinated style of German rearmament.[105] Blomberg was not expected to issue binding directives for rearmament based on a coordinated strategic plan; such directives could come only from Hitler himself. Though it can be shown that individual armaments programs went to Hitler for approval, no evidence before summer 1936 indicates that the "Führer and Reich Chancellor" concerned himself with the issue of overall rearmament.[106] Nor were his directives of 1936 and 1938–39 the result of consultations in a lengthy decision-making process; they read as ideological appeals justifying his maximum demands on the individual services.[107] German rearmament from 1933 to 1939 was thus not a masterpiece of strategic organization, but rather a process set in motion by each of the services acting on its own, hindered by bureaucracy, with undefined aims and often chaotic execution. The military establishment, hardly affected by or interested in rearmament's political, economic, and social implications, never came to grips with its consequences for the Wehrmacht or nation.

The Wehrmacht's internal disunity was likewise evident in strategic planning. On 24 June 1937 Blomberg issued a "Directive for the Uniform War Preparations of the Wehrmacht."[108] The directive lay in the tradition of Groener's directive of 16 April 1930, but it showed how much had changed. For Blomberg, France and Czechoslovakia were the Wehrmacht's principal enemies. In the event that Britain, Poland, and Lithuania joined the hostile coalition, the situation for Germany would be, in Blomberg's view, "hopeless." He added that Germany's "political leaders" would do everything possible "to keep England and Poland" neutral. In his directive, Blomberg understood the "war preparations of the Wehrmacht" exclusively in an operational sense, and made no mention of the armaments requirements for the multifront war envisaged in Europe or of the problems the war economy would face during mobilization. The essence of the directive was "purely instrumental, technical thinking."[109]

On 5 November 1937, Hitler conferred with the Foreign Minister and the commanders-in-chief of the Wehrmacht and of the services. As documented in the Hossbach Protocol, Blomberg's expectations about the intentions of the political leadership met with disappointment[110]; Blomberg's dismissal followed. The chief of the army general staff, Beck, who had warned of the

---

[105] Georg Thomas, *Geschichte der deutschen Wehr- und Rüstungswirtschaft (1918–1943/45)*, Wolfgang Birkenfeld, ed., (Boppard, 1966), pp. 62–79.
[106] Several examples can be found in Deist, "Rearmament," pp. 462–65, 490.
[107] For example, the October Program of the Luftwaffe of 1938: Deist, "Rearmament," pp. 500–501.
[108] IMT, Vol. 34, p. 734. See the comprehensive interpretation by Müller, *Beck*, pp. 239–47; Deist, "Rearmament," pp. 528–30.
[109] Müller, *Heer*, p. 237.
[110] See the most recent study by Jonathan Wright and Paul Stafford, "Hitler, Britain and the Hoßbach Memorandum," *Militärgeschichtliche Mitteilungen*, 42 (1987), pp. 77–123; Messerschmidt, "Foreign Policy," pp. 636–39.

military consequences of Hitler's goals, was the next to face – in March 1938 – Hitler's determination to decide the timing and shape of military action personally. In summer 1938 Beck sought to reclaim the voice in strategic matters that the Wehrmacht had surrendered since 1933. He failed.[111] Blomberg's June 1937 directive was the last "for the uniform war preparations of the Wehrmacht," despite later attempts to promote one by Wilhelm Keitel, Hitler's principal military assistant after the dictator had made himself commander-in-chief of the Wehrmacht.[112] Hitler believed that he could do without a concrete strategic orientation for the armed forces.

Between 1933 and 1939 the Wehrmacht and its leaders in no way conformed to Ludendorff's concept of a military leader and "defense staff" (*Wehrstab*) who would direct and supervise preparation for war. The services' complete absorption in organizing a rearmament unprecedented in speed and scale, their traditional inability to transcend the rivalries that separated them, and the reassuring belief that the political leadership had a firm grip on all issues related to the conduct of war except "strictly military" ones, led to the domination of "purely instrumental, technical thinking" and to an exclusive focus on operational art. The Wehrmacht and its leaders neither generated nor sought strategic ideas.

HITLER'S STRATEGY

A few days after becoming chancellor, Hitler partially disclosed his political aims and the strategic conceptions that they entailed in an address to the Reichswehr's commanders.[113] His announced aim of "regaining political power" was for the moment primarily a reference to domestic politics. But in his address to the Reichswehr leadership, it also meant the reestablishment of Germany's position as a European great power. And near the end of his address Hitler announced in unequivocal fashion that his aims went far beyond revision. After reestablishing Germany's great power position, the choice would be "perhaps to fight for new export openings, perhaps – and probably better – to conquer and ruthlessly Germanize new living space in the East." Here Hitler departed from the long-term policy objectives familiar to Reichswehr leaders. Hitler's remarks were also noteworthy for their clear linking of means and ends. Everything – from the suppression of domestic dissent, to overcoming the great depression, to the struggle against Versailles, to the buildup of the Wehrmacht – aimed at establishing Germany's position as the greatest European power and at using German power for conquest in the East. The beginnings of a strategic conception were unmistakable.

[111] See Müller, *Beck,* pp. 254–311.
[112] Deist, "Rearmament," pp. 531–37.
[113] Vogelsang, "Neue Dokumente."

Intensive historical study of Hitler and the Third Reich has shown that the *Weltanschauung* that shaped Hitler's thoughts and actions as "Führer and Reich Chancellor" had assumed its final, programmatic form in the second half of the 1920s.[114] Despite their heterogeneous quality, his speeches and writings from the 1920s, especially *Mein Kampf*, make clear that the social-Darwinist notion of the human "struggle for survival" and the pseudobiological concept of race formed the central, axiomatic basis of his *Weltanschauung*. His views were typical of one broad stream of contemporary thought in Germany from the end of the nineteenth century, a *Weltanschauung* that the experiences of the First World War seemed to have confirmed.[115]

It is impossible to overestimate the influence of this *Weltanschauung* on Hitler's political actions. One of its basic components, the unshakeable belief in the distinctive qualities and superiority of the so-called Nordic or Aryan race, involved a struggle to the death with world Jewry, whose putative aim was the "enslavement of productive, creative peoples." The "most bitter struggle" of this kind ever attempted was currently underway in Germany, and the task of the National Socialist movement was to apply "in the area of practical politics the knowledge and scientific insights of the race doctrine as well as the explanation of world history it provides."[116]

Here also Hitler expressed in an extreme form thoughts that preoccupied his contemporaries. From the perspective of his racist, social-Darwinist *Weltanschauung*, politics was "in reality the struggle for survival of a *Volk*."[117] He did warn against war as a permanent condition: constant losses of the best specimens endangered the "race value" of a people. But he viewed the "peaceful struggle of economic competition" as "the most inhuman war" of all. The task of policy was always to "choose for its struggle the weapons in such a way that life in the highest sense" would be served. From this he concluded that no distinction existed between peace and war and that Germany should make no alliances without the thought of war.[118]

The task of German policy was simple: to conduct the struggle for *Lebensraum* ("living space") in the East. Only conquest could make good the mistakes of the past and preserve the "race value" of the German people. The nation should concentrate all efforts on the struggle for living space, which meant that domestic and foreign policy had to be interlocking and,

114 See above all Eberhard Jäckel, *Hitlers Weltanschauung*, rev. ed. (Stuttgart, 1981).
115 See Hans-Günter Zmarzlik, "Der Sozialdarwinismus in Deutschland als geschichtliches Problem," *Vierteljahreshefte für Zeitgeschichte*, 11 (1963), pp. 246–73; the last chapter of Arno J. Mayer's book, *The Persistence of the Old Regime* (New York, 1981).
116 *Hitler's Secret Book*, with an introduction by Telford Taylor (New York, 1962), pp. 127, 220, 221. See also, Hamid Moghareh-Obed, "Rassenhygiene/Eugenik: Ideologisches Prädispositiv und Handlungsmotivation zum Genozid," in Wolfgang Michalka, ed., *Der Zweite Weltkrieg: Grundzüge, Analysen, Forschungsbilanz* (Munich, 1989), pp. 798–813.
117 *Hitler's Secret Book*, pp. 46–52.
118 Ibid., p. 155.

above all, that the nation must prepare for war. Hitler demanded the "complete, thorough training and education of the nation for war." Only then would Germany's future security be "almost guaranteed."[119]

This brief outline leaves no doubt that Hitler began preparing for war from his first day in office. In accordance with his long-term aims, his strategy in these years was comprehensive and, despite a bewildering tactical versatility, purposeful and consistent. The domestic political measures of the regime,[120] the almost total, organized militarization of the nation with the help of the National Socialist Party and its organizations – as well as the persecution and elimination of all groups and persons considered a danger to *Volk* unity – fulfilled the domestic political conditions for conducting war that Stülpnagel and Ludendorff had described. From the beginning, this campaign consisted of relentless indoctrination, forcible "coordination" (*Gleichschaltung*) of state bureaucracies and private voluntary organizations, destruction of the rule of law, measures of "racial hygiene," and the persecution, dispossession, and expulsion of Germany's Jews. Yet the population, haunted by the immense and useless sacrifices of World War I, followed the regime into war with only "reluctant loyalty" in September 1939.[121] That provided a warning that the leadership took seriously, and placed limits on the economic sacrifices it felt it could demand in the first phase of the war. Only the Wehrmacht's impressive victory over France gave the regime's propaganda the credibility needed to meet Hitler's demands for "inner unity."

Why did Hitler devote so little attention to planning a rearmament that would serve his aims better, and why did he fail to coordinate the divergent efforts of the three services? The apparent answer, judging from his "Second Book" of 1928, is that he privileged psychological and ideological preparation for war over its material aspects.[122] From a tactical and political point of view, Hitler probably welcomed the Reichswehr's complete absorption in the rearmament that he had made possible, and saw no reason to doubt the desire of the military leaders for swift and comprehensive rearmament. In the first years after 1933, he therefore limited himself in essence to urging the acceleration of rearmament. Nor did he change that approach in 1937–38, when rearmament had developed its full momentum. His attitude precluded comprehensive armaments planning for the German armed forces.

[119] Ibid., p. 69. See Rainer Zitelmann, "Zur Begründung des 'Lebensraum'-Motivs in Hitlers Weltanschauung," in Michalka, ed., *Der Zweite Weltkrieg*, pp. 551–67.
[120] See Martin Broszat, *The Hitler State* (New York, 1981); Thamer, "Verführung," pp. 338–446.
[121] Wolfram Wette, "Ideology, Propaganda and Politics as Preconditions for the War Policy of the Third Reich," in *Germany and the Second World War*, Vol. 1, *The Build-up of German Aggression* (London, 1990), pp. 114–24; Wilhelm Deist, "Überlegungen zur 'widerwilligen Loyalität' der Deutschen bei Kriegsbeginn," in Michalka, ed., *Der Zweite Weltkrieg*, pp. 224–39.
[122] *Hitler's Secret Book*, p. 69.

That lack of planning was all the more remarkable given the bottlenecks that slowed the pace of rearmament after 1935 at the latest and imposed drastic policy changes. For Hitler and his party, economic strains were all the more dangerous because economic success – in overcoming the great depression – had been indispensable to consolidating the regime. National Socialism's massive spending had stimulated the economy to such an extent that unemployment fell by 50 percent within two years.[123] But the economic upswing, intertwined with rearmament from the beginning, in turn summoned up long-term inflationary risks uncontrollable even through the financial sleight of hand of Reichsbank President Hjalmar Schacht. The regime virtually exhausted its foreign exchange reserves as early as 1935.[124] That in turn endangered the imports of raw materials vital for rearmament and of food essential to public contentment.

Hitler's reaction was both decisive and typical: he sought to mobilize the German economy with the Four Year Plan of September 1936.[125] His insistence on the exploitation of all mineral deposits within Germany, however uneconomic, and for the establishment or expansion of synthetic materials plants simply suspended economic law. In his August 1936 memorandum on the Four Year Plan, Hitler made clear that the function of all economic activity was preparation for war. At the end of the memorandum he flatly demanded that: "1) The German army must be ready for combat in four years. 2) The German economy must be ready for war in four years."[126] Such a program could only aggravate rather than relieve the bottlenecks and conceal inflation from which the economy now suffered; the result of Hitler's further acceleration of rearmament was the system of drastic raw materials quotas introduced in 1937.[127] In the end, only conquest could maintain the pace of rearmament.

Economic considerations thus played an important role in the decision to annex Austria and move against Czechoslovakia in 1938,[128] and the economic spoils from these actions temporarily relieved economic strain. Germany began the war in a precarious economic situation that resulted directly from the pace and scale of rearmament. Yet the structural weaknesses described did not prevent the Wehrmacht from fielding the most modern armed force in Europe at the outset of the war. In the final analysis, Hitler ignored bottlenecks and the threat of economic catastrophe in the short term in pursuit of his long-term solution to Germany's difficulties, the conquest of living space in the East. Seen in the light of his ideological premises, his

---

123 Volkmann, "National Socialist Economy," p. 235.
124 Ibid., p. 255.
125 Ibid., pp. 273–79.
126 Ibid., pp. 277–79; Wilhelm Treue, "Hitlers Denkschrift zum Vierjahresplan 1936," *Vierteljahreshefte für Zeitgeschichte*, 3 (1955), pp. 194–210.
127 Deist, "Rearmament," pp. 449–54.
128 Volkmann, "National Socialist Economy," pp. 323–36.

strategy had consistently and successfully integrated domestic, economic, and military policy.

What was the effect of this ideologically inspired policy of war preparation upon foreign policy, an area at least in theory dominated by cool calculation? In his February 1933 address to the Reichswehr's commanders, Hitler stressed that the buildup of the Wehrmacht would be the "most dangerous time." Foreign policy had to provide a diplomatic shield until Germany was strong.[129] Hitler and the Foreign Ministry succeeded in avoiding isolation by offering apparently advantageous bilateral deals to selected neighbors, and by propagating the misleading notion that the National Socialist regime was simply continuing the Weimar policy of revision with greater noise and emphasis. This policy of camouflage made possible the reintroduction of conscription in March 1935 and the remilitarization of the Rhineland a year later. That act marked the final break with the system of collective security created by the treaties of Versailles and Locarno; as before 1914, German security now rested solely on German might.

Hitler had assumed that Britain would tolerate his policy of German continental hegemony, which implied the defeat of France, if British interests overseas remained safe.[130] In that way he hoped to eliminate any threat in western Europe and then concentrate on the decisive phase of his political program, the war for *Lebensraum* in the East. At the Hossbach conference of 5 November 1937, he described Britain as a "hate-inspired antagonist" but also indicated that he did not expect British resistance to the absorption of Czechoslovakia.[131] The feeble British and French reaction to the *Anschluss* apparently confirmed his assessment, for that coup in turn markedly improved Germany's strategic position against Czechoslovakia. He therefore decided on war, until frustrated by the cession of Czechoslovak border areas to Germany under the Munich Agreement. That surrender, however, was yet another confirmation of his assessment of British policy.[132] Far into World War II, Hitler hoped for an Anglo-German bargain that would condone German continental hegemony. A wish elevated into dogma precluded realistic, rational calculation.

Britain's adverse reaction to Germany's occupation of Prague in March 1939 made clear how badly Hitler had misconstrued the principles underlying British acceptance of the *Anschluss* and the partition of Czechoslovakia. On 31 March, Chamberlain declared that Britain would help Poland if its independence appeared threatened. That guarantee meant that Hitler had failed in his attempt to use Poland as an instrument of his strategy.[133] He now determined to solve the "Polish question" by force, and set 1 September

[129] Messerschmidt, "Foreign Policy," pp. 581–89.
[130] Ibid., pp. 594–604.
[131] Ibid., pp. 636–39.
[132] Ibid., pp. 663–72.
[133] Ibid., pp. 692–96.

as the Wehrmacht's planning date for readiness to act. That deadline made still more acute the self-inflicted time pressure that rearmament and its economic consequences had imposed since 1937–38, while the political conditions for action against Poland visibly worsened.

The most striking consequence of Hitler's fixation on Poland was the increase in influence of the Soviet Union, Hitler's ultimate target. As expansion remained his unchanging goal and British resistance hardened, he felt compelled to free himself to strike Poland by concluding the nonaggression pact and secret protocol with Stalin. That bargain made him dependent on Soviet support yet failed to deter Britain and France from declaring war on Germany on 3 September 1939.[134]

The reaction of the Western Powers represented Hitler's first serious strategic defeat. The war to conquer living space in the East – the core of his policy – had begun under a constellation of forces incompatible with his objectives. Only Germany's military and industrial might – applied for the moment against the Western Powers rather than against Soviet Russia – could now serve to correct this situation. The axioms of Hitler's ideology, not rational calculation, had determined strategy; the result corresponded neither to his ideological aims nor to rational economic or military goals.

WAR AND RUIN

Germany's strategic decisions during World War II initially centered on Europe. The strategic turning point came in December 1941 with the failure of the German attack on Moscow and Hitler's declaration of war on the United States.[135] Thereafter the military policies and tactics of Germany's enemies, along with the increasing determination of the National Socialist regime to maintain "inner unity" at the front and at home, explain the war's continuation for three and a half years amid losses in the millions on all sides.

The regime continued and intensified the manifold methods of influencing public opinion with propaganda it had tested in the years before 1939. After the still-vivid experience of "hunger-blockade" in the First World War, the regime sought to guarantee stability at home by providing a dependable food

---

[134] Ibid., pp. 707–17. See also Gottfried Niedhart, "Sitzkrieg versus Blitzkrieg: Das attentistische Konfliktverhalten Großbritanniens in der Krise des internationalen Systems am Vorabend und bei Beginn des Zweiten Weltkriegs," in Michalka, ed., *Der Zweite Weltkrieg,* pp. 49–56.

[135] Jürgen Förster, "Das Unternehmen 'Barbarossa' – eine historische Ortsbestimmung," in Horst Boog, et al., *Das Deutsche Reich und der Zweite Weltkrieg,* Vol. 4, *Der Angriff auf die Sowjetunion* (Stuttgart, 1983), pp. 1079–88; Enrico Syring, "Hitlers Kriegserklärung an Amerika vom 11. Dezember 1941," in Michalka, ed., *Der Zweite Weltkrieg,* pp. 683–96: Bernhard R. Kroener, "Der 'erfrorene Blitzkrieg'. Strategische Planungen der deutschen Führung gegen die Sowjetunion und die Ursachen ihres Scheiterns," in Michalka, ed., *Der Zweite Weltkrieg,* pp. 133–48; Bernd Wegner, "Hitlers Strategie zwischen Pearl Harbor und Stalingrad," in Horst Boog, et al., *Das Deutsche Reich und der Zweite Weltkrieg,* Vol. 6, *Der globale Krieg* (Stuttgart, 1990), pp. 97–100.

supply for the German population. The National Socialists foresaw and accepted the catastrophic consequences of their policy in the German-occupied areas, from which they also sought to extract food for the Wehrmacht.[136] The regime likewise sought to avoid demanding too many sacrifices from Germans in terms of wages, prices, and working conditions.

Yet only the war opened the way to creation of a militarized *Volksgemeinschaft* based on the ideology of the National Socialist rulers. The regime undertook ever more rigorous efforts to remove "un-German elements" (as Stülpnagel had put it) from the militarized *Volksgemeinschaft*. These efforts affected primarily Germans of Jewish religion or descent, whose isolation and deprivation of rights ended in deportation from Germany and physical annihilation in the ghettos and death camps of the East.[137] The elimination of "un-German" elements also affected handicapped and insane Germans, who were considered "unworthy of life" and eliminated through National Socialist "euthanasia" programs.[138] After the German attack on the Soviet Union and the ensuing radicalization of the conduct of the war, constant surveillance and terror struck pitilessly at deviations from the line dictated by regime propaganda. Within a perverted legal system, special courts, military courts, and drumhead courts martial dispatched tens of thousands of Germans with relentless efficiency and ever greater speed.[139] Hitler's efforts to avoid a repetition of the trauma of 1918 were successful. Despite massive Allied bombing of German cities and an ever more hopeless military situation, the "inner unity" of the *Volksgemeinschaft* at home and at the front lasted to the bitter end.

Yet in the economy the shortcomings of the polycratic Führer-state were all too evident even before the war's strategic turning point. It proved impossible to unite all the diverse groups, institutions, and special interests involved in the war economy in a common effort. The result was an incomplete economic mobilization – a "peacetime war economy" or "transition economy" – which ended only with Albert Speer's appointment as armaments minister in February 1942. The Wehrmacht itself bore a major share of responsibility for this situation, thanks to the continued absence of a coordinated tri-service armament program and to the persistent illusion of military

---

136 Hans Umbreit, "Auf dem Weg zur Kontinentalherrschaft," in *Das Deutsche Reich und der Zweite Weltkrieg*, Vol. 5, pt. 1, *Organisation und Mobilisierung des deutschen Machtbereichs*, pp. 321–27; Rolf-Dieter Müller, "Die Konsequenzen der "Volksgemeinschaft": Ernährung, Ausbeutung, Vernichtung," in Michalka, ed., *Der Zweite Weltkrieg*, pp. 240–48.

137 See Raul Hilberg, *The Destruction of the European Jews* (Chicago, 1961); Eberhard Jäckel and Jürgen Rohwer, eds., *Der Mord an den Juden im Zweiten Weltkrieg: Entschlußbildung und Verwirklichung* (Stuttgart, 1985); Arno J. Mayer, *Why Did the Heavens Not Darken? The Final Solution In History* (New York, 1988).

138 Ernst Klee, *"Euthanasie" im NS-Staat: Die "Vernichtung lebensunwerten Lebens"* (Frankfurt/M., 1985); idem, Dokumente zur "Euthanasie" (Frankfurt/M., 1985).

139 Manfred Messerschmidt and Fritz Wüllner, *Die Wehrmachtjustiz im Dienst des Nationalsozialismus* (Baden-Baden, 1987).

leaders that the economy would simply produce on command. Dr. Fritz Todt, appointed armaments minister in March 1940, failed to increase efficiency and production by imposing structures modeled on private industry. The incompatible interests of the regime's rapidly expanding economic bureaucracies and the general euphoria after victory over France made the required radical measures seem less than urgent.

The German leadership never achieved optimal control of war production, nor did it fulfill the requirements of a clearly defined strategy – which in any case did not exist. This inability to master the problems of economic mobilization meant that by summer 1941 Germany had already lost the "war of the factories" against Britain and America. As World War I had shown, that war was in the long run the decisive one.

Nor could Speer's astonishing successes in the final phase of the war reverse defeat.[140] His achievements resulted not only from a purposeful organizational structure, but also from the general radicalization of the war, which expanded to the home front after the defeat before Moscow in December 1941, and reached a high point in Goebbels' fanatical Sportspalast speech of 18 February 1943, "*Wollt Ihr den totalen Krieg?*" Radicalization also affected production; the regime adopted brutal measures to mobilize labor for the war economy. In May 1941, the German economy employed 1.7 million foreign laborers; by May 1944, the figure was 5.2 million in the *Grossdeutsches Reich*, entirely apart from the millions of prisoners of war. Despite the great differences in their formal status, all workers – including the Germans – felt constant pressure to increase production. Coercion ranged from the compulsory assignment of German workers to specific plants to slave labor and annihilation through work in the concentration camps.[141] The system and its functionaries predictably expressed their race ideology in repulsive and criminal form by ranking slave laborers hierarchically, with Soviets and Jews at the bottom. In the final phase of the war, Allied bombing significantly accelerated Germany's exhaustion and economic paralysis.

On the battlefield, victory over Poland changed Germany's strategic situation only by making Hitler's partner and ideological archenemy, the Soviet Union, into Germany's immediate neighbor along a broad eastern border. In contrast, the spectacular successes in the north and in western Europe in spring 1940 decisively improved Germany's strategic situation. In the Scan-

140 See the summary by the authors of *Das Deutsche Reich und der Zweite Weltkrieg*, Vol. 5, pt. l, *Organisation und Mobilisierung des deutschen Machtbereichs* (Stuttgart, 1988), pp. 1003–16; Rolf-Dieter Müller, "Die Mobilisierung der Wirtschaft für den Krieg – eine Aufgabe der Armee? Wehrmacht und Wirtschaft 1933–1942," in Michalka, ed., *Der Zweite Weltkrieg*, pp. 349–62.

141 See Ulrich Herbert, *Fremdarbeiter: Politik und Praxis des 'Auslander-Einsatzes' in der Kriegswirtschaft des Dritten Reichs* (Berlin, 1985); the articles by Christian Streit, Gerhard Schreiber, Rolf-Dieter Muller, and Falk Pingel, in Michalka, ed., *Der Zweite Weltkrieg*, pp. 747–97.

dinavian phase, Britain was the sole enemy. The navy was the originator of WESERÜBUNG, the bold operation against Denmark and Norway.[142] Raeder, navy commander-in-chief, followed Wegener in his awareness of the strategic importance of the northern European flank to Germany's naval war against Britain. The army achieved operational triumph in the campaign against France using the plan of Lieutenant General Erich von Manstein, who won out against the World War I conceptions of the army high command only with Hitler's support.[143] By June 1940, Germany had conquered the positions that Wegener had identified as prerequisites for war against Britain: the Norwegian and French Atlantic coasts.

The new strategic position appeared to offer Germany a chance to eliminate the one remaining enemy still in the way of a war for living space in the East – Britain. Yet the Germans were unable to seize this chance because they lacked the necessary forces. WESERÜBUNG had so depleted the surface navy, and the seagoing submarine force was so small, that any attempt to isolate Britain by cutting its sea links was doomed to failure.[144] The German air offensive against Britain failed even more conspicuously. Had the Luftwaffe succeeded, a landing operation against Britain would still have been risky, but no such operation was possible without air superiority over the Channel.[145] Hitler's decision to postpone operation SEA LION on 14 September 1940 acknowledged a strategic defeat.

A few months earlier, in his euphoria over imminent victory in France, Hitler had assumed that he could "negotiate with Britain on the basis of a partition of the world."[146] That events did not fulfill that expectation showed the gap between the hubris of summer 1940 and Germany's actual strategic situation. The German leadership passed summer and fall 1940 examining a variety of strategic options, especially ones against Britain.[147] After Hitler's original hope of an understanding with Britain had collapsed, German leaders recognized that even a direct attack would not force the British to come to terms. Only two possibilities remained: the strategic defensive, to hold Germany's position on the continent against Britain and the United States, or to attack Britain indirectly by threatening its Empire and lines of communication. The Germans could not carry out either strategy

---

[142] See Klaus A. Maier, et al., *Germany and the Second World War,* Vol. 2, *Germany's Initial Conquests in Europe* (Oxford, 1991), pp. 181–96.

[143] Hans Umbreit, "The Battle for Hegemony in Western Europe," in ibid., pp. 238–54, 281–304.

[144] Bernd Stegemann, "The First Phase of the War at Sea up to the Spring of 1940," in ibid., pp. 176–78, 218.

[145] Klaus A. Maier, "The Battle of Britain," in ibid., pp. 374–407; idem, "Die Luftschlacht über England," in Michalka, ed., *Der Zweite Weltkrieg*, pp. 513–22.

[146] Gerhard Schreiber, "Die politische und militärische Entwicklung im Mittelmeerraum 1939/40," in Gerhard Schreiber et al., *Das Deutsche Reich und der Zweite Weltkrieg,* Vol. 3, *Der Mittelmeerraum und Südosteuropa: Von der "non belligeranza" Italiens bis zum Kriegseintritt der Vereinigten Staaten* (Stuttgart, 1984), p. 166.

[147] Ibid., pp. 162–222.

without the agreement and cooperation of Spain, Vichy France, and Germany's alliance partners Italy and Japan. Yet insistent negotiations and Hitler's October 1940 pilgrimage to meet Laval, Pétain, Franco, and Mussolini produced nothing of significance. Mussolini indeed took the occasion to inform Hitler of his imminent attack on Greece, which portended difficulties for an indirect strategy against Britain. The unyielding attitude of Britain and the pointed reserve of Spain, Vichy, and Italy confronted Hitler with a strategic situation that had serious implications in the long run, given the increasing support of the United States for Britain.

For German leaders, however, an alternative to the anti-British strategy had always existed. The army general staff had begun in late June and early July 1940 to study a possible attack on the Soviet Union.[148] On 21 July, in view of British intransigence, Hitler directed the commander-in-chief of the army to look into the "Russian problem." Brauchitsch was able to sketch immediately the details of the proposed operation. During a conference with senior Wehrmacht commanders on 31 July 1940, the German decision to turn East took a concrete, although not absolutely definitive form. Hitler's ideological aims, the struggle for living space in the East and against "Jewish Bolshevism," came to the fore once more and combined with the strategic necessity of creating an autarkic continental world power position against Britain and the United States. The decision of 31 July was a symbiosis of dogma and calculation.[149] It marked the beginning of comprehensive military preparations for the attack on the Soviet Union in the spring of 1941, and Hitler took the first steps to secure the northern and southern flanks of that operation.[150]

In its military and economic preparations for this campaign, the German leadership grossly underestimated Soviet resources and abilities and just as grossly overestimated its own.[151] The attack on the Soviet Union, operation BARBAROSSA, was actually the only German military effort in the Second World War planned as a Blitzkrieg campaign to be completed within limited time and with limited forces. In accordance with Hitler's aims, it was also planned as a racist war of annihilation.[152] Military leaders, far from oppos-

---

[148] Ernst Klink, "Die militärische Konzeption des Krieges gegen die Sowjetunion," in *Das Deutsche Reich und der Zweite Weltkrieg*, Vol. 4, *Der Angriff auf die Sowjetunion* (Stuttgart, 1983), pp. 202–16.

[149] Jürgen Förster, "Hitlers Entscheidung für den Krieg gegen die Sowjetunion," in ibid., p. 16. See also the definitive work by Andreas Hillgruber, *Hitlers Strategie: Politik und Kriegführung 1940/41*, 2nd ed. (Munich, 1982).

[150] Förster, "Hitlers Entscheidung," pp. 13–18.

[151] Bernhard R. Kroener, "Blitzkrieg oder totaler Krieg?" in *Das Deutsche Reich und der Zweite Weltkrieg*, Vol. 5, pt. 1, *Organisation und Mobilisierung des deutschen Machtbereichs* (Stuttgart, 1988), pp. 990–1001; Rolf-Dieter Müller, "Von der Wirtschaftsallianz zum kolonialen Ausbeutungskrieg," in *Das Deutsche Reich und der Zweite Weltkrieg*, Vol. 4, *Der Angriff auf die Sowjetunion* (Stuttgart, 1983), pp. 113–89.

[152] Helmut Krausnick and Hans-Heinrich Wilhelm, *Die Truppe des Weltanschauungskrieges: Die Einsatzgruppen der Sicherheitspolizei und des SD 1938–1942* (Stuttgart, 1982); Christian Streit, *Keine Kameraden: Die Wehrmacht und die*

ing the ideological barbarization of warfare, supported and even promoted it. Germany's conduct of the war in the East served the racist aim of conquering living space for the "Aryan master race" and claimed as its victims not only Red Army troops and Soviet political officers, but millions of Soviet civilians, especially Jews, as well.

The devastating initial advance seemed to confirm the German leadership's optimistic assessment. The head of the army general staff, Colonel General Franz Halder, concluded as early as 3 July that the Wehrmacht had in essence achieved its main campaign objective.[153] But the situation rapidly deteriorated; it was soon clear that the war against the Soviet Union would not end in 1941. The beginning of the Soviet winter offensive on 5 December, in conjunction with Japan's attack on Pearl Harbor and Hitler's declaration of war on the United States on 11 December, caught Germany in a strategic vice between the Soviets and the Americans. The strategic initiative in all areas now passed to the Reich's enemies, who broke the German will to fight in three and a half more years of bitter struggle.

In 1942 German leaders tried to compensate for their loss of strategic freedom by operational successes aimed at Russia's vital oil fields and at Suez; thereafter, Allied pressure compelled them to concentrate on defending what they held. Despite further offensives on land and water, Germany failed to regain the strategic initiative.[154] Hitler's refusal even to consider a political settlement of the conflict, and his continued insistence on "all or nothing," made it impossible to develop a successful defensive strategy; in effect, Hitler forced the Wehrmacht to continue a war it could not win. War had become an end in itself.

As developments since November 1937 had shown, Hitler's ideological fixation on war and his racist war aims made the time factor increasingly important; he feared that old age or assassination might deflect him from accomplishing his "mission," and was increasingly conscious of Germany's

sowjetischen Kriegsgefangenen 1941–1945 (Stuttgart, 1978); Jürgen Förster, "Das Unternehmen 'Barbarossa' als Eroberungs- und Vernichtungskrieg," in *Das Deutsche Reich und der Zweite Weltkrieg*, Vol. 4, *Der Angriff auf die Sowjetunion* (Stuttgart, 1983), pp. 413–47; ibid., pp. 1030–78; idem, "The German Army and the Ideological War against the Soviet Union," in Gerhard Hirschfeld, ed., *The Politics of Genocide: Jews and Soviet Prisoners of War in Nazi Germany* (London, 1986), pp. 15–29; Mayer, *Heavens*, chapters 7 and 8.

153 Ernst Klink, "Die Operationsführung," in *Das Deutsche Reich und der Zweite Weltkrieg*, Vol. 4, *Der Angriff auf die Sowjetunion* (Stuttgart, 1983), pp. 486–87.

154 Bernd Wegner, "Hitlers zweiter Feldzug gegen die Sowjetunion: Strategische Grundlagen und historische Bedeutung," in Michalka, ed., *Der Zweite Weltkrieg*, pp. 652–66; Werner Rahn, "Der Atlantik in der strategischen Perspektive Hitlers und Roosevelts 1941," in ibid., pp. 667–82; see also Horst Boog, et al., *Das Deutsche Reich und der Zweite Weltkrieg*, Vol. 6, *Der globale Krieg. Die Ausweitung zum Weltkrieg und der Wechsel der Initiative, 1941-1943* (Stuttgart, 1990). On the operational and tactical aspects of the conduct of war, see Jürgen Förster, "The Dynamics of *Volksgemeinschaft*: The Effectiveness of the German Military Establishment in the Second World War," in Allan R. Millett and Williamson Murray, eds., *Military Effectiveness*, Vol. 3, *The Second World War* (Boston, 1988), pp. 199–212.

shrinking lead in armaments. Self-imposed time pressure inhibited rational strategic calculation, which also suffered from the ideological distortions evident in his wishful misjudgment of Britain's tolerance for German continental hegemony and his gross underestimation of Soviet power. If the term "strategy" still had meaning under these conditions, amid the ever-present confusion of the polycratic Führer-state, three factors in Hitler's wartime policies further reduced its importance.

Scholars usually overlook the coalition aspects of Germany's war. Hitler's personal loyalty to Mussolini is well-known, but it did not extend to conceding Italy a voice in the conduct of the war.[155] The partners never agreed on fundamentals such as the relative strategic importance of the various theaters; for Germany, the Mediterranean and North Africa remained secondary, and Italian wishes usually received scant consideration. Hitler and his advisers treated Germany's other allies similarly. The negative effects of that policy in the final phase of the war were obvious – but German refusal to treat coalition partners fairly on the basis of mutual interests was unsurprising, given Hitler's *Weltanschauung*.

The racist core of National Socialist ideology, the resulting belief in German superiority, and the consequent aim of exterminating entire groups and so-called "inferior races" proved of decisive strategic importance in other ways as well. German racism and ruthless exploitation of the material and human resources of the occupied areas increasingly inclined their populations to resistance rather than collaboration – with disastrous consequences for Germany's conduct of the war.[156]

Finally, Hitler's social-Darwinist conviction that "struggle in all its forms" determined the development of peoples further reduced the role of rationality in Germany's wartime policy. Although well aware that the strategic initiative had passed to his enemies, he rejected all peace feelers and remained determined to carry the war to a barbaric end.[157] Relentlessly consistent in his belief in the "right of the strongest," he sacrificed his own nation to that "law."[158] For someone with such a mentality, strategy was a concept from a bygone age.

---

[155] See the conclusion by Gerhard Schreiber and Detlef Vogel, in *Das Deutsche Reich und der Zweite Weltkrieg*, Vol. 3, *Der Mittelmeerraum und Südosteuropa*, pp. 683–94.

[156] Umbreit, "Kontinentalherrschaft," in *Das Deutsche Reich und der Zweite Weltkrieg*, Vol. 5, pt. 1, *Organisation und Mobilisierung des deutschen Machtbereichs* (Stuttgart, 1988), pp. 265–345; Christopher R. Browning, "Wehrmacht Reprisal Policy and the Mass Murder of Jews in Serbia," in *Militärgeschichtliche Mitteilungen*, 31 (1983), pp. 31–47.

[157] Bernd Martin, *Friedensinitiativen und Machtpolitik im Zweiten Weltkrieg 1939–1942* (Düsseldorf, 1974); Ingeborg Fleischhauer, *Die Chance des Sonderfriedens: Deutsch-Sowjetische Geheimgespräche 1941–1945* (Berlin, 1986).

[158] On 21 January 1942, Hitler said: "On this as well I am ice-cold: if the German people is not prepared to fight for its survival, fine; let it vanish." Werner Jochmann, ed., *Adolf Hitler: Monologe im Führerhauptquartier 1941–1944, Die Aufzeichnungen Heinrich Heims* (Hamburg, 1980), p. 239; see also Hitler's scorched earth order of 19 March 1945, in *Kriegstagebuch des Oberkommandos der Wehrmacht*, Vol. 5, pt. 8, pp. 1580–81.

German strategic thought and action had changed radically on the road from Ludendorff to Hitler, the road from the dominance of the military specialist to the absolute priority of politics and ideology. Clausewitz had written that "the first, the supreme, the most far-reaching act of judgment that the statesman and commander have to make is to establish by that test the kind of war on which they are embarking; neither mistaking it for, nor trying to turn it into, something that is alien to its nature. This is the first of all strategic questions, and the most comprehensive."[159] Hitler was well aware of the kind of war on which he was embarking. But Germany's military leaders, except for the retired Beck, simply ignored that central strategic issue. For them, war remained limited to actual combat, and the political and strategic aspects of industrialized warfare were of very limited interest. Their operational virtuosity and supreme tactical skill merely helped prolong the German national apocalypse and the devastation of Europe.

[159] Carl von Clausewitz, *On War*, Michael Howard and Peter Paret, trans. and eds., rev. ed. (Princeton, 1984), pp. 88–89.

13

The collapse of empire: British strategy, 1919–1945

WILLIAMSON MURRAY

THE BACKGROUND

If World War I had shaken Britain's position and confidence, the succeeding three decades proved even less kind. During that period, Britain lost its economic and political position as a great power. Much of "the collapse of British power" lay beyond the control of Britain's statesmen.[1] Nevertheless, certain decisions contributed substantially to the decline and almost resulted in national catastrophe, and those decisions were as important as factors beyond the control of those who cast national policy. This essay will seek to diagnose the causes, inevitable as well as preventable, that led to the end of empire and the decline in national importance.

For much of this period, World War I exerted a powerful influence on British strategic policy. In the last decade of the twentieth century, we now tend to see the period 1919–1939 as the prelude to the next great war, but for those making British strategy and defense policy during that period, the fearful catastrophe just past was the primary influence on policy; even after Britain had embarked on the next great struggle to thwart German ambitions, memories of the last conflict cast dark shadows over policymaking.

Winston Churchill, in his monumental *World Crisis,* best caught the impact of World War I on Britain:

> It was the custom in the palmy days of Queen Victoria for statesmen to expatiate upon the glories of the British Empire, and to rejoice in the protecting Providence which had preserved us through so many dangers and brought us at length into a secure and prosperous age. . . .
>
> Children were taught of the Great War against Napoleon as the culminating effort in the history of the British people, and they looked on Waterloo and Trafalgar as the supreme achievements of British arms by land and by sea.

---

[1] Correlli Barnett, *The Collapse of British Power* (London, 1972).

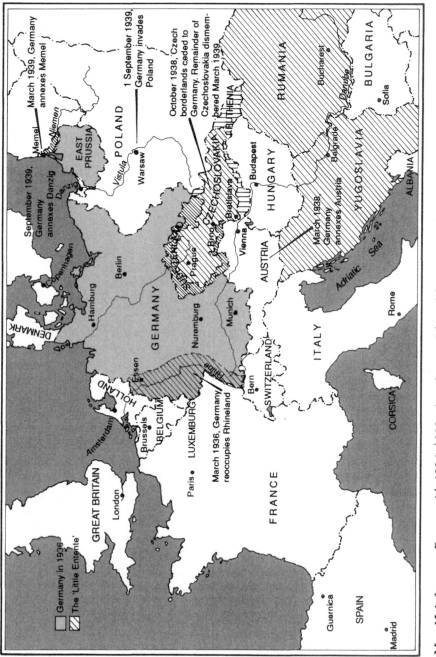

Map 13.1. Interwar Europe with 1936–1939 crises. *Source.* Adapted from Peter Calvocoressi and Guy Wint, *Total War: The Story of World War II* (New York: Pantheon, 1972), 68.

These prodigious victories, eclipsing all that had gone before, seemed the fit and predestined ending to the long drama of our island race, which had advanced over a thousand years from small and weak beginnings to a foremost position in the world. Three separate times in three different centuries had the British people rescued Europe from military domination. . . . Always at the outset the strength of the enemy had seemed overwhelming, always the struggle had been prolonged through many years and across awful hazards, always the victory had at last been won: and the last of all the victories had been the greatest of all, gained after the most ruinous struggle and over the most formidable foe. Surely that was the end of the tale as it was so often the end of the book. History showed the rise, culmination, splendor, transition and decline of States and Empires. It seemed inconceivable that the same series of tremendous events through which since the days of Queen Elizabeth we had three times made our way successfully, should be repeated a fourth time and on an immeasurably larger scale. Yet that is what has happened, and what we have lived to see.[2]

Several pages later as he mused on whether British statesmen might have prevented World War I, Churchill noted: "I cannot tell. I only know that we tried our best to steer our country through the gathering dangers of the armed peace without bringing her to war, and when these efforts failed, we drove through the tempest without bringing her to destruction."[3]

The cost of that "success" haunted British statesmen throughout the next three decades. In the war 744,702 British soldiers had died; the number of wounded was 1,693,262.[4] The best of a generation had disappeared on the Western Front.[5] And if those casualties had brought victory, success hardly seemed commensurate with the costs: Britain had gained a few worthless German colonies. The Turkish collapse in the Middle East brought the oil of Mesopotamia under British control, but along with expansion came the problems and costs involved in administering Arab territory from Palestine to Iraq. That commitment further stretched British forces, while conflict between Jews and Arabs in Palestine soon exacerbated Britain's problems in the Middle East, particularly after Hitler gained power in Germany.

From our perspective, one can understand the enormous difficulties confronting Allied statesmen at Paris in 1919. However, for those who had survived the war and had held high expectations throughout its terrible trials, the petty squabbles surrounding the drafting of the treaty caused terrible disillusionment. The Versailles treaty settled few of the great issues for which the allies had fought. John Maynard Keynes's devastating attack on the alleged greed and opportunism of the victors reinforced popular disillusionment. *The Economic Consequences of the Peace* appeared in fall 1919 after

2 Winston S. Churchill, *The World Crisis* (Toronto, 1931), p. 3.
3 Ibid., p. 6.
4 C.R.M.F. Cruttwell, *A History of the Great War* (Oxford, 1934), p. 630.
5 See particularly Vera Brittain's *Testament of Youth, An Autobiographical Study of the Years 1900–1925* (London, 1978) for a moving portrait of the impact of the terrible casualties on the women of Britain.

the ink on the treaty had barely dried[6]; few in Britain doubted thereafter that the peace was a monument of immorality.

Beyond disillusionment, the 1920s brought literary outpourings of memoirs, novels, and poetry underlining the horror of the trenches and the meaningless sacrifice of a generation of British youth.[7] By 1930 much of Britain's elite, not merely intellectuals but the political and governing classes as well, had become convinced that no victors had emerged from the Great War; rather all had lost. The corollary to this view was that there would be no victors in a future war – that in fact there was no cause, no conflict that justified the sacrifice of a nation's youth. The Oxford resolution of 1934 (when Oxford students ratified their refusal to fight for "King and country" regardless of the circumstances) underlined the extent to which Britain's "best and brightest" subscribed to this world-view.

In the stable 1920s the delusions of Britain's elites represented little danger to British security; in the harsher 1930s such views were exceedingly dangerous, blinding the British to the full extent of the threat. Worse still, those who held such views also assumed that the other powers no longer regarded war as an instrument of policy and would shun it if offered a reasonable compromise.

British statesmen all too often introduced misguided notions of fair play and moral principle into their calculations about the international arena. In the 1920s, this led to efforts at playing the honest broker on the continent between France and Germany. By the 1930s it led to an explicit rejection of the balance-of-power approach to strategic and diplomatic issues. In July 1938, for example, Lord Halifax, Foreign Secretary, announced to the Cabinet that he had debated "whether it was worthwhile to draft an appeal to the contending sides in Spain to stop the war. Such an appeal would, of course, be based on grounds of humanity, Christianity, the peace of the world and so forth. He feared that it would not be likely to succeed, but it would strengthen the moral position of His Majesty's Government and might put them in a position to take helpful action later on."[8] Nevile Henderson, ambassador to Germany, wrote Halifax during the same summer:

> Personally I just sit and pray for one thing, namely that Lord Runciman [Chamberlain's and Halifax's special arbitrator in the Sudetenland] will live up to the role of impartial British liberal statesman. I cannot believe that he will allow himself to be influenced by ancient history or even arguments about strategic frontiers and economics in preference to high moral principles. The great and courageous game which you and the Prime Minister are playing will be lost in

---

6   J. M. Keynes, *The Economic Consequences of the Peace* (London, 1919).
7   This is hardly the place to give a comprehensive list of the antiwar literature, but the unfamiliar reader might begin with Guy Chapman, *A Passionate Prodigality* (London, 1933); Frederick Manning, *The Middle Parts of Fortune* (London, 1930); and Siegfried Sassoon, *Memoirs of an Infantry Officer* (London, 1930).
8   PRO CAB 23/94, Cab 32 (38), Meeting of the Cabinet, 13.7.38 p. 134.

my humble opinion if he does not come out on this side of the higher principles
for which the British Empire really stands.[9]

The German foreign office and government reinforced these British attitudes through a massive disinformation campaign. The Germans systematically distorted the historical record and presented World War I as a conflict
in which no nation bore any greater share of responsibility than any other by
careful editing, alteration, and suppression of documents, patronage of aca-
demics with "the right point of view," and skillful polemics that "proved"
Germany innocent of "war guilt."[10] This disinformation campaign succeeded beyond the wildest expectations of its perpetrators. By 1930 a substantial portion of the Anglo-American intellectual community and of informed opinion in general had concluded that Germany held no more
responsibility for the war than any other major power. It required only a
short step to the conclusion that the Versailles settlement had seriously
wronged Germany. For much of the interwar period, many British leaders
consequently perceived their policy to be morally wrong whenever it sought
to uphold the strategic status quo by maintaining the Versailles treaty.

Such pro-German attitudes directly affected Anglo-French relations, and
often led to callous and mean-spirited treatment of Britain's continental ally.
As early as 1920, even Maurice Hankey, the Cabinet's often far-sighted
secretary, had written off a British continental commitment to France.[11] A
substantial portion of what passed for strategic thinking in Britain during the
interwar period was thus an effort to legitimize this flight from the continent.
B. H. Liddell Hart's *The British Way in Warfare* argued this point ad nau-
seam: According to him, Britain's traditional strategic policy involved attacks on the periphery while allies shouldered the burden of defeating the
threat on the continent, a strategy he termed one of "limited liability" and
one that Neville Chamberlain seized upon as the foundation of British strategic policy in the late 1930s.[12] At best, the British tolerated the French and
refused to recognize that they had legitimate security fears in the face of a
recovered and rearmed Germany. Not until the great scare of early 1939 over
German "plans" for a surprise air attack based on control of Holland did the
British awake to the possibility that France might be as important to British
security as Britain was to French security.[13]

---

[9] *Documents on British Foreign Policy (DGFP)*, 3rd. Ser., Vol. 2, Doc. #590, 6.8.38., letter
from Henderson to Halifax.
[10] See particularly, Holger Herwig's brilliant article, "Clio Deceived, Patriotic Self-Censorship
in Germany After the Great War," *International Security* (Fall 1987).
[11] See Stephen Roskill, *Hankey, Man of Secrets*, Vol. 2, *1919–1931* (Annapolis, 1972) pp.
209–10.
[12] B. H. Liddell Hart, *The British Way in Warfare* (London, 1932). For the best discussion of
Liddell Hart as a military and strategic thinker, see: Brian Bond, *Liddell Hart, A Study of
His Military Thought* (New Brunswick, N.J., 1977).
[13] As an example of British cavalier insensitivity to French feelings, see Chamberlain's
December 1938 remark in the House of Commons that Britain had no obligation to come

Yet the British enjoyed substantial advantages. Geography – particularly the position of the British Isles off the continent – afforded them time and perspective to recover from their errors when the day of reckoning came in 1939. As important was the British form of government: no matter how willfully naive Anglo-American democracies can be, they do permit the replacement of incompetent leadership. Thus Neville Chamberlain lost his position in early May 1940, overtly because of the Norwegian debacle, but in reality because his strategic policies had failed so dismally. Halifax and Churchill were the alternatives; Halifax's unwillingness to take responsibility gave the mantle to Churchill. It is worth contrasting this situation with that in the Soviet Union a year later. There, on 22 June 1941, *no* alternative remained but to soldier on under the leadership of the man whose diplomatic, strategic, and military policies had thrust the Soviet Union into the jaws of defeat.

THE ADMINISTRATIVE MACHINE

At the beginning of the twentieth century, the British erected a system for analyzing strategic and military problems confronting the empire. Before World War I, they created the Committee of Imperial Defence (CID) to bring together military, financial, economic, diplomatic, and governmental perspectives to achieve a coherent and coordinated defense policy. The initial efforts involved some stumbling, yet in stark contrast to Wilhelmine Germany, the British addressed the crucial issues that confronted them in the decade before the war.[14] During the war itself, the system broke down (the CID no longer met after 1915), and British difficulties in evolving a coherent wartime strategy partially reflected that institutional breakdown.

After the war, Hankey pushed Lloyd George to reestablish the CID, but his efforts met with little initial success.[15] When Lloyd George fell, Hankey found himself and the Cabinet Secretariat under siege. Bizarre attacks by the Beaverbrook and Rothermere press argued that efficient, effective coordination of Cabinet decisions was distinctly "unconstitutional" and un-British – muddling through was the ideal.[16] Hankey, however, not only survived to resurrect the CID, but by the 1930s created a whole set of subcommittees under the CID, which included the Chiefs of Staff (COS), the Joint Intelligence Committee, and a Joint Planning Committee made up of the chief planners of the three services. Hankey's biographer has quite rightly praised this system as a major factor in Britain's survival in World War II.[17] This

to the aid of France in case of Italian attack (PRO FO 371/21593, C 15385, 15505/13/17).

[14] For the best study of the CID, see Franklyn Arthur Johnson, *Defence by Committee, The British Committee of Imperial Defence, 1885–1959* (London, 1960).

[15] Roskill, *Hankey*, pp. 156–57.

[16] Ibid., p. 309.

[17] Stephen Roskill, *Hankey, Man of Secrets*, Vol. 3 (London, 1974), p. 419.

carefully structured system of intertwined committees and subcommittees allowed the British to prepare thorough and intelligent analyses of the strategic situation. Above all, the system rested on the accumulation of knowledge and experience in assessing the world balance of power since the end of the previous century. It is worth contrasting the output of the British system with the amateurish products of the OKW (*Oberkommando der Wehrmacht*) and OKH (*Oberkommando des Heeres*) during the same period. Even allowing for the idiosyncracies of Hitler's regime, the Germans were simply out of their league.[18] So too were the Americans, as George C. Marshall and his planners from the American Chiefs of Staff discovered at the Casablanca Conference in January 1943.

But problems existed. When the Prime Minister failed to exercise strong leadership, the bureaucracy could tie itself in knots. Britain's response to the rising threat from Nazi Germany suggests the dimensions of the problem. Beginning in November 1933, Hankey, Robert Vansittart, and Warren Fisher, together with the COS, formed the Defence Requirements Committee to work out a rearmament program to address the more glaring mismatches between British military strength and commitments.[19] After much wrangling, the committee recommended four months later that Britain spend 71 million pounds over five years to upgrade the armed forces.[20] The Cabinet then ignored the report for a month before referring its recommendations to another committee, the Committee on the Disarmament Conference. After more argument, particularly from the Treasury, the Cabinet finally agreed to an amended set of recommendations on 31 July 1934.[21] The process had consumed eight months, countless discussions, and vast amounts of paper to achieve an insignificant increase in defense expenditure. The endless discussions reflected the lackadaisical style of the MacDonald-Baldwin years.

But strong leadership could also move the system toward faulty strategic decisions. Chamberlain clearly manipulated strategic assessments toward conclusions congruent with his policies. After the occupation of Austria, the Prime Minister's terms of reference to the COS for evaluating Czechoslovakia's strategic prospects assumed the "worst case" in every respect. Chamberlain simply removed the Soviet Union from the strategic equation; the Prime Minister and Halifax then used the resulting survey to "prove" that the Soviet Union could not affect the balance.[22] In the post-Munich period, when much of British public opinion even within the Conservative Party favored accelerating defense programs, Chamberlain used Hankey's commit-

---

[18] See my article "Net Assessment in Nazi Germany in the 1930s," in *Calculations, Net Assessment and the Coming of World War II*, Allan R. Millett and Williamson Murray (New York, 1992).

[19] PRO CAB 16/109, 14 Nov. 1933, 1st Meeting of the D.R.C.

[20] PRO CAB 24/247, CP 64 (34), 5.3.34.

[21] Robert Paul Shay, Jr., *British Rearmament in the Thirties* (Princeton, 1977), p. 44.

[22] See Williamson Murray, *The Change in the European Balance of Power, 1938–1939, The Path to Ruin* (Princeton, 1985), pp. 156–162.

tee system to thwart substantial changes in policy. The bureaucracy's blizzard of reports led a frustrated Vansittart to proclaim:

> The other point which I wish to make is that relating to procedure. . . . It seems clear that all the machinery here contemplated will involve the maximum delay and accumulation of papers. We surely do not want any more written "European Appreciations." We have been snowed under with papers from the Committee of Imperial Defense for years. Moreover, this procedure by stages implies a certain leisureliness which is not what we want at the present moment.[23]

In addition to bureaucratic delay, the conflicting and fiercely argued agendas of the participants frequently got in the way of accurate assessment:

> [P]olitical decision makers were confronted with an amalgam of *service generated* data and assumptions, which it was difficult for busy Cabinet ministers to challenge with any great knowledge of their own. Even the creation of the Minister for the Coordination of Defense did not fully grapple with this fundamental problem, that the "building blocks" of information and judgement came not from objective, independent sources. To be sure, the Minister could often recommend to the Cabinet *spending priorities,* as between the various services' bids, but it was much more difficult to contest the Admiralty's assessment of the Japanese navy or the army's plans to deal with the Wehrmacht on the battlefield. Those were internal matters on which the military was fully unchallengeable.[24]

The bureaucratic process generally allowed the British to focus on their long-term goals: preservation of the Empire and maintenance of economic and political power. Upholding these goals in the face of the challenge of the late 1930s and early 1940s may well have been impossible. Cultural and social factors made the British slow to recognize the virulence of the threat; Chamberlain's policies failed because Hitler's aims were unlimited.

The appointment of Churchill as prime minister, ironically on 10 May 1940, supplied the crucial element in making Hankey's system work. Widely read in history, a practicing historian of skill and eloquence,[25] a man with extraordinary experience in government, Churchill possessed a great store of accumulated wisdom upon which to draw. Moreover, he had had twenty years to reflect on the failures of government in World War I. Consequently, he was able to extract the most from the British system of government.[26]

---

23 PRO FO 371/22922, C 1545/281/17, Minutes by Sir Robert Vansittart, 10.2.38., criticizing CP 40 (39), "Staff Conversations with France and Belgium."

24 Paul Kennedy, "British 'Net Assessment' and the Coming of the Second World War, 1935–1941," in *Calculations, Net Assessment and the Coming of World War II.*

25 For a perceptive critique of Churchill's histories, see Maurice Ashley, *Churchill as Historian* (New York, 1968).

26 For two excellent short studies of Churchill as a strategist see Eliot A. Cohen, "Churchill and Coalition Strategy in World War II," in *Studies in Grand Strategy,* Paul Kennedy, ed., (New Haven, 1990) and Eliot A. Cohen, "Churchill at War," *Commentary,* May 1987. The massive volumes by Martin Gilbert, *Winston S. Churchill,* Vol. 6, *Finest Hour, 1939–1941* (Boston, 1983) and Vol. 7, *Road to Victory, 1941–1945* (Boston, 1986) are crucial to understanding Churchill as statesman and strategist in World War II.

Churchill's relationship with the system was not an easy one, as the wartime diaries of the Chief of the Imperial General Staff (CIGS), Field Marshal Alanbrooke, attest.[27] Churchill badgered, cajoled, and often hounded subordinates, although he never drove them to make decisions against their better judgment. By and large, his judgment proved superior, and he provided inspiration not only to the British but to the Americans as well. Moreover, he listened to the ideas and warnings of the scientific establishment. Thus, R.V. Jones, a scientist in his twenties, convinced the Prime Minister of the existence and danger of *Knickebein* (a German blind bombing device), despite disbelief from scientific and military authorities.[28] As one commentator has noted:

> It must be conceded, in addition, that Churchill *enjoyed* leading a nation at war, and delighted in grappling with the myriad challenges of supreme command. By no means bloodthirsty, . . . he did have the ruthlessness required of a warlord. In the dilemmas and perplexities of strategy he found problems which summoned forth the prodigious energies of his mind. He had also trained his intellect in peacetime to deal with these problems through his writings as a historian. . . . A Churchill is not merely a rarity, but a phenomenon: no politician could hope to become such through study or self-conscious imitation, and indeed our times and world position can hardly produce his like.[29]

Part of Churchill's brilliance lay in his innate ability to separate the essential from the inessential; part rested on his restless, unceasing diligence and energy; and part on experience. A short memorandum of late December 1939, written in response to COS opposition to mining the Norwegian Leads and in favor of massive intervention in northern Scandinavia, suggests his power of argument as well as his ability to get to the heart of the matter:

> The self contained minor operation of stopping the ore from Narvik and at Oxelsund must not be tried because it would jeopardize the larger plan. The larger plan must not be attempted unless Sweden and Norway cooperate. Not merely must they not resist militarily or adopt a purely passive attitude, but they must actively cooperate. . . . But is there any prospect of Sweden and Norway actually cooperating with us of their own free will to bring about a series of operations which as is well set out in their [Chief of Staffs'] paper will (a) ruin the trade of their ironfield and the shipping which carries it. (b) involve them in a war with Germany. (c) expose the whole southern part of both countries to German invasion and occupation? Left to themselves they will certainly refuse, and, if pressed diplomatically, they will protest loudly to the

---

27 See Arthur Bryant, *The Turn of the Tide, A History of the War Years Based on the Diaries of Field-Marshal Lord Alanbrooke, Chief of the Imperial General Staff* (Garden City, N.Y., 1957); and Arthur Bryant, *Triumph in the West, 1943–1946, Based on the Diaries and Autobiographical Notes of Field Marshal The Viscount Alanbrooke* (London, 1959).

28 R. V. Jones, *The Wizard War, British Scientific Intelligence, 1939–1945* (New York, 1978), pp. 100–102.

29 Cohen, "Churchill at War," p. 48.

world. Thus, the minor operation is knocked out for the sake of the bigger, and the bigger is only declared practicable upon conditions that will not occur.[30]

Throughout the war British military leaders found their proposals and arguments under constant scrutiny from the Prime Minister; when their responses justified their positions they could move forward, but not until they had satisfied a demanding and knowledgeable taskmaster. British success in grand strategy rested on the partnership of Churchill's energy and insight with a responsive bureaucracy.

THE ECONOMIC CONSTRAINTS ON STRATEGY

Effective strategy demands financial resources and the industrial strength to provide military staying power. Since the late nineteenth century the economic underpinnings of British strategy had steadily eroded. Even before World War I British leaders had recognized that their relative world position was declining.[31] Britain's industrial domination, established in the mid-nineteenth century, had largely disappeared. The post-1918 period further underlined Britain's tenuous position in the emerging economic balance; in fact, decline was no longer relative but in many respects absolute. Moreover, economic recovery from the postwar economic slump was depressingly slow. Table 13.1 on comparative manufacturing production suggests this acceleration of Britain's industrial decline.

Britain's ailing economic infrastructure received a further shock with the Depression and the 1931 financial crisis. Textile production fell by two-thirds; coal by one-fifth; Britain's shipbuilding industry had fallen to 7 percent of its pre-1914 volume by 1933; steel and pig iron production dropped by 45 and 53 percent respectively from 1929 to 1932.[32] This depressing economic situation showed only slight improvement in the late 1930s. Throughout the 1930s the British economy depended on foreign exchange earned by exports to pay for substantial portions of its imports. After 1931, Britain achieved a favorable balance of trade only in 1935 (Table 13.2). The actual balance of trade, not including income from overseas investments, was even less favorable (Table 13.3). Fear of a crisis similar to that of 1931 compounded these trends. Consequently, throughout the late 1930s worries over the economy and over possible overexpenditure on defense dominated rearmament policy. As Chamberlain emphasized in December 1937, "the maintenance of Britain's economic stability represented an essential element in the maintenance of her defensive strength."[33] British fears of economic

---

[30] PRO CAB 66/4, WP (40) 3, 31.12.39., "Swedish Iron Ore," W.S.C.
[31] See Aaron L. Friedburg, *The Weary Titan, Britain and the Experience of Relative Decline, 1895–1905* (Princeton, 1988).
[32] Paul Kennedy, *The Rise and Fall of the Great Powers, Economic Change and Military Conflict From 1500 to 2000* (New York, 1987), p. 316.
[33] PRO CAB 23/90A Cab 49 (37), Meeting of the Cabinet, 22.9.37., p. 373.

Table 13.1. *Annual indices of manufacturing production, 1913–1938*

	World	U.S.	Germany	U.K.	France	USSR	Italy	Japan
	(1913 = 100)							
1913	100.0	100.0	100.0	100.0	100.0	100.0	100.0	100.0
1920	93.2	122.2	59.0	92.6	70.4	12.8	95.2	176.0
1921	81.1	98.0	74.7	55.1	61.4	23.3	98.4	167.1
1922	99.5	125.8	81.8	73.5	87.8	28.9	108.1	197.9
1923	104.5	141.4	55.4	79.1	95.2	35.4	119.3	206.4
1924	111.0	133.2	81.8	87.8	117.9	47.5	140.7	223.3
1925	120.7	148.0	94.9	86.3	114.3	70.2	156.8	221.8
1926	126.5	156.1	90.9	78.8	129.8	100.3	162.8	264.9
1927	134.5	154.5	122.1	96.0	115.6	114.5	161.2	270.0
1928	141.8	162.8	118.3	95.1	134.4	143.5	175.2	300.2
1929	153.3	180.8	117.3	100.3	142.7	181.4	181.0	324.0
1930	137.5	148.0	101.6	91.3	139.9	235.5	164.0	294.9
1931	122.5	121.6	85.1	82.4	122.6	293.9	145.1	288.1
1932	108.4	93.7	70.2	82.5	105.4	326.1	123.3	309.1
1933	121.7	111.8	79.4	83.3	119.8	363.2	133.2	360.7
1934	136.4	121.6	101.8	100.2	111.4	437.0	134.7	413.5
1935	154.5	140.3	116.7	107.9	109.1	533.7	162.2	457.8
1936	178.1	171.0	127.5	119.1	116.3	693.3	169.2	483.9
1937	195.8	185.8	138.1	127.8	123.8	772.2	194.5	551.0
1938	182.7	143.0	149.3	117.6	114.6	857.3	195.2	552.0

Source: Paul Kennedy, *The Rise and Fall of the Great Powers, Economic Change and Military Conflict from 1500 to 2000* (New York, 1987), p. 299.

Table 13.2. *British balance of payments, 1928–1938 (not including gold)*

Year	million pounds	Year	million pounds
1928	+123	1934	−7
1929	+103	1935	+32
1930	+28	1936	−18
1931	−104	1937	−56
1932	−51	1938	−55
1933	0		

Source: R.S. Sayers, *The Bank of England, 1891–1944*, Vol. III (London, 1976), appendix 32, table A, pp. 308–309.

Table 13.3. *British balance of trade, 1929–1938 (in million pounds)*

	1929	1930	1931	1932	1933	1934
Imports	1,117	953	786	641	619	683
Exports	854	670	464	425	427	463
Balance	−263	−283	−322	−216	−192	−220

	1935	1936	1937	1938		
	724	786	950	849		
	541	523	614	564		
	−183	−263	−336	−285		

Source: Sayers, *The Bank of England, 1891–1944*, Vol. III, Table C, pp. 312–313.

vulnerability increased with the passage of neutrality laws in the United States: after all, the British had been able to finance World War I only through American loans. They failed to recognize, however, that the German economy was even more vulnerable than their own, and that their potential opponents had no prospect of outside help.

The German occupation of Prague in March 1939 finally forced Chamberlain to abandon his business as usual approach and to launch a massive program of rearmament, although the Treasury remained adamant in its claims that rearmament would bankrupt Britain. In April 1939 Sir Alan Barlow, Under Secretary of the Treasury, warned that Britain's economic "position had radically changed for the worse from 1914" and that the country could not support a long war.[34] Barlow's warning came true in summer 1940 when the Churchill government, facing the Wehrmacht, also confronted the fact that it lacked the financial resources to pay for further armaments from the United States. Churchill took considerable risks in pushing for maximum production to make good the losses on the continent and to fight the Battle of Britain. Then the successes of summer and fall 1940 persuaded the Americans that Britain was worth supporting through Lend-Lease; that outcome was Britain's most important strategic success of the war. Churchill quite rightly described the resulting Lend-Lease program as "so great an event in the history of our two nations."[35] Only United States financial and economic aid removed the threat of insolvency and allowed full mobilization of industrial and manpower resources.

A report of late 1944 suggests the extent of that mobilization and the level of sacrifice demanded of the British people:

[34] PRO CAB 16/209, SAC/4th Meeting, CID, Strategic Appreciations Sub-Committee, p. 75.
[35] Gilbert, *Winston S. Churchill*, Vol. 6, p. 1,032.

The British civilian has had five years of blackout and four years of intermittent blitz. The privacy of his home has been periodically invaded by soldiers or evacuees or war workers requiring billets. In five years of drastic labor mobilization, nearly every man and every woman under fifty without young children has been subject to directions to work, often far from home. The hours of work average fifty-three for men and fifty overall; when work is done, every citizen who is not excused for reasons of family circumstances, work, etc., has had to do forty-eight hours a month duty in the Home Guard or Civil Defense. Supplies of all kinds have been progressively limited by shipping and manpower shortage; the queue is part of normal life. Taxation is probably the severest in the world, and is coupled with continuous pressure to save. The scarce supplies, both of goods and services, must be shared with hundreds of thousands of United States, Dominion, and Allied troops; in the preparation of Britain first as the base and then as the bridgehead, the civilian has had inevitably suffered hardships spread over almost every aspect of his daily life.[36]

This sacrifice made possible the mobilization of national resources to an extraordinary extent, so much so that industrial production reached a plateau in 1942 from which the economy largely failed to make further advances. Ernest Bevin, Minister of Labour, warned his colleagues as early as May 1941:

The chief conclusion which I draw from these figures is that we have now deployed our main forces and drawn heavily upon our reserves. . . . Further demands for the Forces must in the main be met from production. To make this good and maintain essential service, as well as increase production, something can still be obtained from [the] redistribution of labour within the field of industry and services, but our main reliance must be upon increased efficiency in management to secure the best use of the resources that we have.[37]

Indices of British production are indeed impressive; Britain outproduced Germany for much of the war in many categories of weapons despite the Reich's far larger industrial base. But numbers can be misleading. In the air, Britain held its own against the Luftwaffe's best. The "Lancaster" was the finest heavy bomber of the European war, the "Spitfire" one of the best short-range fighters, and the "Mosquito" the best strategic bomber, photo reconnaissance aircraft, night fighter, and night intruder. Unfortunately, British ground equipment was miserable. The 2-pounder anti-tank gun was completely inadequate, a result of the army's underfunding during the 1930s. Inadequate funding, however, only explains part of the problem; failures in the last half of the war are less easy to excuse. Design and production of British tanks were scandalous even given the weaknesses of the motor industry. The "Covenanter" tank appeared in summer 1940 in such a sorry state

---

36 W. K. Hancock and M. M. Gowing, *British War Economy* (London, 1949), p. 519.
37 Michael Howard, *Grand Strategy*, Vol. 4, *August 1942-September 1943* (London, 1972), p. 3.

that the entire vehicle required reconstruction from the bottom up.[38] When the "Churchill" went into test stage, it had a top speed of only 8–9 mph because of faulty suspension. In 1942 "Churchills" were failing acceptance tests at 150 miles![39] Throughout the war, the British failed to produce a reliable truck to support their mechanized forces.[40] Even more distressing was the fact that while British science led in the development of radar and navigational devices, actual production of electronic equipment depended heavily on American components.[41]

A declining and backward economy impeded the full achievement of Britain's strategic goals in World War II. But these deficiencies were no more severe than the tactical and operational inadequacies that handicapped battlefield performance throughout the war.[42] Similar deficiencies in World War I had resulted in the debacles at Gallipoli and Paschendaele. They also help to explain British difficulties in the Western Desert in 1941–42 and the catastrophe in Malaya. But the British generally avoided such disasters thanks to Churchill's guidance. His strategic approach maximized the potential of a nation already sinking toward second-class status. From our vantage point it is easy to identify Britain's weaknesses in 1945; the mark of Churchill's genius is that so little of that decline was obvious then.

PERCEPTIONS OF THE THREAT

This essay encompasses three distinct periods: 1919–1933, 1933–1939, and 1939–1945. Within each period different perceptions and attitudes guided British strategy. Immediately after World War I, the dominant theme was that such a war must never again happen, and however depressing the postwar world looked, no threat loomed on the horizon. Russia had collapsed into revolutionary chaos; Weimar Germany had its hands full – in the east with its new neighbors and in the west with its old antagonist, France. The Pacific Dominions worried about Japan, but from the British perspective Japan appeared of little immediate concern.

In the early 1920s the British worried most about another naval race, this time with the Japanese and the Americans. None of the contestants had much stomach for the race: the British and the Japanese because they had

---

[38]   M. M. Postan, D. Hay, and J. D. Scott, *The Design and Development of Weapons: Studies in Government and Industrial Organisation* (London, 1964), p. 313.

[39]   Ibid., p. 339.

[40]   Martin van Creveld, *Supplying War, Logistics from Wallenstein to Patton* (Cambridge, 1977), p. 216.

[41]   For an excellent discussion of the failings of Britain's industrial base see Correlli Barnett, *The Audit of War, The Illusions and Reality of Britain as a Great Nation* (London, 1986), Chapter 9.

[42]   See Williamson Murray, "British Military Effectiveness in the Second World War," in *Military Effectiveness*, Vol. 3, *The Second World War*, Allan R. Millett and Williamson Murray, eds., (London, 1989).

little prospect of winning against the Americans; the Americans because an electorate eager to return to "normalcy" was reluctant to support massive naval expenditures. The outcome was the 1922 Washington Naval Treaty, which established a battleship ratio of 5–5–3 between the three great naval powers, Britain, the United States, and Japan.[43] In the long run, the treaty contributed to the obsolescence of the British battle fleet (most British battleships had been laid down earlier than their Japanese and American counterparts). But it is hard to see how a British government could have enlisted popular support to match even the Japanese in a naval race.

As early as summer 1919, the British Cabinet had decided on what later came to be called the "Ten Year Rule" – the Cabinet instructed the services to plan their budgets on the assumption that no major conflict would occur for ten years. The ten year date moved forward every year until the early 1930s. Even if it were hard to see any prospective threat, the rule led British governments to evade their responsibility of providing a minimum base from which rearmament might begin. A further result was the shattering of any common strategic approach for the three services: the RAF planned "strategic" bombing campaigns against continental enemies (either Germany or France)[44]; the Royal Navy looked to the Pacific; and the army stuck pigs on the Indian frontier.

This relatively placid environment altered radically in the 1930s as the Japanese invasion of Manchuria in 1931 underlined the weaknesses of the League of Nations. Ironically, the dismal strategic results of the Manchurian crisis only confirmed many Britons in their belief in the efficacy of the League.[45] Then the arrival of Adolf Hitler in January 1933 thoroughly upset the European balance. Within three years, the Abyssinian crisis added Fascist Italy to the list of Britain's potential enemies. As Paul Kennedy suggests:

> Perhaps the greatest difference between British net assessment in the 1930s and American net assessment in (say) the 1960s was the extraordinary *fluidity and multipolarity* of the international scene in the earlier period. At the beginning of the 1930s, the British widely regarded the Soviet Union as the greatest land enemy of the Empire, while in naval terms the chief rivals were the United States and Japan. They saw Mussolini's Italy as tempermental, France as unduly assertive and difficult (but not hostile), and Germany as still prostrate. Five or eight years later, Japan appeared as a distinct challenge to British interests in the Far East, Germany had fallen under Nazi rule and was assessed as the "greatest long-term danger," and Italy's policies appeared aggressive and hostile, whereas the United States was more unpredictable and isolationist than ever [my italics].[46]

---

43 See Roskill, *Hankey, Man of Secrets*, Vol. 2, pp. 238–57.
44 See Trenchard's comments about a possible air war between Britain and France in Sir Charles Webster and Noble Frankland, *The Strategic Air Offensive Against Germany, 1939–1945*, Vol. 4, Annex and Appendice (London, 1961), Appendix 1.
45 The most thorough discussion of the Manchurian Crisis is Christopher Thorne, *The Limits of Foreign Policy* (London, 1972).
46 Kennedy, "British 'Net Assessment' and the Coming of the Second World War," p. 35.

Senior British ministers and their advisers quite rightly regarded the Germans as the most serious potential opponent.[47] Nevertheless, getting to Singapore to face the Japanese posed intractable logistical difficulties for the Royal Navy, while the Italians lay across Britain's line of communications to India and Asia.

One of the inexplicable aspects of Britain's response to the increasingly dangerous strategic environment lay in how military and intelligence experts evaluated the threats. Until 1935, their assessments were gloomy but did not project immediate catastrophe. In the event of German rearmament, they calculated that the Germans, confronting many of the same problems as Britain, would not pose a serious threat until the early 1940s.[48] In 1936 a substantial about-face occurred as the British recognized that the Germans were expanding at breakneck speed, taking military and economic risks that no British government would have dared take.

For the next three years British analysts painted the strategic picture in the gloomiest colors. Not only did they ascribe extraordinarily high military capabilities and potential to Germany, but they also denigrated their own capabilities and those of prospective allies such as the French. The Soviet Union and the United States might as well as not have existed. Moreover, the British expected Germans, Japanese, and Italians to act in unison in any future conflict, even though the "China incident" bogged the Japanese down after summer 1937.[49] Military appreciations almost uniformly exaggerated Italian strength.[50] Estimates of German aircraft production were generally accurate, but Air Staff depictions of Luftwaffe combat potential erred wildly.[51] Similarly, estimates of the German army's size were accurate, but figures on reserve forces and armament production were enormously exaggerated.[52] In

---

[47]   See Norman Gibbs, *Grand Strategy,* Vol. 1, *Rearmament Policy* (London, 1976).

[48]   Wesley Wark, *The Ultimate Enemy, British Intelligence and Nazi Germany, 1933–1939* (Ithaca, 1985) presents a useful study of shifts in assessments during this period.

[49]   See PRO CAB 53/8, COS/227 the Meeting, 19.1.38., COS Sub-Committee, Minutes, Annex: Memorandum by the CNS; CAB 23/90A, CAB 46(37), Meeting of the Cabinet, 8.12.37.; CAB 53/51, CP 30(36), 7.2.36., Cabinet, CID, Defense Coordination Paper written by Hankey; CAB 16/181 DP(P) 2nd Meeting, 11.5.37., "New Naval Construction," CID, Defense Plans (Policy) Sub-Committee; CAB 16/183A, DP(P) 48, 19.4.39., CID, "The Dispatch of the Fleet to the Far East in the Event of War Against Japan," Memorandum by the DCNS.

[50]   From the beginning of the Abyssinian crisis, the COS and particularly the naval staff under Chatfield gave inflated estimates of Italian military power; see among others: PRO CAB 53/26, COS 421 (JP), 19.12.35., COS Sub-Committee, "Defense in the Eastern Mediterranean and the Middle East: Report by the Joint Planning Sub-Committee."

[51]   See Williamson Murray, "The Change in the European Balance of Power, 1938–1939," Ph.D. dissertation, Yale University, 1975, pp. 74–77.

[52]   PRO CAB 55/8, JP 155, 12.10.36., Joint Planning Sub-Committee, "Appreciation of the Situation in the Event of War Against Germany in 1939;" CAB 24/27, 1921/B, 22.4.38., CID, "The German Army: Its Present Strength and Possible Rate of Expansion in Peace and War."

contrast, British estimates of French capabilities through 1938 were thoroughly pessimistic.[53]

The conclusion to the gloomy March 1938 COS study on the prospects of the West in a war over Czechoslovakia best sums up the military's notions about the strategic environment of the late 1930s:

> We conclude that no pressure that we and our possible allies can bring to bear, either by sea, on land or in the air could prevent Germany from invading and overrunning Bohemia and from inflicting a decisive defeat on the Czechoslovakian army. We should then be faced with the necessity of undertaking a war against Germany for the purpose of restoring Czechoslovakia's lost integrity and this object would only be achieved by the defeat of Germany and the outcome of a prolonged struggle. In the world situation today it seems to us [that] . . . Italy and Japan would seize the opportunity to further their own ends and that in consequence the problem we have to envisage is not that of a limited European war only, but of a World War. On this situation we reported as follows some four months ago: "Without overlooking the assistance we should hope to obtain from France and possibly other allies, we cannot foresee the time when our defense forces will be strong enough to safeguard our territory, trade and vital interests against Germany, Italy, and Japan simultaneously."[54]

Appeasement was the result of symbiosis between the "worst case" analysis of German capabilities by Britain's military experts and the "best case" analysis of German intentions by Britain's political leadership. By nature, Chamberlain and Halifax could not understand men like Hitler and Mussolini; Chamberlain actually believed, as he once remarked to his Foreign Secretary, that the dictators "were men of moods – catch them in the right mood and they will give you anything you ask for."[55] After visiting Hitler at Berchtesgaden in mid-September 1938, Chamberlain told his Cabinet colleagues that "the impression left on him was that Herr Hitler meant what he said."[56] One week later, after the disastrous second meeting with Hitler at Bad Godesberg, Chamberlain suggested to the Cabinet that

> Herr Hitler had certain standards. (He spoke now with greater confidence on this point than after his first visit.) Herr Hitler had a narrow mind and was violently prejudiced on certain subjects; but he would not deliberately deceive a

53 Compare the figures for French Army Strength given in CAB 53/37, COS 698 (Revise), COS Sub-Committee, 28.3.38., "Military Implications of German Aggression Against Czechoslovakia"; and CAB 53/40, COS 747(JP), 15.7.38., COS Sub-Committee, "Appreciations of the Situation in the Event of War Against Germany in April 1939: Joint Planning Sub-Committee Appreciation" with the estimate of French military strength in CAB 55/16, JP 407, 15.5.39., Joint Planning Sub-Committee, "Staff Conversations with Poland."

54 PRO CAB 53/37, COS 698 (Revise) (also see paper DP[P] 22), CID, COS Sub-Committee, "Military Implications of German Aggression Against Czechoslovakia," 28.3.38., p. 152.

55 PRO PREM 1/276, Chamberlain to Halifax.

56 PRO CAB 23/95, Cab 39(38), Meeting of the Cabinet, 17.9.38., p. 64.

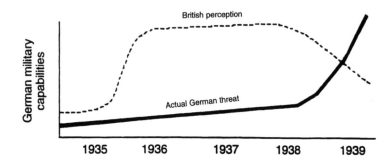

Figure 13.1. British perception of the German threat.

man whom he respected and with whom he had been in negotiations, and he was sure that Herr Hitler now felt some respect for him. When Herr Hitler announced that he meant to do something it was certain that he would do it.[57]

These attitudes, when combined with "worst case" analyses of the military situation, produced Britain's tragic policies of fall 1938, and almost led to defeat without struggle.

In 1939 a major shift occurred in British assessment. Popular pressure forced an unwilling Chamberlain government finally to embark on a rearmament program that addressed British military weaknesses, and to seek to contain Hitler through aggressive diplomacy. Ironically, these changes, which led to an extension of British commitments, resulted in more optimistic assessments of the strategic balance despite a marked deterioration of the military situation (see Figure 13.1). The explanation for this curious phenomenon apparently lies in the services' belief that the government had at last recognized the severe deficiencies of the military establishment and had begun serious rearmament. Moreover, the intelligence reports that filtered through a wall of disbelief in September 1938 had considerable impact on British assessment: everything indicated that the Germans would have confronted enormous organizational and operational problems had war come in fall 1938.[58]

Churchill's world-view was enormously different from that of the individuals who had guided British policy from 1919 to 1940. From the earliest days of Hitler's appointment as Chancellor, he recognized that the Nazis represented both a moral *and* a strategic danger. As he warned the readers of the *Daily Mail* in 1934:

[57] PRO CAB 23/95, Cab 42(38), Meeting of the Cabinet 24.9.38., p. 178.
[58] For an assessment of the military balance in the Czech crisis see Williamson Murray, *The Change in the European Balance of Power*, Chapter 7.

I marvel at the complacency of ministers in the face of the frightful experiences through which we have all so newly passed. I look with wonder upon the thoughtless crowds disporting themselves in the summer sunshine, and upon this unheeding House of Commons, which seems to have no higher function than to cheer a Minister; [and all the while, across the North Sea], a terrible process is astir. *Germany is arming!*[59]

Churchill made the difference in British strategy after assuming the prime ministership in May 1940. Yet by the time he took power, his predecessors had lost nearly all the advantages that Britain had once possessed. Germany had avoided a two-front war with the Hitler-Stalin pact, and the Western Powers had undertaken *no* action against the Nazis during the winter of 1939–1940. The degree of Allied strategic miscalculation became clear in the first weeks of the spring campaign.

For many, if not most on the continent, the French defeat presaged a similar British collapse. Churchill, however, estimated that the United States would not allow Britain to fall under Nazi control, nor did he believe that the unholy alliance between the Soviet Union and Nazi Germany could last. Hitler saw the situation in similar terms: British refusal to make peace in summer 1940 rested on the hope of eventual American and Soviet intervention.[60]

Churchill and his strategic advisers identified Germany as the greatest strategic threat, and after the beginning of BARBAROSSA, the Soviets came to the same conclusion. With the Americans, matters were not so easy. Roosevelt and Marshall had agreed on a "Germany first" strategy even before the United States found itself dragged into the conflict. But the event that brought the United States into the war, Pearl Harbor, also made concentration on Germany that much more difficult, for American opinion and the U.S. Navy inevitably regarded Japan as the main enemy. Nevertheless, Hitler's declaration of war on the United States immediately after Pearl Harbor suggested that an intimate alliance linked Germany and Japan.

Churchill easily maintained a close relationship with the United States, but the Soviets were more difficult partners. Unlike most of his military advisers, Churchill calculated that the Soviet Union would prove indigestible even to the Wehrmacht. Despite his long hostility to the Soviet regime, Churchill quickly embraced the opportunity that Barbarossa provided:

But all this fades away before the spectacle which is now unfolding. The past with its crimes, its follies and its tragedies, flashes away. . . . I see also the dull, docile, brutish masses of the Hun soldiery plodding on like a swarm of crawling locusts. I see the German bombers and fighters in the sky, still smarting from many a British whipping, delighted to find what they believe is an easier and safer prey. Any man or state who fights on against Nazidom will have our aid.

[59] Quoted in Gilbert, *Winston S. Churchill,* Vol. 5, p. 550.
[60] See the Franz Halder, *The Halder War Diary, 1939–1942,* Charles Burdick and Hans-Adolf Jacobsen, eds. (Novato, CA., 1988), p. 242.

Any man or state who marches with Hitler is our foe. . . . The Russian danger is therefore our danger, and the danger of the United States, just as the cause of any Russian fighting for his hearth and home is the cause of free men and free peoples in every quarter of the globe.[61]

But unlike most in the Western alliance, Churchill never entirely lost his suspicions of Stalin,[62] nor did he expect the tensions of international politics to disappear after Hitler's destruction. Given the dangers that Britain had faced in 1940, victory over the Reich was the overarching goal, but one that did not entirely obscure the realities of the emerging postwar world.

THE IMPLEMENTATION OF BRITISH STRATEGY

The strategic world confronting the British in 1919 was indeed a daunting one. Britain had carried the burden of fighting in 1918, and its troops, heavily reinforced by the dominions, had broken the German army in the great battles of late summer and fall. But while German military and naval power collapsed in revolution, the Reich's long-range prospects had improved compared with those of 1914. Germany now bordered on only one great power, a debilitated French Republic. In the east, the post-1919 successor states shielded postwar Germany from an exhausted Soviet Union.[63] To the south, Austria-Hungary's collapse had created a jumble of weak and quarreling states – a region open to German economic and political penetration as soon as the Reich regained its strength.

Only France remained steadfastly anti-German, and only French financial and political support maintained an anti-German front in East-Central Europe.[64] But France's prospects for holding Germany at bay rested on a weak economy, an exhausted population, and the dubious card of British support. Churchill caught the French mood accurately: "Worn down, doubly decimated, but undisputed master of the hour, the French nation peered into the future in thankful wonder and haunting dread. Where then was that SECURITY without which all that had been gained seemed valueless, and life itself, even amid the rejoicing of victory, was almost unendurable? The mortal need was Security. . . ."[65]

The failure to settle the German problem was the greatest weakness of the 1919 settlement, although that failure resulted more from the manner in

---

[61] Winston S. Churchill, *The Grand Alliance* (Boston, 1950), pp. 371–73.

[62] Gilbert, *Winston S. Churchill*, Vol. 7, p. 239.

[63] One of the astonishing aspects of postwar German reaction to their strategic situation was the consistent efforts of German leaders, military as well as civilian, from Seeckt to Hitler, to reach a compact with the Soviets to destroy Poland and reestablish a frontier with revolutionary Russia.

[64] See particularly, Piotr Wandycz, *France and Her Eastern Allies* (Minneapolis, 1962) and *The Twilight of French Eastern Alliances, 1926–1936* (Princeton, 1988).

[65] Winston S. Churchill, *The Gathering Storm* (Boston, 1948), p. 6.

which the war had ended than from the mistakes of Versailles. Hankey noted in his diary after visiting the sick Woodrow Wilson in 1921 that

> The ex-President was also very bitter against the French, who, he said were "up to their old games." Even for Foch he would not have a good word. He regards him as the ultimate author of all our difficulties. I said he was a first-rate General. To that he replied "That may be, but at the time of the armistice the Germans had broken his spirit and he would not fight on." This, no doubt, was harking back to Pershing's idea that we ought to have gone on with the war.[66]

In fact, the British had suggested even easier terms than the French in 1918 – Haig had proposed a withdrawal from Belgium and the surrender of the High Seas Fleet.[67]

By allowing the German army to return home "with honor," the allies helped propagate the infamous *Dolchstoss* legend – that German troops, unbeaten in the field, had been "stabbed in the back" by the Jews and the socialists – and allowed the preservation of the unitary German state. In the long run, few stabilizing factors prevented a renewed German attempt to gain hegemony on the continent. Unfortunately, British policies contributed to a weakening of France's position.

Yet the most ominous trends in Britain's position were economic and political. The war had eaten up a substantial portion of its financial reserves; its industrial decay had begun before the war; and victory failed to bring quick recovery. Economic and industrial decline struck at Britain's military potential. Illusions about the League of Nations and pious hopes that nations would reject the utility of military power also affected British potential. The Ten Year Rule reflected only the reality of British politics, for no consensus existed in support of even minimal defense spending levels. The elections of the mid 1930s sent politicians scurrying for cover from fear that the public might think the nation had embarked on a serious program of rearmament. Some form of appeasement was thus inevitable given popular attitudes and the British economic and strategic predicament.

Historians have tended to see the history of the 1930s as a logical progression: refusal to stand up against Japanese aggression in Manchuria in 1931 led to Italian aggression against Abyssinia; failure to resist in 1935–1936 led to the troubles of the late 1930s. In fact, few connections linked these separate crises. There were strategic reasons for nonintervention in Manchuria (the distance to the Far East and weaknesses in the British military establishment) and for seeing the Japanese move as a strategic advantage to British interests (involvement in China robbed the Japanese of much of their flexibility in the late 1930s).

---

[66] Roskill, *Hankey*, Vol. 2, p. 245.
[67] Sir Llewellyn Woodward, *Great Britain and the War of 1914–1918* (Boston, 1970), pp. 424–25.

The Abyssinian crisis was more troubling, for it directly involved British interests. Given Mussolini's megalomaniacal goals, no Anglo-French policy could have guaranteed Italian friendship.[68] British policy was torn in two divergent directions: on the one hand, Realpolitik appeared to suggest that Italy was necessary to offset Germany, while on the other, British public opinion *demanded* support for the League and for Abyssinia. Moreover, the national mood clearly opposed actions that might lead to military confrontation. As if those divergent trends were not enough, the COS weighed in with strategic appreciations suggesting that Italy could severely damage Britain's military and naval forces. Such an outcome, they argued, would adversely affect the precarious balance of forces Britain already faced.[69] The multiple pressures tugging at a government irresolute by nature produced a strategic policy that fell between two stools. The British failed to save Abyssinia; they thoroughly confused the French; and they antagonized the Italians. Thereafter Britain confronted a hostile Italy in the Mediterranean, a militant Japan in East Asia, and a swiftly arming Germany on the continent.

The failure of the League of Nations in the Abyssinian crisis did little to alter the course of British strategic policy. The public remained firm in its preconceptions of how the international arena worked. As crisis loomed in 1938, some on the Left argued for a complete abandonment of Britain's responsibilities: "Today if Mr Chamberlain would come forward and tell us that his policy was really one not only of isolation but also of Little Englandism in which the Empire was to be given up because it could not be defended and in which military defense was to be abandoned because war would totally end civilization, we for our part would wholeheartedly support him."[70]

Given a combination of depressing military assessments, optimistic estimates of German intentions, and public naivete, the British, not surprisingly, pursued appeasement when the Czech question arose in spring-summer 1938. Ironically, Chamberlain's policies succeeded in smoking out Hitler. British diplomacy, from Lord Runciman's attempt at mediation to Chamberlain's flights to Germany, underlined the pacific policies of the Western Powers and the aggressive dishonesty of Nazi foreign policy.

The real surrender of Czechoslovakia occurred during Chamberlain's first visit to the Führer at Berchtesgaden in September 1938. Some Cabinet members had already sensed the drift of Nazi policy; they instructed the Prime Minister that 1) if Hitler refused to make a settlement until Hungarian and Polish demands were met, he should return home at once; 2) the proposed guarantee should be multilateral; 3) Germany should sign a nonaggression

---

[68] For Mussolini's long-range aims and ideological goals, see MacGregor Knox, *Mussolini Unleashed* (Cambridge, 1982), and "Conquest, Foreign and Domestic, in Fascist Italy and Nazi Germany," *Journal of Modern History*, (March 1984).
[69] See Arthur Marder, *From the Dardanelles to Oran* (London, 1974), Chapter 3.
[70] Quoted in N. Thompson, *The Anti-Appeasers* (Oxford, 1971), pp. 156–57.

pact with Czechoslovakia; and 4) an international force should be created to monitor the territorial exchange.[71] When the Prime Minister then flew to Bad Godesberg to offer the peaceful surrender of Czechoslovakia, he met outright refusal from Hitler; upon his return to Britain, Chamberlain attempted to persuade his colleagues to crawl even further. This time he met opposition even from Lord Halifax, and a substantial number of ministers came close to revolt.[72] At the last moment, Hitler backed away from the brink of war, thus saving Chamberlain from the unpleasant need to act in the face of Germany's extraordinarily bad behavior. By now both public opinion in Britain and even in the Dominions had moved well beyond the government's position.

But Munich did not rescue Chamberlain from the need to face the German challenge and to speed the lethargic pace of British rearmament. Since coming to power in May 1937, the Prime Minister had placed strong restraints on defense expenditure. As he told the Cabinet in 1937:

> He could not accept the question at issue as being a purely military matter. Other considerations entered into it. He himself definitely did challenge the policy of [the government's] military advisors. The country was being asked to maintain a larger army than had been the case for very many years; a great air force, which was a new arm altogether; and, in addition, an army for use on the continent; as well as facilities for producing munitions which would be required not only for our forces but also for our allies.[73]

By fall 1938 the government was trapped; it had argued throughout the crisis that Britain was unprepared for war. Now, in view of German behavior and with distrust for the Nazi regime rising in the electorate, British unpreparedness was obvious to all. The government had to act.

Yet despite his public pronouncements, Chamberlain had no intention of accelerating the rearmament program. On 3 October, the Prime Minister informed the Cabinet that since his term as Chancellor of the Exchequer he had felt that "the burden of armaments might break our backs." He had thus embarked on appeasement to resolve the conflicts causing the armaments race.[74] The government did ask the services what they needed to repair major deficiencies; but almost immediately Thomas Inskip, Minister for Coordination of Defense, challenged the service proposals on two grounds. First of all, did Munich call for revision of authorized programs? Second, did not "the financial implications even of the present programs . . . threaten that stability which is, after all, in our experience probably our strongest weapon of war?"[75]

---

[71] PRO CAB 23/95, Cab 41 (38), Meeting of the Cabinet, 21.9.38., p. 163.
[72] Murray, *The Change in the European Balance of Power*, pp. 206–209.
[73] PRO CAB 23/88, Cab 20 (37), 5.5.37.
[74] PRO CAB 23/95, CAB 48 (38), Meeting of the Cabinet, 3.10.38., p. 304.
[75] PRO CAB 24/279, CP 234 (38), 21.10.38., "Defense Preparations Forecast."

Inskip's objections opened a prolonged period of deliberation – in which the Prime Minister won as much by delaying tactics as by the use of his authority. The navy got some escort vessels; the RAF lost its bid for heavy bombers and received an increase in fighters, but only by extending existing contracts from 1941 into 1942, not by speeding production. The army received nothing – until finally in February, under intense Cabinet pressure, Chamberlain agreed to a small continental commitment.[76] Thus from Munich to the German occupation of Prague the tempo of rearmament hardly changed.

Hitler's bad faith in occupying the remainder of Czechoslovakia finally triggered a long overdue reassessment of Britain's armament needs. As during the Czech crisis, the government followed public opinion. When word came of Hitler's move, Chamberlain stressed to his colleagues that "the state whose frontiers we had undertaken to guarantee against unprovoked aggression had now completely broken up." He suggested further that Hitler might have acted because of his disappointment at not having achieved a victory in September. "He thought therefore that military occupation was symbolic more than appeared on the surface."[77] But public opinion was no longer willing to tolerate such explanations. The Prime Minister's whining defense of appeasement in the House that evening did not strike a responsive chord: "It is natural, therefore, that I should bitterly regret what has now occurred. But do not let us on that account be deflected from our course."[78]

A storm of popular outrage forced major changes in both rearmament and foreign policy. It did not, however, force a reassessment of strategic assumptions. Chamberlain now aimed to prevent war by diplomacy rather than place Britain in the best strategic position should one occur. Consequently, British diplomacy distributed guarantees throughout Eastern Europe – guarantees for which no military backing existed. As Churchill noted about the Polish guarantee:

> When every one of these aids and advantages has been squandered and thrown away, Great Britain advances, leading France by the hand to guarantee the integrity of Poland. . . . But this [the defense of Czechoslovakia] had been judged unreasonable, rash, below the level of modern intellectual thought and morality. Yet now at last the two Western Democracies declared themselves ready to stake their lives upon the territorial integrity of Poland. History, which we are told is mainly the record of crimes, follies, and miseries of mankind, may be scoured and ransacked to find a parallel to this sudden and complete reversal of five or six years' policy of easy-going placatory appeasement, and its transformation almost overnight into a readiness to accept an obviously imminent war on far worse conditions and on the greatest scale.[79]

76 Murray, *The Change in the European Balance of Power*, pp. 271–78.
77 PRO CAB 23/98, Cab 11 (39), Meeting of the Cabinet, 15.3.39., pp. 9–13.
78 Hansard, *Parliamentary Debates*, 5th Ser., Vol. 345, House of Commons (London, 1939), Cols. 437–40.
79 Winston S. Churchill, *The Gathering Storm* (London, 1948), p. 347.

Unfortunately, Churchill was wrong: the government did not accept the possibility of war. Nothing illustrates Chamberlain's attitude better than his tardy, hesitating approach to the Soviet Union. Given the nature and goals of Stalin's regime, it is unlikely that the British could have reached a satisfactory agreement with the Soviets; the crucial point is that the British hardly tried.[80] After word arrived in London of the signing of the Nazi-Soviet Non-Aggression Pact, Halifax mused that the agreement would be of little strategic significance, although its moral effect would, he admitted, be enormous.[81]

Chamberlain's road to Canossa petered out in the Ball-Wohltat talks of summer 1939, during which the British offered the Nazis a large loan in return for promises of good behavior. One suspects that the looming general election constrained the government. Then the German invasion of Poland forced Chamberlain to declare war or face defeat in the House of Commons. The declaration of war did not represent a change of heart. The government, the bureaucracy, and the French failed to agree on any action against Germany. Over the summer, Chamberlain had suggested that the Italians represented a significant weakness in the Axis position.[82] The military, however, talked the Cabinet out of its assessment of Italy's vulnerability; the Joint Planning Committee went so far as to argue fancifully that Italy might "be in a position to hit us more effectively at the outset than we can hit her. . . ."[83] The COS urged that "Italian neutrality, if it could by any means be assured [that it could *not* be assured was precisely the point], would be decidedly preferable to her active hostility."[84]

By their refusal to undertake any action – from crushing Italy, to cutting German supplies from Scandinavia, to attack on the Western front – the democracies allowed Germany to evade the consequences of its desperate economic and strategic position after the conquest of Poland. As a result, the Wehrmacht could husband its scarce resources for one great throw of the dice in spring 1940.[85] As an allied strategic survey suggested in April of that year:

> Hence, the Reich appears to have suffered relatively little wear and tear during the first six months of war, and that mainly as a result of the allied blockade. Meanwhile, it has profited from the interval to perfect the degree of equipment

---

80 For a fuller discussion of these issues see Murray, *The Change in the European Balance of Power*, pp. 297–307.
81 PRO CAB 23/100, Cab 41 (39), Meeting of the Cabinet, 22.8.39., p. 320.
82 PRO CAB 2/8, CID Minutes of the 360th Meeting held on 22.6.39., p. 232.
83 PRO CAB 55/18, JP 470, 12.7.39., CID, Joint Planning Committee: "The attitude of Italy in war and the problem of Anglo-French support to Poland," p. 3.
84 PRO CAB 53/31, COS 939 (Revise), CID, Chiefs of Staff Committee: "The attitude of Italy in war and the problem of Anglo-French support to Poland," p. 200.
85 For a fuller discussion of the Reich's overall strategic and economic situations in fall 1939, see Murray, *The Change in the European Balance of Power*, pp. 326–38.

of its land and air forces, to increase the officer strength and complete the training of its troops, and to add further divisions to those already in the field.[86]

Churchill's appointment as prime minister in May 1940 was one outcome of the catastrophic failure of Chamberlain's policies. This essay has already underlined Churchill's crucial role in the formulation of British strategy; nevertheless, Hastings Ismay's discussion with Field Marshal Claude Auchinleck after the latter had assumed command of the Middle East may help make Churchill's contribution even clearer. Ismay noted:

> The idea that he was rude, arrogant, and self-seeking was entirely wrong. He was none of those things. He was certainly frank in speech and writing, but he expected others to be equally frank with him. To a young brigadier from Middle East Headquarters who had asked if he might speak freely, he replied: "Of course. We are not here to pay each other compliments. . . . " He had a considerable respect for a trained military mind, but refused to subscribe to the idea that generals were infallible or had any monopoly of the military art. He was not a gambler, but never shrank from taking a calculated risk if the situation so demanded. . . . I begged Auchinleck not to allow himself to be intimidated by these never ending messages, but to remember that Churchill, as Prime Minister and Minister of Defense, bore the primary responsibility for ensuring that all available resources in shipping, man-power, equipment, oil, and the rest were apportioned between the Home front and the various theaters of war, in the best interests of the war effort as a whole. Was it not reasonable that he should wish to know exactly how all these resources were being used before deciding on the allotment to be given to this or that theater?[87]

As another military assistant characterized the change from Chamberlain to Churchill, "The days of mere 'coordination' were out for good and all. . . . We were now going to get direction, leadership, action with a snap in it."[88] And Churchill played a major role in the selection of British field commanders. While he did not hesitate to relieve those who failed to meet his standard, he protected competent commanders from service and political pressures. In summer 1940 he stood steadfast against pressure from the Air Ministry and Air Staff to remove Sir Hugh Dowding from Fighter Command.[89] That fall, despite sustained opposition from the CIGS, Dill, and the future CIGS, Alanbrooke, Churchill forced the army to bring back Percy Hobart, the armor pioneer. The Prime Minister made clear his point of view:

> I am not at all impressed by the prejudices against him [Hobart] in certain quarters. Such prejudices attach frequently to persons of strong personality and original view. In this case General Hobart's original views have been only too tragically borne out. The neglect by the General Staff even to devise proper

[86] PRO CAB 85/16, M.R. (J) (40) (3) 2, 11.4.40., Allied Military Committee, "The Major Strategy of the War, Note by the French Delegation."
[87] Lord Hastings, *The Memoirs of General the Lord Ismay* (London, 1960), pp. 269–70.
[88] General Sir Leslie Hollis, *One Marine's Tale* (London, 1956) pp. 66–71.
[89] Martin Gilbert, *Winston S. Churchill*, Vol. 6, p. 658.

patterns of tanks before the war has robbed us of all the fruits of this invention.[90]

By no means, however, was Churchill's appointment inevitable. King George VI and Chamberlain would have preferred Halifax. Moreover, Churchill's authority met stiff resistance in the first days of his stewardship. A substantial number within the government hoped to reach some accommodation with the Germans. In late May, Halifax expressed disgust at the relish with which the new Prime Minister approached his task.[91] One month later, "Rab" Butler, Under Secretary of State for Foreign Affairs, informed the Swedish ambassador that "no opportunity would be neglected for concluding a compromise peace, if the chance [were] offered on reasonable terms."[92]

But the mood in Britain had changed. Churchill, furious at Butler's indiscretion, passed a biting note to Halifax.[93] Churchill, as he subsequently claimed, only reflected the national mood. In late June, Admiral Dudley Pound, Chief of Naval Staff, told the French Admiralty's liaison officer: "the one object we had in view was winning the war and . . . it was as essential for them [the French] as for us that we should do so. . . . All trivialities, such as questions of friendships and hurting people's feelings, must be swept aside."[94] Indeed they were, when for cold, hard, strategic reasons, Force H from Gibraltar attacked the French fleet at Mers-el-Kabir after it refused to comply with British demands aimed at keeping it out of German hands. The attack destroyed the new battle cruiser *Dunkerque* and two older battleships and killed 1,500 French sailors.[95]

Churchill had enunciated clear strategic goals upon assuming office, though those goals seemed more and more difficult to attain as German armor swept all before it in France. "You ask, what is our policy? I will say: It is to wage war by sea, land and air, with all our might and with all the strength that God can give us; to wage war against a monstrous tyranny, never surpassed in the dark lamentable catalogue of human crime. That is our policy."[96] He stuck to this goal with tenacity over the next five years.

Churchill's immediate problem was keeping the French in the war. When that failed, he confronted the problem of defending Britain. But from the first, he moved decisively and effectively to establish close relations with President Roosevelt and the United States. That relationship, along with victory in the Battle of Britain, were his greatest triumphs. Yet blunting the

---

90 Ibid., p. 862
91 The Earl of Birkenhead, *Halifax* (Boston, 1966) p. 458.
92 Llewellyn Woodward, *British Foreign Policy in the Second World War* (London, 1962), p. 53.
93 See PRO FO 371/24859 and FO 800/322.
94 PRO ADM 205/4 undated and unsigned memorandum.
95 See P.M.H. Bell's excellent study: *A Certain Eventuality, Britain and the Fall of France* (Edinburg, 1974).
96 Winston Churchill, *Hansard*, 13 May 1940, cols. 1501–1502.

German air offensive and securing financial support from the United States were in themselves not enough to defeat the "Greater German Reich."

At the highest level, Churchill aimed to draw the United States into the conflict at Britain's side while reaching accommodation with the Soviet Union. That regime, however, maintained its steadfast support of Nazi Germany, quite literally flooding the Third Reich with deliveries of grain, oil, and raw materials until 22 June 1941.[97] Molotov's fulsome congratulations for the splendid successes of the German Wehrmacht in Western Europe sum up Soviet strategy and diplomacy policy during this period.[98] The Germans were nevertheless moving to remove this impediment to Britain's survival. In early June 1940 the German army began planning for an invasion of the Soviet Union in 1941; by the end of July, Hitler ordered preparations for BARBAROSSA. The Führer reasoned that Britain remained in the war only out of hope of American and Soviet intervention. As yet he could do little about the United States, but the Soviet Union offered an inviting target, particularly given the Nazi *Weltanschauung*.

Churchill believed that British strategy could affect the outcome of the war in a few crucial areas. The battle to protect the North Atlantic sea lanes was the most important fought by British forces – on its success rested support for the great bomber offensive, the deployment of British air and ground forces in the Mediterranean and eventually onto the continent, and the feeding of the British Isles. Churchill himself wrote: "How willingly would I have exchanged a full-scale invasion for this shapeless, measureless peril, expressed in charts, curves and statistics!"[99] Only German unpreparedness saved an equally unprepared Royal Navy from defeat in 1939–1941.[100] Deployment of four-engine aircraft might have helped alleviate the submarine menace earlier, but the growing weight of evidence suggests that ULTRA was the decisive element in the victory over the U-boats.[101]

As to allocations between theaters, that depended not only on internal decision-making and the course of the war, but on Allied pressures as well. With memories of World War I casualties and the destruction of Allied ground forces in spring 1940 still fresh in mind, a bombing campaign against Germany appeared particularly attractive. The Air Ministry made extravagant claims that echoed the writings of interwar air power theorists. The public's sense that something had to be done against the Germans while the Soviets bore the brunt of the ground war also supported the allocation of

---

[97] See particularly Ferdinand Friedensburg, "Die sowjetischen Kriegslieferungen an das Hitlerreich," *Vierteljahrshefte für Wirtschaftsforschung* (1962).

[98] *DGFP*, Series D, Vol. IX, Doc. #471, 18.6.40.

[99] Winston S. Churchill, *The Hinge of Fate* (London, 1950), pp. 100–01.

[100] Murray, *The Change in the European Balance of Power*, pp. 45–47, 73–77.

[101] Among a whole host of works on "Ultra," two of the most important on its impact on the war at sea are Patrick Beasley, *Very Special Intelligence* (London, 1978), and F. H. Hinsley, et al., *British Intelligence in the Second World War*, Vol. 1 (London, 1978), Vol. 2 (London, 1982), Vol. 3, pt. 1 (London, 1984), and Vol. 3, pt. 2 (London, 1987).

resources to "strategic" bombing. Yet Churchill himself, however strongly he supported Bomber Command's efforts, never fully accepted the argument that the air campaign by itself could be decisive. As he noted to the Chief of Air Staff, Air Marshal Charles Portal, in September 1941:

> It is very disputable whether bombing by itself will be a decisive factor in the present war. On the contrary, all that we have learned since the war began shows that its effects, both physical and moral, are generally exaggerated. There is no doubt that the British people have been stimulated and strengthened by the attack made upon them thus far. Secondly, it seems very likely that the ground defense and night fighters will overtake the air attack. Thirdly, in calculating the number of bombers necessary to achieve hypothetical and indefinite tasks, it should be noted that only a quarter of our bombs hit the targets. . . . [The] most that we can say is that it [the bomber offensive] will be a heavy, and, I trust, a seriously increasing annoyance.[102]

In nearly every respect Churchill was on the mark. While Bomber Command's offensive played a crucial role in Germany's defeat,[103] it was only one among several factors. Ironically, in view of prewar air power claims that "strategic" bombing would provide an escape from the catastrophe of attrition warfare, the bombing offensive provided attrition in another milieu – attrition that was more costly in national treasure and just as costly in terms of the sacrifice of "the best and the brightest."[104]

As in the Great War, the British experienced the greatest difficulty in executing the operations necessary for effective strategy on the ground.[105] The 1940 battles in France hardly represented a fair trial for British operational and tactical capabilities; it was the Mediterranean theater that gave British ground forces their first notable test. Unfortunately, British aims in the Middle East were not entirely clear in 1940. Field Marshal Archibald Wavell emphasized Abyssinia as the most important strategic target for British forces. It was not; Italian forces in Ethiopia possessed neither the aggressiveness, nor the operational reach, nor the logistical support to threaten anything more valuable than British Somaliland. In effect, they were in a gigantic internment camp. Nevertheless, Wavell broke off the attack on Italian forces in the Western Desert for two weeks to support his East African campaign, and pulled out the 4th Indian division to send it to Abyssinia.[106]

---

102   Quoted in Gilbert, *Winston S. Churchill*, Vol. 6, p. 1,205.
103   For a further discussion of this point, see Williamson Murray, *Luftwaffe*, (Baltimore, 1985), pp. 270–72.
104   See Murray, *Luftwaffe*. For the impact of attrition on Bomber Command see Max Hastings, *Bomber Command* (London, 1978).
105   See Paul Kennedy, "Britain in the First World War," in *Military Effectiveness*, Vol. 1, *The First World War*, and Williamson Murray, "British Military Effectiveness in the Second World War," *Military Effectiveness*, Vol. 3, *The Second World War*, Allan R. Millett and Williamson Murray, eds., (London, 1988).
106   The best account of British actions in the Western Desert is in I.S.O. Playfair, *The Mediterranean and the Middle East*, Vol. 1, *The Early Successes Against Italy*, (London, 1974).

Those two weeks gave the Germans time to get Rommel to Tripoli and prolong the war in North Africa for three years.

Like most senior British officers, Wavell never understood the imperative of speed in pursuit of a beaten enemy, nor did he grasp the tactical and operational concepts that turned Richard O'Connor's raid against Italian forces in Egypt and Libya into one of the few overwhelming British ground victories of the war. When O'Connor's forces reached El Agheila (within striking distance of Tripoli), Wavell stopped the advance and broke up O'Connor's experienced XIII Corps.[107]

By this time, the British also felt the tug to intervene on the continent. The fierce resistance of Greek forces to the ill-timed and worse-led Italian invasion of October-November 1940 had inspired much of the Anglo-Saxon world. Churchill was torn between finishing off the Italians in Libya and helping the Greeks against imminent German attack. He did make clear to his advisers that they should not consider themselves under any obligation "to a Greek enterprise if in your hearts you feel it will be another Norway fiasco. If no good plan can be made please say so. But of course you know how valuable success would be."[108] Wavell, Dill, and Eden, all on the scene in the Middle East, urged support for Greece. British aid, unfortunately, resulted in catastrophe that hustled the British off the continent. The subsequent loss of Crete magnified the disaster. Crete was the real prize, for its airfields would have allowed British attacks on the Achilles heel of the German war effort: Rumanian oil.

Defeat on the mainland was not surprising given the balance of forces in the Balkans; the defeat on Crete, however, raises questions about the competence of British military leaders and the operational and tactical performance of British troops. ULTRA intelligence fully informed the defenders of Crete that the Germans were coming by air and sea.[109] Given Royal Navy superiority, any major German effort would have to come mainly by air. Moreover, the day before MERKUR began the Greeks found the operation orders for the Luftwaffe's 3rd Parachute regiment in a BF 110 shot down in Suda Bay.[110] Nevertheless, Freyberg and his subordinate commanders concentrated on defending the beaches rather than the airfields. As a result, the Germans seized Maleme airfield after a desperate struggle and then drove British and Dominion troops off the island.

The performance of British and Commonwealth troops and their commanders on Crete underlines a major problem in executing British strategy: tactical and operational weakness compared to similar German units. In the Western Desert, the Eighth Army consistently outnumbered Rommel's forces

---

[107] Playfair, *The Mediterranean and Middle East,* Vol. 1, pp. 364–65.
[108] Gilbert, *Winston S. Churchill,* Vol. 6, p. 1,013.
[109] Hinsley, *British Intelligence in the Second World War,* Vol. 2, pp. 419–421.
[110] G. C. Kiriakopoulos, *Ten Days to Destiny, The Battle for Crete 1941* (New York, 1985), p. 87.

by a substantial margin. The fact that Churchill had regular access to German strength returns for the *Afrika Korps* (through ULTRA) and could thus calculate the balance of forces in the Middle East, explains why he so vigorously pushed his desert commanders to attack the outnumbered Germans. But Churchill did not understand the weaknesses in doctrine, training, leadership, and weapons of British troops when matched against the Germans.

Hitler's declaration of war on the United States after Pearl Harbor removed the last impediment to victory.[111] As Martin Gilbert has suggested:

> The widening of the war, so frightening a prospect for those countries not previously closely engaged in it, such as Australia, was for Churchill a miracle of deliverance from more than two years of British isolation, weakness, and omnipresent danger of defeat. The accession of the United States as a "full war partner," he telegraphed to . . . the Prime Minister of Australia, on December 12, "makes amends for all and makes the end certain."[112]

The road to victory, however, proved long indeed. In Southeast Asia, British ground forces collapsed before the drive and execution of inferior Japanese ground forces – Malaya, Singapore, and Burma all succumbed in the most humiliating fashion. The great Singapore naval base, supposedly the cornerstone of British defenses in East Asia, fell with the loss of several hundred thousand troops as well as the *Prince of Wales* and *Repulse*. The British defeat resulted from the incompetence of the commanders, the poor training of troops, and gross underestimation of the Japanese.[113] It took two years of hard training and preparation before the British army could match the Japanese in jungle fighting; Field Marshal Lord Slim, one of the greatest of Britain's soldiers, eventually made the British army in Burma the most responsive and combat-effective British force of the war. His achievement makes clear that training and doctrine were the source of Britain's battlefield deficiencies.

It was the Mediterranean that Churchill saw as the theater of opportunity for the Anglo-American allies. Even before he arrived in the United States in December 1941 he suggested to his naval advisers that an American landing at Casablanca would "decide the action of French North Africa" and draw Vichy France into the allied camp.[114] Churchill initially worried whether the pull of the Pacific might distract the Americans from Europe. In fact, the

---

111   Hitler's declaration of war on the United States was one of the Germans' worst strategic mistakes in World War II. It was a mistake committed with some forethought by the Führer, for in fact the Kriegsmarine had been pressuring him to declare war on the United States since summer 1941. See in particular, Holger Herwig, *The Politics of Frustration, The United States in German Naval Planning, 1889–1941*, (Boston, 1976) pp. 232–34.
112   Gilbert, *Winston S. Churchill*, Vol. 7, p. 4.
113   For the underestimation of the Japanese, see Christopher Thorne, *Allies of a Kind: The United States, Britain and the War Against Japan, 1941–1945* (London, 1978); and H. P. Willmott, *Empires in the Balance: Japanese and Allied Pacific Strategies to April 1942* (Annapolis, 1982).
114   Gilbert, *Winston S. Churchill*, Vol. 7, p. 5.

Americans proved all too eager to come to grips with the Wehrmacht. In May 1942, Roosevelt promised the Soviets that Anglo-American forces would re-create the second front that Stalin and his henchmen had watched the Germans destroy in May and June 1940. That promise forced Churchill to undertake a most unpleasant journey to Moscow to explain why there would be no second front in 1942.

The argument between British and American strategists over a Mediterranean strategy as opposed to landings on the French coast formed much of the strategic framework for the middle portions of the war. In dealing with the Americans, the British chiefs proved particularly effective in creating a common point of view, although in 1942 it took the direct intervention of Franklin Roosevelt, using his constitutional powers as commander-in-chief, to force the American senior leadership to agree to the landings in North Africa. While TORCH was successful, the Germans reacted quickly enough to seize Tunisia. That action forced a sustained campaign to clear Axis troops from North Africa that lasted throughout the first half of 1943. The campaign in Tunisia, as American military leaders had feared, prevented a second front in 1943. But scant prospect existed for a successful Anglo-American landing on the coast of France in 1943 in any event. The victory in Tunisia destroyed a quarter of a million German and Italian troops, imposed a terrible attrition rate on the Luftwaffe that pushed it toward eventual collapse in early 1944, and gave the Americans needed experience against a first-class opponent.[115] The savage pounding that German troops gave U.S. GIs at Kasserine Pass taught the Americans that defeating the German Army would *not* be easy.

Meetings between American and British senior leaders at Casablanca established Allied grand strategy in the last half of the war. As historians have pointed out, thoughtful British preparations made American proposals look amateurish by comparison, but they did provide the Americans with useful lessons in staff work at the strategic level. The conditions for a successful landing on the European continent had yet to be achieved. Moreover, given the stresses and sacrifices that British society had borne thus far, the last thing Churchill could afford was a failed landing, especially since the great majority of invading troops in 1943 would have been British. It also made global strategic sense to finish off the Germans in Tunisia and then clean up Sicily so that convoys could pass directly through the Mediterranean instead of taking the long route around the Cape of Good Hope.

As early as summer 1942, Churchill had seen even greater potential for the Mediterranean:

> If, however, we move from "Gymnast" northward into Europe, a new situation must be surveyed. The flank attack may become the main attack, and the main attack a holding operation in the early stages. Our second front will, in fact, comprise both the Atlantic and the Mediterranean coasts of Europe, and we

[115] See Murray, *Luftwaffe,* pp. 154–61.

can push either right-handed, left-handed, or both-handed as our resources and circumstances permit.[116]

The American chiefs remained skeptical of the advantages of opportunism. Nevertheless, the careful, well-prepared briefs of the British COS brought the Americans around to a limited Mediterranean strategy for 1943. The British failed in their argument that a more aggressive Mediterranean strategy could reap greater dividends; the most they could extract from the unwilling Americans was a continuation of the HUSKY attack on Sicily on to the Italian peninsula. The attack was not so much a further exploitation of the Sicilian operation as it was an attempt to meet the demands of American airmen for control of the southern Italian airfields around Foggia needed for operations against northern Italy and southern Germany.

By fall 1943 the move away from the Mediterranean theater was in full swing. Eisenhower, Tedder, Montgomery, Spaatz, and Doolittle among others transferred to England to execute OVERLORD. By now Churchill, like Stalin, was beginning to focus on the emerging postwar world. His concerns ironically led to a strange alliance with "Bomber" Harris to prevent diversion of Bomber Command from its area bombing campaign to precision attacks on French marshaling yards. Harris's intellectually dishonest case rested on his claim that Bomber Command would hit thousands of French houses in addition to the marshaling yards (in postwar interviews he admitted that he had no qualms about slaughtering French civilians since "they had run away in 1940").[117] Churchill worried legitimately that heavy French casualties would permanently scar Anglo-French relations; however, Bomber Command was now a far more flexible and accurate instrument than its commander admitted. It soon demonstrated that its navigational devices would allow it to reduce the marshaling yards with minimal damage to surrounding civilians.

The execution of OVERLORD was the great operational triumph of the Anglo-American partnership. It represented an extraordinary logistical and organizational success; it also reflected the tactical and operational weaknesses of the allied armies.[118] General N. Ritchie, who had lost so dismally in the desert in spring 1942 as Eighth Army Commander, led the British corps that failed to trap the fleeing Germans at Falaise. Montgomery's conduct of the buildup and the attrition battle in Normandy was his finest hour, especially considering the weakness of his instrument. But the lethargic British pursuit from Normandy ended the chance for victory in 1944. As Liddell Hart suggested, Montgomery was probably right in arguing for a single thrust into Germany, but he and the British army were hardly the ones to

116 J.R.M. Butler, *Grand Strategy*, Vol. 3, pt. 2, *June 1941–August 1942* (London, 1964), p. 638.
117 Oral Interview with Air Marshal Sir Arthur Harris, Bracknell, RAF Staff College Library.
118 Max Hastings, *Overlord* (London, 1984), pp. 315–17. See also, Murray, "British Military Effectiveness in the Second World War," pp. 124–29.

execute such a strategy. With Operation MARKET GARDEN, Montgomery largely got his wishes; unfortunately, the operation was fundamentally flawed. At the moment that planning for MARKET GARDEN began, ENIGMA decrypts indicated that the Germans were moving 9th and 10th SS Panzer divisions into the area for rest and refit.[119] At that time, Montgomery also halted Lieutenant General Brian Horrocks' XXX Corps even though it possessed enough gasoline to advance another 100 kilometers.[120] As a result, the German Fifteenth Army slipped across the Scheldt; Antwerp remained blocked for another two months; and the Germans gained nearly two weeks to reknit their defenses – something that they had had plenty of experience in doing.

In the last year of the war, Churchill paid considerable attention to shaping the postwar world. Despite internal political opposition and a lack of understanding among the Americans, the Prime Minister intervened in Greece to block a communist bid for power. However, the Allies could do little to influence the settlement in Eastern Europe. Stalin's strategy insured that Soviet troops occupied all areas in Eastern Europe and the Balkans that fell within the Soviet Union's war aims. Moreover, by launching the December 1944 Ardennes offensive (which required stripping the Eastern Front of reserves), Hitler pinned the Western Powers on the far bank of the Rhine while Soviet troops rampaged up to the Oder. Consequently, at Yalta in February 1945 the actual military situation had a decisive influence on negotiations for the postwar frontiers of Central Europe. The advance of the Allies to either Berlin or Vienna, both of which Churchill advocated, would have only had symbolic value. With Prague it was a different story. It is indeed hard to explain American attitudes, particularly those of Marshall and Eisenhower; one nevertheless wonders even in this case how much difference American liberation would have made, given the weakness and illusions of Beneš and his cohorts.

CONCLUSION

Once again Britain emerged from a world war at the head of a victorious coalition. But the impact of that war resulted in the loss of Britain's empire and its great power position. Failure to recognize that outcome only exacerbated Britain's postwar economic and political decline. Yet the British strategic story is not one of complete failure: the British, their values, and their independence survived the war. Given Churchill's starting point in May 1940, that was no mean accomplishment.

[119] Two Ultra messages underlined this German movement in the clearest possible fashion. These messages are dated September 5 and 6; MARKET GARDEN did not occur until 17 September: PRO DEFE 3/127/XL 9188, 5.9.44., 11 52 Z and DEFE 3/128, XL 9245, 6.9.44., 0103Z.

[120] J. L. Moulton, *Battle for Antwerp, The Liberation of the City and the Opening of the Scheldt, 1944* (London, 1978), pp. 52–53.

In the interwar period, Britain had faced an alarming world. The empire that previous generations had bequeathed to British statesmen was the result of centuries of accretion, not of strategic grand design. Although the empire extended from Asia to Europe and the Americas, and despite British pride in the fact that the sun never set on it, its very size represented a nightmare to British strategists. In the relatively quiet era of the 1920s, the British dealt effectively with the United States and Japan to prevent a naval race. But in the 1930s, Britain faced a harsh world with little room for maneuver. Public and official blinkers and naivete exacerbated Britain's difficulties in formulating successful strategic policies. The Italians and especially the Japanese were serious threats to the empire; Germany's rise placed Britain itself in mortal danger. The failure of British policy came not from appeasement per se; rather it was Chamberlain's dogged adherence to that policy, which ended only when Churchill replaced Chamberlain on 10 May 1940.[121]

Churchill picked up the pieces. He did so with a verve and wisdom rarely seen in human history. And although he could not correct the deeply imbedded operational and tactical deficiencies of Britain's military organizations, he did keep a firm hand on the strategic tiller. Correlli Barnett has severely criticized the social, economic, and educational policies that Churchill's coalition laid out while the struggle continued.[122] Yet whatever the validity of Barnett's criticisms in retrospect, it is hard to see how the British people could have maintained the struggle without the promise of the "New Jerusalem." However unrealistic such dreams might have been in the harsh light of the emerging postwar world, the British government had little choice but to make such promises given the need to survive the war. In the final analysis, the British brought the state "through the tempest without bringing her to destruction."[123]

[121] See Peter Ludlow's outstanding article, "The Unwinding of Appeasement," in *Das "Andere" Deutschland im Zweiten Weltkrieg*, L. Kettenacker, ed., (Stuttgart, 1977).

[122] Correlli Barnett, *The Audit of War, The Illusion and Reality of Britain as a Great Nation* (London, 1986).

[123] Churchill, *The World Crisis*, p. 6.

14

The strategy of innocence? The United States, 1920–1945

ELIOT A. COHEN

INTRODUCTION

America's evolution into the first among the great powers culminated between 1920 and 1945.[1] Until then, American power had remained largely latent, although the Civil War had revealed the magnitude of U.S. potential strength. By the turn of the century, the United States had become a respected sea power, but the European powers doubted that it possessed the constancy of purpose and the political skill to play a major role in world politics. The abrupt withdrawal of the United States into isolation after World War I only confirmed that skepticism. By 1945, however, no one could doubt the reality of American power or the ability of American democracy to handle extraordinary tests.

American national security policy still bears the imprint of the 1920–45 period. The experience and memories of those years help account for the otherwise inexplicable willingness of the American people to tolerate during the Cold War what were, by historical standards, vast peacetime military establishments; the premium on readiness and avoidance of surprise attack; the willingness to conceive of national security in global rather than local terms; and the American military's persistent preference for excessively neat patterns of civilian-military relations.

The period under discussion poses particular historical problems. Many issues demand consideration in a single essay: isolation on the one hand, and involvement in literally every corner of the globe on the other; a peacetime

---

[1] For useful surveys of American strategy from 1920 to 1945, see Allan R. Millett and Peter Maslowski, *For the Common Defense: A Military History of the United States* (New York, 1984), pp. 361–470; Ronald Spector, "The Military Effectiveness of the U.S. Armed Forces, 1919–1939," and Allan R. Millett, "The United States Armed Forces in the Second World War," in Allan R. Millett and Williamson Murray, eds., *Military Effectiveness*, (Boston, 1988), Vol. 2, pp. 70–97 and Vol. 3, pp. 45–89.

professional army two-thirds the size of the marine corps of the early 1990s, and a wartime conscript army more than three times the size of the U.S. armed forces at the end of the Cold War. But although this periodization makes for difficulties, it has important benefits. First, it reveals underlying continuities in a strategic culture that historians all too often treat as beginning in 1941 or 1945. Second, it forces attention on the transition between peace and war and leads to a better comprehension of wartime achievements. For instance, only an understanding of the painful evolution of military production from 1939 to 1942 can make plain the magnitude of the achievements of 1943–44. This essay will deal, however, more with American participation in World War II than with American strategy in the interwar period. Wars, particularly great wars, reveal national character as it is being forged, and there are few better ways of understanding the strengths and weaknesses of American strategic culture than by examining it through the lens of the greatest war in history.

LEGACIES

In the 1920s and 1930s, most Americans viewed World War I as a grievous exception to a long-standing policy of noninvolvement in European affairs. To most the war represented a terrible mistake. A happy reversion to an ante bellum strategic outlook seemed the logical outcome.

In some respects this reversal occurred, although the armed forces remained considerably larger by American standards than before the outbreak of war in 1914.[2] By 1920, the U.S. army had declined to 200,000 men from nearly two and a half million in 1918. Within a few years it reached a postwar nadir of 132,000. Yet even this was one-third larger than the prewar army of fewer than 100,000. The U.S. navy also failed to shrink to prewar levels; at its postwar nadir of 91,000 men in 1933 it was over two-thirds larger than the navy of 1914. Despite the Hoover administration's economy drive, the United States retained fifteen battleships, three aircraft carriers, eighteen cruisers, seventy-eight destroyers, and fifty-five submarines in 1931. This fleet was numerically superior to Japan's and was on a par with the Royal Navy. The marine corps, 10,000 strong in the prewar period, declined to an interwar low of 16,000 men in 1933; it too had emerged from World War I with permanent gains.

Strategy is not only a matter of choice about when and where to fight, but of the organizations and institutions that prepare for it. American involvement in World War I transformed the army and navy. The army reverted to its prewar constabulary duties, garrisoning the Philippines and protecting American interests in China. And some lessons of World War I were inapplicable to the challenges of the next war – for example, the preference for a

---

[2] Numbers: *Historical Statistics of the United States, Colonial Times to 1970*, p. 1141.

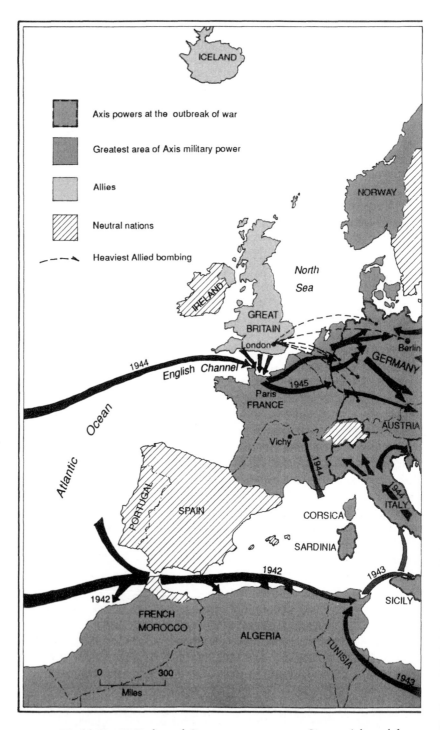

Map 14.1. World War II: Defeat of Germany, 1942–1945. *Source.* Adapted from Knox et al. *The Mainstream of Civilization Since 1500*, 5th Edition (New York: Harcourt Brace Jovanovich, 1989), 961.

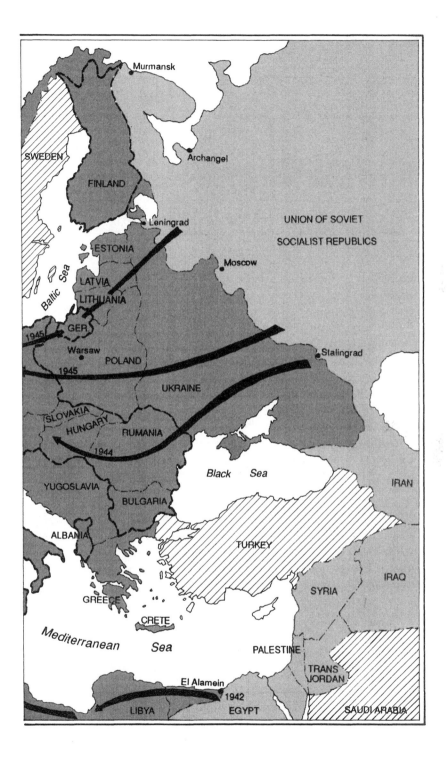

strong field commander over a powerful chief of staff in Washington.[3] Nonetheless, for the first time since the Civil War the army had fought a first-rate foe; it had also experienced the frustrations of coalition warfare. It had recognized the need for industrial mobilization to support a mass army. It could not devise solutions to all these challenges in the interwar period, and some paper solutions (for industrial mobilization, for example) proved unworkable. But at least it recognized the problems.

World War I likewise profoundly affected the navy. The Naval Act of 1916 promised the creation of a "navy second to none," and although many of the resulting ships bore no relevance to the impending struggle against Germany, they did lay the basis for a permanent commitment to naval power. After World War I, the navy conceived itself as the equal of the Royal Navy, and secured the resources to achieve that equality.[4]

World War I, in which a large, albeit foreign-equipped air force had deployed in France, made the army receptive to the development of a semi-independent aviation arm, even if not swiftly enough for the impatient aviators of the army air corps. The establishment in 1934 of the GHQ Air Force – the immediate predecessor of the Army Air Forces – underlined the army's commitment to air power.[5]

The world war also invigorated the American system of high command. On 24 July 1919, by joint order, the Secretaries of War and Navy revived the Joint Board, an organization that had proved less than efficient in the preceding decade and a half and that had exercised little control over American forces during World War I.[6] The Joint Board consisted of the head of each service (the chief of staff of the army and chief of naval operations), the assistant chief of each service, and the directors of the war plans divisions. In July 1941 the deputy chiefs for aviation also joined. The Joint Board established a Joint Planning Committee (1919), a Joint Economic Board (1933), and a Joint Intelligence Committee (1941). In addition to its other functions, the Board formulated and debated joint war plans. The regular meetings of the Board and its subcommittees created a forum for comprehensive strategic reviews such as the January 1929 assessment of U.S. prospects in a war with Japan. The Board fell short of the integrated mechanisms of military plan-

---

3 See Mark S. Watson, *Chief of Staff: Prewar Plans and Preparations* (Washington, 1950), pp. 2–3.

4 By 1918, the U.S. Navy still had only sixteen battleships to Britain's thirty-three and nine battle cruisers, but the U.S. had thirteen more battleships and six battle cruisers under construction compared with Britain's three battleships and one battle cruiser under construction. On the Navy's condition during this period, see Thomas C. Hone, "The Effectiveness of the 'Washington Treaty' Navy," *Naval War College Review* 32:6 (November-December 1979), pp. 35–59.

5 See John F. Shiner, "Birth of GHQ Air Force," *Military Affairs* 42:3 (October 1978), pp. 113–20.

6 The records of the Joint Board (henceforth cited as *JB*) cover this matter. (National Archives, Microfilm Publications, *Records of the Joint Board 1903–1947* [Washington, D.C., 1986], Microfilm Publication M-1421). On the history of the Joint Board see *JB* 301.

ning that the services required, but it represented a substantial advance over the pre-1914.

As for the home front, "World War II was largely fought . . . on the basis of the constitutional law of World War I."[7] World War I set the pattern for "the delegation of vast discretionary powers to the President to deal with a broadly defined subject-matter in furtherance of objectives equally broad."[8] A brilliantly conceived Selective Service System, for example, reconciled Americans to wide-ranging and nearly unlimited national conscription, a system equally effective in World War II.[9]

What about the impact of World War I on the American decision to participate in World War II? Some historians have argued that the world wars were a single great conflict, a war broken by a long armistice and turning on the German effort to grasp hegemony in Europe. Many lines of continuity exist between the First and Second World Wars in Europe. But these continuities appear less sharp in the case of the United States.

The United States had entered World War I at the end of the conflict. Its productive potential never exercised a decisive influence on the battlefield; only half of the aircraft flown by American pilots were American-made, and barely one in seven artillery pieces were of American manufacture.[10] American forces in the field, although large in number (2 million men left for France in eighteen months), arrived in strength late, and did not bear the brunt of even the offensives that crushed Wilhelmine Germany. Initially, America's wishes carried great weight at the prolonged negotiations concluding the war. But this influence reflected America's potential as much as its actual strength; it also reflected the financial and agricultural power of the New World. By the end of 1919, the United States clearly had the *potential* to be a superpower, but it had not yet achieved that status. Only the American navy was a mark of present as opposed to latent strength.

But America's participation in World War I was indispensable to Allied success. Without the promise of vast, fresh armies, the Allies could not have hung on in the desperate spring of 1918. The threat and subsequent reality of the American Expeditionary Force eventually convinced the Germans that resistance into the winter of 1918–19 would be hopeless. But although the American intervention was decisive in the last year of the war, it had not shaped the first three quarters of the conflict.

The U.S. experience in World War II was quite different. A much earlier mobilization, beginning in 1940, but with origins in 1938 and before, made the United States a major military power by the mid-point of the war. The

---

7 Edward S. Corwin, *Total War and the Constitution* (New York, 1947), p. 173 and passim.
8 Ibid., p. 39.
9 See Eliot A. Cohen, *Citizens and Soldiers: The Dilemmas of Military Service* (Ithaca, NY, 1985), passim.
10 Leonard P. Ayres, *The War With Germany: A Statistical Summary* (Washington, 1919), p. 81.

United States had matched and was surpassing British war production by 1942. This time, the United States supplied not only men but machines in vast quantities. At the strategic level, the American war effort was also quite different. In World War I, the United States had little opportunity to control the war's shape; the dominant theater remained the Western Front. In World War II, by contrast, the United States set the pace of the Pacific War from the beginning, and by 1943 had achieved at least equality in setting strategy in Europe. Finally, at the deepest psychological level, the American high command appears to have escaped the emotional scars that the World War I slaughter inflicted on Britain.

Yet this account fails to acknowledge the lines of continuity between the American experiences in the two world wars. The element of continuity in leadership is critical. Barely twenty-four years separated the end of one conflict and the beginning (from the American point of view) of the second; senior officials and commanders, including Roosevelt and the Joint Chiefs of Staff had participated in the last war, and it had shaped them. Equally important, the experiences of the first war left institutional legacies that persisted into the next conflict.

One legacy was a relentless drive for autonomy and independence. The suspicion, occasionally bordering on paranoia, that the American military harbored toward Churchill and the British Chiefs of Staff grew in part from the experiences of 1917–18, when the United States was clearly a junior partner at the tactical and operational level. Lieutenant General Stanley Embick, for example, the army's representative on the Joint Strategic Survey Committee, was attached to the American delegation at the Allied War Council during the first war. There he contracted an abiding mistrust of the British, reflected in his caustic comments on the merits of aid to Great Britain in 1940 and of operations in the Mediterranean in 1943.[11] The effort of the military intelligence services to deny the forerunner of the Office of Strategic Services access to any information from British intelligence – presumably slanted and hence dangerous – likewise suggests the strength of this feeling.[12]

World War I experiences also shaped individual conceptions of command. Admiral Ernest J. King acquired much of his willingness to delegate responsibility from his World War I service on the staff of Henry T. Mayo, commander of the Atlantic Fleet.[13] General George C. Marshall derived a number of lessons from his experience on Pershing's staff in France, although, interestingly, many of these lessons stemmed from his view that the experience of the American Expeditionary Force had been atypical. In the late

[11] See Forrest C. Pogue, *George C. Marshall*, Vol. 2, *Ordeal and Hope 1939–1942* (New York, 1965), pp. 132–33; Ronald Schaffer, "General Stanley D. Embick: Military Dissenter," *Military Affairs* 37 (October 1973), pp. 89–95.

[12] See "Report to the Joint Board on 'Memorandum of Establishment of Service of Information,'" JB 329, Serial 699.

[13] Ernest J. King and Walter Muir Whitehill, *Fleet Admiral King: A Naval Record* (New York, 1952), pp. 144–45.

1920s he argued that World War I, with its methodical attacks supported by detailed intelligence, could mislead the army about future challenges.[14] Moreover, Marshall had a keen sense that training methods and operational principles of a small, professional peacetime army were radically unsuited to creation of a massive, draftee wartime force, a view that his subsequent work as a National Guard adviser reinforced.[15] To oversimplify, then, American military leaders approached World War II mindful of their 1917–18 experiences and with a desire to "this time, do it right." They intended to fight a mobile, aggressive war on fronts of their own choosing, to draw more thoroughly on the vast industrial productive capacities of the nation, and not to fall prey to the duplicity of wily European allies.

Finally, American policy remains incomprehensible without reference to Wilsonian ideals and to a mistrust of colonialism dating back considerably further than 1914. Otherwise, it is hard to understand such episodes as FDR's persistent, condescending, and – to Churchill – infuriating pressure for Indian independence in the midst of the war.[16]

THE AMERICAN REGIME, 1920–1945

The U.S. Constitution was a prime force in shaping American strategic culture between 1920 and 1945. Laid down in the last decades of the eighteenth century, it had shown remarkable resilience even in the face of extreme stress during the Civil War, chiefly, though not exclusively, through its delegation of vast powers to the president in wartime. "Energy in the executive is a leading character in the definition of government," Alexander Hamilton had written. "It is essential to the protection of the community against foreign attacks."[17] Abraham Lincoln found the vague and flexible "war power" in the Constitution, and his successors continued to exploit it, none more skillfully than Franklin D. Roosevelt. In time of war Roosevelt became a virtual though benign dictator. Unlike Churchill he was commander in chief as well as head of state and head of government, an enormous concentration of power. The judicial and legislative branches of government hardly suspended operation, but they did not intervene in the making of strategy. "The grand strategy of the war, to take one example, was almost totally executive in concept, and even the execution of the war strategy was not seriously attacked in Congress."[18] Roosevelt did not consult Congress about war aims, refused the legislators either a major presence or influence at the great war-

14 Lecture at Fort Benning, n.d. (1927–1933), in Larry I. Bland, Sharon R. Ritenour, and Clarence E. Wunderlin, Jr., eds. *The Papers of George Catlett Marshall*, Vol. 1, 'The Soldierly Spirit' December 1880-June 1939 (Baltimore, 1981), pp. 334–338.
15 Ibid, p. 708.
16 For Roosevelt's desire to achieve Wilson's goals without making Wilson's mistakes, see James McGregor Burns, *Roosevelt: The Soldier of Freedom* (New York, 1970), passim.
17 *The Federalist Papers*, No. 70.
18 Roland Young, *Congressional Politics in the Second World War* (New York, 1956), p. 5.

time conferences that forged strategy, and even failed to provide Congress with much more information than it could glean from newspapers. From time to time – as with Pearl Harbor, procurement scandals, or relations with Admiral Darlan in 1942 – Congress investigated aspects of the war effort, but it had little impact on the direction of the conflict.

Although by today's standards this state of affairs was extraordinary, it was fortunate for the conduct of strategy. Under the first War Power's Act, passed days after the attack on Pearl Harbor and subsequently renewed, Congress granted Roosevelt virtual carte blanche to reorganize the federal government as he saw fit. Given his mistrust of established bureaucracies, he exploited this power to its fullest, creating by executive order new agencies such as the War Production Board reporting directly to him rather than to established cabinet departments.

But this extraordinary concentration of power in the executive branch represented an artifact of war rather than a condition of peace. Throughout the interwar years, Congress had taken an active role in shaping American strategy by its control of the budget and by passing so-called neutrality legislation designed to keep the United States out of war.[19] Yet Congressional suspicion of foreign entanglements simply reflected a broad stream in American opinion. In September 1939, one poll asked Americans whether "there are any international questions affecting the United States so important to us in the long run that our government should take a stand on them now, even at the risk of our getting into war?" Almost 55 percent said no, barely 20 percent said yes, and the remainder either said they did not know or that it would depend on the circumstances.[20]

Yet even in peace a President had discretionary power to shape American strategy. FDR's use of the Federal Bureau of Investigation (FBI) to break up pro-Nazi activities, and his cooperation with British secret service agencies, revealed a great deal of flexibility in the covert side of peacetime strategy-making. As early as 1940 the FBI, without the State Department's knowledge, had begun quietly cooperating with representatives of what became a large British intelligence establishment in the United States.[21] Roosevelt's use of the navy to prosecute an undeclared war in the North Atlantic in 1941 is even more suggestive.

Neither the pluralism of the American political system nor the system of checks and balances designed to prevent tyranny hampered the war effort. Like Churchill, Roosevelt had enormous powers at his disposal, although constraints of legislative and collegial opinion bound both to some extent. Yet in one key respect American politics did shape strategy: through the

---

19 See Robert A. Divine, *The Illusion of Neutrality* (Chicago, 1962), and Robert Dallek, *Franklin D. Roosevelt and American Foreign Policy 1932–1945* (New York, 1979).
20 Hadley Cantril and Mildred Strunk, eds., *Public Opinion 1935–1946* (Princeton, 1951), p. 949.
21 See H. Montgomery Hyde, *Room 3603* (New York, 1963).

system of regular elections for the Congress and Presidency. The negative aspect of this system was obvious – for example, in the election year of 1940 FDR hesitated to take open measures that might involve the United States in the war. But there was a positive side as well. Unlike Churchill, Roosevelt never feared a vote of no confidence. Electoral victory guaranteed presidential power for four years.

How did Americans approach the formulation of strategy? A long postwar tradition suggests that Americans approached such matters with a double-edged naiveté. Isolated by the oceans, cocooned in a political system devoted to preservation of liberty rather than exercise of state power, Americans were innocents in making strategy. "This unearned security during a long century had the effect upon our national habits of mind which the lazy enjoyment of unearned income so often has upon the descendants of a hard-working grandfather."[22] In peace they had failed to see the German and Japanese challenges to the balance of power or the need for engagement in European affairs. In the midst of war, which Americans invariably viewed as a crusade, they adopted an unreasonable doctrine of unconditional surrender. They failed to foresee the necessity of balancing Soviet encroachments in Europe until it was too late because they could only conceive of other nations as friends or foes. The complaint is similar to one made in an official history:

> In their preliminaries, developments, and immediate sequels World War I and World War II followed a cycle whose phases are well marked: (1) prior to the war, insufficient military expenditures, based on the public's prewar conviction that war could not come to America; (2) discovery that war could come after all; (3) a belated rush for arms, men, ships, and planes to overcome the nation's demonstrated military weakness; (4) advance of the producing and training program, attended by misunderstandings, delays, and costly outlay, but gradual creation of a large and powerful army; (5) mounting successes in the field, and eventual victory; (6) immediately thereafter, rapid demobilization and dissolution of the army as a powerful fighting force; (7) sharp reduction of appropriations sought by the military establishment, dictated by concern over its high cost and for a time by the revived hope that, again, war would not come to America.[23]

The gravamen of the charge, then, is that American democracy in the twentieth century has proven itself ill-suited to steady and sound strategy.

This indictment has some merit. America's unwillingness to participate in the League of Nations surely deprived that organization of what little vitality it might have developed. Without an American willingness to keep the balance in both Europe and Asia favorable to the Western democracies, the dictatorships could and did gamble on expansion. It was folly, but not groundless folly, for Hitler and the Japanese militarists to believe that the

---

22 Walter Lippmann, *U.S. Foreign Policy: Shield of the Republic* (Boston, 1943), p. 49. See also his *U.S. War Aims* (Boston, 1944).
23 Watson, *Chief of Staff*, p. 23.

United States would be unable and unwilling to throw its weight behind Britain.

But the critics of American strategy-making often overdraw the charge of strategic fecklessness.[24] For example, the funding of the navy during the interwar period was sufficient to maintain a formidable force. The navy may not have reached parity with the Royal Navy until the outbreak of war, but it did receive the resources to build a substantial fleet, and more importantly, to experiment with new forms of naval power such as the aircraft carrier.[25] American naval strength reached its low point in the late 1920s when the foreign threat was lowest. Beginning in 1933 with authorization for two aircraft carriers and several dozen smaller vessels, the navy grew steadily through additional appropriations in 1934, 1938, and 1940 that included 10,000 naval aircraft in the last year. Even at its weakest, the navy was the second largest in the world and one of the most efficient.

Few countries could lay claim to great statesmanship during the 1930s; yet here too the usual charges against the United States seem excessive. If the European powers, which had the military resources and interests refused to confront Hitler, why should the United States have done so? And in the Pacific, the United States attempted to walk a fine line between condoning Japanese behavior in China and provoking war. Yet, when the leaders of Japan decided to attack a country vastly superior in military potential and their near-equal in current strength, the groundwork already existed for victory. The Two Ocean Navy Act of 1940 had already authorized many of the aircraft carriers that swept Japan from the seas.

The modern presidency and modern American government in fact evolved during the 1920–45 period. The Reorganization Act of 1939 played an important role in consolidating presidential power by creating the Executive Office. Even more important were changes in the military command structure after the outbreak of war. At the top, the single most important step occurred with the creation in 1942 of the Joint Chiefs of Staff (JCS) to replace the Joint Army and Navy Board. The Joint Board had been reasonably effective, but it dealt with the intersection of service interests rather than with strategic decisions.[26] Army chief of staff Douglas MacArthur summed up the prevailing view in his 1932 report to the Secretary of War:

> The ultimate mission of the two services is, in a very true sense, the only element in common between fighting on the land and on the sea. The line between the army and navy fields of activity, namely, the coastline, is an insur-

---

24 For a particularly cogent argument, see John Braeman, "Power and Diplomacy: The 1920's Reappraised," *The Review of Politics* 44 (July 1982), pp. 342–69.
25 See the discussion of early American carrier aviation in Norman Friedman, *U.S. Aircraft Carriers: An Illustrated Design History* (Annapolis, 1983), pp. 31–78.
26 See the brief discussion in Watson, *Chief of Staff,* pp. 79–81.

mountable geographical obstacle for each. . . . So the line of demarcation between the army and navy is clear-cut and permanent in character.[27]

Some modification of this attitude of course occurred. "Joint Action of the Army and the Navy," the official statement of doctrine for control of joint operations, included provisions for unified command under certain circumstances in its 1935 and later versions.[28] But until war broke out, agreements between army and navy for command of joint operations resembled carefully negotiated treaties rather than working organizational links.

The JCS soon became a far more effective body than the Joint Board. Created in January 1942, it included the chief of staff, the Chief of Naval Operations (CNO), the commander in chief of the United States Fleet (COMINCH), and the commanding general of the Army Air Forces. By summer the organization had evolved further through the consolidation of the positions of CNO and COMINCH in the hands of Admiral Ernest J. King, and the addition of a new member, Admiral William D. Leahy, who became the President's chief of staff. Characteristically, FDR never described the functions and duties of the JCS.[29] He did, however, make clear to the chiefs that they worked for him as commander in chief. As the war continued, the service secretaries lost their influence over the formulation of strategy; instead, the JCS alone hammered out strategic decisions under the direction of a President who paid close attention to the day-to-day running of the war.

The war also enforced major reforms of the army and navy departments. In both cases, the positions of the chief of staff and CNO gained strength in ways not envisioned until the war. Before the war, for example, the CNO was to control overall war planning and training, while the commander-in-chief U.S. Fleet (COMINCH) was to run operations. This arrangement proved unworkable. With the consolidation of the two offices, King acquired unusual power over the usually independent bureaus of the navy, but the President blocked any formal reorganization of the department. In the army,

---

27 Report of the Chief of Staff to the Secretary of the Army, in *Report of the Secretary of War to the President, 1932* (Washington, 1932), p. 95. Interestingly enough, MacArthur argued that "The national strategy of any war - that is, the selection of national objectives and the determination of the general means and methods to be applied in attaining them, as well as the development of the broad policies applicable to the prosecution of war - are decisions that must be made by the head of the State, acting in conformity with the expressed will of Congress. . . . The issues involved were so far reaching in their effects, and so vital to the life of the Nation, that this phase of coordinating Army and Navy effort could not be delegated by the Commander in Chief to any subordinate authority." Ibid., p. 97.

28 *JB* 350, Serial 514.

29 For a good brief overview of the JCS system, see the summary account in National Archives, *Federal Records of World War II*, Vol. 2, *Military Agencies* (Washington, 1951), pp. 6–13; also William D. Leahy, *I Was There* (New York, 1950), pp. 95–107, and more generally Eric Larrabee, *Commander in Chief: Franklin Delano Roosevelt, His Lieutenants & Their War* (New York, 1987).

Marshall overhauled the high command structure when the war began, and assigned most of the general staff's administrative duties to three new commands: army ground forces, army service forces, and army air forces. He slashed the size of the general staff and at the same time created the operations division (OPD) to formulate strategy and control the war.[30]

THREATS AND CHALLENGES

By the 1920s new dimensions of national security not seen in earlier periods of U.S. history had emerged. Some Americans argued that the preservation of the European balance of power was now a national interest, and although this concern had not provided the decisive motivation for intervention in World War I, it did carry weight among a small but influential group.[31] A parallel school of thought perceived American colonies in the Pacific as an extension of national interests; naval planning, in particular, took into account the need to defend those colonies. Finally, the American consciousness had absorbed the notion that it might be necessary to fight for democracy as a principle. Whereas traditional American exceptionalism had suggested that the United States could flourish as the sole republican regime in a world of monarchies and tyrannies, Woodrow Wilson had implicitly argued that isolation was no longer possible.

When Wilson presented the Versailles Treaty to the Senate he made a different case, telling its members that "America may be said to have just reached her majority as a world power" and that "there can be no question of our ceasing to be a world power."[32] Less than six months later he told Congress that "a fundamental change has taken place with reference to the position of America. . . . No policy of isolation will satisfy the growing needs and opportunities of America."[33] Yet few people accepted that expansive definition of national security in the 1920s and 1930s. For most, the prospects of a serious war seemed remote; the purpose of the armed forces was to control colonies, to preserve military expertise, and to discourage potential aggressors. As the neutrality legislation of the 1930s revealed, many in Congress were willing to contract American rights overseas in order to avoid war.

As war clouds gathered in Europe and the Pacific, Americans began to recognize the threat of Nazi Germany and to accept some of the burdens

[30] For Marshall's reforms, see James E. Hewes, Jr., *From Root to McNamara: Organization and Administration 1900–1963* (Washington, 1975), pp. 57–103.
[31] See Robert Osgood, *Ideals and Self-Interest in America's Foreign Relations* (Chicago, 1953), pp. 307–428.
[32] Address to the Senate, 10 July 1919, in Ray Stannard Baker and William E. Dodd, eds., *The Public Papers of Woodrow Wilson: War and Peace* (New York, 1922), Vol. 1, pp. 550–51.
[33] Ibid., Vol. 2, pp. 430–31.

required to stop Hitler. From summer 1940, for example, two-thirds of Americans supported a year's compulsory military service – although in August 1941, Congress came within a vote of denying the administration an extension of compulsory military service.[34]

How did army and navy planners view the long-term threats to national security?[35] Throughout the 1920s, they saw no immediate threat: the armed forces were rather a form of insurance.[36] Since "economic and racial struggle" caused wars and since such competition apparently continued, the armed forces must prepare against undefined future emergencies.[37] In the meantime, they garrisoned key defensive positions and prepared to aid imperiled American citizens and interests. In general, planners throughout the late 1920s maintained a sanguine view not only of America's economic strength but of its social cohesiveness and its political efficiency.

This confidence was evident in the "Blue-Orange Estimate of the Situation" completed in January 1929 and accepted by the Joint Board (although only the navy accepted the implied decisions). The Estimate provided a comprehensive net assessment of the balance between America and Japan, and noted that "The United States is now the richest nation in the world with practically no foreign debt and with almost unlimited credit."[38] Noting its near autarky in raw materials and industrial potential, planners calculated that a year after mobilization the United States could produce 1,500 aircraft a month – compared with a Japanese maximum of 700 a year. Confident of the quality of American equipment, the planners were also confident about the resilience of a country they viewed as "mainly Anglo-Saxon in race and institutions. Our government is democratic and the world war showed that a strong President can assume autocratic powers with the consent of the people." That background of confidence inspired war plans even against potential adversaries as powerful as an Anglo-Japanese combination.

By the mid-1930s American military planners correctly understood that Japan had embarked on a campaign of expansion in East Asia and that world politics had entered a period of turmoil.[39] By the late 1930s, the sense of threat was acute. In his annual report of 1938, the Secretary of War suggested that the danger of a second world war "made essential a reorientation of our military policy." Moreover, he argued, "in the military sense the Americas are no longer continents" and referred to "the simple unadulterated fact that the range and destructive potentialities of weapons of warfare, primarily those whose realm is the skies, have, in recent years, so shortened the elements of distance and time that any hostile air base established anywhere within

---

34 See the polling data in Cantril and Strunk, eds., *Public Opinion*, p. 459.
35 See Fred Greene, "The Military View of American National Policy, 1904–1940," *American Historical Review*, 66:2 (January 1961), pp. 354–77.
36 See *Report of the Secretary of War to the President, 1923* (Washington, 1923), pp. 6–7.
37 Ibid., p. 18.
38 JB 325, Serial 280.
39 See *Report of the Secretary of War to the President, 1937* (Washington, 1937), p. 1.

effective striking proximity of the Panama Canal would prove a vital threat to that waterway – and therefore, a threat to the very security of these United States."[40] The requirements of hemispheric defense suggested mobile and flexible forces.[41]

At the same time the navy moved toward a two-ocean standard of naval power. Where it had previously emphasized operations in the Pacific, by 1940 it aimed at having "forces sufficient to enable us to have complete freedom of action in either ocean while retaining forces in the other ocean for effective defense of our vital security."[42] The possibility of a Nazi occupation of Britain and of German control of the Royal Navy represented serious threats to the United States.

For the navy, particularly after the early 1930s, the likely enemy was Japan. Unlike their army counterparts, navy planners believed that in case of war the navy should mount a serious effort to rescue or recover the Philippines.[43] By 1941, the navy had assembled the building blocks for a successful operation against Japan: a long-range and balanced fleet increasingly centered on aircraft carriers; the concepts for seizing, building, and defending island bases; and long-range submarines to attack enemy lines of communications. The navy knew that the coming war would be long and hard and that victory would probably not come through a cataclysmic battle but through a prolonged series of campaigns.[44]

The army never managed to focus on a clearly defined enemy in the interwar period. Army planners did not know until the late 1930s that they would have to fight the Germans in Europe; therefore they targeted a generic enemy. The result was a preference for forces designed for the Western Hemisphere; when war came, the army adjusted its organization and equipment slowly. In 1940, for example, Marshall defended a program for modernizing the army's 75mm guns rather than investing more heavily in 105mm howitzers on the grounds that "concrete fortifications and masonry villages of European battlefields may dictate a need for a weapon firing a heavier projectile than . . .

---

40   *Report of the Secretary of War to the President, 1939* (Washington, 1939), p. 2. See also the annual report of the Chief of Staff for that year, pp. 23ff.

41   General Marshall's biennial report of 30 June 1941, in Walter Millis, ed., *The War Reports of General of the Army George C. Marshall, General of the Army H.H. Arnold, Fleet Admiral Ernest J. King*, (Philadelphia, 1947), p. 35.

42   *Report of the Secretary of the Navy to the President, 1940* (Washington, 1940), p. 2.

43   On interwar planning, see Russell Weigley, "The Role of the War Department and the Army," and Waldo H. Heinrichs, Jr., "The Role of the United States Navy," in Dorothy Borg and Shumpei Okamoto, eds., *Pearl Harbor as History: Japanese-American Relations 1931–1941* (New York, 1973), pp. 165–88, 197–224. On ORANGE, the plan for war with Japan, see Louis Morton, "War Plan ORANGE: Evolution of a Strategy," *World Politics*, 11 (January 1959), pp. 221–50.

44   See Philip T. Rosen, "The Treaty Navy, 1919–1937," and John Major, "The Navy Plans for War, 1937–1941," in Kenneth J. Hagan, ed., *In Peace and War: Interpretations of American Naval History 1775–1978* (Westport, CT, 1978), pp. 221–62.

the 75-mm gun, but our forces would rarely be confronted with such targets in this hemisphere."[45]

As a result of this limited strategic vision and a predilection for mobility – misunderstood as a plenitude of motor transport and a dearth of cumbersome equipment (rather than ability to move on the battlefield) – the army created infantry divisions too light for Europe.[46] Even the revised tables of organization of 1942 and 1943 did not compare favorably with the firepower of comparable German units at full strength. In tank and anti-tank warfare, the stubborn adherence of the army ground forces to the mobile and reliable but undergunned and under-armored Sherman tank, and their insistence on independent battalions of largely useless tank destroyers, suggests the dominance of the prewar misunderstandings of what mobility required.[47]

The threats to American security changed as war approached. American decision-makers worried briefly but intensely about defending the Western Hemisphere against direct assault by Germany and by Nazi sympathizers. These fears had real consequences, for in 1939 and 1940 the army and navy prepared for intervention in Brazil to forestall the creation of a Nazi regime there.[48] Until summer 1942, the United States stood on the strategic defensive to protect itself against direct attacks, while shoring up the countries fighting Hitler. American strategic decision-makers faced two critical problems during this phase: how to build a domestic consensus to support intervention on the Allied side, and how to expand U.S. military forces while sustaining the Allies and keeping sufficient forces ready to deter enemy aggression.

The first problem was less serious than decision-makers thought at the time, although its severity is a matter of dispute. The second involved a series of painful tradeoffs. The barter of fifty American destroyers for British bases in the Western Hemisphere and the shipment of "surplus" army equipment in summer 1940 (including 500,000 rifles, 900 field guns, and 80,000 machine guns) bit deep into the growing armed forces, particularly the army.

[45] Quoted in Janice McKenney, "More Bang for the Buck in the Interwar Army: The 105-mm Howitzer," *Military Affairs,* 42 (April 1978), p. 84.
[46] Kent Roberts Greenfield, Robert R. Palmer, and Bell I. Wiley, *The Organization of Ground Combat Troops* (Washington, 1947), pp. 274–75; Robert M. Kennedy, *The German Campaign In Poland* (1939) (Washington, 1956), pp. 30–31; W.J.K. Davies, *German Army Handbook 1939–1945* (New York, 1974), pp. 37, 40–42. German light and heavy machine guns were basically the same weapon, the redoubtable MG 34: most of the American machine guns were the less effective but still adequate 30 caliber. German mortars were 50mm and 81mm, American mortars 60mm and 81mm; antitank guns the same; German heavy howitzers were 150mm vs. 155mm for the Americans.
[47] See Constance McLaughlin Green, Harry C. Thomson, and Peter C. Roots, *The Ordnance Department: Planning Munitions for War* (Washington, 1955), pp. 275–87; Christopher R. Gabel, *Seek, Strike, and Destroy: U.S. Army Tank Destroyer Doctrine in World War II,* Leavenworth Papers #12 (Ft. Leavenworth, KS, 1985).
[48] Watson, *Chief of Staff,* pp. 94–95.

Appropriately, it required presidential decisions to force the services to surrender even obsolescent but nevertheless valuable weapons to countries that
seemed on the verge of collapse.

After Midway, the United States embarked on a strategic offensive that
continued until the end of the war. In this respect, the American strategic
experience was unique; where other countries faced mortal perils during
periods of strategic defense – the Battle of Britain and the invasion of the
Soviet Union, for example – the United States was at no time vulnerable to
direct enemy action. In order to avoid defeat, the United States had to sustain
its allies on a vast scale; in order to win, it had to embark on the most
extensive strategic offensives in history.

From mid-1942 the American armed forces confronted the challenge of
storming two continent-sized citadels. It would not suffice to blockade the
enemy and thus reduce him; both Nazi-occupied Europe and Japan's Asian
empire were virtually autarkic. Nor could one hope to cause the enemy's
collapse by protracted attrition. Rather, the United States had to pierce a
thick crust of defenses and penetrate into the enemy heartlands. The United
States had to project its power along extraordinarily long and vulnerable
lines of communication – nearly a month's sailing time from San Francisco to
Sydney, more than two weeks from New York to Liverpool, and over two
months from New York to the Persian Gulf.[49] It then required completely
new combinations of men and machines that included multidivision amphibious assaults to batter its way into Europe and up the Pacific island chains
toward Japan.

RESOURCES

Peace and war posed radically differing challenges to American strategists.
The problem in peace was to balance scanty resources between current requirements and the demands of long-term investment in bases and evolving
technologies. In war the problem was vastly different: resources available
swelled astonishingly. But it was also similar, for the armed forces likewise
confronted difficult tradeoffs between near- and long-term requirements.

Throughout the interwar period, peacetime budgets for the services remained comparatively low as a percentage of Gross National Product (Table
14.1). The army reacted by adhering to its traditional preference for a cadre
force, along the lines Emory Upton had advocated after the Civil War.[50]
Rather than forming small full-strength units, it maintained the cadre for
much larger forces that would fill out upon mobilization. On the whole, this
effort was less than successful, particularly when compared with the immense
expansion that turned the Weimar Republic's 100,000-man *Reichswehr* into

---

[49]	From Marshall's second biennial report, 1941–1943, in Millis, ed., *War Reports*, p. 77.
[50]	See Russell F. Weigley, *History of the United States Army* (New York, 1967), pp. 400ff.

Table 14.1. *Interwar army and navy budgets*[51] *(excluding veterans compensation and pensions)*

	1920	1925	1930	1935	1940
Percent of GNP	2.8	.7	.9	1.2	1.8
Percent of federal outlays	37	24	25	14	20

Hitler's army. Still, the army succeeded in maintaining an elaborate school system that expanded extremely fast in 1940–42 to accommodate the influx of recruits. The navy was altogether luckier; it received authorization in 1933 and 1934 to build three aircraft carriers, seven battleships, eleven cruisers, over a hundred destroyers, and more than forty submarines. But the navy did not gain real superiority over Japan even after passage of a ten-year $1.1 billion expansion program in 1938. The Japanese had their own expansion program, and the navy lacked adequate overseas bases and manpower.

Despite the stringent budgets of the 1930s, all three services developed successful weapons systems at least in prototype form during this period. Perhaps the greatest successes came in the Army Air Forces, which "fought during World War II with aircraft which were all either in production or under development prior to December 7, 1941."[52] Similarly, in 1940 the navy ordered the first of its *Essex* class carriers, and had even earlier developed submarines suitable for long-range operations against Japanese lines of communication.[53] Even the army achieved notable successes with its M-1 rifle and 105mm howitzer. Scanty as the interwar budgets were, they did not preclude the services from performing two essential tasks: developing the weapons needed and preparing a mobilization base for larger wartime forces.

Peacetime thinking about mobilization, particularly in the army, nevertheless had several important flaws.[54] It envisioned an orderly process beginning from a definite M-Day.[55] Yet the thinking behind all plans before 1940 flowed from "the assumption that a nation passed from a peace status to a war status as quickly and as decisively as one passes from one room to another. No provision whatsoever had been made for the maze of corridors, blind alleys and series of antechambers – labeled 'Phoney War,' 'cash and

---

[51] Percentages derived from *Historical Statistics*, pp. 224, 1114.

[52] Wesley Frank Craven and James Lea Cate, eds., *The Air Forces in World War II*, Vol. 6, *Men and Planes* (Chicago, 1955), p. 193.

[53] See Ernest Andrade, Jr., "Submarine Policy in the United States Navy, 1919–1941," *Military Affairs*, 35:2 (April 1971), pp. 50–56.

[54] On interwar mobilization planning, see Marvin A. Kreidberg and Merton G. Henry, *History of Military Mobilization in the United States Army 1775–1945* (Washington, 1955), pp. 377–540.

[55] See R. Elberton Smith, *The Army and Economic Mobilization* (Washington, 1959), pp. 73–86.

Table 14.2. *Resources and military power, 1940*[56]

	Population (millions)	Raw Steel (000s metric tons)	Electricity (gigawatt hours)
United States	132	60.7	178
Germany	70	21.5	63
Japan	73+	6.8	9
Britain	46+	13.1	28
Soviet Union	170	18.3	48

carry,' 'more than mere words,' 'Lend Lease,' etc. – which the United States was compelled . . . to traverse between September 1, 1939, and December 7, 1941."[57] Moreover, the army's high command was not ready to cope with rapidly changing demands for forces capable of intervening in Latin America, or for large air forces with which to impress the dictators.

Once war began the latent power of the United States came into its own. What were its resources? (Table 14.2.)[58] The United States was virtually self-sufficient in many important areas: it produced some 1.35 billion barrels of crude petroleum in 1940, for example, and met its needs without importing more than 3 percent of that amount.[59] Yet even in those areas where raw materials fell short (rubber was the critical example), conservation and new technologies remedied shortages. Synthetic rubber production, a negligible source in 1942, reached nearly 800,000 long tons by 1944, or only slightly less than all rubber production in 1940.[60]

More fortunate than either friends or foes, the United States was the only major participant in the war whose homeland did not become a battleground, and this security was a major help in maximizing production. The United States did not tower over its competitors with respect to population alone; its strength lay rather in the size, versatility, and productivity of its economy. The last point is particularly important; the latent power of the American war machine was vast not merely because of its size, but because of its ability to draw on extraordinary ingenuity and organizational skill. Table 14.3 on motor vehicle production suggests the relative potential of the American economy. The U.S. aircraft industry similarly dwarfed that of every

[56] Sources: *Historical Statistics of the United States;* United States Strategic Bombing Survey, *The Effects of Strategic Bombing on Japan's War Economy* (Washington, 1946); B. R. Mitchell, *European Historical Statistics,* 2nd rev. ed. (New York, 1980).

[57] Robert Sherwood, *Roosevelt and Hopkins: An Intimate History* (New York, 1948), p. 280.

[58] In what follows, I have relied heavily on U.S. Bureau of the Budget, *The United States at War* (Washington, 1946).

[59] *Historical Statistics,* p. 593.

[60] *The United States at War,* pp. 293–97.

Table 14.3. *Production of motor vehicles (000's)*[61]

	1929	1937
United States	5,358	4,810
Europe (without Soviet Union)	637	1,109
Germany	105	327
France	224	200
Britain	217	493
Soviet Union	1	200
Japan	0	10+

other country. In 1936, for example, the Americans possessed approximately five times as many civil aircraft as Germany, despite Lufthansa's phenomenal success as an airline; only a few years later American planes were flying almost eight times as many miles.[62] Figures such as these reinforced the underlying confidence of American planners as war approached in 1940 and 1941.

Wartime productivity of the American economy matched or surpassed that of peacetime. In 1944, it produced four times as much munitions as the British with fewer than twice the workers (13.4 million workers in the U.S. vs. 7.8 million in the U.K. in mid-1944).[63] When all is said and done, the effort remains a remarkable testimony to American business organization; the explosion of military production in 1942 and 1943 came as a surprise to Americans and foreigners alike.[64] In his pioneering study of the American corporation in its heyday, Peter Drucker has noted that

> The experience which directly shows the true nature of modern mass production was, of course, the American industrial conversion to war in 1942 and 1943. It has by now become clear that most of the experts in this country, including the majority of industrial engineers and managers, underestimated our productive capacity so completely in 1940 and 1941 precisely because practically all of us failed to understand the concept of human organization

[61] League of Nations, *Bulletin of Monthly Statistics*, 19:6 (June 1938), p. 268.
[62] Heinz J. Nowarra and Karlheinz Kens, *Die deutsche Flugzeuge 1933–1945*, 5th ed. (Munich, 1977), p. 9.
[63] W. K. Hancock and M. M. Gowing, *British War Economy* (London, 1949), pp. 367–68. One wartime economist has argued that "the munitions production of the major belligerents at full mobilization was roughly proportional to the size of their prewar industrial labor force combined with the prewar level of productivity in industry." Raymond W. Goldsmith, "The Power of Victory, Munitions Output in World War II," *Military Affairs*, 10 (Spring 1946), p. 79.
[64] For interesting comparisons with the British effort, see M. M. Postan, *British War Production* (London, 1952), pp. 243–48, and Correlli Barnett, *The Pride and the Fall: The Dream and Illusion of Britain as a Great Nation* (New York, 1986), passim.

which underlies mass production. We argued in terms of *existing* raw material supplies and *existing* plant capacity and failed to realize that we are capable of producing new raw materials, of designing new machines for new purposes, and of building new plants in practically no time *provided the human organization is in existence.*[65]

Drucker drives home this point with the story of how, during the war, Cadillac mass-produced bombsights using a labor force of superannuated prostitutes from Detroit's slums – a workforce that intelligent management made effective.[66]

If bringing hitherto marginal workers into war production represented one kind of managerial success, the mobilization of the nation's scientific capacities was another.[67] Roosevelt created the National Defense Research Committee (NDRC) in summer 1940, and one year later the Office of Scientific Research and Development, of which NDRC became a part. Despite inevitable friction and difficulties, the services worked closely with thousands of civilian scientists. The results included not only such weapons as the atomic bomb, but a stream of innovations such as the DUKW (an amphibious truck), a wide range of tropical medicines and pesticides, and the stunningly lethal proximity fuze. The enemy outmatched the United States in selected weapons, in some cases throughout the war – German tanks were clearly superior, as was the German light machine gun. Yet American forces had an overall edge in the technology of war, an edge that a combination of quality *and* quantity created and that neither enemies nor allies could match. This advantage was particularly true in the mundane devices that made American forces mobile and sustainable. After the war General Dwight D. Eisenhower singled out five pieces of equipment as vital to success in Europe: the DUKW, bulldozer, jeep, 2½-ton truck, and C-47 transport aircraft. "Curiously enough," he noted, "none of these is designed for combat."[68]

Some industries grew virtually from scratch during the war; in 1941, for example, U.S. merchant ship construction was some 1.1 million deadweight tons. Shipyards produced over 8 million tons in 1942 and over 19 million tons in 1943; without this construction the U.S. could not have sustained the war in the Pacific or the Normandy invasion. To achieve this growth the U.S. Maritime Commission standardized a particular design – the so-called Liberty Ship – slow, obsolescent, and simple. In 1941 the ship took nearly a year to build; by the end of 1942 less than two months.[69] Part of the explanation for

---

65 Peter F. Drucker, *The Concept of the Corporation* (1946; New York, 1983), p. 32. Emphasis in the original.
66 Drucker, *Adventures of a Bystander* (New York, 1978), pp. 270–71. Postan, *British War Production*, pp. 394–95, notes the ways in which chronic shortages of skilled managers afflicted British war production.
67 For a good short account, see James Phinney Baxter, *Scientists Against Time* (1946; Cambridge, MA, 1968).
68 Dwight D. Eisenhower, *Crusade In Europe* (Garden City, NJ, 1948), pp. 163–64.
69 *The U.S. at War*, pp. 135–43.

Table 14.4. *Relative magnitude of munitions production, 1944*

United States	100
Germany	40
USSR	35+
Britain	25
Japan	15
Canada	5–

Table 14.5. *Trend of combat munitions production of the major belligerents (1944 = 100)*

Country	1938	1939	1940	1941	1942	1943	1944
United States	2	2	5	11	47	91	100
Canada	0	2	6	27	73	102	100
Britain	4	10	34	59	83	100	100
USSR	12	20	30	53	71	87	100
Germany	16	20	35	35	51	80	100
Japan	8	10	16	32	49	72	100

these successes stems from increased worker productivity, which rose by 25 percent between 1939 and 1944.[70] Shortly after the war ended, one economist calculated the relative magnitude of the munitions production of the major belligerents in 1944 (Table 14.4).[71] If one factors in nonlethal but nonetheless critical goods (food, merchant ships, trucks, and so forth), the dominance of American war production becomes even more striking. The American productive surge was startling in both scale and rapidity, as Table 14.5 shows.[72]

The chief shortage throughout the war was manpower. Unlike any other power in the war, the United States committed itself to four efforts: a great army, navy, air force, and productive base. The manpower shortage hurt the army most of all, leading it to take what Maurice Matloff has called the "90 Division Gamble," in effect to settle for a relatively small army.[73] The crisis caused by the German offensive in the Ardennes in December 1944 stripped the United States of all strategic reserves. The result was a "photo finish" in

[70] Goldsmith, "The Power of Victory," p. 71.
[71] Ibid., p. 72.
[72] Civilian Production Administration, *Industrial Mobilization for War: History of the War Production Board and Predecessor Agencies 1940–1945*, Vol. 1, *Program and Administration* (Washington, 1947), pp. 964–66.
[73] Maurice Matloff, "The 90-Division Gamble," in Kent Roberts Greenfield, ed., *Command Decisions* (Washington, 1960), pp. 365–81.

Table 14.6. *Mobilization of the labor force of the U.K. and the U.S. for war, June 1944*[74] *(percentages)*

	United Kingdom	United States
A. Armed forces	22	18.5
B. Civilian war employment	33	21.5
C. Total A + B	55	40
D. Other employment	45	58
E. Unemployed	—	2
F. Total labor force	100	100

which by V-E day every active U.S. division had been deployed overseas and all but two had been in battle. Moreover, the demands on high-quality manpower and the ability of potential soldiers to volunteer for the other services through 1942 degraded the quality of American infantrymen. One 1943 sample of infantrymen was over a half-inch shorter and six pounds lighter than the army average and had a smaller percentage of top-grade scorers on the intelligence tests.[75] Such deficiencies had a bearing on the general inferiority of American infantry units vis-à-vis their German counterparts.

Yet the American manpower pool was never as strained as that of the British (Table 14.6). The British war mobilization was not necessarily more efficient: "the British people were compelled to undergo, irrespective of the shipping shortage, a sharp decline in their domestic standard of living, their export trade, and their capital inheritance."[76] Unlike the reasonably well-fed and clothed American workers, whose productivity actually increased, that of British workers fell in a number of critical sectors.

Remarkably, the United States paid for the war with a low level of inflation – barely 30 percent between 1939 and 1945.[77] American leaders performed this feat with comprehensive price controls, a less successful effort to stabilize wages, and, with the exception of 1943, heavy taxation. In 1945, for example, roughly 45 percent of governmental funding came from taxes. But taxation covered only one quarter of overall war expenditures, as opposed to more than half in Britain and Canada.[78] Price, rent, and to a lesser extent wage controls provided economic stability, but the Chairman of the War Production Board, Donald Nelson, held "that the highest levels of industrial production come only from an economy that is well supplied with

[74] Hancock and Gowing, *British War Economy*, p. 370.
[75] Robert R. Palmer, "The Procurement of Enlisted Personnel: The Problem of Quality," in Robert R. Palmer, Bell I. Wiley, and William R. Keast, *The Procurement and Training of Ground Combat Troops* (Washington, 1949), p. 3.
[76] Ibid., p. 373.
[77] *The U.S. at War*, p. 236.
[78] Ibid., p. 259.

machinery, repair parts, power, and transport facilities, homes for workers, water, sewers, and utilities, and a generous standard of necessities."[79] As a result, although production of most consumer durables stopped, food, clothing, and repair items remained at prewar levels or slightly increased.

The chief instrument of mobilization was the War Production Board. Although the services controlled procurement, this agency was responsible for overall production. It allocated scarce raw materials through a variety of mechanisms and scheduled production of common items such as valves and engines. The WPB was initially responsible to the President, and it served a particularly important role in balancing the requirements of the services, Allies, and civilian economy – a function in which it met bitter opposition from the services. The WPB contributed substantially to the war effort through its insistence in 1942 on scaling down production goals that would have exceeded the economy's capacity by 20 percent and have led to even worse bottlenecks than actually occurred.[80] The WPB's action involved a struggle with the military, since the JCS declared early in the war that "production of war materials should be governed by military requirements and not on the productive capacity of the country."[81] But the WPB did not generally base its production decisions in the early part of the war on strategic considerations – of which the military generally failed to inform it.

The production effort sustained not only burgeoning American forces but those of the allies as well. Some $48 billion went to lend-lease, two-thirds to the British Empire, over one-fifth to the Soviet Union, and the rest to others.[82] Lend-lease to the Soviet Union included no fewer than 430,000 jeeps and trucks by 1944, a transport fleet indispensable to Soviet advances from 1943 on.[83] The British Empire and Commonwealth drew close to half of its tanks, nearly one-fifth of its combat aircraft, three-fifths of its transport aircraft, and nearly two-fifths of its landing craft and ships from American sources.[84]

What of Allied contributions to American resources? Throughout most of the 1920s and 1930s, American planners expected that the Allies would contribute little to an American war effort. This attitude changed in 1938 when American and British planners first discussed operations in the Pacific. But in practical terms, no real benefit from the Allies appeared until 1940, when Roosevelt authorized a clandestine but extensive liaison with the British. With some exceptions – the 1940 destroyers-for-bases deal – the United

---

[79] Ibid., p. 128.

[80] See Donald M. Nelson, *Arsenal of Democracy: The Story of American War Production* (New York, 1946), pp. 368–90; Civilian Production Administration, *Industrial Mobilization*, pp. 273–92.

[81] Minutes, 9th Meeting of the JCS, 6 April 1942. In Paul Kesaris, ed., *Records of the Joint Chiefs of Staff, Part I: 1942–1945* (Frederick, MD, 1980–1983), henceforth JCS.

[82] James A. Huston, *Sinews of War: Army Logistics 1775–1953* (Washington, 1966), p. 454.

[83] See John Erickson, *The Road to Berlin* (Boulder, CO, 1983), p. 81.

[84] Postan, *British War Production*, p. 247.

States gained little quantitative advantage from its allies, at least early in the war. British Empire wartime aid to the United States amounted to between 25 and 30 percent of American lend-lease, according to British sources, although less than 20 percent according to American sources.[85] Much of this aid came in the form of direct support to troops in Britain, Australia, and other staging areas. Yet a comparison of relative aid figures does not tell the full story of America's gain from its wartime alliances.

The United States could not have successfully fought the war without Britain and the Soviet Union. Soviet forces pinned down two-thirds and sometimes three-quarters of German ground forces on the Eastern Front after June 1941, while the British Empire provided the jumping-off points for successful attacks on the German and Japanese empires. Although the eventual American drive through the Central Pacific owed little to Australian and New Zealand support, that effort would have been far more difficult without the attritional battles of 1942 along the lines of communication to the Antipodes that had worn the Japanese down. The drive from the Southwest Pacific used Australia as its base and involved large Dominion forces. And without the time that British and Soviet resistance to Nazi Germany bought, the United States would not have had the breathing space to arm.

Less obvious, perhaps, is the extent to which the American war effort benefited from the pooling of Anglo-American resources. One of the greatest advantages of the Allies throughout the war lay in the area of intelligence, particularly signals intelligence. Even before the war, the Americans and British shared some decrypted messages, and once the United States entered the war, the most remarkable coordination of intelligence efforts in history began. The British code-breaking establishment at Bletchley Park absorbed new American recruits, while American signals intelligence dominated the Pacific. Although some overlap occurred, it was far less than if the two nations had not cooperated so closely.

In addition, the United States benefited from the use of British designs either adapted to American needs or simply mass-produced in this country. Britain shared its designs for landing craft, merchant ships, and such indispensable devices as the cavity magnetron that made microwave radar possible. The Merlin engine made the American P-51 the best piston engine fighter of the war, and the United States also gained from British experience in operating a wide range of antisubmarine equipment, including sonar. Perhaps most remarkable was the institutionalization of logistical cooperation between the United States and the Empire.[86] The first such organization, created in early

---

[85] Hancock and Gowing, *British War Economy*, p. 376; Huston, *Sinews*, p. 454.
[86] See Richard M. Leighton and Robert W. Coakley, *Global Logistics and Strategy 1940–1943* (Washington, 1955), pp. 247–94. Although inevitably somewhat slanted, the British official histories are particularly good on this subject: H. Duncan Hall, *North American Supply* (London, 1955); Hall and C. C. Wrigley, with J. D. Scott, *Studies of Overseas Supply* (London, 1956); Postan, *British War Production*.

1942, was the Munitions Assignment Board, served to render the munitions industries of both countries a "common pool." The two allies made the same arrangement for raw materials and shipping. Although the combined boards never achieved the grip over production for which the British had hoped – the Americans, as chief producers, were too canny for that – they symbolized the cooperation of two great states. When Britain faced a critical shortage of shipping for imports in Spring 1943, the President allocated increased shipping at the expense of U.S. services and over the vociferous objections of his military advisers.[87] Both in emergencies and over the long haul the United States sustained its principal ally throughout the war.

STRATEGIC DECISION-MAKING

The goals of American national security policy throughout the 1920s and 1930s were quite simple: to ensure the physical security of the continental United States. Outlying possessions such as the Philippines also came under the American security umbrella, although this situation changed in 1934 after the United States officially declared its intention to grant Philippine independence within twelve years. More important was the Panama Canal, to which American planners devoted increasing attention in the late 1930s. In the 1920s, the elaborate coastal fortifications at each terminus of the Canal seemed adequate for its defense; by the end of the 1930s, however, the spread of airfields in Latin America suggested a new threat that the army, in particular, prepared to meet.[88] Growing concern in the late 1930s over the Panama Canal reflected a similar extension of the basic concepts of continental defense.

Throughout the nineteenth and early twentieth centuries the United States had resolutely opposed extension of European influence in the Western Hemisphere. But World War II, particularly after summer 1940, was qualitatively different. For a brief time, four factors came together to make the military threat to the Western Hemisphere appear direct and serious. These factors were the appeal of Fascism and Nazism in Latin America; the prospect of a Vichy French-Nazi alliance that could give the Germans bases in Dakar, only a short distance from Brazil; the advent of new military technologies, particularly long-range aviation; and the possible collapse of Britain. In addition, American decision-makers used force throughout the interwar period to protect their citizens and possessions abroad, and although the deployments required were not large by today's standards they were substantial given the forces maintained at the time. The United States was a small power in terms of military force, but it was not purely isolationist. It pos-

---

[87] This episode is well described in Richard M. Leighton, "U.S. Merchant Shipping and the British Import Crisis," in Greenfield, ed., *Command Decisions*, pp. 119–224.

[88] See Stetson Conn, Rose C. Engelman, and Byron Fairchild, *Guarding the United States and Its Outposts* (Washington, 1964), pp. 300–27.

sessed a considerable navy, and its forces operated overseas with some regularity; nearly one-third of the United States army, for example, was in service outside the continental United States throughout the 1930s.

American decision-makers came to see in the experience of the depression and the spread of militaristic and totalitarian regimes a confirmation of Wilson's basic view that a liberal world order was the only guarantee of American safety. For that reason, their long-term objective became the removal of the causes of war by creating such an order. American strategy in World War II is understandable only within the context of such a vision. The United States sought not merely to defeat particular enemies, but to reconstruct enemy polities and the larger world order.

American strategy focused on containing Japanese expansion in East Asia and thwarting German hegemony in Europe. In Roosevelt's casual words at Casablanca, once war had begun, America's objective became the "unconditional surrender" of the Axis Powers. Yet it soon became apparent that – with occasional exceptions – the United States sought not the obliteration of its opponents but their reconstruction in its own image. MacArthur's startling words at the Japanese surrender, "it is for us, both victors and vanquished, to rise to that higher dignity which alone befits the sacred purposes we are about to serve," pointed directly toward the reconstruction and rehabilitation that followed.[89]

In addition, the United States developed objectives that concerned its own allies. The Americans, and in particular the President, wished to see the British Empire abandon imperial preference and begin to decolonize. Roosevelt's badgering of Churchill over the Indian revolt of 1942 is a particularly telling example of this interest.[90] While American decision-makers hoped that other colonial empires would follow suit, most, like Wilson, preferred gradual rather than radical emancipation. As for the minor allies, of which Free France was the most important, FDR's antipathy to De Gaulle represented not only personal dislike, but a larger fear of postwar military dictatorship in France. Although American leaders did not see democracy as immediately and universally suited for implantation abroad, they intended to foster it where they thought it had a chance.

Throughout much of the war the United States viewed its two other great allies, the Soviet Union and China, with particular anxiety. Both bore the brunt of the Axis onslaught, both were in danger of collapse or, worse, of concluding separate and unfavorable peace agreements with the enemy, and both had been outsiders in the prewar international system. Without the vigorous participation of both, American planners feared, the war could not

---

89   Quoted in D. Clayton James, *The Years of MacArthur*, Vol. 2, 1941–1945 (Boston, 1975), p. 709.

90   See in particular, Christopher Thorne, *Allies of a Kind: The United States, Britain, and the War Against Japan 1941–1945* (New York, 1978) and William Roger Louis, *Imperialism at Bay: The United States and the Decolonization of the British Empire 1941–1945* (New York, 1978).

be won; China and the Soviet Union were clearly combating the overwhelming bulk of Japanese and German ground forces. Planners considered the Soviet attrition of German forces essential to victory in Europe, and Chinese air bases and, eventually, ports vital to success in the Pacific. American strategy therefore aimed at keeping these two staggering allies in the war. In addition, the American vision of a liberal world order required that both states play a part as guarantors of stability in their war-shattered regions.

American objectives were thus not simply "unconditional surrender." In fact, American strategic objectives were extremely complex and involved numerous tradeoffs between short- and long-term goals. Consider only American relations with Britain. In 1940 and 1941 the tradeoff was between support for a Britain in desperate straits or the conservation of resources for defense of the Western Hemisphere. Later, American leaders sought to support and work in close harmony with the British while ensuring that the Empire would not block the creation of the new world order. The fact that public sympathies and antipathies were not infinitely malleable complicated the formulation of long-term objectives ever more. Popular attachments, dislikes, and suspicions, along with anxiety about casualties and the progress of the war, all exercised an influence on the translation of objectives into action.

Peacetime strategic decision-making in the United States looked very different from the making of strategy in war. Most notable was the role of Congress, which through a variety of actions – for example, the Neutrality Acts that restricted overseas arms sales, or a refusal to authorize funds to fortify Guam – exercised a substantial restraint on the wielding of military power. In peacetime the individual services rather than a joint organization dominated military planning.

Wartime decision-making was quite different. The President and the Joint Chiefs of Staff dominated the process. The service secretaries, despite one or two early attempts to participate in the formulation of strategy, soon found themselves excluded, an evolution that had parallels in the British War Cabinet as well. Congress virtually dropped out of sight from the point of view of strategic decision-making. The JCS normally met without the President although under the chairmanship of his personal chief of staff, Admiral Leahy. In this arrangement, the American system differed greatly from the British, in which the Prime Minister presided over many of the meetings of the Chiefs of Staff. Marshall indeed sometimes went weeks at a time without meeting the President. After the war, he confided that he had never visited Roosevelt at Hyde Park or Warm Springs and that he had rejected Hopkins's advice to strike up a personal relationship with the President. Rather, "he persisted in the belief that it was the best policy to keep away from the President as much as possible."[91] His chief colleague, Admiral King, tended

91 Robert Emmett Sherwood Papers, Houghton Library, Harvard University, Folder 1899, "Interview with George Catlett Marshall, 23 July 1947."

to agree, and saw in the "decentralized" American system far less civilian control than in Britain – and a good thing too.

King's picture was both inaccurate and a testimony to Roosevelt's skill as a manipulator. Before the war FDR had taken a close albeit erratic interest in military and naval affairs. In spring 1937, for example, he gave detailed orders for a joint exercise designed to test the services' ability to detect and destroy a fleet attacking either the east or west coasts.[92] During the war Roosevelt overruled the JCS far more frequently than Churchill ever did his Chiefs of Staff. The President had no compunction about ordering his military commanders to divest themselves of sorely needed weapons to bolster the British in 1940. In 1942 he instructed them to undertake the invasion of North Africa, of which they heartily disapproved. At Cairo in 1943, he ignored their advice and canceled operations in support of Chiang Kai-shek (the Andaman Islands invasion). In 1944 he conferred at Pearl Harbor with the Pacific theater commanders, MacArthur and Nimitz, in the absence of the JCS, whom he had pointedly not invited to the meeting on the invasion of the Philippines. These examples are only a few of the more notable times that FDR asserted his position as commander in chief, a title he regarded not as an honorific but as a job description.[93]

Roosevelt's wartime Chief of Staff concluded that FDR and Churchill "really ran the war . . . we were just artisans building definite patterns of strategy from the rough blueprints handed to us by our respective Commanders in Chief."[94] The difference in their control over the military was less of degree than of style. If Roosevelt did not keep the JCS by his side day in and day out, neither did Churchill use someone like Harry Hopkins as his surrogate. Hopkins, a man without formal position in the government or experience in military affairs, possessed unswerving loyalty to FDR and penetrating common sense. He accompanied the JCS on many of their travels and eased many of their dealings with the President. As Harold Smith, Director of the Bureau of the Budget put it, "Hopkins' sole job was to see everything from the President's point of view. He was bound by no preconceived notions, no legal inhibitions and he certainly had absolutely no respect for tradition."[95] Roosevelt's preference for indirection and informality led him to manipulate the military leadership, rather than, as in Churchill's case, to confront, cajole, or bully it. He maximized his own leverage, for example, by denying King's request to reorganize the Navy Department. The result was an unswerving civilian control that frequently extended downward to the details of policy.

---

[92]   JB 350, Serial 608.
[93]   Kent Roberts Greenfield, *American Strategy in World War II: A Reconsideration* (Baltimore, 1963), pp. 49–84; see also Larrabee, *Commander in Chief*.
[94]   Leahy, *I Was There*, p. 106.
[95]   Quoted in Sherwood, *Roosevelt and Hopkins*, p. 159.

The JCS organization itself grew enormously throughout the war, and JCS responsibilities consumed most of the senior leaders' time. After the war King estimated that he spent fully two-thirds of his time on JCS or Combined Chiefs of Staff business rather than purely Navy affairs.[96] As befited a body without formal charter, the JCS grew and changed as the war progressed. In late 1942 the Joint Deputy Chiefs of Staff emerged to relieve the Chiefs of some of their crushing administrative burden. The creation of a Joint Strategic Survey Committee in November 1942 provided advice on long-range strategic planning from a group of military "elder statesmen." In 1943 a Joint Logistics Committee began to handle logistical problems not tied to immediate war planning. Interestingly, the impetus for the creation of the JLC came from the President who, even while rejecting a JCS proposal to grant a written charter, informed them that "joint logistics planning should parallel joint strategic planning." Despite the protests of the Joint Staff Planners, that parallel planning began.[97]

As for the JCS itself, its members met regularly on Wednesdays over lunch, and almost invariably alone.[98] According to its chairman, it processed an average of 130 papers a month, an enormous burden. Compounding these burdens was a frustrating isolation from the rest of government. Coordination with the civilian agencies that controlled war production was frequently poor; even liaison with the President was sometimes unsatisfactory. The official historian notes that "the War Department was frequently indebted to the British Joint Staff Mission for copies of correspondence between the President and the Prime Minister dealing with future military operations or related matters."[99] In the end, informal arrangements of this kind or new organizations overcame these gaps. Marshall best expressed his colleagues' views in a memorandum written in summer 1943:

> The U.S. Chiefs of Staff have been aware for a long time of a serious disadvantage under which they labor in their dealings with the British Chiefs of Staff. Superficially, at least, the great advantage on the British side has been the fact that they are connected up with other branches of their Government through an elaborate but most closely knit Secretariat. On our side there is no such animal and we suffer accordingly . . .

In the end, Marshall proposed the creation of "some form of a Secretariat for keeping all these groups in Washington in an automatic relationship one with the other."[100]

96 King and Whitehill, *Fleet Admiral King*, p. 368.
97 See the discussion in Robert W. Coakley and Richard M. Leighton, *Global Logistics and Strategy 1943–1945* (Washington, 1968), pp. 91–100.
98 Leahy, *I Was There*, p. 104.
99 Ray S. Cline, *Washington Command Post: The Operations Division* (Washington, 1951), p. 314.
100 Memo, General Marshall for James F. Byrnes, 10 July 1943, quoted in Cline, *Washington Command Post*, p. 106.

Marshall's comments raise the broader issue of civil-military relations. The claim that the American political leaders left military alone to fight the war falls apart on close inspection. Roosevelt controlled high-level military decision-making in a variety of ways while giving the appearance of allowing the military a loose rein. British observers noted that American planners labored under greater political responsibilities than their British counterparts, and this perception was in some measure accurate. The absence of true Cabinet government and Roosevelt's tendency to bypass the State Department forced upon American generals and admirals a variety of essential political issues by default, for lack of integrated policymaking machinery along British lines. Not until the end of 1944 did a major advance occur with the creation of a State-War-Navy Coordinating Committee (SWNCC).[101]

At the heart of modern civil-military relations in war lies a paradox of military professionalism. On the one hand, military organizations have become extraordinarily complex and require the leadership of individuals with extensive experience and training in the art of war. On the other hand, this professional expertise supports an activity that is permeated by politics. The senior military leaders of World War II entered the war with a belief that "civilian authorities determine the 'what' of national policy and the military confine themselves to the 'how.'"[102] They accepted civilian supremacy as axiomatic; none succumbed to the pre-1918 German conception of war as the exclusive province of generals and admirals. Eisenhower's cable of 7 April 1945 to General Marshall explaining his reluctance to think of Berlin as a major military objective concludes with the revealing sentence, "I am the first to admit that a war is waged in pursuance of political aims, and if the Combined Chiefs of Staff should decide that the Allied effort to take Berlin outweighs purely military considerations in the theater, I would cheerfully readjust my plans and my thinking so as to carry out such an operation."[103] The views of the American military lay somewhere between those of Moltke and Bismarck. They believed strategy to be an autonomous art; political considerations might legitimately override purely military strategy, but purely military strategy did exist.

That view was questionable, for in the end few major American wartime decisions were purely military. That circumstance created friction but did not cripple the war effort or even embitter civil-military relations, although it later obscured a full understanding of how America had in fact waged war. In many cases Roosevelt's decisions did not involve a "political" over a "military" choice, so much as choosing the least unpleasant among several politico-military options. After the war Marshall said of Roosevelt's decision

---

[101] Ibid., pp. 312–32; Maurice Matloff, *Strategic Planning for Coalition Warfare 1943–1944* (Washington, 1959), pp. 106–111.

[102] Matloff, *Strategic Planning 1943–1944*, p. 110.

[103] Eisenhower to Marshall, 7 April 1945, in Alfred D. Chandler, ed., *The Papers of Dwight David Eisenhower, The War Years* (Baltimore, 1970), Vol. 4, p. 2592.

to invade North Africa in 1942: "We failed to see that the leader in a democracy has to keep the people entertained. That may sound like the wrong wording but it conveys the thought."[104] To the end, American military leaders found it hard to reconcile themselves to the fact that they could not divorce war from politics.

The American strategic decision-making apparatus was directly linked to that of the alliance with Britain, perhaps the most remarkable coalition in history. It was the American military that succeeded in establishing the Combined Chiefs of Staff organization and rooting it in Washington during the ARCADIA conference of 1941–42. The CCS soon spawned a web of Anglo-American committees to control and direct the war. Anglo-American strategic coordination developed chiefly, however, through the extraordinary connection between Roosevelt and Churchill. The President initiated the contacts upon Churchill's return to the Admiralty in 1939, and their correspondence amounted to no fewer than 950 messages from the Prime Minister and some 750 from the President – an exchange, on average, every three days. The correspondence covered a wide variety of subjects and, to the end, showed a camaraderie that was both useful and genuinely felt. Still, in Robert Sherwood's words:

> neither of them forgot for one instant what he was and represented or what the other was and represented. Actually, their relationship was maintained to the end on the highest professional level. They were two men in the same line of business – politico-military leadership on a global scale – and theirs was a very limited field and the few who achieve it seldom have opportunities for getting together with fellow craftsmen in the same trade to compare notes and talk shop. They appraised each other through the practiced eyes of professionals and from this appraisal resulted a degree of admiration and sympathetic understanding of each other's professional problems that lesser craftsmen could not have achieved.[105]

In addition to smaller visits back and forth across the Atlantic, the great wartime conferences supplied overall direction to the war. The Anglo-Americans conferred most frequently in 1943, and the four conferences that year were the longest of the war, ten days or more, remarkably protracted periods of strategic deliberation. Although the conferences varied in format and in the issues considered, several points are notable. First, throughout the war, the Combined Chiefs of Staff alternated between their own meetings and meetings in the presence of Churchill and Roosevelt, who also conducted their own private discussions. Discussions ranged over a variety of issues; a representative example is the meeting of the Combined Chiefs of Staff on 23

104 Quoted in Larrabee, *Commander in Chief*, p. 9.
105 Sherwood, *Roosevelt and Hopkins*, pp. 363–64. For the correspondence, see Warren F. Kimball, ed., *Churchill and Roosevelt: The Complete Correspondence*, 3 vols. (Princeton, 1984).

January 1943 in Casablanca.[106] At this session the assembled leaders, including Roosevelt and Churchill, discussed aid to the Soviet Union, the invasion of Sicily and Mediterranean strategy, the buildup of American forces in Britain, and the prospects of operations in Burma. The two political leaders quizzed their military advisers on production rates for various kinds of military equipment, merchant ship tonnage remaining to the Japanese, and the time required to train amphibious forces for operations against Italy. In other words, the President and Prime Minister did not confine themselves to issuing sweeping policy guidelines. Rather they were civilian leaders who believed that victory was possible only by weaving strategic decisions, thread by thread, into a cloth of their own unique design.

Once top civilian and military leaders had made strategic decisions, the services implemented them as executive agent for the JCS or the Combined Chiefs of Staff. Although the Army Air Forces were virtually an independent service in many respects, in this area they were wholly subordinate to the army. The staffs of King and Marshall were the "Washington command posts" from which theater commanders received direction. King served, as discussed previously both as commander in chief, U.S. Fleet (COMINCH), and as Chief of Naval Operations (CNO). He controlled current operations and plans primarily in the former capacity, with the office of the CNO serving to manage the raising of the naval forces.[107] The COMINCH staff was organized as a fleet headquarters and divided into intelligence, plans, operations, and readiness (or training) sections, plus a special antisubmarine unit. King kept the COMINCH office small, an establishment of barely 600 (half enlisted) throughout the entire war. In addition, with only two exceptions he rotated senior officers through the COMINCH organization, and often sent them back to the fleet after little more than twelve months in Washington. The result was a compact and efficient staff generally familiar with wartime conditions in the fleet. In addition to his other responsibilities, King conferred regularly, usually twice a month, with the Navy's principal theater commander, Admiral Chester Nimitz, and made many key personnel decisions in the Pacific.

Marshall's command post was OPD, the Operations Division of the General Staff. It too was a relatively small organization of some 200 officers divided into four main groups: strategy and policy, theater, logistics, and

---

106 What follows is based on JCS files, reprinted in Department of State, *Foreign Relations of the United States: The Conferences at Washington, 1941–1942, and Casablanca, 1943* (Washington, 1968), pp. 707–19.
107 What follows is based largely on Julius August Furer, *Administration of the Navy Department In World War II* (Washington, 1959), pp. 102–70, and Robert William Love, Jr., "Ernest Joseph King," in Robert William Love, Jr., ed., *The Chiefs of Naval Operations* (Annapolis, 1980), pp. 137–80.

current.[108] Marshall rotated his officers less frequently than King. Like King, Marshall periodically conferred directly with theater commanders; but he administered guidance for the war effort chiefly through voluminous correspondence, particularly with Eisenhower. It was no coincidence that Eisenhower had served, however briefly, as the head of OPD.

Just as Roosevelt and Churchill concerned themselves with many of the details of future military operations, so did the service command posts. The operational staffs in Washington had to deal not only with high-level planning but with a constant stream of decisions concerning deployments and allocation of resources. When, for example, an OPD officer, sent to the South Pacific in 1942, reported back on the problems of army troops in New Caledonia, "a series of about a dozen interrelated staff actions resulted, dealing with everything from the activation of a new combat division to the dispatch of a mobile laundry unit."[109] On supreme occasions the Combined Chiefs of Staff did the same. The Joint Chiefs of Staff flew to London immediately after D-Day so that the CCS could be together "for major decisions on the spot in the event that Allied forces suffered serious reverses."[110]

Owing in large part to Marshall's insistence at the first Washington conference, the JCS created theater commands on the basis of unity of command. Rather than adopting the British committee system of theater control under which commanders of the different services cooperated with one another, the Americans established the principle of a single commander for each theater. This principle was amended in practice, for the navy was often unwilling to permit large naval forces to operate under army control. And in the Pacific, interservice disputes did prevent creation of a single theater command, or even two pure theater commands – Admiral Nimitz served as Commander in Chief of the Pacific Fleet (and hence King's direct subordinate) as well as Commander in Chief Pacific Ocean Areas.[111]

RESULTS

War was the test of America's strategy from 1920 to 1945. American strategists did not flatter themselves with the belief that they could, by their own exertions, prevent war from starting. They hoped rather to prepare forces that would enable them to bring a war to a successful conclusion. To assay their efforts, one needs to consider three different kinds of strategy in this period: *prewar strategy* – plans prepared in peacetime; *improvised strategy* –

---

108   Cline, *Washington Command Post*, p. 193. There was also an executive (administrative) group and a Pan-American group, as well as several smaller committees.
109   Ibid., p. 142.
110   Sherwood Papers, Folder 1894, "Interview with Admiral Ernest J. King, 24–25 August 1946."
111   The tangled question of command in the Pacific is discussed in Louis Morton, *Strategy and Command: The First Two Years* (Washington, 1962), pp. 225–33, 240–63, 294–300, 352–63, 472–501.

campaigns devised on short notice in the war; and *planned strategy* – campaigns planned under the pressures of war but with time to mature before implementation.

The ORANGE Plan for war with Japan best exemplifies *prewar strategy.* Planners drew up ORANGE in the 1920s, modified it repeatedly through the 1930s, and ultimately replaced it with the RAINBOW Plans, first conceived in 1939.[112] The ORANGE Plan envisioned a prolonged, step-by-step return to the Philippines, the path subsequently taken by Nimitz's Central Pacific offensive in late 1943: attacks first on the Gilberts, then the Marshalls, and finally the Marianas. ORANGE did not guide American planning in 1942 and 1943 in any direct sense; new plans written in Washington determined those operations. But ORANGE served two vital purposes. First, it familiarized a generation of naval officers with the basic problems involved in prosecuting a war against Japan. Although Nimitz's subsequent claim that officers forecast all the problems involved in a war against Japan on the gaming tables at the Naval War College is overstated, there is some truth in it. Second, the requirements of ORANGE forced the navy and marine corps to confront fundamental and highly complex technical and organizational problems. During the interwar period, the marine corps began working out essential techniques for conducting amphibious landings on opposed beaches and the navy had begun to grapple with the logistical problems of a fleet operating far from its home bases.[113] In both cases, the navy and marine corps failed to find detailed solutions in the interwar period, design or procure the proper equipment, or adequately train large forces. But they had raised the problems and prepared the minds of future leaders for the broad strategic issues that they would confront.

The RAINBOW Plans, far less detailed than the ORANGE Plan, served a different purpose: the establishment of basic strategic principles, of which the most important was the identification of Germany as the main enemy.[114] It was characteristic of the strength of purpose of the President and his chief planners that they attempted to adhere to this principle even after the Japanese attack on Pearl Harbor. In practice, however, "Germany First" in the beginning proved both untenable and, in some respects, unnecessary. By the end of 1942, for example, the army had deployed roughly the same number of troops in the Pacific as in the European and Mediterranean theaters.[115]

[112] On ORANGE and its importance for World War II strategy see Morton, "War Plan ORANGE," Morton, *Strategy and Command,* pp. 21–44, 434–53, Grace P. Hayes, *The History of the Joint Chiefs of Staff in World War II: The War Against Japan* (Annapolis, 1982), pp. 4–25.

[113] See Jeter A. Isely and Philip A. Crowl, *The U.S. Marines and Amphibious War: Its Theory and Its Practice in the Pacific* (Princeton, 1951), pp. 3–71, and Duncan S. Ballantine, *U.S. Naval Logistics in the Second World War* (Princeton, 1947), pp. 25–37.

[114] Louis Morton, "Germany First: The Basic Concept of Allied Strategy in World War II," in Greenfield, ed., *Command Decisions,* pp. 11–47.

[115] See Matloff and Snell, *Strategic Planning for Coalition Warfare 1943–1944,* p. 555.

The flood of American war production enabled the United States to undertake simultaneous full-scale offensives in 1944 in both theaters. In 1942, the navy commissioned four new battleships and one large and eleven escort carriers; in 1943 it commissioned two more battleships and no fewer than six large, nine light, and twenty-four escort carriers.[116] As a result, sufficient forces existed to launch no fewer than four major offensives in 1944: the Central and Southwest Pacific offensives against Japan, the bomber offensive against Germany, and the invasion of Normandy, as well as lesser operations in Italy, southern France, and China.

Much of American strategy was *improvised strategy,* and here the U.S. high command performed well although it preferred, on the whole, *planned strategy* of the kind described later. The military leadership reluctantly adopted unforeseen or opportunistic operations such as the Solomon campaign of 1942, the assault on North Africa in the same year, the invasion of Italy in 1943, and the submarine campaign against the Japanese merchant marine. In August 1942, with barely a month's preparation, the marines attacked Guadalcanal and inaugurated the prolonged and brutal struggle for the Solomons. This series of battles, lasting more than six months, broke the back of Japanese air power and wrested the initiative from the enemy. It ran counter to the letter of Germany First, and although not foreseen before the war, proved a tremendous success.

In other areas the United States was less willing to seize strategic opportunities. American planners stubbornly opposed the British desire to exploit Allied success in North Africa and instead argued forcefully for an invasion of France in 1943. Similarly, the navy took nearly two years to fully discover that its submarines were more usefully employed against Japanese merchant ships than fleet units.[117] The case of the submarine offensive suggests that broad directives for a change in strategy are not enough. Within hours of Pearl Harbor the order went out to execute unrestricted submarine warfare against Japanese merchantmen. But to do so, submariners had to accept a new doctrine, overcome technical problems, and devise new tactics that included wolfpack and surface attacks.

Throughout the war *planned strategy* was supposed to be the American forte. "The overall strategic concept," a phrase beloved of American planners, won some favor with Churchill, although the British Chiefs of Staff regarded it as fatuous. Of all long-range strategy conceived during the war, the most important were the plans to invade France, defeat Japan, and bomb Germany. But all three concepts required important modifications. Much against their will, the Joint Chiefs deferred an invasion of France from 1943 to 1944. Through early 1944 long-range plans for the defeat of Japan envisioned occupation of the South China coast to secure harbors, airfields, and

---

[116] Millis, ed., *War Reports,* pp. 738–41.
[117] For a brief discussion, see Spector, *Eagle Against the Sun,* pp. 478–87.

access to Chinese manpower for the climactic battles on the Home Islands. The daylight bomber offensive against Germany was initially successful because it forced the Luftwaffe to come up and die, not because it destroyed German fighter production.

Yet the stubbornness with which American planners fought for their strategic conceptions had a payoff. Ultimately, Allied forces implemented these strategies even if later or in rather different form than initially envisioned – and they worked. Had American planners *not* been so rigid in their insistence on basic concepts, and had they simply acceded to the British wishes, the war might well have lasted considerably longer. In the event, the strategic biases of the two Allies complemented one other. Although compromise is rarely thought of as a sound basis for strategy, World War II casts some doubt on that aspect of conventional wisdom.

How well did American strategists assess threats to their strategy? On the whole, American planners gauged the likely reactions of their enemies reasonably well. They enjoyed the aid of superb intelligence-gathering and analytical organizations that were in high gear by 1943. But even more, they understood, as did Churchill, that the chief threat lay not in any particular Axis counterblow but in the possibility of stalemate or a prolongation of the war. After the war, Marshall recalled that the Joint Chiefs had been particularly "conscious of the morale of our forces in the Pacific – that they could not go on indefinitely in the Pacific taking heavy casualties and enduring great hardships. . . ."[118]

World War II both shaped and revealed American strategic culture as no other war with the exception of the Civil War. Two dominant characteristics stand out: the preference for massing a vast array of men and machines and the predilection for direct and violent assault. The war was, at many levels, a war of mass production fought by the country that had used that concept to forge the world's largest and most productive economy. It was neither elegant nor subtle, but it worked. A British officer who fought alongside the Americans wrote:

> The Americans were analytic. They approached warfare as they approached any other large enterprise; breaking it down to its essentials, cutting out what was superfluous, defining tasks and roles and training each man as if he was about to take an individual part in some complicated industrial process. Indeed, the American system for basic training resembled a conveyor belt, with soldiers instead of motor-cars coming off the end.[119]

He termed the result "soulless" but effective. Erwin Rommel arrived at a similar judgment on the American war effort:

> What was astonishing was the speed with which the Americans adapted themselves to modern warfare. In this they were assisted by their extraordinary sense

---

118 Sherwood Papers, Folder 1899, "Interview with George Catlett Marshall, 23 July 1947."
119 Shelford Bidwell, *The Chindit War* (New York, 1979), p. 45.

for the practical and material and by their complete lack of regard for tradition and worthless theories. . . . European generals could certainly have executed the invasion [of Normandy] with the forces available, but they could never have prepared it – neither technically, organizationally, nor in the field of training.[120]

The most successful American commanders believed that an intimate link existed between the nature of American society as manifested in the economy and America's preferred way of war: "The Americans, as a race, are the foremost mechanics in the world. America, as a nation, has the greatest ability for mass production of machines. It therefore behooves us to devise methods of war which exploit our inherent superiority."[121] At a time when critics belabor American military leaders for being "managers" rather than "warriors," it is wise to remember that a certain kind of managerial skill produced victory in 1945. Churchill's physician, Lord Moran, observed in Marshall "that remarkable gift for organization which is everywhere behind American production. But I would not call it a work of genius."[122] He was wrong in that last remark; what Marshall had and typified was a certain, no doubt limited, kind of genius, but genius nonetheless.

On the whole, American strategy was a resounding success. Decision-makers, especially Roosevelt, achieved their objectives, although the full fruits of their accomplishment became visible only in succeeding decades. The end of the war and the years to follow brought the defeat of the Axis Powers and their rehabilitation, the establishment of an open world order outside the Communist bloc, and the restoration of free institutions to some countries and their introduction to others. In winning the war, America suffered nowhere near as heavily, in lives, material, or psychological trauma as any of the other participants; indeed, victory in 1945 transformed the United States within less than five years into the unquestioned leader of the noncommunist world. Although better outcomes are conceivable, it is difficult to see how different American strategic choices could have brought the war to an end more than a few months earlier or prevented the communization of Eastern Europe and China. Americans – and many other peoples – are the beneficiaries today of the strategies constructed and implemented with such success nearly half a century ago. If innocence gave birth to those strategies, it was a peculiarly providential brand of innocence.

[120] B. H. Liddell Hart, ed., *The Rommel Papers,* Paul Findlay trans. (New York, 1953), pp. 521–23.
[121] George S. Patton, *War As I Knew It* (Boston, 1947), p. 366.
[122] Moran, *Churchill: The Struggle for Survival 1940–1965* (Boston, 1966), p. 120.

15

The illusion of security: France, 1919–1940

ROBERT A. DOUGHTY

The overriding goal of French policy remained fixed throughout the interwar period: security. Between August 1914 and November 1918, Germany had killed 1.35 million of France's young men, ravaged France's countryside and industrial regions, and imposed on France a war effort that had consumed national wealth and resources on an unprecedented scale. With French victory came the burning desire to avoid another such victory. But unlike other Western leaders after 1918, those who made French strategy lacked confidence in disarmament as a route to security. They believed security had to precede disarmament. The greatest and most obvious threat came from a resurgent and aggressive Germany; consequently the overiding goal of French grand strategy was protection against France's eastern neighbor.

In the first decade after World War I, France followed two strategic paths. One pursued collective security through the Treaty of Versailles and League of Nations, the other sought national security through military agreements and alliances. Although the quest for alliances somewhat weakened the effort at collective security, the French expected their network of alliances and agreements to generate sufficient military power to punish any state upsetting the European status quo. They also hoped to curtail Germany's aggressiveness by threatening a two-front war. Unfortunately for France, no common interests welded its intricate network of allies and clients together, and Britain declined either to participate in or to tolerate for long French efforts to enforce Versailles.

As France developed a military strategy to support its grand strategy, the need to maintain links to its Eastern European allies and to its imperial possessions – particularly those in North Africa – complicated its task. If Italy became an enemy, France's links with Eastern Europe and North Africa would be gravely threatened. In the quest for a military strategy, the French had to balance the conflicting requirements of organizing and equipping military forces that could simultaneously protect their frontiers, provide assistance to their eastern friends, and defend their lines of communication in the Mediterranean. Unfortunately, France did not have sufficient military forces for all these requirements. In the final analysis, French grand strategy proved inadequate because France was too weak to mold a strong alliance, and because its military forces were too defensively minded to challenge German power directly.

NATIONAL SECURITY INSTITUTIONS

Throughout the interwar period, the French accepted the need to subordinate military strategy to grand strategy. Military and political thinkers sometimes distinguished between military and political strategy by describing their subordination to the "general direction of war," which established objectives.[1] When they spoke of "strategy," however, they usually meant the use of military forces to achieve a wartime goal. The July 1938 law on the organization of the nation for war explained that "The general direction of war belongs to the government. The government determines the objectives to be attained by force of arms and assures the establishment of necessary measures to provide for the needs of the Army and for those of the Nation."[2] By "government," the French meant the civilian leadership of the nation, primarily the Council of Ministers but also including the Chamber of Deputies and Senate.

As a consequence of France's system of government, men such as Georges Clemenceau, Louis Barthou, and Edouard Daladier exercised great influence over French grand strategy, but numerous other officials affected its details. France relied on a formal bureaucratic structure to formulate its national security policies, and individuals frequently debated and influenced those policies in a system of committees designed for that purpose. Law prescribed the organization and functioning of this structure, and identified duties and responsibilities. Though political questions always remained important, the French expected this "system of committees" to ensure that their grand strategy, military strategy, and military capabilities were in harmony.

The framework of France's system for coordinating national defense originated before World War I and stemmed from the belief that modern warfare inevitably involved the entire nation and therefore required governmental coordination of all national efforts. The highest committee was the Superior Council of National Defense (*Conseil supérieur de la défense nationale*),

---

[1] On the different levels of strategy, see Henry Dutailly, *Les problèmes de l'Armée de Terre française (1935–1936)* (Paris, 1980), p. 25. For a fuller treatment of the evolution of the French bureaucratic structure, see Robert Vial, "La défense nationale: son organisation entre les deux guerres," *Revue d'histoire de la deuxième guerre mondiale*, 5 (Avril 1955), pp. 11–32.

[2] *Journal officiel de la république française: Lois et décrets*, 13 Juillet 1938, p. 8330 (hereinafter *J.O. Lois et décrets*).

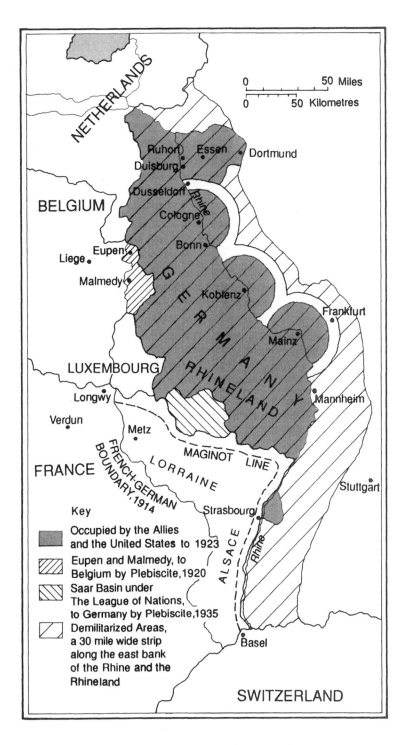

Map 15.1. French interwar strategy of defense: The Maginot Line and the occupation of Germany. *Source.* Adapted from Kagan, Ozment, and Turner, *The Western Heritage Since 1300*, Fourth Edition (New York: Macmillan, 1991), 976.

founded in 1906 to address military problems. The Council had played a limited role before 1914, but its responsibilities and influence increased after 1918. Most French leaders agreed that the experience of World War I proved that exclusively military efforts no longer sufficed to prepare the nation for war; coordination of economic and industrial planning was indispensable. To ensure that preparedness, the membership of the Council grew after 1918. Its members were the ministers of the government of the day and, as advisers, the highest-ranking officers in the army, navy, and – later – air force. The Council's purpose was to assist the government in the mobilization and preparation for total war. The 1938 law explained that the government received advice during peacetime from the Superior Council of National Defense on "measures pertaining to the organization of the nation for wartime."[3]

Though the Council avoided directly addressing questions of grand strategy, which were the government's responsibility, its discussions were wideranging. In the session of 26 December 1921, for example, it considered the questions of naval tonnages raised in the Washington Conference.[4] The session on 15 November 1924 discussed the proposed Geneva Protocol on the peaceful resolution of international differences.[5] And the session on 3 November 1930 resulted in formal advice to the government on armaments limitation policy.[6] Despite the wide variety of topics it considered, the limitations of the Council were apparent. As early as 13 November 1922, several members emphasized its advisory role, and one of them noted that only the government could "make decisions."[7] Military members of the Council understood that the responsibility for providing advice was different from having the power to make decisions.

Such limitations, nevertheless, did not preclude the military from influencing the government over strategic questions. The Superior Council of National Defense served as a major forum for the expression of the military's concerns about the means available for achieving strategic goals. Though after the war some military figures complained of the gap between ends and means, meetings of the Superior Council provided sufficient opportunities for military figures to express reservations about French grand strategy. They failed to do so.

Below the Superior Council, France created the High Military Committee (*Haut comité militaire*) in 1932 to engender closer contact and harmony among the three services. This body had the narrow responsibility of coordinating the activities of the services. But it also allowed the military leaders to communicate their views and concerns to civilian leaders. The joint com-

---

3 *J.O. Lois et décrets*, 13 Juillet 1938, p. 8330.
4 Procès-verbaux (hereafter P.V.), C.S.D.N., 26 Décembre 1921, S.H.A.T. 2N5.
5 P.V., C.S.D.N., 15 Novembre 1924, S.H.A.T. 2N6.
6 P.V., C.S.D.N., 3 Novembre 1930, S.H.A.T. 2N7.
7 P.V., C.S.D.N., 13 Novembre 1922, S.H.A.T. 2N5.

mittee consisted originally of the president of the Council of Ministers (the Premier), the vice-president of the superior councils of war for the three services, the three chiefs of the general staffs, and the inspector general of aerial defense. The ministers of the three services joined shortly after its creation.

During its short existence from 1932 to 1936, the committee met infrequently – except for a busy year in 1935 – and concentrated on the problems of command in wartime and of friction between the services. Despite the best of intentions, no unity of opinion or command emerged and no equivalent to the post-World War II Joint Chiefs of Staff system in the United States evolved. The committee nevertheless had some influence over military strategy and grand strategy. At the meeting of 5 April 1935, for example, it examined the effect of German rearmament and possible French responses to a German occupation of Austria, Memel (Lithuania), or the Rhineland demilitarized zone.[8]

The government of Léon Blum abolished the High Military Committee in 1936 and replaced it with the Permanent Committee of National Defense (*Comité permanent de la défense nationale*). The 1938 law on the organization of the French military stated simply that the Committee studied "employment of ground, sea, and air forces."[9] The minister of national defense or the president of the Republic presided over the new committee, which consisted of the ministers, the three vice-presidents of the services' superior councils of war, and the three chiefs of the general staffs, along with representatives of the Ministry of Foreign Affairs. The Committee met infrequently: four meetings in 1936, six in 1937, two in 1938, and only one in 1939.

The Committee nevertheless discussed a range of strategic issues. In the 5 December 1938 meeting, General Maurice Gamelin, Chief of Staff of National Defense, presented an overview of French national security needs. Gamelin underlined the importance of aviation and said that first priority should go to fighters rather than bombers, since anti-aircraft technology and German fighters made the success of the bomber "uncertain." He went on to stress the importance of the "maritime domain": control of the Mediterranean was "indispensable" for communications with French possessions and allies, and the French navy, "with the cooperation of the [Royal] Navy," must therefore be its "master."[10]

The meeting of 15 March 1938 dealt with the complexities of providing military support for France's allies in Eastern Europe. The point of the meeting was to answer an impertinent British question about French strategy in the growing Czech crisis: "You say that you will go to the aid of Czechoslovakia, but practically [speaking] what can you do?" Discussions in the meet-

8 P.V., Haut Comité Militaire, 5 Avril 1935, S.H.A.T. 2N19.
9 *J.O. Lois et décrets*, 13 Juillet 1938, p. 8331.
10 P.V., C.P.D.N., 5 Décembre 1938, S.H.A.T. 2N25.

ing underlined the small chance of support from other Eastern European states and suggested the weaknesses of France's alliances in that area. And on France's own military capabilities, General Joseph Vuillemin, the senior air force officer, made his infamous statement that any German air offensive would "annihilate" the French air force within fifteen days. The meeting inevitably concluded that France could do virtually nothing to assist Czechoslovakia.[11] Colonel Pierre Le Goyet has argued that this meeting greatly affected Daladier's decision to accept Munich.[12]

Another important committee was the Superior Council of War (*Conseil supérieur de la guerre*). Established by presidential decree in July 1872, the council consisted of the Minister of War, the chief of the general staff, and the leading general officers of the French army. The air force and navy also had councils, but they had less influence than the army's. Even though the government had the final word, the council played a remarkably important role in the decisions to build fortifications on the northeastern frontier and to move forces forward into Belgium in the event of war. In a meeting on 22 May 1922, Marshal Joseph Joffre supported the thesis of Marshal Ferdinand Foch: too great an emphasis on fortifications would be "doomed to defeat for seeking to establish a new wall of China."[13] On 15 December 1925, however, the council concluded that France should erect a discontinuous system of fortifications along the northeastern frontiers, and on 12 October 1927 the council adopted Marshal Philippe Pétain's concept for the design and location of what eventually became the Maginot Line.[14] The council in effect dominated the formulation of France's continental military strategy.

Except for the sharp conflict in 1919 between Clemenceau and Foch over separating the Rhineland from Germany, the most heated debates between civilian and military leaders occurred over resources rather than over strategic goals or methods. General Maxime Weygand openly complained that the government had failed to use the Superior Council of National Defense intelligently, but his criticism did not suggest that the military needed greater influence over strategic issues. In the last days before his retirement in 1935, he charged that the government had not consulted the council about remedying "dangerous insufficiencies," but these deficiencies were above all in personnel and finances.[15] Perhaps the greatest conflicts occurred on the eve of the so-called "hollow years" of the late 1930s, when the low birth rates of 1914–18 sharply reduced the supply of potential conscripts and raised the specter of possible French force reductions – just as Germany rearmed. Yet on the key aspects of France's grand strategy, such as the links to Eastern

11   P.V., C.P.D.N., 15 Mars 1938, S.H.A.T. 2N25.
12   Colonel Pierre Le Goyet, *Munich: Pouvait-on et devait-on faire la guerre en 1938?* (Paris, 1988), p. 119.
13   P.V., C.S.G., 22 Mai 1922, S.H.A.T. 50.
14   P.V., C.S.G., 15 Décembre 1925, S.H.A.T. 50 bis; 12 Octobre 1927, S.H.A.T. 50 bis.
15   Général Maxime Weygand, *Mémoires* (Paris, 1950–1957), Vol. 2, p. 43.

Europe and cooperation with Belgium and Britain, little or no disagreement existed. The military may sometimes have grumbled, but it remained far more concerned about the means of French strategy than the ends.

THE SEARCH FOR SECURITY

In the first decade after World War I, France could pursue several alternative security strategies. Among these were the partition and emasculation of Germany, or a rapprochement with its former enemy. The wisdom of hindsight suggests that either of those stark alternatives might have made France safer than the path ultimately chosen.

Among the strongest and most vocal proponents of dismemberment was Foch, who wanted to sever the Rhineland from the Reich. As commander of the Allied armies, Foch initially requested the occupation of the left bank of the Rhine and the establishment of three bridgeheads on the other. He later suggested the creation of an "autonomous" Rhineland state or states to provide a buffer for France and reduce Germany's economic power and population advantages. Clemenceau realized how unsympathetic the other allies were to this proposal and asserted his control over policy by thwarting Foch. He also curtailed the activities of General Charles Mangin, commander of one of the occupying armies, who tried to promote a separatist movement in the region.[16] In the face of strong British and American opposition, Clemenceau compromised and accepted guarantees of military support from those two countries and the right to occupy the Rhineland for up to fifteen years.

As an alternative grand strategy, France could have sought reconciliation with its vanquished enemy. Given the terrible costs of the war, this alternative was problematic, for neither the opinion of the French elite nor French voters would have tolerated a policy of trust and disarmament. As Marshal Foch exclaimed: "Disarmament . . . gives us only momentary, precarious, fictitious security. It is almost impossible to prevent Germany from rearming in secret." He added, "If . . . [Germany] wants to go to war, nothing will prevent it from finding the means."[17] The elections of 1919 gave a sweeping victory to the French right, which had little sympathy for the "Boches" and no desire for rapprochement. Despite their victory, the French people felt deeply resentful, highly suspicious, and very insecure.[18]

Two considerations affected the French as they constructed their grand strategy in the interwar period. André Maginot explained the first of these in

16 Jere C. King, *Foch versus Clemenceau: France and German Dismemberment 1918–1919* (Cambridge, 1960), pp. 16–17, 21–22, 24, 31, 52, 61–64, 78–88, 92–94, 97–106.
17 Raymond Recouly, *Le mémorial de Foch: mes entretiens avec le maréchal* (Paris, 1929), pp. 242–43.
18 George Bernard Noble, *Policies and Opinions at Paris, 1919* (New York, 1968), pp. 153–85, 220–68.

a debate in the Chamber of Deputies in 1922: "[T]he best and surest way for a people to assure their defense, that is their security, is to be ready at every moment to defend themselves."[19] To prevail in a war against its most likely enemy, Germany, which had a larger population and far greater industrial resources, France had to prepare for the worst case, a long total war. While the French accepted with anguish the possibility of another all-out war on the European continent, they never deviated from the belief that preparation for and the will to fight such a war were essential for their security.

As France completed mobilization planning and organized its forces, it chose not to create a force capable of limited actions in Europe. In 1936, Gamelin insisted upon a general mobilization if France were to send forces into the Rhineland to repulse a German effort to remilitarize that area. In March 1938, French leaders contemplated intervention in the Spanish Civil War, but relented when military officials argued that they required at least a million men for the frontier covering force. At the end of September 1938, France mobilized its covering forces along the northeastern frontier and called more than 750,000 reservists to duty as precaution during the Munich Crises.[20] This emphasis on a total war in Europe did not leave the French unprepared to fight a lower intensity war elsewhere. Nevertheless, the colonial conflicts of the 1920s and 1930s did not cause France to modify its approach in Europe. The basis of its grand strategy, preparation for a long total war, did not change.

The second major aspect of French strategy was linked to the first and also remained unchanged. French strategists believed that only the assistance of allies would allow them to defend themselves against Germany. In a total war, France lacked the resources to prevail against an increasingly industrialized and populous Germany. In addition, the geographic position of the nations surrounding Germany offered France significant advantages if it could secure them as allies. For example, if Italy were an ally, France could establish land communications to its allies in Eastern Europe, enjoy secure communications with North Africa, and force Germany to prepare for a multifront war.

Britain, however, was the ally France most sought. As David Thomson has noted, the French had concluded at the beginning of the century that relations with Britain and Germany were decisive for France's position in Europe.[21] Only Germany's land power exceeded France's; only Britain's naval power exceeded France's. Now that Germany was their most likely enemy, the French no longer had the strategic advantages of earlier centuries, and if

---

[19] *Journal officiel de la république française: Chambre débats* (hereafter *J.O. Ch. Deb.*), 29 Mars 1922, p. 1230.
[20] Robert A. Doughty, *The Seeds of Disaster: The Development of French Army Doctrine 1919–1939* (Hamden, CT, 1985), pp. 36–38.
[21] David Thomson, *French Foreign Policy*, Oxford Pamphlets on World Affairs, No. 67 (Oxford, 1944), p. 13–14.

they were to remain secure, they needed the resources and support of others – especially Britain.

The question was whether the resources of Britain and other allies would be available to France through the mechanism of the Covenant of the League of Nations, or through a traditional alliance system. The international environment of the 1920s and early 1930s favored collective security through the League of Nations and discouraged the establishment of networks of alliances reminiscent of the system that had allegedly contributed to the outbreak of general war in 1914. France was nevertheless reluctant to rely solely on the League, which called for the settlement of international disputes through international conferences, possibly backed by economic sanctions and in extreme cases by force. Although the Covenant seemed to guarantee France's security against Germany, several articles enabled states to make their own judgments about whether sanctions were necessary and thus – in the French view – to use loopholes to escape from the responsibility to act against aggression.

France preferred a system that rested on national interests backed by treaties, guarantees, and automatic sanctions including military action where necessary.[22] Only a system that could assemble sufficient military power to crush any state bent on upsetting the European order would bring peace. But for a time the French traveled both routes: collective security through the League of Nations and later the Locarno Pact, and security through a series of alliances, mutual assistance agreements, and military accords.[23]

For a short period after 1918, France believed the Anglo-American guarantee against German aggression would ensure security. But the guarantee proved an illusion: the United States Senate repudiated it and the British consequently withdrew their support. That was a bitter blow. Worse followed. France's repeated attempts to keep Germany at bay by enforcing the letter of the Versailles Treaty soon put it at odds with Britain, which read apprehension as vindictiveness. The French made their stand on the reparations mandated in the Treaty. Nonpayment was an effective gauge of German intentions; payment was vital to help repair Germany's savage and systematic wartime destruction of northern France. When German stonewalling led the French, with Belgian and Italian assistance, to seize and exploit the Ruhr coal basin in January 1923, the new German government, headed by Gustav Stresemann, abandoned passive resistance and agreed to resume payments. Although the French had apparently gained a victory, they soon abandoned their policy of confrontation and agreed to the Dawes Plan,

---

22 See Arnold Wolfers, *Britain and France between Two Wars: Conflicting Strategies of Peace Since Versailles* (New York, 1940), pp. 25–28. Wolfers argues that France's fear of a defeated enemy was unusual and that its insistence on force as a guarantee of security made "coercion" against an aggressor the "basic principle of international efforts for peace."

23 For an analysis of France's efforts, see Elizabeth R. Cameron, *Prologue to Appeasement: A Study in French Foreign Policy* (Washington, D.C., 1942), pp. 1–15, and René Albrecht-Carrié, *France, Europe, and the Two World Wars* (New York, 1961), pp. 102–16.

which reduced Germany's reparations payments. This change marked the end of a truly independent French policy in Europe.

Following the collapse of the Anglo-American guarantee and the failure of direct action, France fell back on the League Covenant, but the Covenant contained no obligation to act automatically against aggression. French leaders became particularly concerned as increasing evidence of clandestine German rearmament emerged, and as the influence of groups such as the "racist movement of Hitler and Ludendorff" found greater public support.[24] France did attempt to strengthen the League's ability to act against aggression. As early as 1923, it strongly supported the Draft Treaty of Mutual Assistance that sought to require member states to assist fellow members against aggression. When the League Assembly rejected this treaty, France supported the Geneva Protocol of 1924, which reinforced procedures set down in the League Covenant for the settlement of disputes and which strengthened collective security. Even though the Protocol received overwhelming support in the League Assembly, it too died, this time at the hands of the British.

Belated attempts by the new Conservative administration in London to reassure France nevertheless generated renewed talk of an Anglo-French security agreement. The Germans countered, and their proposals led to treaties signed at Locarno in October 1925 that ostensibly established a system of collective security for Western Europe. In the Treaty of Mutual Guarantee between France, Germany, Britain, Italy, and Belgium, the Germans agreed to accept their Versailles Treaty boundaries with France and Belgium. In return, all signatories agreed to settle disputes by peaceful means, thus preventing a replay of the Ruhr crisis. Under Locarno, any act of aggression against one of the signatories would in theory oblige the others to take immediate action, but the extent of that action would inevitably depend on geography and the powers' inclinations. Locarno left Germany entirely free to pursue ambitions in the east against Poland and Czechoslovakia that even moderate Weimar politicians held dear.

Despite Locarno, France never had full confidence in collective security. Along with efforts to strengthen the League, the French launched an entirely separate effort that in many ways undermined the League. Soon after the conclusion of World War I, they began constructing an elaborate series of alliances, accords, and agreements with the powers that surrounded Germany. The French did not purposely undermine the League's system of collective security; they simply established insurance against its possible impotence.

The resulting arrangements were less a formal alliance system than a set of special relationships with Germany's neighbors. France initially saw this

---

[24] For an early analysis of the radical groups in Germany, see André Honnorat, *Un des Problèmes de la Paix: Le Désarmement de l'Allemagne* (Paris, 1924), p. 145. On the general subject of French assessments of German rearmament, see Georges Castellan, *Le réarmement clandestin du Reich 1930–1935* (Paris, 1954), passim.

network primarily as a defense of the status quo rather than a military instrument. The strategic goal was nevertheless to encircle Germany with powers sympathetic to France and thus to prevent Berlin from acquiring allies and expanding its influence in the east. The military objective was to confront Germany with a multifront war. For hard-liners such as Raymond Poincaré, who staunchly opposed concessions to France's enemy, the objective was to surround Germany with a ring of bayonets. For other hardliners, such as André Tardieu, efforts to improve relations with Germany represented the "politics of abdication."[25]

Nevertheless, the French were reluctant – particularly in the 1920s – to threaten the Germans openly with a policy of encirclement. Such action would neither have harmonized with an international environment that preferred conciliation over coercion nor accorded with the views of its two important neighbors, Britain and Belgium. French leaders recognized that too strong an emphasis on the military encirclement of Germany would only further encourage Berlin to seek rearmament and gain them sympathy in the international community. They also knew that British and Belgian leaders had strong reservations about France's links to the turbulent nations of Eastern Europe.

THE ESTABLISHMENT OF THE FRENCH NETWORK OF ALLIANCES AND AGREEMENTS

The first state to enter the French system of alliances was Belgium, whose traditional neutrality Germany had ruthlessly violated in 1914. In summer and fall 1920, the two nations' military leaders negotiated a technical arrangement that committed their states to respond to a German use of military force. They also agreed to an annual meeting of their respective military staffs. In 1931, the Belgians notified their counterparts that this agreement had no other purpose than to provide military cooperation between the nations in case of "unprovoked aggression from Germany," and that the only guarantees of mutual assistance came from the League and Locarno.[26] Until Belgium chose neutrality in 1936, this agreement – though limited – remained an important element of French grand strategy.

French diplomats also established a number of important arrangements in Eastern Europe. They turned first to Poland, whose very existence, along with its acquisition of the Corridor and substantial portions of East Prussia, placed it in a permanent state of hostility with Germany. During the Soviet-

25 André Tardieu, *Sur la pente* (Paris, 1935), p. x.
26 Pierre Renouvin and Jacques Willequet, *Les relations militaires franco-belges de mars 1936 au 10 mai 1940* (Paris, 1968), Annexe II, "Texte des lettres échangées entre M. Hymans et l'ambassadeur de France (Février 1931)," p. 45. For an analysis of Franco-Belgian relations, see Brian Bond, *France and Belgium 1939–1940* (Newark, DE, 1975).

Polish War, France provided much-needed advice and assistance, and on 19 February 1921 the two states signed a treaty that committed them to "take concerted measures for the defense of their territories."

From a strategic point of view, the next most useful ally in the 1920s was Czechoslovakia. Since the Czechs shared a long border with Germany and controlled the most democratic and prosperous state in Eastern Europe, the French viewed them as natural allies. Their well-equipped army and the Skoda armament works made them even more appealing. On 25 January 1924 the two countries concluded a treaty that provided for mutual aid in the event of unprovoked attacks. The final protocol of Locarno, signed in October 1925, contained updated versions of the Franco-Polish and Franco-Czechoslovak treaties as one of its annexes. Thus France firmly anchored its alliance network within the Locarno system and League Covenant.

The French network expanded in the late 1920s and remained of central importance, despite the so-called "spirit" of Locarno. The Kellogg-Briand Pact of August 1928, which renounced war but made no provision for sanctions, hardly replaced alliances. France strengthened its links with Romania in June 1926, and in November 1927 signed a Treaty of Friendship with Yugoslavia. Since three bilateral treaties linked Czechoslovakia, Romania, and Yugoslavia in the Little Entente, French policy toward Eastern Europe tilted toward this group. By 1930 the French appeared close to their goal of encircling Germany with their own friends.

The linchpin of any encirclement of Germany was Italy which, as Pierre Laval once remarked, represented the "bridge" linking France with its allies in Eastern and Central Europe.[27] Military planners believed that Italian railroads would allow the first French troops to reach the Danube in three days and an entire expeditionary corps in three weeks.[28] Additionally, Italy could employ its air force against Germany and provide naval support for a land offensive through the Balkans. Without Italy, logistical bottlenecks would limit French ability to assist Eastern European allies; geography alone argued strongly for a close connection between Italy and France.

French planners between 1932 and 1934 also recognized the dangers of a German-Italian coalition. In addition to the measures required to repel German aggression, France would then have to strengthen its forces along the

[27] Pierre Laval, *Laval parle* (Paris, 1948), p. 245 cited in Robert J. Young, *In Command of France: French Foreign Policy and Military Planning 1933–1940* (Cambridge, MA, 1978), p. 91. On the question of Italy in French foreign policy, see William I. Shorrock, *From Ally to Enemy: The Enigma of Fascist Italy in French Diplomacy* (Kent, OH, 1988).

[28] "Extrait d'une conférence du Général Schweisguth au Collège des hautes études de la Défense nationale, le 20 avril 1937," in Dutailly, *Les problèmes de l'Armée de terre française*, p. 348. In their discussions with the French, the Italians also mentioned the possibility of an attack across Bavaria toward Munich, an operation that would force the Germans to move troops from either their eastern or western frontier: Robert J. Young, "French Military Intelligence and the Franco-Italian Alliance, 1933–1939," *The Historical Journal*, 28 (March 1985), p. 160.

Italian border and in the empire – particularly in North Africa. Italy's geographic position and its possessions in North Africa also represented a significant threat to the maritime routes connecting France to its empire. Politicians and military authorities concurred on the difficulties of successfully defending the German frontier and the Mediterranean with the limited forces available; the military pressed for an alliance with Italy that it hoped would greatly complicate German defense planning.[29]

Amidst growing Italian appreciation for the perils of German expansion into Austria, and following the reintroduction of conscription in Germany in March 1935, relations between France and Italy warmed considerably.[30] During General Gamelin's visit to Italy in June 1935, the French informally agreed that if Germany attacked Italy, they would dispatch an army corps to serve as a link between Italian and Yugoslav forces. Italy agreed that if Germany attacked France, it would send an Italian army corps to strengthen the defenses around Belfort. The military discussed contingencies that included a remilitarization of the Rhineland, a German attack through Belgium against France, and an offensive through Austria against Italy. In air staff talks, the two governments discussed possible air operations and agreed on additional meetings.[31] During informal meetings in May and June 1935, members of the army's Superior Council of War warned of the dangers to the strategic equilibrium if the Italian "friendship" changed into an "uncertain neutrality or . . . hostility."[32]

After remilitarization of the Rhineland and Belgium's withdrawal into neutrality, Italy became even more crucial to France's grand strategy. The French had lost the Rhineland buffer and were unsure of Belgium's future course. Gravely concerned about the new strategic environment, Gamelin argued that war was avoidable only if France, Italy, and Poland offered a united front.[33]

Despite the military's desire for a rapprochement with Italy, the 1935 accord with Rome had little or no prospect of survival. The apparent sympathies between Mussolini and Hitler made a coalition between them seem likely if not inevitable, to most French leaders. Moreover, the planned attack on Ethiopia for which Mussolini had sought diplomatic cover in his agreements with France inevitably forced Paris by late 1935 to choose between

29 Guy Pedroncini, "La stratégie française et l'Italie de 1932 à 1939," Jean-Baptiste Duroselle and Enrico Serra, eds., *Italia e Francia dal 1919 al 1939* (Milano, 1981), pp. 341–47.
30 Robert J. Young, "Soldiers and Diplomats: The French Embassy and Franco-Italian Relations, 1935–1936," *The Journal of Strategic Studies*, 7 (March 1984), pp. 77–79.
31 Pierre Le Goyet, *Le mystère Gamelin* (Paris, 1975), pp. 103–106; Jean-Baptiste Duroselle, *La décadence 1932–1939* (Paris, 1979), pp. 137–38.
32 France, Ministère des Affaires Etrangères, Commission de publication des documents relatifs aux origines de la guerre, 1939–1945, *Documents diplomatiques français* (Paris, 1963), 2nd Série, Vol. 2, No. 357 (25 Juin 1936), pp. 536–37 (henceforth D.D.F.).
33 Pedroncini, "La stratégie française et l'Italie de 1932 à 1939," p. 344.

Italy and Britain. Though Laval's decision was reluctant and subject to quali-fications, the choice of Britain was no choice at all.[34]

With the collapse of the Laval government in early 1936 and the arrival in power of Léon Blum and the Socialist-Communist Popular Front, interest in a rapprochement with Fascist Italy dramatically declined. Hope of having Italy complete the encirclement of Germany died as Italo-German coopera-tion in Spain became obvious and Italy acquiesced to the July 1936 Austro-German agreement that made Austria a German vassal. In an 8 December 1937 meeting of the Permanent Committee of National Defense, the mem-bers glumly noted the strategic consequences of Italy's relationship with Germany; France could not prevail in a long war against Germany if the Italians cut the maritime lines of communication to the French empire. France would therefore have to reduce Italy as quickly as possible in the event of war.[35]

For a brief moment after Munich, hope for agreement with Italy flared anew but soon vanished in the harsh reality of the Pact of Steel. The last meeting of the Permanent Committee of National Defense on 24 February 1939 dwelt on the concentration of Italian troops in Libya and the possibility of an attack on French possessions in North Africa. Daladier summarized the meeting's conclusion, "[T]o reply to an Italian attack . . . , it is necessary to prepare an offensive on Libya. . . ."[36]

As relations with Italy worsened, France loosened its links to the Little Entente. Although the three eastern governments desired a formal agreement with France, the French hesitated in June and July 1936 when Romania formally proposed a mutual assistance pact.[37] That hesitation resulted par-tially from the remilitarization of the Rhineland in March 1936, with its concomitant decrease in the feasibility and likelihood of a French offensive against Germany. But it also grew from the reluctance of the Popular Front government to extend France's military obligations, particularly as it decided not to intervene in Spain. The French foreign ministry concluded that a formal alliance with the Little Entente similar to the Franco-Polish Treaty would add nothing to the French system.[38]

In late 1937, Yvon Delbos, Blum's foreign minister, reversed direction and made another attempt to strengthen relations with the Little Entente. But the opportunity had disappeared. After reflection on the consequences of the remilitarization of the Rhineland and France's failure to act, Romania and

---

[34] Philippe Masson, "Les conversations militaires franco-britanniques (1935–1938)," in Annick Besnard, Jean-Marie d'Hoop, and Patrick Fridenson, eds., *Les relations franco-britanniques de 1935 à 1939* (Paris, 1975), pp. 120–22.

[35] P.V., C.S.D.N., 8 Décembre 1937, S.H.A.T. 2N24.

[36] P.V., C.P.D.N., 24 Février 1939, S.H.A.T. 2N25.

[37] Young, *In Command of France,* pp. 144–45; Anthony Tihamer Komjathy, *The Crises of France's East Central European Diplomacy 1933–1938* (Boulder, CO, 1976), pp. 170–71.

[38] Duroselle, *La décadence,* p. 321.

Yugoslavia rejected a strengthening of the alliance and moved toward closer relations with Italy and Germany. Even the Czechs examined the possibility of rapprochement with Germany. France's policy in Eastern Europe was unraveling.[39]

Of all the states in the east, Poland occupied the foremost place in French grand strategy. As victors in the 1920–21 war with the Soviets, the Poles represented a significant threat to Germany in the event of a Franco-German conflict, especially in the 1920s. Unfortunately, a bitter quarrel between Poland and Czechoslovakia frustrated French diplomatic efforts to build a coherent eastern front against the Germans. Moreover, the Poles viewed the Soviets as a dangerous threat, and on several occasions the Polish government complicated Franco-Soviet relations.[40]

Though Poland's commitment to the defensive alliance seemed real, the possibility of its straying from French influence emerged when it concluded a ten-year nonaggression pact with Germany in January 1934, and thereby acquired some insurance against a German attempt to recover Danzig and the Corridor by force. In the French view, the Poles seemed to be taking a duplicitous path that could only lead to the cutting of ties with France. But during the Rhineland crisis in 1936, Poland was one of the few countries that pledged support. Nevertheless, French officials remained skeptical about the sincerity of Polish commitments, especially given the close personal relations between some German and Polish leaders.[41] France could only hope that Poland's commitment against Germany was real and that friction between Poles and Soviets would not draw France into conflict with the Soviet Union.

Viewed with the advantage of hindsight, the French network of alliances and agreements would have been stronger with the Soviet Union as a full-fledged participant. But the influence of France's own internal politics and the political conservatism of its civilian and military leadership made any such relationship impossible; the specter of Bolshevism and fear of Soviet designs had fostered a deep-seated skepticism of the advantages of a Soviet connection. In the early 1930s relations nevertheless improved, and in November 1932 the two countries concluded a nonaggression pact. However, the process of ratifying the pact occasioned a great debate in France, and Edouard Herriot, the prime force behind the move toward closer relations, reminded the Chamber of Deputies that the devout Francis I had allied himself with Turkish infidels (against the Germans) in the sixteenth century.

Foreign Minister Louis Barthou took the crucial steps toward the Soviet Union. After Moscow proposed a mutual defense pact in January 1934, Barthou attempted to strengthen existing agreements and expand their scope. Although his effort to establish an Eastern European pact modeled on

[39] Ibid., p. 323.
[40] Piotr S. Wandycz, *The Twilight of French Eastern Alliances 1926–1936* (Princeton, 1988), pp. 294–96, 332–35, 395–409.
[41] Duroselle, *La décadence*, p. 173.

Locarno floundered, France and the Soviet Union concluded a new alliance in May 1935, despite Barthou's assassination the previous October.[42] The value of this alliance for France was questionable, even after ratification in February 1936. Because no common Russo-German border existed, the complexities of bringing Russian ground forces to bear against Germany led Paris to harbor serious reservations about the Soviet ability to hold German forces on the eastern front. Other French leaders questioned Soviet motives. They believed that the Soviets sought only to acquire technical assistance from France, and that they would wait out any Franco-German war until both sides had exhausted themselves; then they could step in and pick up the pieces.[43]

Despite formal ratification, military conversations never materialized and the treaty remained without effect. French neglect continued throughout the period of the Popular Front, which could not risk upsetting its already precarious domestic political coalition with close ties to Moscow. Despite Blum's best efforts, his government could not convince a skeptical military of the strategic value of the Soviets.[44] The Socialists themselves disagreed over the wisdom of endorsing the Franco-Soviet Pact because some believed that it would significantly increase France's risk of war. Moreover, they feared that endorsement of the pact would lead to greater defense spending at the expense of domestic programs.[45] Although Blum eventually supported the pact, the treaty remained unexploited and the opportunity for closer relations with the Soviets soon disappeared.

These links to the east represented a pale shadow of the Franco-Russian alliance of 1914. The strength of the French network lay in the combined power of the participating states; its weakness lay in the lack of common interests among the participants, particularly over how to coordinate, organize, and use that power. For example, Poland and Czechoslovakia never put aside their long-simmering dispute over territory.[46] More importantly, Polish intransigence blocked France's desperate attempts in 1939 to win safe passage through Poland for Soviet troops in the event of war against Germany. From the Polish perspective, the Soviet Union was a threat as large, if not larger, than Germany. As a Polish official explained to Georges Bonnet (the

---

[42] William Evans Scott, *Alliance against Hitler* (Durham, NC, 1962), pp. 153–202, 246–50.

[43] For the views of important military opponents of closer relations with the Soviet Union, see Philip Charles Farwell Bankwitz, *Maxime Weygand and Civil-Military Relations in France* (Cambridge, 1967), pp. 249–58; General Victor H. Schweisguth, D.D.F., Série 2, Vol. 3, No. 343, 5 Octobre 1936, pp. 513–14.

[44] Young, *In Command of France*, pp. 145–50. For an analysis of the relationship between Blum and Gamelin, see Martin S. Alexander, "Soldiers and Socialists: the French Officer Corps and Leftist Government, 1935–1937," in Martin S. Alexander and Helen Graham, *The French and Spanish Popular Fronts: Comparative Perspectives* (Cambridge, 1989), pp. 63–78.

[45] Pierre Gombin, *Les socialistes et la guerre* (Paris, 1970), pp. 190–92; Scott, *Alliance against Hitler*, pp. 261, 189–95.

[46] Scott, *Alliance against Hitler*, pp. 80–85.

French foreign minister) in 1939, "My government will never permit the Russians to occupy the territories we took from them in 1921. Would you allow the Germans to enter Alsace-Lorraine?"[47]

The French network of alliances and agreements thus consisted of a jumble of states with widely varied interests that suffered from internal dissent and disagreements. France's limited power and influence could not impose a more coherent and cohesive structure. The network always appeared to possess greater strength than it actually had, and no state understood this fact better than France.

THE UNEASY NEIGHBORS IN WESTERN EUROPE

Among potential allies, the French valued the assistance of states in the west more than those in the east. France's main friends in Western Europe, Britain and Belgium, possessed many common interests with France, but French truculence toward Germany and France's eastern connections made the British and Belgians question the wisdom of their relationship with Paris. These difficulties with its western neighbors created severe diplomatic and strategic problems for France.

France had first established links with Belgium in 1920 with a narrow military agreement that focused on staff cooperation in the event of German aggression. The Belgians kept the accord secret for some time; only a few ministers and the chief of staff knew of its existence. And although the French viewed the agreement as a military alliance that provided for automatic assistance against unprovoked attack, the Belgians did not. Moreover, over time the agreement became less and less popular in Brussels.

Belgian apprehensions had less to do with the relative power of France than with internal differences between Walloons and Flemings. Thanks to their Dutch and Germanic roots, the Flemings resented the tilt of Belgian politics toward France, believing it favored the French-speaking Walloons. They also feared vassalage to their larger neighbor. Throughout the 1920s, as the Flemish population grew and increased its political weight, doubts about the value of the French connection plagued the Belgian political leadership. Inherently suspicious of Eastern Europe, it remained uncomfortable with France's alliances and became more uneasy with conclusion and ratification of the Soviet alliance in 1936. From the Belgian perspective, Eastern Europe was a powder keg that could ignite and suck Belgium into war against Germany.[48]

The Belgians responded to their internal pressures by slowly modifying their relations with France. In that sense, the diplomatic exchange of 1931

---

47 Georges Bonnet, *Le Quai d'Orsay sous trois républiques* (Paris, 1961), p. 279.
48 Jean-Marie d'Hoop, Jacques Willequet, Jean Vanwelkenhuyzen, "Les rapports militaires franco-belges de mars 1936 au 1er septembre, 1939," in Renouvin and Willequet, eds., *Les relations militaires franco-belges*, pp. 19–20.

that linked the defense of the two countries to the League of Nations and the Locarno treaty signaled Belgium's movement toward neutrality. Contacts between military staffs gradually became less frequent, particularly in the early 1930s, and the effectiveness of the accord decreased.

On 6 March 1936, the day before Germany's reoccupation of the Rhineland, the Belgian minister of foreign affairs notified the French that only that portion of the 1920 accord pertaining to the execution of commitments under Locarno remained valid. On 11 March, the Belgian Prime Minister stated that contact between military staffs would "engender no political commitment or obligation" for either country.[49] In a press conference on 11 July, the minister of foreign affairs explained, "I want only one thing, a foreign policy exclusively and completely Belgian."[50] He failed to use the word "neutrality," but Belgium's status clearly had changed.

While contacts between military staffs did not end, they remained infrequent, and Belgium became more secretive about information relating to its national defense. It provided some limited military information and permitted French engineers to do topographic work along its borders, but understanding of Belgian operational planning declined significantly in France. The Belgians had previously purchased much of their military matériel from France but now sought it from other sources, especially Britain. By early 1937, Belgium had adopted a policy of neutrality and had publicly announced its willingness to defend its borders against either France or Germany. Yet despite Belgium's disruption of France's alliance network, French strategists never deviated from their long-standing plan to rush to the aid of their northern neighbor in order to meet a German attack. The French army aimed to conduct a forward defense, not fight on its own territory as in 1914–18.

The other important western neighbor, Britain, also complicated France's strategic designs. The strategic goals of the two nations were dissimilar, and this disjunction first appeared in 1920 when the French supported the Young Turks under Mustapha Kemal while the British backed their Greek opponents. Most French leaders, however, believed that Britain's national interests would push it to support France in any future war with Germany. Unfortunately, convincing the British and getting them to prepare for such an eventuality proved a Herculean task.

While most French leaders desired the continuation of the Anglo-French Entente that had led to victory in World War I, Britain reverted immediately after 1919 to its traditional position of avoiding continental commitments. France watched helplessly as its wartime ally demobilized and virtually

49 Renouvin and Willequet, eds., *Les relations militaires franco-belges,* Annexe III, "Lettre de M. Van Zeeland, ministre des Affaires étrangères, à M. Laroche, ambassadeur de France à Bruxelles, 6 mars 1936," pp. 46–47.
50 Quoted in d'Hoop, Willequet, and Vanwelkenhuyzen, "Les rapports militaires franco-belges," p. 25.

disarmed except for the Royal Navy. Britain's refusal to stand by its guarantee of French security against German invasion proved a shock, but French exasperation with the British increased as they quarrelled over German reparations. Many Frenchmen soon viewed the reluctant British as having lost their national spirit; Paris nonetheless never lost interest in having the British as allies.

The need for British support increased with the departure of French troops from the Rhineland in 1930. France no longer possessed a natural jumping-off point to attack Germany and to assist its Eastern European allies. For leaders such as Herriot, the strategic situation after 1930 added a renewed sense of urgency to reestablishing an effective alliance with Russia. For others, such as Edouard Daladier and Paul Reynaud, it only increased interest in the British link.

Yet Britain remained aloof throughout the early 1930s. Only the Ethiopian crisis revived British interest, particularly once Britain found itself on a collision course with Italy in the Mediterranean. While the Franco-Soviet pact of May 1935 remained unexploited and the ink had yet to dry on the June 1935 military staff accords with Italy, France assessed its alternatives in the Ethiopian crisis and chose Britain. Even though an Italian alliance would permit it to move up to ten divisions from its southeastern frontier to its northern frontier and up to eight divisions from North Africa,[51] Britain was more important strategically.

The French decision represented less a retreat from its allies in Eastern Europe than an acknowledgment of strategic reliance on the British. This preference rested on more than a simple need for soldiers and guns. Lack of British naval support, particularly if Italy were an enemy, would jeopardize France's contact with its empire and with its much-needed manpower, equipment, and natural resources. Without the goods transported on British merchant vessels, France could not meet domestic needs in peacetime, much less wartime. Nor could the French survive in war without British industrial and financial resources. France felt capable of fighting Germany alone for a short period, but doubted that it could wage a successful total war without British assistance. Above all, the French knew they could not wage a successful war against Germany *and* Italy without that assistance. Moreover, given the dictatorial unpredictability and acquisitiveness of Benito Mussolini, the chances of Italy abiding by any long-term commitment to France were scant.

In the wake of Ethiopia, French policy came increasingly under British influence, for Paris now confronted the possibility of conflict with Italy and Germany on two widely separated fronts. By late 1937, the various French committees that dealt with national security affairs were studying the complexities of any such conflict.[52] With France divided internally and conscious

---

[51] Young, "Soldiers and Diplomats," p. 81.
[52] See P.V., C.P.D.N., 8 Décembre 1937, S.H.A.T. 2N24.

of military weakness, the British had the initiative in making decisions that affected both powers, and placed pressure on Paris not to intervene in Spain.[53] Other considerations, however, also shaped French policy. During the 15 March 1938 meeting of the Permanent Committee of National Defense, Blum pointed out that sending substantial shipments of arms to Spain would limit France's ability to mobilize and equip its own forces in a total war.[54] The French thus did not mindlessly relinquish control of grand strategy to the British. But they did increasingly follow Britain's lead.

The strengthening of French ties with Britain resulted in a corresponding loosening of ties to Eastern Europe. In March 1938, the French concluded that despite their obligations to support Czechoslovakia against aggression, they could do little to assist their eastern ally. In the 15 March 1938 meeting of the Permanent Council, Daladier explained, "The only aid that we can furnish is indirect; by mobilizing, we can hold German troops on our borders."[55] Despite this understanding of France's limited capabilities, Daladier insisted during the Franco-British discussions in London a month later that France would keep its commitments to Eastern Europe. He used the threat of Gallic impetuousness to barter with the English for resuming substantive staff talks. But once encouraged by British agreement to the talks, the French foreign minister pressed larger concessions to Germany on the Czechs. He emphasized that Britain and the Little Entente would not aid Czechoslovakia, and that France could not fight Germany alone.[56]

In a painful meeting with the Czechs in Prague on 16 September 1938 the French ambassador explained that given the "insufficiencies" in forces, splits in public opinion, and the uncertainty of British support, France could not defend Czechoslovakia. He concluded, "France intends . . . to act in accord with England. . . ." He added, "[I]t is for Europe that we fight even if we abandon you."[57] Around 0200 hours on 21 September, the French informed the Czechs that in the event of war between Germany and Czechoslovakia over the Sudeten Germans, they would not assist Prague; they had agreed with the British to withhold support. The Czechs had to accept the Franco-British proposal for ending the crisis, and if they did not do so, they "eliminated any practical possibility of assistance from France."[58]

After the war, Bonnet attempted to explain France's actions. "[T]he Czechoslovak army would have been quickly overrun. England could do nothing,

---

53 John E. Dreifort, *Yvon Delbos at the Quai d'Orsay: French Foreign Policy during the Popular Front 1936–1938* (Lawrence, KS, 1973), p. 51. For a contrasting view and for an explanation of the effect of domestic considerations on the decision for nonintervention, see David Wingeate Pike, *Les français et la Guerre d'Espagne* (Paris, 1975), p. 373.
54 P.V., C.P.D.N., 15 Mars 1938, S.H.A.T. 2N25.
55 Ibid.
56 René Girault, "La décision gouvernementale en politique extérieure," in René Remond and Janine Bourdin, eds., *Edouard Daladier: Chef de gouvernement Avril 1938-Septembre 1939* (Paris, 1977), p. 212.
57 Quoted in Le Goyet, *Munich*, p. 93.
58 Ibid., p. 102–103.

France [could do] hardly more. France did not have an air force, and General Gamelin admitted the impossibility of a strong ground offensive 'within at least two years'. . . . It was not the advice of Chamberlain and Daladier which swayed Beneš; it was the military inferiority of the democracies as compared to the Nazis." By supporting the Munich agreements, according to Bonnet, France had avoided an "immediate and catastrophic defeat."[59]

France's abandonment of Czechoslovakia and move toward Britain, however, should not mask its differences with its western partner. In late 1938, for example, Britain feared the growing tension between France and Italy and viewed manifestations of French independence with alarm. Despite these differences, the French followed the British lead on three important issues: the Munich crisis of September 1938, the guarantee to Poland, and the entry into the war.[60]

But the French remained concerned with Eastern Europe. They sent three battalions of R-35 tanks to Poland, Romania, and Yugoslavia and two battalions to Turkey between August 1939 and March 1940. In December 1939, the French sent 36 105mm long-range cannon, their most modern artillery piece, and 15,000 rounds of ammunition to Turkey. At a time when their army desperately needed the equipment, they sent significant numbers of anti-tank weapons to their allies: 520 25mm Model 1934, 310 25mm Model 1937, 78 47mm, and 660,000 anti-tank rounds.[61] By sending equipment to allies that they could not really assist directly, the French weakened their own defenses. But they believed that strengthening other countries, particularly Poland, offered strategic advantages.

STAFF TALKS WITH BRITAIN

Among the inducements that moved France away from its eastern allies was the prospect of the staff talks it had long sought with Britain. From the French perspective, it was the 1935 Ethiopian crisis that had prompted Britain's interest in talks. Until that point, the reluctant ally had firmly resisted military talks similar to those between 1906 and 1914 that had prepared for British intervention on the continent. Many British leaders believed that those discussions had trapped Britain into war. Nevertheless, the British proposed in September 1935 that talks commence, and after some delay over

59 Bonnet, *Quai d'Orsay sous Trois Républiques,* pp. 228, 225.
60 François Bédarida, "La gouvernante anglais," in Remond and Bourdin, eds., *Edouard Daladier,* p. 229.
61 France, Assemblée Nationale, *Rapport fait au nom de la commission chargée d'enquêter sur les événements survenus en France de 1933 à 1945,* Annexes, *Témoignages et documents recueillis par la Commission d'enquête parlementaire* (Paris, 1951–1952), Testimony of Raoul Dautry, V, pp. 2014–2015; Le Général d'Armée Weygand à M. Le Général Commandant les Forces Terrestre, Objet: Livraison de Matériel à la Turquie, No. 1844/2, 7 Décembre 1939, S.H.A.T. 27N78.

the conditions under which France would aid Britain in a war against Italy, the navies met on 29 October. The army and air staffs began meeting on 9 December but discussed little of substance. Only a naval agreement emerged from the talks; it concerned the vital topic of operational responsibilities in the Mediterranean.[62]

Several months later, staff talks began again at France's request during the Rhineland crisis. The British were reluctant to provide guarantees, and the meetings on 15 and 16 April 1936 produced little useful coordination or planning.[63] Another round of staff talks took place in March 1938, but discussions again lasted only a few days. Then France obtained a commitment in April 1938 for more substantive staff talks in exchange for encouraging Prague to grant further concessions to the Sudeten Germans. The talks that followed lasted from May through September 1938 and resulted in the first significant military cooperation between the two powers since World War I.[64]

Although French foreign policy after October 1938 closely followed British policy, French strategy essentially fused into a combined Anglo-French strategy as staff talks progressed and the threat of war increased. In 1939, the most important peacetime staff talks took place in three stages (29 March to 4 April, 24 April to 3 May, and 28 to 31 August).[65] For the first time, the two countries agreed on a "Broad Strategic Policy" for the conduct of a war against the Axis. Although establishment of an Allied joint strategy did not alter France's preparations for a total war against Germany, the possibility of stronger British support, new staff talks, and greater military cooperation caused the French to move toward London. By the end of 1938, the French network of alliances in the east was in disarray.

Given the abandonment of Czechoslovakia in 1938, French armed support for Poland in 1939 is ironic. France was nevertheless reluctant to assume too precise or broad a commitment. In May 1939, Polish leaders came to Paris for diplomatic and military conversations and concluded a new military accord. With both France and Britain wary of being drawn into a conflict between the Poles and Soviets, the French warned their eastern ally of their

---

62 Masson, "Conversations militaires," pp. 121–22; Patrick Fridenson and Jean Lecuir, "L'Aviation dans les projets franco-britanniques de 1935 à 1939," in Besnard, d'Hoop, and Fridenson, *Relations franco-britanniques*, pp. 151–52.
63 Masson, "Conversations militaires," p. 124; Fridenson and Lecuir, "L'Aviation dans les projets," pp. 154–56.
64 Masson, "Conversations militaires," p. 125; P.N. Buckley, E.B. Haslam, W.B.R. Neave-Hill, "Anglo-French Staff Conversations, 1938–1939," in Besnard, d'Hoop, and Fridenson, *Relations franco-britanniques*, pp. 93–99; Brian Bond, *British Military Policy between the World Wars* (Oxford, 1980), pp. 227–29, 269, 272–77, 312–17.
65 Buckley, Haslam, and Neave-Hill, "Anglo-French Staff Conversations," pp. 99–118; Pierre Le Goyet, "Les conversations de 1939 sur la coopération franco-britannique en temps de guerre," in Besnard, d'Hoop, and Fridenson, *Relations franco-britanniques*, pp. 127–48.

intention to consult Britain before acting during a crisis. Reflecting French recognition of their limited ability to assist Poland, the new military accord stipulated that any French attack into Germany in support of Poland would involve only a portion of French forces on the northeastern frontier.[66]

France could not resolve its strategic dilemma simply through British promises. The clearest example of this lay in the question of Italy. When the two allies adopted the formal "Broad Strategic Policy" for the conduct of a war, they emphasized the necessity of remaining on the defensive. Since the enemy would "be more fully prepared . . . for war on a national scale, [and] would have superiority in air and land forces," the two allies had to "face a major offensive" and concentrate their "initial efforts" on defeating this attack. Allied policy, however, also suggested the possible "opportunity for counter-offensives early in the war [against Italian possessions in North Africa], without prejudice to the success of the defense in Europe."[67] The French recognized that if the allies were to prevail against Germany and Italy, they must maintain access to their colonies, particularly in North Africa. If France deflected Germany's first attack but lost North Africa, its chances of winning a long war would decline significantly.

But a French offensive against Italy could not occur until substantial British forces arrived on the continent and freed the French to mass some thirty divisions to attack.[68] An opportunity in North Africa could come earlier, since the French could mobilize over 440,000 soldiers in that area, while the Italians, according to French estimates, could mobilize only 150,000.[69] Despite such favorable force ratios, the British curbed initial French eagerness to launch an immediate offensive in North Africa if Italy joined the war. The French military attaché in London complained that the British were "almost obsessed with the defensive in all theaters."[70]

France may have surrendered its diplomatic and military independence by 1938, but it paid that price willingly in exchange for British support. The Anglo-French strategy developed in the staff meetings irrevocably tied British operations to French military strategy. Since linking the two nations' strategies had long been a goal of its grand strategy, the French felt reasonably satisfied with their strategic situation in 1939. Only the festering problem of Belgium and the issue of operations against Italy remained unresolved.

[66] Henri Michel, "France, Grande-Bretagne et Pologne (Mars-Août 1939)," in Besnard, d'Hoop, and Fridenson, *Relations franco-britanniques,* p. 395.

[67] Lieutenant Colonel B. R. Neave-Hill, "Franco-British Strategic Policy, 1939," in Besnard, d'Hoop, and Fridenson, *Relations franco-britanniques,* p. 339.

[68] Neave-Hill, "Franco-British Strategic Policy, 1939," p. 346.

[69] Pedroncini, "La stratégie française et l'italie de 1932 à 1939," p. 350.

[70] General Albert Lelong, Report for Gamelin, 8 April 1939 quoted in William Gregory Perett, "French Naval Policy and Foreign Affairs 1930–1939," Ph.D. Diss., Stanford University, 1977, p. 409.

THE MAKING OF FRENCH MILITARY STRATEGY

Of the three services, the French army possessed the most influence over the formulation of military strategy because of the obvious German ground threat. The navy nevertheless occupied an important position, for the French believed that only a strong navy could maintain the maritime communications with the colonies on which victory in a long war depended. The navy would also have to play a central role in transporting forces to support allies in the east. In contrast, air force influence over strategy remained subordinate. For a short period in the mid-1930s, notions of swift and easy victories through strategic bombing circulated in Paris, but French air planners soon confronted the unpalatable fact that the Luftwaffe was rapidly surpassing French air strength. France's industries, especially those in the northeast and around the all-important capital, were close to the German border and thus more vulnerable to air attack than many of their German counterparts. Harsh geographic realities thus tied the French air force to the land battle.

The most important discussions on military strategy took place in the army's Superior Council of War. During long meetings in the early 1920s, the council hammered out a framework for military strategy on the continent.[71] One of the most important components of that strategy was its emphasis on an initially defensive stance in a war with Germany. Political and military leaders agreed that only after amassing sufficient forces and defeating Germany's initial offensive could France and its allies attack.

In a 17 May 1920 meeting – the first deliberations after the war to discuss the problem of the frontiers – the Superior Council of War concluded that central Belgium remained the most likely route for a German invasion.[72] If the nation took special measures to protect France's northeastern frontier, the council believed that the Germans would have to attack central Belgium and thus repeat the Schlieffen Plan. They assumed the Germans would make the main attack north of the Meuse between Liège, Namur, and Charleroi, the area that became known as the "Gembloux Gap." That route seemed most likely because of Germany's violation of Belgian neutrality in 1914, the absence of geographic obstacles, and the large network of roads and railways running toward Paris. From this point on the high command demonstrated an unswerving preference for fighting in Belgium rather than in France.

To strengthen France's defenses, senior military leaders agreed on the necessity of fortifying the northeastern frontier. From the time of Vauban, the tradition of permanent frontier fortifications had been stronger in France than in most other countries. After the defeat of 1871, General Raymond A. Séré de Rivières had constructed a series of fortifications along the Meuse

---

[71] For a more detailed treatment, see Doughty, *The Seeds of Disaster*, pp. 41–71.
[72] P.V., C.S.G., 17 Mai 1920, S.H.A.T. 50.

between Verdun and Toul, with the main fortifications centered around those two cities. The most important considerations that led to the Maginot Line, however, lay in a doctrinal preference for a prepared battlefield, the shortage of French manpower, and the need for constant readiness to repel an invader. Only fortifications, in the Council's view, would enable France to overcome its disadvantages against Germany.

The decision to protect the northeastern frontier with a massive system of fortifications also stemmed from the location of much of France's natural resources and industry within easy striking distance of the Germans. Within the triangle formed by Dunkirk, Strasbourg, and Paris lay 75 percent of France's coal, 95 percent of its iron ore, and most of its heavy industry. The Paris-Lille-Rouen area produced nine-tenths of France's cloth, four-fifths of its woolen goods, most of its chemicals, and all of its automobiles and aircraft. The French consequently feared that they would lose the next war if the Germans launched a surprise attack (*attaque brusquée*) and seized a significant portion of this territory.

At the same time, much of France's population resided near these resource and industrial centers. Manpower for the armed forces had long been a source of serious disquiet to French leaders. From the time of the Franco-Prussian War, the ratio of young males favored the Germans. In the late 1860s the ratio of young men between twenty and thirty-four had only slightly tilted toward France's eastern neighbor. But by 1910 the Germans had increased their advantage to 1.6 to 1, and by 1939 the Germans had more than twice as many men of military age.[73] For reasons of manpower as well as of patriotism, France had to protect its citizens living along the frontiers. French leaders had to create their strategy within this important constraint.

At a meeting on 17 May 1920, the Superior Council of War addressed the question of fortifying the frontiers. The session demonstrated a lack of consensus within the army's leadership about the function, form, and location of fortifications for defending the northeastern frontier. But almost all agreed on the necessity of some type of fortifications. By mid-1922, the Council had split between advocates of a continuous line of defensive works reminiscent of World War I and those who argued for fortified regions to act as centers of resistance that would facilitate offensive action or defensive maneuver.

On 12 October 1927, after seven years of debate, the Council adopted the concept of deep underground fortresses to cover key terrain features, with smaller blockhouses and other obstacles protecting the rest of the frontier.[74] The main fortifications were to run parallel to the northeastern frontier, with the largest fortresses located in the Rohrbach-Vosges-Haguenau and

---

[73] Ratios computed from population figures in Dudley Kirk, "Population and Population Trends in Modern France," in *Modern France: Problems of the Third and Fourth Republics,* Edward Mead Earle, ed. (Princeton, 1951), p. 317.

[74] P.V., C.S.G., 12 Octobre 1927, S.H.A.T. 50 bis.

Montmédy-Thionville-Boulay sectors. These two heavily fortified areas would shield the northeastern corner of France and the crucial resources around Metz and Thionville.[75]

When the Superior Council of War addressed the possibility of extending the fortification system to the Ardennes, its members concluded that other areas should receive a higher priority. Pétain, reflecting the views of his colleagues, argued before the Senate Army commission in March 1934 that this sector was "not dangerous."[76] When Gamelin met with the Belgian chief of staff in April 1935 and in May 1936, they discussed coordination between their forces and devoted most of their attention to issues other than defending the Ardennes.[77] In comparison to the vulnerable resources on the northeastern frontier and the absence of easily defensible terrain in western Belgium, the Ardennes seemed to require less defensive preparation. From beginning to end, the high command treated it as a mere connecting sector between the northeastern and northern frontiers.

The southeastern frontier along the Italian border also seemed less significant. Beginning in April 1935, Gamelin and his staff analyzed a possible war against Italy but never became overly concerned about an attack from across the Alps. The likelihood of a war against both Germany and Italy or solely against Germany seemed greater than a war against Italy. Gamelin never seriously considered sending large units into the Alps, particularly when it became clear that a French offensive against Italy could not occur until substantial British forces arrived on the continent.[78] Though construction of a few defensive works on the Italian frontier began in 1931, it proceeded slowly; some key fortresses remained unfinished until 1938.[79]

By September 1939, the broad outlines of France's military strategy were in place, and reflected the decisive influence of geography and resources. French forces would hold the northeastern and southeastern frontiers and move into central and western Belgium to establish a forward defense. The depth of their advance would depend upon luck and circumstances beyond their control. Those circumstances became particularly problematic following Belgium's return to neutrality in 1936.

If the Belgians appealed for aid prior to a German attack, French forces might be able to move forward to defend along the Albert Canal. If not, they had three other possibilities. The first, the farthest forward, ran from the

---

[75] Jean-Yves Mary, *La Ligne Maginot: ce qu'elle était, ce qu'elle en reste* (San Dalmazzo, Italy, 1980), pp. 58–63.

[76] Pétain's testimony is included in Général Maurice Gamelin, *Servir* (Paris, 1946), Vol. 2, p. 128.

[77] "Conférence franco-belge du 5 Avril 1935," Annexe IV, in Renouvin and Willequet, *Relations militaires*, pp. 47–51; "Conversations militaires franco-belges du 15 Mai 1936," Annexe VI, in Renouvin and Willequet, *Relations militaires*, pp. 52–58.

[78] Dutailly, *Les problèmes de l'Armée de terre française*, pp. 96, 98–99, 103, 106, 111–12, 113.

[79] Mary, *La Ligne Maginot*, pp. 15, 62–63, 77–81, 192–4.

border at Givet along the Namur-Dyle-Antwerp line. This possibility eventually evolved into Plan D, or the Dyle Plan. The second alternative was a defense farther to the rear along the frontier to Condé, through Tournai along the Scheldt (Escaut) to Ghent, and then either directly to the North Sea at Zeebrugge, or along the Scheldt to Antwerp. This plan eventually became known as Plan E, or the Escaut Plan. The final alternative was a defense along the entire Franco-Belgian frontier to Dunkirk. Of these three alternatives, a defense along the Namur-Dyle River-Antwerp line would be about 70 kilometers shorter than the other two.[80]

During the first weeks of the war, Gamelin preferred caution and prepared for implementation of the Escaut Plan. Following the rapid and deep thrusts of German forces in Poland, French military leaders worried about whether their mobile forces could reach their designated defensive positions in Belgium before the arrival of German mechanized forces. Less than a month after the beginning of the war, the French high command ordered the commander of First Army Group – who held responsibility for the area from the Channel to the Maginot Line – to assure as his first priority "the integrity of the national territory and [to] defend without withdrawing the position of resistance organized along the frontier. . . ." The directive also noted that the high command could authorize First Army Group to enter Belgium and occupy a defensive position along the Scheldt.[81]

A Gamelin directive of 24 October described the two main alternatives for occupying positions in Belgium, one along the Escaut and the other along the Dyle. The directive argued that an advance beyond the Scheldt depended on the time available for French forces to reach prepared positions.[82] In the first weeks of the war, France thus favored moving no farther than the Scheldt line. But after the French learned that the Belgians were strengthening the defenses along the Albert Canal and were improving their readiness, Gamelin became more optimistic about an advance deep into Belgium.[83] In late October and early November, he concluded that Allied forces could advance to the Dyle without danger. From this point on, Gamelin favored the more ambitious strategy despite warnings from General Alphonse Georges, commander of the northern and northeastern frontiers, about the difficulties of reaching the Dyle ahead of the Germans.

At first the British expressed reservations about *any* move into Belgium, but Gamelin eventually persuaded the British generals. After detailed analysis and discussions, Plan D gained acceptance on 9 November during a

---

[80]   Gamelin, *Servir*, I, pp. 84–88.
[81]   G.Q.G., E.-M. Général, 3ème Bureau, No. 0264 3/FT, 26 Septembre 1939, S.H.A.T. 27N155.
[82]   G.Q.G., E.M. Général, 3ème Bureau, No. 0559 3/N.E., 24 Octobre 1939, S.H.A.T. 27N155.
[83]   Le Goyet, *Le mystère Gamelin*, pp. 281–83.

meeting of senior Allied commanders at Vincennes. In its meeting on 17 November, the Supreme War Council concluded that it was "essential" to hold the Dyle line and ratified that decision. On that same day, Gamelin issued a directive that provided details about occupying the Dyle line from Antwerp in the north to Givet in the south through Louvain, Wavre, the Gembloux Gap, and Namur.[84]

Thus by mid-November the Allies considered the Dyle line as the most suitable position to defend in Belgium. During the next four months, as the Dutch and Belgians improved their defenses, as the British slowly increased their forces, and as French units became better equipped and trained, Gamelin looked farther afield, toward Holland.

While Allied officials still discussed Plan D, Gamelin was considering the possibility of moving into the Netherlands. By sparing the Dutch from German conquest, the Allies would retain ten Dutch divisions, secure North Sea communications, and deny the Germans a staging area for air and sea attacks against Britain.[85] By securing the Scheldt, the Allies could also use the port of Antwerp. A move to link up with the Dutch along the Scheldt, however, represented an extreme variation of Plan D.

On 8 November Gamelin issued a directive that for the first time mentioned the possibility of a German attack on the Netherlands. He emphasized the importance of Allied forces on the south bank of the Scheldt preventing the enemy from bypassing Antwerp to the west. Gamelin then strengthened the left wing of First Army Group with the Seventh Army, which apparently moved into position in December. Prior to its move to the far left flank of Allied forces, the Seventh Army (one light mechanized, two motorized, and four infantry divisions) had served as the essential part of the general reserve behind the advance into Belgium. As part of its new mission, Seventh Army would also move into Holland and secure the Scheldt by occupying the peninsula on the north bank.[86]

Despite worries in the high command, Gamelin then decided shortly before the German offensive that the Dyle Plan and the "Holland Hypothesis" would include an advance of French troops toward Breda, soon known as the "Breda Variant." He planned to have French forces link up with the Dutch along the Scheldt. On 12 March 1940 he issued a directive to General Georges that coupled Seventh Army's mission on the left flank with the Dyle maneuver, and made the move into the Netherlands almost automatic. Georges in turn directed First Army Group to implement any order to enter

---

[84] François Bédarida, *La stratégie secrète de la drôle de Guerre: Le Conseil Suprême Interallié, Septembre 1939-Avril 1940* (Paris, 1979), pp. 149–50, 179; G.Q.G., E.-M. Général, 3ème Bureau, No. 0773 3/N.E., 17 Novembre 1939, S.H.A.T. 27N155.

[85] Le Goyet, *Le mystère Gamelin*, p. 284; D. W. Alexander, "Repercussions of the Breda Variant," *French Historical Studies*, 8, No. 3 (1974), p. 481.

[86] G.Q.G., E.-M. Général, 3ème Bureau, No. 0682 3/N.E., 8 Novembre 1939, S.H.A.T. 27N155.

the Netherlands by moving its left flank to Tilburg, or at least to Breda.[87] Thus by Gamelin's direction the Seventh Army was to occupy a bridgehead between the Belgians and the Dutch. To reach this position, it would have to move past the Belgians along the Albert Canal and then pivot east. For the Seventh Army, the risky Breda maneuver meant traveling about 175 kilometers while the Germans were only approximately 90 kilometers away from Breda.

On 16 April, two months prior to the German invasion, another directive further modified this plan to cover a German attack on the Netherlands that bypassed Belgium. Gamelin altered the area for Seventh Army to occupy, but the directive noted that "in this case, the Belgians may be hostile or passive." However, Georges's directive of 20 March contained the key point: "If circumstances are favorable, our positions will be pushed to the Albert Canal. It is only in the case where the enemy has largely preceded us in Belgium that the Escaut hypothesis will be followed."[88]

In making the Breda Variant and concomitantly weakening his reserves and ability to concentrate elsewhere, Gamelin personally took the final step in the long evolutionary process of deciding how to defend France's frontiers. Several high-ranking officers objected strongly to sending forces to Breda, but none spoke as prophetically as Georges. He emphasized the danger of committing France's mobile forces against a "diversion" when the main German attack might come through the French center. He also asked that a corps with two divisions replace the Seventh Army on the left flank and that the field army return to the general reserve.[89]

As Gamelin's confidence increased, he allowed himself to become enamored of a strategic design of questionable value. In return for the aid of possibly ten Dutch divisions and to deny the Scheldt to the Germans, Gamelin sacrificed his strategic reserves and severely weakened the ability to respond to an unexpected German move. He also committed himself to the Breda Variant despite the absence of staff talks between France and its neutral neighbors.

Because Gamelin designed the Breda Variant, he must personally bear responsibility for the riskiest aspects of an ultimately disastrous military strategy. Though he had reached the highest echelons of the French army by rarely taking chances, he chose a risky alternative when the destiny of his country and its allies depended on his judgment. The irony is that with the exception of the Breda Variant, French strategy was the work of committees

[87] Gamelin, *Servir*, I, pp. 82–83; III, pp. 176–77; G.Q.G., E.-M. Général, 3ème Bureau, No. 790 3/Op, 20 Mars 1940, S.H.A.T. 27N155.

[88] G.Q.G., E.-M. Général, 3ème Bureau, No. 1122 3/Op, 16 Avril 1940, S.H.A.T. 27N155; G.Q.G., E.-M. Général, 3ème Bureau, No. 790 3/Op, 20 Mars 1940, S.H.A.T. 27N155.

[89] Quoted in Pierre Lyet, *La Bataille de France (Mai-Juin 1940)* (Paris, 1947), p. 22; Le Goyet, *Le mystère Gamelin*, p. 295–96.

and thus very conservative. Had the Germans known that Gamelin would squander most of his reserves, they would have launched the 1940 campaign with much greater confidence.

CONCLUSION

Throughout the interwar period, France energetically sought security against a resurgent Germany. By emphasizing collective security through the League and establishment of a series of military accords, agreements, and alliances, the French seemed to have mobilized sufficient power to protect the status quo. The alliance system, however, suffered from a lack of common interests and from Britain's unwillingness to participate. It suffered further from France's failure to raise military forces capable of assisting France's allies either by moving into Eastern Europe or by attacking Germany. As long as Britain remained uncommitted, the French network was little more than a hollow structure because France was too weak to mold a strong alliance and its military forces were too defensively minded to challenge German power directly.

Although French allies and commitments increased as France energetically expanded its network, French security did not. By extending its alliances to the east, France placed itself in a position of having to react to German initiatives. Yet because of its internal politics and the reservations of its western allies, France could not act impetuously in Eastern Europe. Similarly, the more the French expanded their network of eastern alliances, the more apparent the internal disagreements and weaknesses in their network became.

France faced a terrible predicament. The deeper its commitments extended into Eastern Europe, the more their fulfillment relied on the ability of its armed forces to deliver a strong offensive against Germany. Military agreements with its eastern allies were viable only as long as France was militarily capable of providing assistance in the event of war against either Germany or the Soviet Union. To provide such assistance, the French required a military force capable both of strategic maneuver and of offensive action against Germany. The more entrenched the French became behind their fortifications, the more they encouraged German adventurism in the east. And the more the French reinforced, supplied, or strengthened their allies in the east, the more vulnerable they became to a direct German onslaught.

France's strategic predicament became even more complicated once Italy became hostile. The French were torn between successfully defending against a major attack from Germany along their northern and northeastern frontiers or diverting scarce resources and forces to the defense of the Mediterranean, which they had to control if they were to win a long war against Germany. The more France strengthened the northern frontier, the more vulnerable North Africa became to Italian attack. The more it strengthened its forces in the Mediterranean, the more vulnerable the northern frontier became. Ultimately, the making of strategy is about the making of choices, and France faced difficult choices.

Despite the requirement of its grand strategy for a military means to assist the eastern allies, France lost its ability after 1930 to launch an offensive into Germany. In that sense, a yawning gap had opened between the requirements of grand strategy and military capabilities. By September 1939, France was unable to support its allies in the east. Although the French did have plans for conducting an attack into Germany to relieve the pressure on Poland, they only envisaged limited operations. In June 1938 Gamelin issued a directive to guide the conduct of an offensive between the Rhine and Luxembourg, but emphasized the danger of committing major forces into the rough terrain around Saarbrücken. A year later, he issued another directive regarding an offensive into Germany, but the new directive was even more "timid." The detailed instructions to the commanding general of Second Army Group were extraordinarily cautious.[90] Clearly, he had no intention of charging into Germany. France's primary contribution to the security of its eastern allies – as Gamelin suggested at the meeting of the High Military Committee on 5 April 1935 and Daladier reiterated at the meeting of the Permanent Committee of National Defense on 15 March 1938 – was in the mobilization of its forces, which would force Germany to keep some troops on its western border.

Although Lieutenant Colonel Charles de Gaulle had not framed his ideas about the formation of a professional armored corps primarily with the aim of supporting France's eastern allies, his mechanized force might have met that need.[91] The military hierarchy conceded that large armored formations could act as "an instrument of political intervention," but that smacked too much of the infamous Plan XVII which had propelled French forces toward Germany in 1914 without a clear objective. From their perspective, such formations could offer little protection to the frontiers and represented a serious waste of resources.[92] Carefully controlled, methodical attacks seemed much preferable. But the senior military leaders remained aware of their limited ability to support the eastern allies. On 28 August 1939 General Georges explained to Colonel Paul de Villelume, liaison between the Foreign Ministry and Gamelin's staff, that France could defend itself against invasion but that Poland was "lost" because France could not provide any substantial

---

[90] Dutailly, *Les problems de l'Armée de Terre*, pp. 108–11. The first directive is reproduced on pages 379–83.

[91] Charles de Gaulle, *The Army of the Future*, trans. Walter Millis (Philadelphia, 1941), p. 77.

[92] "Note pour le cabinet militaire du ministère (11 juillet 1936)," included in Gamelin, *Servir*, Vol. 3, p. 519; Général Eugene Debeney, *La guerre et les hommes* (Paris, 1937), p. 213.

aid.[93] The initiative had long since passed to Germany. As early as 1936, France could only react to Hitler's actions. Other than returning Britain to its side, French policy had created little more than a fragile shield that the Germans could easily crack. France's best efforts had failed to provide security.

[93] Paul de Villelume, *Journal d'une défaite (23 août 1939 – 16 juin 1940)* (Paris, 1976), pp. 12–13.

16

Strategy for class war: The Soviet Union, 1917–1941

EARL F. ZIEMKE

Soviet strategy ostensibly rested "on a solid Marxist-Leninist ideo-theoretical foundation."[1] V.I. Lenin established that foundation in 1915 when he determined that "war is simply the continuation of politics, [i.e., pursuit of class interests] by other means."[2] He thereby elevated the conduct of war beyond the realm of mere statecraft to which Clausewitz had consigned it by associating war with policy. By Lenin's definition, class interest was equally evident in the wars between imperialist states, but only Soviet military power "[would serve] the most advanced social structure and the cause of the defense of the conquests of the world's workers."[3] The very nature of war, on the one hand, required that strategy emanate from the Communist Party, the repository of Marxist-Leninist theory and protector of working class interests. On the other hand, the Soviet Union was the successor to the Russian Empire and as such, a state within a world system of nation-states, organized on national and territorial bases, in which strategy was an instrument of foreign policy subject to military as well as political requirements. Consequently, from its inception Soviet strategy was a Russian strategy developed within the framework of Marxist-Leninist doctrine.

IN A RING OF FRONTS

Leon Trotskiy's successful engineering of the 7 November 1917 coup brought the Bolsheviks into possession of Petrograd (St. Petersburg) and very little else. They acquired the war and navy ministries, but the Stavka, the general headquarters controlling the army, was 400 miles away in Mogilev.

---

1 Ministerstva Oborony SSR, Institut Voyennoy Istorii, *Sovetskaya voyennaya entsiklopediya* (Moscow, 1976–1980), Vol. 7, p. 560 (hereinafter cited as *SVE*).
2 Ibid., Vol. 2, p. 306; V.I. Lenin, *Polnoye sobraniye Sochineniy* (Moscow, 1961), Vol. 26, p. 224.
3 V.D. Sokolovskiy, *Soviet Military Strategy*, 3d. ed. (New York, 1975), p. 383.

The only military organizations the Bolsheviks controlled were the Military Revolutionary Committee that Trotskiy had organized in the Petrograd Workers' and Soldiers' Soviet to manage the coup, and the sailors, soldiers, and Red Guards (workers militia) that it had employed. Discipline and organization were weak, and except for Trotskiy, who had served as a war correspondent in France early in World War I, knowledge of military affairs was practically nonexistent in the Military Revolutionary Committee and the Bolshevik Party.

When the Stavka sent an expeditionary force against Petrograd in the second week of November, Trotskiy, realizing that the situation required more military proficiency than storming the Winter Palace, gave command of the Military Revolutionary Committee's troops to a tsarist lieutenant colonel and assigned two staunch Bolsheviks to watch over him. The Bolshevik victory on the Pulkovo Heights on 12 November convinced Trotskiy that he had found the mechanism for bending military expertise to party purposes.

But military power was a negligible concern to the Bolsheviks. Although their revolution had skipped its "bourgeois" phase, they were convinced that the Marxist dialectic was at work and that the Bolshevik success represented "a torch that will light the flame all over Europe."[4] In December, they seized control of the Stavka, negotiated an armistice with Germany, and disbanded the already dissolving "old army." But within weeks incipient civil war and devastating German demands reduced the prospects for the revolution's survival without a military force to nil; on 28 January 1918 the Council of People's Commissars issued a decree authorizing "a new army, . . . the Workers' and Peasants' Red Army." This 300,000 man volunteer force was to form "the bulwark of Soviet authority," establish the model for all national armies "in the near future," and provide "support for the impending socialist revolution in Europe."[5] Subsequent decrees authorized a Workers' and Peasants' navy and air force. Four weeks later, after Trotskiy, now Commissar for Foreign Affairs, had rejected German peace terms and the Germans in turn had marched on Petrograd, Lenin summoned what was left of the Stavka (five generals and a few other officers who had not gone off to form White units) to the capital. There they became the nucleus of the Supreme Military Council closely supervised by political commissars.

On the night of 23 February 1918 the Central Committee adopted Lenin's proposal to accept German terms; he had argued that it was better to preserve something than to risk everything. The Treaty of Brest-Litvosk, signed a week later, gave rise to the dominant strategic problem of the Civil War, the ring of fronts. Germany now controlled the Ukraine, western Byelorussia, the Baltic States, and Finland. The Allies intervened in response to rebuild an eastern front against Germany and to eliminate the Bolsheviks. Without

---

4 V.I. Lenin, *Collected Works* (Moscow, 1964), Vol. 26, p. 492.
5 N.I. Savinkin, ed., *KPSS o vooruzhennykh silakh sovetskogo soyuza* (Moscow, 1981), p. 25.

Map 16.1. The Russian Civil War, 1917–1922. *Source.* Adapted from Arthur Banks, *A World Atlas of Military History, 1861–1945* (London: Seeley Service & Co., 1978), 104.

agreeing on a common purpose or plan, they sent expeditions to Murmansk, Arkhangel, and Vladivostok. By late summer, White armies, some with Allied and others with German encouragement, held the Urals, a 300-mile-long bridgehead on the Volga east of Moscow, the Don Basin, and the Caucasus. The Bolsheviks held only a rough 400-to-600-mile circle around Moscow, which they had made their capital.

After Brest-Litvosk, Trotskiy became the People's Commissar for Military and Naval Affairs. From the outset, he discarded the idea of a small volunteer force in favor of a conventionally organized, trained, and disciplined mass army, predominantly composed of conscripted peasants commanded by "military specialists" (former officers of the old army). He proceeded cautiously because he was adopting what the party had always considered the worst features of bourgeois military practice and because the peace treaty with Germany prohibited armed forces of any kind. Consequently, he waited six months before installing a fully centralized command structure.

Regulations published in late September 1918 established the *Revvoyen-sovet Respubliki* (Revolutionary Military Council of the Republic) as the "organ of supreme national military authority." The *Revvoyensovet* consisted of the People's Commissar (Trotskiy) as chairman, the commander in chief of all armed forces, and five other members, all of whom were experienced political commissars. Trotskiy believed that the commander in chief had to be a military specialist, and his choice was Ioakim Vatsetis, a colonel of Latvian troops in the old army. The regulations gave the commander in chief "full independence in all strategic-operational questions," but one other member had to countersign his orders.[6] The aim, Trotskiy explained to Lenin, was to institute "strict separation of operational-command functions from political functions" as well as to ensure that the political members in the *Revvoyensovet* "enjoy[ed] equal authority and [bore] equal responsibility."[7] To provide a general staff – without using that politically repellant designation – Trotskiy converted the Supreme Military Council into the Field Staff and subordinated it to the *Revvoyensovet*.

Trotskiy's purposes were to centralize command in the hands of military professionals, watch them closely, but shield them against random interference from other state and party authorities. Those who wanted to – and many did – saw the *Revvoyensovet* as the old Stavka revived to serve Trotskiy's ambitions. One such was Josef Stalin, although as a member of the Central Committee and the nascent Politburo as People's Commissar for Nationalities he was, compared with Trotskiy, on the fringes of power. At Tsaritsyn (later Stalingrad and later still Volgograd), Stalin assembled an entourage of guerrilla detachment commanders who despised military specialists and disliked the thought of adjusting to a military system.

6 Institut Marksizma-Leninizma, *Dekrety sovetskoy vlasti* (Moscow, 1959–1972), Vol. 3, p. 372f.
7 Jan M. Meijer, ed., *The Trotskiy Papers 1917–1922* (The Hague, 1971), Vol. 1, p. 119.

Kliment Voroshilov, a former mechanic long on ambition and short on talent, was the most vocal of this group and most dedicated to Stalin. Through this group and its contacts within the party, Stalin generated a campaign against Trotskiy to which the latter responded with a demand that the Central Committee "declare publicly whether the policy of the War Department is my personal policy . . . or the policy of our party as whole."[8] In response, the Central Committee declared on 25 December 1918 that ". . . the policy of War Department, like that of all other departments, is carried out on the precise basis of general directives issued by the party through its Central Committee and under its direct control. . . ."[9] The declaration, in its initial context a statement of confidence in Trotskiy, regulated the whole subsequent course of Soviet civil-military relations.

The armistice of November 1918 surprised and shocked the Bolsheviks. They had regarded the world war as their decisive strategic asset, the *deus ex machina* that would open the floodgates of revolution throughout Europe. The armistice, negotiated after barely a flicker of revolution, presaged instead a long-continuing, solitary struggle for survival for the Bolshevik state.

December 1918 began the period of war communism, the distinguishing feature of which was "democratic centralism," the concentration of governmental and political authority in a few hands. "Full power to mobilize the country's manpower and resources for defense" became vested in the Council of Workers' and Peasants' Defense, and all state agencies other than the *Revvoyensovet* were directly subject to its orders. Lenin, the chairman, and Trotskiy were its dominant members. The food, railroad, and army supply commissariats held seats; at Lenin's behest Stalin was a member without portfolio.[10] Although Trotskiy, who wrote the council's charter, had exempted the *Revvoyensovet* from its orders, Lenin's chairmanship formalized a personal prerogative to intervene in military matters. Democratic centralism also extended to the armed forces, where Trotskiy installed within the *Revvoyensovet* a "bureau," consisting of himself, Vatsetis, and the chief of intelligence in the field staff. The Politburo officially took charge in the party, and its five members, Lenin, Trotskiy, and Stalin included, could act for the Central Committee.[11]

The armistice terminated the German occupation, but the ring of fronts quickly reformed. British and French military missions arrived in the Black Sea to monitor the German withdrawal, and stayed to support Ukrainian separatists and General Anton Denikin's White Army. In Paris the peace conference recognized the independence of Poland and looked favorably on

---

[8] Ibid., p. 207.
[9] Savinkin, *Silakh*, p. 42.
[10] *Dekrety*, Vol. 4, pp. 92–94.
[11] Stalin's presence in the highest bodies was Lenin's idea. Although neither Lenin nor the party regarded him as a particularly significant figure, Stalin seldom opposed Lenin openly and never voted against him, in contrast to the other members.

independence movements in Latvia, Lithuania, Estonia, and Finland. A British fleet entered the Baltic; at the gates of Petrograd General Nikolay Yudenich activated a White army with British money and munitions. At Omsk, Admiral Aleksandr Kolchak formed a unified command for White forces in Siberia and the Urals and proclaimed himself supreme ruler of all Russia. However, Allied public opinion showed little support for intervention, while the national independence movements were as hostile to the Whites as to the Reds, and Kolchak, Denikin, and Yudenich failed to coordinate their operations or cooperate with the breakaway nationalities.

The Red Army, with 1.8 million men on its rolls in February 1919, could claim to be a mass army but not a true workers' and peasants' army: 85 percent of the troops were conscripted peasants. Although it substantially outnumbered its enemies, it could not function as had the mass armies of World War I. It lacked weapons to arm more than one-third of its troops and could only concentrate about two-thirds of those at the front, which the field staff estimated as 4,800 miles long. The Field Staff may well have stretched the facts, but the ratio of troops to frontage was indeed low on both sides.[12] On fronts frequently several hundred miles long, the *Revvoyensovet* deployed armies that seldom exceeded 40,000 troops – and the desertion rate consistently ran over 50 percent. Nevertheless, the Red Army held two great strategic advantages: interior lines against enemies who could not and would not coordinate their operations, and possession of the Russian heartland against opponents holding only the ethnically diverse fringes.

Three out of four Red Army commanders were military specialists. Some had volunteered; most were drafted. All, particularly former generals, worked under intense suspicion. Trotskiy preferred those who had not gained recognition in the old army on the theory that they would be less subject to pressure from former colleagues. Vatsetis was one of those. Another was Boris Shaposhnikov, a former colonel who had volunteered in early 1918 and had found a place on the Field Staff. Shaposhnikov was a general staff officer of the old school, self-effacing, diligent, and not overly ambitious. The so-called communist commanders served, in the main, at the company and lower levels, but a few who rose to become legendary figures in a manner military specialists could not. Vasiliy Blyukher, a former corporal who led a partisan detachment on a long raid behind the enemy front, became the first to receive the Order of the Red Banner, the Soviet Union's highest decoration. He went on to command a division.

Two communist commanders, Mikhail Tukhachevskiy and Mikhail Frunze, began their careers directly in the upper command echelon. At age twenty-five, Tukhachevskiy gained Lenin's confidence and received command of the First Army. Success in the field, membership in the Communist

---

[12] S.M. Klyatskin and A. F. Gorlenko, "*Doklady I.I. Vatsetisa V.I. Leninu,*" *Istoricheskiy Archive*, 1 (1958), pp. 41–71.

Party, and a bent for self-promotion made him a rising star. But some, notably Stalin, saw him as a mere soldier flying false colors because he was a newcomer to the party (1918), had served as a guards lieutenant, and came from the lower nobility. Frunze, however, was a model communist commander. He had no military training but possessed excellent party credentials and benefited from the view that party experience should come before military experience in command appointments. By exploiting a quirk in the regulations, he had made himself the commander of the army to which he was assigned as commissar. Unlike Voroshilov who was also for a time a self-made army commander, he had the sense to rely on military specialists and to comport himself in a disciplined manner.

The battles of 1919 decided the Civil War. The principal Soviet goal was the recovery of the grain, coal, ores, and oil of the Ukraine and Caucasus that were critical to the state's survival. Fierce internecine quarrels and maneuvers to acquire power, position, and influence within the party paralleled the war against the Whites and the Allies. The first conflicts occurred on the East Front, the group of armies facing Kolchak, "the main *front* of the Republic," a designation first made in summer 1918 and again in February 1919. Vatsetis's successor was Sergey Kamenev, a former colonel of mediocre ability who was pleased to receive so important an appointment. His commissar was S.I. Gusev, important enough in the party to be a candidate for the Central Committee, but like Stalin without a state appointment commensurate with his party rank and resentful of the power base that Trotskiy, a newcomer to the party, had created in the *Revvoyensovet*. Gusev's attitudes towards Trotskiy soon found echoes from other commissars and commanders who saw both political and personal advantages in warring on the People's Commissar for Military and Naval Affairs. The East Front, beside setting the political tone, achieved the first major Bolshevik victory of the Civil War. Kolchak's offensive, a threatening lunge toward Moscow in the winter, lost its momentum; by June he was in retreat toward Siberia in considerable disarray.

Meanwhile, Trotskiy's military policy had generated a crisis within the party. His efforts to strengthen the military specialists' authority and regularize the chain of command distressed the commissars and other party figures with military ambitions. Stalin, Gusev, and others had planted suspicions in the Central Committee that Trotskiy and the *Revvoyensovet* were more concerned with serving their own interests than those of the party. Unfavorable strategic developments heightened intraparty tension. In May, Denikin launched an offensive out of the Caucasus and Crimea toward Moscow, and Yudenich staged a thrust toward Petrograd. By conventional standards, the odds were against them, but those standards did not apply in the Civil War. Consequently, the speed of their advances and the Red Army's rapid disintegration gave ample reason to fear.

At this point Bolshevik squabbling came close to losing the war. Vatsetis proposed shifting sizeable forces from the East Front to the South Front, which was retreating through the Ukraine from the Volga to the Dnepr. Gusev and his commissars protested directly to Lenin that such a change in emphasis was committing "a massive fatal error that could cost us the revolution." Stalin then added to the trouble by suggesting from Leningrad that Trotskiy had brought a group of traitors into the *Revvoyensovet* and that it was high time that the Central Committee summoned up "the fortitude to draw appropriate conclusions."[14] At this point, Lenin brought the Central Committee into play, and Trotskiy and the military experts lost. Gusev's plan to shift only an army to attack Denikin's offensive in the flank and rear from Tsaritsyn received Lenin's and the party's blessing.[15] In a series of votes the Central Committee approved Gusev's proposal, dismissed Vatsetis, named Kamenev as commander in chief, appointed Gusev to the *Revvoyensovet,* and put Trotskiy on notice that it, not he, would henceforth set military policy.

All of this was disastrous. The Red Army had neither the strength nor the expertise to launch a flank attack, and the situation rapidly approached catastrophe. Only at the last moment, as Denikin's army approached Tula, the final obstacle on the road to Moscow, did the Politburo override the Central Committee and the commander in chief. It halted the East Front and shifted the emphasis to the south. Ironically, Stalin had just become the chief commissar at South Front. There he exhibited scant interest in cooperating with the military specialists but built up his own gang around the original Tsaritsyn group with such stunningly unoriginal minds as Budennyy and Voroshilov. But the Whites had shot their bolt, and the Denikin offensive collapsed from its own weight and incompetence as well from the Bolshevik shift in emphasis. Stalin immediately devoted himself to the propagation of a myth that depicted himself as guiding an invincible and wholly Bolshevik development in the art of war, the 20,000-man cavalry army.

By the end of 1919 the ring of hostile fronts had disintegrated. The allies evacuated Arkhangel and Murmansk in September. Kolchak's government and army collapsed in November, while Estonia accepted a Soviet peace offer, thereby ending the White threat to Petrograd. On 5 December, Lenin could predict a complete victory in the Civil War within the next few months.[16] By April the Whites had retreated to the Crimea and held no other territory from which they could dispute control of the Russian heartland.

But by now Lenin had bigger fish to fry; he announced to the Ninth Party Congress that the long-awaited world revolution had broken out with the declaration of a "Soviet Republic" in Saxony and revolution in the Ruhr.

14 Meijer, *Trotskiy,* Vol. 1, pp. 521–25; Leon Trotskiy, *My Life* (New York, 1970), p. 452.
15 Trotskiy, *Life,* p. 454; Ya. P. Krastynya, *Istoria latyvshskikh strelkov* (Riga, 1972), p. 448; Meijer, *Trotskiy,* Vol. 1, p. 587.
16 Lenin, *Works,* Vol. 30, p. 219.

"The Proletarian Soviet power in Germany," Lenin told the delegates, "is spreading irresistibly. The time is not far off when we shall be marching hand-in-hand with a German Soviet Government."[17] But the Soviets had first to handle the problem of Poland, while the German bourgeoise was proving surprisingly resistant to being discarded on the rubbish heap of history. On 25 April the Poles mounted a major offensive aimed at stealing the Ukraine from the Soviets. Pilsudski had waited until the Bolsheviks had removed the embarrassment of the Whites so that he would not have to share his spoils. The Bolsheviks were likewise eager to take on the Poles, spread the revolution to the west, and link up with their German "brothers." The Politburo designated West Front to execute a counteroffensive that would destroy Poland as a bourgeois state. Moreover, the party proclaimed a "patriotic war" and called on "all workers, peasants, and honorable Russian citizens" to join in repulsing the Polish invaders.[18]

The ensuing Polish-Soviet War involved wild changes of fortune, underlining both the weaknesses of the opposing forces and their ambitious appetites. From the first Budennyy and Voroshilov showed scant interest in cooperating with or taking directions from anyone else. Soviet forces soon regained Kiev, but Stalin's ill-disciplined protéges allowed Polish forces to escape, something that the future dictator ignored as he proclaimed a great victory for the cavalry army. Soviet forces now advanced into Poland, where they seemed to have the prospect of installing a communist government in Warsaw. Pilsudski and his forces, however, put up a spirited defense. Political infighting contributed to the Soviet defeat: Tukhachevskiy advanced to the gates of Warsaw, but once there faced a concentrated Polish counteroffensive, while Stalin and his henchmen disobeyed orders and in effect refused to support the main attack.

In the end the army and party failed disastrously in the full view of the world; no amount of talk about Allied intervention and Polish aggression could obscure the fact that the humiliation was largely self-inflicted. Because Lenin, the party's highest authority, was deeply involved, the question of responsibility remained unresolved. It lingered as a permanent irritant in civil-military relations. Stalin thereby escaped his share of responsibility for the disastrous mishandling of the Polish offensive. Nevertheless, the Soviets destroyed the last White stronghold and declared victory in the Civil War by the end of the year.

The experiences of World War I exercised a decisive influence over the strategic paths the other European powers travelled. But in the case of the Soviet Union, Russia's experiences in World War I played a relatively smaller role in the formulation of Soviet policy in ensuing decades. It was to the Civil War that most of Stalin's military looked for the lessons from which to

[17] Ibid., 442.
[18] Institut Marksizma-Leninizma, *Istoriya grazhdanskoy voyny v SSR* (Moscow, 1960), Vol. 5, p. 68.

formulate strategic policies. Those lessons were particularly important in forming the *Weltanschauung* of Joseph Stalin. First, the Civil War had confirmed the Bolshevik regime in its conspiratorial instincts about the nature of the outside world. Second, Stalin drew the conclusion that military experts were a dangerous lot whom the regime must watch closely. Third, the soon-to-emerge Stalinist regime emphasized the political and ideological nature of the future defense of the Soviet Union. Finally, the various civil-military conflicts over how the war should be waged resulted in a deep cleavage between the political generals, many of them beholden to Stalin, and those who had displayed some minimal level of military competence. That fault line existed within the Red Army until Stalin resolved the cleavage by shooting most of the competent in 1937.

FRUNZE AND MILITARY REFORM

Although fighting continued in the Ukraine, the Caucasus, and the Far East for almost two more years, the Tenth Party Congress in March 1921 adopted a peacetime program. War communism, or legalized extortion to support the war, had wrecked the economy and driven the peasantry to desperation. Intensified conscription during the Polish war had increased the Red Army to 5.5 million men, a body of unproductive consumers. Only 1.8 million men were in organized units, and barely 600,000 of them were combat effective. Trotskiy admitted that the navy, which had played an insignificant part in the Civil War, had 180,000 men "on the books." The air force had about 23,000 men assigned to a small training and supply establishment and various army commands.[19] While the Congress was in session, Tukhachevskiy suppressed the great mutiny at the Kronshtadt naval base. Although the 27,000 mutineers constituted a significant segment of the navy's personnel, Lenin dismissed the mutiny as an insignificant incident. But his opaque party jargon betrayed a tacit awareness that the sailors, predominantly peasant conscripts, had reacted to their class's economic distress.[20]

During the Congress, Lenin announced the New Economic Policy (NEP), which offered limited free enterprise. It could not be effective unless the state stopped confiscating output, and that could not occur without drastic cut backs in military demand. Trotskiy had a solution: to convert the army to a militia system in which the troops would simultaneously provide labor, support themselves, contribute to the economy, and perform military service. But many delegates, including some earlier opponents of a regular army, had

[19] S.A. Tyushkevich, *The Soviet Armed Forces: A History of Their Organizational Development* (Washington, 1978), p. 93; Karyaeva, *Direktivy frontov*, Vol. 4, p. 219; Meijer, *Trotskiy*, Vol. 2, p. 577.
[20] Lenin, *Works*, Vol. 30, pp. 183–85; S.S. Kromov, ed., *Grazhdanskaya voyna i voyennaya interventsiya v. SSSR* (Moscow, 1983), p. 306.

found careers in the military and did not see a militia as affording sufficient scope to their ambitions.

The congress approved Trotskiy's motion on condition of its gradual implementation. Economic pressure, however, pushed the conversion along at some speed. Army strength dropped to 1,600,000 men by autumn 1921, to 800,000 by the next year, and to 600,000 by early 1923. The navy, which Lenin had wanted abolished after the Kronshtadt mutiny, fell to 35,000 by September 1921.[21]

Trotskiy was by no means bent on demilitarization. In fact, he was working with General Hans von Seeckt, the German Army's commander in chief, to overcome Soviet deficiencies in military technology. Seeckt, for his part, looked to evade the peace treaty's restrictions on German weapons development. On 7 May 1921 Trotskiy informed Lenin that the Germans were willing "to cooperate with us in restoring our war industry" and help in building an air force and submarine fleet.[22] Owing to financial and political problems, collaboration progressed haltingly; nevertheless, it was the most significant Soviet military achievement of the 1920s. The Germans built a Junkers aircraft factory and a poison gas plant, provided assistance in submarine construction, and established testing and training facilities for aircraft and tanks. They also gave general staff training to a few Soviet officers.[23]

The Tenth Party Congress elected Frunze, Gusev, and Voroshilov to the Central Committee. Frunze and Gusev were Voroshilov's rivals because of their association with the East Front group and not Stalin's Tsaritsyn group, but mutual opposition to Trotskiy constituted an overriding bond. At the Congress, Frunze and Gusev introduced a set of theses designed to undercut Trotskiy's position. Frunze contended in the ensuing year-long debate with Trotskiy that communists like himself with no formal military education could derive a specifically communist military doctrine from Marxism.[24] Trotskiy replied, in essence, that "war is a practical art, a skill" that "requires a certain schooling," and therefore, "we must reject all attempts at building an absolute revolutionary strategy with the elements of our limited experience. . . ."[25] The debate climaxed at the Eleventh Party Congress in March and April 1922 – and died. As Lenin warned Frunze in private, "it seems to

21 Tyushkevich, *Armed Forces*, p. 123; Meijer, *Trotskiy*, Vol. 2, pp. 415, 573–77.
22 Meijer, *Trotskiy*, Vol. 2, p. 441.
23 F.L. Carsten, *The Reichswehr and Politics 1918–1933* (Oxford, 1966), pp. 135–47; Helm Speidel, "Reichswehr und Rote Armee," *Vierteljahrshefte für Zeitgeschichte*, 1 (1933), p. 18.
24 Frunze never quite managed a precise definition of that doctrine. For a recent Soviet exposition, see M.A. Gareev, *M.V. Frunze: Military Theorist* (Washington, 1988), pp. 95–107. Walter D. Jacobs, *Frunze: The Soviet Clausewitz* (The Hague, 1969) follows the debate in detail (pp. 24–99).
25 Leon Trotskiy, *Military Writings* (New York, 1969), pp. 56, 73.

me that our military communists are still insufficiently mature to pretend to the leadership of all military affairs."[26]

Though the party did not adopt the unified military doctrine, neither did it reject it. Lenin and even Trotskiy had conceded that it might be attainable in the future and that it rested on premises acceptable to the party. Marxism might thus confer superiority in war as well as in politics, and be the essential qualification for military leadership. Moreover, Frunze used the Civil War to buttress his theory with sweeping and attractive assumptions. He argued that the Red Army had solved the problems of mobility and maneuver that had baffled western armies in World War I; working class influence in the Red Army would now provide the maneuverability, decisiveness, and offensive spirit that no bourgeois army could match.

No one doubted that workers (and working peasants) should command the Red Army. When the Civil War ended, about 60 percent of command personnel were communists, but few held appointments above company level, and even fewer were workers or peasants. In 1921, the Red Army's Military Academy, which Trotskiy had created in 1918 to give general staff training to workers and peasants, graduated its first class. Its mission was twofold: to instruct and to keep abreast of developments in the art of war. To do either properly, it had to catch up with the mainstream of European military thought. A.S. Svechin, an instructor of strategy and military history and the academy's foremost theorist, headed a commission to analyze the World War I experience.[27] That did not prevent Frunze, as commandant, from imposing a heavy emphasis on the Civil War experience.

In 1922, the Soviet system entered a period of profound change. In May Lenin suffered a stroke, and by late 1923 was almost totally incapacitated. The contest for succession commenced. Its earliest manifestation was an all-out attack on Trotskiy's position. In February 1924, a Central Committee commission called for appointment of a strong figure to reform the military establishment. Gusev chaired the commission, of which Stalin and Frunze were both members. The choice fell on Frunze, and during the year, he became deputy commissar of military and naval affairs, deputy chairman of the *Revvoyensovet,* chief of the army staff, commandant of the Military Academy, and a candidate member of the Politburo. In January 1925, he replaced Trotskiy as People's Commissar of Military and Naval Affairs. Voroshilov followed close behind, becoming commander of the Moscow Military District, a member of the *Revvoyensovet* in 1924, and Frunze's deputy in the defense commissariat and the *Revvoyensovet* in 1925. In November 1925,

[26] Jacobs, *Frunze,* p. 92; I.A. Korotkov, *Istoriya sovetskoy voyennoy mysli* (Moscow, 1980), p. 80.
[27] A. Ageev, "*Voyennyy teoretik i voyennyy istorik A.A. Svechin,*" *Voyenno-istoricheskiy Zhurnal,* 8 (1978), pp. 127–29.

after Frunze's death, Voroshilov became commissar of military and naval affairs.[28]

In the traditional Soviet view, Frunze ranks as a *polkovodets* (an outstanding field commander, a *Feldherr*), the true father of the Soviet military system. He gained that stature because he reformed and reorganized the armed forces in accordance with communist principles and thereby guaranteed the politico-military superiority that they enjoyed until the Soviet collapse in 1991. In other words, he provided an example, guidance, and a structure on which this new type of armed forces, born in 1918, could build to full maturity.

Frunze received credit for eliminating Trotskiy's allegedly pernicious influence in the armed forces. In doing so, he gratified his own ambition by making himself the tool of the troika, of which Stalin was a member, that had taken control after Lenin's death. With the troika's support, he supplanted Trotskiy's long-time deputy, E.M. Sklyanskiy, and exploited the position so effectively that Trotskiy lost control of the commissariat before he resigned.[29]

Ironically, Frunze implemented and made Trotskiy's militia scheme marginally palatable to his fellow military communists. The economy, not Frunze, had the deciding voice, and it could not sustain regular armed forces much larger than half a million men. The navy survived Lenin's effort to abolish it, but continued under a political cloud with the surviving odds and ends of the old Baltic fleet. The imperial naval shipyards were now in Estonia, and Vrangel' had taken the remaining ships of the Black Sea fleet in evacuating the Crimea. Likewise, lack of an aircraft industry limited the air force despite a commitment to air power. The Soviets could finance purchases abroad only from the imperial gold reserve, and the German connection was still only at its beginning.[30]

The new militia was to give basic infantry training to two annual conscription classes, approximately 1.8 million men. The regular (cadre) army could accommodate about 30 percent of one annual class. In a long disquisition, "Cadre Army and Militia," published in 1925, Frunze promised a reconversion to a regular army after economic conditions improved, and pointed out that the militia divisions would, in the meantime, carry cadre strengths of 16 percent, providing spaces for career personnel.[31] Although the regime could still not do without military specialists, the reorganization diminished their role and strengthened the position of military communists.

[28] F.N. Petrov, ed., *M.V. Frunze* (Moscow, 1962), pp. 298–300; SVE, Vol. 2, pp. 363–65, Vol. 8, pp. 342–45.

[29] Isaac Deutscher, *The Prophet Unarmed* (New York, 1959), pp. 134f, 160–63.

[30] See M.V. Zakharov, ed., *50 let vooruzhennyk sil SSSR* (Moscow, pp. 169, 181, 182; S.S. Lototskiy, et al., *Armiya sovetskaya* (Moscow, 1969), pp. 103–107.

[31] M.W. Frunze, *Ausgewählte Schriften* (Berlin, 1955), pp. 408–28.

In the command structure, Frunze completed reforms that had, in the main, begun before he became people's commissar. The Defense Council (the former Council of Workers' and Peasants' Defense), continued as the highest state body concerned with military affairs. But after Lenin's death it no longer exercised unlimited power, and became a cabinet committee under the Chairman of the Council of People's Commissars that confined itself to matters affecting armed forces development. The *Revvoyensovet* continued, with significant changes in its makeup. After the abolition of the post of commander in chief in March 1924, the *Revvoyensovet,* as a collegial high command with the people's commissar as head, acted as commander in chief. The commissar's deputy and the chief of the army staff, the chief of the army political directorate, and other military and political figures also sat on the *Revvoyensovet.* Voroshilov's 1924 appointment and Budennyy's in 1923–24 suggests that the initial objective was to undermine Trotskiy's power.

The armed forces' executive organs were the army staff and the army's main administration. This arrangement restored a division between Field Staff and Main Staff that had existed during the Civil War but had disappeared in 1921 when the two merged. As with the Field Staff, the army staff was a planning agency for the armed forces, including navy and air force. The main administration was responsible for force development, training, and general administration.

Like Trotskiy before him, Frunze had to confront the party's antipathy to three standard features of military organizations: personal rank, unity of command, and the general staff. The idea of the general staff as a military institution proved profoundly disturbing to the party and to many communist commanders who served in the Civil War. They saw it as an elite possessed of arcane knowledge acquired only through long initiation, a confraternity capable of dominating and manipulating the military system. The military communists had signified their disdain by calling the Field Staff the general staff. On the other hand, the *Revvoyensovet* had given Tukhachevskiy, Frunze, Yegorov, and I.P. Uborevich "appointment to the general staff" as a mark of signal distinction, and the Military Academy was capable of turning out enough graduates to make general staff training a requirement for advancement to higher level command.[32] Frunze avoided the words "general staff," but he proclaimed that the army staff "must not only be the brain of the Red Army; it must be the military brain of our entire Soviet state. . . ."[33]

In carrying out reforms and in his voluminous commentaries on them, Frunze undertook to establish a rationale for armed forces in a communist state that would afford the military a secure place and autonomy within its

[32] V.M. Ivanov, *Marshal Tukhachevskiy* (Moscow, 1985), p. 207.
[33] Zakharov, *50 let,* p. 175.

professional sphere without infringing on party prerogatives. The army staff, as the brain of the army and the military brain of the state, was limited to providing "that material which lies at the basis of the work done by the Defense Council."[34] Military strategy was subordinate to party politics, not to policy in the Clausewitzian sense. "Only the person who possesses all this knowledge" – that is, of military art and of politics – could make strategy.[35]

Frunze's strategic conceptions combined political assumptions, elements of the unified military doctrine, the Civil War experience, and the World War I experience as General Erich Ludendorff and other foreigners assessed it. Concurring with Lenin's prediction of the inevitability of "a series of frightful clashes with the bourgeois states," Frunze assumed a constant and compelling requirement for a strong standing army.[36] War in the future would be prolonged, and the rear, the source of industrial and agricultural support, would be as important as the front in deciding the outcome.[37] Future wars could involve attrition as well as annihilation, position and maneuver, defense and offense. They would also be class wars; hence, the Soviet forces, exploiting their class orientation and Marxist guidance, would display a natural propensity for the most decisive forms: annihilation, maneuver, and the offensive.[38]

THE TUKHACHEVSKIY ERA

A new day dawned sooner than Frunze could have imagined. The First Five-Year Plan for industrial development and collectivization of agriculture took effect in May 1929, and in July, the Central Committee decided that "the five-year-plan . . . provides favorable conditions for significant qualitative and quantitative improvement in defense."[39] By now Stalin's voice dominated party and state affairs.

With one exception, the world outside appeared as hostile as Lenin had predicted. Germany was the exception; military collaboration continued although Soviet support for German communists periodically disturbed relations. Poland remained an enemy by mutual agreement, and France's association with Poland, Czechoslovakia, Hungary, Romania, and Yugoslavia sustained the impression of a "capitalist" alliance aimed at the Soviet Union. The United States had not yet recognized the USSR, while Britain resumed relations in 1929 after a two-year break. Japan, which had been the last to withdraw its troops from Vladivostok, was establishing military footholds in North China. The Chinese Nationalist Government expelled its Soviet ad-

---

34   Ibid., p. 175.
35   Gareev, *Frunze*, p. 149.
36   David Shub, *Lenin* (Garden City, NY, 1948), p. 394; Frunze, *Schriften*, p. 424.
37   Ibid., pp. 248–59.
38   See M.V. Zakharov, ed., *Voprosy strategii i operativnogo isskusstva v sovetskikh voyennykh trudakh 1917–1940* (Moscow, 1965), pp. 16, 41–53.
39   Savinkin, *Silakh*, p. 258.

visers in 1927; in July 1929, Nationalist troops seized the Soviet-owned Chinese Eastern Railroad.

Tukhachevskiy inherited Frunze's place as the foremost Soviet military theorist. He could not match Frunze in political stature and appeal, but his military reputation was high and growing. In foreign military circles, the Polish war had made Tukhachevskiy the only consequential name in the Red Army leadership. Given, like Frunze, to self-promotion through writing, Tukhachevskiy had published his own account of the operations in Poland, entitled *March Beyond the Vistula*. In it, he suggested that the First Cavalry Army could have saved the day had it followed orders; that assessment did nothing to improve his relations with Stalin, Voroshilov, and Budennyy.[40] His position in the military hierarchy, consequently, depended heavily on his membership in the East Front Group and on his connection to Frunze. In 1924, he became Frunze's deputy in the army staff, and in November 1925, he became chief of staff, probably because the selection occurred before Frunze's death.

With dutiful obeisance to Frunze, Marxism, class struggle, and the Civil War, Tukhachevskiy concentrated on foreign military developments, particularly those in Germany. After analyzing production and manpower figures for World War I, he concluded in 1926 that "we must be prepared to encounter large heavy forces, armies numbering in the millions and armed with the last word in technology."[41] In 1927, he proposed setting up a scientific-technological center to conduct research and development for all kinds of advanced weaponry.[42] *War As a Problem of Armed Struggle*, published in 1928, took the dramatic increases in artillery pieces, machine guns, and aircraft that occurred during World War I and projected them into the future, concluding that the "increase in weapons and auxiliary means" would "sharply alter the conduct of war." War would become a train of successive operations aimed at destroying the enemy's armed forces, his industry, and his territory.[43] After Stalin repeatedly dismissed his proposals for a technological buildup as "harebrained schemes," Tukhachevskiy asked for a transfer, and in May 1928, Shaposhnikov replaced him in the army staff.[44]

Stalin had always regarded the military profession as a low calling whose members' expertise did not qualify them to make strategy. He had divided strategy-making into two essential elements: determine the site and direction of the main effort, and assure stability in the rear. He ranked party experience as the most relevant to the first and an absolute requirement for the second, because military professionals themselves represented a possible threat to

40 See M.N. Tukhachevskiy, *Izbrannye proizvedeniy* (Moscow, 1964), Vol. 1, pp. 115–68.
41 Ibid., Vol. 1, p. 253.
42 Ivanov, *Tukhachevskiy*, p. 262.
43 Tukhachevskiy, *Izbrannye*, Vol. 2, pp. 3–23.
44 Ivanov, *Tukhachevskiy*, p. 82; N.I. Koritskiy, et al., *Marshal Tukhachevskiy* (Moscow, 1965), p. 131.

stability in the rear. At the boss's behest, Voroshilov rewrote the history of the Civil War to give Stalin sole credit for determining the direction of the main effort against Denikin, Yudenich, and Vrangel'. He also showed – and far more credibly – how Stalin, in partnership with the chief of the *Cheka* (political police) Felikhs Dzerzhinskiy, had ensured stability in the rear by rooting out actual, potential, and imagined opposition, both civilian and military.[45]

Stalin, as Lenin's successor and soon to be dictator, delivered the Central Committee report, a kind of state-of-the-union address, at party congresses. At the Fourteenth Congress in 1925, he regarded the Soviet Union as in an extended period of "equilibrium . . . and peaceful coexistence" with the capitalist world.[46] Two years later, he began his report with "Our country, Comrades, is living and developing in a capitalist encirclement." He predicted that the worldwide economic boom then at its height would soon bring the capitalist states into conflict with each other. He added that although war with the capitalist world was necessary and inevitable, the Soviet Union would adopt a peaceful policy to "buy off the capitalists" while strengthening its defenses. The policy would change when revolutionary movements had "matured" or "at the moment when the capitalists come to blows over the division of the colonies."[47]

When the Sixteenth Congress met in June 1930, the Great Depression had begun and political turmoil was spreading across the globe. Stalin told the delegates that the world economic crisis was "laying bare and intensifying the contradictions and antagonisms between the major imperialist countries. . . . " Capitalism was in decay, and would result in "an epoch of wars and revolutions." He foresaw a possibility that their common antagonism toward the Soviet Union would lead the capitalists to consider "whether it would not be possible to solve this or that contradiction of capitalism, or all the contradictions together, at the expense of the USSR." As deterrents to "adventurous attacks," the Soviet Union would have to rely on sympathy and support from the workers in capitalist countries, growth in Soviet economic and political strength, increasing Soviet military power, and "undeviating pursuit" of the peace policy. In view of this threatening situation he asked for and received a major acceleration in the five-year plan, above all in heavy industry.[48]

Armament had been a major component of the five-year plan since July 1929. At that time, the Central Committee decided to "accelerate technological advancement in the Red Army" by having test models of artillery

[45] K. Voroshilov, "*Stalin i krasnaya armiya,*" in *Lenin, Stalin i krasnaya armiya* (Moscow, 1934), pp. 41–61.
[46] Stalin, *Collected Works* (Moscow, 1953), Vol. 7, p. 268.
[47] J. Stalin, *Political Report of the Central Committee to the Fifteenth Congress of the CPSU(B)* (Moscow, 1949), pp. 1–30.
[48] J. Stalin, *Political Report of the Central Committee to the Sixteenth Congress of the CPSU(B)* (Moscow, 1951), pp. 7–39.

and tanks and armored vehicles "of all types" developed within the next two years. In January 1931, the Central Committee promulgated the first phase (1931–33) of a comprehensive "technological reconstruction" (*perestroyka*) that would equip the army and navy with the latest in modern armaments, build up the air and armored forces, and motorize the infantry, cavalry, and artillery.[49]

Although an armaments chief, Uborevich, joined the *Revvoyensovet* in 1929, Tukhachevskiy had kept and enlarged his image as the foremost Soviet authority on technological warfare. Leningrad afforded the best stage outside of Moscow for that purpose. Its party organization possessed a certain autonomy and it still had some appurtenances of a capital, among them the F.E. Dzerzhinskiy Military Academy, founded in the early nineteenth century as the Mikhaylovskiy Artillery Academy. Tukhachevskiy undertook to convert the academy, which had a tradition of research, into the scientific-technological center that he had envisioned as chief of the army staff.[50] Stalin and Voroshilov ignored him, but others did not. Sergey Kirov, as party chief in Leningrad and next in rank to Stalin, took an active interest in military affairs. Two of Tukhachevskiy's early patrons, Valerian Kuibyshev and Grigoriy Ordzhonikidze, were in the Politburo and the Defense Council. In 1930, Kuibyshev became head of *Gosplan,* the economic planning agency, and Ordzhonikidze became Commissar for Heavy Industry.[51] Stalin could not yet disregard such men, who had staunchly supported him in his struggle for power. In June 1931, Tukhachevskiy returned to Moscow to direct the technological reconstruction as armaments chief and deputy people's commissar.

Concurrently with Tukhachevskiy's appointment, the Central Committee adopted a resolution on command in the army. It claimed that the "main immediate requirements for raising the army's combat capabilities" were the "decisive improvement of military-technological competence in the command staffs and their mastery of advanced combat techniques and the intricacies of contemporary battle."[52] The resolution assumed a consensus that did not exist. Groups within the army staff, the M.V. Frunze Military Academy (named for Frunze in the week he died), the branch inspectorates, and the higher commands followed Tukhachevskiy. Vladimir Triandafillov, who had served under Tukhachevskiy in the army staff, had completed an extensive study in 1929 entitled "Characteristics of Army Operations in Contemporary War." Drawing on German and French examples from World War I and a few from the Soviet-Polish War, he described a war in which army groups composed of shock armies, each with four or five infantry corps and strong

49 Ministerstva Oborony SSSR. Institut Voyennoy Istorii, *Istoriya vtoroy mirovoy voyny 1939–1945* (Moscow 1973–1979), Vol. 1, p. 258 (hereinafter cited as *IVMV*).
50 *SVE,* Vol. 2, p. 176; Koritskiy, *Tukhachevskiy,* p. 206.
51 *SVE,* Vol. 4, p. 513f, Vol. 6, p. 107f.
52 Savinkin, *Silakh,* pp. 262–65.

artillery, tank, and air elements, would oppose each other on broad, deeply echeloned fronts. Matériel and manpower, he concluded, would determine "all of tactics, operational art, and strategy."[53] Yet political orthodoxy dictated that all future wars would be class wars, and many in the party and the army as a whole were convinced that the Civil War had established a permanent model for class war. The Central Committee itself straddled the issue; it instructed the military not to overvalue traditional service arms while exercising caution in regard to bourgeois mechanization theories.[54]

Hitler's rise to power in January 1933, coupled with the Japanese takeover in Manchuria in 1931, substituted actual for hypothetical strategic problems. Germany became the main potential enemy, and Stalin eventually instructed foreign communist parties to form Popular Fronts with other antifascist parties. During 1933 he concluded neutrality and nonaggression treaties with other European states, accepted American recognition, and opened negotiations for treaties with France and Poland. The Seventeenth Party Congress in early 1934 sought to position the Soviet Union at the head of a world coalition against German fascism. Those who tried "to poke their pig noses into our Soviet garden," Stalin declared, would receive "a crushing repulse." The Soviet Union would pursue its "peace policy" resolutely and was prepared to conclude nonaggression treaties with all countries, including, he hinted, Germany.[55]

The Seventeenth Congress initiated a three-year period in which the Soviet Union attempted to make its military system compatible with those of prospective bourgeois allies. Tukhachevskiy addressed the Congress and received a candidate membership in the Central Committee, rare and signal honors for a military professional. In March 1934, the People's Commissariat for Military and Naval Affairs assumed the more up-to-date appellation of People's Commissariat of Defense. The *Revvoyensovet*, which smacked too much of revolution, expired in June 1934. A year later, the army staff became the general staff, and Voroshilov, Budennyy, Tukhachevskiy, Yegorov, and Blyukher acquired the rank of Marshals of the Soviet Union. Although Voroshilov's and Budennyy's qualifications were minimal, military professionalism appeared to have won significant recognition.

Tukhachevskiy told the Seventeenth Congress that "to deploy sufficiently gigantic technological resources to smash any country intruding on us," the industrial base required expansion and greater emphasis on armament production.[56] Tank production thereafter rose from 2,000 to 3,000 vehicles per year, aircraft from 2,000 to 4,000 planes, and artillery from 2,500 to 6,000 pieces. By late 1934, lines of permanent fortifications comparable to the

53 Zakharov, *Strategii,* pp. 291–345.
54 *SVE,* Vol. 1, pp. 262–64.
55 J. Stalin, *Report to the Seventeenth Congress of the CPSU(B) on the Work of the Central Committee* (Moscow, 1951), pp. 29–37.
56 Nikulin, *Tukhachevskiy,* p. 177.

Maginot Line were nearing completion on the western border and in the Far East.[57] After Germany reintroduced conscription in 1935, the Soviets began to phase out the militia system and increased the regular army to over 1.5 million men.[58]

Tukhachevskiy and Triandafillov (who died in 1931) had manifestly studied "The Attack in Positional Warfare" (the basic offensive doctrinal manual of the German army in 1918) and concluded that the deep operation represented the key to victory in contemporary warfare. Tukhachevskiy's objective in the years after 1931 was to adapt the *rassekayushchiy udar*, the cleaving blow that Red infantry and cavalry had sometimes employed in the Civil War, to conflicts involving mechanized forces and solid, deep defenses. He had means – tanks, aircraft, and even parachute troops – that no other army possessed in comparable numbers and variety. In 1932 he activated two mechanized corps, each with 500 tanks and over 200 other armored vehicles, and a year later, established a corps-type organization (enlarged in 1936 to an army) for the TB-3s and other bombers that were coming into service.[59] PU 36, the 1936 field service regulations issued early the next year, gave the Red Army a deep operations doctrine. It established surprise, close coordination of combined arms, and maneuver as first principles, and made the breaking of the enemy's defense throughout its entire depth the objective.[60]

Whatever the prospects for the future, the Tukhachevskiy era ended with deadly finality in spring 1937. His career collapsed swiftly with his dismissal as deputy defense commissar and reassignment to the command of the Volga Military District on 11 May. Then on 26 May came his expulsion from the army and arrest. On 11 June, Tukhachevskiy was executed along with Yakir, Uborevich, and five others. Over the next four years, at least 43,000 others, among them Yegorov and Blyukher, followed. Stalin applied his principle of stability of the rear within the armed forces according to criteria, if there were any, known only to himself. The senior ranks were the hardest hit, creating a stream of swift promotions to fill the vacancies – and not infrequently leading to even swifter exits. The only exemptions from the purge went to Stalin's own, the veterans of the First Cavalry Army. They rose to the top in numbers disproportionate to their professional qualifications.

STALIN'S SCHOOL

Germany and Italy formed the Rome-Berlin Axis in October 1936. A month later, Germany and Japan joined in the Anti-Comintern Pact. In April 1937, the Central Committee abolished the Council of Labor and Defense and

---

57 *IVMV*, Vol. 1, p. 262.
58 Zakharov, *50 let*, p. 198.
59 V.A. Anfilov, *Proval blitskrige* (Moscow, 1974), p. 117; Olaf Groehler, *Geschichte des Luftkriegs* (Berlin, 1980), p. 135.
60 See Narodnyy Komissariat Oborony, *Vremennyy polevoy ustav RKKA 1936* (Moscow, 1936), passim.

replaced it with a seven-member collegium, the Defense Committee Under the Council of People's Commissars. Vyacheslav Molotov, Chairman of the Council of People's Commissars and Stalin's dutiful servant, was the chairman and Voroshilov and Stalin were members. The identity of other members remains in question, most likely because the purges in the civilian sector made tenures short. Charged with "coordinating all measures pertaining to questions of defense relating to the intensifying military threats against the USSR," the Defense Committee was the highest government body exclusively concerned with military affairs, the primary conduit through which Stalin transmitted his orders.[61]

Stalin restored the commissar system throughout the armed forces in May 1937, and three-man military councils again came into existence in the field commands. Voroshilov chaired the Main Military Council, of which Stalin was a member. Mekhlis, Stalin's former secretary, was the chief army commissar, and Shchadenko, who had been a commissar in the First Cavalry Army, became the chief of the army's command personnel directorate in November 1937.[62]

The Main Military Council was Stalin's general headquarters. In his memoirs, Marshal Kirill Meretskov, who was its secretary in 1938, gave a guarded glimpse inside the council. It met, he says, two or three times a week, usually to hear the reports of military district commanders. Stalin attended frequently and often invited the members and military district commanders to continue discussions over dinner. He was more than just a member of the council, however. "Virtually every military or military-economic issue," Meretskov states, "was settled with the direct participation of the General Secretary of the CPSU." The council sent all of its recommendations to Stalin and received the results of his action through party and government channels in the form of directives.[63]

Democratic centralism had arrived at its ultimate stage: all authority in the state and the party emanated from a single source, the General Secretary of the Communist Party. He exercised, in its name, the Central Committee's responsibility for decision-making in military affairs and its control over domestic and foreign intelligence gathering. The NKVD, the People's Commissariat for Internal Affairs, like its predecessor the *Cheka,* protected the party against counterrevolutionary activities and enforced stability in the rear. The capitalist world, counterrevolutionary by definition, gave the NKVD a mandate in foreign intelligence as well, and Stalin directed its operations through a personal secret chancellery in the Central Committee

[61] SVE, Vol. 4, p. 266, Savinkin, *Silakh,* p. 268.
[62] SVE, Vol. 2, p. 566. Biographical information of the persons mentioned is found in SVE under their name entries.
[63] K.A. Meretskov, *Serving the People* (Moscow, 1971), p. 95.

secretariat, the Special Section. The General Staff's Intelligence Directorate, the RU (later GRU), was also tied to the Special Section.[64]

In the three and a half years from October 1936 to March 1940, the Soviet Union engaged in wars in Spain and Finland, responded to Japanese provocations on Manchuria's eastern border and in Outer Mongolia, and "reunited" Poland's eastern provinces with the Ukraine and Byelorussia. Those undertakings profoundly affected Soviet strategy-making after 1936.

The Spanish Civil War, which began in July 1936, was the first armed conflict since World War I to involve major military powers (Germany and Italy on the Nationalist side, the Soviet Union on the Republican). Military theorists and planners everywhere – but nowhere more intently than in the Soviet Union – looked to it for answers to the questions about contemporary war that had troubled them for almost two decades. It continued long enough to provide seemingly solid evidence.

In 1939, the General Staff Academy issued a volume of "operational-tactical conclusions" on the experience in Spain. The compiler, Brigadier General S. Lyubarskiy, followed mainstream thought and drew a single fundamental lesson: "History repeats itself." The war in Spain had "decisively demonstrated the growing strength of the defensive" and had become a war of position after an even shorter period of maneuver than was true in World War I. Neither side conducted deep operations except in a fragmentary way. While the quantities of tanks, aircraft, and artillery had remained limited, they were sufficient to demonstrate that "even if the forces have enormous strength and the most advanced technological means, operations will assume a prolonged character."[65] In practical terms, according to Lyubarskiy, history had again proved the value of the mass army in which infantry was the "decisive arm" and artillery the main support element. Fortifications had demonstrated "great importance" as well, but tanks had displayed strengths and weaknesses in about equal proportions.[66]

In the *Air Army*, Brigadier General A.N. Lapchinskiy, a professor of air tactics in the Frunze Academy, analyzed the bombers' performance. Lapchinskiy identified three primary types of missions: long-range (strategic), to destroy the enemy civilian population's morale; interdiction, directed against the enemy's bases and communications lines; and direct battlefield support. Spain, he concluded, had proved the last to be by far the most important. Only the destruction of the adversary's armed forces "secured victories." Bombing cities did not impair the "armed mass's will to fight" and

---

[64] See Niels Erik Rosenfeldt, *Knowledge and Power: The Role of Stalin's Secret Chancellery* (Copenhagen, 1978), passim.
[65] S. Lyubarskiy, *Nekotorye operativno-takticheskiye vyvody iz opita voyny v. Ispanii*, (Moscow, 1939), pp. 7, 16, 33, 37, 47, 62.
[66] Ibid., pp. 10, 12, 14, 15, 19, 24, 49, 53, 57f.

interdiction was worthwhile only if it did not detract from direct battlefield support.[67]

New field service regulations, PU 39, incorporated such analyses and elements of Frunze's class war doctrines. PU 39 designated the infantry as the chief arm and all others as subsidiary to it. Artillery possessed "the most powerful and farthest reaching fire of all the ground arms." The tank's "fundamental mission" was to support the infantry; in a mobile battle, tanks could "be utilized for deeper blows into the enemy's deployment." The air force's mission was "to assist the ground troops in battle and operations." Class-war doctrine, somewhat Stalinized, reappeared in such aphorisms as "The Red Army's greatest asset is the new man of the Stalinist epoch. He will have the decisive role in battle. If an enemy unleashes a war on us, the Workers' and Peasants' Red Army will be the most offensive-minded of all the attacking armies that ever existed."[68]

The purge kept the entire strategy-making apparatus in turmoil. Blyukher was executed in November 1938, Yegorov and Fedko in February 1939, and their positions on the Main Military Council went unfilled. Meretskov, who had served under Blyukher in 1935-36 but was associated with the First Cavalry Army, received command of the Leningrad Military District in 1939. Command of the Kiev Special Military District went to S.K. Timoshenko, who had commanded a division in the First Cavalry Army. "Volunteers" returning from Spain in some instances faced execution, but in others received spectacular advancement for reasons that remained opaque to all but Stalin.

At the Eighteenth Party Congress in March 1939, Stalin initiated another strategic turnabout. Alluding to the September 1938 Munich Agreement, he told the delegates that Britain, France, "and the United States" were "egging on the Germans to march east" but that the Soviet Union would frustrate their schemes by "strengthening business relations with all countries."[69] A month later, after Germany had occupied the remainder of Czechoslovakia and begun a violent propaganda campaign against Poland, the Soviet ambassador pointed out to the German Foreign Ministry that "ideological differences of opinion" had not interfered with Soviet-Italian relations and there was no reason why Soviet-German relations should be any different. Out of normal relations, he added, "better ones could grow."[70] German and Soviet representatives opened negotiations in June to "strengthen business relations." In Moscow on 23 August, nine days before Germany invaded Poland, the Soviet Union and Germany concluded a nonaggression pact that

---

[67] A.N. Lapchinskiy, *Vozdushnaya armiya* (Moscow, 1939), pp. 94, 144.
[68] Narodnyy Komissariat Oborony SSSR, *Polevoy ustav RKKA 1939* (Moscow, 1919), pp. 9, 11, 20-22, 24.
[69] J. Stalin, *Report to the Eighteenth Congress of the CPSU(B) on the Work of the Central Committee* (Moscow, 1951), pp. 22, 28.
[70] Karl Hoffkes, ed., *Deutsch-Sowjetische Geheimverbindungen* (Tübingen, 1988), p. 39.

took effect immediately and specified that each partner was to remain neutral if the other went to war with a third party or parties. Reverting to the strategy of buying off potential enemies to gain time, Stalin had given Germany relief from its greatest strategic problem, the two-front war.

Stalin paid an enormous price, but from the Soviet point of view time was a crucial strategic asset. Stalin paid even more for it under a September 1939 treaty of friendship with Germany in which the Soviet Union committed itself to supply grain, oil, and other essential materials to the Reich. Involvement in Spain had resulted in a profoundly alarming assessment: most of the arms in the Soviet inventory were or would soon be obsolete. An almost complete second technological reconstruction was in the offing. The Red air force needed high-performance aircraft of all types, and those demanded more sophisticated production techniques than Soviet industry possessed. Soviet tanks were too lightly armored and armed and of too many different types for effective battlefield maintenance. A military-industrial conference held in August 1939 settled on two new and advanced tanks, the medium T-34 and the heavy KV-1, but they required advanced production methods. The conclusions drawn from the experience in Spain about the importance of infantry and artillery established requirements for modernization and expanded production of everything from submachine guns to the heaviest artillery.[71] To all this, Stalin, apparently far overestimating his ability to buy time, added a naval building program that besides destroyers and submarines, included four battleships in the 60–70,000 ton range and a dozen heavy cruisers.[72]

In September 1939, on the Khalkin-Gol (Halha River) in Outer Mongolia, Major General Georgiy Zhukov concluded the second border conflict with the Japanese Kwantung Army. Zhukov, commanding 57,000 troops, encircled and crushed a roughly equal Japanese force in a 50-mile-wide, 10-mile-deep stretch of disputed territory between the Khalkin-Gol and the Mongolian settlement Nomanhan.[73] Although Lake Khasan and the Khalkin-Gol were the first large Red Army engagements against foreign troops since 1920, they did not influence Soviet strategic thinking nearly as much as did the Spanish Civil War, probably because experience against the underequipped Japanese appeared to count for little. Nevertheless, later expe-

---

[71] Groehler, *Luftkriegs*, pp. 298–300; Tyushkevich, *Armed Forces*, pp. 225–31; N.N. Voronov, *Na sluzhbe voyennoy* (Moscow, 1963), p. 114; Lototskiy, *Armiya*, p. 144f.

[72] N.G. Kuznetsov, *Nakanune* (Moscow, 1969), p. 227; Donald W. Mitchell, *A History of Russian and Soviet Sea Power* (New York, 1974), p. 366; Jürg Meister, *Soviet Warships of the Second World War* (New York, 1977), pp. 20f, 22, 39–43, 59–65, 184–208.

[73] On Lake Khasan, see *IVMV*, Vol. 2, pp. 211–13; and Alvin D. Coox, *The Anatomy of a Small War* (Westport, CT, 1977). The current official Soviet estimate on Japanese troops in the Khalkin-Gol battle is 75,000 (*IVMV*, Vol. 2, p. 216; *SVE*, Vol. 8, p. 253). An earlier Soviet account (M.V. Novikov, *Pobeda na Khalkin-gola* (Moscow, 1971), p. 67) gives the Japanese strength as 55,000, which is somewhat lower than a Japanese figure, 58,925, given in Alvin D. Coox, *Nomanhan* (Stanford, 1985), Vol. 2, p. 916.

rience showed that the Soviets had made an impression on the Kwantung Army.

Two days after the battle on the Khalkin-Gol, the Soviet Union began an eight-day "march of liberation" to occupy eastern Poland, which the nonaggression pact placed in the Soviet sphere of interest. That act of unprovoked aggression had a notable strategic impact. It created a German-Soviet boundary, shifted the Soviet frontier 150 to 200 miles west (necessitating another round of frontier fortification), and led to a major change in the projected role of armor. In a commission on armor organization, Kulik and Pavlov had argued against tank corps, of which there were then four with 560 tanks apiece, because such large aggregations of armor had not occurred in Spain. Two of the corps committed in the "march of liberation" gave shockingly poor performances, and on 21 November, the Main Military Council abolished all the tank corps.[74]

A cross between another "march of liberation" and a Blitzkrieg began against Finland on 30 November 1939. This strike became an embarrassing four-month war in which the outnumbered and lightly armed Finns outperformed four (later six) Soviet armies. The secret protocol to the nonaggression pact had placed Finland in the Soviet sphere of influence, and the general staff, expecting Finnish resistance, had worked up a comprehensive operations plan. Stalin shelved it and instead ordered the commander of the Leningrad Military District to mount a "short and swift" drive on short notice, keeping in mind "the full strength of the USSR."[75] The Finns were well aware of Soviet strength, but their skill, and persistent Soviet command and supply problems, prevented a triumphal march on Helsinki. On 12 March, having advanced sufficiently to impose severe terms and fearful of Franco-British intervention, Stalin accepted an armistice.

To commemorate the "victory" Stalin appointed Timoshenko, who had assumed command in Finland in January, as People's Commissar of Defense; gave him, Kulik, and Shaposhnikov marshal's stars; and "advanced" Voroshilov to the deputy chairmanship of the Council of People's Commissars. The Central Committee held a special plenary session in late March "to discuss the results and lessons of the armed conflict in Finland thoroughly." The Main Military Council did the same in April in a four-day conference.[76]

The lessons were obvious. Commands at all levels had lacked responsibility, initiative, flexibility, and a capacity for independent decision-making, qualities fundamentally incompatible with the Soviet system. Consequently, the changes in thought and behavior patterns required were monumentally

---

[74]	Anfilov, *Proval*, p. 117f.
[75]	A. Vasilevskiy, *Delo vsey zhizni* (Moscow, 1976), pp. 95–97; Meretskov, *Serving*, pp. 102–17.
[76]	*IVMV*, Vol. 3, p. 409.

difficult to promote, especially under Stalin's aegis. As a sign of intent, the Supreme Soviet decreed the abolition of the commissar system in August 1940 and proclaimed that "full unity of command" would prevail throughout the Red Army and Navy.[77] PU 40, published later in the year, significantly altered the class war tone that had characterized PU 39. The former political commissars' functions fell under the rubric, "Sections for Political Propaganda."[78]

THE RACE AGAINST TIME

The German Blitzkrieg in Poland surprised Soviet strategic analysts, but appeared to be explicable as a hopeless mismatch in which a vast superiority in matériel and manpower produced an inevitable result. The Soviets expected the fighting in Western Europe to be more telling. In June 1940, at the time of Dunkirk, the Defense Commissariat submitted an assessment to Stalin that again attributed German success to superior mass, but this time specifically in terms of armor. On 9 June, Timoshenko approved a plan to organize nine mechanized corps, each with 36,000 troops and 1,031 tanks.[79]

The fall of France was an unmitigated strategic calamity for the Soviet Union. Nikita Khrushchev commented later that when word of the French request for an armistice came over the radio, Stalin and the others present realized instantly that "the most pressing and deadly threat in all history faced the Soviet Union."[80] Stalin was already hastening to bring the Baltic states and Bessarabia into his hands, but their possession would do little to improve his position. Hitler controlled Europe from the North Cape to the Mediterranean and from the Vistula to the Bay of Biscay. The market value of Soviet neutrality had taken a sharp plunge, and the two-front war was now, if anything, more Stalin's problem than Hitler's.

Nevertheless, Churchill's refusal to come to terms with Hitler and the continuation of the "imperialist" war gave Stalin some comfort. In September, he told the British Ambassador, Sir Stafford Cripps, that even though a German victory over Britain would put the Soviet Union in a difficult and dangerous position, "it was impossible at the present time to invite the certainty of a German invasion of the Soviet Union by any alteration of Soviet policy." He added that he preferred to risk fighting Germany alone because he believed a victory over Britain would "appreciably weaken"

[77] Savinkin, *Silakh*, p. 289.
[78] Narodnyy Komissariat Oborony SSSR, *Polevoy ustav Krasnoy Armii 1940 g.* (Moscow, 1940), pp. 10, 15–22, 25, 26.
[79] Anfilov, *Proval*, p. 118; I.E. Krupchenko, et al., *Sovetskiye Tankovye voyska* (Moscow, 1973), p. 13.
[80] N.S. Khrushchev, *Khrushchev Remembers* (Boston, 1970), p. 134.

German military power and possibly prevent Hitler from launching another major campaign.[81]

Stalin remembered that the Finns had cultivated a close relationship with Germany during World War I, and would not tolerate their doing so again, but his position was delicate. He could keep the Finns aware of Soviet power, which he did by making Meretskov chief of the general staff and giving M.P. Kirponos command of the Leningrad Military District. Both had contributed decisively to breaking the Finnish Mannerheim Line, and both held the highest decoration, Hero of the Soviet Union.

However, the Finns were not ready to submit to the Soviet pressure, and pursued closer ties to Germany. In July, the I.G. Farben concern contracted for 60 percent of Finland's vital nickel output. In August, Germany began shipping arms to Finland, and Finland granted the Wehrmacht transit rights across its territory from the Gulf of Bothnia to northern Norway.[82] Vyacheslav Molotov, since 1939 the Soviet Foreign Minister as well as chairman of the Council of People's Commissars, went to Berlin in November to find out whether Germany proposed to abide by the 1939 agreement regarding Finland. He received a mishmash of vague reassurances, promises, and denials – except on one point. Hitler told him he did not want another armed conflict in the Baltic Sea area, and if one were to occur, it would severely strain German-Soviet relations.[83]

The general staff had been working since early summer on the assumption that war with Germany was inevitable, and Meretskov presented its strategic estimate to Stalin in September. The estimate embodied conclusions on three basic concerns: the two-front war, the probable location of the enemy's main effort, and the location of the Soviet main effort. The problem of such a war had changed in two respects: after the Lake Khasan and Khalkin-Gol incidents, Japan was likely to behave more circumspectly, but Germany had become a more dangerous enemy. Consequently, the issue would be decided in Europe. There, powerful though it was, Germany could not stage equally strong attacks north and south of the Pripyat Marshes, and the lure of land and mineral resources in the Ukraine and oil in the Caucasus would draw its main effort to the south. However, because Soviet doctrine required the carrying of the war to the enemy's territory, the Red Army main effort would have to be on the most direct line to Germany, which was north of the Pripyat Marshes.[84] The general staff's conception – to tie down the enemy main

---

81   U.S. Department of State, *Foreign Relations of the United States 1940*, Vol. 1 (Washington, 1959), p. 611 (hereinafter cited as *FRUS*).

82   See Earl F. Ziemke, *The German Northern Theater of Operations 1940–1945* (Washington, 1959), pp. 114–16.

83   See U.S. Department of State, *Nazi-Soviet Relations 1939–1941* (Washington, 1948), pp. 217–47.

84   S.P. Ivanov, *The Initial Period of War* (Washington, 1986), pp. 174, 175. The strategic estimate has surfaced only in the form of scattered allusions; see Earl F. Ziemke and Magna E. Bauer, *Moscow to Stalingrad: Decision in the East* (New York, 1989), pp. 16, 17.

force and strike in its rear – was sophisticated, but Stalin rejected it and required that the Soviet main force stand in the south.[85] The general staff complied, and thereafter considered the main efforts, German or Soviet, closed subjects.

Another issue was closed from the outset: the possibility of exploiting the vast Russian space. The German general staff regarded the immensity of the Soviet land mass as its most difficult strategic problem. Unfortunately, "as a practical matter the military leadership left a strategic defense out of consideration and assumed that all future Red army operations would be almost exclusively offensive."[86] No doubt the military leadership knew what Stalin would not tolerate.

The People's Commissariat of Defense sponsored a weeklong conference in Moscow from 23 to 29 December, in which military district commanders, chiefs of staff, branch chiefs and inspectors, army commanders, and some corps and division commanders participated. Central Committee and Politburo members were present, but Stalin did not attend. In what could be termed the keynote speech, Zhukov analyzed modern offensive operations. He attributed German victories in Poland and France primarily to surprise and the shock of powerful blows against weak and irresolute opponents. Since the same collapse was unlikely in the Soviet Union, the problem, as he saw it, was not a whole new style of warfare; instead, it was how the Soviet Union could bring matériel and manpower to bear most effectively in a prolonged war of attrition.[87] Timoshenko's summation confirmed that Zhukov had spoken for the Defense Commissariat. German victories in Poland and Western Europe, he said, had "in no way been surprising in strategic respects." Soviet military leaders and theoreticians, he added, "in contrast to the Hitlerite leadership, do not rely on lightning war." They believed, instead, that a major war "in the present epoch" would be "intense and protracted" and that individual operations would achieve "finite aims," resulting in the securing of strategic goals only in the long-term.[88]

The actual main theme of the conference, and Stalin's paramount strategic concern, was war readiness. Meretskov provoked a long, sometimes acrimonious discussion when he asserted that training was still not close enough to the actual requirements of battle and that "shortcomings in operational and general military proficiency exist in the upper command structure, the troop commands, army and *front* staffs, and especially in aviation."[89] Debates also arose over whether or not the Red Army needed to activate heavily armed and armored shock armies and whether the air force ought to acquire a

85 Vasilevskiy, *Delo,* p. 106.
86 *IVMV,* Vol. 3, p. 415.
87 Anfilov, *Proval,* p. 136.
88 Korotkov, *Voyennoy mysli,* p. 137; Anfilov, *Proval,* p. 167.
89 Meretskov, *Serving,* p. 124f; M.I. Kazakov, *Nad kartoy bylykh srazhenniy* (Moscow, 1971), p. 52.

capacity to execute the kind of bombing offensive Germany was then conducting against England.[90]

After the conference ended, the military district commanders and their
chiefs of staff stayed in Moscow to observe war games on 11 and 12 January.
The games, one north and one south of the Pripyat Marshes, dealt only with
single operations in conformity with the thinking Timoshenko had expressed
at the conference.[91] Zhukov and Pavlov were the chief players, and each
took the "red" (Soviet) side in his own district. Although participants and
observers have written a good deal about the games, who won or lost remains uncertain; however, Zhukov appears to have displayed the greater
offensive-mindedness in both.[92]

Stalin summoned the participants of the war games to a meeting in the
Kremlin with the Main Military Council and the Politburo on 13 January. He
appears to have gone into the meeting having already decided that the army
was not ready. First, he took Meretskov sharply to task over the weaknesses
in the "red" performances in the war games, which were in accordance with
general staff calculations. Later, he turned on Kulik, whose single-minded
drive to expand the artillery he had encouraged for the past two years. When
a question arose about reducing the artillery's budget share to provide for
more tanks, Kulik insisted tanks were a "sheer waste" because artillery
would "make scrap" of them. In response, Stalin asked the military district
commanders how many more mechanized corps each believed he needed.
The total came to between fourteen and twenty, and Stalin thereupon
declared Kulik "wrong" and added, "contemporary war will be a war of
motors, on land, in the air, on water and underwater."[93]

In his final remarks, Stalin reproached the general staff for not having
given "the military districts problems they will have to solve in actual war,"
and laid down specific requirements: to prepare for a two-front war, to learn
how to conduct "a war of fast movement and maneuver," and to "work out
the organizational questions" devolving from the other requirements.
"War," he added, "is approaching fast and now is not distant. . . . We must
gain a year-and-a-half to two-years' time to complete the armament plan."[94]
Meretskov said Stalin told him on 18 January that "of course we would not
be able to keep out of war until 1943 . . . but it was conceivable that we

---

90 Ibid., p. 53f; Korotkov, *Voyennoy mysli*, p. 172f; Anfilov, *Proval*, p. 121; A. Eremenko,
    The Arduous Beginning (Moscow, 1966), p. 31f.
91 Although Soviet literature describes the war games as strategic, they were merely elements
    of a strategic plan. Strategic war gaming was apparently not a Soviet practice at that time.
92 Anfilov, *Proval*, p. 170; Kazakov, *Nad kartoy*, p. 56f; Meretskov, *Serving*, p. 126; G.K.
    Zhukov, *The Memoirs of Marshal Zhukov* (New York, 1971), p. 184f.
93 Eremenko, *Beginning*, p. 34; Kazakov, *Nad kartoy*, p. 59.
94 A.I. Eremenko, *Pomny voyny* (Donetski, 1971), p. 129f. The last of Eremenko's three
    memoirs, *Pomny voyny* (War Recollections), in some respects contradicts the account of
    the Kremlin meeting he gives in *The Arduous Beginning*. On the differences, see Earl F.
    Ziemke, "Stalin as a Strategist," *Military Affairs* (Dec. 1983), p. 176.

would not be involved until 1942."[95] Stalin gave Zhukov, whom he had appointed to succeed Meretskov in the general staff, an order to activate twenty additional mechanized corps.[96]

By early 1941 Stalin was the odd man out. Britain had nothing to offer except an invitation to make the Soviet Union an alternative German target, and diplomatic sallies designed to clarify the state of relations with Germany confirmed the impressions Molotov had brought from Berlin. In negotiations begun in January on a Soviet demand for a partnership in the Finnish nickel mines, the Finns obviously counted Germany as a third party in the bargaining.[97] Also in January, a Soviet warning that the Soviet Union would regard a German troop presence in Bulgaria as a violation of its security interests brought a German reply that if it needed to, the Reich would send troops into Bulgaria.[98] On 1 March, Bulgaria joined the Axis, and a day later, German troops entered the country on their way south to Greece.

During the winter and spring, the general staff refined and implemented two strategic plans: MP-41, a mobilization plan, and Plan 9, which is described as "a covering plan for the state frontier."[99] MP-41 was the latest in a series of annual plans based on an assumption, accepted since 1934, that in future wars, mobilization would occur before, not after a declaration of war. Mobilization, consequently, had already been going on for some years, and the Red Army's active-duty strength had more than doubled in 1939–40. MP-41 added 800,000 troops in the first five months of 1941, which brought the total strength to 5 million by 1 June.[100]

Plan 9, the covering plan, embodied conceptions developed over the past ten years about the start and initial conduct of contemporary wars. The general staff believed war between countries as large and powerful as Germany and the Soviet Union would necessitate that both sides conduct operations in essentially the same way. The initial objective was to carry the war to the enemy's territory. Forces would deploy covertly before the declaration of war. Surprise would be impossible. And after the declaration of war, a two-to-three-week period of "creeping war" would ensue during which the parties would test each other and make adjustments before delivering their main blows.[101] When fighting began in earnest, "the war would inevitably become long and intense, and the achievement of victory would depend to a decisive degree on the ability of the rear to supply the front with human and material resources longer than the enemy could."[102] Plan 9 called for 170 divisions

[95] Meretskov, *Serving*, p. 125.
[96] Zhukov, *Memoirs*, p. 198.
[97] See Ziemke, *Northern Theater*, p. 118.
[98] Gerhard L. Weinberg, *Germany and the Soviet Union 1919–1941* (Leiden, 1954), p. 152f.
[99] *IVMV*, Vol. 3, pp. 438, 439.
[100] Ivanov, *Initial Period*, p. 177f.
[101] Zhukov, *Memoirs*, p. 215; Vasilevskiy, *Delo*, p. 101; Ivanov, *Initial Period*, p. 106; Sokolovskiy, *Strategy*, p. 134.
[102] Ivanov, *Initial Period*, p. 174.

and two brigades in two strategic echelons: the first, on and near the border, to stop the enemy, deal "answering blows," and possibly begin carrying the war to the enemy's territory; the second, on the line of the Dnepr and Western Dvina rivers, to complete the job of carrying the war to the other side's territory.[103]

While the general staff followed its schedule for implementing Plan 9, Stalin worked even more intensively than he had in 1939 to buy time. The German Foreign Ministry observed that Soviet deliveries under the trade agreements, which were slow in January and February, grew "by leaps and bounds" in March.[104] The Soviet tone toward Finland became progressively milder until, by early May, the Finnish Foreign Minister was finding he could chide the Soviet ambassador for the "psychologically unfavorable effect" his government's past behavior had on Finnish public opinion.[105] In April, Stalin negotiated a neutrality treaty with Japan. This treaty secured an uncertain degree of relief from the two-front war threat but gave Japan freedom to exploit the political vacuum in Southeast Asia. On the day the treaty was signed, Stalin made public his willingness to accommodate the Axis powers by seeing the Japanese Foreign Minister off at the railroad station and there singled out the German ambassador from the other dignitaries and told him, "We must remain friends, and you must now do everything to that end."[106]

To send an unmistakable signal that he was prepared to deal in person, Stalin, who had not held any post in the government since 1922, became Chairman of the Council of People's Commissars (prime minister) on 6 May. The signal was obviously not meant for the Western Powers. Acting United States Secretary of State Sumner Welles sent warnings of an impending German attack to Moscow on 1 and 4 March and through the Soviet Ambassador in Washington on 20 March. The U.S. Ambassador reported that such messages were only arousing Soviet suspicions.[107] Churchill sent a personal letter to Stalin, on 22 April, and on 11 May, British Foreign Secretary Anthony Eden instructed Cripps to emphasize the "many signs" of a German attack in talking to the Russians.[108] Cripps later commented that for several months before the Soviet-German war started, "not only Stalin, but even Molotov avoided me like grim death" and "did not want to have anything to do with Churchill.[109]

Churchill attributed Stalin's apparent refusal to take up the warnings to "the purblind prejudice and fixed ideas which Stalin raised between himself

103 Ibid., pp. 187–91; Vasilevskiy, *Delo,* pp. 107–14.
104 *Nazi-Soviet Relations,* p. 318; Weinberg, *Germany,* p. 161.
105 H. Peter Krosby, *Finland, Germany, and the Soviet Union 1940–1941* (Madison, 1968), pp. 161–63.
106 *Nazi-Soviet Relations,* p. 324.
107 *FRUS 1941,* Vol. 1, pp. 702, 712–15, 723.
108 Winston S. Churchill, *The Grand Alliance* (Boston, 1950), p. 316; F.H. Hinsley, et al., *British Intelligence in the Second World War,* Vol. 1 (New York, 1979), p. 455.
109 Alexander Werth, *Russia at War 1941–1945* (New York, 1964), p. 276f.

and the terrible truth."[110] In fact, however, Churchill and Stalin were likely receiving the same intelligence, interpreting it the same way, and only attempting to exploit it differently. From northern Norway to the Pyrenees, the Germans in spring 1941 conducted Operation HARPOON, an elaborate deception designed to divert attention, Stalin's particularly, from the deployment against the Soviet Union by simulating one against England.[111] As far as British Military Intelligence (MI) could discern, ULTRA (decrypts of German intelligence) intercepts not withstanding, invasion of England was about as likely as an attack on the Soviet Union, and MI regarded another Soviet-German compact similar to that of August 1939 or a Soviet capitulation to a German ultimatum just as likely.[112] Stalin apparently thought so too, and on 14 June, signified his willingness to open a dialogue with Berlin by having TASS, the Soviet news agency, issue a communique stating that "Germany is unswervingly observing the provisions of the Soviet-German nonaggression treaty as is the Soviet Union."[113] Churchill and a number of others have cited the TASS communique as conclusive evidence of Stalin's purblindness. But as late as 22 June, the day the German invasion began, the British Foreign Office had "no conclusive evidence that Germany intended to attack Russia and not merely to use diplomatic and military threats to intimidate her."[114]

The 170 divisions and two brigades of Plan 9 were in place in the western military districts by early June. The first strategic echelon formed into two subechelons: one, fifty-six divisions and two brigades, sat within thirty miles of the border and the other, fifty-two divisions, was thirty to sixty miles farther back. The second strategic echelon, sixty-two divisions, remained in reserve at distances up to 180 miles behind the border. Additionally, the defense commissariat retained four armies under its control just east of the Dnepr River.[115] Sometime between 14 and 19 June, Stalin permitted Timoshenko to order the western military districts to set up command posts from which they could exercise their appointed wartime functions as *front* commands and to camouflage air fields, military units, and "important military objectives."[116] But he continued efforts in Berlin and Moscow to start talks, and did not allow a war alert order until the night of 21 June.[117]

[110] Winston S. Churchill, *The Gathering Storm* (Boston, 1949), p. 367.
[111] See Ziemke, *Northern Theater*, p. 138; Ivanov, *Initial Period*, p. 165f.
[112] Hinsley, *Intelligence*, pp. 463–81.
[113] *FRUS 1941*, Vol. 1, p. 149.
[114] Llewellyn Woodward, *British Foreign Policy in the Second World War*, Vol. 1 (London, 1970), p. 623.
[115] Zakharov, *50 let*, p. 252; *IVMV*, Vol. 3, p. 440, 441; B.S. Tel'pulhovskiy, *Velikaya otechestvennaya voyna sovetskogo soyuza* (Moscow, 1984), p. 50; Ivanov, *Initial Period*, p. 181, 184.
[116] Institut Marksizma-Leninizma, *Istoriya velikoy otechestvennoy voyny sovetskogo soyuza* (Moscow, 1960–1965), Vol. 2, p. 10.
[117] Weinberg, *Germany*, p. 167; *IVMV*, Vol. 4, p. 28.

At 0400 on 22 June Zhukov reported that the German attack had begun, and Stalin summoned him and Timoshenko to the Kremlin. After a three-hour discussion during which the German declaration of war arrived, Stalin allowed Timoshenko to issue a directive ordering the field commands to engage enemy forces that had violated the frontier. At a second lengthy session later in the morning, Timoshenko and Zhukov urged Stalin to name himself supreme commander in chief, since the de facto authority was his anyway and neither of them could make decisions without consulting him. Stalin said he would have to consider the matter further. At the end of the day he authorized a third and completely unrealistic directive ordering the frontier forces to mount "offensives in the main directions for the purposes of destroying the enemy's assault groupings and carrying the war to his territory."[118] According to Zhukov, Stalin, under the shock of the first day, could not get a grip on himself; his voice faded, he could not deal coherently with events, and "his orders regarding organization of the armed struggle did not always conform to the situation."[119]

THE FRAMEWORK OF STRATEGY

The Soviet approach to the conduct of war stemmed from two bases – one theoretical, the other pragmatic. Lenin's conversion of war from an act of state policy into a manifestation of class interests supplied the first. Lenin, writing in 1915 when war was not yet a real concern of his, dismissed Clausewitz's reference to "other means" with the parenthetical remark, "namely, violence."[120] Trotskiy, the pragmatist, maintained that the "other means" imposed an array of practical requirements not subject to Marxist analysis. Acting on that basis – at the cost of his standing in the party – Trotskiy won the Civil War.

But the military communists and those who, like Stalin, saw Trotskiy as a threat to themselves, preferred to judge the result in ideological terms. A corollary to Lenin's thesis on war formed the basis of this judgment. Lenin had asserted that henceforth war would inevitably generate class conflict. Although he was mistaken with regard to both World War I and the Polish War, the victory in the Civil War seemed to provide more than sufficient proof that future wars, no matter how they originated, would become class wars. From there it was a short step to the assumption that the Red Army's political orientation had guaranteed victory in the Civil War, and properly developed, would do so again in any future wars.

Frunze tried to eliminate the dichotomy altogether by subordinating the practical aspect of war to the ideological and by attributing special characteristics, such as aggressiveness, mobility, and decisiveness to the ideological

[118]   Ivanov, *Initial Period*, p. 224.
[119]   G.K. Zhukov, *Vospominaniya i razmyshleniya* (Moscow, 1990), Vol. 2, p. 106.
[120]   Lenin, *Sochineniy*, Vol. 26, p. 224.

component in the Civil War. However, the introduction of unity of command and the conception of the Red Army staff as the military brain of a state that was, after all, supposed to have a single brain, skirted the edge of renewed separation. The military's position in the state, moreover, underwent a substantial permanent downgrading during Frunze's incumbency. Trotskiy had been Lenin's partner, the head of a *Revvoyensovet* that had a definite strategy-making function, and people's commissar. The military did not again stand that high in the power structure.

Frunze, no doubt, believed he was building an ideologically and professionally correct military system on a solid Marxist-Leninist foundation. Like most in the party and the military, he was not aware that ideological orthodoxy was becoming insufficient. Stalin would not tolerate even semi-autonomy in the military sphere, much less a potential Trotskiy. Frunze's sudden death – under circumstances sufficiently unusual to cast suspicion on Stalin – enabled the general secretary to let Frunze's reforms stand for the time being. Through Voroshilov he could prevent them from advancing in unwanted directions.

Stalin's military policy after 1925 maintained two fixed goals: sufficient power to decide the issue in European and world terms *after* the bourgeois states had exhausted themselves in imperialist wars, and his absolute control of that power. The first required force modernization commensurate to the world standard and technologically competent management. The second, which stood first on Stalin's agenda, necessitated his preventing the technological influx from spawning a military technocracy.

Voroshilov provided exactly the type of leadership that Stalin needed in the military and naval affairs commissariat. Insulated by ignorance and indifference and owing his position entirely to Stalin, he applied his considerable skill at bureaucratic infighting to keep would-be technocrats in their proper places. In 1930, however, the industrialization program injected a complication: the armed forces had to be prepared to absorb advanced weapons and equipment that their current mixed structure of primarily regular cavalry and territorial militia infantry could not deploy effectively. Voroshilov was obviously unsuited for this assignment. Kirov, Kuibyshev, and Ordzhonikidze, who were the Politburo members most concerned, had each developed confidence in Tukhachevskiy through contacts dating back to the Civil War. Their support brought him to the fore in the technological reconstruction.

As organizers of the tightest knit military-industrial complex ever conceived, Tukhachevskiy and his sponsors drew national and international attention. The professional-minded in the military gravitated toward Tukhachevskiy, while Kirov and Kuibyshev, although professed Stalinists, acquired strong personal followings in the party. They did not comprehend Stalin's priorities. Kirov's assassination in December 1934 and Kuibyshev's death three months later, whether coincidence or design, gave an indication of those priorities.

Tukhachevskiy's career peaked in 1935–36, ironically, because Stalin, for once, needed him. The technological reconstruction was in full swing. More importantly, Stalin was angling for bourgeois allies, and to that end the Red Army had to display at least a patina of conventional military respectability. The broader mandate that Tukhachevskiy assumed certainly did not come from Stalin or Voroshilov. In the post-Stalin era, Tukhachevskiy has received praise as an innovator and original thinker who would have revolutionized the art of war had he lived. His actual achievement was to promote conformity with foreign military thinking and to emphasize beating potential enemies at their own game.

With the creation of the Defense Committee in April, the reinstatement of the commissar system, and Tukhachevskiy's arrest in May 1937, Stalin initiated the most ruthless, thoroughgoing and – by his terms of reference at least – effective military reform since Peter the Great. Thereafter, military professionals literally existed by his grace alone and were judged according to his subjective standards. Hardly any whose reputations originated outside of association with him survived the test during the next two years, and subsequently survival remained a revocable dispensation for all. The Defense Committee and the Main Military Council provided the mechanism for enforcing similarly subjective standards across the whole range of military affairs.

Concurrent developments on the world scene appeared to confirm that the reform was on the right track. The Spanish Civil War persuaded nearly all observers that advancing technology would enhance the defensive and prolong war; numbers, not art, would prevail. Those circumstances potentially conferred an advantage in endurance directly proportional to the firmness with which a nation held its military instrument. They also decidedly favored the last entrant in a conflict, which Stalin had always meant to be, and for which he positioned himself in August 1939. The first year of war in Europe, however, upset his calculations. The Winter War with Finland exposed deep-seated military weaknesses at all levels, while the German victory in France almost simultaneously demolished his strategic policy.

The German invasion proved his reform a phenomenal success in one respect: the Soviet forces could not function without him. That was a negligible consolation in the midst of an onrushing disaster that was likely to become total with or without him. According to Zhukov, Stalin's depression passed in a day. The progression of Stalin's responses to the crisis indicates that the recovery took longer. On 23 June, the Main Military Council became the Stavka (general headquarters) of the High Command but with Stalin still only a member. A week later, possibly seeking to distance himself somewhat from the direct military command, Stalin converted the Defense Committee into the State Defense Committee, a war cabinet of which he took the chairmanship. In late July, after restoring the commissar system in full force and initiating a minipurge that eliminated the entire top air force command, he assumed the chairmanship of the defense commissariat and the Stavka. Having finally ventured that far, on 8 August he named himself Supreme High Commander of the armed forces, converted the Stavka into his general headquarters, and thereby unified the political and practical-military aspects in his own person. He had created the command structure that won the war – at horrendous cost.

17

The evolution of Israeli strategy: The psychology of insecurity and the quest for absolute security[1]

MICHAEL I. HANDEL

Since its war of independence in 1948, Israel has repeatedly defied the odds to achieve remarkable operational and tactical successes against its Arab neighbors. But this impressive record has also served to conceal Israel's fundamental strategic inadequacies – serious flaws borne of an unremitting sense of vulnerability and the constant threat and occurrence of war. Even without the Jewish people's history of diaspora, persecution, and annihilation, Israelis have had little reason to feel secure in their territorially-shallow nation surrounded by enemies with far greater populations, financial resources, military forces, and access to military technology. Israel has known no formal peace except for the 1979 peace treaty with Egypt. With short-range survival as the watchword, undue reliance on military solutions was inevitable, as was the concomitant neglect of longer-range planning and diplomatic options. Ironically, then, the development of strategy and policy for one of the foremost military performers of the twentieth century has often been marked by confusion, indecision, and a lack of vision (Table 17.1).

GEOGRAPHICAL FACTORS: THE TERRITORIAL IMPERATIVE

In strategy, as in real estate, three critical considerations to keep in mind are location, location, and location. Nations must adapt to their environments by devising strategies calculated to capitalize on geographic assets and compensate for vulnerabilities. Nevertheless, modern technology has made strategy less dependent on geographical conditions by "shrinking space," "accelerating time," and increasing firepower beyond the previous limits of the

---

[1] I would like to thank Major-General (Ret.) Shlomo Gazit for his comments and suggestions, and my wife, Jill Handel, for her tough questions and for editing this essay.

Table 17.1. *Four possible combinations of offensive or defensive strategic and operational doctrines*

		Strategic doctrines (or policies)	
		Offense	Defense
Operational doctrines	Offense	1. Offensive Offensive	2. Defensive Offensive
	Defense	3. Offensive Defensive	4. Defensive Defensive

imagination. Therefore, much depends on the capacity of a nation to dictate the type of war (whether guerrilla or conventional) most suited to its technological level of development and situation as a whole.

Even though geographical factors are no longer as important as in the past, national strategies are still mainly the product of a long evolutionary process shaped by generations of strategic thinkers and perpetuated through national political traditions. Yet national fears and centuries of conditioning are clashing more and more frequently with the revolutionary developments in modern technology.

Israel is a classic case of a nation whose strategy has been dominated by geographic considerations. The territory between the Jordan River and the Mediterranean Sea has always been extremely vulnerable, for its location at the crossroads of major routes between Africa and Asia long made it the natural strategic objective of major powers to the north, east, and southwest.[2] Israel's location in the midst of the Arab world creates a buffer zone between Egypt on the one hand and Syria, Jordan, and Iraq on the other. Israel has also supported the autonomy of Jordan and, in the past, that of Lebanon. As the geographical vortex of the region, Israel was instrumental in protecting Jordan from a Syrian invasion in 1970,[3] and could have interfered with much of the support sent to Iraq by way of Aqaba during the Iran-Iraq war. During the last forty years, Israel reached the Suez Canal twice (in 1956 and 1967) and through its presence there from 1967 to 1976 caused the Egyptians to block the Canal for ten years.

But to the Israelis, who face intense "border pressure" – to use a time-honored concept from geopolitics[4] – their nation's location is hardly an asset. In addition to considering the nations directly on Israel's frontier, the Israeli

[2] George Adam Smith, *The Historical Geography of the Holy Land* (London, 1897).
[3] See Henry Kissinger, *White House Years* (Boston, 1979), pp. 594–631.
[4] Michael I. Handel, *Israel's Political-Military Doctrine* (Cambridge, MA, 1973), pp. 1–6; idem, *Weak States in the International System* (London, 1981), pp. 70–6.

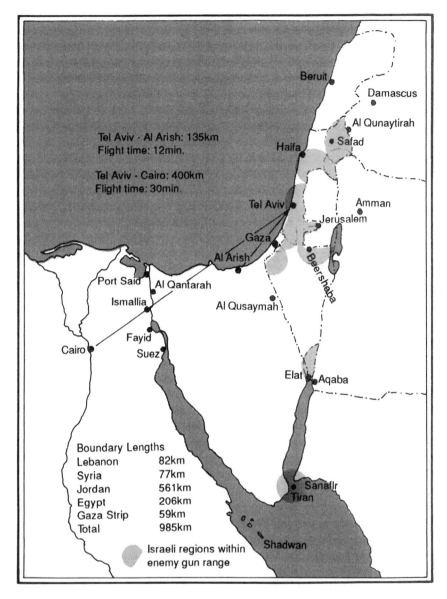

Map 17.1. Israel's vulnerability.

military has always had to regard a number of other Arab states as hostile: Saudi Arabia, Iran, and Iraq to the east; and Libya, Tunisia, Algeria, Morocco, and Sudan to the west. Although not bordering on Israel, Iraq has participated directly in all major Arab-Israeli wars and fired over 40 SCUD missiles at Israel during the 1991 Gulf War. In the Yom Kippur War (1973), Moroccan soldiers fought on the Golan Heights, while Libyan forces were stationed along the Egyptian front in the Sinai. Most recently, Israeli strategists have become concerned about Iranian intervention in support of radical Islamic groups in southern Lebanon, as well as about the Iranian acquisition, in North Korea and China, of missiles capable of reaching Israel. Iranian plans to acquire nuclear weapons and long-range delivery systems have also added to Israel's worries about Iranian participation in a future Arab-Israeli war. As a unifying force in the Arab world, a war against Israel will attract more Arab states *after* it has already begun, particularly if Israel appears to be falling behind. Given its past experience, the Israeli Defense Force will base its plans on a worst case analysis even if it is unlikely that all the Arab states would unite against Israel and even though the dynamic political, economic, and technological changes constantly taking place in the region make such calculations unreliable (Table 17.2). The intention here, though, is not so much to precisely define the regional balance of power as it is to illustrate the type of psychological pressure felt by Israeli strategists.

Israeli strategists and operational contingency planners must weigh a wide range of unpredictable and complex factors such as political elements and the motivations of various parties; considerations of military and technological quality including command and control, quality of planning, manpower, and hardware; and the presence, whether verified or assumed, of nuclear or chemical weapons. In view of the quantity and combined wealth of the Arab states arrayed against them, Israeli strategists have always recognized the impossibility of a final victory. In 1955, Ben Gurion wrote " . . . From our point of view there can never be a final battle. We can never assume we can deliver one final blow to the enemy that will be the last battle, after which there will never be the need for another clash or that the danger of war will be eliminated. The situation for our neighbors is the opposite. They can assume that a final battle will be the last one, that they may be able to deliver such a blow to Israel that the Arab-Israeli problem will be liquidated."[5]

Israel's narrow coastal strip has no territorial depth whatsoever. Within its old borders, the distance from the Jordanian frontier to the Mediterranean Sea was only about ten miles, but even the current border along the Jordan River leaves both Jerusalem and all of the airfields in the Negev within range of Jordanian heavy artillery. All Israeli airfields are within three to five minutes flying time of Syria and Jordan, while long-range Syrian surface-to-air

---

[5] Ilan Amit and Naomi Avigadol, "Notes on the History of the Israeli Concept of National Security," mimeographed (Haifa, October 1987), p. 14.

Table 17.2. *The Arab-Israeli balance of power: Different possible estimates*

	Israel	Direct eastern front		Ratio of SY + JO
		Syria	Jordan	
*Population (1989)	4.40 Jews 3.61 Arabs 0.79	12	2.9	1:4.1
GDP, ($ billion, 1985)	22.9	20.27	3.99	1:1
Defense expenditure ($ billion, 1986)	4.3	3.47	0.735	1:1
Armed forces personnel (thousands, 1987/1988)	440	606	115	1:1.6
Combat aircraft (1987/1988)	682	650	107	1:1.1
Tanks (1987/1988)	3790	4100	1.025	1:1.35
APCs (1987/1988)	5000	3800	1.465	1:1

Sources. A. Levran (ed.) *The Middle East Military Balance 1967–1988* (Tel Aviv: Tel
*CIA, *The World Factbook, 1989.*

missiles (SAM-5) or Jordanian Hawk missiles can cover most of Israel's airspace.[6] And recently, Egypt, Syria, Iraq, Saudi Arabia, and other Arab states have acquired surface-to-surface missiles capable of hitting any target in Israel.

As might be expected, Israel's lack of depth has exerted a powerful influence on the formation of its strategic doctrine. Before 1967, Israeli strategists adopted a preemptive strategy, for the combination of densely populated areas and no territorial depth made it imperative that Israel fight all wars outside its own borders. But the volatility of preemptive or "interceptive" strategies, which are offensive on both the tactical and operational levels, makes them more likely than others to trigger unplanned confrontations, escalation, and war.[7] In Israel's earlier years, peripheral defense (*haganah*

[6] Amiram Nir, *SAM-5 Batteries for Syria: Background and Possible Implications,* Memorandum No. 9 (Tel Aviv, February 1983); see also Aharon Yariv, "Strategic Depth," *Jerusalem Quarterly,* 17 (1980), pp. 3–12; Aryeh Shalev, "Security Dangers From the East," *Jerusalem Quarterly,* 27 (1983), pp. 15–27 and, 30 (1984), pp. 132–44; Yael Yishai, "Israel's Territorial Predicament," *Jerusalem Quarterly,* 40 (1986), pp. 73–88.
[7] See Handel, *Doctrine,* and Ariel Levite, *Ha'Doctrina Ha'Tzvait Shel Yisrael: Hagana ve Hatkafa* [The Israeli military doctrine: defense and offense] (Tel Aviv, 1988), pp. 44–52.

according to fronts, coalitions, or worst case analysis (an Israeli view) *

Western front Egypt	Ratio of EG + S + JO	Extended eastern front		Ratio of SY + JO + IR + S	Ratio of east & west fronts SY + JO + IR + S + EG	Libya	Ratio of east & west SY + JO + IR + S + EG + LY
		Iraq	Saudi Arabia				
54.7	1:19.3	18	15	1:13.3	1:28.4	4	1:29.6
46.56	1:3.1	36.5 (1986)	77.4 (1986)	1:6	1:8	26.76 (1974)	1:9.2
5.2	1:2.2	10	16.2	1:7.1	1:8.2	1.4 (1986)	1:8.6
980	1:3.9	1,035	72	1:4.2	1:6.4	115	1:6.6
600	1:2	705	190	1:2.4	1:3.3	537	1:4.1
2400	1:2	5500	550	1:2.9	1:3.6	2800	1:4.3
4100	1:1.9	5000	3140	1:2.7	1:3.5	2000	1:3.9

Aviv University, The Jaffe Center for Strategic Studies, 1988).

merchavit) seemed the best solution to the problems of inadequate strategic depth and a small regular army. "Peripheral defense" was based on the establishment of paramilitary (*nahal*) and fortified civilian border settlements designed to provide the first line of defense.[8] In the event of a surprise attack, they were supposed to repel and contain the enemy until the army and reserves had fully mobilized. Because Israel had failed to recapture a number of evacuated settlements in the War of Independence and could not afford to trade space for time, the policy of "not yielding an inch" (*af sha'al*) was essential.

Nevertheless, the importance of the "peripheral or territorial defense" strategy declined in most areas following expansion of Israel's territory after the 1967 war, the enlargement of the regular army, and improvements in intelligence and early warning systems. But the mentality of "peripheral defense" and "not yielding an inch" left an indelible impression on the

---

8   Yehezkiel Dror, "Bitachon ve Hityashvut" [Security and settlements], *Mibifnim* (September 1987), pp. 83–8; Lt. Col. Dr. Elchanan Oren, "Ha'Hityashvut, Yeuda ve Yeadea – ve Ha'Bitachon," [Establishing settlements – goals and defense aspects] *Ma'arachot* [Campaigns], 49 (October 1979), pp. 109–25.

outlook of Israeli strategists.[9] Rather than developing a more appropriate doctrine based on mobile defense on the newly acquired Suez Canal position, Israeli strategists insisted on constructing an expensive, but easily penetrable, line that did not capitalize on their advantage in dynamic, fast-paced mobile warfare. Yet long after Israel had reached the Suez Canal, its strategists still favored a heavily offensive strategy that was no longer dictated to the same extent by geographical concerns. Between the Six Day War (1967) and the Yom Kippur War (1973), the continued absence of depth on the Lebanese, Syrian, and Jordanian borders gave rise to a military doctrine based on both static defense *and* a modified version of mobile warfare.[10] Israeli military planners could not reconcile a defensive strategy along the Suez Canal (the Bar Lev Line) and a heavily offensive strategy on the eastern borders. But when the time came to implement a defensive strategy, the Israelis felt more secure with the idea of implementing an entirely offensive strategy on both fronts; they still felt pressured to take the war to Cairo, Amman, or Damascus rather than allow it to occur within or near their new borders.

During the first two or three days of the Yom Kippur War, this strategy fell somewhere between static and dynamic defense. The failure of the Bar Lev Line to halt the Egyptian advance across the Suez Canal and into the Sinai in turn hastened the collapse of the mobile counterattack. In contrast, the static defense was very effective in the northern section of the Golan Heights, where the defending troops, unlike those on the Bar Lev Line, were on full alert – the Syrian Army lost up to 800 tanks in an unsuccessful attempt to break through the defensive line.

During the late 1980s and early 1990s, Israeli military planners recognized the advantages of a more defensively oriented conventional military doctrine. Yet any withdrawal on the eastern fronts as part of a peace agreement will revive Israel's reliance on a much less stable strategic and operational offensive doctrine and increase the incentive to preempt in crisis situations (see Table 17.1, page 535).

The absence of territorial depth has also caused Israeli military thinkers to emphasize intelligence as a first line of defense.[11] Indeed, Israel is the only

---

9   Major-General (Ret.) Yisrael Tal, "Offense and Defense in Israel's Wars," *Ma'arachot*, 49 (February/March 1988), pp. 4–8; idem, "The Offensive and the Defensive in Israel's Campaigns," *Jerusalem Quarterly*, 51 (1989), pp. 41–7.

10 Ya'acov Bar-Siman-Tov, "The Bar-Lev Line Revisited," *Journal of Strategic Studies*, 11 (1988), pp. 149–77.

11 Tal, "Offense and Defense in Israel's Wars," p. 6. In this article, Major-General (Ret.) Tal assigns top priority to intelligence warning and a preemptive or offensive strategy. He believes that in preparing for war, Israel should order its priorities as follows: (a) intelligence; (b) air force; (c) armor; (d) parachutists or high quality infantry; (e) all others. See also Major-General (Ret.) Yisrael Tal, "Torat Ha'Bitachon: Reka ve Dynamica" [Israel's military doctrine: background and dynamics], *Ma'arachot*, 253 (December 1976), pp. 2–9. Very little has been published on Israeli intelligence. A number of journalistic reports published in recent years shed some light on this subject, but they must be taken with more than a grain of salt: see Ian Black and Benny Morris, *Israel's Secret Wars: A History of Israel's Intelligence Services* (New York, 1991); Dan Raviv and Yossi Melman, *Every Spy*

country in the world in which the status of the intelligence branch is comparable to that of the air force, army, and navy. Israelis often ask themselves what might have happened if the Arab countries that achieved strategic surprise in 1973 had done so in 1967, before Israel had obtained any strategic depth. Yet although Israeli intelligence is considered to be of high quality, it nevertheless failed to give effective warning of the approach of war in 1967 and 1973,[12] and was also caught unawares by the Iraqi invasion of Kuwait in 1990 and the ensuing SCUD attacks on Israel. Hence the need to preempt when in doubt, and the importance of making the best use of available space.

For the purposes of strategic planning, therefore, Israeli strategists established a strategic sphere of influence outside Israeli territory, an extended "border" for operational purposes. For example, the Litani River inside Lebanon is considered a trip wire – or red line – across which any large movement of forces constitutes a *casus belli*. Equally serious threats have included any large-scale movement of Iraqi troops into Jordan and the possibility of Egyptian troops moving into Jordan before the Sinai Campaign and on the eve of the Six Day War. Similarly, any significant movement of Egyptian troops into the Sinai in breach of the Israeli-Egyptian peace treaty would be viewed as a cause for war. The Israelis have also considered freedom of communication and transport to and from Israel by way of the Mediterranean, the Red Sea, or the Suez Canal as vital interests to be defended by the use of force. The closing of the Suez Canal and the Straits of Tiran in contravention of international law in large part caused the 1956 and 1967 wars.

Israel's central location does, however, allow it the advantage of interior lines, which permit a more economical use of force, enhance the possibility of effectively concentrating at the decisive point, and allow swift movement from one front to another. In 1967, when Egypt and Jordan posed the most serious threats, Israel followed an offensive strategy on both fronts but made no effort along the Syrian border. After pressure on the Egyptian and Jordanian fronts had eased, Israeli troops moved to the Syrian front. When caught off guard by the Arab surprise attack that opened the Yom Kippur War in 1973, Israel could not at first pursue its preferred strategy of simultaneous offensives. Instead, the Israelis initially concentrated the majority of their troops against Syria, the most serious threat, while remaining on the defensive or conducting only limited offensive operations elsewhere. In the future, interior lines of communication may no longer be as valuable, since modern communications technologies and longer-range weapons expose more of Israel's territory to attack or neutralization from much greater distances.

A Prince: The Complete History of Israel's Intelligence Community (Boston: 1990); Victor Osrarovsky and Claire Hoy, *By Way of Deception: The Making and Unmaking of A Mossad Officer* (New York, 1990); Samuel M. Katz, *Soldier Spies: Israeli Military Intelligence* (Novato, CA, 1992). The most reliable source on Israeli intelligence methods is still Efraim Dekel, *Shai: The Exploits of Hagana Intelligence* (New York, 1959).
12 Handel, *Perception, Deception and Surprise: The Case of the Yom Kippur War* (Jerusalem, 1976).

Geographically, Israel's strategic outlook has improved in recent years. The peace agreement with Egypt created a buffer zone that shortened Israel's lines of communication, and it placed a U.S. observation/early warning system in the Sinai. In addition, Israel also made significant improvements in its warning and alert system: in the event of war on the eastern front, Israel could concentrate most of its troops in the east where it has less strategic depth, and maintain only a small force on the border with Egypt. Should the Egyptians decide to enter the war, the IDF would still have enough time to bring in reinforcements before the Egyptians could move their troops to the Israeli border.

PSYCHOLOGICAL FACTORS

The history of the Jewish people magnifies the Israelis' sense of insecurity. Following the destruction of the First and Second Temples (the first and second politically independent Jewish states), the Jews were expelled from their homeland. This left them at the mercy of other nations and taught them that the destruction of a state and the ensuing enslavement, expulsion, or annihilation of its inhabitants was not merely an abstract possibility. Life in the diaspora for almost two millennia was an unceasing struggle for survival. In the twentieth century, the trauma of the holocaust – the wholesale destruction of European Jewry by Nazi Germany – made it plain that the possibility of annihilation as a people was as real in the modern age as it had always been. For Zionists, then, the quest for a State of Israel was part of a quest for security.

The psychological and cultural influences of Jewish history have also shaped the environment in which Israeli strategy has been formulated. Jewish isolation by choice or gentile decree in the ghettos of Europe discouraged interest in or respect for the hostile environment of the outside world. Generations of isolation taught a distrustful self-reliance. Much of this outlook was brought to Israel, which from its declaration of independence experienced serious problems in finding and keeping allies. This was made inevitable by Arab control of oil and strategically important areas. Israel enjoyed some fleeting diplomatic success in establishing friendly relations with other states during the 1950s and 1960s, but its early ties with the Soviet Union and France soon dissolved. Votes in the United Nations often went against Israel, while the Arab oil embargo of 1973–74 and rapidly escalating oil revenues raised Arab influence to new heights and increasingly isolated Israel. This not unexpected turn of events fueled the Israelis' search for self-reliance, if not withdrawal, fostering a ghetto mentality that precluded an emphasis on the political and diplomatic dimensions of strategy. And after two millennia in the diaspora, the Jews had little experience in managing a large political entity such as a state. Such attitudes, combined with a strong sense of individualism and a democratic tradition, undermined the orderly conduct of government affairs and decision-making procedures.

On the other side of the Arab-Israeli conflict, strong ethnocentric biases and perceptions have made communication difficult and mutual understanding virtually impossible. Arab attitudes toward Israel reinforced the Jewish settlers' most deep-seated fears: Arab states would not recognize the Jewish state's existence, refused to negotiate directly with Israel, worked through the Arab League to impose an international boycott on it,[13] and pressured other nations not to recognize Israel or to sever diplomatic relations. After the collapse of the Soviet Union and the Gulf War, however, many third world and East European countries established or reestablished diplomatic relations with Israel.

At the United Nations, the acceptance of Israel as a member proved to be one of the last decisions favorable to it. From the mid-1950s onward an intensive Arab campaign led to a series of decisions culminating in the 1975 General Assembly resolution branding Zionism as a form of racism. Such policies only exacerbated the longstanding ghetto mentality, as have the endless Arab threats to drive the Jews into the sea and the relentless anti-Semitic propaganda in Arab publications and media.[14] The PLO's national charter, which calls for the establishment of *one* secular state between the Jordan River and the sea, further confirmed Israeli fears that their opponents were bent on annihilation.

Although most Israelis felt elated over President Anwar Sadat's visit to Jerusalem, the tough negotiations that ensued, the cold attitude of Egypt after the signing of the peace treaty, and Egypt's treatment at the hands of the Arab states after the negotiations quickly extinguished hopes of a radical change in Arab attitudes. Cynical observers believed that Sadat's initiative was merely a tactic to corner Israel into returning the Sinai. Such skepticism is still prevalent, and despite the peace agreement, Israeli planners believe they cannot afford to ignore the potential threat of the Egyptian armed forces.

Although several generations of Israelis have now been born in an independent and strong Jewish state, the psychology of insecurity persists.[15] Fear of Arab neighbors is so ingrained that most Israelis still prefer security to taking risks for peace.[16] For while geographical and demographic conditions made it comparatively easy for Israel to conclude a peace agreement with Egypt, they are the greatest obstacles to similar agreements with Syria, Jordan, or a Palestinian state. The Sinai, which separates Israel and Egypt, is a

---

13 Dan S. Chill, *The Arab Boycott of Israel: Economic Aggression and World Reaction* (New York, 1976).
14 Yehoshafat Harkabi, *Arab Attitudes To Israel* (New York, 1972).
15 Asher Arian, Ilan Talmud, Tamar Hermann, *National Security and Public Opinion in Israel*, JCSS Study no. 9 (Tel Aviv, 1988), pp. 80–8.
16 Handel, *Doctrine*, p. 64.

barren, unpopulated area which, after being cleared of Israeli settlements without much trouble, could serve as a strategic buffer zone. But in the case of a disengagement agreement with Syria, Jordan, or a Palestinian state, Israel would lose what little strategic depth it has acquired in the West Bank and the Golan Heights (which is also Israel's largest water resource). Whether Israel can evacuate the numerous Israelis now living in East Jerusalem and the West Bank in order to create a Palestinian autonomous zone remains to be seen.[17]

The Khartoum decisions of 1967, wherein the Arabs refused to negotiate with Israel, led the Israelis to establish many settlements along the Jordan River, the strategically important highway from Jericho to Jerusalem, and on the Golan Heights. In an almost reflexive way, Israel has clung to its policy of "peripheral defense" and "not yielding an inch." What began as an attempt to establish *faits accomplis* and to signal the Arabs that Israel would proceed with the settlement of these areas unless there were serious peace negotiations, ended in the establishment and steady growth of Jewish settlements. Unlike the Sinai, the cities of Jerusalem, Hebron, and Bethlehem are also important to most Israelis for religious and sentimental reasons. By now, settlers in the occupied areas and their relatives living inside Israel proper make up a powerful political constituency that will lobby vigorously against any withdrawal from the occupied territories. The influx of about 400,000 Russian immigrants since 1990 has made the idea of territorial concessions and relinquishing control of water resources even more difficult. Moreover, while an evacuation would be accompanied by the risk of attacks from a more radicalized Arab population, a continuation of the status quo has propelled the *intifada* – or passive resistance punctuated by terrorism in the occupied areas – from it popular beginnings in 1987 increasingly toward Algerian-style violence supported by Islamic fundamentalists.[18]

THE DEMOGRAPHIC FACTOR: THE HANDWRITING ON THE WALL

Demography adds another important dimension to the feelings of insecurity. Since its independence, Israel has included a relatively large, unsympathetic Arab population and certain areas in which the Arabs have always constituted a majority. Before the 1967 war, however, the Israeli Arabs were thought to have developed their own identity after almost twenty years of separation from the rest of the Arab world; certainly they had benefited

---

17   For two such proposals, see Yeroham Cohen, *Tochnit Allon* [The Allon Plan] (Tel Aviv, 1973); and Aryeh Shalev, *Kav Hagana Beyehuda u'ba'Shomron* [The West Bank: line of defense] (Tel Aviv, 1982). For the English version, see Aryeh Shalev, *The West Bank: Line of Defense* (New York, 1985).

18   See Report of a JCSS Study Group, *The West Bank and Gaza: Israel's Options for Peace* (Tel Aviv, 1989); and Report of a JCSS Study Group, *Israel, the West Bank and Gaza: Toward a Solution* (Tel Aviv, 1989).

materially if not politically from the advanced Israeli economy and welfare society. But after the 1967 war and the occupation of large Arab-populated areas, contact between the Israeli Arabs and the Arabs of the occupied territories radicalized the Israeli Arabs. Thus, the growing number of Arabs under Israeli control means that a high percentage of its total population cannot be relied upon in wartime. By the year 2000, it is expected that Israeli Arabs will make up from 23 to 27 percent of the population.[19]

The demographic changes that have taken place within Israel since 1967 have therefore added a serious *internal* security problem to that already faced externally. Although Israel's Jewish population grew rapidly during the 1950s, expectations of slow population growth have now changed to predictions of actual decline. This imposes a limit on the maximum size of the armed forces Israel can mobilize from its 4.0 million Jewish citizens. Israel's Military Participation Ratio (MPR) has remained high throughout its short history[20]: once eighteen, every male must serve three years on active duty and remain in the reserves until the age of fifty-five. Each reservist usually serves more than one month a year either on active duty or in training. While the Israeli reserve system can rapidly swell the ranks of the army in times of war, it places an enormous burden on the economy. In addition, the level of training and hence performance of reserve units cannot match that of the regular army. Dependence on reservists has determined the basis of Israel's strategy and military doctrine: wars must end quickly and decisively to avoid or minimize the economic paralysis caused by total mobilization. Preemptive attacks offered the best way to achieve surprise and reduce a military conflict to the shortest possible duration. Israel's total mobilization of its reserves during the 1967 crisis brought the economy to a halt, which in turn exerted a powerful destabilizing pressure in favor of launching a preemptive war. In the same way, a prolonged period of mobilization during and after the Yom Kippur War in 1973 crippled Israel's economy.

Israel has also expanded the size of its armed forces through the compulsory service of women in noncombat duties in administration, training, intelligence work, maintenance, and radar operation. Women serve for two years and remain in the reserves up to age twenty-five unless they marry earlier. In the age of high technology, the role of women in noncombat duty will become increasingly important since this is the only source of manpower that the Israelis have not yet fully tapped.[21]

---

[19] JCSS Study Group, *The West Bank and Gaza*, pp. 203–4. For an excellent and detailed study of Israel's demographic trends, see Arnon Soffer, "Demography in Eretz-Israel in 1988 and the Year 2000," *Jerusalem Quarterly*, 51 (1989), pp. 115–44.

[20] This concept was suggested by Stanislav Andreski in *Military Organization and Society* (Berkeley, 1967), pp. 33–9. See also Handel, *Doctrine*, p. 7.

[21] See Lt. Col. Margalit, "Nashim be'Tzahal – Mashaav Shelo Mutzaa," [Women in the IDF – an untapped resource] in Zvi Offer and Major Avi Kober, eds., *Eychut ve Kamut: Dilemot be Binyan Ha'Koach Ha'tzvai* [Quality and Quantity in Military Buildup] (Tel Aviv, 1985),pp. 331–41 (hereinafter cited as Offer and Kober, eds., *Quality and Quantity*).

Nevertheless, demographic constraints set an upper limit on the size of the armed forces Israel can mobilize.[22] The small number of new recruits each year has, for example, restricted the number of pilots Israel can train. Manpower limits rather than the number of aircraft available therefore determine the size of the Israeli Air Force (IAF). From 1973 to 1987, the Israeli army expanded by about 25 percent, reaching its upper limit in manpower during the growth spurt following the Yom Kippur War. During the same period, almost all of the opposing Arab armies at least doubled in size.

The Arab demographic advantage has always prompted the Israelis to seek qualitative solutions. Indeed, the issue of quantity versus quality obsessed Israeli strategic planners even before independence.[23] The high caliber of Israeli manpower offered qualitative solutions,[24] along with intangibles such as Israel's military doctrine and planning, maintenance of the initiative, offensive doctrine, planning of military operations, interior lines, indirect approach, and stratagem and deception. Since 1967, the Israelis have increasingly turned to technological solutions and state-of-the-art weaponry. As the trends in manpower and demography became unfavorable after 1973, modern weapons technology came to the fore as a potent force multiplier at a time when the quality of the IDF's leadership, planning, and doctrine had begun to deteriorate. This development was not entirely a coincidence, since Israel's growing reliance on technology encouraged the "neglect" of many nonmaterial qualitative dimensions as well as the increased bureaucratization and higher tooth-to-tail ratio of the IDF.[25]

In modern conventional warfare, however, population size as a traditional indicator of military strength has declined in importance relative to technological developments. Israeli military planners were quick to identify this trend in the early 1970s. Yet demographic trends cannot be ignored in low-intensity warfare and daily coexistence. With a rapidly increasing population of Arabs and Jews, conflict and a lower quality of life are inevitable even in the event of a peace settlement. While the immigration of more than 400,000 Russian Jews is not enough to reverse demographic trends, it has added a pool of highly educated professional and skilled manpower that will increase Israel's *qualitative* edge over its neighbors. The influence of the Russian immigrant population has already been felt through its contribution to the

---

22 See Jacob Kop, "Ha'Chesem Ha'Demographie – Musag Muchlat?" [The demographic barrier – an absolute concept?] in Offer and Kober, *Quality and Quantity*, pp. 313–21.
23 For an excellent discussion from an Israeli perspective, see Offer and Kober, *Quality and Quantity*.
24 For an excellent study, see Reuven Gal, *A Portrait of the Israeli Soldier* (New York, 1986).
25 For a detailed discussion arguing that the quality of manpower, particularly on the middle and higher echelons of command, has been deteriorating since the 1967 war, see Immanuel Wald, *Klalat Ha'Kelim Ha'Shvurim (1967–1982)* [The decline of Israeli military and political power (1967–1982)] (Jerusalem and Tel Aviv, 1987) (hereinafter cited as *The Decline of Israeli Military and Political Power*).

election of a moderate Labor government under Prime Minister Rabin in 1992. In general, these immigrants will exert a more secular, moderate influence on Israeli domestic politics.

But overall demographic trends working against Israel will only continue to worsen. According to a World Bank estimate, by the year 2000, the combined populations of Syria, Jordan, Egypt, Iraq, and Saudi Arabia will number 132 million compared with Israel's 6 million. And by the year 2025, the gap will widen to 224 million Arabs and 8 million Israelis.[26]

ECONOMIC MIRACLES

Waging war places tremendous burdens on any society, particularly a society that has since 1948 fought no fewer than five major wars interspersed with interminable low-intensity conflicts. Israel is short of almost all natural resources – it controls few minerals, has little water, and its small territory is half desert. Only the boost provided by large infusions of financial aid and economic support enabled Israel to prepare for war while building a relatively advanced industrial base. For a number of reasons, Israel was more successful in this type of endeavor than any other modern state. Since independence, it has received extensive economic aid from three principal sources: the United States, the Jewish diaspora, and German reparations. Until the 1967 war, the comparatively limited scope of the Arab-Israeli conflict allowed Israel to invest a lower percentage of its GNP in defense and more in the development of the economy.

While the 1948 and 1956 wars were followed by relatively tranquil periods, the Six Day War in 1967 led to large-scale guerrilla and terror operations against Israel and a war of attrition on the Egyptian border. Combined with a flood of Russian arms to the Arabs and the Arab states' greatly increased oil revenues, this constant pressure made American financial, economic, and military support essential. Israel alone could no longer bear most of the economic burden of war as it had prior to 1967; and without U.S. support, Israel could not have purchased weapons comparable to those of the Arab states. As the Arab capacity to support much higher military expenditures reached unprecedented levels, Israel was forced to invest a higher and higher proportion of its GNP in defense and in its military industry: in 1954, Israel spent 6.3 percent of its GNP on defense; in 1963, 10.8 percent; in 1972, 20.8 percent (peacetime); and in 1979, approximately 30 percent (Figure 17.1).

Since the late 1980s, Israel's military expenditures as a percentage of GNP have declined from well over 20 percent to just over 12 percent, even as its

---

[26] The World Bank, *World Development Report 1992* (New York, 1992), Table 26, pp. 268–269.

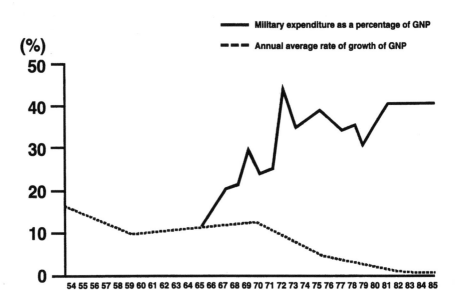

Figure 17.1. Comparison of the rate of growth of Israeli GNP and military expenditure as a percentage of GNP.

GNP has grown at a slow but steady pace. The fact that any major military effort would immediately reverse these favorable trends certainly operates as a strong restraint on Israeli military planners.

Although much of the U.S. economic assistance to Israel has been in the form of grants and forgiven aid, Israel has accumulated a national debt of over $25 billion – an amount exceeding its annual GNP.[27] At least 33 percent of the Israeli GNP must service the national debt.[28] In 1984, Israel's reliance on foreign assistance resulted in its ranking second in the world – after Bahrain – in aid received per capita ($313.50 per capita). In the same year, Israel's public expenditures per soldier amounted to $45,582, putting it in sixteenth place, behind many of the Arab oil-producing countries.[29] As Israel's economy became more dependent on U.S. aid, the IDF, paradoxically, was expanding, and appears to have reached its peak strength on the eve of the war in Lebanon. Israel can sustain this level of relative strength in the long run *only* if it continues to receive significant foreign aid, conserves its strength, avoids a major war or intensive lower-level military effort, and maintains or increases its technological lead.

[27] Ma'ayan, "Gevul Ha'Koach," [The limits of power] in Offer and Kober, eds., *Quality and Quantity*, p. 299.
[28] Ma'ayan, "Gevul Ha'Koach," [The limits of power], pp. 298–9.
[29] These data are from Ruth Leger Sivard, *World Military and Social Expenditures 1987–1988* (Washington, 1987).

Although Israel has developed one of the strongest and most modern military organizations in the world, its military strength depends on foreign aid. The flaws in its decision-making processes and diplomacy have thus far not prevented it from being consistently successful in mobilizing the financial and military support of at least one major power during each critical phase of its existence. Since its independence, Israel managed to obtain military or financial support from the USSR (through Czechoslovakia) between 1947 and 1949; France between 1955 and 1968; and West Germany, which paid reparations from 1953 on and supplied military equipment between 1959 and 1967. As their French and German weapons connections dissolved, the Israelis approached the United States. Limited American financial support began in the 1950s, and ballooned in and after the early 1970s.[30] Short periods of isolation in the early 1950s and late 1960s generated fears that Israel would soon be without external military or financial support. From 1950 to 1955, Israel purchased weapons abroad with extreme difficulty, until the French agreed to supply weapons as part of their cooperative effort in preparing for the Sinai-Suez Campaign. The second period began after the 1967 war, when President de Gaulle used the accusation that Israel had fired the first shot in the war as a pretext for imposing a French arms embargo against Israel. For a period of almost two years after the embargo, which was never fully implemented, the United States would not supply Israel with major weapons systems. Meanwhile, the Arab states easily acquired the best weapons systems on the market either from the West or the Soviet Union. Consequently, all Israeli governments since that of Prime Minister Ben Gurion have stressed the importance of self-reliance in weapons production. Developing a strong weapons industry became a national obsession that absorbed enormous amounts of energy and resources. Israel's historic fears also lay behind the decision to produce nuclear weapons that was apparently taken by Prime Minister Ben Gurion.[31] Their potential for allowing Israel to maintain a smaller conventional standing army and for deterring an all-out Arab attack seemed to provide the ultimate guarantee for survival.[32]

TECHNOLOGY AS A PANACEA IN ISRAEL'S STRATEGY

From the War of Independence through the early 1960s, Israel emphasized planning and doctrine, maintenance of the initiative, preemption, motivation, fighting spirit, and other qualitative factors to compensate for its in-

---

[30] David Pollock, *The Politics of Pressure: American Arms and Israeli Policy Since the Six Day War* (Westport, CT, 1982), and Nitza Nachmias, *Transfer of Arms, Leverage and Peace in the Middle East* (Westport, CT, 1988).

[31] See Uri Bar Joseph, "The Hidden Debate: The Formation of Nuclear Doctrines in the Middle East," *Journal of Strategic Studies*, 5 (June 1982).

[32] This is the thesis of Shai Feldman, *Israeli Nuclear Deterrence: A Strategy for the 1980s* (New York, 1982).

feriority in hardware. During the 1950s, Israel's military doctrine and weapons technology lacked synchronization, for the infantry-oriented IDF did not yet appreciate the potential of armored warfare. Following the 1956 Sinai Campaign, top priority went to the development of the tank corps, to the neglect of other important dimensions such as artillery, mechanized infantry, and the combination of arms. Between 1956 and 1967 Israel acquired its first state-of-the-art military technology through its French purchases, and began to build its own military industry. This evolutionary rather than revolutionary process involved weapons construction under license from other countries, the upgrading or modification of existing obsolete equipment (which was elevated to an art), and the design and production of weapons needed to match certain Soviet equipment.

The economic recession that preceded the Six Day War of 1967, the subsequent French arms embargo, and the flood of cheap labor from the newly occupied territories hastened the rapid expansion of Israel's military industry. Other favorable conditions were a low rate of inflation, a closer relationship with the United States, worldwide economic prosperity, and above all the national euphoria that followed Israel's victory.[33] There were strategic and military reasons as well. Policymakers felt the combination of Israeli combat experience and ingenuity would put Israel on the "cutting edge" of weapons production and ensure a market abroad. They hoped that Israeli industry could produce indigenous weapons – tailored to the IDF's military doctrine and local conditions – at a lower cost than the prevailing prices in the foreign weapons market.[34]

After the French arms embargo, the Israelis decided to replace the engines of the Mirage III with more powerful U.S. engines. The experience gained from this complex industrial operation proved to be invaluable when Israel began producing its own jet fighters (Kfir C-2, Kfir C-7). In the early 1970s, the Israelis began to design and then manufacture a domestic, state-of-the-art tank (Merkava, now MKIII) that incorporated lessons learned from the 1967 war and later those of the 1973 and 1982 wars. By the early 1970s, Israel was able to produce almost all its light weapons and ammunition, as well as a number of major weapons platforms and jet engines under license.[35]

With renewed confidence in its capabilities, Israel pressed on toward its goal of full autonomy in weapons production with little regard for expense. Nevertheless the small-scale production of major weapons proved costly and still depended on foreign sources for know-how, composite materials, engines, and tooling equipment. Thus although the quest for autarky in weapons production was a powerful motivating force, it remained unrealistic.

[33] Naftali Blumental, "The Influence of Defense Industry Investment on Israel's Economy," in Lanir, ed., *Israeli Security Planning in the 1980s*, pp. 166–77.
[34] Berglas, "Defense and Economy," p. 185.
[35] See *Jane's Defense Weekly*, 24 June 1989, p. 1299.

Major weapons platforms such as the Lavi fighter aircraft were so expensive that they absorbed funds earmarked for development of other sophisticated weapons systems, an area in which Israel enjoyed a relative advantage. While Israel successfully exported smaller types of equipment and munitions whose origin was difficult to trace, sluggish sales of major weapons platforms drove up production costs and prevented savings through economies of scale. Exceeding the reach of its economy, Israel has thus invested hundreds of millions of dollars in state-of-the-art weaponry of uncertain effectiveness.[36]

Israel's military industry is now among the most sophisticated in the world: it combines technological proficiency with combat experience, and can produce new and highly innovative weapons in a relatively short time. Usually, by the time a new weapons system has been made public, the next generation of that weapon is already in production or in service. Since the mid-1970s, the military industry's share of Israeli exports has climbed steadily, making virtue out of necessity. But the pressure to expand sales and reduce its foreign debt led the Israeli government to approve the sale of new, highly classified weapons that might otherwise have enabled the IDF to achieve numerous technological surprises.

With manpower resources fully tapped, Israel now relies heavily on capital-intensive warfare – that is, on automation, technological surprise, massive, accurate firepower, area munitions, and standoff weapons – to reduce casualties and minimize the destruction of expensive weapons platforms. As the war in Lebanon demonstrated, the Israelis surprised the Syrian army and its ally, the Soviet Union, by introducing a wide range of new weapons. But in the process, Israel disclosed the existence of many technological innovations in a war that was not essential to its survival. Many of the weapons were so innovative that the superpowers had not yet produced them.

To guard against catastrophe in a conventional war, the Israelis embraced the ultimate technological panacea: nuclear weapons. Historical fears and the difficulties in obtaining conventional weapons during the 1950s form the backdrop to Israel's nuclear weapons policy. The program to acquire nuclear weapons probably began after the Sinai Campaign, as a technological challenge whose solution would provide the "ultimate answer" to its security problems. There was little time to ponder the longer-range complications inevitably created by nuclear weapons. Only in later years was more careful thought given to problems of delivery, the development of a second-strike capability, the acquisition of nuclear weapons by Arab states, and the possession of nuclear weapons as a way of reducing the size of Israel's conventional

---

36 Major General (ret.) Edward B. Atkeson, *A Military Assessment of the Middle East, 1991–1996* (Carlisle, PA, 1993), pp. 19–22. See also references to an essential but unnamed weapons system, which is possibly an intelligence satellite system (Amos) or microwave weaponry. Aluf Ben, "[A System] Fighting for Its Life," *Haaretz*, 28 January 1993.

army in order to ease the nation's economic burden. By the early 1970s intelligence suggested that Israel possessed an arsenal of nuclear weapons and today has the technological know-how and fissionable material to produce all types of nuclear weapons from A-bombs to neutron bombs. No doubt Israel currently has a moderate second-strike capability and a variety of regional strategic and tactical means of delivery.[37]

Israel's nuclear policy has always been responsible. Even when its survival was most seriously jeopardized, as on the eve of war in 1967, or during the early setbacks of the Yom Kippur War (1973), Israel made no direct threats to use nuclear weapons. The most visible manifestation of Israeli nuclear strategy to date was when Israel unambiguously signaled that it had already acquired or could acquire nuclear weapons at any time. More recently, the "Vanunu Affair" (1987–1988) – in which an Israeli employee from the nuclear reactor in Dimona disclosed highly classified evidence of Israel's potential to produce nuclear weapons – was apparently part of an Israeli deception plan intended to remind neighboring countries of its nuclear status.[38] Israel launched satellites (OFEK 2 in September 1988 and OFEK 3 in April 1990) not long afterward, yet another signal that it possessed medium-range missiles capable of delivering nuclear weapons to any target in the Middle East.

Despite early concerns over the reactions of the superpowers and the Arabs, Israel's successful nuclear strategy may have helped push President Sadat into seeking peace between Egypt and Israel. Even earlier, the existence of Israeli nuclear weapons may well have influenced the Egyptian and Syrian decision to pursue limited rather than total goals during the 1973 war. Nuclear weapons also provide Israel with an excellent bargaining card as other nations try to restrain nuclear proliferation. The United States has undoubtedly been aware that as long as the Israelis could defend themselves by conventional means, they would issue no open statements regarding their nuclear capabilities. No doubt this is an important motivation behind the U.S. policy of maintaining the "balance of power" in the Middle East. Since the Gulf War, however, references to nuclear weapons production plans since

37 On Israeli nuclear strategy, see Yair Evron, *Ha'Dilemma Ha'Ga'arinit Shel Yisrael* [Israel's nuclear dilemma] (Yad Tabenkin, Israel, 1987); Feldman, *Israeli Nuclear Deterrence;* Peter Pry, *Israel's Nuclear Arsenal* (Boulder, CO, 1984); Shlomo Aronson, "The Nuclear Dimension of the Arab-Israeli Conflict," *Jerusalem Journal of International Relations,* 7 (Jan./Feb. 1984); Bar Joseph, "The Hidden Debate: The Formation of Nuclear Doctrines in the Middle East" in Louis Rene Beres, ed., *Security or Armageddon: Israel's Nuclear Strategy* (Lexington, MA, 1986); Leonard S. Spector, *The Undeclared Bomb: Between Protest and Compliance* (Cambridge, MA, 1988), pp. 164–93; and Yuval Ne'eman, "Yisrael ve Ha'Harta'a Ha'Ga'arinit: Mediniut Ha'Ga'arin Shel Yisrael 1948–1986," [Israel and nuclear deterrence: the nuclear policy of Israel 1948–1986] *Ma'arachot,* 48 (April 1987), pp. 19–21.
38 "Hijack or high jinks," *The Economist,* 24 September 1988, p. 50. For other indications, see Hersh, *The Samson Option.*

Prime Minister Ben Gurion's time have become more common in the Israeli press.[39] American observers estimate that Israel has acquired between 200 and 300 nuclear weapons mostly for tactical use.[40]

Nuclear weapons are not, however, a panacea. They are not much help against low-intensity violence, nor can they credibly deter irrational opponents, or provide much comfort in a prolonged "border" war of attrition or an indecisive conventional war. For Israeli strategists, nuclear weapons must be seen in a psychological context as the "ultimate guarantee" that their nation can, if necessary, prevent a major conventional defeat and protect itself from annihilation.

THE DOMESTIC ENVIRONMENT AND THE FORMATION OF STRATEGY

Until the war in Lebanon, the Israeli public's long-standing consensus on national security affairs gave the government considerable leeway in determining its policies in close cooperation with the IDF. When the war in Lebanon broke out in 1982, 66 percent of the population supported the government because they believed it would be a limited war of short duration. By June 1985, however, a public opinion poll showed that only 15 percent of the population still supported the war.[41] But while public support of the unity government, the Knesset, and the press was at a low ebb, the IDF continued to enjoy strong public support even after its withdrawal from Lebanon.[42]

A privileged few – mainly to preserve secrecy – make Israeli strategy and the most important decisions about major military operations. This group includes the prime minister, defense minister, and – depending on the prime minister – a few confidants, normally other ministers. The chief of staff, chief of intelligence, and a few aides considered to be above party politics have also

---

[39] See, for example, the leading article in *Davar*, "Yehoshafat Following Yeshiahu," 24 January 1993.

[40] Atkeson, *A Military Assessment of the Middle East 1991–1996*, pp. 22–24.

[41] See Asher Arian, *Israeli Public Opinion and the War in Lebanon*, JCSS Memorandum No. 15 (Tel Aviv, October 1985), pp. 1, 4, 13, 29; Arian, Talmud, and Hermann, *National Security and Public Opinion in Israel*.

[42] Arian, *Israeli Public Opinion and the War in Lebanon*, pp. 2, 13. See also, Shai Feldman and Heda Rechnitz-Kijner, *Deception, Consensus and War: Israel in Lebanon*, Paper No. 27, JCSS (Tel Aviv, October 1984). For longer range trends and the decline in the Israeli public's consensus on national security matters, see Dan Horowitz, "Ha'Kavua ve Ha'Mishtane Be Tifisot Ha'Bitachon Shel Yisrael," [The permanent and the transitory in the Israeli concept of national security] in *Milchemet Breira* [War by choice] (Tel Aviv, 1985), pp. 57–117, in particular pp. 77–82; also Dan Horowitz, "Ha'Milchama ba Nishbar Ha'Consensus Ha'Leumi," [The war in which the national consensus broke] in *Milchemet Levanon: Bain Mecha'a le Ha'skama* [The Lebanon war: between protest and compliance] (Tel Aviv, 1983), pp. 135–53 (hereinafter cited as *The Lebanon War: Between Protest and Agreement*).

participated ex officio in most national security decisions.[43] Such a small number of participants has made the process much more sensitive to individual attitudes, perceptions, and wishful thinking.

Israel has never adopted a constitution and lacks a formal definition of the decision-making process in national security matters. In the absence of a clear understanding of who was responsible for national security policy, the prime minister and his cabinet assumed this task. Only in 1976, for example, did the enactment of a basic law concerning the army formally establish a direct link between the cabinet and the chief of staff by stating that the minister of defense was responsible for the IDF. Without a specific formal structure to define the decision-making process in national security matters, the system that evolved under Ben Gurion, who was both prime minister and defense minister, was highly centralized, secretive, and authoritarian. The offices of prime minister and defense minister became separate only later, on the eve of the Six Day War, when public pressure prompted the appointment of Moshe Dayan as minister of defense. The formation of national strategy was then left, with minor changes over the years, in the hands of the prime minister, defense minister, chief of staff, and a few others. At times, a smaller number of cabinet ministers formed a Ministerial Defense Committee (MDC), or even less formally, a kitchen cabinet.[44] And while the Knesset can theoretically deal with national security matters, it has rarely done so because of the national consensus on this subject, the lack of information, and the need for secrecy.

Without formal institutions such as a national security council, the cabinet ministers and the prime minister depend almost exclusively on the IDF, its chief of staff, and the intelligence community to provide information on and analyses of national security issues. As a result, according to General (ret.) Aharon Yariv, the viewpoint of the military has been most influential on Cabinet ministers; "[o]nly the military possessed the staff requisite for strategy development."[45] General (ret.) Avrasha Tamir, former head of strategic planning for the IDF general staff, has also noted that "what influences the decisions more than anything else are the papers of the general staff, and they are tailor-made to the needs, the conceptions, and the viewpoints of the army."[46] In Israel, the major source of intelligence and the sole coordinating agency of all intelligence estimates and reports is the military intelligence organization. "It is the director of military intelligence who bears the overall responsibility both for military as well as political intelligence. Military intelligence prepares the national estimates and its director serves as a de facto

---

[43] See Yehuda Ben-Meir's excellent critical study, *National Security Decision Making: The Israeli Case,* JCSS Study No. 8 (Tel Aviv, 1986), in particular pp. 67–71, 84–91.
[44] Ibid., pp. 104–8.
[45] Ibid., p. 84.
[46] Ibid.

intelligence adviser to the prime minister and to the Cabinet."[47] "In effect, the director of military intelligence has become the national security adviser. This is both unprecedented and dangerous."[48] Despite a succession of committees specially appointed to examine the structure and functioning of the Israeli intelligence community (for example, Yadin-Sherf [1963], the Agranat Commission [1973–1974], the Zadock Committee [1974], and the Cahan Committee [1982–1983]) that have all recommended establishment of a strong and independent civilian intelligence organization, the government has taken no such action.

Professor Daniel Shimshoni's argument that "a disproportionate concern with the military aspects of security could lead to a neglect of diplomacy, or to inadequate questioning of the demands and strategies of the military establishment,"[49] understates the danger. Strategic and defense issues received little coverage in the Israeli press until the Yom Kippur War in 1973 and national security affairs was not taught at the universities. Only in 1978 was a noteworthy thinktank, the Jaffee Center for Strategic Studies, established at Tel Aviv University. It attracted many former senior military men, who produced the first solid body of position papers and analytical studies of Israel's national security problems.

Another feature of Israeli politics is the high percentage of former senior military officers who entered politics and assumed senior government positions: among others Moshe Dayan, Ezer Weizman, Chaim Bar Lev, Yitzhak Rabin, Yigal Allon, Yigal Yadin, Ariel Sharon, Meir Amit, Aharon Yariv, Mota Gur, and Mordechai Zipori. Although this movement into government positions has raised questions about the nature of civil-military relations in Israel, it is not an entirely negative phenomenon. Former military men are in a better position to analyze and discuss the proposals and plans of the IDF; and their firsthand knowledge of the costs and risks of military operations often leads them to adopt a more cautious position. Their contacts in the military and the defense ministry also enable them to obtain more in-depth information on military plans. Finally, they are in a stronger position than civilians to recommend budgetary cuts and austerity measures for the IDF.

Because of the presence of numerous retired officers in government and the IDF's monopoly in the analysis of military affairs and strategy, a narrow military view of national security affairs and strategy inevitably prevails at the highest levels. Consequently, the Israeli government has frequently ignored important considerations such as economics, diplomacy, and negotiations. It has often taken a military approach to problems with no military solution, and it has frequently seen military operations or war as choices of the first – rather than last – resort. Finally, the Israeli system places too much

---

47 Ibid., p. 86.
48 Ibid., p. 87.
49 Daniel Shimshoni, *Israeli Democracy: The Middle of the Journey* (New York, 1982), p. 156.

emphasis on short-run, day-to-day operational matters including weapons acquisition, counterterror operations, and reprisal raids at the expense of long-term political-strategic plans, national goals, and greater thought about the relationship of the economy and foreign policy to national security.

Success despite great odds in the War of Independence, the Sinai Campaign, and the brilliant 1967 victory seemed to confirm the feeling that all was well in Israel's strategy-making process. But this was far from true. Military success was also attributable to such factors as the ability to maintain the initiative and achieve surprise (1956, 1967), Arab weakness and disunity, and serious Arab misestimates of Israeli power and motivation (mistakes that the Arabs may not repeat in the future).

Indications of the inherent weaknesses of the Israeli strategic decision-making system were evident long before near-disaster in 1973, which finally exposed the dangers of a limited "military" approach. Nevertheless, the system subsequently underwent few reforms, although failure in the Lebanon war and the *intifada* once more demonstrated its inadequacies. Former senior government officials and military officers have described this decision-making process as "amateurish, based on improvisation and lacking institutionalization" (Abba Eban) or as "irresponsible, haphazard, not thought out and not based on any examination and evaluation of alternatives . . . (It was) only by chance that good or correct decisions were arrived at" (Shlomo Gazit, former director of military intelligence). And as Meir Amit, former IDF chief of operations and head of the Mossad has said, " . . . In Israel there is no systematic decision-making process in any area. . . . From economic and social issues to national security, there is no orderly process, everything is pulled from a hat. . . . We are a country that runs itself instead of being run."[50]

Yossi Beilin, the Cabinet Secretary from 1984 to 1986, "was astounded by the lack of any preparation for Cabinet meetings. The preparations are more lacking than anyone from the outside could imagine. The ministers are not presented with sufficient information enabling their vote to take into account all the ramifications of these decisions." In an essay on the organization of the Israeli national security system, Benyamin Amidror, one of the most perceptive Israeli military analysts, stated that "Israel is the only advanced nation in the world which does not have a distinctive system organized and defined as a national security establishment."[51]

Several brief examples demonstrate the truth of these statements. In the early 1950s, Israeli military intelligence, which controlled much of the flow of information to the government, rejected a number of apparent peace "feelers" from Egypt. This rejection sprang from the pessimism of habitual worst-case analysis and from the IDF's desire to monopolize all major na-

[50] Ben-Meir, *National Security Decision Making: The Israeli Case*, p. 67, 69.
[51] Ibid., p. 70.

tional security decisions,[52] for an emphasis on diplomacy and peace would by definition have relegated the IDF and its commanders to a secondary role. The Lavon Affair is a classic example of the damage inflicted by a national security decision-making process gone awry. In 1954, Israeli intelligence became alarmed at the prospect of an Anglo-Egyptian agreement concerning British withdrawal from the Suez Canal area. Such an agreement would have given Egypt direct control of all shipping traffic in the Suez Canal as well as control over half a dozen British airfields in the Canal Zone. After completion of the negotiations, Israeli military intelligence wrongly concluded that such an agreement would boost Egypt's military strength to an unacceptable level. As a result, the Minister of Defense, Lavon, in coordination with Gibli, the head of Israeli intelligence, developed a cloak-and-dagger plan that called for Israeli agents in cooperation with a number of Egyptian Jews to blow up British and American installations. This operation was intended to sabotage Anglo-Egyptian negotiations by casting suspicion on the Egyptians and demonstrating that their government was incapable of controlling internal security let alone the Suez Canal region. However, the Egyptians caught the agents red-handed, and the scandal clearly implicated Israel in the whole affair.

A broader analysis not based exclusively on military considerations would have made it evident from the start that (a) preventing the British and Egyptians from reaching an agreement would be *impossible;* (b) even if an agreement were reached, it would not radically alter the balance of power; and (c) the inordinately high risks of the operation far exceeded any possible gains. This operation brought an abrupt end to the early attempts of Egypt's President Nasser and Israel's Prime Minister Sharett to establish a dialogue, and jeopardized Israeli-British-American relations. Not for the last time, the Israeli government and prime minister were excluded from the planning of the operation, and first learned of it as a fait accompli. Only the fact that the civilian defense minister was deeply involved in the affair prevented it from being a purely military takeover of policy. In any event, the whole operation – which went to the very core of Israeli national security and foreign policy – was decided upon and orchestrated by a small circle of Israeli military leaders. This irrational project, which was at worst naive and at best romantic, could not have taken place if a system incorporating broader groups of experts with wider perspectives had existed.[53]

Victory in 1967 falsely validated Israel's confused and improvised process: the Israelis presented their haphazard approach to decision-making as a

---

52 For some consequences of the military tendency to emphasize worst-case analysis, see Raymond Cohen, "Israeli Intelligence Before the 1956 Sinai Campaign," *Intelligence and National Security* (January 1988), pp. 100–40.

53 Uri Bar Joseph, "Out of Control: Intelligence Intervention on Politics in the U.S.A., Britain, and Israel," 2 Vols., Ph.D. diss., Stanford University, 1990, pp. 229–408. See also Shabtai Teveth, *Onat Ha'Gez: Kitat Yorim Be' Beit Giz* [Shearing Time: Firing Squad At Beth-Jiz] (Tel Aviv, 1992).

triumph of rationality and careful deliberation that had exhausted all peaceful means of resolving the crisis before the resort to war.[54] Israel's outstanding military planning, a highly efficient and well-trained military machine, and surprise had secured a quick and decisive victory, and the world assumed that comparable excellence in the strategic decision-making process underlay it all. It did not. Because it is all the more difficult to criticize one's own performance in the aftermath of a decisive victory, the flaws in the Israeli decision-making process went uncorrected.

The outcome of the 1967 war provides a good example of poor long-range planning. Defense minister Moshe Dayan made a major contribution to the war with his last-minute decision to abandon a planned limited attack in favor of an all-out preemptive attack on the Egyptians. Dayan also participated in a deception plan that concealed Israel's intention to go to war, and this achievement of strategic surprise was critical to ultimate success. (Dayan publicly stated that it was too late for Israel to go to war because the element of surprise had been lost. As part of the ruse, Israeli soldiers were "sent on leave" the day before their planned attack.) And although Dayan instructed IDF field commanders to stop short of the east bank of the Suez Canal before their attack on the Egyptian front, Israeli troops proceeded all the way to the canal. The government then accepted this military fait accompli without examining its strategic or operational implications. The IDF remained on the banks of the Suez Canal.

Israel's presence at the canal was a strategic thorn in Egypt's side that led in turn to the war of attrition,[55] in which the IDF suffered heavy casualties. Only in retrospect was it realized that this was one of the first serious strategic setbacks in Israeli history. Inadequate strategic planning and the predominance of a narrow military view had again taken their toll. The decision to allow Israeli bombers to "buzz" Cairo and other cities as a warning to Egypt rapidly expanded into a more extensive deep-penetration bombing operation. In a process that policymakers had never thought through, ad hoc tactical and operational decisions replaced long-range strategy. The Israeli Cabinet and the Ministerial Defense Committee (MDC) did not know the implications of the decisions, nor the intentions of IDF planners.[56] The minister of defense and the IDF obtained approval for their plans through a selective disclosure of information that played down the risks involved. Instead of ending the war of attrition, the stepped-up bombing campaign re-

54 Janice Gross Stein and Raymond Tanter, *Rational Decision-Making: Israeli Security Choices, 1967* (Columbus, OH, 1980). See also Michael Brecher, *The Foreign Policy System of Israel* (New Haven, 1972), Chapters 15, 16; and Shimshoni, *Israeli Democracy: The Middle of the Journey.*

55 Yaacov Bar-Simon-Tov, *The Israeli-Egyptian War of Attrition, 1969–1970* (New York, 1980); also Jonathan Shimshoni, *Israel and Conventional Deterrence: Border Warfare from 1953 to 1970* (Ithaca, NY, 1988), pp. 123–212; and Dan Schuftan, *Hatasha* [Attrition: Egypt's post-war political strategy, 1967–1970] (Tel Aviv, 1989).

56 Ben Meir, *National Security Decision Making*, p. 66.

sulted in increased Soviet involvement, and eventually led to direct confrontation with Soviet military advisers. The Israelis strengthened the Soviet Union's commitment to defend Egypt by threatening Soviet prestige, and they hardened Egypt's determination to fight Israel in the future. Israel's ill-considered actions also had serious repercussions at home – namely, greater dependence on the United States and the first wavering of public support for the government's military decisions.

Although the IDF's high command provided partially misleading information, the government was remiss in not insisting on a critical examination of the entire spectrum of the problems and risks involved. By failing to explore other options, the government de facto relinquished its responsibility to the IDF, the defense minister, and the ambassador in Washington (Rabin).[57] The IDF's approach was also short-sighted: a search for "quick fixes" that appeared cheap and promised to save lives. Apparently, the possession of new weaponry such as the F-4 Phantom fighter-bomber led to this approach; weapons determined strategy, not the other way around.

Despite the failure of strategic bombing and the war of attrition, the government did not reexamine its decision-making process. Furthermore, there was no independent staff or advisory body to examine the IDF's influence on the government and question its one-sided approach to the formation of strategy. Even the shock of 1973 was not traumatic enough to bring effective reform.

The war in Lebanon is the best example of how personal ambitions can subvert a faulty national security decision-making process.[58] When the focus of PLO operations shifted from Jordan to Lebanon, Israel could not resist the temptation to become entangled in Lebanon's civil war. In the mid-1970s, the Israeli government gradually increased its support of the Christian factions, a commitment that widened in scope when Ariel Sharon became Israel's minister of defense. Sharon planned to use the war in Lebanon to solve Israel's problems with the PLO once and for all.

A system in which small unofficial circles deal with all matters, including national security affairs, without effective checks and balances can magnify the influence of individual leaders far out of proportion and in contradiction to democratic processes. This effect is even more pronounced if the personalities of the participants reinforce rather than restrain each other.[59] In proposing to invade Lebanon, Israeli leaders believed that military power and

[57] See Yitzhak Rabin with Dov Goldstein, *Pinkas Sherut* [An Autobiography], 2 vols., (Tel Aviv, 1979), 1: 213–315. An abbreviated version published in the United States is entitled *The Rabin Memoirs* (Boston, 1979); see also Dan Margalit, *Sheder Min Ha'Bayit Ha'Lavan* [A message from the White House] (Tel Aviv, 1971).

[58] See Ze'ev Schiff and Ehud Ya'ari, *Israel's War in Lebanon* (New York, 1984); also Arye Naor, "The Israeli Cabinet in the Lebanon War (June 5–9, 1982)," *Jerusalem Quarterly*, 39 (1986), pp. 3–16.

[59] Alouph Hareven, "Disturbed Hierarchies: Israeli Intelligence in 1954 and 1973," *Jerusalem Quarterly*, 9 (1978), pp. 3–19.

swift action could solve any problem; they were confident of Israel's military superiority, and not in the habit of making rational, long-range calculations. Ostensibly, Sharon proposed to invade Lebanon for the purpose of establishing a 40 kilometer security zone along Israel's northern border, although actually he and Chief of Staff Raful had prepared a far more ambitious plan in cooperation with the Christians in Beirut. Unbeknownst to the government, their scheme had the following objectives: attack as far as Beirut, eliminate the PLO as a force in Lebanese affairs, attack the Syrian army if possible, and eventually sign a peace treaty with a Lebanese Christian government. Sharon hoped that once the PLO was out of Lebanon, the Palestinians would seek to fulfill their political ambitions in Jordan.

He managed to get approval in stages by first revealing only fragments of his plan, then later presenting the government with a series of faits accomplis in the field.[60] This approach enabled him to launch an all-out offensive war although the Israeli Cabinet thought it had approved a limited operation that would last from twenty-four to forty-eight hours and not involve Syria.[61] The scope of the supposedly limited operation increased from the radius of a 40 kilometer raid, all the way to Beirut, then on to a large-scale war with the Syrian army. Prime Minister Begin was not privy to the full extent of Sharon's intentions.[62] But by neglecting to scrutinize Sharon's plans, the government forfeited its responsibility and became an accomplice, especially since neither Begin nor the government had the courage to halt the operation.

Rational analysis would have shown that the IDF could not control Lebanon, and that such a war could only drag on at a high cost in life and economic resources. There were no attempts to estimate realistically the price of such a war to the Israeli economy, which is now conservatively thought to have lost no less than 5 billion dollars because of the invasion.[63] The idea of signing a peace agreement with a Christian Lebanese government was at best wishful thinking; the Christian government was not in control and was generally unreliable. Finally, Sharon's plan risked touching off a full-scale war with Syria, antagonizing the United States, alienating world public opinion, and dissolving the Israeli public's traditional consensus on matters of national security. Only Israeli intelligence considered these eventualities, and its advice went unheeded.[64]

As Rabin argued, Israel had never before worked on the assumption that through a decisive victory it could impose its own conditions for peace on the enemy – let alone arrive at a comprehensive political solution to the Arab-

60 Schiff and Ya'ari, *Israel's War in Lebanon*, p. 302.
61 Naor, "The Israeli Cabinet."
62 Schiff and Ya'ari, *Israel's War in Lebanon*, pp. 58–9.
63 Haim Barkai, "Reflections on the Economic Cost of the Lebanon War," *Jerusalem Quarterly*, 37 (1986), pp. 95–106.
64 Shlomo Gazit, "Intelligence Estimates and the Decision Maker," in Handel, ed., *Leaders and Intelligence* (London, 1989), pp. 261–88; Appendix, pp. 282–87.

Table 17.3. *Number of Israelis killed in road accidents and terror attacks,*
1973–1987

Year	Road accidents	Terror attacks
1973	683	—
1974	716	62
1975	648	33
1976	602	3
1977	636	5
1978	619	56
1979	566	21
1980	434	9
1981	436	11
1982	385	3
1983	436	9
1984	399	6
1985	387	13
1986	415	8
1987	493	—
Total	7,855	239

Israeli conflict.[65] Yet this was Sharon's impossible objective. In actuality, the PLO in Lebanon had never been more than a minor irritant: on the average, fewer than ten Israeli citizens were killed a year in attacks from Lebanese territory, while by the end of the war in Lebanon about 800 Israeli soldiers had lost their lives (Table 17.3).

The first entirely offensive war initiated by Israel ended in military, economic, and political disaster. As two of Israel's preeminent strategic observers have commented: "Born of the ambition of one willful, reckless man, Israel's 1982 invasion of Lebanon was anchored in delusion, propelled by deceit, and bound to end in calamity. . . . There is no consolation for this costly, senseless war. The best one can do now is to learn its lessons well."[66] But this devastating experience had no salutary effect. No committee thoroughly investigated the decision-making process that led to the war, and the Israeli Cabinet continued to formulate its policies in the same unsystematic fashion.

[65] Yitzhak Rabin, "Ashlayot Mediniot u'Mechiran," [Political Illusions and Their Price] in *The Lebanon War: Between Protest and Compliance* (Tel Aviv, 1983), pp. 12–23, 13.
[66] Schiff and Ya'ari, *Israel's War in Lebanon*, p. 301. For Sharon's version, see Ariel Sharon with David Chanoff, *Warrior: An Autobiography* (New York, 1989).

Unfortunately, Israeli democracy has given rise to a tangle of fractious small parties that cannot agree even among themselves. The resulting coalition governments usually require the support of the smaller religious political parties that have, especially in recent years, exercised power far out of proportion to their size. A national security council might recommend long-range strategic policies such as proposals to recognize and/or negotiate with the PLO, evacuate the occupied territories, and impose economic austerity – proposals that some of the parties or the population (and hence any government) would find unacceptable. This also explains why the Israeli government has consistently avoided painful long-range decisions and focuses on day-to-day decisions. Such an approach forecloses long-term options and ineluctably leads to the loss of control and to paralysis. By default, it has left longer-range initiatives in the hands of Israel's enemies.

CIVIL-MILITARY RELATIONS, DIPLOMACY, AND NATIONAL SECURITY

Despite the powerful influence of the IDF on every facet of Israeli life, Israel has remained a solidly Western-style democracy. Democracy is deeply rooted in Jewish tradition, and is reflected in Israel's electoral system, freedom of speech, and general political culture. The Israeli army is a citizen army, and the military elite is not a distinct class seeking to perpetuate its own interests. Rather, it is a heterogeneous group that conforms to the values of Israeli society as a whole. The professional army includes a balanced cross-section of the community, while senior officers return to civilian life relatively young. Unlike other armies, the IDF has never developed right-wing views nor has it wasted much time on pomp and circumstance.

Despite its influence on national security decisions, on intelligence, and the political system, the IDF has remained aloof from domestic politics. Yoram Peri describes the unique state of civil-military relations in Israel as a "'military democracy' . . . in which the army operates, firstly, as a major channel of mobility to the power elite and secondly, as partner of the politicians. . . . [Although] the civil establishment bears the formal constitutional responsibility . . . it is widely felt that the army may legitimately assume an important role within the political system."[67] Such participation is not unexpected in a

---

67 All quotations are from Yoram Peri, *Between Battles and Ballots: The Israel Military in Politics* (Cambridge, 1983), pp. 279, 280. See also Yoram Peri, "Defusei Ha'Zika Shel Zahal L'Ma'arechet Ha'Politit be Yisrael," [The relationship pattern of the IDF to the Israeli political system] in *Milchemet Breira* [War by choice] (Tel Aviv, 1985), pp. 31–56; Moshe Lissak, ed., *Israeli Society and Its Defense Establishment*, Special Issue, *Journal of Strategic Studies*, 6 (September 1983); Dan Horowitz, "The Israeli Defense Forces: A Civilianized Military in a Partially Militarized Society," in R. Kolkowitz and A. Korbonski, eds., *Soldiers, Peasants and Bureaucrats* (London, 1982), pp. 77–106; Dan Zamir, "Generals in Politics," *Jerusalem Quarterly*, 20 (1981), pp. 17–36; Dan Horowitz and Moshe Lissak, "Democracy and National Security in a Protracted Conflict," *Jerusalem Quarterly*, 51 (1989), pp. 3–40.

society where concern for national security dominates, but it is surprising that Israel has remained a viable democracy in which the military has rarely interfered in the domestic political arena.

Instead, it is Israel's civilian leaders who have on occasion deviated from democratic procedures. The Lavon Affair, although initiated by IDF intelligence, reached its full magnitude through the actions of Defense Minister Lavon. (In fact, an important part of the aftermath of the Lavon Affair and Ben Gurion's involvement was to protect the IDF's reputation as an institution that was above politics.) Likewise, Sharon was a civilian at the time that he led a government unaware of the precise nature of his plans into the debacle in Lebanon. The only instance in which the IDF sought to force the government's hand was on the eve of the Six Day War in 1967, when the senior leaders of the IDF pressured Prime Minister Eshkol to launch the war. This was, however, an extreme situation in which the pressures applied by the military accurately reflected the general public mood.

But in the area of foreign policy, the military view has exercised extensive influence. Israel's leaders too often viewed diplomacy as an instrument to support the military, rather than the reverse. The struggle to obtain weapons dominated foreign policy until 1969–70, when Israel finally established a stable procurement relationship with the United States. The traumatic experience of being unable to purchase weapons essential for defense in the 1950s left an enduring mark on the Israeli psyche. The need to buy weapons prompted Israel to approach France, a move that eventually resulted in the joint decision of Israel, England, and France to launch the Sinai-Suez Campaign. The Israeli Defense Ministry, not the Foreign Office, almost completely managed the diplomacy behind the 1956 war.

Israel has always been diplomatically isolated.[68] It has never signed a formal military treaty with any power and has almost always stood alone in the United Nations. Many countries have been hesitant to establish formal diplomatic relations with Israel for fear of Arab economic and political sanctions, and until recently, Arab states have refused to negotiate with it. Consequently, most high-level Israeli officials gave up on diplomacy, which became "militarized" and was almost completely discounted as an instrument of national security. Negotiations and mediation appeared to weaken Israel's position vis-à-vis the Arabs.

For diplomacy to have a chance, the Arabs will have to drop their notion of diplomacy as a means of coercion and see it also as a road to genuine compromise. Israel will view diplomacy as only another weapon in the Arab arsenal until nations outside the region, particularly European ones, adopt a more objective view of the situation in the Middle East. Moreover, until the IDF recognizes that the Israeli foreign ministry is more than a weapons-

---

[68] The most comprehensive studies of Israeli foreign policy are still Michael Brecher's *The Foreign Policy System of Israel* (New Haven, 1972); and *Decisions in Israeli Foreign Policy* (New Haven, 1975).

purchasing agency or a debating society, the Israeli foreign ministry will be unable to emphasize the diplomatic dimension of national security.

THE "SEVENTH WAR": LOW-INTENSITY CONFLICT AND COUNTERTERROR OPERATIONS

Because this is not the proper context for a detailed examination of the five wars (or six if we include the war of attrition from 1968 to 1970) in which Israel has been involved over the last forty years, the place of each war in Israel's history has instead been summarized in Table 17.4 according to the following criteria: the strategic initiative leading to each war; Israel's casualties; its allies or the support received; its operational strategy; the immediate objectives to be achieved; unintended longer-range consequences; the level of military technology employed; the compatibility of technology and military doctrine; and finally, the major military strengths and weaknesses revealed. This section examines Israel's "seventh" war – that is, the protracted ongoing war against terrorism – according to the same criteria.

Since the Six Day War in 1967, Israel has invested much time and effort in the development of a counterterror and antiguerrilla strategy. Consistent with the IDF's normal practice in the planning and preparation for conventional warfare, this strategy has been heavily offensive and purely military on all levels. It removed terrorist attacks from Israeli territory and put the PLO, other Palestinian terrorist organizations, and Arab governments generally on the defensive. As a result, terrorist attacks on Israelis moved to Europe and elsewhere while incidents on Israeli territory remained tolerably low. Israel's borders have been effectively blocked, although not hermetically sealed. Even before the 1973 war, Israel had "convinced" neighboring Arab states, most notably Syria and Jordan, not to allow their countries to become bases for direct operations against Israel. Since 1973, casualties have gradually dropped from an average of a few dozen to between ten and twenty annually (Table 17.3). Over the years, Israel convinced other nations that international cooperation and the adoption of an aggressive, uncompromising strategy are the most effective means of combating terrorism. But it has not successfully mobilized much political support within international organizations and has failed to isolate and delegitimatize organizations and states that support terrorism.

The IDF's focus on low-intensity conflict and counterterror operations has caused a corresponding reduction in the time and resources available for the improvement of its conventional infrastructure. The political and operational relationships between conventional and low-intensity conflicts are frequently misunderstood. Pursuit of low-intensity, counterguerrilla, and counterterror operations often led to unintended escalations and wars while diverting attention from more serious threats and incurring costs far exceeding any potential benefits. Despite Israel's military success in countering low-level violence, politicians have remained extremely sensitive to terrorist activities and have often overreacted to incidents that they could either have ignored or dealt with routinely. Such hypersensitivity has worked to the advantage of Arab terrorists, allowing them to accomplish their political goals despite their mediocre operational achievements.

From the perspective of military strategy – imposing their preferred terms of war or relative military advantages on the enemy – the Israelis have been very successful in conventional war, guerrilla warfare, and even counterterrorism. This forced Israel's Arab opponents to search for a new strategy after each setback until, after the PLO's failure in Lebanon, the Palestinians in the occupied territories discovered the advantages of political war and passive resistance. This development surprised the Israelis, who were ill-prepared to respond to such an approach. Although the Israelis have been partially successful in limiting the impact of the *intifada* since it began in 1987, they have realized that this problem has no exclusively military solution. The only effective answer to the *intifada* is political – that is, direct negotiations with the Palestinians on the occupied territories. This process began in the early 1990s and is continuing today. Early in 1993, Prime Minister Rabin's new Labor government took the previously inconceivable step of approving direct meetings between Israelis and PLO representatives; a PLO-Israeli agreement on Palestinian self-rule in Gaza and Jericho was the result. As a strategy, the *intifada* is likely to succeed if it remains on the level of political resistance combined with direct negotiations. But if the *intifada* turns into an Algerian-style guerrilla war controlled by radical Islamic fundamentalists, it will prevent any Israeli-Palestinian rapprochement. Ironically, the *intifada* has, for the first time, created an incentive for both the PLO and Israel to come to terms. The PLO has been weakened by internal tensions over leadership and by the Gulf states' withdrawal of financial support in retaliation for PLO backing of Iraq in the Gulf war. On the Israeli side, the prospect of the *intifada* becoming an extremely violent, costly, and militarily unresolvable conflict has provided a strong motivation to negotiate. The danger for both sides is that delay favors the radical Islamic and Jewish groups whose objective is to prevent any peaceful settlement. Islamic fundamentalism, which after all poses the greatest threat to Arab leaders, also creates a common interest for countries such as Egypt, Syria, Jordan, and Saudi Arabia in supporting a Palestinian-Israeli solution.

ISRAELI STRATEGY: FROM ABSOLUTE SECURITY TO RISKS FOR PEACE

On the highest plane, the purpose of strategy is to enhance the *long-range* survival and power of a nation by employing all diplomatic, economic, and

Table 17.4. *A summary: Israeli strategy in six wars*

	War of Independence 1947–1948	Sinai Campaign 1956	Six-Day War 1967	War of Attrition 1968–1970	Yom Kippur War 1973	War of Lebanon 1982–June 85
Strategic initiative	Arab states and Palestinians	Israel (France and UK)	Egypt	Egypt and Syria	Egypt and Syria	Israel
Casualties (killed)	6,074	177	803	721 (594 soldiers)	2,569	Over 657
Allies and/or outside support	USSR, Czechoslovakia, U.S. Jewish community	France (and UK)	Tacit U.S. support	U.S.	U.S.	Initially U.S.
Israeli operational strategy	Defensive, later offensive	Offensive	Offensive	Primarily offensive but also defensive (Bar-Lev Lin)	Defensive, later offensive	Offensive
Immediate strategic objectives	Survival, territorial expansion and integrity	• Preemptive move against increased Egyptian strength (imbalance in arms procurement) • Remove Nasser from power, establish/acquire buffer zone in Sinai	Survival, removal of threat. No other general strategic objectives. Dayan and IDF decide to switch from limited operational to all-out operational objectives	Maintenance of status quo, dictate battle on Israeli terms (maintain operational initiative, force opponent to stop fighting)	Survival, maintenance of status quo, improve bargaining position	1. Eliminate PLO presence in Lebanon 2. Expel Syria from Lebanon 3. Peace with Lebanon 4. Create conditions for favorable political settlement in West Bank

	War of Independence 1947–1948	Sinai Campaign 1956	Six-Day War 1967	War of Attrition 1968–1970	Yom Kippur War 1973	War of Lebanon 1982–June 85
Objectives not achieved	Peace and recognition by Arab states	None of the immediate objectives achieved	Recognition, negotiations or peace	Deterrence, reduced casualities	Maintenance of status quo, reduced cost of war, deterrence	Most immediate objectives not achieved with exception of expelling PLO leadership and Forces from Lebanon
Unintended results achieved (both negative and positive)	Palestinian refugee problem	Created self-confidence, image of deterrence projected until mid 1960s	• Strategic depth and defendable borders • Unfavorable demographic changes	• Illusion of success and of effective deterrence • Diversion of Egyptian military assets to air defense • Direct Soviet involvement • Increased dependence on U.S.	• Loss of self-confidence • Collapse of image of invincibility • In long run, peace with Egypt • Considerable increase in defense burden and dependence on U.S.	• Prolonged war, heavy casualties, increased economic problems, destruction of domestic consensus regarding security, lower self-confidence. • Tarnished image in World, friction with U.S. • Caused Syrians to double size of their army. May have convinced PLO that diplomatic nonmilitary struggle is only effective strategy and led to "recognition" of Israel.

continued

Table 17.4. (*continued*)

	War of Independence 1947–1948	Sinai Campaign 1956	Six-Day War 1967	War of Attrition 1968–1970	Yom Kippur War 1973	War of Lebanon 1982–June 85
Overall	Passive/active short range, opportunistic, greater use of diplomacy	Active opportunistic, short range, primarily military (diplomacy with French and British)	Reactive, short range little political direction	Short range, military capabilities dictate operations, narrow military view	Reactive, less realistic, almost exclusively military (with exception of policy toward U.S.)	Active, unrealistic, irrational, presumably long range but actually short range. Primarily military and power considerations pseudopolitical, opportunistic
Military technology	Obsolete mostly pre-World War II	World War II (except in air)	Modified second world war (except in air)	Increasingly modern technology (almost state-of-the-art)	Most modern weapons technology in particular in air and sea	State-of-the-art, most advanced technology, available.
Matching of technology and military doctrine	Overall good	Infantry oriented role of tanks, fire power, etc. Not yet fully recognized	Perfect, ideal match	Imperfect, lessons of 1967 war overlearned. Understanding of defensive war overall limited.	Poor, mismatch	Excellent in air, good otherwise

	War of Independence 1947–1948	Sinai Campaign 1956	Six-Day War 1967	War of Attrition 1968–1970	Yom Kippur War 1973	War of Lebanon 1982–June 85
Major sources of military strength	Motivation, creative planning, indirect approach, night fighting, ends and means carefully matched, improvisation, learning of lessons good	Excellent use of time motivation, speed, good planning, night fighting, ends and means carefully matched, learning of lessons very good	Excellent planning, excellent use of time, speed, good matching of ends and means, motivation, night fighting. Ideal size formations, good C³	Motivation, good in raids, small commando operations	Motivation, excellent in air and sea warfare, fast and good in learning technological lessons, adaptation	Excellent in air good use of artillery, good understanding of technology
Major weaknesses	Little understanding of military technology, poor in operating larger formations	Poor understanding of modern weapons technology	Over-learning of lessons, over-confidence, too much reliance on improvisation	Poor matching of ends and means, "strategy" is too reactive (not so operations), misunderstanding of opponent, poor learning of lessons	Too much improvisation, poor C³, overall mediocre middle and higher level leadership, confused military doctrine, poor understanding of defensive warfare, no night fighting, poor staff work, poor in operating large size formations, poor use of time	Poor matching of ends and means, no night operations, poor use of time, low motivation, very low tolerance for taking casualties, poor leadership on higher and middle levels, relatively weak in fighting in built up areas, poor C³ and operating large formations, poor staff work.

military means at its disposal. Yet with the exception of the Sinai Campaign and the war in Lebanon, Israeli strategy has simply reacted to opponents' initiatives. As a result, Israel has never really developed a coherent long-term strategy, as opposed to a military-operational doctrine. The combination of its geographical vulnerability, fear of annihilation, political isolation, and domestic political system gave priority to the immediate problem of national survival. Historically, top Israeli decision-makers have acted according to operational imperatives without a clear conception of long-range objectives and without assessing the ultimate consequences of operational success. Instead of strategy governing the use of force, the logic of military operations often determined that of strategy. The domination of military considerations and the fact that the Israeli military determined national security policy and strategy, restricted the scope of Israeli strategy and permitted short-range operational pressures to take precedence over key long-range considerations. This phenomenon is referred to by Y. Harkabi as the "tacticization of strategy."[69]

Although Israeli casualties have been proportionately high by American standards, they have been much lower than those of the Soviet Union or Finland in World War II or North Vietnam during the Vietnam War. In fact, if averaged over the years since 1948, the rate of casualties attributable to military action has only slightly exceeded that of casualties resulting from automobile accidents. Further, the rate of casualties per day was not much higher under the worst circumstances in 1973 than it was in 1967. The Israeli hypersensitivity to casualties must thus be considered from the standpoint of Jewish history in general (of avoiding conflict, war, and casualties whenever possible). Also, since no end to the Arab-Israeli conflict is in sight, Israelis feel that casualties and other costs should be minimized as part of the general effort to conserve energy and resources for the future. Viewed in these terms and considering the fact that each war has left Israel more dependent on outside support, every war *avoided* must be considered a victory. Consequently, the war in Lebanon was an enormous strategic blunder – an unnecessary self-inflicted disaster.

Lack of strategic depth, the economic difficulties created by the mobilization of reserve forces, and external political pressure to bring any war to a quick end has led Israeli strategists to choose a purely offensive doctrine on all levels. The IDF's two most successful wars, in 1956 and 1967, fall into this category. Wars initiated by the Arabs – 1947–1949, the war of attrition, and 1973 – at least initially imposed a defensive strategy on Israel, which increased both costs and casualties. The war in Lebanon is the exception, for

---

69 For a brilliant analysis of this phenomenon and of Israel's current strategic predicament as a reflection of trends in its domestic politics since 1973, see Y. Harkabi, *Ha'chra'ot Goraliot* [Fateful decisions] (Tel Aviv, 1986). For the abbreviated and revised American edition, see *Israel's Fateful Hour*, trans. Lenn Schram (New York, 1988).

although the Israelis employed an offensive doctrine on all levels, they could not bring this war to a quick or decisive conclusion.

Although Israel did not initiate the War of Independence and was willing to accept the United Nations partition decision, the Arab declaration of war gave the Israeli government the opportunity to expand both its territory and its chances for survival. Prime Minister Ben Gurion's opportunistic decision to launch the 1956 war failed to accomplish any of its immediate objectives: Israel acquired no territory, created no buffer zone in the Sinai, did not destabilize Nasser's regime, and did not open the Suez Canal to Israeli shipping. Moreover, Israel probably missed an opportunity for a rapprochement with Egypt. The Sinai Campaign deepened Egyptian animosity and the Arab perception that Israel was a "foreign body" implanted in the Middle East in order to work with the colonial powers. The opportunity to collaborate with the French, however, was too tempting to resist. For the first time, Israel received an adequate supply of weapons as well as French air and naval cover. Israel never considered remaining neutral, and the enhancement of Israeli self-confidence and the establishment of Israel's image of power were unintended but useful achievements.

Surprised by the crisis that preceded the Six Day War in 1967, the Israeli government decided to launch a preemptive attack and improvised overall strategic plans at the last minute. A planned limited offensive against the Gaza Strip and northern Sinai changed into an attack intended to destroy the Egyptian army and air force and to occupy the entire Sinai. The improvised offensive against Jordan began *only* after Jordan attacked first, while the decisions concerning the Golan Heights operation came only after much hesitation and under strong pressure from the settlers in the area.

The government in effect allowed the IDF to determine the immediate objectives of the war, and lower-level field commanders made many critical decisions. As we have seen, the decision of the latter not to halt until reaching the banks of the Suez Canal had serious consequences. In military terms, Israel's victory in the Six Day War was an event of the greatest strategic moment, yet Israel did not translate this military triumph into comparable political success. There were no serious attempts to begin a dialogue with the vanquished or to make any moderate Bismarckian or Churchillian peace offers. The desire to secure greater strategic depth, defensible borders, and the unification of Jerusalem superseded all else. The trauma of the prewar crisis and Arab threats of genocide conditioned Israeli decision-makers to seek absolute security[70] before political dialogue. Yet immediately after the 1967 war, Dayan did make the famous and telling statement, "We are waiting for a telephone call." Under the circumstances and with human nature being what it is, Israel's hubris and fear on the one hand and Arab humilia-

---

[70] Wald refers to Israel's quest for absolute security as obsessive in *The Decline of Israel's Military and Political Power*, p. 18.

tion on the other might have rendered even the most magnanimous and openminded diplomacy irrelevant.

The fruits of this victory inevitably added to the burden on Israeli national security. The Arabs vowed to avenge their loss and restore their dignity by force, while Israel embraced a false sense of security and strength. The euphoria of victory led most Israelis to overlook the drastic demographic problems that came with their military success. Moreover, Israel's world image had changed from that of an underdog to that of a powerful, aggressive state, and Palestinian national aspirations received increased support. Unlike the halcyon days following the Sinai Campaign in 1956, Israel has not known a day of peace since the 1967 victory and must divert increasingly scarce resources to its defense. Clearly, it is dangerous to evaluate a strategic victory (or defeat) in *military terms alone*. Military victories have ensured Israel's survival and "bought time," but they have not produced any lasting political solutions. As Clausewitz observed, the results in war are never final unless consolidated by political agreements. Despite its decisive and overwhelming *military* victory in 1967, Israel failed to "compel the enemy to do its will."[71]

The war of attrition of 1969–70 initiated by Israel's neighbors actually consisted of two distinct military conflicts: one on the eastern front against the PLO and the Jordanian and Iraqi armies, and another more intensive one against the Egyptian army along the Suez Canal. As if nothing had changed since 1948, Israel tried to transfer the war to the opponent's territory. While this strategy worked on the eastern front, it caused a prolonged and escalating campaign of attrition in the war against Egypt. By overemphasizing the "military lessons" of the Six Day War, the Israelis had built an imbalanced force that relied too heavily on tanks and air power and too little on artillery and combined operations. The availability of certain military capabilities largely determined Israel's strategy in the war of attrition. Israel made the decision to commence a "strategic bombing" campaign against the Egyptian hinterland when it acquired long-range F-4 Phantom aircraft. The "yield no inch" policy that had inspired the establishment of the Bar Lev Line meant forsaking the possibility of mobile defense and maneuver; and while a defensive doctrine across the board was feasible on the conventional level, Israel nevertheless by force of habit continued to rely exclusively on an offensive doctrine on all levels. Furthermore, Israel refused to negotiate a partial withdrawal from the Suez Canal, a step that could have opened the Canal and perhaps allowed Egypt to disengage from the conflict. Instead, operational military considerations took precedence over longer-range political objectives, which eventually brought direct Soviet involvement and increased Israeli economic and military dependence on the United States.

Even after Israel had acquired a modicum of territorial depth, it did not

---

[71] Both references are to Carl von Clausewitz, *On War*, ed. and trans., Michael Howard and Peter Paret (Princeton, 1976), Book 1, Chapter 1.

switch from an all-out offensive military doctrine to a partly or fully defensive one. Habit prevailed even though political constraints and increased dependence on the United States discouraged the choice of a preemptive strategy. At the same time, changes in military technology temporarily shifted the advantage from the offense (air power and tanks) to the defense (anti-aircraft and anti-tank missiles). For the first time, Israeli strategists misread the trends in weapons development and failed to match their doctrine to the state of technology in the region. Although Israel might have benefited from a totally or partly defensive doctrine in 1973, it failed to plan, train, and develop an army for this purpose.[72] This lack of preparedness and mismatch between political conditions, technology, and military doctrine combined to produce initially disastrous results.

The "moment of truth" occurred on 6 October 1973 when the Israelis discovered that by increasing their dependence on U.S. military and economic support, they had also mortgaged their strategic freedom of choice. Until 1973, Israeli decision-makers had tacitly assumed that they were still free, as in 1967, to decide when and under what circumstances to preempt an attack; this option was, after all, a central element of their political-military doctrine. Israel took American aid for granted, as something they deserved for services rendered; they did not consider it as conditional aid that would require some accommodation to U.S. interests. Thus, Israel's national policy strayed from the reality and the self-sufficiency required by its quest for absolute security. Moreover, Israel's victory in the Six Day War and the perception of success in the war of attrition had caused both the Israelis and Arabs to overestimate Israel's strength – a miscalculation that fostered Israeli overconfidence and led the Arabs to underestimate their own strength. As a result, Egypt and Syria failed to exploit fully the strategic and operational surprise they achieved in 1973. Israel initially suffered a serious setback from the unanticipated Arab attack but managed to regain its equilibrium and win a purely military victory. Its former self-confidence did not, however, emerge unscathed.

American pressure prevented Israel from securing a more decisive victory over Egypt in 1973 – a move that made subsequent Israeli-Egyptian negotiations easier. Similarly, American pressure led to the so-called disengagement agreements with Egypt and Syria, and eventually to the Egyptian-Israeli peace treaty. Although Prime Minister Begin and Dayan made considerable contributions to President Sadat's decision to visit Jerusalem, it was, in the end, Sadat's initiative. As an Arab leader, Sadat had "the ball in his court" by definition, since the same type of gesture by an Israeli leader was unlikely to succeed. Showing great strategic creativity, Sadat used diplomatic means to achieve the objectives he had set out to accomplish in the Yom Kippur War;

---

72 On this point, see Wald, *The Decline of Israeli Military and Political Power,* pp. 101ff; Levite, *Offense and Defense in Israeli Military Doctrine,* pp. 106ff; and Efraim Inbar, "Israeli Strategic Thinking After 1973," *Journal of Strategic Studies,* 6 (1983), pp. 36–60.

the Sinai was returned to Egypt's control.[73] Despite the fact that this was an Egyptian initiative, Israel benefited as well. Sadat's initiative resulted in one of Israel's most singular strategic accomplishments; it evacuated the Sinai without losing the strategic depth acquired in 1967. With American and United Nations troops stationed in the Sinai and elaborate warning systems in place, the peninsula was largely demilitarized, which shortened Israeli lines of communication and created a genuine buffer zone between Egypt and Israel. Had Egypt ever attempted to move against Israel through the Sinai, Israel would have received ample warning. In addition to these benefits, Israel and Egypt also received generous American military and economic aid of about 3 billion dollars a year. Above all, the peace agreement at least partially eliminated the most powerful Arab state as a potential enemy, freeing the IDF to concentrate on the eastern front.

Ironically, the Egyptian-American strategic initiative helped Israel more than any policy it had devised itself. Israel took certain risks by withdrawing from the Sinai, but these were reduced to a tolerable level. The passage of time without a direct confrontation with Egypt has further bolstered Israeli confidence, making similar agreements, perhaps with Syria or Jordan, possible. Unfortunately, while the empty desert of the Sinai is an excellent buffer zone, the same cannot be said of the Golan Heights and the West Bank, the evacuation of which would surely be a nightmare for Israeli strategists.

After concluding the peace treaty with Egypt, Israel could have reduced its military burden and concentrated on badly needed economic development and reconstruction. But Prime Minister Begin and especially Defense Minister Sharon had other plans. Until June 1977, when Begin's conservative Likud Party unexpectedly came to power, Labor governments had always run Israel. The Likud's victory reflected the backlash from the 1973 war and the Israeli public's disappointment with the Labor leadership, but it was above all the consequence of demographic changes in Israeli society.[74] Begin and his government adopted policies very different from those of the previous thirty years' Labor-led governments. In regard to national security, foreign policy, and the Arabs, Begin's government was nationalistic and "heroic," with an emphasis on "Jewish pride." It viewed Jewish power as an idealized value in its own right; it considered the use of power not as the *ultima ratio,* but as a sign of sovereignty and in fact as the *prima ratio* – the preferred instrument of policy. Begin did not base his policies on rational and systematic calculations, but more and more on sentiment and emotion.[75]

Under Begin, Israel's national security policy became even further removed from an objective evaluation of its situation. The shift to more ethnocentric policies made it much harder for Israeli leaders to understand their enemies.

---

[73]   See Handel, *The Diplomacy of Surprise* (Cambridge, MA, 1981), Chapters 5 and 6, pp. 241–354.
[74]   Harkabi, *Ha'chra'ot Goraliot* [Fateful decisions], pp. 197–275.
[75]   Ibid., pp. 110–96.

Even more so than in the past, military strength defined strategy, and leaders rejected the complexities of longer-range, broadly based assessments. Israel's invasion of Lebanon exposed the folly of this unrealistic evaluation of means and ends.

Paradoxically, both Israel's early military weakness and subsequent military strength gave rise to a strategy dominated by military considerations. Until 1967, Israeli weakness, geographical vulnerability, and diplomatic isolation meant that military considerations were given top priority. And while Israel could afford to pay more attention to nonmilitary considerations after 1967, patterns of strategic thought changed little. Military strength had become *the* solution. Had Israel felt militarily vulnerable after 1967 and 1973, the incentive to resort to force instead of politics would not have seemed as compelling. Although the Yom Kippur War shook its self-assurance, Israel had won the war militarily and therefore remained confident that military solutions could solve political and strategic problems. A less confident Israel would never have seriously considered the invasion of Lebanon to be the best solution to the Palestinian and Lebanese "problem."

The idea of a partly defensive doctrine or strategy was unthinkable to the generation conditioned by Israel's pre-1967 geography and the impressive military successes of 1956 and 1967, although the generation that emerged after the 1973 and 1982 wars may ultimately support it. In 1973, Israel achieved its greatest successes in purely defensive tank battles against Syria in the northern sector of the Golan Heights and against an Egyptian tank attack on 14 October 1973. Likewise, the Israeli Air Force discovered that attacking Egyptian and Syrian airfields was costly and ineffective. In contrast, the "defensive" interception of Egyptian and Syrian aircraft allowed Israeli fliers to hit both the aircraft and its less easily replaceable pilot. Israel implemented this same doctrine during the war in Lebanon.

Ignoring the advice of Israeli military intelligence, which warned against any large-scale military operations in Lebanon, Sharon charged ahead in 1982. The peace with Egypt had removed the threat on Israel's southwestern border, and neither Begin nor Sharon cared much about the political embarrassment the invasion would cause Egypt. Instead they saw it as a test of Egypt's intent to adhere to the peace agreement. Perhaps Sharon also assumed that the Egyptians would prefer that the PLO disappear from the Middle East political scene. The United States government seemed to support a quick military solution to the chaos in Lebanon, while Israel had an army considerably stronger than its possible opponents.

In the invasion of Lebanon, the IDF and Sharon adhered to a purely offensive doctrine despite geographic, demographic, and political circumstances that made a quick and decisive victory impossible. If such a victory was unlikely, then a defensive approach offered a better chance to reduce casualties and increase stamina. Sharon's plan was implausible. Neither the Lebanese nor the Syrians had successfully imposed order on Lebanon's chaotic situation. How, then, could 30,000 to 40,000 Israeli soldiers do so? How could the IDF occupy a major, densely populated Arab capital? How could such a war end quickly when the difficult mountainous terrain and dense urban population were ideal for defense? Why should the PLO leadership evacuate Beirut – and if they did, what would stop them from returning a year or two later? Why should the Syrians leave Lebanon without a prolonged fight? Would the United States support Israel in a protracted, bloody, and unnecessary war that would certainly involve heavy civilian casualties? No one asked these questions because all blithely assumed that Israeli "willpower" and military proficiency would ensure a quick and decisive victory. The invasion of Lebanon provided a classic example of the failure to understand that military power alone cannot win a war.

The war in Lebanon was the first open and direct Israeli intervention in the internal affairs of an Arab country, and the first clear Israeli setback. Before 1982, Israel lost on average about ten to twenty citizens a year to hostile guerrilla activities from Lebanon; the war cost the lives of almost 700 soldiers. Israel failed to expel the Syrians from Lebanon, did not achieve peace with Lebanon, alienated most of its allies, and missed an ideal opportunity to strengthen its economy. Instead, Israel became more dependent on the United States, tarnished its international image, lost the longstanding national consensus on national security, and demoralized its own military. It undermined the Egyptian-Israeli peace treaty by embarrassing the Egyptian government, caused the Syrians to double the size of their army, and exacerbated international hostility toward itself.

Israel's experience in the Gulf War (1991) indicates that its strategists had learned some of the lessons of the war in Lebanon and even the 1973 war. Despite Iraq's firing of over forty SCUD missiles at Israel, the "nationalistic" right-wing Likud government refrained from responding militarily.[76] This unprecedented decision was adhered to only under considerable U.S. pressure as well as promises of military aid. (The United States sent Patriot anti-aircraft/missile batteries to Israel as a symbolic gesture.) Israel's rational decision not to intervene demonstrated its understanding that every war *not* fought leads to greater strength. For the Israelis, Iraq's defeat by the U.S.-led coalition was another miracle in a year of miracles (the disintegration of the Soviet Union along with its military and economic support for Arab states, and the massive immigration of Jews from Russia). The Gulf War eliminated the strongest potential Arab threat to Israel, in a world that had up to that point seriously underestimated Iraqi strength and progress in its nuclear weapons programs. Had Israel suffered greater devastation from the SCUD missiles or felt itself in greater peril, it would have retaliated in kind and even used nuclear weapons in the last resort. In this scenario, the United States and

[76] Laura Zittrain Eisenberg, "Passive Belligerency: Israel and the 1991 Gulf War," *The Journal of Strategic Studies*, 15 (September 1992), pp. 304–329.

the United Nations would probably have brought the escalating conflict to an abrupt and indecisive end; and Iraq would have been left to carry on with its nuclear and other unconventional weapons programs. More than ever before, the Gulf War demonstrated the limits on Israeli military power, with its ultimate dependence on outside support primarily from the United States.

CONCLUSION

Having reached the bottom of its manpower reserves after the 1973 war, Israel will have to rely increasingly on the most advanced military technology as a force multiplier. Hence correct identification of and timely adjustment to the latest trends in weapons technology will be more critical than in the past. Although the Israeli military performed poorly in this respect in 1973, it did very well in 1982, giving Israeli strategists reason to be optimistic for the future. Yet state-of-the-art weapons systems have become prohibitively expensive, and it is not clear how Israel could continue to carry this economic burden while absorbing hundreds of thousands of Russian immigrants. Increased reliance on technology may also encourage neglect of the non-material aspects of war such as the quality of planning and training, the proper selection of commanders, and the tooth-to-tail ratio. High-technology weapons favor the defense over the offense, reduce the possibility of maneuver on the battlefield – an area in which the Israelis have always had an advantage, and eliminate the preemptive strike option that many Israeli strategists believe provides them with the best chance of victory. Furthermore, the investment in preparations for high-tech war may become self-negating as the Arab states identify their relative advantage in low-tech warfare, passive resistance, and public relations – areas that Israeli strategists have not yet dealt with effectively.[77]

Despite numerous flaws, Israeli national security policy or strategy cannot be considered a failure. Israel has managed to survive in an ongoing conflict including no fewer than six wars and an intense terror and guerrilla campaign. It has more than proven that it is capable of self-defense, and has so far won against any possible regional coalition while developing economically and securing a reasonable standard of living for its population.

Israel's ability to defend itself even under the most difficult circumstances, as in 1973, has in the end convinced some of its neighbors that the Jewish state is a fact of life. Such a realistic assessment probably contributed to President Sadat's decision to recognize Israel and conclude a peace treaty. Other Arab states such as Morocco and Jordan have also maintained a continuous dialogue with the Israeli government. In this respect, the disastrous invasion of Lebanon in 1982 was the second important strategic

[77] See Stuart A. Cohen, "Changing Emphases in Israel's Military Commitments, 1981–1991: Causes and Consequences," *The Journal of Strategic Studies* 15 (September 1992), pp. 330–50.

turning point for Israel. The invasion represented the first time in its history that Israel planned and executed an entirely offensive war. From the start, the war never stood a chance for success, but Israel's eventual military failure did create conditions favorable for the opening of an Israeli-Palestinian dialogue. It convinced the PLO of the futility of its attempt to defeat Israel by military means. Unfortunately, Israel's complicated political system and national psychology made it difficult to take advantage of this opportunity. Changes in the regional and international environment have now created a convergence, however precarious, of Israeli and Arab interests that could lead to a peace agreement: the Arab states no longer have Soviet support, Iraq is no longer a threat, the *intifada* has shown the necessity of a political solution, and Islamic fundamentalism menaces Israelis and Arab leaders alike.

If Israel can now demonstrate that it is able to cope with the Palestinian uprising in the occupied territories – that "passive resistance" has indeed led to a mutually acceptable settlement on Palestinian autonomy – then it can be said that a reactive, short-range, militarily dominated strategy has succeeded despite itself. But adherence to a similar strategy in the future is bound to fail. Israel's heavy dependence on foreign aid limits its strategic freedom of action, and the Arabs cannot be expected to continue making the mistakes that Israel exploited in the past. For the first time, Israel must develop a more balanced, farsighted political strategy to complement its military might, for military power without political wisdom is ultimately sterile.

18

Strategy in the nuclear age: The United States, 1945–1991

COLIN S. GRAY

The American way of statecraft and strategy is distinctive. The system is not elegant, but it has endured because it works and because it is sufficiently true to American culture to be socially tolerable. The socially transmitted attitudes, beliefs, and preferred modes of action that collectively constitute culture are neither casual nor random choices. Cultural attributes usually point to ideas and activities that have worked well for a society. The United States could probably have achieved its successes – whether conquering the internal frontier, defeating Nazi Germany, or containing the Soviet Union – in more elegant ways. But the nation still did the job.

Americans collectively are better at some activities than others. They are better engineers than diplomats,[1] and they lack many of the qualities important for imperial governance. But the American system of statecraft is no accident. Administrations may change in Washington, but the deeply pragmatic perspective they bring to strategic questions does not. Successive presidents have favored the same kind of solution to enduring problems and have committed the same errors in a rich variety of ways.

This essay represents neither a history nor a critique of American strategy in the Cold War. Instead it seeks to explain why the United States designed, or at least adopted, its particular strategic approaches, how it manifested that strategy, and how well that strategy worked. The period covered extends from the dawn of the nuclear age in July 1945 until the formal dissolution of the USSR in December 1991.

THE UNITED STATES AND THE BALANCE OF POWER

The course of world politics since 1945 and the grand-strategic choices of the United States are intertwined. As *the* global superpower, the United States

---

1 Except during the Revolutionary War period, in which diplomacy secured the French alliance and formal recognition of independence through the 1783 Treaty of Paris.

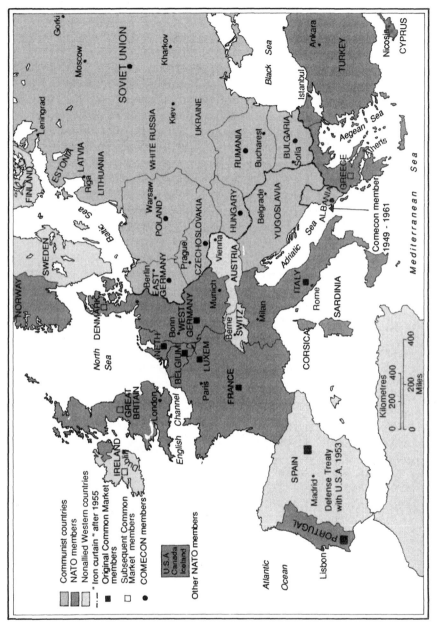

Map 18.1. Cold War Europe, ca. 1949–1989. *Source.* Adapted from McKay, Hill, and Buckler: *A History of Western*

has determined the geometry of the balance of power since 1945. Washington has played so powerful a role that its policy choices have forever altered the world's security environment.[2]

Americans have never been comfortable with the notion that their foreign policy should follow the logic of the balance of power. The sustaining national myth that the United States is a blessed *and divinely commissioned* polity allows scant room for the expedient compromises with evil that maintaining the balance of power requires. Nonetheless, the logic of that balance was crucial in creation of the winning alliance with France in the 1770s. After 1945, albeit with second thoughts, the United States joined the ranks of states *permanently* and actively engaged in the harsh competition of international politics.

U.S. policies after 1945 originated in the urges that produced American belligerency in 1917 and 1941. From late 1916, when Britain, the banker of the allied coalition, faced imminent bankruptcy[3] until 1991 – with the exception of the brief interwar era of German disarmament – no balance of power could exist in Eurasia without active U.S. participation. Despite their unreadiness in 1917 and 1941, U.S. forces were essential for the defeat of Germany in both world wars. Indeed for many years after 1945, the United States served as the sole Western end of the balance of power. The material basis for American hegemony in the West declined after the late 1960s, but the U.S. as organizer and guardian of the West's security did not decline politically, psychologically, or militarily on a scale commensurate with the shifting balance of economic strength.[4]

Historical accident produced the mutually antagonistic roles of the United States and the Soviet Union. The Axis powers first created and then waged a losing battle against a grand alliance blessed with overwhelming material strength. The resulting peace left only two states of the first rank. The superpowers' rivalry provides the context, but to understand American strategy and strategic performance from 1945 to 1991, four facts are of enduring importance.

---

[2] In 1945 the United States had the world's largest air force, navy, and marine corps and the world's second largest army. It was the only atomic power – if temporarily out of ammunition after Hiroshima and Nagasaki; it owned two-thirds of the world's gold reserves; and it produced fully half of the world's industrial output. It should be unnecessary to add that the 1940s were quite extraordinary years. See Paul M. Kennedy, *The Rise and Fall of the Great Powers: Economic Change and Military Conflict from 1500 to 2000* (New York, 1987), pp. 357–59.

[3] In the words of David French, "[b]y November 1916 the end of British credit was within sight but victory was not." *British Strategy and War Aims, 1914–1916* (London, 1986), p. 248.

[4] Kennedy makes this obvious point strongly in *Rise and Fall of the Great Powers*, particularly pp. 514–40. For some flavor of what is wrong with Kennedy's argument, see the persuasive critique in Samuel P. Huntington, "The U.S. – Decline or Renewal?" *Foreign Affairs* (Winter 1988–1989), pp. 76–96.

First, before 1945 the United States had no extensive peacetime experience in playing the central role in balance of power politics, unlike other great powers in the modern state system, which had often made yesterday's enemy into today's ally and vice versa. A consequence of the limited, if intensive, U.S. exposure to great power politics was that American leaders focused unduly on the security relationship with Moscow as the key to a healthy balance of power.

Second, notwithstanding the organized chaos of its "policy process," the United States had had little practical experience of rough equality with other polities. America on its continent and in its hemisphere was hegemonic since the mid-nineteenth century. In statecraft as in strategy, experience becomes habit. The closing years of World War II did little to dent American expectations of hegemony or anticipation of the deference due that hegemony. Americans' self-important view of themselves as the legatees of the "city on a hill" did not encourage respect for the values and opinions of others, and the insular physical and political geography of the United States encouraged this lack of empathy for alien *Weltanschauungen.*

Third, the United States has faced criticism for focusing its grand strategy unduly upon the military instrument to the detriment of alliance diplomacy. Indeed in its competition with the Soviet Union the United States had bowed to the influence of its allies to a remarkably small extent. The emergence of true superstates after 1945 both guaranteed their mutual antagonism and meant that the gain or loss of an ally would be unlikely to upset the balance.

Fourth, nuclear weapons devalued the importance of allies relative to that of national armaments. The promotion of the United States to a superpower was coincidental with, not a product of, the success of the Manhattan Project. Nuclear weapons rendered some of the negative tasks in statecraft easier than before, but once other powers acquired them they also introduced a new set of limitations upon the use of force, the *ultima ratio* of powers greater than other powers.

STRATEGY BEGINS AT HOME

America's warlike but unmilitary society frustrates the national security rationalist. Disorder characterizes the "process" from which policy emerges, although the country has performed steadily on national security fundamentals. It is difficult to comprehend why *the* preeminent guardian state of the West, with its wealth of competence in analytical techniques, makes and irregularly unmakes decisions on matters of peace, war, and survival in an undisciplined and deeply astrategic manner.[5]

---

[5] Arnold Kanter, *Defense Politics: A Budgetary Perspective* (Chicago, 1979), has merit, but there is no adequate monograph on the subject of national security policymaking, let alone military strategy-making, in the United States.

In the period reviewed in this essay, fourteen broad official strategy reviews took place, from NSC 20/4 of 23 November 1948 to the Bush administration's national security review in spring 1989.[6] Such reviews often repackaged orthodox opinion under the guise of new strategic thought.[7] But strategy remains a word of power in Washington. Periodically, an administration will rediscover strategy, more often than not when it is accused of lacking one.[8] American politicians and senior officials tend to view strategy-making as optional; not that the United States has lacked for strategy, it has only lacked a purposeful strategy centrally directed. It is possible, of course, to overvalue the strategic art; at times no strategy can deliver success. In addition, many situations arise in which the fine-tuning of means with ends does not necessarily serve policy. Once the American republic had survived its shaky first decades, it found little need to be subtle and agile in its application of force. The United States failed to develop and nurture a tradition of excellence in strategy because it did not need one.

As with all polities (and to extend Edward N. Luttwak's advocacy of the salience of paradox),[9] the United States has the vices of its virtues and the virtues of its vices. For example, the American urge to reform the world in its own democratic self-image sometimes confuses the desirable with the feasible. The openness of the processes of American government – attributable to the constitutionally mandated separation of powers – and the relatively extensive sharing of what other polities treat as secrets of state, can stimulate a well-informed public debate. But that same pluralism and democratization of expertise also fuels protracted delay in the making of strategy. Nevertheless, in time of crisis and in the hands of competent figures who share common assumptions about national priorities, foreign dangers, and society's

---

6 See "NSC 20/4: U.S. Objectives with Respect to the U.S.S.R. to Counter Soviet Threats to U.S. Security," in Thomas H. Etzold and John Lewis Gaddis, eds., *Containment: Documents on American Policy and Strategy, 1945–1950* (New York, 1978), pp. 203–11. Aaron L. Friedberg: "The Making of American National Strategy, 1948–1988," *The National Interest* (Spring 1988), pp. 65–75, analyzes the purposes and consequences of such broad policy reviews.

7 George Washington is the honorable, if largely out-of-period exception to this generalization. This may be unfair to Ulysses S. Grant, although it is not unfair to Grant's legacy as interpreted authoritatively for three quarters of a century. Russell F. Weigley observes as follows: "Studying strategy from the Grant of the Wilderness, Spotsylvania, Cold Harbor, and Petersburg, American soldiers entered the twentieth century and the time of America's emergence into world power believing that the superior weight of military force that America could bring to bear against almost any rival could be their only sure military reliance." "American Strategy from its Beginnings through the First World War," in Peter Paret, ed., *Makers of Modern Strategy: From Machiavelli to the Nuclear Age* (Princeton, 1986), p. 440.

8 See Ronald Reagan: *National Security of the United States* (Washington, January 1987); and *National Security Strategy of the United States* (Washington, January 1988). The habit was catching, see George Bush: *National Security Strategy of the United States* (Washington, March 1990); and *National Security Strategy of the United States* (Washington, August 1991).

9 Edward N. Luttwak, *Strategy: The Logic of War and Peace* (Cambridge, MA, 1987), passim.

ability to pay, the U.S. government can perform wonderfully. The practice of politics in a pluralistic democracy with the executive and legislative branches designated as separate and co-equal requires ad hoc coalition-making, a comprehensive willingness to compromise, and generally a need to accommodate (or appear to accommodate) many of the organized interests with access to government.

By and large, the executive must propose, but it is the Congress that disposes. Moreover, just as the concept of the executive conjures up a misleading image of unity of purpose, so casual reference to the legislative branch of government obscures the parallels between the functioning of that branch and that of high feudalism. Congressional barons protect their fiefs against each other and against the executive branch. By the nature of their interests and responsibilities, they often approach issues that bear upon strategy-making idiosyncratically.

The influence of individual offices, agencies, departments, branches of government, and public opinion over national security policy and strategy has thus varied. Because this essay spans four and a half decades, it is important to seek answers to the following questions. First, in what ways did the domestic setting for U.S. strategy-making change from 1945 to 1991? Second, what can be said about that setting that is valid for the entire period?

THE CHANGING LANDSCAPE

First, American society accepted a high level of defense effort as normal after 1950–51, when the North Korean invasion of June 1950 – and particularly the Chinese intervention in November – served as the lever for a peacetime military mobilization that had enduring budgetary and force-level consequences. The scale of U.S. defense effort – in part to keep pace with the USSR – rose dramatically in 1950–51, and did not return to the level of the late 1940s, in terms of percentage of GNP, until 1978–79.[10] This matter of sheer quantity is of the utmost importance because it is the defense budget that transforms strategic ideas into steel, high explosive, and plutonium.

Second, successively in 1947, 1958, and 1986, the executive branch of the U.S. government reorganized itself in ways that favored either centralized civilian control over the armed services, or – in the case of the Goldwater-Nichols Defense Reorganization Act of 1986 – the centralized control of the Chairman of the Joint Chiefs of Staff (JCS) over military strategy, force planning, budget requests, and advice to civilian superiors. Since 1945, the institutional landscape of the defense community has changed with the or-

---

10   In the last pre-Korean War fiscal year, 1950, Department of Defense outlays stood at 4.4% of GNP. In FYs 1978 and 1979 outlays were at 4.7%, prior to the Carter-Reagan spending surge – and even the peak year of the Reagan increase registered only 6.3% on the GNP scale. See Dick Cheney, *Report of the Secretary of Defense to the President and the Congress*, (Washington, January 1991), Table A-3, p. 111.

ganization in 1947 of a Department of Defense, with the establishment of an independent air force that same year, with legislative recognition of the committee of the Joint Chiefs of Staff and its chairman, and with the creation of the National Security Council (NSC) for cabinet-level determination and coordination of policy and grand strategy as part of the Office of the President. The NSC acquired a staff with a National Security Adviser to the president at its head.

Third, large numbers of civilians joined the ranks of defense professionals. Civilian defense intellectuals contributed massively, for good or ill depending on one's point of view, in managing the gigantic U.S. military enterprise and providing ideas on the threat and use of force for consideration by policy-makers and defense planners.[11] No historical precedent exists in modern times for the penetration and intellectual domination of civilian theorists over defense policy that occurred in the United States during the late 1950s and the 1960s.

In 1945–46 civilian defense intellectuals began to grope toward understanding the strategic meaning of atomic weapons. In the 1950s their leading members manned the RAND Corporation, an organization that worked for the guardian of The Great Deterrent, the recently independent U.S. Air Force.[12] The influence of the civilian strategic theorists depended on the issue, but they nevertheless had a pervasive effect upon the terms of discussion of central defense questions.

Fourth, Congress was not always a compliant partner in the 1940s, 1950s, and 1960s; in the 1970s and 1980s the imperial presidency of the early and mid-1960s declined in stature vis-à-vis a more active and skeptical Congress. That Congress came to regularize the novel practice of inviting expert testimony by persons critical of official proposals. It demanded more, and more timely, information on executive plans and actions of all kinds; and it generally conceived of itself as a partner in the determination and management of national security policy, although never did it willingly shoulder blame for errors. The post-Vietnam emergence of a Congress deeply distrustful of executive competence and probity had important implications for the political feasibility of changes in military missions, major programs, and policy. By nature a fragmented body reflective of American social trends, the Congress does not function well as a policy leader.

---

[11] With particular reference to the nuclear questions that attracted their attention most heavily, see Lawrence Freedman, *The Evolution of Nuclear Strategy* (1981; New York, 1989); Colin S. Gray, *Strategic Studies and Public Policy: The American Experience* (Lexington, KY, 1982); Fred Kaplan, *The Wizards of Armageddon* (New York, 1983); Barry H. Steiner, *Bernard Brodie and the Foundations of American Nuclear Strategy* (Lawrence, KS, 1991); and John Baylis and John Garnett, eds., *Makers of Nuclear Strategy* (New York, 1991).

[12] For an early and friendly assessment, see Bruce L.R. Smith, *The RAND Corporation: Case Study of a Nonprofit Advisory Corporation* (Cambridge, MA, 1966). There is merit in the balancing view of Kaplan, *Wizards of Armageddon*.

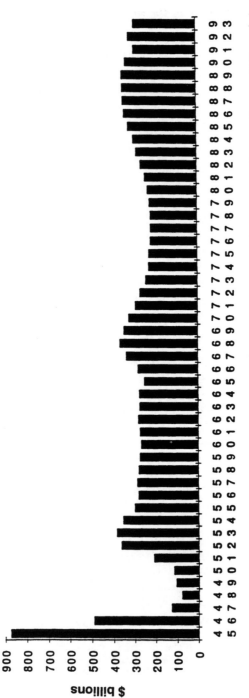

Figure 18.1. National defense outlays. Constant (1993) dollars. Outlays for 1992 and 1993 are estimates. *Source.* Office of the Assistant Secretary of Defense (Comptroller), National Defense Budget Estimates for FY 1993, March 1992, pp. 36 (deflator), 126–127.

A CONSTANT LANDSCAPE

Domestically, what remained largely constant throughout this period for U.S. strategy-making? First, popular and official security fears are analogous to a wave train in the deep ocean.[13] Defense outlays since 1945 (Figure 18.1) provide a convenient graphical representation of rising and falling alarm. Irregular though the cycles have been, enough of a pattern emerges – and the reasons for the pattern are sufficiently apparent – for the student of American defense behavior to perceive a unity in the surge-and-coast, wave-train phenomenon. Since new, or refurbished old, strategic ideas of major relevance to policy choice usually require weapons and force structures different from those extant, they are unlikely to be realized unless they can catch a rising wave of American security alarm – with its permissive budgetary climate. This was how the Air Force purchased its nuclear equipment in the 1950s; it was how the services could practice – albeit reluctantly – limited war in Southeast Asia in the 1960s; it was how the U.S. Navy could schedule – if not actually obtain or maintain – a 600-ship force structure for its revamped maritime strategy in the 1980s; and, for the future, it is how the United States one day assuredly will obtain a multilayered strategic defense system.

Second, a recent study of the history of the JCS offers the judgment that Goldwater-Nichols "ended forty years of service ascendancy."[14] That opinion is questionable because, in Carl Builder's words: "[t]he most powerful institutions in the American national security arena are the military services – the army, navy, and air force – not the Department of Defense or Congress or even their commander in chief, the president."[15] As Builder plausibly notes:

> The roots of modern American military strategies lie buried in the country's three most powerful institutions: the army, navy, and air force. Though many people outside the military institutions, including academics and presidents may propose military strategies and concepts, these can be implemented only if and when military institutions accept and pursue them.[16]

No matter what strategic theorists write about strategic deterrence and limited war, there are four distinctive physical environments for combat. Americans do not wage, or plan to wage, limited war; rather they plan to fight on land, at sea, in the air, or in and for space. The environments largely determine the technologies, the tactics, and the character of the operational goals. Unity in policy, in overall planning, and in crisis and wartime direction

---

13　Then Deputy Secretary of Defense Donald Atwood made the same point, but his analogy is with "the rollercoaster pattern of defense spending." See "Atwood Says More Imagination Needed in Defense," *Defense Daily*, 4 May 1989, p. 192.

14　Mark Perry, *Four Stars* (Boston, 1989), p. 339.

15　Carl H. Builder, *The Masks of War: American Military Styles in Strategy and Analysis* (Baltimore, 1989), p. 3.

16　Ibid., p. 4.

has always made sense. But unification of the armed forces in an attempt to transform soldiers, sailors, and airmen into generic "military persons" does not make sense, given geographic and technological realities.

Third, strategic discussion has been rare in the United States since 1945. The foreign policy goals that military power served seemed so obvious, and the military instrument so awesome, that useful strategic study and discussion rarely occurred. From the early 1950s to the late 1980s, the dominant school of strategic theory followed an ahistorical, apolitical method of calculating purportedly correct "answers" to defense problems. Both liberal and conservative analysts in the defense community showed a naive faith in the tradition of Baron Antoine Henri de Jomini. They believe in the veracity and power of basic axioms (concerning stability and instability and first and second strikes and so forth). They maintained a confidence in their ability to calculate right answers to the key questions of deterrence and war.[17] From Albert Wohlstetter's study of *Selection and Use of Strategic Air Bases* (R-266, April 1954),[18] to *A Calculus of First-Strike Stability* by John Glenn et al (N-2526-AF, June 1988),[19] the American engineering spirit sought to reduce strategic problems to equations.[20] In his penetrating study of RAND's approach to strategic theory, Fred Kaplan notes that "the study [of strategic air bases by Wohlstetter] was among the first attempts, to abstract the 'nuclear exchange,' to place it like one of Wohlstetter's exercises in mathematical logic from earlier days, in a rarified universe all its own, apart from the world of political leaders and their appreciation of horrible risk, apart from the broader issues of how nuclear weapons fit into an overall strategy."[21]

Notwithstanding the flowering of strategic thought between 1955 and 1965 and the subsequent growth of a permanent defense studies cottage industry, the defense community more often praised than practiced strategy. In 1982 the United States sent marines to serve as targets in Lebanon without a strategic rationale or any realistic appreciation of the risks involved. In 1983 President Reagan committed the country to a Strategic Defense Initiative (SDI) without the benefit of a supportive strategic rationale. In 1988, the Intermediate-Range Nuclear Forces (INF) treaty went into force even though its terms undermined the credibility of NATO's strategy of flexible response. In effect the United States has not had a true strategy-making system, at least

17 See John Shy's apposite comments in "Jomini," in Paret, ed., *Makers of Modern Strategy,* particularly pp. 183–85.
18 (Santa Monica, CA, April 1954).
19 (Santa Monica, CA., June 1988). In addition, see Dean Wilkening and Kenneth Watman, *Strategic Defenses and First-Strike Instability,* R-3412-FF/RC (Santa Monica, CA, November 1986).
20 Colin S. Gray, *War, Peace, and Victory: Strategy and Statecraft for the Next Century* (New York, 1990).
21 Kaplan, *Wizards of Armageddon,* p. 109. Like arguments are advanced in Marc Trachtenberg, *History and Strategy* (Princeton, 1991) ch. 1.

one that enjoys commanding leverage over other related and competing systems. The American government did have adequate procedures for developing defense budgets and for conducting force planning. But the relationship between policy and military power, the realm of strategy, remained sorely neglected. During long periods of peace, errors in strategy are apparently cost-free because the correct empirical basis for judging whether the United States has enough of the right kind of forces remains uncertain. The field test of military forces during Operation DESERT STORM in 1991 did suggest that the American military were unusually competent in theater strategy and almost unprecedently effective in operational art and tactics. To be strong and effective in both, however, is not necessarily to be wise in war. Fourth, the surge-and-coast style in defense preparation is symptomatic of a society which does not regard its military establishment as a great institution of state. And it has long been axiomatic that the general public neither cares nor knows much about military affairs. The consequences of Vietnam, environmentalism, resentment at increasingly affluent allies, and the sheer length of time since the country faced a mortal threat had all cut into public support for high levels of national defense spending by the end of the Reagan era. The implosion of the Soviet empire in 1989–90, and the demise of the Soviet Union itself in 1991, had the effect of accelerating an existing trend toward a much reduced defense effort.

Defense, if not strategic, expertise is relatively easy to acquire in the United States. No society ever has provided such detailed information on national security issues. Nevertheless, the United States is no more likely to become a country of defense experts than are those Western democracies that practice less openness in government. The American public's ignorance on questions of national security has important implications. Above all else, it has meant that one cannot reliably secure shifts in public policy through rational strategic argument. The American public and its representatives have a history of rising admirably to clear and present dangers, but they tend to respond pragmatically to events and developments on their current merits rather than to foresee and address long-term trends.

HISTORY AND STRATEGIC CULTURE[22]

Cultural characteristics are not carved in stone; they evolve gradually. Even a social, political, economic, and military event as immense as World War II had – in the American case – the net effect of only reinforcing existing

---

[22] This section is an extension, but not a repetition, of arguments that the author has developed elsewhere. See Colin S. Gray: *Nuclear Strategy and National Style* (Lanham, MD, 1986), ch. 2; *The Geopolitics of Super Power* (Lexington, KY, 1988), chs. 5–6; and particularly "U.S. Strategic Culture: Implications for Defense Technology," in Asa A. Clark IV and John F. Lilley, eds., *Defense Technology* (New York, 1989), pp. 31–48.

tendencies. The experience of the seventeenth, eighteenth, and nineteenth centuries formed a strategic culture with roots in five interdependent factors.

First, as Denis Brogan noticed, "[s]pace determined the American way in war, space and the means to conquer space." Brogan points out that

> Into empty land the pioneers moved, feeling their way slowly, carefully, timidly if you like. The reckless lost their scalps; the careful, the prudent, the rationally courageous survived and by logistics, by superiority in resources, in tenacity, in numbers. Americans who did not learn these lessons were not much use in the conquest of the West.[23]

The American military has not always been well directed strategically or operationally, its tactical skills frequently have left much to be desired, and its weapons have not always been state-of-the-art.[24] But it has always shown a mastery of logistics. The insouciance with which German staff officers approached the supply planning and execution of great campaigns in two world wars – and the consequences of that casualness – stand in significant contrast to the twentieth century logistical triumphs of the United States. American soldiers have not always capitalized on their superior supply services; indeed, a fine line runs between the prudent exploitation of logistical excellence and dependence on logistical systems at the expense of operational initiative. Nevertheless, the national experience of coping with continental geography has bred a respect for physical distance that has invariably improved U.S. military performance.

Second, the experience of a moving frontier had a lasting influence upon the American strategic personality. The American fascination with technology, particularly with mechanical means of transportation, resulted from conquering the wilderness. The relative absence of societal support on the frontier bred a pragmatism that translated into an engineering, problem-solving approach – an approach that at times has dismissed conditions as merely problems. American society responded sensibly to its shortage of labor, particularly highly skilled labor, by embracing machines and taking the lead in producing machine tools. The American preference for the use of machines in war lies rooted in the sparse people-to-space ratio of frontier America, and in the acute shortage of skilled artisans that lasted well into the nineteenth century.

Third, contemporary American strategic culture is the product of a society that has embraced the myth of well-merited national success. Notwithstand-

---

23 Denis W. Brogan, *The American Character* (New York, 1944), p. 150. Emphasis in original. See also, Oscar and Lilian Handlin, *Liberty in America, 1600 to the Present,* Vol. 1, *Liberty and Power 1600–1700* (New York, 1986), ch. 2, "Space, 1600–1690."

24 For example, see the negative judgment on U.S. armor in 1944–45 in Allan R. Millett, "The United States Armed Forces in the Second World War," in Millett and Williamson Murray, eds., *Military Effectiveness,* Vol. 3, *The Second World War* (Boston, 1988), pp. 61, 72–74, 79–80.

ing some blemishes,[25] the pages of world history, at least for those who live north of the Mason-Dixon Line, generally read well for Americans. It is therefore understandable that many Americans have confused success with virtue. In the national experience, thirteen squabbling colonies evolved into a world power that succeeded in most important national endeavors up to the Vietnam war. Such a history fostered an optimism that inevitably influenced national security issues.

Fourth, the country that emerged from its geostrategically tenuous colonial origins resulted in a nation of unusual size in all relevant measures of power.[26] The scale of resources influenced both the national security enterprises undertaken and the manner in which Americans approached those enterprises. For example, from 1941 to 1945 the United States waged two geostrategically distinct wars logistically half a world apart, out-produced friends and enemies alike, developed the atomic bomb, and created in the fabulously expensive B-29 Superfortress the instrument for its delivery. The United States was able to wage a rich man's war.[27]

Fifth, American society is deeply convinced that the world is destined to be governed by the precepts of American liberal democracy. Some influential Americans have taken the Soviet collapse as proof of the superiority of American ideas on good governance and enlightened economics over those of the forces of darkness and evil.[28]

Culture, whatever the forces that have shaped it, is by definition slow to change. But it is neither immutable nor unitary: American society accommodates subcultures; each service has an institutional personality that speaks to the unique features of different missions[29]; many countries share some cultural characteristics; and policymakers do exercise choices outside the traditions of their strategic culture. Britain decided in World War I to field a continental-size army, and after August 1915 to wage as much land combat as should prove necessary to defeat the enemy. Second, the United States elected in 1917 to intervene massively in a European war, and in 1965 decided to wage war in Southeast Asia but not according to some theory of victory via decisive battle. In all three cases, British and American societies

[25] At the risk of appearing ungenerous, one could cite the significant contributions of Bourbon France to American independence (see Jonathan R. Dull, *The French Navy and American Independence: A Study of Arms and Diplomacy, 1774–1787* [Princeton, 1975]); British war-weariness, Royal Navy overconfidence, and limited motivation in 1812–14; the less than first-class character of nineteenth century opponents; and the prior and simultaneous attrition that America's allies imposed upon the Germans twice in this century.

[26] See Allan R. Millett and Peter Maslowski, *For the Common Defense: A Military History of the United States of America* (New York, 1984), ch. 1 ("A Dangerous New World").

[27] See Millett, "United States Armed Forces in the Second World War," pp. 60–61, 82–84.

[28] For what amounts to a self-parody of this pleasing thesis, see Francis Fukuyama's unduly celebrated article, "The End of History?" *The National Interest* (Summer 1989), pp. 3–18, and the somewhat amended book-length version, *The End of History and the Last Man* (New York, 1991).

[29] See Builder, *Masks of War.*

eventually punished the policymakers who had affronted the strategic norms, even though the first two enterprises were successful.

Eight characteristics of American strategic culture are readily discernible.

Indifference to history

In myth and to some extent in practice the United States is still the New World. The study of history is not popular in the United States. America is the land of new beginnings, apparently endless horizons, and infinite possibilities. When an American politician says of his country's achievements that "the best is yet to come," his words are not banal to American ears. History and historical experience suffer an equal lack of respect from Americans. The United States is not only indifferent to historical experience – its culture is actively antihistorical. With a minimum of baggage from the past, each new policy review tackles the future boldly and rediscovers the obvious, committing old errors in new ways.

The engineering style and the technical fix

The true parent of American thinking on national security is Jomini, not Clausewitz. Jomini wrote of war as an art, but his quest for certainty and his obsession with reducing the complex and ambiguous to a few apparently simple principles has also characterized American military thought and practice. The domestic historical experience yielded the belief that American know-how will find a solution – generally technical – to every problem. The RAND school of strategic analysis, with its "fixes" for an arguably vulnerable Strategic Air Command, epitomized this engineering approach to security.[30]

The same national security community that believed in 1941 that it could calculate precisely the number of heavy bomber sorties needed to defeat Germany and Japan[31] is just as capable of believing calculations of World War III nuclear damage. In his classic study of *The American Way of War,*

---

[30] See Gray, *War, Peace, and Victory,* ch. 4. The vulnerability analyses produced in the RAND style and the stability precepts which appear to flow from them showed virtually no recognition of the dominant role of politics in decisions over war or peace. Similarly reductionist in effect have been the writings of the past decade that purported to demonstrate systemic connections between offensive strategies and the risks of war. A leading representative of this mechanistic approach to strategic issues is Jack Snyder, *The Ideology of the Offensive: Military Decision Making and the Disasters of 1914* (Ithaca, NY, 1984). Snyder renders explicit the historical connection with more modern problems in his "Civil-Military Relations and the Cult of the Offensive, 1914 and 1984," *International Security* (Summer 1984), pp. 108–46.

[31] Respectively, 66,045 sorties for the nine critical German target systems and 51,480 sorties for Japan. Cited in R.J. Overy, *The Air War 1939–1945* (1981; New York, 1985), p. 310. For essential background, see W.F. Craven and J. L. Cate, *The Army Air Forces in World War II,* Vol. 1, *Plans and Early Operations, January 1939 to August 1942* (Chicago, 1948), particularly chapters 4,7 and 16.

Russell F. Weigley discerned a national tendency "to seek refuge in technology from hard problems of strategy and policy, . . . [a tendency] fostered by the pragmatic qualities of the American character and by the complexity of nuclear-age technology."[32]

Weigley was careful to distinguish this resort to the technical from the sensible quest for better weapons, and for technical answers to technical issues. The American way in defense preparation as well as war has emphasized the technical and logistical rather than the politically well-informed and operationally agile. Mobility, particularly at strategic and operational levels, has been the long suit of American military power. But full exploitation of transportation technologies represents a necessary but not sufficient ingredient of military effectiveness. Operation DESERT STORM appeared to illustrate that the art of war had attained new heights in the United States. But it so far stands as an exception to the usual ponderousness of American military style.

Impatience

For better or for worse, the United States is a society with a low tolerance for lengthy investment with distant payoffs. Policymakers at home and abroad should take seriously the affirmation in the Declaration of Independence that the United States of America is, inter alia, about "the pursuit of Happiness." It is not the American way to live with problems and worry about them until they become more tractable. American society confronts problems, or conditions, in the engineering spirit of the resolute problem-solver. Whether the problem is poverty at home, nation-building in South Vietnam, teaching respect for multiparty democracy in El Salvador and Panama, or reducing the risks of war through arms control, American policymakers seek near-term results. Since major weapons systems can take a decade or more from gestation to initial operational capability, the lack of foresight ingrained in culture and institutions can render even the idea of long-range planning mildly humorous.

Blindness to cultural differences

The continental isolation of American society and its success against weaker adversaries bred a lack of awareness of strategic (inter alia)-cultural diversity that has major consequences for its choices in national military strategy. Notwithstanding the heritage of immigration, Americans have generally failed to study the strategic cultures of other societies. In the most serious of America's wars – the Revolutionary War and the Civil War – the strategic

---

[32] *The American Way of War: A History of United States Military Strategy and Policy* (New York, 1973), p. 416.

culture of the two sides was too similar to make much difference.[33] U.S. involvement in both world wars was vital for victory, but fortunately American armed forces did not have to win either war on their own. In neither world war were American soldiers obliged to purge their strategic culture of habits that undermined military effectiveness and that might have proven fatal even to the best armies of the day.

Global victory in 1945 provided apparent confirmation of cultural superiority, and a heady sense of being a superpower. Pride in recent military achievements and in the potency of new and largely American weapons technologies did nothing to encourage strategic empathy in the postwar world. For many years, American officials and theorists believed that they could enlighten the backward Russians with the gospel of strategic stability.[34] But one cannot admire or criticize a national strategic culture like a Byzantine mosaic, according to its aesthetic logic and compatibility with its setting. Although a society cannot function effectively for long in a manner that offends national cultural preferences, forces from without ultimately determine the measure of a strategic culture's worth. Strategy by definition is a comparative subject.

American strategic culture has to function in a world populated with many different strategic cultures. A lack of empathy that betrays both superpower hubris and insularity often blinds policymakers to the trend and meaning of events. The sustaining myth of American national exceptionalism, the notion that *we* are a truly unique society, fostered a dangerous strategic-cultural arrogance.

Continental Weltanschauung, maritime situation

The United States is the world's greatest naval power. The U.S. Navy has inherited many of the former duties of the Royal Navy, but the United States cannot wage war beyond North America – with the exception of long-range bombardment – unless it enjoys a working control of the relevant sea lines of communication. Despite those facts, the United States is neither a natural sea power nor does a maritime perspective and precepts dominate its strategic culture. Because of its size, its historical experience of success, and the impatient temper of its people, the American way of war has been quintessentially continentalist. Americans have favored the quest for swift victory through

---

33 See Ira D. Gruber, "The Anglo-American Military Tradition and the War for American Independence," in Kenneth J. Hagan and William R. Roberts, eds., *Against All Enemies: Interpretations of American Military History from Colonial Times to the Present* (Westport, CT, 1986), pp. 21–47; and, for a different twist, John Shy, "The Military Conflict Considered as a Revolutionary War," in Shy, *A People Numerous and Armed: Reflections on the Military Struggle for American Independence* (New York, 1976), pp. 193–224.

34 Albert J. Wohlstetter, "The Delicate Balance of Terror," *Foreign Affairs* (Jan. 1959), pp. 211–34; Thomas C. Schelling, "Surprise Attack and Disarmament," in Klaus Knorr, ed., *NATO and American Security* (Princeton, 1959), ch. 8; and Thomas C. Schelling and Morton H. Halperin, *Strategy and Arms Control* (New York, 1961).

the hazards of decisive battle rather than the slower approach of maritime encirclement. This preference long antedated the impact of nuclear weapons upon American assumptions about the likely duration of major wars.

The spirit of the American way is captured in the exhortations "On to Richmond!" and "On to Berlin!" The eagerness to come to grips with the still formidable Wehrmacht of 1942–43, as revealed in the Anglo-American strategy disputes of those years,[35] suggests a country inclined to believe that the shortest distance between friendly bases and the enemy's center of gravity was the highroad to victory.

The mixed continental and maritime heritage of the United States had intriguing consequences for strategy choice. The United States had the basis for a thoroughly maritime view of national security and of its international security duties. Instead, because of Western Europe's value in the balance of power and because of strategic policy habits formed in the 1950s, the U.S. adhered through the 1980s to a Eurocentric, continentalist strategy that equated *war* with war in Europe. Flexible response permitted little flexibility in the sense of treating war in Europe as only one campaign within a global conflict.

Indifference to strategy

Nuclear weapons appear to many Americans to have made strategy obsolete.[36] All too often, tactics have masqueraded as strategy. For example, plans for using weapons according to explicit measures of effectiveness (MOE's) are often described as targeting strategy. The utility of the threat of force or actual use of force have by contrast tended to attract little interest. Until the unpleasant and confusing experience in Korea in the early 1950s, American society and its military experts had little experience dealing with conflicts that required high-order strategic skills. American society might have performed more effectively and ultimately more economically had it functioned more strategically, but until the 1960s the country did well enough without.

Indifference to strategy is not simply the natural consequence of a national security community's material abundance. Reinforcing factors are the ideological character of most American conflicts, the insulating strategic benefits of oceanic distance, weak continental neighbors, a partial European surrogate in the form of Britain and its navy, and the sloppiness bred by success.[37]

---

[35] See Michael Howard, *Grand Strategy*, Vol. 4, *August 1942–September 1943* (London, 1970), passim.

[36] See Freedman, *Evolution of Nuclear Strategy*, pp. 432–33. This negative view of nuclear strategy as strategy also pervades McGeorge Bundy, *Danger and Survival: Choices About the Bomb in the First Fifty Years* (New York, 1988).

[37] On the subject of what Americans have learned from their experience, see John Shy's pathbreaking essay "The American Military Experience: History and Learning," in Shy, *A People Numerous and Armed*, pp. 224–58.

Strategically, it is much less stressful to wage a materially profligate war and defeat an enemy decisively, than to use national military power to prop up uncertain allies in enterprises whose outcomes are often questionable. Traditionally, it has been the American way to reduce war and strategy to narrow military undertakings, a proclivity as evident in the Gulf in 1991 as it had been in Europe in 1944–45.

But powers neglect the essential characteristics of strategy at their peril. The United States was fortunate in that its day of reckoning occurred in Southeast Asia rather than in a World War III. The weaknesses in much of American limited-war theory and strategy manifested themselves in a "limited" war waged without benefit of a theory of victory, much less clear goals.[38] The weaknesses in NATO's longstanding "strategy" (or antistrategy) of flexible response could have had similar consequences on a much grander and more dangerous scale.

But strategy is not a magical elixir that a properly fortified society can use to accomplish its ends. That U.S. strategic performance in Vietnam was so lamentable does not mean that a better strategy could have produced success. Unsuitable policy choices can frustrate strategy just as much as operational incompetence or tactical ineptitude.

The resort to force, belated but massive

As a popular democracy whose system of government is uniquely influenced by societal pressures, the United States is not well suited to an agile use of armed force for limited political purposes. The United States is a large country that tends to perform extremely well on large tasks when its citizenry accepts their necessity.[39] But attempts to wage war without the blessings of American society are likely to fail.[40] For any enterprise lacking obvious life or death implications, the government of a popular democracy can expect public support only if the military operation is brief, successful, and attended by few casualties. A quarter century after General George C. Marshall said that "a democracy cannot fight a Seven-Years War," Presidents Johnson and Nixon proved him correct.[41] The traditional American mindset has viewed

---

38 A few works of outstanding value study the booming volume of literature on the American war in Vietnam. Of particular interest in the context of this essay are Harry G. Summers, Jr., *On Strategy: A Critical Analysis of the Vietnam War* (Novato, CA, 1982); Bruce Palmer, Jr., *The 25-Year War: America's Military Role in Vietnam* (Lexington, KY, 1984); Shelby L. Stanton, *The Rise and Fall of an American Army: U.S. Ground Forces in Vietnam 1965–1973* (1985; New York, 1988); and Andrew F. Krepinovich, Jr., *The Army and Vietnam* (Baltimore, 1986).

39 In the inimitable words of Samuel P. Huntington, "the United States is a big country, and we should fight wars in a big way. One of our great advantages is our mass; we should not hesitate to use it." *American Military Strategy*, Policy Papers in International Affairs No. 28 (Berkeley, CA., 1986), pp. 15–16.

40 A point hammered home as a major theme in Summers, *On Strategy*.

41 See Weigley, *American Way of War*, p. 5.

peace as the normal and self-evidently desirable condition of humankind. It follows then to most Americans that only evil men or evil causes promote wars for aggressive reasons. Americans do not resort to force quickly, but when they do, as citizens of *the* exceptional polity, they expect a thumping triumph. With few exceptions, American forces have been relatively inept at the start of war,[42] but as John Shy has observed, the experience of the Revolutionary War taught Americans to expect as much.[43] Nor do Americans expect their armed forces to be committed to morally dubious battle.

In the late 1950s and early 1960s, some influential civilian defense intellectuals constructed a theory that promised just that: the Korean experience had shown that U.S. society must learn how to wage "limited" war in the nuclear shadow.[44] Then Lyndon Johnson discovered that this theory fit the real American polity poorly. The public would not tolerate sacrifice without decision.

Apart from shallow rationalism and built-in incomprehension of alien strategic cultures, U.S. strategic theory on the use of nuclear weapons is deeply and characteristically insular rather than continental. Julian Corbett's and B.H. Liddell Hart's notions of a British way in warfare, which centered around the limited national liability of offshore powers,[45] find their echoes in modern American speculation about the controlled use of nuclear weapons.[46] How well such theorizing would fit military-technical realities, would function amidst the friction and fog of crisis and war, and could persist in the face of the deep gulf between American and Soviet/Russian strategic cultures,[47] will remain a mystery forever.

The evasion of politics

The enforcement of continental Manifest Destiny and the belated yet vital participation in crusades against Kaiser*ism* and Nazi*ism* have not encouraged Clausewitzian approaches to the use of force. The United States transformed

---

[42] See Charles G. Heller and William A. Stofft, eds., *America's First Battles, 1776–1965* (Lawrence, KS, 1986).

[43] Shy, "American Military Experience," p. 239.

[44] See William W. Kaufmann, "Limited Warfare," in Kaufmann, ed., *Military Policy and National Security* (Princeton, 1956), ch. 4; Robert E. Osgood, *Limited War: The Challenge to American Strategy* (Chicago, 1957); and Morton H. Halperin, *Limited War In the Nuclear Age* (New York, 1963).

[45] Julian S. Corbett, *Some Principles of Maritime Strategy* (Annapolis, MD, 1972), ch. 3; and Basil Liddell Hart, *The British Way in Warfare* (London, 1932). Michael Howard performs too thorough a demolition of the allegedly "British way in warfare" in his essay, "The British Way in Warfare: A Reappraisal," in Howard, *The Causes of Wars and other Essays* (1983; London, 1984), pp. 189–207.

[46] For example, see Kaplan, *Wizards of Armageddon;* and Albert Wohlstetter, "The Political and Military Aims of Offense and Defense Innovation," in Fred S. Hoffman et al., eds., *Swords and Shields: NATO, the U.S.S.R., and New Choices for Long-Range Offense and Defense* (Lexington, MA, 1987), pp. 3–36.

[47] See Stephen M. Meyer, "Soviet Nuclear Operations," in Ashton B. Carter et al., eds., *Managing Nuclear Operations* (Washington, 1987), pp. 470–531.

into military problems – and inelegantly but definitively solved through machine warfare – the political challenges that American Indians or menacing empires in Europe and Asia had posed.

American strategic studies in the Cold War years – with three central theoretical pillars of deterrence, limited war, and arms control – was deeply respectful of Clausewitz. Defense theorists tended to parrot the arguable proposition that "war is simply a continuation of political intercourse, with the addition of other means."[48] Those same theorists, however, proceeded to design and elaborate ideas on stable deterrence, crisis management, the conduct of limited war, and approaches to arms control that were utterly apolitical. Studies over the last several decades specified the requirements of stable deterrence with scant acknowledgment of the political motives that generate crises and wars. The U.S. defense community has found comfortable certainty in the application of a few elementary apolitical principles for the determination of strategic sufficiency. Fortunately, the awesome potential of nuclear weapons and the Soviet inclination to avoid high-risk military adventure probably saved the United States from the bloody refutation of the apolitical and astrategic simplicities of its favorite theories.[49]

The United States has a strategic culture more comfortable with administration than with politics, and centered upon the quaint belief that the country can purchase the right weapons in the right numbers to serve both as a deterrent in peacetime and as an adequate arsenal in crisis or war. The American literature on force planning quite resolutely declines to recognize that its subject is an art and not a science. "How much is enough" strategic-nuclear firepower will forever remain indeterminate, because that firepower is required to deter rather than to assure victory.[50]

THREATS, POLICY GOALS, AND RESOURCES

After 1946–47, and for the third time in this century, the United States contended against an evil empire with most of the instruments of grand strategy. The overriding goal in the Cold War, as in 1917–18 and 1941–45, was to maintain the balance of power *in* Eurasia rather than risk the nearly impossible task of balancing power *with* an effectively united Eurasia.[51] NSC 20/4 of 23 November 1948 judged that "Soviet domination of the potential power of Eurasia, whether achieved by armed aggression or by political and subversive means, would be strategically and politically unac-

48   Carl von Clausewitz, *On War*, (1832; Princeton, 1976), p. 605.
49   For densely packed, culturally founded strategic errors, see Jerome H. Kahan, *Security in the Nuclear Age: Developing U.S. Strategic Arms Policy* (Washington, 1975).
50   For example: Henry C. Bartlett, "Approaches to Force Planning," *Naval War College Review* (May–June 1985), pp. 37–48; and Robert P. Haffa, Jr., *Rational Methods, Prudent Choices: Planning U.S. Forces* (Washington, 1988).
51   Nicholas J. Spykman, *America's Strategy in World Politics: The United States and the Balance of Power* (1942; Hamden, CT, 1970).

ceptable to the United States."[52] And in January 1988, President Ronald Reagan offered the following familiar thought:

> The first historical dimension of our strategy . . . . is the conviction that the United States' most basic national security interests would be endangered if a hostile state or group of states were to dominate the Eurasian landmass – that area of the globe often referred to as the world's heartland. We fought two world wars to prevent this from occurring. And, since 1945, we have sought to prevent the Soviet Union from capitalizing on its geostrategic advantage to dominate its neighbors in Western Europe, Asia, and the Middle East, and thereby fundamentally alter the global balance of power to our disadvantage.[53]

The security wards of the United States in Eurasia distracted Soviet power and attention, served as physical barriers against Soviet access to the high seas, provided U.S. bridgeheads in Europe and Asia, and fielded useful, if not critical, "continental swords" complementary to U.S. maritime, air, and central-strategic striking power. Despite much rhetoric to the contrary, military security was the top priority. The U.S. government did not allocate 4.9 percent of its GNP (FY 1991) to the Department of Defense for the purpose of advancing American-style democracy abroad.

After 1945, fear of what the USSR might choose to do with its increasingly formidable military power drove the level, shape, and much of the detail of the U.S. defense effort. The capabilities, declarations, and actions that comprised U.S. national security policy made sense only with reference to the Soviet threat. That threat, as variously defined over the years, was not *a* factor helping to define the purposes of U.S. policy, grand strategy, and military strategy. It was *the* factor.

In retrospect it is easy to criticize a defense community prone to equate political intentions with military capability. A neglect of strategic reasoning and an effective disdain for political context permeated much of the analytic defense literature in the United States. It is unlikely that the USSR could have reaped sufficiently great reward from a hard-target counterforce duel to warrant a leap from peace to nuclear war in one fell swoop, a scenario suggested in some defense literature. With probable errors in commission and omission readily admitted, it is still easy to forget that sound national security policy should and can function as a self-negating prophecy. When successfully designed and executed, a U.S. policy that aims to prevent Soviet aggrandizement is hard to justify in hindsight. The USSR was contained, and more, *much more*. Does that mean that the USSR did not really require containing? Or does it mean that U.S. policy was successful?

Given the strategic-cultural framework for this discussion, American society performed remarkably in terms of the measure of effectiveness that Edward N. Luttwak described: "During four decades and more, therefore,

---

52 Etzold and Gaddis, eds., *Containment*, p. 208.
53 Reagan, *National Security Strategy of the United States* (1988), p. 1.

the strategic virtue most required of Americans and their government has been sheer tenacity."[54] Tenacity is not the most obvious description of American culture in the twentieth century. Perhaps it is more accurate to say that Americans are tenacious in applying American-style solutions to problems. Nonetheless, the tenacity to which Luttwak refers is the tenacity required to stay the long open-ended course. When Luttwak writes "that Soviet conduct so far has *not* been the normal conduct of a normal Great Power; it has resembled, rather, that of a Great Power at war,"[55] he points accurately to long-standing and authoritative American perceptions of threat.

The dissolution of the Great Russian empire, whether temporary or permanent, in no way diminishes the extent of Soviet power in the past. The political, economic, and military circumstances of Eurasia in the mid-to-late 1940s, the recent as well as more distant Soviet record of aggressive self-defense, and the grim character of Soviet imperialism, all pointed to a problem deserving of attention. Even in retrospect, it seems unlikely that the United States could have achieved "normal" political relations with Stalin's Russia after World War II. American leaders may have exaggerated the military menace behind the overt political hostility, but who really knows? The USSR certainly had suffered vast economic and demographic damage as a consequence of its foreign and self-inflicted domestic catastrophes of the first half of the century. Nonetheless, the destruction of the Axis powers created vacuums in Europe and Asia that the USSR appeared strongly motivated to fill. Politics, not engineering, is the master science. Soviet political hostility toward a United States with the ability to thwart a Soviet bid for bicontinental hegemony – let alone territorial conquest – was no figment of diseased conservative imaginations. It was not unreasonable for American policymakers to infer real danger from Soviet statements of political hostility, unfriendly political actions, and military deployments; an apparent match existed between those events and the formal goals of Soviet political ideology.

With regard to high policy and its fit with military strategy and grand strategic resources of all kinds – national, allied, and functionally friendly – U.S. performance is hard to fault. With benefit of hindsight it is clear that many Americans exaggerated Soviet military power in the late 1940s and 1950s. But during the 1960s and 1970s the United States systematically underestimated Soviet military power. In general it is difficult to deny the results of U.S. strategic performance. Any responsible American government had to assume that the undisguised latent Soviet threat might take active form. The issue was not whether Moscow needed to be deterred, but whether Washington prudently could assume otherwise. Furthermore, the United States and its allies always had ample resources (political, demographic,

---

54 "Do We Need a New Grand Strategy?" *The National Interest* (Spring 1989), p. 3.
55 Ibid. Emphasis in original.

material, economic, scientific, geopolitical) for the *onshore* containment of the Soviet empire. Indeed, American national preferences have played a large role in the choice of grand and military strategy precisely because resources have been sufficient to give those preferences scope.

A STRATEGY SKETCH: THE NUCLEAR FACTOR

The need to design and maintain a strategy that extends American protection over allies and friends around the rimlands of Eurasia has remained the geostrategic corollary of Eurasian onshore containment. Quite properly, the United States has worried periodically about attacks upon itself. But the nature, difficulty, and likely consequences of such attacks probably rendered them relatively easy to discourage.[56] Ultimately, U.S. strategy is about the advancement of American interests and most certainly about the security of the American people. But historical experience, geopolitical reasoning, and the momentum of events produced a postwar era wherein the driving force behind U.S. strategy was the need – certainly the perceived need – to protect the Eurasian periphery against Soviet land power.

From the dawn of the nuclear age a strong thread of American opinion held that although nuclear threats have deterrent value, the concept of nuclear strategy is an oxymoron. Yet for reasons of coalition geography and of the proximity of its security clients in Europe to Soviet land power, the United States had to assume that nuclear weapons were instruments of policy capable of functioning in the traditional means-ends context of strategy in time of war as well as in the deterrence of war. American strategists presumed that interlocking East-West strategic, operational, tactical, and technological choices would determine whether or not nuclear weapons were weapons and nuclear war was war as generally understood. Both Soviet and NATO governments regarded nuclear weapons as useable instruments of war. There is no good reason to believe that either side was bluffing about its willingness to use nuclear force in the direst circumstances. Nevertheless, the perceived utility of nuclear weapons declined as ownership became bilateral in 1949, as the USSR acquired a large retaliatory capability in the second half of the 1960s,[57] and as the political fuel behind East-West antagonism lost its potency in the 1980s.

Ironically, the 1990s are bringing a functional return to the strategic conditions of the late 1940s. In that period, the Truman administration had not decided how to use atomic weapons. Indeed, for several years it was not clear

---

[56] For many years, the deterrence of attack upon one's homeland received the label "passive," in contrast to the "active deterrence" presumed necessary to persuade a deterree not to assault one's friends and allies.

[57] See Richard K. Betts, *Nuclear Blackmail and Nuclear Balance* (Washington, 1987). It is important that one should not read back uncritically into the 1950s and 1960s the attitudes and opinions about the inutility of nuclear weapons that belong more properly to a later period.

if the government would grant political sanction for the prompt use of those weapons.[58] Even after the Berlin Blockade had compelled official scrutiny of the use of atomic weapons, the balance of expert opinion held that execution of SAC's proposed emergency war plan (HALFMOON) would not defeat the USSR.[59] The 1990s may not be the literal beginning of a "post-nuclear era,"[60] but they are the decade of the elaboration and maturing of strategic theories, military plans, and force postures that accord nuclear capability a strictly residual deterrent role. Given the certainty of the return of a major Eurasian threat to U.S. interests and the likelihood of greater nuclear proliferation in the Third World, the idea of a "post-nuclear era" is fallacious.

Strategic air power has been both the symbol and the embodiment of American preferences in the deterrence and conduct of war. The success of the Manhattan Project and the B-29 program – and their marriage in the Western Pacific – appeared to choke off argument about the efficacy of aerial bombardment. Certainly Hiroshima and Nagasaki preempted any potential public debate among the services over the wartime record of the Combined Bomber Offensive in Europe.[61] The fit of long-range air-atomic striking power with American strategic culture was almost perfect. From Anglo-American colonists who waged locally unprecedentedly "savage" warfare against Indian societies,[62] to General William Tecumseh Sherman's 1863 observation that "Madam . . . war is cruelty . . . the crueler it is, the sooner it will be over,"[63] to the U.S. Navy captain who reflected in 1954 that SAC's war plan would reduce the USSR to "a smoking radiating ruin at the end of

---

58 On U.S. nuclear weapons policy in the late 1940s and 1950s, see David Alan Rosenberg, "The Origins of Overkill: Nuclear Weapons and American Strategy, 1945–1960," *International Security* (Spring 1983), pp. 3–71.

59 In addition to Rosenberg, "The Origins of Overkill," the history of U.S. nuclear war planning is approachable via Trachtenberg, *History and Strategy;* Kaplan, *Wizards of Armageddon;* Jeffrey Richelson, "PD-59, NSDD-13 and the Reagan Strategic Modernization Program," *The Journal of Strategic Studies* (June 1983), pp. 125–46; Leon Sloss and Marc Dean Millot, "U.S. Nuclear Strategy in Evolution," *Strategic Review* (Winter 1984), pp. 19–28; Desmond Ball and Jeffrey Richelson, eds., *Strategic Nuclear Targeting* (Ithaca, NY, 1986), particularly Rosenberg's and Ball's essays; Scott D. Sagan, "SIOP-62: The Nuclear War Plan Briefing to President Kennedy," *International Security* (Summer 1987), pp. 22–51; and idem, *Moving Targets: Nuclear Strategy and National Security* (Princeton, 1989), ch. 1.

60 Edward N. Luttwak, "An Emerging Postnuclear Era?" *The Washington Quarterly* (Winter 1988), pp. 5–15.

61 See the United States Strategic Bombing Survey, *Over-all Report (European War)*, Washington, D.C., 30 September 1945.

62 Not having training in proper concepts of personal and societal honor or sportsmanship, Indian warriors tended to decline to stand and fight in pitched battles that would maximize the effectiveness of the colonists' firepower. It followed that – after European diseases – punitive raiding was a far more effective way of controlling the Indian menace than was the pursuit of decisive engagements.

63 Quoted in Herman Hathaway and Archer Jones, *How the North Won: A Military History of the Civil War* (Urbana, IL, 1983), p. 548.

two hours,"[64] to the air campaign against Iraq in 1991, the exercise of maximum violence for swift results has been the American way.[65]

Beginning with Truman, and then with a rush after Eisenhower took office, the United States and its global coalition elevated nuclear weapons to a dominant position in national and coalition military strategy. Economically, this course was not strictly necessary. As envisaged in the decisive planning document, NSC 68 of 14 April 1950,[66] the West could have chosen a different way to cope with the impending problem of *mutual* nuclear deterrence. The Western Powers could have exploited their economic superiority to generate large general purpose forces. The consequences of the 1953 decision to rely heavily on nuclear weapons for extended deterrence posed questions that became more and more difficult to answer as the overall balance of Soviet-American military power shifted towards rough equality.

In the early 1950s, the geostrategic structure of the Soviet-American conflict amounted functionally to an exchange of hostages. The physical survival of the Soviet Union depended on tolerable Soviet behavior toward American allies on the Eurasian periphery. SAC would literally execute the USSR in the event – or perhaps merely in strong anticipation[67] – of a Soviet military adventure against Western Europe. Similarly, the heavily armed land power and medium-range nuclear weapons of the USSR held Western European societies hostage to tolerable U.S. behavior. The stability of this asymmetrical standoff theoretically declined after the Soviet Union acquired a nuclear striking force capable of negating the deterrent effect of U.S. nuclear forces.[68] From the mid-1950s to the late 1980s the central thread in the history of American military strategy was therefore the problem of extending nuclear deterrence over distant allies in the face of increasingly robust Soviet nuclear capabilities. That problem was the central thread because the United States chose to contain Soviet power onshore in Eurasia and was unable or politically unwilling to reduce its reliance on nuclear forces for deterrence.

The decision to rely primarily on nuclear weapons to deter and, if need be, to compel was both inevitable and successful.[69] The United States enjoyed systemic competitive advantages over the USSR in high-technology weapons. Nuclear-armed forces were and remain cheaper than general purpose forces, while the nuclear deterrent appeared to offer a higher quality of assured

[64] Quoted as the title to David Alan Rosenberg, "A Smoking Radiating Ruin at the End of Two Hours: Documents of American Plans for Nuclear War with the Soviet Union, 1954–1955," *International Security* (Winter 1981–82), pp. 3–28.

[65] See Michael S. Sherry, *The Rise of American Air Power: The Creation of Armageddon* (New Haven, 1987).

[66] "NSC 68: United States Objectives and Programs for National Security, April 14, 1950," in Etzold and Gaddis, eds., *Containment*, pp. 385–442.

[67] Throughout the 1950s and at least the early 1960s, SAC was strongly committed to the preemptive attack option. Sagan, *Moving Targets*, p. 24.

[68] See Betts, *Nuclear Blackmail and Nuclear Balance.*

[69] See Thomas C. Schelling, *Arms and Influence* (New Haven, CT, 1966).

success in prevention of war than did any conventional alternative. The problem after the mid-1950s was the anticipated lack of credibility of U.S. nuclear threats. If these threats were ever exercised in action, either in the large dosages that planners envisaged from the 1950s through the mid-1970s or in the relatively modest quantities that were in theory feasible after the adoption of SIOP-5 in 1976,[70] U.S. strategic forces would license and all but guarantee a Soviet response that created an intolerable amount of nuclear damage.

In the second half of the 1950s and the early 1960s an American preemptive attack on the USSR would have resulted in *relatively* small damage in North America – for a nuclear war. However, the period when theoretical victories in central nuclear war still seemed possible was vanishing by the mid-1960s. The U.S. government consistently tried to enhance the credibility of its extended nuclear deterrent. Those endeavors progressed from the early 1960s – when the Kennedy administration ordered major revisions in the nuclear war plans (from SIOP-62 to SIOP-63) in favor of flexibility (city and country withholds) – through the next major revision in 1974–75 (SIOP-5) in favor of "(very) limited nuclear options," to SIOP-6 (1983) with its focus on the Soviet leadership and renewed emphasis on countermilitary targeting.[71] As the theoretical ability to disarm Soviet long-range nuclear striking power disappeared after the mid-1960s, the central question that emerged was whether or not the Western Alliance was seeking to perpetuate a structure of coalition strategy – extended deterrence through threats of controlled nuclear coercion – long rendered obsolete because of Soviet modernization.

The misnamed nuclear "war-fighting" philosophy allegedly enshrined both in the Carter administration's Nuclear Targeting Policy Review (NTPR) of 1977–79 and PD-59 of 25 July 1980 and was a theory of deterrence and not a plan for victory.[72] Unfortunately, it is not clear that high officials understood the importance of a theory of victory in nuclear war. Governments should employ nuclear force, like other kinds of force, only for the purpose of gaining strategic objectives that support policy goals. President Reagan's SDI plainly had cultural appeal to those who welcomed it as the only means to impose a technological peace vis-à-vis Soviet long-range ballistic missiles.[73] American scientists and engineers could provide a workable

---

70 See Lynn Etheridge Davis, *Limited Nuclear Options: Deterrence and the New American Doctrine*, Adelphi Papers No. 121 (Winter 1975–1976); and Desmond Ball, "The Development of the SIOP, 1960–1983," in Ball and Richelson, eds., *Strategic Nuclear Targeting*, pp. 70–75.

71 See Sagan, *Moving Targets*, ch. 1; and Desmond Ball and Robert C. Toth, "Revising the SIOP: Taking War-Fighting to Dangerous Extremes," *International Security* (Spring 1990), pp. 65–92.

72 See Colin S. Gray, "War-Fighting for Deterrence," *The Journal of Strategic Studies* (March 1984), pp. 5–18; idem, *Nuclear Strategy and National Style*, ch. 9; and Robert A. Levine, *Still the Arms Debate* (Brookfield, VT, 1990).

73 But in a generally positive assessment of SDI, Michael Vlahos concludes with the interesting point that "[d]efenses are a way of meeting both the cultural and the military

alternative to the political peace that had no longer seemed attainable. The appearance of Mikhail Gorbachev and his advertisements in words and deeds of radical "new thinking" on foreign affairs further discouraged an astrategically inclined American society from thinking strategically about the crisis of relevance over nuclear weapons that menaced the integrity of U.S. and NATO strategy.[74] Then the collapse of the Soviet position throughout East-Central Europe in 1989–90 sidelined the damage to NATO's nuclear-oriented strategy that the INF treaty of 1987 otherwise would have wrought.

The United States learned to depend upon latent nuclear threats. Since 1945 American officials and defense theorists conducted a dialogue among themselves. The inferable success of deterrence has ensured an absence of historical experience that would settle the most vital, persisting issues of nuclear strategy.[75] In theory, almost all kinds of war and war outcomes are possible. But in the fortunate absence of experience in nuclear war, the weapon and weapon-support technologies of the past four decades evolved without benefit of serious intellectual challenge. Strategic debate proceeds for mundane reasons such as institutional interests, but it also continues because events do not settle key issues. What are those issues?

- The usefulness of major war between nuclear-armed states and coalitions.
- The strategic utility of nuclear weapons for deterrence and defense.
- The controllability of nuclear conflict.
- The relevance of a classical approach to strategy, which seeks advantage through the defeat of the enemy's military forces.
- The integrity of the concept and practice of *nuclear* strategy.

The making and exercise of strategy comprise a practical art. With a keen sense of the obvious, the scholarly critic of American nuclear strategy can point to the horrors of nuclear war, the uncertain benefit for deterrence of various weapon systems, and the difficulties that would impede efforts to end nuclear war speedily on mutually acceptable terms.[76] In peacetime the U.S. government is given to indecision, a lack of clarity of conception, an absence of unity of thought and action, and disorganization in policy performance; nevertheless, it is not prone to the commission of great errors in statecraft and strategy. The cultural and other factors that shape the larger decisions on national security policy tend to be relatively tolerant of fault. As

imperatives of national security." *Strategic Defense and the American Ethos: Can the Nuclear World Be Changed?* SAIS Papers in International Affairs No. 13 (Boulder, CO, 1986).

74 For the intriguing although considerably overstated argument that some have greatly exaggerated the accomplishments of nuclear deterrence, see John Mueller, *Retreat from Doomsday: The Obsolescence of Major War* (New York, 1989).

75 When convenient in this essay the author has followed standard practice and referred to "nuclear strategy." However, for the record, the author agrees with Edward N. Luttwak: strategy is strategy and there is no distinctively nuclear form of strategic logic (See Luttwak, *Strategy*, ch. 11).

76 The classic study remains Fred Charles Iklé, *Every War Must End* (New York, 1971).

noted, historical experience has not resolved the key issues in nuclear strategy. That fact alone is arguable, but still powerful, testimony that U.S. strategy has been good enough.

One need not look too closely at nuclear policy debates to appreciate that the *theoretical* grounds for criticizing U.S. practice are overwhelming.[77] It is historically unprecedented for the most potent weapons of the greatest state of an era to have utility only in nonuse.[78] Yet common sense, elementary prudence, institutional habits, and strategic logic have obliged defense professionals to behave as if nuclear weapons were employable in a manner that would advance U.S. policy goals.

No one can assume that nuclear deterrence is an existential phenomenon, an automatic result of the presence of nuclear weapons. Good grounds exist for wondering whether nuclear targeting plans matter any more for deterrence than they would for the course and outcome of such a war. Nevertheless, the fact remains that a nuclear-armed state has targeting problems to resolve. A nuclear arsenal involves technical choices over tradeoffs between yield (and weight) and number of warheads, and over the characteristics of its delivery vehicles. The inventory of nuclear delivery systems represents the product of strategy in the service of policy.

What follows is a point-by-point summary of the collective and perhaps to some degree cumulative wisdom that inspired the practice of American nuclear strategy. Many theoretical and some practical difficulties attend any approach to nuclear strategy, but a practicable consensus has formed in support of these points. In its protracted historical "strategic moment" of international preeminence, the United States faced no more baffling problem than how to deal with the new and emerging technologies of nuclear weapons and their means of delivery. The ten points below summarize the U.S. response to those problems.

1. **Nuclear armed forces should be large rather than small.** Generously proportioned forces are less susceptible to technological, tactical, or operational ambush than are more modest forces. Moreover, large nuclear arsenals are more tolerant of negotiating error in arms control and of an adversary's noncompliance. A strategic nuclear arsenal with 12,000–13,000 warheads is a case of excessive insurance, but no identifiable connection links negotiated strategic arms *reductions* and national safety.

2. **Nuclear armed forces should be diversely, rather than simply, postured.** The triad of ICBMs, SLBMs, and manned bombers was not planned in advance as the most desirable way to deploy central nuclear systems. But

---

77 For example, see Nigel Blake and Kay Pole, eds., *Dangers of Deterrence: Philosophers on Nuclear Strategy* (London, 1983); Robert Jervis, *The Illogic of American Nuclear Strategy* (Ithaca, NY, 1984); Robert Jervis et al., *Psychology and Deterrence* (Baltimore, 1985); Richard Ned Lebow, *Nuclear Crisis Management: A Dangerous Illusion* (Ithaca, NY, 1987); and "The Rational Deterrence Debate: A Symposium," *World Politics* (January 1989), pp. 143–237.
78 See Bernard Brodie, *War and Politics* (New York, 1973).

every administration during three decades found the case for the triad persuasive. It provided complementary threats and a diversity of targets near-certain to thwart the ingenuity of would-be attackers.

3. **Command, control, communications, and intelligence (C3I) that support nuclear-armed forces should be as survivable as those forces.** Only in the 1980s did budgets match official rhetoric in praise of survivable C3I and flexibility in nuclear use. Analysts and defense officials long appreciated that the idea of nuclear war as a spasm of violence limited only by the size and combat readiness of forces could be a self-fulfilling prophecy unless they made careful provision for the continuing wartime command and control of those forces. If the only plan required for a nuclear war was a single pulse of destruction, then C3I requirements would be greatly simplified; the ability to order an attack would represent the only requirement. The need to build an intelligence and command system capable of performing the minimum essential missions while under surprise attack complicated matters somewhat, but in practice, the United States decided wisely that the minute risks of overconfidence in strategic control on the part of policymakers were vastly less dangerous than the temptations that vulnerable C3I might offer. The representatives of a deeply technically oriented strategic culture considerably overstated the problems, both real and alleged, of "command instability."[79] However, this is not an area in which policymakers should take avoidable risks.

4. **Forces and plans for the contingent use of nuclear armed forces should allow for flexibility in employment.** No one knows whether public explanation of some of the facts of, and intentions behind, flexibility in nuclear war planning really would enhance the credibility of nuclear threats, the strategic effectiveness of tailored nuclear use, and the prospects for terminating a nuclear war with an outcome short of general holocaust. It was an enduring fact of postwar history, however, that successive administrations voted for more, rather than less, flexibility in nuclear war plans. The actual plans have not always matched the policy expressed in guidance documents,[80] nor

---

[79] Scenarios of command "decapitation" abounded in the classified and unclassified worlds of U.S. defense debate in the 1980s. Such scenarios always pointed to the technically and tactically *possible*, but they tended to entail heroic assumptions and required implausible skill on the part of the attacker. This is an important subject and it does need to be studied constantly. However, when viewed operationally, strategically, and politically the problems of strategic C3I were less daunting than some of the unclassified literature of the 1980s suggested. Superior examples of this literature, which would benefit from a strategist's perspective, include Desmond Ball, *Can Nuclear War Be Controlled?* Adelphi Papers No. 169 (1981); John Steinbruner, "Nuclear Decapitation," *Foreign Policy* (Winter 1981), pp. 16–28; Paul Bracken, *The Command and Control of Nuclear Forces* (New York, 1983); Bruce G. Blair, *Strategic Command and Control: Redefining the Nuclear Threat* (Washington, 1985); Ashton B. Carter et al., eds., *Managing Nuclear Operations* (Washington, 1987); and Kurt Gottfried and Bruce G. Blair, eds., *Crisis Stability and Nuclear War* (New York, 1988).

[80] See Janne E. Nolan, *Guardians of the Arsenal: The Politics of Nuclear Strategy* (New York, 1989).

could policymakers necessarily use U.S. forces and their C3I support in as flexible a manner as they might wish. But for decades, presidents insisted on the possibility of employing strategic nuclear weapons with some discrimination and flexibility.

5. **Targeting policy for nuclear forces matters.** It is not certain that the details of U.S. nuclear threats decisively affect the perceived quality of deterrence in the minds of enemy policymakers. It may be that fear of nuclear war is *the* statesman's reaction to nuclear peril, rather than a concern to understand what an enemy's nuclear forces might attempt, or be able, to do.[81] Since there is no way of knowing in advance just how sensitive policy outcomes would be to targeting policies, the prudent have to assume that targeting could matter. For this reason, American strategic nuclear forces have held at risk Soviet political and military leadership assets, strategic nuclear forces, other military capabilities, and war-supporting industry. Although the overall design and the detail of targeting matters, the defense community needed to remember that algorithms are not the nuclear targeteers' only means of determining the adequacy or inadequacy of nuclear forces. Above all, deterrence does not necessarily result from acquiring nuclear firepower or from posing particular kinds of technically credible threats. The intended deterree has to *choose* to be deterred.

6. **Successful military action alone cannot enforce the limitation of damage.** Nuclear armed forces of the United States in the 1980s could not win a war in the classical sense against the USSR. Even if they had inflicted disproportionate damage on their Soviet counterparts, they could not have protected the American homeland from an intolerable level of retaliation. Desire for military advantage or for the denial of military advantage to the enemy certainly helped drive the process of strategic force modernization. But it is unclear how much counterforce capability was worth purchasing, given the restrictions on the technically, tactically, and operationally possible. Whether or not the United States would have suffered light, heavy, or annihilating damage in a nuclear war would have depended on the willingness and ability of Soviet political leaders to be deterred from exercising much of their nuclear firepower. U.S. ability to help shape the relevant Soviet choices (to fight or not to fight, escalate or not to escalate, retaliate symbolically, substantially, or massively) remained problematic. Wisely, the United States behaved as if perceptions of negative and positive sanctions could have influenced Moscow's actions: the alternative to this assumption was unacceptable.

7. **Nuclear weapons have a declining but still major strategic usefulness.** The U.S. defense community entered the last decade of the twentieth century with a belief in the declining utility of nuclear weapons; a new defense policy

---

[81] So awesome are the grim possibilities of a nuclear war and so approximate are the approximations that pass for working knowledge of a nuclear wartime environment that targeting choice might prove to be politically inconsequential.

aims to contain regional disputes as its first priority now that the Soviet threat has foundered.[82] But that task does not lend itself to easy translation into identifiable demands for strategic utility. Moreover, U.S. policymakers have sensibly embraced the notion that conventional deterrence lacks full strategic integrity in a nuclear age and that nuclear weapons prospectively have a permanent strategic role as a deterrent. Since complete nuclear disarmament could never be verified and the rewards for cheating could be boundless, the United States will always have to maintain a nuclear arsenal to dissuade others from using nuclear weapons.

8. **All polities would use nuclear weapons in a manner that expressed consequentialist policy logic.** In other words, Russian nuclear strategy may be distinctively Russian, reflecting the strategic culture of that particular historical entity. But nuclear holocaust represents a transcultural phenomenon, an outcome with no policy or strategic interest to any culture. At least in the 1970s and 1980s, the United States endeavored to shape its nuclear strategy to fit the structure and details of a uniquely Soviet Russian adversary. It may not matter for the prevention or control of war whether the United States has nuclear war plans of any particular character. But if that is not the case, the price of such an error might be a war that could have been deterred and a race to oblivion that a politically more intelligent nuclear campaign plan might have arrested.

9. **The technical details of nuclear force posture and operating procedures are important for decisions for peace and war.** It is sensible to worry about the technical details, for they can make a critical difference. However, the inclination to technicity, to the exaggeration of technical significance, as well as indifference to strategic reasoning, frequently misleads American policymakers. The technical rather than political, aspects of stability receive too much emphasis. The inclination – indeed eagerness – to recognize some weapons as inherently defensive or offensive and as stabilizing or destabilizing suggests a national security community attempting to avoid the perils of politics and strategy by concentrating on the calculable and settled worlds of administration and engineering.[83]

10. **In practice the United States prefers offensive to defensive deterrence.** In the 1980s, ballistic missile defense in particular, and strategic defense in general received official accolades. But the U.S. government did not explain the consequences for foreign policy and military strategy of superpower transitions to truly defensive strategic postures.[84] It is possible that an im-

---

82 President George Bush, "In Defense of Defense," Speech to the Aspen Institute Symposium, 2 August 1990, reprinted in Cheney, *Report of the Secretary of Defense*, pp. 131–34.
83 See Colin S. Gray, *Weapons Don't Make War: Policy, Strategy, and Military Technology* (Lawrence, KS, 1993).
84 See Samuel F. Wells, Jr., and Robert S. Lutwak, eds., *Strategic Defenses and Soviet-American Relations* (Cambridge, MA, 1987); Colin S. Gray, "The Transition from Offense to Defense," *The Washington Quarterly* (Summer 1986), pp. 59–72.

practicality of coercive first-use of nuclear weapons imposed by missile defences could have posed a fundamental challenge to the integrity of NATO's strategy of flexible response. Similarly, the possibility of strategic defense posed a challenge to the structure of Western grand and military strategies.

CONCLUSIONS: THE QUESTION OF PERFORMANCE

The only test of the quality of national performance that really counts is the test of success or failure. Did American grand strategy achieve its policy objectives? More than four and a half decades after the end of World War II, the most important problems facing U.S. policymakers and military strategists are the problems of success. Adapting American national security policy and military strategy to international conditions radically different from those of the late 1940s and early 1950s may be more difficult than the 1950s-style containment of the USSR. Many of the means and methods of U.S. performance in national security since 1945 merit criticism,[85] but that criticism, whether from left or right, from defense-minded military reformers or disarmament-minded peace activists, exists in the context of U.S. success.

First, the United States organized and maintained a generally healthy imbalance of power in favor of the Western world for more than forty-five years. The postwar preeminence of the United States and the Soviet Union may have ensured their mutual suspicion; nevertheless, the United States functioned as the leading, indeed essential, guardian of the non-Soviet world against whatever might have transpired in the absence of that guardianship. The job needed to be done, although in some cases the United States may have overdone it, and may have supported regimes that would have failed any audit of democratic virtues. But given American strategic culture and international conditions after 1945, the United States performed more steadily and effectively than any close student of American history would have dared predict. And America sustained that steadiness despite a cultural inclination toward impatience with open-ended tasks, a proclivity to define conditions as problems to be solved, and a propensity to assume goodwill on the part of other polities simply because they had not recently demonstrated contrary tendencies.

Second, the United States helped organize and did not tire of leading the most successful coalition in history, an alliance that survived despite enor-

---

[85] Edward N. Luttwak, *The Pentagon and the Art of War: The Question of Military Reform* (New York, 1984); Asa A. Clark IV et al., eds., *The Defense Reform Debate: Issues and Analysis* (Baltimore, 1984); Arthur T. Hadley, *The Straw Giant* (New York, 1986); Fen Osler Hampson, *Unguided Missiles: How America Buys Its Weapons* (New York, 1989); and Daniel Wirls, *Buildup: The Politics of Defense in the Reagan Era* (Ithaca, NY, 1992).

mous differences between the states involved.[86] In common with Athens after the Persian Wars, postwar America established and led what could only be a client-states' organization thinly disguised as a multilateral alliance. But unlike the Delian League, the alliance system of the United States did not evolve into an overbearing imperial power. It was no mean feat to lead rather than direct a coalition for forty years in strategic conditions in which the coalition leader ran the extraordinary risk of total annihilation. It is not surprising that NATO seemed perennially "troubled" or at "the crossroads." What was truly remarkable was that NATO retained its vigor for so long.

Third, the near-term focused, astrategic, and still impatient United States outlasted the USSR in the postwar competition for power and influence. Mikhail Gorbachev and his Russian successors acknowledged that their country requires a lengthy period of relief from external struggle if it is to compete in the prospectively complicated balance-of-power system of the twenty-first century.

Fourth, whether through quality of strategic ideas, skill in policy execution, the quantity and quality of military forces, or some element of luck, U.S. strategy has done the largest part of the job that American society asked of it. It deterred a *grande guerre* or at least avoided one with honor and geopolitical advantage.[87] The United States surrendered no vital national values, and the economic and social burdens of peacetime defense preparation were far short of crippling. Given that the United States had to function as the last line of its own defense, the last line of defense for all of the non-Soviet world, and was able to share, historically speaking, relatively little of its total military duty with its allies, its strategic performance was generally admirable.

It is difficult, probably impossible, to distinguish competence in policy when conditions are unusually favorable. For example, Lawrence Freedman has noted correctly that extended deterrence in the form of the American nuclear guarantee to NATO "is one of those areas where a policy has worked far better in practice than an assessment of . . . theory might lead one to expect."[88] It is possible that this essay may allocate credit to U.S. policies and strategies that would have had difficulty failing. In large measure, nuclear deterrence might have been existential[89] and required little maintenance of a balance of terror that was really indelicate. Furthermore, nuclear deterrence may have been redundant. Perhaps the Soviet Union was generally satisfied

---

86 Calls for an end to the longstanding U.S. role in NATO have not been in short supply. See Melvyn Krauss, *How NATO Weakens the West* (New York, 1986); and David P. Calleo, *Beyond American Hegemony: The Future of the Western Alliance* (New York, 1987).

87 But see Mueller, *Retreat from Doomsday*.

88 Freedman, *Evolution of Nuclear Strategy*, xx.

89 McGeorge Bundy, "Existential Deterrence and Its Consequences," in Douglas MacLean, ed., *The Security Gamble: Deterrence Dilemmas in the Nuclear Age* (Totowa, NJ, 1984). Lawrence Freedman provides a useful critique in "I Exist; Therefore I Deter," *International Security* (Summer 1988), pp. 177–95.

with its postwar imperial holdings and with its prospects for success in political competition far short of major war.

The United States has not performed well in arms control negotiations, but to date little harm has resulted. The strategic forces that the United States chose to maintain or develop under arms control restraints have been adequate to meet the minimal demands placed upon them in the 1970s and 1980s. Moreover, even including the ballistic missile defenses prohibited under the ABM treaty of 1972, it is reasonably clear that the United States has not denied itself capabilities that might have affected the balance over the past two decades. In short, arms control simply has not been vital to national and international security.[90]

In Vietnam, U.S. military leaders abdicated too much responsibility to a theater commander in whom they held less than full confidence, and they failed to provide an overall strategic framework for the conduct of the war. They thus made success unlikely, flouting most of the much-maligned principles of war.[91] There was a plausible political rationale for each of the more important prohibitions upon operational flexibility, as there was for each of the major tendencies in academic theories of limited war and crisis management. But those politically attractive operational restrictions had the practical effect of permitting the enemy in Hanoi to wage the several wars in Vietnam on its own terms. This is not to say necessarily that the United States could have won in Vietnam at an acceptable price even by following a much more astute strategy. But the JCS and the Secretary of Defense, by their silence, knowingly collaborated in the unsound conduct of the war. Whatever can be said in praise or criticism of Operation DESERT STORM, the conduct of the 1991 Gulf War exposed an unmistakable and healthy rejection of the 1950s' and 1960s' theories of limited war.[92]

If there is a major lesson in the Vietnam experience, it is that the U.S. government should only select policy objectives that it can plausibly attain through socially acceptable means and methods. In Vietnam, President Johnson willed the end, indeed courageously willed the end given the heroically ambitious scale of his domestic program. But he failed to will suitable

---

[90] For the argument that arms control can be modestly useful, see Albert Carnesale and Richard N. Haass, eds., *Superpower Arms Control: Setting the Record Straight* (Cambridge, MA, 1987) and Bruce D. Berkowitz, *Calculated Risks: A Century of Arms Control, Why It Has Failed, and How It Can Be Made to Work* (New York, 1987). Frontal assaults on that view are launched in Patrick Glynn, *Closing Pandora's Box: Arms Races, Arms Control, and the History of the Cold War* (New York, 1992); and Colin S. Gray, *House of Cards: Why Arms Control Must Fail* (Ithaca, NY, 1992).

[91] A point made painfully clear in Summers, *On Strategy*, passim; and Palmer, *25-Year War*, pp. 192–93.

[92] *Reportedly*, the entire JCS, including its chairman, General Earle G. Wheeler, decided on 25 August 1967 that it would resign en masse the next day over the issue of Vietnam war policy and over plain evidence of double-dealing by the Secretary of Defense, Robert S. McNamara. It is even more impressive to recall that the JCS finally decided not to resign on 26 August 1967. See Perry, *Four Stars*, pp. 160–66. The absence of scholarly apparatus in Perry's book reduces the confidence with which this point can be made.

military actions. Furthermore, his most senior military and civilian advisers on the war failed to tell him the truth. The Vietnam experience certainly showed American strategic culture in full dress, including the ignorance of and indifference to other cultures, the waging of an attritional struggle with excessive reliance on machines and firepower, and the inability to function strategically. The fighting prowess of the U.S. Army in Vietnam was no better and no worse than it had been in previous wars except in the final stages, when no one saw much point in being the last American to die in Vietnam. The difference was that the strategic and operational contexts precluded a victory that would obscure and even excuse tactical and organizational flaws. If a military instrument wins or at least is an important factor in a coalition victory, the very fact of victory tends to discourage criticism.

The "strategy school" of American military reformers argued, reasonably enough, that America's failure in Vietnam stemmed from the absence of sound strategy. But as this essay has sought to explain, there are deep-seated, historically based reasons why the U.S. government has great difficulty thinking, let alone behaving, in a truly strategic manner. God's anointed people, blessed with success in the application of their arms in a long series of just causes, are not prone to careful management of means-ends relationships.

U.S. military power, like American society, is a powerful but blunt instrument. U.S. strategic culture performs certain military enterprises admirably. Fortunately, those enterprises include virtually all of the larger, more orthodox tasks that bear upon war and peace between states and coalitions. Planning and execution of a D-Day landing, of nuclear deterrence, of SIOP-level nuclear war, or of large-scale nonnuclear war all exploit America's strengths and avoid the worst of America's weaknesses. The larger and more violent the endeavor, the more effectively the United States is likely to perform. Some American military reformers, as well as strategic theorists have forgotten that "a country has the kind of army its total ethos, its institutions, resources, habits of peaceful life, make possible. . . . So the American way of war is bound to be like the American way of life."[93]

93 Brogan, *American Character*, pp. 162, 163.

19

Conclusion: Continuity and revolution in the making of strategy

MACGREGOR KNOX

Our sources for the making of strategy – the rational and reciprocal adjustment of ends and means by rulers and states in conflict with their adversaries – cover 2,400 years and a bewildering range of societies.[1] Much has changed since Thucydides wrote of the greatest war he knew, the war between Athens and Sparta. Yet as his Athenians emphatically predicted, the quest for domination has proved an enduring feature of human existence:

> Of the gods we believe, and of men we know, that by a necessary law of their nature they rule wherever they can. And it is not as if we were the first to make this law, or to act upon it when made: we found it existing before us, and shall leave it to exist forever after us . . .[2]

In the ceaseless conflict from this law described – as Thucydides also repeatedly stressed – uncertainty, chance, friction, and the will of the enemy place extraordinary demands on the makers of strategy and those led or driven to carry it out.[3] And as a disenchanted aristocrat from the greatest democracy of the ancient world, Thucydides saw far better than later counselors of princes or emperors the intimate connection between politics – the internal

---

[1] This essay rests in large part on those of the other contributors, to whom I gratefully acknowledge a considerable debt; when I touch on the subjects of their essays, the reader should simply assume an appropriate footnote. Eliot Cohen, Don Kagan, Richard Kaeuper, Michael Handel, Bernard Knox, Williamson Murray, Paul Rahe, Brian Sullivan, and Perez Zagorin have been generous with criticism and encouragement. Sins of omission or commission in what follows are entirely my own.

[2] Athenian delegation to the Melian oligarchs, V:105 (Crawley translation). Thucydides – whose insistence that human affairs were subject to recurring patterns led him to describe his book as "a possession for all time" – underscored that same historical "law" in the crucial early speech of the Athenian delegation at Sparta: "And it was not we who set the example, for it has always been the law that the weaker should be subject to the stronger" (I:24, 75–76).

[3] For chance as a central theme of the History, see Lowell Edmunds, *Chance and Intelligence in Thucydides* (Cambridge, MA, 1975).

and external policies of a *polis* ruled by the sovereign assembly of warrior-citizens – and war.

Thucydides would thus have been wholly at home with Clausewitz's notion of conflict as the unpredictable escalatory "collision of two living forces" governed by the "paradoxical trinity" of violence, chance, and politics.[4] Most of the central insights of both Thucydides and Clausewitz have stood the test of the greatest leap in human history, the transition – underway as Clausewitz wrote – from the cyclical quasistagnation of the agrarian age to the permanent revolution of science, technology, and industry. But that leap and its apparently still-accelerating consequences have nevertheless transformed irrevocably the framework within which strategy is made. And those consequences continue to transform it on an almost daily basis. Marx was wrong about many things, but not about the dynamics of the industrial age: "The bourgeoisie cannot exist without constantly revolutionizing the instruments of production" – and of war. One approach to understanding the ever-changing landscape that now faces the strategist is to seek to dissect the forces that have driven the transformation of strategy in the last 2,400 years, and seem likely to do so in the future. Those forces have interacted reciprocally, but categories – bureaucracy, mass politics, ideology, and technology and economic power – may best serve to separate them for analysis.

BUREAUCRACY

"War is a matter of vital importance to the State; the province of life or death; the road to survival or ruin." The first sentence in the strategic manual of Thucydides' great Chinese near-contemporary, Sun Tzu, puts it candidly. The making of strategy is the domain of *states,* those remorseless monsters whose central characteristic is the monopoly of violence on their own territory and whose pivotal institutions are armed forces and bureaucracy. The growth of bureaucracy is bound up with war, for in pre-industrial states the chief government expenditure was normally defense or aggression. That expenditure drove taxation, which in turn required increasingly large bureaucratic machines for collection and disbursement. Yet strategy remained obstinately unbureaucratized until the twentieth century, thanks to the jealous resistance of rulers against the encroachment of experts, to the relative simplicity of pre-industrial strategic issues, and to the nature of bureaucracy itself.

Bureaucracies are neatly *zweckrational:* swift and precise – in theory and surprisingly often in practice – in executing orders. But they inevitably define national purpose in terms of bureaucratic rather than national survival. They are happiest with established wisdom and incremental change. They cherish the myth that virtually all strategic problems are soluble in and through their own element – be it diplomacy, economic power, covert knowledge and

---

4 Carl von Clausewitz, *On War,* ed. and trans. Michael Howard, Peter Paret (Princeton, 1984), pp. 77, 89.

action, ground combat, naval supremacy, or air bombardment – and that problems not thus soluble are not problems. When faced with the incommensurate or unquantifiable alternatives that are the stuff of strategy, they usually retreat to incoherent compromise with their fellows or take flight into strategy by intuition – unless the structure of strategic decision-making forces them to defend all choices in rational terms. And in the absence of driving political leadership, even structured debate may produce only paralysis.

The assembly and the elected generals made the strategy of democratic Athens. Imperial Rome's strategy-making machinery – if any semipermanent institutions existed – has left no trace in the sources before the late empire.[5] In the incoherent snake pits of early "feudal" Europe, the great medieval monarchies, and the princedoms of the Renaissance, the rulers and a few trusted advisers made strategy without benefit of systems analysts or option papers. In theory, the monarchs of the early modern absolutist states likewise monopolized the making of strategy. Commanding figures such as Philip II of Spain, Louis XIV, and Frederick the Great did so in practice, relegating their sometimes elaborate staffs to advisory roles. But in the ever more competitive world of early modern statecraft, no power could avoid for long the predicament inherent in centralized hereditary power: what saved the state when the ruler offered catastrophic leadership or none at all?

For the two great or near-great powers that were not absolutist the question did not arise. The Dutch republic took shape through wars in which merchant oligarchies, aristocratic generals, and piratical seamen alternated or cooperated in providing strategic leadership. England's emergence as the hegemonic sea-power owed much to the final collapse of Stuart absolutist pretensions in 1688. That made possible an unprecedented mobilization of landed and commercial financial might and a remarkably effective strategic leadership by a small Admiralty bureaucracy in consultation with key parliamentary figures and interests. The French sought to resolve the issue of strategic leadership, and much else, through a revolution fueled in part by the manifest strategic incompetence that their monarchy had displayed in the Seven Years' War. The paradoxical result was a disastrous twenty-two years' struggle against most of Europe and a dictatorship whose protagonist, Napoleon, incarnated operational brilliance – and strategic lunacy.[6]

Prussia took another path, especially after its crushing defeat at Jena-

---

[5] For the *making* of strategy in imperial Rome, see especially Fergus Millar, "Emperors, Frontiers and Foreign Relations, 31 B.C. to A.D. 378," *Britannia* 13 (1982), particularly pp. 4–7; Edward N. Luttwak, *The Grand Strategy of the Roman Empire* (Baltimore, 1976) offers a brilliant reconstruction of the substance of that strategy, but see also Arthur Ferrill, *The Fall of the Roman Empire: The Military Explanation* (London, 1986).

[6] Napoleon, like his German successors in the "thirty years' war" of 1914–45, resolved strategic issues by battlefield virtuosity and harbored apparently unlimited aims. The outcome in both cases was defeat by a "world of enemies."

Auerstädt in 1806 revealed the full price of absolutism without a Frederick the Great. A reforming "bureaucratic absolutism" emerged to save the state even from monarchical incompetence.[7] Yet bureaucratic absolutism did not lead to the bureaucratization of Prussian strategy. Thanks to Prussia's geographic situation wedged between potential adversaries, to its tradition of battlefield distinction, and to the Napoleonic example of deciding strategic issues exclusively by battle, the result was the bureaucratization of *operations*. The elder Moltke's general staff was bereft of strategic insight; left to themselves, the generals and king would have gone on to Vienna in 1866 and thrown Prussia into a hopeless coalition struggle that might have spared the world the thirty years' war of 1914–45. But fortunately for Prussia, Bismarck made its strategy, and so astutely combined diplomacy and force that he secured central European hegemony without provoking counteraction from the powers on the wings.

His achievement proved impossible to repeat. The army's victories in 1866 and 1870 so unbalanced Prusso-German politics and society that even Bismarck's civilian successors came to see the German sword as the exclusive remedy for strategic obstacles. Bismarck's success fortified bureaucratic absolutism even against the new universal suffrage Reichstag. The Germany he left behind had neither civilian control, nor interservice coordination, nor machinery for making strategy other than a general staff whose collective wisdom after 1912 was "war the sooner the better."[8] In the end, Prussian bureaucratic absolutism offered a strategic leadership less coherent – and no less dependent on great leaders – than the system of Frederick the Great that it had replaced.

The Imperial Japan of the 1930s, Imperial Germany's East Asian analogue from its Bismarckian constitution to its Ludendorffian civil-military relationship, likewise failed to develop decision machinery capable of avoiding disaster. In the interminable conferences that preceded the Pearl Harbor attack, Japan's military bureaucracies showed themselves incapable of framing a national strategy that proposed a convincing relationship between the three widely separated theaters in which they faced the Soviet Union, China, and the American-British-Dutch coalition. Japan's armed forces also suffered from an extreme and peculiar form of bureaucratic diffusion of power, the "rule of the higher by the lower" through which ideologically exalted junior and mid-level officers further accelerated the rush toward ruin. Finally, the navy's control mania precluded discussion of the political aspects of the Pearl Harbor attack. In the minds of the planners, the target of the carrier striking

---

7   See Hans Rosenberg, *Bureaucracy, Aristocracy, and Autocracy: the Prussian Experience, 1660–1815* (Cambridge, MA, 1958), Chaps. 8, 9.
8   Moltke the younger, at the "council of war" of 8 December 1912: John C.G. Röhl, "Admiral von Müller and the Approach of War, 1911–1914," *Historical Journal* 12:4 (1969), p. 662.

force was a mere operational detail, to be veiled by security not merely from civilians and generals, but even from the navy's own intelligence staff.[9]

Nor did decision machinery grace the great dictatorships of the interwar era; their rulers revived the secretive guardianship of strategic decision of the absolute monarchs. Unsurprisingly, Imperial Japan and its Führer-dictatorship allies failed to formulate a global coalition strategy – and even Hitler and Mussolini, despite long association and constant meetings, failed to agree or even seek agreement on strategic essentials.[10]

It was the democratic great powers – Britain, France, and the United States – that pioneered "defense by committee" amid swift technological change, gathering threats, a growing need for interservice coordination, and friction between civilians and "brass hats." France's efforts were tentative and ineffectual; the national *esprit de système* did not extend to the realm of strategic decision-making. The *Conseil Supérieur de la Défense Nationale* (CSDN) failed to provide much-needed coordination of strategy, diplomacy, and resource mobilization in its few years of operation before 1914. It was merely an occasional forum for inconclusive discussion between high military figures and the cabinet, and it ceased to operate in wartime. After 1918 it became a "monster" too large for useful debate, and its terms of reference confined it to the integration of military and economic mobilization. Neither the CSDN nor the lesser defense planning committees of the 1930s made, or were intended to make, French strategy. That remained the prerogative of the ever-changing cabinet, which lacked the necessary orderly procedures and weight of experience.[11]

---

[9] See Michael A. Barnhart, "Japanese Intelligence before the Second World War: 'Best Case' Analysis," pp. 424–55 in Ernest R. May, ed., *Knowing One's Enemies: Intelligence Assessment before the Two World Wars* (Princeton, 1984); Alvin Coox, "The Effectiveness of the Japanese Military Establishment in the Second World War," in Williamson Murray and Allan R. Millett, eds., *Military Effectiveness*, v. 3 (Boston, 1988), pp. 11–16; and Akira Iriye, *The Origins of the Second World War in Asia and the Pacific* (London, 1987), especially pp. 170–72. Maruyama Masao, "Thought and Behaviour Patterns of Japan's Wartime Leaders," in his *Thought and Behaviour in Modern Japanese Politics* (Oxford, 1969), pp. 84–134 is still useful on the decision-making process (see especially the astounding eyewitness account of a key meeting in October 1941, p. 88 note) and for the parallel to Imperial Germany. For navy secrecy about its target, Barnhart, "Japanese Intelligence," p. 446 and Scott D. Sagan, "The Origins of the Pacific War," *International Security*, 18:4 (1988), pp. 916–17.

[10] Mussolini and his service chiefs, for instance, did their best to keep the Wehrmacht out of the Mediterranean until the disasters of December 1940-February 1941 forced them to implore German aid. Hitler consulted the Italians on no major strategic decisions, and gave little or no warning of forthcoming actions such as the invasion of the Soviet Union (see in general MacGregor Knox, *Mussolini Unleashed, 1939–1941* [Cambridge, 1982] and Lucio Ceva, *La condotta italiana della guerra. Cavallero e il Comando Supremo 1941/1942* [Bologna, 1975]).

[11] Seventeen individuals in forty-one cabinets served as minister of war (of national defense in 1932 and after 1936) between 1919 and June 1940; stretches of continuity under Clemenceau, Painlevé, Maginot, and Daladier hardly guaranteed a coherent process of decision. On the system's failure to function, see especially Jean Vial, "La défense nationale: son

The empirical British, drawing on experience in improvising global strategy that stretched back to the War of the Spanish Succession, developed the first and perhaps the most supremely effective strategic decision machinery. Britain's world-spanning responsibilities and shrinking margin for error led in the 1890s to proposals for interservice coordination and the centralization and rationalization of decision-making. Then stinging defeats at the hands of Boer backwoodsmen and the difficulties of coordinating that unexpectedly large imperial "small war" provided a catalyst; the result was the Committee of Imperial Defence. And in the last years before 1914 Britain's peculiar predicament as a sea power facing both an overwhelming land challenge and a growing sea threat led to unparalleled interservice strategic debate. Remarkably, debate worked. The navy's strategy by intuition cut a poor figure at the decisive meeting in August 1911. The army, despite the tactical dimwittedness that characterized its trajectory from Balaclava to Colenso and Passchendaele, developed and defended the one strategy that fit Britain's overriding need to preserve France from German vassalage, and thus save Britain's own independence. The BEF would go to Maubeuge – and *be there* to stagger into the gap between German First and Second Armies on the Marne.

The system broke down in war. The belated centralization of political and economic war leadership in Lloyd George's War Cabinet failed to bring civil-military harmony or coherent strategic decision-making, which remained as rare in 1914–18 Britain as in the other great powers. But between the wars the moving spirit behind the prewar CID, Maurice Hankey, succeeded in expanding the system into the now-familiar structure of CID, Chiefs of Staff Committee, Joint Planning Committee, Joint Intelligence Committee, and Cabinet and CID subcommittees. All were under the aegis of the Cabinet, and charged with hoarding the accumulated experience of 1914–18 and imposing coherence on British strategy through study, closely argued position papers, and face-to-face debate.

Yet bureaucratic structures alone were not enough to impose strategic coherence when politicians of the stamp of Stanley Baldwin and Ramsay MacDonald were determined not to have a strategy. In 1935–36 the structures themselves helped rule out the obvious step of squashing Mussolini, whose own military warned him in August 1935 that collision with Britain would bring "a disaster that would plunge us to a Balkan level." Hitler noted with interest what both he and the commander of the British Mediterranean fleet took as Whitehall's pusillanimity.[12] And Neville Chamberlain's wish-

organisation entre les deux guerres," *Revue d'Histoire de la Deuxième Guerre Mondiale*, April 1955, pp. 11–32.

12 Badoglio to Mussolini, 14 August 1935, in Giorgio Rochat, *Militari e politici nella preparazione della campagna d'Etiopia* (Milan, 1971), p. 229; Fisher, Commander-in-Chief, Mediterranean Fleet, on the "pusillanimity" of the C.O.S. and Admiralty: Arthur

fulfillment fantasies about Hitler's intentions then combined fatefully with the Chiefs of Staff worst-case judgment of German capabilities to paralyze Britain in 1938. The Chiefs of Staff themselves dampened Chamberlain's uncharacteristic interest in attacking Fascist Italy in summer-fall 1939, a step that might have offset German victory in Poland, distracted Hitler from the Western Front at small cost to the allies, and saddled the Germans suddenly with a major economic drain. But with Churchill in the driver's seat, the rationality and clarity of war cabinet and subcommittee decision-making proved an immense force multiplier, and may have spelled the difference between survival and catastrophe in 1940–41.[13]

Britain's example was decisive for the United States. The army-navy Joint Board established in 1903 to remedy deficiencies uncovered in war against Spain offered a sometimes effective vehicle for interservice coordination after 1919. But it fell short of the needs of high command in the war that made the United States the successor of Britain as the only global great power. The apparently mortal threats of 1941–42, the British staffs as exemplars and fiercely distrusted competitors, and the autocratic war powers that Roosevelt wielded with relish and skill combined to create a structure resembling that of Britain's. Its greatest peculiarity lay at its apex. Whereas in Britain – despite Churchill's commanding position – the collegial cabinet or war cabinet made the most vital decisions through discussion after the COS and the subcommittees had relentlessly parsed the alternatives, open debate in the American system normally took place only at the Joint Chiefs of Staff level if at all. That placed immense responsibilities on the president; the quality of his strategic leadership was in the final analysis all-important. When it was good, as Roosevelt's arguably was in seeking to crush Hitler as swiftly and convincingly as possible, the results were stunning. When it was indecisive or colored by wishful thinking, as in Roosevelt's dealings with Stalin or Chiang Kai-Shek, the outcome could be less happy.

When the wartime system gave birth – in the face of a new global threat – to the much expanded bureaucratic structures of the 1947 National Security Act, the elective monarchy at the summit retained at least some of the war powers that Lincoln, Wilson, and Roosevelt had wielded to such effect. The National Security Council in theory provided a forum for the debate of fundamental alternatives, and for discerning the full range of strategic choices available to the United States. In practice, it only debated when presidents wanted debate. And whatever its uses in cold war peacetime, war leadership without a president with the necessary education and experience

Marder, "The Royal Navy and the Ethiopian Crisis of 1935–36," *American Historical Review*, 75:5 (1970), p. 1339.

[13] On all of this, see also Williamson Murray, *The Change in the European Balance of Power, 1938–1939* (Princeton, 1984); on war with Italy in 1939, see ibid., pp. 314–21; Murray, "The Role of Italy in British Strategy 1938–1939," *RUSI Journal*, 124:3 (1979), pp. 43–49 (Chamberlain for action, p. 47); and Knox, *Mussolini Unleashed, 1939–1941*, pp. 44–45.

was far beyond the system's powers, as the Vietnam misadventure demonstrated. The majestic structure of the Joint Chiefs of Staff proved capable only of interservice brokerage of targets, missions, and budgets. McNamara and his civilian analysts confused bean-counting with strategic judgment, and infected their military-bureaucratic antagonists with their own shallow rationalism. Neither Johnson nor his advisers evolved a strategy less supinely dependent on the enemy than the "hope that [America's] will to continue . . . would cause the Communists to relent."[14] The services, left without guidance except for presidential restrictions on where they could fight, mounted wars of attrition against the enemy's capillaries, while choking off evidence and strategic advice that contradicted their perceived bureaucratic interests. The subsequent reinforcement of the powers of the theater commanders and of the chairman has checked interservice brokerage – and eliminated debate – by cutting the Joint Chiefs out of the process of strategic decision. The most elaborate military bureaucracies in history thus retain a wide preserve of absolutism at their summit and undiminished scope for bureaucratic autism below.

MASS POLITICS

Bureaucracy has transformed the processes by which the "few" at the summit make strategy; the revolution of mass politics has given the "many" a voice in the selection of the few, and has fused strategy with domestic politics. The ancient republics briefly prefigured this transformation. In the Athens of Thucydides, free citizens decided commanders, forces, and missions, and then in many cases served as hoplites or rowers in executing decisions they had helped make. The Roman assembly controlled the right to declare war, and senate and consuls were the central organs of strategic direction; the position of Rome's elite was vastly stronger than that of its Athenian counterpart. Yet in both cases, as the speeches in Thucydides, the sinister Roman rituals proclaiming a *bellum iustum,* and the Senate's record of diplomatic-strategic deliberation suggest, popular and elite participation demanded moral legitimation for war and some justification of proposed strategy by argument. Those limitations were unique to republics, although by modern standards the need for moral legitimation weighed lightly on the warrior-citizens of the ancient world.

Both direct democracy and the Roman balanced constitution proved incompatible with units larger than the *polis.* Athens came to rule its allies and subjects as "tyrant city"; Rome's far larger and more cohesive empire

14 U.S. strategy to 1968, as summarized by the most astute defenders of the process that produced it: Leslie H. Gelb with Richard K. Betts, *The Irony of Vietnam: the System Worked* (Washington, 1979), p. 26; for a less sympathetic view, see Robert L. Gallucci, *Neither Peace nor Honor: The Politics of American Military Policy in Viet-Nam* (Baltimore, 1975).

evolved into an autocracy with republican forms; medieval and early modern republics tended to be either city-states or small mountain communities of egalitarian warriors. The modern revival of republicanism in the Netherlands revolt and the English, American, and French revolutions required representative institutions; these were units too large for direct democracy. Yet those institutions either began with or evolved toward universal male suffrage. That revived the close interaction between domestic politics and foreign policy and strategy found otherwise only in the ancient *polis* and in tribal societies.

Before the coming of mass politics, monarchical makers of strategy were not entirely exempt from domestic background influences. Even absolutist princes governed in part through the aristocracy that they headed and whose values they shared. Military success reinforced elite loyalty to monarch and state; defeat might lead to aristocratic revolt or the monarch's assassination. Nor was troop morale and loyalty a matter of indifference to princely strategists. Yet absolutist "state-building" and military art sought to neutralize these forces: to make aristocrats into court poodles or military-bureaucratic professionals, troops into automatons, burghers and peasants into docile sources of money and recruits, diplomacy and strategy into algebraic calculation with known quantities, and war into a geometric exercise decided and directed from the royal *Kabinett*. "The king has lost a battle; calm is the first duty of the subject" – the Prussian proclamation after Jena-Auerstädt neatly summarized the divorce between strategy and domestic politics under absolutism.

Those barriers began to erode in the seventeenth and eighteenth centuries in the Dutch republic and in Britain, where commercial and landed elites achieved power through parliamentary institutions. Commercial interests working through parliaments powerfully influenced the making of maritime strategy in both states. But the masses remained as yet largely mute. Britain's professional army conformed to the continental absolutist model except in its commanders' dependence on parliament. The navy's lower deck likewise had no political voice – although it was sometimes less than docile, as in the 1797 mutinies that briefly paralyzed British strategy.

The American and French revolutions erased the barriers between domestic politics and strategy. Despite fundamental differences in ideology and practice, both revolutions gave all male adults a political voice and made them citizen-soldiers. Absolutism could not compete with the resulting "juggernaut of war, based on the strength of the entire people."[15] As a Prussian reformer wrote after Jena, the power of France's egalitarian principles – once they found bayonets – was so great "that the state that fails to take them up voluntarily will either suffer destruction or be compelled from outside to

---

[15]   *On War*, p. 592 (pp. 585–94 offers a brilliant sketch of the relationship between types of regime and scale of military effort from antiquity to the French revolutionary wars).

accept them."[16] Thereafter even dictatorships, from Napoleon to Hitler and Stalin, rested on a measure of mass support.

Mass politics and the mass warfare that was its logical consequence meant that opinion became a decisive strategic factor, a vital component of fighting power.[17] As in the ancient *polis* and in republican Rome, makers of strategy after 1792 consciously or unconsciously sought to act on the two essential components of national morale: faith in victory and belief in the justice of the nation's cause. Both increasingly required propaganda and censorship or self-censorship, justified by the undoubted need for military secrecy but equally necessary to parry enemy propaganda, silence domestic dissent, and abolish unpalatable facts. Both worked best for states that were the incarnation of a total ideology, for such ideologies claim mastery of the historical process – and thus of victory – while by the same logic depriving opponents of moral legitimacy and even humanity. Finally, both combined exceedingly well with a measure of terror.

Faith in victory or defeat was not entirely an empirical matter, but strategists could generate it best by doing their traditional job of placing the enemy in a hopeless situation. Propaganda might help steel opinion for the long wait for the *Endsieg*, as in Germany in 1914–18 and 1939–45. But contrary evidence – from the shipwreck of Ludendorff's 1918 offensives to the steady retrograde movement of German armies after Stalingrad – was beyond the control of the leadership. Not so with the justice of the national cause; facts in no way proved an impediment to belief. Indeed the manipulation of facts to provide a morally satisfying cloak for *raison d'état* emerged as one of the most vital requirements of strategy in the age of mass politics.

Bismarck's success in provoking a French declaration of war in 1870 with the Ems telegram was not lost on his successors. Moltke the younger, in urging war against France and Russia after 1912, insisted that the age of cabinet wars was over. Victory in the war for which he relentlessly pressed rested upon "so formulating the *casus belli* that the nation unanimously and fervently takes up arms."[18] That moment came in August 1914, in an outpouring of enthusiasm without parallel among Germany's rivals, a moment that marked all who passed through it, from Prussian generals to social

---

16 Hardenberg memorandum, September 1807, in Georg Winter, ed., *Die Reorganisation des Preussischen Staates unter Stein und Hardenberg* (Leipzig, 1931), vol. I, pp. 305–06.
17 For the concept, Martin van Creveld, *Fighting Power: German and U.S. Army Performance, 1939–1945* (Westport, Connecticut, 1982), but see also Omer Bartov (*The Eastern Front, 1941–1945. German Troops and the Barbarization of Warfare* [London, 1985], and *Hitler's Army: Soldiers, Nazis, and War in the Third Reich* [Oxford, 1991]) which demonstrate that ideological indoctrination was a decisive ingredient in German *Kampfkraft*.
18 Moltke memorandum in Röhl, "An der Schwelle zum Weltkrieg: eine Dokumentation über den 'Kriegsrat' vom 8. Dezember 1912," *Militärgeschichtliche Mitteilungen* 1/77 (1977), p. 118; see also the Kaiser's contemporary remark on "constructing" provocations à la Bismarck: marginalia on d. 15560, *Die grosse Politik der europäischen Kabinette 1871–1914* (Berlin, 1922–27), 39:11.

democrats.[19] Yet the foundation of that enthusiasm, the claim that Germany was the victim of unprovoked attack by a ring of fiendish enemies driven by Cossack bloodlust, French thirst for revenge, and British "trade-envy," was entirely bogus. Its fabrication was the one intelligent German *strategic* act of the war: "The mood is brilliant. The government has been very skillful in making us appear as the attacked," the chief of the Kaiser's naval cabinet noted happily as Germany mobilized on 1 August 1914.[20]

In the second round of the German war, the government was less skillful. In preparing for war, Hitler drew on the sense of victimization by diabolical rivals created before and during 1914–18, and nurtured thereafter through the barrage of official and semi-official lies aimed at clearing Germany of "war guilt."[21] He exploited the axiom, affirmed equally by Ludendorff and by the social democrats in 1918, that the German army remained undefeated in the field. He used popular "war-fatalism" and the aversion to defeat rather than to war itself that distinguished Germany from its western neighbors. Yet even his uninterrupted run of bloodless prewar successes failed to instill the desired fanatical belief in final victory.[22] Neither Goebbels' 1939 hate-barrages against the despised Poles nor Germany's claims that it had invaded its many victims in self-defense stirred the self-righteous passions of 1914. It was the crushing victories in spring 1940 that rescued the German people temporarily from forebodings of a renewal of the relentless attritional *Weltkrieg* of 1914–18. The disappearance of doubters behind Himmler's barbed wire, the regime's monopoly of information and propaganda, and its ceaseless and successful efforts to indoctrinate Germany's fighting youth with the consciousness of superiority helped mightily. And in the end, the universal complicity of the German people in arms in the regime's immense crimes in the East left little choice but a fight to the last cartridge.

[19] In France, the major combatant most comparable to Germany, enthusiasm seems to have been far more qualified than that attested to in virtually all German accounts: see Jean-Jacques Becker, *1914. Comment les français sont entrés dans la guerre* (Paris, 1977).

[20] Müller diary, quoted in Röhl, "Admiral von Müller," p. 670 and note 99. For German premeditation in 1914 and European and world domination as the war aim from the outset among both soldiers and civilians, see *Kurt Riezler: Tagebücher, Aufsätze, Dokumente*, ed. Karl Dietrich Erdmann (Göttingen, 1972); Fritz Fischer, *War of Illusions: German Policies from 1911 to 1914* (New York, 1975) and *Germany's Aims in the First World War* (New York, 1967); Röhl, "Der militärpolitische Entscheidungsprozess in Deutschland am Vorabend des Ersten Weltkriegs," in his *Kaiser, Hof und Staat* (Munich, 1987); and Adolf Gasser, *Preussischer Militärgeist und Kriegsentfesselung 1914* (Frankfurt, 1985).

[21] See Holger Herwig, "Clio Deceived: Patriotic Self-Censorship in Germany after the Great War," *International Security* 12 (1987), pp. 5–43.

[22] Wolfram Wette, "From Kellogg to Hitler (1928–1933). German Public Opinion Concerning the Rejection or Glorification of War," pp. 71–99 in Wilhelm Deist, ed., *The German Military in the Age of Total War* (Leamington Spa, 1985), and "NS-Propaganda und Kriegsbereitschaft der Deutschen bis 1936," *Francia* 5 (1977), pp. 567–90; for Hitler on the as yet insufficient fanaticism of public and elites, see Wilhelm Treue, ed., "Rede Hitlers vor dem deutschen Presse (10. November 1938)," *Vierteljahrshefte für Zeitgeschichte* 6:2 (1958), p. 189.

Stalin faced a lesser strategic challenge than Hitler in managing opinion and morale. He and Lenin before him had inherited a society that war and defeat had in part decapitated; civil war and famine finished the job.[23] With Russia's already frail civil society crushed, the regime could rest – as in Lenin's famous definition of dictatorship – "directly on force." Terror outweighed consent; fear was the primary fuel of Soviet economic growth. And terror largely insulated Stalin's foreign policy and strategy from domestic politics, as his instantaneous reversal of course toward Germany in 1939 suggests. The major exception was 1941: Stalin's stubborn and disastrous refusal to trade space for time was a confession of the limits of terror. German penetration of Soviet soil was inadmissible because it might break Soviet terror's spell. Yet it was *German* terror that saved Stalin: at least *with* Stalin his subjects had some small chance of biological survival. But in other respects Stalin showed his customary contempt for domestic opinion; witness his cautious interest in yet another lightning reversal, a separate peace with Germany in 1941–43.[24]

Parliamentary democracies have had a less easy time. The chronic inability – for both good and ill – of modern mass electorates to judge strategic issues by *raison d'état* has almost invariably hobbled their strategists in initiating and fighting wars of national effort. In 1914 Britain went to war to avert French defeat, German continental hegemony, and Britain's probable loss of independence. But that cold calculation scarcely moved the earnest social reformers who held the balance in Asquith's Liberal cabinet, much less the masses. It was the Germans who launched the BEF in August 1914 by invading Belgium and giving both cabinet and electorate a cause that seemed moral.[25] Likewise in 1938–39 Hitler made Britain's case for war, although the initially sluggish British electorate showed more insight in the end than its political masters. Public and parliament ran ahead of Chamberlain after Munich, and imposed war once Hitler attacked Poland.

Since 1917 the United States has likewise relied on its most dangerous enemies to strike. Imperial Germany's submarine attacks alone might not have generated the domestic quasi-unanimity necessary for a European land war. Nor did the public see or accept the pressing strategic need to prevent German domination of Eurasia. It took Zimmermann's amazing offer of

23 For this conceptual framework, see above all Martin Malia, *Comprendre la Révolution russe* (Paris, 1980).
24 See in general Vojtech Mastny, "Stalin and the Prospects of a Separate Peace in World II," *American Historical Review* 77:5 (1972), pp. 1365–88; also Ingeborg Fleischhauer, *Die Chance des Sonderfriedens. Deutsch-sowjetische Geheimgespräche 1941–1945* (Berlin, 1986), pp. 68–172, 284–89; Soviet archives apparently contain as yet undisclosed material on Stalin's approaches to the Germans.
25 Zara Steiner, *Britain and the Origins of the First World War* (New York, 1977), Chap. 9 and especially pp. 236–37; Cameron Hazlehurst, *Politicians at War: July 1914 to May 1915* (New York, 1971), chaps. 2–9; David French, *British Strategy and War Aims, 1914–1916* (London, 1986), pp. 21–22; for the strategic imperative of supporting France, see especially Michael Howard, *The Continental Commitment* (London, 1972), pp. 53–59.

Texas and the southwest to Mexico to finally enrage American opinion. Imperial Japan bettered Zimmermann's performance in 1941. Beneath the absurd paranoid theories of the American revisionists who sought to link Roosevelt to the Pearl Harbor debacle lay a strategic truth. Had Roosevelt set out to design an event that would guarantee domestic unanimity and steel America to devastate Japan, he could scarcely have improved on the work of the Japanese naval staff. Nor could he have improved on Hitler's subsequent declaration of war, which spared a potentially bruising Congressional debate about the Atlantic naval measures and incidents through which Roosevelt had sought to implement "Germany First" from early September 1941. Finally, Stalin in his more prosaic way likewise made the case for United States resistance after 1945 by his failure to control his Eastern European appetites until the "Yanks" had gone home, and by the permission he gave Kim Il-Sung to "prod South Korea with the point of a bayonet" in 1950.[26] If the makers of strategy in modern democracies can rarely count on mass support for preemptive defense, they may sometimes hope that their apparent flabbiness may lure dictatorships to overreach.

And once a democracy is embarked on war, mass politics places sharp restrictions on its strategists' ability to steer. Democracies have so far fought limited wars happily if they were brief. But without enemy cooperation, brevity may be attainable only by transgressing limits. The diplomatic and strategic flexibility of the *ancien régime* is long gone; witness the outcry over Eisenhower's 1942 "deal" with Darlan, or the inability of the British and United States governments to prepare public opinion for the possibility that their Soviet ally might soon prove almost as great a threat as their Nazi enemy. Mass politics likewise imposes the need for constant action and success – in George Marshall's apologetic comment on the 1942 North African landings – "to keep the people entertained."[27] Finally, the mobilization of passion required for success generates immense momentum. Enraged citizens do not think in the bloodless abstractions of contemporary social science. They seek not "war termination" but total victory. Nor are they necessarily wrong. The fatal defect of Versailles may simply have been that the Allied and Associated Powers failed to do to Germany what their publics demanded – and ultimately received in 1945.

IDEOLOGY

The complement to mass politics is ideology, a term invented in the aftermath of the French revolution. Its most common twentieth-century mean-

---

26 *Khrushchev Remembers* (Boston, 1970), pp. 367–69.
27 Eric Larrabee, *Commander-in-Chief* (New York, 1987), p. 9. From a strategic and operational viewpoint, TORCH was certainly preferable to Marshall's alternative: a landing with green troops in France in summer 1943 against an unshaken Luftwaffe and some of the armor that Hitler otherwise squandered at Kursk.

ings run along a continuum, from any widely held set of notions about how the world works to the all-encompassing, all-explanatory systems of belief sometimes called "total" ideologies. The concept of ideology could only originate once religion ceased to hold a monopoly of the interpretation of the world. But for the purposes of this essay it may usefully include religion; militant Christianity and Islam, in particular, have rivaled in intensity and sometimes reinforced in effect the allegedly secular total ideologies of the nineteenth and twentieth centuries.

Ideology influences the making of strategy in two principal ways: it shapes the expectations and goals of those who decide and the ferocity and stamina of those who fight.[28] In Jihad and Crusade, belief set illusory goals that ranged from limitless expansion to the conquest of Jerusalem. Belief – "*Gott mit uns*" in every one of humanity's innumerable languages – defined the just war, assured victory, and promised eternal salvation or fleshly delights to those who suffered or fell. Yet until the Reformation, ideological warfare involving entire populations was conspicuous only along the fiery border between Christendom and Islam.

The Reformation ended that. In the long run it emancipated the individual and opened the road for the revolution of modern mass politics. In the short term it generated pitiless religious wars fought not merely by ideologically driven princely strategists such as Philip II, but by much of the population of contested areas such as Bohemia and Germany. The force of ideology – from Philip's sense of mission and confidence that God would provide to the Norse Protestant fury of the troopers of Gustavus Adolphus – sustained a long century of massacre that helped discredit all religion and made Europe after 1648 briefly safe for rationalist cabinet war. "From fanaticism to barbarism is but a single step," wrote Diderot, summing up the wisdom of the following century.

Diderot's phrase also unintentionally summed up the Revolution of 1789–94, which gave political shape to two secular religions of world redemption. The first was the religion of class that demanded the deaths of France's king

---

[28] Since 1914–18, Western and especially American intellectuals have found it increasingly hard to imagine dying for an idea. Hence – perhaps – the popularity of the "group dynamics" model of combat motivation put forward by sociologists (for an influential early example, see Edward A. Shils and Morris Janowitz, "Cohesion and Disintegration in the Wehrmacht in World War II," *Public Opinion Quarterly* 12 (1948), pp. 280–315). Yet the Germans – and many others before and since – failed to conform to the model. As Omer Bartov has demonstrated (*Hitler's Army*, Chap. 2: "The Destruction of the Primary Group") the Germans in Russia died too fast to form stable "primary groups." Their cohesion derived above all from racist belief and from fear of Soviet revenge. Nor has ideology at the unit level been lacking in American wars: see James M. McPherson, "Ideology and Combat Motivation in the Civil War," typescript (I am grateful to Robert Westbrook for a copy of that work, which summarizes a book in progress). Even in Vietnam, an underlying if rarely articulated belief that the war in some obscure way served the defense of the "American way of life" helped maintain cohesion and discipline until well after withdrawal began (see for instance Charles Moscos, "Behavior of Combat Soldiers in Vietnam," pp. 134–56 in his *The American Enlisted Man* [New York, 1970]).

and nobles and priests – and soon by extension those of France's neighbors – not for what they had done, but for what they were. The second was the cult of the nation-state. The Revolution fused the two; the Abbé Sieyès presented the clergy and nobility with their death-warrant when he described them in 1789 as outside *la nation*.[29]

The Girondin visionaries who launched France against Europe in April 1792 provided a brief foretaste of the ideological warfare of the twentieth century. Their war was to be an international class-war of unlimited aims, a war of "peoples against kings" for the salvation both of France and of the human race. It was to be a national war by the French people to reconquer at sword-point its "dignity, greatness, security, and credit." It was equally to be a war of internal conquest against the remaining powers of the monarchy and the remnants of the aristocracy, a war "necessary to consummate the revolution." And those who demanded war were also prepared for *Götterdämmerung:* "we want equality, even if we must seek it in the grave; but before descending ourselves, we shall hurl all traitors into it."[30] If ideological lunacy filled the place of strategy among those who imposed war, ideological motivation among the troops – along with the highly professional NCO corps of the old army – made possible the new style of warfare that swamped France's enemies with numbers and élan. Clausewitz saw it firsthand in 1793–94, and summed it up in one unforgettable sentence: "the colossal weight of the whole French people, unhinged by political fanaticism, came crashing down on us."[31] That example, rationalized and routinized first by Napoleon and then by Prussia, forced other great powers to follow or go under. Mass warfare was almost inevitably ideological warfare. That was why the "old regime" imperfectly restored after 1814–15 sought assiduously to avoid great power wars, and in part why the U.S. Civil War, the bloodiest Western struggle between 1815 and 1914, escalated inexorably until the losers crumbled.

Of the twin political religions that emerged from 1789–94, that of class acquired the most elaborate body of doctrine. The struggles of few and many, aristocrats and *demos,* which Thucydides had analyzed as one concomitant of his war, had at their root "the lust for power arising from greed and ambition."[32] That motivated the extermination of adversaries, but as a practical measure, not as the fulfillment of supposed historical laws. The

---

29 Emmanuel Sieyès, *Qu'est-ce que le Tiers état?* (Geneva, 1970 [1789]), pp. 124–26; see also pp. 195, 203.

30 Quotations: Isnard, 29 November 1791, *Archives Parlementaires de 1787 à 1860,* première série, vols. 35–37 (Paris, 1890–91), 35:442; Cloots, 13 December 1791, 36:79; Brissot, 29 December 1791, 36:608; Isnard ("Une guerre est près de s'allumer, guerre indispensable pour consommer la révolution"), 5 January 1792, likewise Brissot, 17 January 1792, 37:85, 471; equality in the grave: Isnard, 20 January 1792, 37:547, but see also 35:442, 36:79, 37:413–14. I have profited greatly from Timothy Blanning, "Nationalism and the French Revolution," lecture at Princeton University, 21 April 1989.

31 *On War,* p. 518.

32 III:82, revolution on Corcyra and throughout the Greek world.

French Revolution and Marx between them changed that. The guillotine, "sword of equality," leveled France's privileged orders in the name of abstract justice and the happiness of all humanity. Principles proved even more pitiless than powerlust, although the latter was not absent. Then Marx built the logic of revolutionary terror into a Hegelian mechanism that claimed the objectivity of science while promising release from history itself through the dictatorship of the class he had chosen as most oppressed. Lenin applied that logic in creating his "party of a new type," and the doctrine's subsequent trajectory as a political religion for backward societies further reinforced its terrorist character. In states without a civil society, without middle classes and institutions independent of the state machine, "order through terror" was simultaneously an imperative and an irresistible temptation to those who seized power.[33]

The foremost consequences of Marxism-Leninism for the making of strategy were three. The imminent prospect of world revolution inspired Lenin and at least some of his associates until defeat at Warsaw in 1920. Thereafter it receded to the status of quasitheoretical final goal, but remained the ultimate source of party legitimacy and definitive proof of Marxism-Leninism's claim to command history. Stalin, often hopefully depicted as a "pragmatic" expansionist and certainly no enthusiast for revolutions independent of Red Army control, saw on the horizon in the 1920s the prospect of replacing "capitalist encirclement" of the Soviet Union with "socialist encirclement" by a ring of satellites. By 1940 close subordinates such as Molotov and Dekanosov apparently harbored visions of a two-stage progress toward world revolution: first European domination by the end of the war, then final victory and world mastery. And Stalin himself reportedly agreed to Kim Il-Sung's 1950 adventure because it "appealed to his convictions as a Communist."[34]

The second strategic effect of the ideology qualified faith in world revolution by counseling patience. Marxism-Leninism's greatest internal successes – the seizure of power and military-industrialization through terror – were products of the brutal voluntarism that was one strand in Marx's legacy. But it was the other main strand of Marx – the belief in the determining effect of the material base and in the gradual ripening of historical forces – that apparently inspired much of Stalin's foreign policy. Willing-

---

33   For the phrase, Hélène Carrère d'Encausse, *A History of the Soviet Union, 1917–1953*, v. 2, *Stalin: Order through Terror* (London, 1982); the most incisive analysis of the origins, implications, and later development of Marx's system is Leszek Kolakowski, *Main Currents of Marxism*, 3 vols. (Oxford, 1978).

34   See Robert C. Tucker, "The Emergence of Stalin's Foreign Policy," *Slavic Review*, 36 (1977), especially p. 571; R.C. Raack, "Stalin's Plans for World War II," *Journal of Contemporary History*, 26 (1991), pp. 219–20; Kreve-Mickevicius report of June 1940 conversations with Molotov and Dekanosov, in U.S. House of Representatives, *Select Committee to Investigate Communist Aggression and the Forced incorporation of the Baltic States into the U.S.S.R., Third Interim Report*, 83rd Congress, 2nd Session (Washington, 1954), pp. 458, 459, 462. Kim Il-sung: *Khrushchev Remembers*, p. 368.

ness to defer in the present to superior military-economic power and confidence in the ultimate result gave his policy a relentlessness that Hitler'the gambler could not match. As Stalin boasted – not entirely truthfully – to the British in 1941, he unlike Hitler always knew "where to stop." For a time that cautious acquisitiveness helped make Communism – in the words of one disenchanted ex-admirer of Cuban and Vietnamese Stalinism – a "successful Fascism."[35]

Finally, Marxism-Leninism was uniquely suited to serve as an imperial ideology in the age of nationalism.[36] Class struggle might not in practice be the mainspring of history, but it did offer a fiction that transcended the nation. It legitimized rule over the disparate nationalities and tribes of the former Tsarist empire, then control of the hapless peoples of Eastern and East-central Europe conquered in 1944–45, and finally hegemony over the far-flung "second Soviet empire" acquired by Khrushchev and Brezhnev. Marxism-Leninism and the shared hatred for the "capitalist" West that the ideology proclaimed as the stuff of human progress shaped the Newspeak of empire. That language and its shared assumptions bound together figures as disparate as Brezhnev, Castro, Mengistu Haile Mariam, and the rulers in Hanoi. It welded naïve provincial Leninisms such as the Grenada "New Jewel Movement" to Soviets, Bulgarians, Cubans, Czechoslovaks, East Germans, Nicaraguans, and North Koreans.[37] It also helped mold a wide variety of syncretic party despotisms, from Kwame Nkrumah's Ghana to the pan-Arab national socialisms of Iraq and Syria.[38] What the language could not do was explain the failure of history to fit. The collapse of Soviet industrial growth – in direct proportion to the ebbing of terror after Stalin's death – and mortifying defeat in Afghanistan ultimately deprived those who ruled of belief in anything but their own privileges, and stripped Marxism-Leninism of imperial binding force and strategic effect.

All that remained was nationalism – the final stage of Communism – and its enduring support in adversity throughout. Stalin the Georgian had never disdained Great Russian myths: Alexander Nevsky routing the Teutonic Knights, Ivan the Terrible cementing the state with blood, the cannons of Borodino and Tsar Alexander riding triumphant into Paris in 1814. In the dark days of 1941 Stalin frantically sought to mobilize that nationalism to

---

[35] Stalin to Eden, in Sumner Welles, *Seven Decisions that Shaped History* (New York, 1951), p. 200; Susan Sontag, in *The New York Times*, 27 February 1982, p. 27.

[36] For the useful term "imperial ideology" (although applied to Roosevelt, not Lenin and Stalin), see pp. 16–17 of Franz Schurmann's eccentric yet often perceptive *The Logic of World Power* (New York, 1974).

[37] The captured internal documents of the Grenadan regime offer in vivid miniature much insight into the ideological dimensions of "second Soviet empire": Paul Seabury and Walter A. McDougall, eds., *The Grenada Papers* (San Francisco, 1984). For a brilliant overview, see Helène Carrère d'Encausse, *Ni Paix Ni Guerre: Le nouvel Empire soviétique ou du bon usage de la détente* (Paris, rev. and expanded ed., 1987).

[38] On the Iraqi Ba'th debt to Stalinism, see Samir Al-Khalil, *Republic of Fear* (New York, 1990), pp. 96–109, 246–57.

provide the staying power that "proletarian internationalism" – powerless against the German "workers" of the steadily advancing Wehrmacht – could not offer. And in his 1945 victory congratulations to the Great Russian people, he implicitly recognized his heavy debt to their nationalism. Stalin's emulators in Peking, Pyongyang, and Hanoi subsequently created national socialisms in which nationalism and Marxism-Leninism interacted dialectically in the mobilization of hatred and the generation of immense fighting power.

Nationalism was also the fate of the non-Communist advanced world in the age of mass politics, with the partial exception of Britain and the United States. An invention of French revolutionaries and German romantics, spread by industrialization's demand for literacy (which could only be literacy in a national language and culture), it has divided humanity far more convincingly than the class struggle.[39] Its central fiction is the segmentation of the species into ethnic-linguistic units that in the words of the Abbé Sieyès "exist before everything" and are "at the origin of everything" and express a will that is "always legal, [that] is the law itself."[40] That conception of the nation was and remains sharply different from the Lockean belief in popular government in the service of *individual* liberty within a freely associating community found across the Channel, and even more strongly across the Atlantic.[41] Nationalism is the belief in the historic rights, wrongs, hatreds, and mission of one's own ethnic-linguistic *group,* and in individual self-realization through subordination to that group. National self-determination is antithetical not equivalent to democracy, despite frequent self-interested equation of the two. It merely means the "right" to be ruled by one's own ethnic-linguistic group. Self-determination thereby also entails the "right" to oppress other ethnic-linguistic groups located on the "national territory," or as a minimum to thwart – in the inimitable words of one representative of the German Left in 1848 – "the efforts of puny little nationalities to found their lives in our midst and like parasitic growths to extinguish our existence."[42]

---

[39] On the origins, nature, and spread of nationalism, see the apparently contradictory – but in reality complementary – accounts of Elie Kedourie, *Nationalism* (London, 1960) and Ernest Gellner, *Nations and Nationalism* (Ithaca NY, 1983).

[40] "La nation existe avant tout, elle est à l'origine de tout. Sa volonté est toujours légale, elle est la loi elle-meme." (*Qu'est-ce que le Tiers état?*, p. 180): a statement as breathtaking in its totalitarian implications as Rousseau's more famous remark that "whoever refuses to obey the general will shall be compelled to do so by the whole body. This means nothing less than that he will be forced to be free."

[41] For this essential distinction, see Kedourie, *Nationalism*, pp. 73–74. The Founding Fathers' pre-1789 use of the term "nation" to describe the United States and "national" to mean belief in a strong federal government has unfortunately tended to blind historians of the United States to the ethnic-linguistic, anti-individualist core of the nationalist phenomenon.

[42] Wilhelm Jordan (Berlin), 21 June 1848, *Stenographischer Bericht über die Verhandlungen der deutschen constituirenden Nationalversammlung zu Frankfurt am Main* (Leipzig, 1848–49), 1:419.

Nationalism does not come in two kinds, "good" and "bad," Mazzini and Mussolini.[43] Nor does it become virtuous through underdog status or wrongs suffered. It operates along a continuum running from the brothers Grimm to Auschwitz, from philology and folklore and poetry in the service of the national idea to the extermination of neighbors. Not all nationalisms reach extremes. Some national mythologies are more explosive than others. Some political cultures offer greater scope for extremism than their fellows. Weakness or defeat teaches limits. But the doctrine's logic drives all impartially toward domination and extermination.

The consequence of nationalism – a doctrine, like Marxism, whose adherents proclaim it merely a recognition of the nature of things – for the making of strategy has been to foster fanaticism in leaders and followers, in goals and methods alike. The heirs of the Girondins in nationalist extremism were the middle-class "professors" of the 1848 Frankfurt parliament whose example then galvanized, in fear and emulation, the many nationalities of east-central Europe. The "Greater Germany" outlined at Frankfurt stretched from Strasbourg to Riga and from the Danish Belts to Trieste; it might reclaim Holland, Flemish Belgium, and Switzerland; it would assuredly challenge Britain for world mastery by sea. History decreed rule over millions upon millions of non-Germans. Language enjoined a Germany that stretched "as far as the German tongue resounds." For the moment, that vision remained a "sweet academic pipe-dream": monarchical Prussia would not stake its existence for German nationalism in a war against all Europe.[44] Bismarck then bent that nationalism to his own limited "great-Prussian" purposes.

But German nationalism took revenge. The doctrine's peculiar compound of Teutomaniacal ancestor-worship, apocalyptic Lutheran state-theology, and Hegelian determinism was a decisive background influence on the making of German strategy after 1890. Germany chose war against overwhelming odds in 1914 in part because the general staff was as convinced as overheated Prussian pastors that "nations are not numbers and God is not bound by the laws of arithmetic."[45] Geist – the German spirit – would overcome both the effete and high-strung "Gauls" and the despised Slavs that the German elite thought it knew well from its Polish borderlands. "The army with the stronger resolve [Wille] will win in the end," was the verdict of

[43] A myth characteristic of but not confined to Italian historiography; for its most elegant and influential formulation, see Luigi Salvatorelli, Pensiero e azione nel Risorgimento (Turin, 6th. ed., 1963), Chap. 7.

[44] See in general Günter Wollstein, Das "Grossdeutschland" der Paulskirche (Düsseldorf, 1977) ("pipe-dream" – a Danish view – p. 334 note 73). For Frederick William IV's refusal to fight, see Ludwig von Pastor, Leben des Freiherrn Max von Gagern 1810–1889 (Munich, 1912), p. 234.

[45] Chaplain Reetz of Bromberg, quoted in A. J. Hoover, "God and Germany in the Great War: The View of the Protestant Pastors," Canadian Review of Studies in Nationalism, 14:1 (1987), p. 75.

Wilhelm Groener, that least ideologically exalted member of the high command, on the *Materialschlacht* at Verdun. And at the end, in October 1918, Ludendorff insisted that defeat was above all in the mind: "the *Geist* of the troops had failed."[46] Moral forces had indeed served Germany well at rifle company level. The troops had fought until mid-1918 with unparalleled conviction and effectiveness in part through the belief, drummed into them in innumerable sermons from military chaplains and itinerant field-pastors, that this greatest of all wars was the Last Judgment, to be consummated upon Germany's demonic enemies by the German people in God's service. But that culmination of a long tradition of "national self-deification" (as a not unsympathetic social democrat had described it before 1914) was no substitute for strategic judgment. Nor was it enough to ensure victory against the 6:1 odds in weight of metal that the general staff, on the verge of choosing its last immense offensive gamble, foresaw for spring 1918.[47]

A like contempt of Spirit for numbers in a kindred political context produced a parallel result in Imperial Japan. There in the late nineteenth century the government had in essence commissioned its intellectuals to invent an ideology to fit the nation for its world role.[48] The result blended emperor-worship with Confucian piety toward authority and the samurai ethic of frenzied pugnacity, implicit obedience, and merciless self-sacrifice, "democratized" and bestowed upon the entire Japanese people. That people the ideologues declared a unitary *Volk* with mythic origins and bonded by blood.

Japan's national ideology had spectacular strategic effects. It inhibited the armed services, which long before 1941 had through military activism in China and assassinations at home made themselves arbiters of the nation's course, from confessing even in private to doubts about taking on the United States. It gave them a justified confidence that the *Volk* would wholeheartedly follow. And long before America's de facto oil embargo of July 1941 it loaded the dice for war – despite or because of an American military-industrial superiority of 10 or 13 to 1. Future American superiority was

46 Groener diary, June 1916, quoted in Michael Salewski, "Verdun und die Folgen. Eine militär- und geistesgeschichtliche Betrachtung," *Wehrwissenschaftliche Rundschau*, 25 (1976), p. 91; Ludendorff memorandum, 31 October 1918, in Herbert Michaelis and Ernst Schraepler, eds., *Ursachen und Folgen* (Berlin, 1958–64), 2:451 (the remark refers to the "black day" of 8 August 1918).

47 On the Last Judgment as the meaning of the war, see Klaus Vondung, *Die Apokalypse in Deutschland* (Munich, 1988), pp. 189–207 and W. Pressel, *Die Kriegspredigt 1914–1918 in der evangelischen Kirche Deutschlands* (Göttingen, 1967), especially pp. 159–74; for the slightly less potent brew served the Catholic minority, see Heinrich Missalla, *"Gott mit uns": Die deutsche katholische Kriegspredigt 1914–1918* (Munich, 1968). For the OHL on Allied munitions superiority, see Erzberger (quoting Max Bauer) to Bethmann Hollweg, 16 June 1917, in Wilhelm Deist, ed., *Militär und Innenpolitik im Weltkrieg 1914–1918* (Düsseldorf, 1970), 2:766.

48 See Carol Gluck, *Japan's Modern Myths* (Princeton, 1985), above all pp. 120–27; pp. 6–8 and 315–16 also contain a useful summary of anthropological and Marxist literature on the relationship of ideology to culture and society.

immaterial, given Japan's present advantage in mobilized forces and the nature of the enemy: "Americans, being merchants, would not continue for long an unprofitable war."[49]

Conversely, Japanese values appeared to decree the rejection not merely of mercantile rationality but of strategy itself. "Calculating people are contemptible . . . " ran the *Way of the Warrior*, an eighteenth-century distillation of the samurai ethic widely popular in the 1930s and 1940s; "common sense will not accomplish great things. Simply become desperate and 'crazy to die.'" The empire stood "at the threshold of glory or oblivion," remarked Tojo on 1 December 1941, unconsciously echoing the well-tried German theme of all or nothing, world mastery or ruin. Japan's position was untenable. Acquiescence to American demands was unthinkable. *Therefore* Spirit would overcome matter or perish in the attempt. Leaders and followers alike, as a military slogan had it, yearned "to match our training against their numbers and our flesh against their steel."[50] That was a wish abundantly granted.

In Germany, defeat and humiliation in 1918 left a vacuum. German nationalism lost its monarchical focus; Protestant theology's promise of *Gott mit uns* rang hollow amid the disgrace of revolution and the shattered fragments of Germany's claim to world domination. What filled the ideological vacuum and helped make possible a far greater war than 1914–18 was the pseudoscientific strand of nineteenth-century Teutomania. The notion of race, like so much else, was a product of the Enlightenment with less than enlightened results.[51] In political cultures presided over by Locke, its political and social results were lethal enough, as the example of the nineteenth century United States suggests. In Germany, largely untouched by notions of natural rights and already fiercely nationalist, the concept of race, equipped after the 1870s with a Darwinian pseudoscientific aura, ultimately produced a nationalism that left rivals in the shade.[52]

To a society already more anti-Semitic than any other in Europe, unhinged by the claustrophobia of two-front war, the British "hunger-blockade," and

---

[49]   Odds in munitions, coal, and steel: Coox, "Effectiveness of the Japanese Military Establishment," p. 21; "merchants": army planner quoted in Barnhart, "Japanese Intelligence," p. 447.

[50]   *Hagakure* and Japanese strategy in 1941: Coox, "Effectiveness," pp. 14–15; Tojo: Nobutaka Ike, *Japan's Decision for War* (Stanford, 1967), p. 283 (similarly p. 272); flesh and steel: Ruth Benedict, *The Chrysanthemum and the Sword* (New York, 1946), p. 87. The many recorded remarks of this kind refute the claim of Sagan ("Origins of the Pacific War," p. 894 and passim) that Japanese decision-making in 1941 was "rational" in the sense of "conscious calculation to maximize utility based on a consistent value system." A central strand of Japan's *ideology* – a category indispensable to understanding cases of this kind – was the rejection of calculation as unworthy of the warrior.

[51]   For European notions of race and their intersection with nationalism, see especially Léon Poliakov, *The Aryan Myth* (New York, 1974).

[52]   On the pseudo-Darwinian admixture, see particularly Daniel Gasman, *The Scientific Origins of National Socialism* (London, 1971).

interminable heavy losses at the front, the encounter with the alien-seeming Jews of Poland and western Russia in 1915–18 proved unsettling. Germany's *völkisch* prophets immediately mobilized opinion even against German Jews, charging them unjustly with shirking battlefield service. The rise of "Judeo-Bolshevism" in Russia and a German revolution in 1918 that included Jews among its leading figures made the supposed connection plain to the thickest provincial pub-dweller: history was race-history, and Germany's defeat in 1918 was the work of a Jewish global conspiracy orchestrating the ring of enemies without and the purported "dagger-stab in the back" of the fighting troops from within.[53]

Hitler neither invented nor was the first to exploit these themes; adherents of the monarchy preceded him in designating the Jews as a "lightning rod" in 1917–19. But he was the most effective. Once in control of the Wehrmacht, his strategy, like that of the Girondins, relied on the dialectical interaction of war and revolution. War would not merely overthrow the existing external order. It would also consummate the National Socialist revolution at home through the total barbarization of the German people and the extermination of the "Jewish world-pestilence."[54] Girondin strategy rested on the mirage of world revolution against kings and aristocrats; Hitler's was a nationalist-racist "bio-strategy." Germany must win, he proclaimed in a secret speech to general officers in early 1938, through its unique combination of numbers and putative racial worth:

> There is only one *Volk* on this earth that with great compactness, united by race and language, lives narrowly confined in the heart of Europe: that is the German people with its 110 million Germans in *Mitteleuropa* . . . [C]omparison [with the populations of other states] fills me with joyous hope – and this compact block will and must ultimately possess *Mitteleuropa* and the world.[55]

The ideology's racist dimension made it slightly less limited than conventional nationalism: it could serve as an imperial ideology for "Aryans." Had Germany defeated the Soviet Union in 1941, the Swiss, Flemings, Dutch, Scandinavians, and "germanizable" Eastern Europeans would presumably have found themselves handed over to Himmler for brain-washing and resettlement in an East cleared by the extermination of Slavs. Hitler even held a place in his heart for the British, should they "see reason."

[53] See Werner Jochmann, "Die Ausbreitung des Antisemitismus," in Werner E. Mosse, ed., *Deutsches Judentum in Krieg und Revolution 1916–1923* (Tübingen, 1971), pp. 409–55, and Uwe Lohalm, *Völkischer Radikalismus* Hamburg, (1970), pp. 46–56.

[54] For more on this thesis, Knox, "Conquest, Foreign and Domestic, in Fascist Italy and Nazi Germany," *Journal of Modern History* 56 (1984), 1–57.

[55] Speech of 22 January 1938, cited in Jost Dülffer, *Weimar, Hitler und die Marine* (Düsseldorf, 1972), p. 547 (the figure of 110 million presumably includes Germany's racially suitable small neighbors); similarly Treue, ed., "Rede Hitlers vor dem deutschen Presse (10. November 1938)," pp. 190–91.

Yet by the end of Hitler's run of success, the ideology had so twisted his perceptions of risk that it helped destroy him.[56] In August 1939 his contempt for democracy's apparent flabbiness – a sentiment he did not monopolize, then or later – caused misjudgment of the British in the long run, if not in the present: "I saw Chamberlain and Daladier, those pathetic worms, at Munich. They lack the guts to attack; blockade is their limit."[57] And in 1941 he completely discarded the tactical cunning gleaned from his analysis of Imperial Germany's failed challenge to a world of enemies in 1914–18. In the 1920s he had argued and practiced the pursuit of great goals by "step-like sections," dividing "the road to be conquered into separate stages" to be dealt with "one by one, systematically, with the sharpest concentration of all . . . forces."[58] But in the pivotal year 1941 he chose to treat the Slavs as slaves from the outset, rather than pose as their liberator from Bolshevism. Dividing the Soviet peoples along ethnic and political cleavages – as Imperial Germany's agents had done effectively in 1914–18 – and exterminating all impartially *after* victory might well have worked.[59] Forcibly uniting most of them with Stalin cost Hitler the war. Yet his destruction scarcely ended nationalism's infinite possibilities for virulent mutation.

The regime-ideologies of Stalin and Hitler were closed systems that touched all aspects of human existence, and were of central importance in setting strategic goals and dictating methods. Yet ideologies that are less than total may also have dramatic strategic effects. The European aristocratic ethos dictated both the ruinous calculations of *gloire*, honor, and "reputation" of sixteenth and seventeenth century princely strategists and the foolhardy contempt for Yankee tenacity and materiel of the Confederate planter-gentry. Eccentric notions of caste and service-honor furnished Hin-

56 The triumph of racist "dogma" over power-political "calculation" is one major theme of Klaus Hildebrand, *The Foreign Policy of the Third Reich* (Berkeley, 1973) (pp. 110–12, 140–41).

57 *Akten zur deutschen auswärtigen Politik*, Serie D, (Baden-Baden, Frankfurt, 1950 –), 7:171 note.

58 *Mein Kampf*, trans. Ralph Manheim, (New York, 1943), p. 250; for the much-debated notion of a *Stufenplan* as the key to Hitler's foreign policy, see above all Andreas Hillgruber, *Hitlers Strategie* (Frankfurt a.M., 1965), and his postscript to the second edition (Munich, 1987), pp. 717ff.

59 The apparent view of Michael Geyer ("German Strategy in the Age of Machine Warfare, 1914–1945" in Peter Paret, ed., *Makers of Modern Strategy from Machiavelli to the Nuclear Age* [Princeton, 1986], p. 592) that extermination in 1941 was less an ideological choice than an escalatory consequence of the meeting between German operational methods and bitter Russian resistance seems doubtful, given Hitler's well-known March 1941 directives to the generals to erase the "Judeo-Bolshevik intelligentsia" and his explicit coupling of "Final Solution" measures with campaign planning. The bitterness of Soviet resistance was in large part a consequence of German terror against civilians and POWs, as the German officer corps soon learned. And that terror's only military use was to force Germans to die rather than surrender to an enraged enemy (see Helmut Krausnick, "Kommissarbefehl und 'Gerichtsbarkeitserlass Barbarossa' in neuer Sicht," *Vierteljahrshefte für Zeitgeschichte* 25 (1977), pp. 686, 737–38; Bartov, *Hitler's Army*, pp. 74–75, 87, 101, 104).

denburg and the German naval leadership with the language for justifying bitter-end resistance in fall 1918.[60] American and British opinion, once roused, willingly made the immense sacrifices that liberal principles demanded, from the battlefields of northern Virginia to those of France and Flanders. But since prospective allies are so rarely both virtuous and powerful, those same principles have routinely faced democratic statesmen with the hard choice between hypocrisy and strategic impotence.

True believers in economic liberalism – in the market as the measure of all things and the motor of human progress – have frequently proved blind both to the realities of power and to the possible use of markets themselves as engines of conquest. They regularly fail to appreciate that the rationality, "moderation," and "pragmatism" they yearn to find in adversaries – and therefore do find, until brutally disillusioned – is a figment of *their own* ideology. And their persistent delusion that their own values are inherent in the historical process – a delusion shared with totalitarians of all stripes – has repeatedly lured them toward disaster.

A deep-rooted Cobdenite faith in the supremacy of economics and the tranquilizing effects of free trade helped disarm the interwar democracies, especially Britain and the United States. In the best-selling 1919 indictment of the Versailles settlement that stripped it of moral validity for a broad Anglo-American public, John Maynard Keynes offered a uniquely innocent prescription for the pacification of Europe: to hand over Russia and Austria-Hungary's successor states to German economic domination. He mocked predictions of a new German bid for mastery by force as "the anticipations of the timid."[61] Keynes's high-minded *Weltanschauung*, acquired as a sheltered citizen of Victorian and Edwardian Britain, filled him with childish petulance toward a state system that so thwarted economic rationality and human progress. The thought that states "by a necessary law of their nature" deal in goods incommensurate with that rationality – in mastery and survival – he rejected out of hand.

Keynes partially redeemed himself later by shocking Neville Chamberlain's treasury with the thought that Britain could afford to rearm on credit. But his naivete about German power was both an expression of and reinforcement for the ideology that moved figures such as Baldwin, MacDonald, and Chamberlain. The death rolls of the Great War intensified beyond measure the belief, in Chamberlain's doleful words, that "war wins nothing, cures nothing, ends nothing."[62] That world-view made it almost fatally difficult for British leaders to understand Hitler, his generation of Germans, and his

---

60 Maurice Pearton, *Diplomacy, Technology, and War since 1830* (Lawrence, KA, 1984), pp. 28–30, is useful on "honor" as a key category in nineteenth century statecraft and strategy.
61 *The Economic Consequences of the Peace* (New York, 1920), pp. 293–94, 291, 290; on Keynes's influence, see Étienne Mantoux, *The Carthaginian Peace, or the Economic Consequences of Mr. Keynes* (Pittsburgh, 1952).
62 Quoted in Keith Feiling, *The Life of Neville Chamberlain* (London, 1946), p. 320. War did end Hitler.

regime, born from war and bound for war, "the father of all things."[63] It was indeed no accident that the man who in the end led Britain in battle against evil was no Cobdenite quasipacifist, but that imperialist student of war and politics, Winston Churchill. But where would British leaders have found the conceptual framework for strategy against Germany – whose cartels even before 1914 made it the world's closest approximation to the predatory "capitalist developmental states" of a later era – had it chosen to conquer Europe with the checkbook rather than the sword?[64]

TECHNOLOGY AND ECONOMIC POWER

The making of strategy in the agrarian age was far from independent of tools and money. Key inventions, from bronze and iron metallurgy to the compound bow, crossbow, stirrup, war galley, ocean-going sailing ship, Greek fire, and gunpowder gave their possessors tactical and operational advantages with often far-reaching strategic effects. Military engineering, from the Romans roads and *limes* to the fortifications of the Ming and of Vauban, sometimes gave its possessors a decisive edge. Agrarian logistical achievements occasionally rivaled those of the following age: agents of the emperor Constantius II assembled 6 million bushels of wheat to feed his army on its march west to suppress Julian the Apostate.[65] And states from the Athenian "tyrant city," to the great agrarian empires of Rome and China, to the Western medieval monarchies and the warring cities of the Italian Renaissance, saw money as the nerve of war. Yet as Machiavelli pointed out, under the conditions of his age it was equally plausible to argue that "gold is not always able to get good soldiers, but good soldiers are always able to find gold."[66] Mongol power struck devastating blows from Poland, Hungary, and Mesopotamia to Annam without resting on an agricultural economy of its own, although agricultural empires held the advantage in staying power.

Warriors, horses, food, fodder, and weapons produced by hand – along with silver and gold – were thus the material base of war in the agricultural era. The pace of man or animal determined mobility; sea transport was a gamble.[67] Technological change was almost imperceptible except to those few who looked back over long stretches of time; Thucydides' history of

---

63 "War, the father of all things, is also our father; it has hammered, chiselled, and tempered us into what we are" (Ernst Jünger – following Heraclitus – 1922: *Der Kampf als inneres Erlebnis*, in *Sämtliche Werke* [Stuttgart, 1978–83], 7:11).
64 For the concept, Chalmers Johnson, *MITI and the Japanese Miracle* (Stanford, CA, 1982).
65 Arthur Ferrill, *The Fall of the Roman Empire*, p. 26.
66 *Discorsi sopra la prima deca di Tito Livio*, X.
67 On the inapplicability of the concept of "interior lines" to the Mediterranean world, and on strategic mobility under pre-industrial conditions, see Luttwak, *The Grand Strategy of the Roman Empire*, pp. 47–48, 80–84.

human progress as the history of naval power and ship design in Book I is one of the strongest of his many claims to modernity. As late as the 1820s, despite his brilliant analysis of the changes in war that the French Revolution's "transformation of politics" had wrought, Clausewitz was mute on the revolution in the mills and iron-foundries that had kept Britain fighting until triumph at Waterloo.[68]

Yet even the sluggish pace of change of the age of agriculture had shown that technology was capable of altering the balance between offense and defense. Armor had countered the "cruel bronze"; the ram had given naval combat new decisiveness; fortifications and roads had blunted barbarian forays; longbow and crossbow and arquebus had dispatched mounted knights and cannon had cracked their hilltop strongholds; and absolutism had in turn perfected a new art of gunpowder-proof fortification that gave the advantage to the strategic defensive.

The Industrial Revolution – best understood not as a distant eighteenth-century event but as a continuously accelerating process – brought an immense qualitative leap, from leisurely and largely unperceived change to frenetic and increasingly planned innovation. Technology advanced in waves: steam power and iron smelted with coal through the 1830s; industrial chemicals, cheap steel, and electricity from the 1830s through the 1890s; the internal combustion engine, powered flight, and electronics during the first half of the new century; and then the blessings of nuclear weapons, jet propulsion, rocketry, semiconductors, lasers, composite materials, and primitive thinking machines.[69] Those waves interacted with the greater or lesser imagination of the military elites of the industrialized states to produce ever-new weapons and classes of weapons, each directed against the weaknesses of predecessors and rivals. Continuous innovation made clear that the relationship between offense and defense was dialectical. The defense retained its "negative object" but the technological balance determined the extent to which it remained Clausewitz's "stronger form of war."

The first great wave of technologies privileged above all firepower, strategic mobility, and strategic communications. The result in the First World War was tactical and operational immobility and the horror of immense losses for virtually no visible gain. In that war's far bloodier sequel, the perfection of wireless tactical communications and the proliferation of the internal combustion engine in all its infinite possibilities spurred the offensive at all levels.

---

68 *On War*, p. 610; Clausewitz admitted that in the past states had gained "great *psychological* advantage" (my emphasis) through superior organization, equipment, or mobility, but affirmed that rough technological balance between contenders was characteristic of "modern war" (p. 282). Michael I. Handel's "Clausewitz in the Age of Technology," pp. 53–94 in his *War, Strategy and Intelligence* (London, 1989) has sharpened my understanding of many of the issues covered in this section.

69 The most fruitful conceptualization of the process, which lays great stress on its dialectical nature, remains David S. Landes, *The Unbound Prometheus* (Cambridge, 1969).

The result was a global war of movement that hid under gaudy maneuver an attrition even more deadly than that of 1914–18.[70] Then came atomic and thermonuclear weapons, intercontinental rockets, and precision guidance, offering a form of war in which the offensive was so dominant that it seemed to *guarantee* reciprocal damage disproportionate to any conceivable political objectives.

The Industrial Revolution thus progressively abolished time and distance in war, made weapons ever more destructive and precise, and allowed the instantaneous collection of ever-greater amounts of information about both enemy and friendly forces. The consequences for the making of strategy were at least four.

First, any war fought between great powers for vital objectives now turns as much on total economic power and technological innovation as on immediate battlefield success – provided only that the defending side survives the initial onslaught, as the French did not in 1870 and 1940. Economic power and innovation in turn depend on "human capital," from mathematicians and "pure" scientists to engineers and literate line workers; on the state's skill at organizing education, research, and the framework of production; on installed and potential industrial plant; and on control or possession of vital raw materials. The calculability of many of these factors has created a new inter-state pecking order, generated by uneven economic development, that overlays and in part cancels traditional inequalities in numbers, agricultural production, and geography. That pecking order has helped "post-dict" the outcome of conventional wars long in duration and unlimited in aim, and has informed a prescient few in advance: Churchill saw Pearl Harbor as the immense strategic blessing it was. By November 1941, as his thrust on Moscow slowed, even Hitler conceded spitefully that "all wars are first of all not racial [*völkischer*] but economic in structure . . . The huckster determines the production of cannon, armor, and munitions." That insight was presumably the source of the unease that his closest military adviser detected a few weeks later: "long before anyone else in the world, Hitler suspected or knew that the war was lost."[71]

Second, the range of strategic choice, already often narrowed by bureaucratic timidity or self-will, the political requirements of mass mobilization, and ideological tunnel vision, suffers in addition from constraints that long-term military-economic planning imposes. The industrial revolution first made possible and ultimately displaced the general-purpose "armed hordes" of 1792–1815, 1870–71, and 1914–16. Since the great *Materialschlachten* of

---

[70] On attrition, see particularly Murray, *Luftwaffe* (Baltimore, 1985) and Bartov, *Hitler's Army*, Chaps. 1–2.

[71] Gerhard Engel, *Heeresadjutant bei Hitler* (Stuttgart, 1974), p. 115; Jodl memorandum, October 1946, in Percy Ernst Schramm, *Hitler: The Man and Military Leader* (Chicago, 1971), p. 204. For the imbalances in manufacturing output and "total industrial potential" that ultimately decided the outcomes of the two world wars, see Paul Kennedy, *The Rise and Fall of the Great Powers* (New York, 1987), pp. 201–02, 259, 271, 330, 332.

1916, even infantrymen have come to fight in, through, and against machines.[72] And machines need an inordinate time for their development, tend by their nature toward specialization, and require time-consuming adjustment to fit into the integrated "weapons systems" needed to crush or counter the "systems" of potential enemies. The fanatical and expert young *Kämpfer* of 12th SS *Panzerdivision* "Hitler Jugend" wept in frustration when their counterattacks failed in Normandy – but fail they did.[73] The victors were the American and British staffs that coordinated the immense logistical effort and the specialized organizations and machines – from Bletchley Park's decryption units and the navies' underwater demolition teams, to Mulberry harbors and undersea pipelines, to hedgerow-cutting tanks and fighter-bombers – that put overwhelming firepower across the beaches and sustained it. Those fruits of a long-term effort inconceivable before 1944 cracked the Wehrmacht. Thereafter, lengthening lead time, "systems integration," specialization of weapons function and training, ever-increasing unit expense, and the ever-greater primacy of the scientific-industrial base have merged "peace" into war even for those who still perceive a dichotomy between the two. Technological, organizational, economic, and even educational decisions taken or evaded in peacetime always constrain strategic choices, and may at the limit dictate defeat without struggle.

Third, strategists in states facing hostile neighbors now have to live – in both peace and war – in a condition of radical uncertainty surpassing that of earlier ages. That uncertainty has two principal sources and one main consequence for the making of strategy. It stems in part from the dialectical movement of technology, the constant danger that innovation will degrade or nullify key weapons systems or suddenly transform the balance between offense and defense. Even worse for strategists of status quo states, the new mobility after 1918 has given wings to the strategic offensive. Strategic surprise, which Clausewitz dismissed as unfeasible, is now virtually the rule in the "conventional" as well as the nuclear realm. 22 June and 7 December 1941 were no accident. Germany achieved strategic surprise – through deception – under virtually worst-case conditions after amassing 3 million men on Stalin's borders. Japan struck devastatingly at the fleet of a government and people that fully expected attack, although not at Pearl Harbor. Egypt's initial success in 1973 demonstrated that even a force under constant overhead and signals surveillance can achieve surprise if held indefinitely poised to strike.[74]

---

72 On 1916 as a turning point, see especially Geyer, "German Strategy in the Age of Machine Warfare," pp. 535–45.
73 Max Hastings, *Overlord: D-Day and the Battle for Normandy* (New York, 1984), p. 127.
74 Handel, "Clausewitz in the Age of Technology," pp. 64–68, 71–74 and "Intelligence and the Problem of Strategic Surprise," also in his *War, Strategy and Intelligence*, pp. 229–81; Barton Whaley, *Codeword BARBAROSSA* (Cambridge, MA, 1973); and the careful dissection of Israeli failure in Eliot A. Cohen and John Gooch, *Military Misfortunes* (New York, 1990), Chap. 5.

The result is that intelligence, which Clausewitz derided, has become increasingly vital to strategists, just as imaging and surveillance and decryption systems have multiplied in effectiveness and scope. What has been absent, however, is machinery to handle swiftly the resulting masses of data, much less to sift putative "signals" from "noise" and deception, to make judgments about the enemy's effectiveness and intentions, and to discern his doctrinal and ideological blind spots while neutralizing those of analysts and strategists. Continued and ever-deeper uncertainty, aggravated rather than relieved by the obligatory pedestrian tallies of enemy "capabilities," is the result. And intelligence-collection devices obey the same dialectical law as weaponry. Counteraction or evasion or deception may at any point surprise even – or especially – those made slothful by seemingly effortless technological superiority.

Finally, the new technologies of communications and imaging that have revolutionized war and intelligence-gathering have massively intensified the connection between strategy and mass politics. In World War I the telegraph and telephone already allowed each coalition to steel domestic and military morale with news of the other's war aims. Transparency hurt the Central Powers most; the world-conquering rapacity of the German middle classes helped convince the Entente peoples that negotiation was futile, and ultimately undermined the German masses' faith in the defensive nature of their war.[75] The dictatorships that followed devised a defense: centralized control of information, relentless indoctrination, and terror. But even in the 1930s communications technology caught the Fascist and Nazi regimes in the "glass house effect," the almost instantaneous disclosure of the inconsistencies between messages aimed at different audiences. Words and images designed to mold the warrior masses leaked across borders to predestined victims, leading to countermobilization. Conversely, throttling bellicosity back somewhat (as Hitler grudgingly did until 1938) to avoid triggering foreign counteraction also had costs: once crisis came, the masses might lack the necessary warlike fanaticism and pig-headed conviction of the justice of their cause. Democratic statesmen such as Churchill who urged preparedness or defensive action faced even worse difficulties. They immediately became targets for concentric assault by enemy media barrages and domestic pacifist agitation.

The subsequent development of global television has effected a qualitative leap in transparency. Closed societies that live in a state of internal war and latent (or actual) external war can still hope to limit damage from foreign "messages" by terror and censorship, although the technological balance between jamming and transmission may yet change. But open societies in peacetime have no such recourse. In limited wars they have only the crude

---

[75] See the wonderful contemporary document collection of S. Grumbach, *Das annexionistische Deutschland* (Lausanne, 1917).

partial remedy of direct attack on enemy broadcast systems. Television's unique ability to manipulate emotion through symbols and pictures, its shocking immediacy and built-in selectivity of presentation, offer amazing opportunities to aspiring Goebbelses. Despotisms need no media of their own to manipulate opinion in democracies, for commercial television executives merrily trample each other to secure exclusive transmission rights for propaganda. And even in the absence of propaganda, images of the death and devastation that are the essence of war may be enough to sap the confidence in victory and conviction of righteousness that are the essence of national morale. Of all of technology's heavy constraints on the makers of strategy, media transparency is far from the lightest.

FROM THE ROAD BEHIND TO THAT AHEAD

That "generall inclination of all mankind, a perpetuall and restlesse desire of Power after power, that ceaseth onely in Death" that Thomas Hobbes – Thucydides' translator – once postulated is still with us. Violence, chance, and politics; danger and friction; escalatory interaction between adversaries remain the terrain of those who make strategy. But the revolutionary new world of bureaucracy, mass politics, ideological fanaticism, and ceaseless economic and technological flux has clothed all in new forms.

The restraints on great-power conflict that have defined the post-1945 era are hardly inherent in the historical process. The collapse of the Soviet Union merely means the death of only *one* ideological challenge to democratic capitalism. Outside the West, religion still inspires universal claims and genocidal loyalties; the passing of European wars of religion has not ended religious war. Nationalism remains deeprooted even in the placid and opulent industrial societies of Western Europe. In societies born in poverty from the debris of empires great and small, the national cult retains all its primitive force. Unless bribed with swift prosperity, societies molded by Tsarist and communist autocracy may well produce new regimes founded on terror and belief. Great Russian nationalism – in the past anti-Western, anti-Semitic, and hungering for great leaders with an iron hand – remains a potential imperial ideology for the lands between the Vistula and the Pacific. Chinese nationalism may yet claim a similar role both within and beyond the Chinese empire's traditional sphere.

Latent ideological rivalry has also come to dog Japan's relationship with the West. The Japanese "capitalist developmental state" imperfectly camouflaged under MacArthur's constitution has so far proved neither democratic nor capitalist. The lines between public and private, state and society are blurred. No one can say where the ruling party leaves off and the bureaucracy and great corporations begin. And in ideological continuity – and much else – Japan resembles Germany after 1918 far more than Germany after 1945. Japan's subjects have retained much of the quasiracial sense of mission that the Meiji oligarchs sought to instill long ago. A widely read pseudoscientific literature trumpets the uniqueness of the Japanese brain; myths of Jewish world-conspiracies attract wide interest; Japanese wartime atrocities in China, Southeast Asia, and the Pacific are Orwellian un-facts. Japanese pacifism, embodied in the cult of Hiroshima and Nagasaki, has a sharp nationalist edge; in the minds of its adherents, Japan is as unique in victimhood as in all else. An unrivaled record of post-1945 economic conquest has hardened these notions into the certainty of systemic superiority. Yet concurrently, as Japan's most discerning interpreter has suggested, even the immense defeats of 1931–45 have failed to give the Japanese state the steering and brakes needed to ward off future collisions.[76]

Economics likewise offers small comfort to those hoping for a release from conflict. The slow decline of United States economic leadership may yet produce an interregnum as catastrophic as that which followed Britain's 1914–17 demise as hegemon of the world market. Japan's advance, based on a domestic market so far impermeable except to token competition, led by corporations shielded from bankruptcy, fueled by the fierce devotion of its work force, and aimed at limitless expansion, appears to offer grim choices. One – perhaps extreme – alternative is the gradual reduction of Japan's trading "partners" to thinly disguised vassalage. Another is the redivision of the world into two or more quasi-autarkic blocs such as the Americas and German-Europe, while leaving Japan to rule alone its Greater East Asia Co-Prosperity Sphere.

Either outcome could swiftly lead to more than economic conflict. In the second case the resulting implosion of world trade would cut even industrial democracies loose from their domestic moorings. Victory in war and prosperity, not historical inevitability, have legitimated democracy since 1945. Economic catastrophe or uncontrolled immigration or national humiliation can still summon nationalism forth in something resembling the fury of 1914–45. And "Weimar Japan's" almost total dependence on external energy and markets, its bizarre nationalist myths, and its absence of a center and a source of legitimacy other than success all hold potential for terrifying mutation in the event of world economic collapse.

Finally, the continuing acceleration of science and technology seems unlikely to make the strategist's world more stable or predictable. Science has expanded war to give the "nonmilitary" aspects of security – and aggression – a weight as great or greater than "purely" military ones. States with appreciable and growing scientific-industrial-military bases have proliferated relentlessly, while the Western democracies are likely to decline from

[76] For this and following remarks on Japan (except the Weimar parallel), see Karel van Wolferen, *The Enigma of Japanese Power. People and Politics in a Stateless Nation* (New York, 1989), and "No Brakes, No Compass," *The National Interest*, fall 1991, pp. 26–35. Van Wolferen's Japan appears to refute Francis Fukuyama's well-known suggestion that "the Western *idea*" no longer has "viable systematic alternatives."

their present 12.4 percent of world population to roughly 11 percent by 2000 and 8.8 percent by 2025.[77] Weapons of mass destruction hitherto reserved to the great have spread inexorably to despots, fanatics, and ambitious midsized powers through the ostensibly innocuous routines of foreign trade. If the survival-logic of states sometimes offends economic rationality, the workings of economic rationality can retaliate by threatening survival. Technology has also opened the prospect of reprofessionalizing war as the exclusive preserve of specialists wielding ever-more automated weaponry; democracies too can now look forward to "cabinet wars." Even the prematurely christened "absolute weapon" shows signs of relativity, of conforming to the dialectical relationship between offense and defense that has governed technologies of violence in the past.

In this bewildering world, the search for predictive theories to guide strategy has been no more successful than the search for such theories in other areas of human existence. Patterns do emerge from the past, and their study permits educated guesses about the range of potential outcomes. But the future is not an object of knowledge; no increase in processing power will make the owl of history a daytime bird. Similar causes do not always produce similar effects, and causes interact in ways unforeseeable even by the historically sophisticated. Worse still, individuals – with their ambitions, vanities, and quirks – make strategy. Machiavelli's *Prince* is sometimes a better guide than Clausewitz to the personal and institutional vendettas that intertwine unpredictably around the simplest strategic decisions. Finally, conflict is the realm of contradiction and paradox. The most successful analytical – but not predictive – framework for contemporary strategists identifies five levels and two dimensions in which the reverse logic of conflict operates, and asks with calculated irony: "can strategy be useful?"[78]

Ultimately, makers of strategy must narrow their focus; too much complexity makes the mind seize. At a minimum they must see clearly both themselves and potential adversaries, their strengths, weaknesses, preconceptions, and limits – through humility, relentless and historically informed critical analysis, and restless dissatisfaction even in victory. They must weigh imponderables through structured debates that pare away personal, organizational, and national illusions and conceits. They must squarely address issues that are bureaucratic orphans. They must unerringly discern and prepare to strike the enemy's jugular – whether by surprise attack or by attrition, in war or in political and economic struggle. And in the end, makers of strategy must cheerfully face the uncertainties of decision and the dangers of action.

77 Percentages calculated from the 1990 figures in World Bank, *World Development Report 1992* (Oxford, 1992), p. 269 (West: high-income OECD members less Japan). With Japan the percentages are 14.7 (1989), 13.2 (2000), and 10.4 (2025).
78 Luttwak, *Strategy: the Logic of War and Peace* (Cambridge, MA, 1987), pp. 231–36

Index

Most writing about strategy – the balancing of ends and means by rulers and states in conflict with their adversaries – has focused on individual theorists or great military leaders. That approach has its uses, but it normally ignores the messy process through which rulers and states have actually framed strategy. Understanding how that process has worked or failed to work in the past is nevertheless of vital practical importance to strategists, and of the greatest interest to students of strategy and statecraft.

The Making of Strategy is about the strategic process. It consists of seventeen case studies that range from fifth-century Athens and Ming China to Hitler's Germany, Israel, and the post-1945 United States. The studies analyze, within a common interpretive framework, precisely how rulers and states have made strategy. The introduction emphasizes the constants in the rapidly shifting world of the strategist. The conclusion tries to understand the forces that have driven the transformation of strategy since 400 B.C. and seem likely to continue to transform it in the future.

Made in the USA
Middletown, DE
10 January 2023

21840350R00387